Lecture Notes in Computer Science 14762

Founding Editors

Gerhard Goos
Juris Hartmanis

The series Lecture Notes in Computer Science (LNCS), including its subseries Lecture Notes in Artificial Intelligence (LNAI) and Lecture Notes in Bioinformatics (LNBI), has established itself as a medium for the publication of new developments in computer science and information technology research, teaching, and education.

LNCS enjoys close cooperation with the computer science R & D community, the series counts many renowned academics among its volume editors and paper authors, and collaborates with prestigious societies. Its mission is to serve this international community by providing an invaluable service, mainly focused on the publication of conference and workshop proceedings and postproceedings. LNCS commenced publication in 1973.

Amon Rapp · Luigi Di Caro · Farid Meziane ·
Vijayan Sugumaran

Editors

Natural Language Processing and Information Systems

29th International Conference on Applications
of Natural Language to Information Systems, NLDB 2024
Turin, Italy, June 25–27, 2024
Proceedings, Part I

 Springer

Editors
Amon Rapp
University of Turin
Turin, Italy

Luigi Di Caro
University of Turin
Turin, Italy

Farid Meziane
University of Derby
Derby, UK

Vijayan Sugumaran
Oakland University
Rochester, MI, USA

ISSN 0302-9743   ISSN 1611-3349 (electronic)
Lecture Notes in Computer Science
ISBN 978-3-031-70238-9   ISBN 978-3-031-70239-6 (eBook)
https://doi.org/10.1007/978-3-031-70239-6

This Springer imprint is published by the registered company Springer Nature Switzerland AG
The registered company address is: Gewerbestrasse 11, 6330 Cham, Switzerland

If disposing of this product, please recycle the paper.

Preface

This volume comprises the full papers presented at the main research track of NLDB 2024, the 29th International Conference on Natural Language and Information Systems, held on June 25–27, 2024, at the University of Turin, Italy. The successful on-site participation at the recent two editions motivated this year's organizers to maintain the traditional face-to-face format, a preference shared by many authors. In exceptional cases, online presentations were permitted.

The conference was managed through the EasyChair system, as in previous years. We received 141 submissions, each assigned to reviewers for a double-blind review, on the basis of the competence of the Program Committee members. We provided two different tracks: one main research track and one industry track.

The General Chairs acted as meta-reviewers to complete missing reviews, provide additional reviews for papers with missing reviews, and take a decision on submissions with significantly conflicting reviews. To ensure fairness and transparency, all Program Committee members declared any conflicts of interest through the conference management system. Based on the reviews, the Program Chairs accepted papers with an average score of approximately 1.0 or higher as full papers, and papers with scores between 0 and 1.0 as short/demo papers, as done in previous editions. The confidence scores indicated by the reviewers, the content of the reviews, and the relevance of the papers to the conference scope were also considered for borderline cases. No poster papers were accepted this year.

We accepted 35 long papers, 26 short papers and 3 demo papers. The final acceptance rate counting the number of full papers was thus 24.8%, similarly competitive in comparison to previous years. Following the publisher's advice, long papers were allotted up to 15 pages, which was well received by authors. This allowed long paper authors to include more results and discussions. Among the acceptances, 4 long papers and 4 short papers were from the industry track.

The NLDB conference continues to attract high-quality, cutting-edge research and keeps pace with developments in applying natural language to databases and information systems broadly. Established as a leading conference, NLDB now attracts participants worldwide and has evolved from focusing on Natural Language, Databases, and Information Systems to embracing recent advancements in data and language engineering. The current proceedings reflect these advancements and support studies related to languages previously underrepresented, such as Arabic, Romanian, Italian, and Japanese languages.

We extend our gratitude to all reviewers for their diligence and timely completion of their assignments, and to the authors for their valuable contributions.

June 2024   Amon Rapp
                                                              Luigi Di Caro
                                                              Farid Meziane
                                                         Vijayan Sugumaran

Organization

General Chairs

Amon Rapp   University of Turin, Italy
Luigi Di Caro   University of Turin, Italy
Farid Meziane   University of Derby, UK
Vijayan Sugumaran   Oakland University, USA

Program Chairs

Amon Rapp   University of Turin, Italy
Luigi Di Caro   University of Turin, Italy

Local Chair

Claudio Schifanella   University of Turin, Italy

Diversity, Equity and Inclusion Chair

Francesca Grasso   University of Turin, Italy

Web and Publicity Chair

Federico Torrielli   University of Turin, Italy

Program Committee

Ana-Maria Bucur   University of Bucharest, Romania
Davide Audrito   University of Bologna, Italy
Stefano Locci   Università degli Studi di Torino, Italy
Adela Ljajić   Institute for Artificial Intelligence, Research and
           Development of Serbia, Serbia
Emilio Sulis   University of Turin, Italy

Philipp Cimiano   Bielefeld University, Germany
Emmanuel Cartier   European Commission, Joint Research Centre,
                                     Belgium
Francesco Cannarile   Eni SpA, Italy
Roberto Nai   University of Torino, Italy
Elisabetta Fersini   University of Milano-Bicocca, Italy
Valeriya Goloviznina   Vyatka State University, Russia
Federico Torrielli   University of Turin, Italy
Andrea Acquaviva   Polytechnic University of Turin, Italy
Raquel Martínez   UNED, Spain
Manuela Sanguinetti   Università degli Studi di Cagliari, Italy
Isabelle Comyn-Wattiau   ESSEC Business School, France
Khaled Shaalan   British University in Dubai, UAE
Attilio Fiandrotti   Università di Torino, Italy
Fouzi Harrag   Université Ferhat Abbas de Sétif, Algeria
Marco Polignano   Università degli Studi di Bari Aldo Moro, Italy
Gennaro Vessio   University of Bari, Italy
Sunil Vadera   University of Salford, UK
Praveen Bushipaka   University of Pisa, Italy
Marco Viviani   Università degli Studi di Milano-Bicocca, Italy
Paloma Martínez Fernández   Universidad Carlos III de Madrid, Spain
Imene Bensalem   Constantine 2 University, Algeria
Lucia Siciliani   University of Bari Aldo Moro, Italy
Irene Siragusa   Università degli Studi di Palermo, Italy
Greta Damo   Université Côte d'Azur, France
Esau Villatoro-Tello   Universidad Autónoma Metropolitana, Mexico
Thomas Mandl   University of Hildesheim, Germany
Davide Picca   University of Lausanne, Switzerland
Muhammad Okky   Ibrohim University of Turin, Italy
Gábor Berend   University of Szeged, Hungary
Jacky Akoka   CEDRIC-CNAM, France
Vladimir A. Fomichov   Moscow Aviation Institute (National Research
                                     University), Russia
Tiberio Uricchio   University of Macerata, Italy
Giancarlo Sperlì   University of Naples, Italy
Pier Felice Balestrucci   Università degli Studi di Torino, Italy
Somnath Banerjee   University of Tartu, Estonia
Jader de Sá   Luxembourg Institute of Science and Technology,
                                     Luxembourg
Muhammad Rashid   University of Turin, Italy
Francesca Grasso   University of Turin, Italy

Miloš Košprdić	Institute for Artificial Intelligence Research and Development of Serbia, Serbia
Nada Mimouni	CEDRIC lab – Conservatoire National des Arts et Métiers, France
Carlos A. Iglesias	Universidad Politécnica de Madrid, Spain
Eleonora Mancini	University of Bologna, Italy
Yasir Arfat	University of Turin, Italy
Benedetta Muscato	University of Pisa, Italy
Helmut Horacek	Saarland University, Germany
Luca Anselma	Università di Torino, Italy
Epaminondas Kapetanios	University of Hertfordshire, UK
Sabrina Villata	University of Turin, Italy
Alaa Alzoubi	University of Derby, UK
Elena Cabrio	Université Côte d'Azur, CNRS, Inria, I3S, France
Rafael Muñoz	University of Alicante, Spain
Soto Montalvo	Universidad Rey Juan Carlos, Spain
Krishnaprasad Thirunarayan	Wright State University, USA
Arianna Graciotti	University of Bologna, Italy
Lucia Cascone	University of Salerno, Italy
Marco de Gemmis	University of Bari Aldo Moro, Italy
Alessio Miaschi	Institute for Computational Linguistics "A. Zampolli" (CNR-ILC), Italy
Muhammad Yasir Shabir	University of Turin, Italy
Mathieu Roche	Cirad, TETIS, France
Vincenzo Calderonio	University of Pisa and IGSG-CNR, Italy
Alessandro Bondielli	Università di Pisa, Italy
Christian Di Maio	QuestIT, Italy
Giovanni Siragusa	University of Turin, Italy
Roman Schneider	IDS, Germany
Veda Storey	Georgia State University, USA
Patrizio Bellan	Fondazione Bruno Kessler and Free University of Bozen-Bolzano, Italy
Dan Tufis	Institutul de Cercetari pentru Inteligenta Artificiala, Academia Romana, Romania
Danilo Croce	University of Rome Tor Vergata, Italy
Komal Florio	Università di Torino, Italy
Matteo Ferrara	University of Bologna, Italy
Giovanni Puccetti	ISTI CNR, Italy
Dino Ienco	IRSTEA, France
Christian Kop	Alpen-Adria-Universität Klagenfurt, Austria
Maristella Matera	Politecnico di Milano, Italy
Natalia Loukachevitch	Research Computing Center of Moscow State University, Russia

Contents – Part I

Contents – Part II

Fine-Tuning BERT on Coarse-Grained Labels: Exploring Hidden States for Fine-Grained Classification

Aftab Anjum[1] and Ralf Krestel[1,2]([envelope])

[1] Kiel University, Kiel, Germany
{afa,rkr}@informatik.uni-kiel.de
[2] ZBW - Leibniz Information Centre for Economics, Kiel, Germany

Abstract. In recent years, pre-trained language models such as BERT (Bidirectional Encoder Representations from Transformers) have demonstrated exceptional performance across various natural language processing tasks. However, its effectiveness of encoding and capturing fine-grained distinctions within the hidden latent space during fine-tuning on coarse-grained labels remains relatively unexplored. To investigate this, we performed two distinct tasks: clustering and few-shot classification on fine-grained labels. The representations extracted from BERT's hidden layers are utilized as input for these tasks. In the few-shot classification task, we demonstrate that the BERT model encodes valuable information about fine-grained labels during its fine-tuning on coarse-grained labels, allowing the few-shot classifier to classify fine-grained classes accurately even with a limited number of data samples. Additionally, in the clustering analysis, a thorough examination of the hidden layers is conducted to identify clusters that align with fine-grained label distinctions. The identification of such patterns further proves that the BERT model indeed encodes fine-grained label information within its hidden layers even when fine-tuned on coarse-grained labels. The findings contribute to a deeper understanding of the capabilities of the BERT model and provide valuable insights into harnessing its hidden latent space for fine-grained classification tasks.

Keywords: BERT · Fine-tuning · Hidden representations · Latent space · Fine-grained labels · Interpretability · Few-shot learning

1 Introduction

The emergence of deep learning models, particularly BERT [7], has significantly advanced the field of natural language processing (NLP) and facilitated breakthroughs in various downstream tasks. BERT's pre-training mechanism, which involves unsupervised learning on vast amounts of unlabeled text, enables it to capture rich contextual information from diverse linguistic patterns, allowing

A. Rapp et al. (Eds.): NLDB 2024, LNCS 14762, pp. 1–15, 2024.
https://doi.org/10.1007/978-3-031-70239-6_1

it to achieve state-of-the-art results across various NLP tasks, including text classification, named entity recognition, and question answering.

Despite the remarkable success of the BERT model in numerous downstream tasks, its inherent architecture complexity, lack of transparency in pre-training, high-dimensional hidden representations, and challenges in probing and interpreting these representations contribute to its characterization as a black box model. This has led to research on the interpretability of transformer models in recent years. Various approaches have been explored to illuminate the inner workings of these models, including research on BERT's attention weights, probing tasks, and layer-wise analysis. Attention weight exploration [4] aims to understand how BERT assigns importance to different input tokens. Probing tasks [10,21] involve designing specific evaluation tasks to assess the linguistic information captured by BERT's hidden representations. Layer-wise analysis [1,2,15,17] delves into the properties and transformations of BERT's representations across its layers to gain insights into its information processing mechanism.

In this work, we explore and analyse hidden representations of the BERT model for fine-grained text classification by fine-tuning on coarse-grained labels. Many real-world NLP applications require a more nuanced understanding, necessitating fine-grained classification without having the corresponding fine-grained labeled training data. Fine-grained classification entails categorizing text into multiple subcategories or classes that possess subtle distinctions. The primary objective of our work is to investigate whether fine-grained class information is encoded within BERT's latent space. To achieve this, we employ a two-step methodology. Firstly, we fine-tune the BERT model on classification using coarse-grained labels. Secondly, we extract the hidden representations from BERT's hidden layer and examine whether any information pertaining to fine-grained labels is present within these representations. To address these questions, we employ a combination of fine-tuning and extraction of hidden representation, enabling us to delve into the intricacies of BERT's underlying architecture and assess its potential for fine-grained classification. These fine-grained classification and clustering techniques offer valuable contributions to the field of NLP.

The remainder of this paper is organized as follows: Sect. 2 provides a comprehensive review of related work of transformer-based language models interpretability and applications. Section 3 presents the methodology part, where we explain the proposed general framework. Section 4 describes the experimental setup and the datasets used for evaluation. Section 5 presents and discusses the results based on two approaches: few-shot classification and clustering. Finally, Sect. 6 concludes the paper by summarizing the findings, discussing their implications, and suggesting future directions for research.

2   Related Work

In our research, we have directed our attention towards BERT [7]—a member of the transformer architecture family which derives its name from the manner in which representations undergo a series of transformations across various network layers. Although other transformer-based language models such as Roberta, Big-Bird, Longfomer, and Universal Transformer exist, our research focuses solely on the analysis of the BERT model. It is worth noting that conducting similar analysis on other models could yield intriguing findings as well.

2.1   Interpretability

Research in neural model explainability and interpretability has grown, with a focus on transformer-based language models. Among the studies, [16] analyze BERT as a ranking model, probing attention values across layers and assessing representations' performance. smilary, [12] conduct a layer-wise analysis of BERT's token representations, mainly on pre-trained models, without considering fine-tuned ones or specific phases. In contrast, [9] challenge the notion that attention mechanisms offer meaningful insights, cautioning against equating attention weights with informative explanations.

Moreover, [1] provides an in-depth examination of BERT's functioning in question answering, elucidating the contributions of different layers. A similar work [5] propose an unsupervised method to uncover latent concepts within BERT, exploring their alignment with linguistic hierarchy and evolution across layers, thus enriching our understanding of neural network knowledge representation.

2.2   Coarse-Grained to Fine-Grained Text Classification

Text classification is a well-established field in natural language processing (NLP) where extensive research has been conducted on various tasks, including binary, multi-class, and multi-label classification. However, it is true that relatively less researchers have focused on different granular levels of classification beyond the conventional approaches. Granular level classification involves coarse-grained and fine-grained text classification which can provide deeper insights and more nuanced understanding of the data.

In another work [3] they use coarse-grained labels to train shallow layers of BERT to learn some surface knowledge, then they propose a weighted self-contrastive module to train deep layers of BERT to learn more fine-grained knowledge based on the learned surface knowledge. The proposed method leverages self-contrastive learning, where representations of similar instances are pulled together and dissimilar instances are pushed apart in a contrastive learning framework. The proposed approach incorporates a hierarchical clustering strategy and introduces weighted instance selection to handle the imbalance between coarse and fine-grained classes.

A similar investigation [19], aims to enhance coarse-grained classifiers by prioritizing accurate identification of fine-grained labels, addressing hidden stratification issues. Their two-stage framework ensures subclasses aren't overlooked or misclassified during coarse-grained classification, even without subclass labels.

Another similar work proposes Coarse2Fine [14] aims to enhance coarse-grained classifiers by prioritizing accurate identification of fine-grained labels, addressing hidden stratification issues. The methodology unfolds through two phases: initially implementing weak supervision, which leverages the entire corpus and user-provided label hierarchy to generate data, subsequently fed into pre-trained language models like GPT-2 to produce the Generated Pseudo Training Data. In the second stage, the classifier is trained using this Pseudo Training Data, and the output of the classifier is once again subjected to weak suppression. This iterative process progressively enhances the classifier's performance with each cycle.

Despite extensive research in the field of text classification, it is notable that no previous study has utilized the BERT hidden representation for the classification of text based on its fine-grained labels. Therefore, in this work, our focus is on fine-tuning the BERT model specifically for the task of classifying coarse-grained annotated datasets. We intentionally do not incorporate any external information regarding fine-grained labels into the BERT model. Additionally, we investigate how the BERT model transforms these conceptual distinctions into the latent space during the fine-tuning process.

3 Inspected BERT Model

In this section, we will provide an overview of the proposed a general framework and its functioning. Subsequently, we will delve into the specifics of each component within the general framework, such as the fine-tuning of the BERT model (which we refer to as "inspected BERT model") for coarse-grained labels, the extraction of hidden, encoded representations at different layers for each test sample in the fine-tuned model, and the identification of varying levels of granularity associated with the same concepts. To this end, we conduct clustering and few-shot classification.

Fine-tuning the BERT model is a critical step in adapting it for specific downstream tasks. The Fig. 1 serves as a comprehensive illustration demonstrating the entire framework. The general framework comprises two steps: firstly, fine-tuning the BERT model using coarse-grained labels (inspected BERT model), and secondly, evaluating the fine-tuned model using fine-grained labels. Before fine-tuning, we pre-process the data, namely performing stop word removal, tokenization, and padding. This ensures that the input data is properly formatted according to the BERT model's requirements. Then, we initialize the BERT model with pre-trained weights from a masked language modeling objective trained on a large-scale corpus. We then extend the architecture by adding a classification head on top of the pre-trained BERT model to enable coarse-grained classification.

During the fine-tuning phase, our sole focus is on the coarse-grained labels. We explicitly do not fine-tune the BERT model on the fine-grained labels and do not provide any external information regarding the fine-grained labels. The purpose of this approach is to investigate how the fine-tuned BERT model, despite not being directly trained on fine-grained labels or having external fine-grained information, encodes and captures nuanced information related to fine-grained labels within its hidden representations. In-order to demonstrate it, we conducted two separate tasks: clustering and few-shot classification.

In the second part of our framework (evaluation of the fine-tuned model using fine-grained labels), we extract the different hidden layer representations of the samples in the test dataset from the fine-tuned BERT model. In order to obtain fixed-dimensional representations, we apply different pooling techniques, which allow to aggregate the contextualized representations of words (and sub-words) produced by the model. This aggregated contextual representations serve as input for both, clustering and few-shot classification. The clustering analysis provides insights into the fine-grained structure present within the encoded data. Additionally, we analyze the results of few-shot classification to further investigate the usefulness of the latent space representations. This approach allows us to leverage the model's encoded information to classify instances with fine-grained labels, even with minimal training data.

4   Experiments

To assess the effectiveness of our framework, we conducted experiments on hierarchical datasets. Each document within these datasets are associated with a single coarse-grained label and a corresponding fine-grained labels.

The 20News dataset [11], a widely recognized collection of newsgroup documents, comprises six overarching classes, encompassing a total of 20 fine-grained classes. For the purpose of our study, we focused on four specific groups, namely Computer, Religion, Sports, and Automotive, which served as coarse-grained labels. Each of coarse-grained labels was subdivided into two distinct fine-grained labels, as showcased by the Computer category consisting of the IBM and Graphics subcategories. The dataset consists of 7444 samples from the selected four coarse-grained classes.

The Harvard USPTO Dataset [20] is a large-scale, well-structured, and multi-purpose corpus of utility patent applications and grants from the United States Patent and Trademark Office (USPTO). It encompasses five coarse-grained classes paired with their respective fine-grained labels. In this work, we focused on four coarse-grained classes: human necessities, chemistry, physics, and mechanical engineering. Each coarse-grained label was further classified into two distinct fine-grained classes. For instance, within the chemistry class, these fine-grained labels include organic macro-molecular compounds and biochemistry. Detailed information regarding the fine-grained classes for both datasets can be found in Table 1.

4.1   Experimental Setting

This section presents a detailed description of the experimental setup utilized for training both, the baseline (refered to as vanilla BERT) and the inspected BERT model.

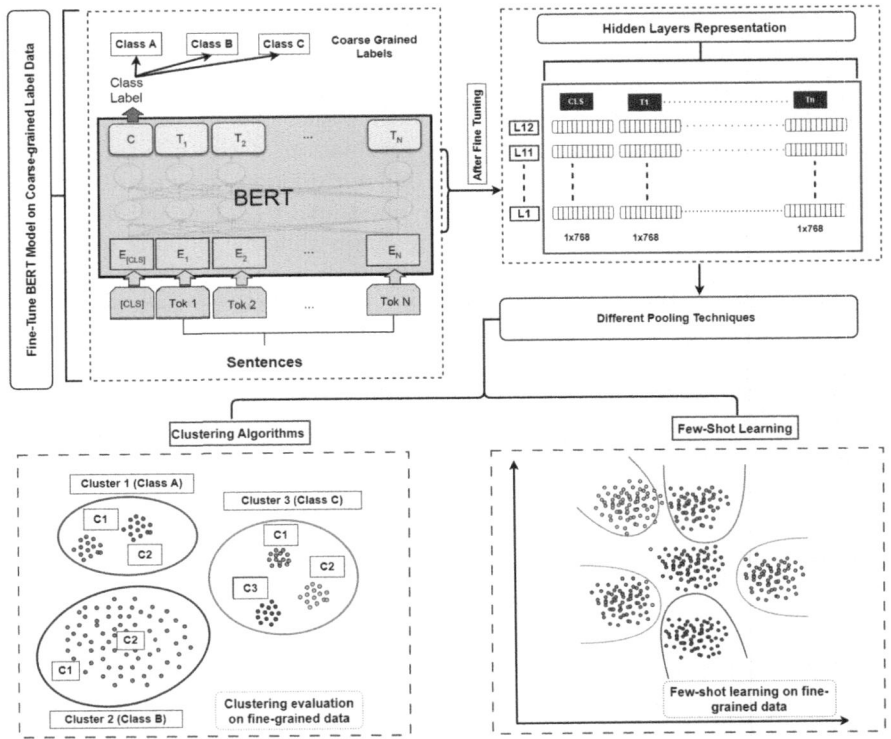

Fig. 1. Proposed general framework

Baseline: Vanilla BERT. The BERT-base [7] model encompasses 12 transformer layers and 110 million parameters. We use this model as our baseline and refer to it as vanilla BERT. For fine-tuning vanilla BERT on the fine-grained labels, we employed a learning rate of 1×10^{-5}, dropout between 0.2 to 0.4 and trained the model using a GPU for a total of 25 epochs with the adam optimizer. To balance computational efficiency and model performance, we utilized a batch size of twelve during training. To facilitate the fine-grained multi-class classification task, we incorporated a linear classification layer on top of the BERT model.

Inspected BERT. Our inspected BERT model is based on the BERT-base model as well. We leveraged BERT-base last layer pooler output as the input for the classification head. To fine-tune the inspected BERT model using coarse-grained labels, we utilized the same set of parameters employed for Vanilla BERT, with the exception of batch size and training epochs. In this case, we employed a batch size of 12 and a maximum training epoch of 15. As for data splitting, we partitioned the data into an 80% training set and a 20% testing set. These specific configurations enabled us to conduct comprehensive evaluations

Table 1. Selected Coarse- and Fine-grained Classes

20News Group Dataset Labels		Harvard USPTO Dataset Labels	
Coarse-grained	Fine-grained	Coarse-grained	Fine-grained
Computer	IBM graphics	human necessities	furniture med. or vet. science
religion	christian atheism	chemistry	organic macro-mol. comp. biochemistry
sports	hockey baseball	physics	measuring photography
automotive	motorcycles autos	mech. engineering	combustion engines dev. for fastening/mach. parts

and accurately assess the performance of the BERT model in the context of the coarse-grained multi-class classification task.

5   Results

We performed two experiments: clustering and few-shot classification. For few-shot classification, our aim is to train a model to achieve accurate predictions using a limited amount of labeled training data. In the clustering task, our objective is to identify different clusters.

5.1   Clustering

To assess the performance of our proposed model, we employed three distinct types of clustering algorithms: centroid-based clustering using k-means, hierarchical clustering employing agglomerative clustering, and graph-based exemplar assignment utilizing affinity propagation. This allows us to explore the robustness and consistency of the observed patterns (encoded information about fine grained labels) across different clustering approaches.

The clustering analysis conducted on different hidden layer representations yields consistent results and trends, aligning closely with the findings from our few-shot classification analysis (see Table 2). To compute accuracy and F1 scores of the clustering algorithms, we followed established methodologies outlined in literature [13]. Among the various clustering algorithms evaluated, affinity propagation emerges as the top-performing method, demonstrating superior accuracy, F1 score, and homogeneity score. However, it does not perform as well in terms of adjusted mutual information because of its preference for generating numerous clusters. This often leads to assignments of data points to multiple clusters simultaneously, which can result in lower adjusted mutual information values.

On the other hand, agglomerative clustering exhibits the second-best performance in terms of accuracy, F1 score, and homogeneity score. Notably, it outperforms other clustering algorithms in the adjusted mutual information metric. These findings highlight the effectiveness of different clustering algorithms in capturing the fine-grained label information present within the hidden representations of the BERT model.

I have discovered two significant aspects of the BERT model's hidden state representations. Firstly, these representations exhibit a complex and

Table 2. Clustering Results for the Inspected BERT Model

Clustering Methods	20News Group Dataset				USPTO Dataset			
	Acc	F1	Hom	AdjMI	Acc	F1	Hom	AdjMI
k-means	0.86	0.60	0.65	0.69	0.89	0.62	0.63	0.64
Agglomerative clustering	0.85	0.63	0.65	**0.72**	0.91	0.64	0.63	**0.65**
Affinity propagation	**0.94**	**0.71**	**0.72**	0.68	**0.98**	**0.75**	**0.80**	0.60

dense encoding [18] capturing intricate details of the input data. Secondly, the encoded data (hidden representation) showcases noticeable non-linear relationships among its features. Given these key observations, we find that the affinity propagation model surpasses other clustering algorithms in performance. Due of its property of handling complex structures and dense clusters [8]. It demonstrates the ability to capture intricate relationships and identify meaningful clusters, even in scenarios where the data points are closely packed. Moreover, affinity propagation exhibits the capability to capture non-linear relationships within the data, enabling it to detect and represent complex patterns and dependencies that may not conform to linear relationships. Considering these properties, affinity propagation proves to be well-suited for our clustering task.

Furthermore, to support our arguments that during fine-tuning of BERT, the model encodes distinct contextual representations of various subcategories in a high-dimensional hidden representation which can be further utilized to classify the data to its fine-grained classes, i conduct visualizations. I visualize the clusters that are present in our encoded data based by applying dimensionality reduction techniques UMAP. These techniques reduce the high-dimensional feature space to a two-dimensional feature space; enabling visual inspection of the clusters.

The Figs. 2 and 3 reveal the successful capturing of intricate distinctions within both, coarse-grained and fine-grained labels by the model. As the model is fine-tuned on four coarse-grained labels, the four classes can be easily distinguished. Although the model is not specifically fine-tuned on fine-grained labels, it still exhibits encoded information that enables the differentiation of clusters, as indicated by the coloring based on the fine-grained labels. However, it is evident that the boundaries between the fine-grained label clusters are not clearly separable, primarily due to two key observations: Firstly, the application of dimensionality reduction techniques in order to visualize the high-dimensional space into a lower-dimensional space inevitably leads to some loss of information. These techniques aim to capture the maximum amount of information in the reduced space but are limited in preserving the complete details of the original high-dimensional space. Secondly, some data are not separable in low dimensional spaces but might be separable in the original high-dimensional space.

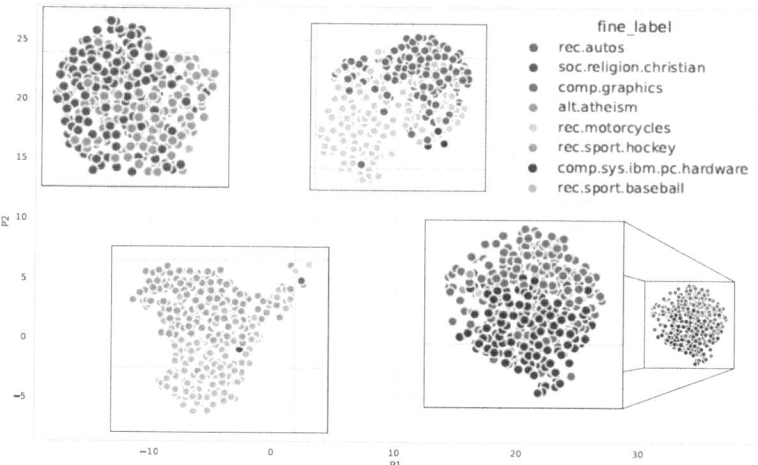

Fig. 2. The cluster visualization for 20news group dataset of four distinct coarse-grained clusters, each enclosed within a separate box.

Despite these challenges, we can still observe that similar fine-grained clusters tend to be in close proximity to each other, while distinct fine-grained labels are positioned farther apart. This implies that the transformer-based models, during fine-tuning, not only encode information related to high-level categories but also capture detailed information about subcategories or fine-grained classes within their hidden high-dimensional representations.

5.2 Few-Shot Classification

The few-shot classification results of our Inspected BERT model and the baseline is presented in Tables 3. The Inspected BERT model was fine-tuned on coarse-grained labels, and its hidden representations on the test data were extracted. Subsequently, an ensemble model (random forest), was trained on these hidden representations based on fine-grained labels in a few-shot scenario. The main objective of this experiment was to demonstrate that during fine-tuning, the Inspected BERT model not only encodes information about coarse-grained labels but also incorporates information about fine-grained labels within its hidden layers' representations. In contrast, the Vanilla BERT model was fine-tuned on fine-grained labels using a few-shot classification. For the 20news group dataset, 1750 (20% test dataset) samples have been used for testing with a variable number of training samples (few-shot scenario). Similarly, within the Harvard USPTO patent dataset, a test subset comprising 4331 samples (equivalent to 20% of the dataset) has been utilized for testing, alongside a variable number of training samples according to the few-shot learning scenario.

The findings in Table 3 clearly indicate that the performance of the Inspected BERT model is significantly better to that of the Vanilla BERT model under all

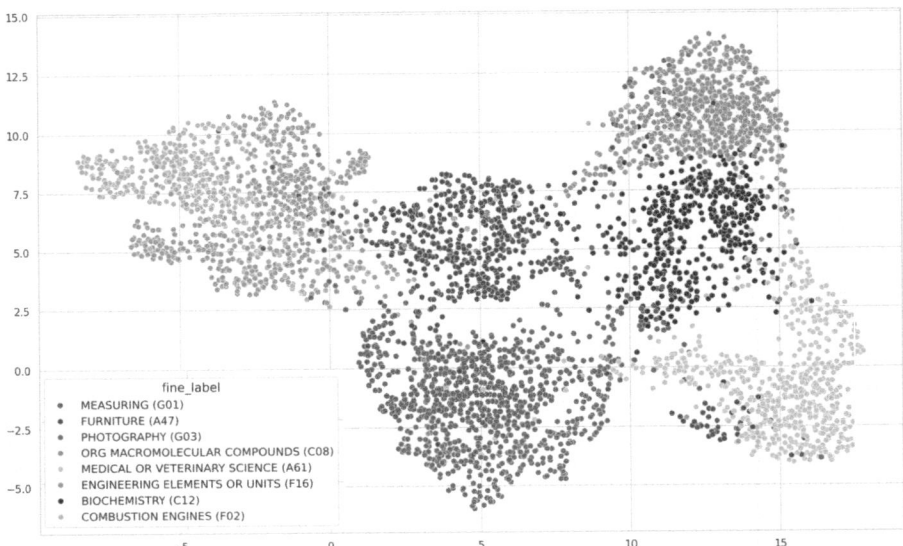

Fig. 3. The cluster visualization for the USPTO dataset for four distinct coarse-grained clusters.

conditions. An analysis of the performance of both models based on the number of training samples reveals that, at the lowest training data size of 8 (one sample per class), the Inspected BERT model outperforms the baseline model to a significant degree. By increasing the amount of labeled data, the baseline BERT model gradually showcases its strengths and attains commendable outcomes. However, they still fail to surpass the performance of the inspected model.

Table 3. Few-shot Classification Results

Train Data Size	20News Group Dataset				USPTO Dataset			
	Inspected BERT		Vanilla BERT		Inspected BERT		Vanilla BERT	
	Acc	F1	Acc	F1	Acc	F1	Acc	F1
8	0.36	0.36	0.02	0.04	0.27	0.31	0.06	0.05
16	0.40	0.41	0.17	0.26	0.39	0.43	0.10	0.12
24	0.50	0.55	0.41	0.43	0.49	0.56	0.11	0.15
32	0.59	0.62	0.49	0.51	0.60	0.64	0.19	0.24
64	**0.70**	**0.74**	0.55	0.55	**0.74**	**0.80**	0.24	0.29

6   Discussion

6.1   Analysis of [CLS] Token

In the BERT model, the [CLS] token serves as a vital component for storing and evolving information across layers. Positioned at the beginning of input sequences, it represents the entire context and provides a context-aware summary. Through the self-attention mechanism, the [CLS] token receives contributions from all tokens, enabling it to gather information from the entire input. As the information progresses through the layers, the representation of the [CLS] token becomes increasingly refined, capturing intricate patterns and semantic nuances. To conduct a thorough analysis of the [CLS] tokens within BERT, we carried out two sets of experiments.

In the first experiment, [CLS] token embeddings were exclusively taken from the hidden layers for few-shot classification using the Random Forest algorithm. Results (Figs. 4a and 4b) showed that lower layers (L1-L4) primarily extract basic features [18] and local context, linear word order, and local context, lacking deeper semantic understanding. Middle layers (L5-L7) progressively capture more complex and abstract information but still fall short on higher-level context comprehension. In contrast, higher layers (L8-L12) demonstrate richer semantic insights and syntactic details, resulting in superior performance for fine-grained classification tasks compared to lower layers.

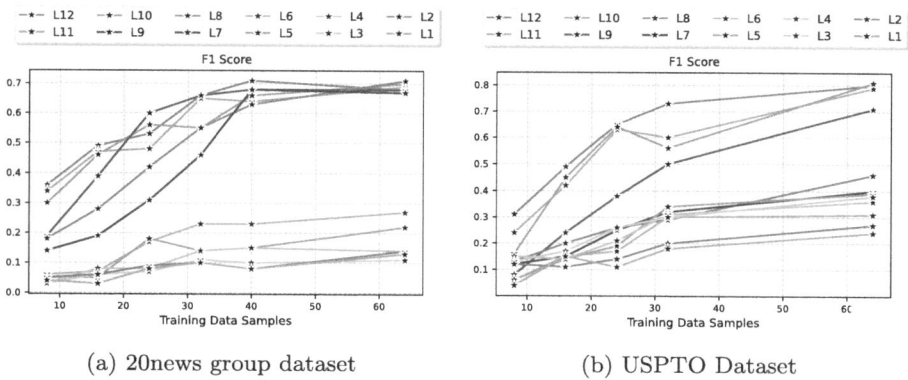

(a) 20news group dataset   (b) USPTO Dataset

Fig. 4. Hidden layers [CLS] tokens

This analysis led to two key findings: firstly, between the seventh and ninth layers, all [CLS] tokens' performance converged, suggesting that a BERT model with 7 to 9 layers suffices for competitive classification results. Secondly, contrary to some researcher claims [6, 10]. BERT does not demonstrate distinct lower, middle, and upper layer distinctions, as seen in Figs. 4a, 4b, 5a, and 5b. Lower layers focus on low-level linguistic attributes [18], such as word morphology and syntax,

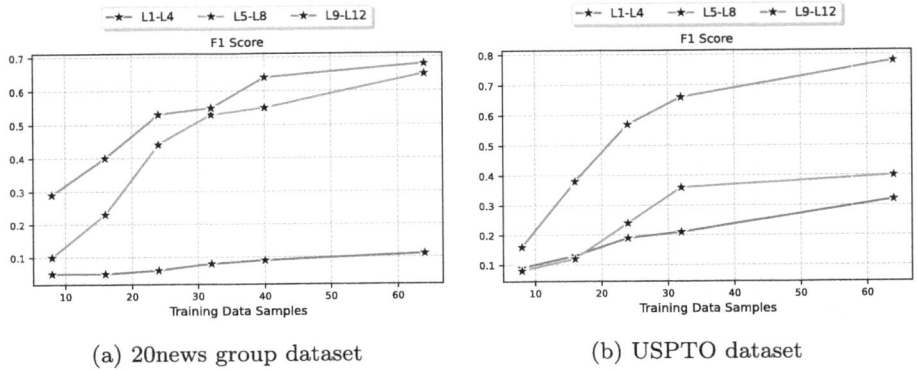

(a) 20news group dataset   (b) USPTO dataset

Fig. 5. Concatenation of hidden layers [CLS] tokens

which may possess lesser significance for downstream tasks. The higher layers excel at capturing task-specific information (coarse- or fine-grained classes) and domain-specific knowledge, enabling them to effectively identify task-relevant patterns and enhance overall performance in our few-shot classification task.

6.2   Analysis of Hidden Layers

In this section, i applied weighted average pooling techniques to hidden layers to extract information for both dataset. The key objective of these experiments is to investigate whether the BERT model solely encodes rich linguistic patterns, contextual dependencies, and local/global semantic relationships of the input sequence solely within the [CLS] token or if other hidden state tokens also contain such valuable information.

The analysis presented in Figs. 6a and 6b sheds light on the information encoded within hidden layers tokens in the BERT model. It reveals that these tokens carry rich information about the input sequence, although there are distinct differences compared to the [CLS] token. Specifically, the information encoded in hidden state tokens is more widely distributed throughout the latent space or hidden representation of the BERT model.

Each hidden state tokens captures context-specific information based on its position within the input sequence. This includes local context, word-level semantics, and syntactic relationships, which collectively contribute to a more granular understanding of the input text. This distributed information allows BERT to capture fine-grained distinctions and nuanced patterns within the sequence. However, utilizing this information effectively poses a challenge, as it needs to be compacted and integrated for model training. I employed various pooling techniques, which involve aggregating high-dimensional vectors (token representation) into single vectors, which can lead to a slight loss of information and a marginal decrease in the F1 score.

The observed hidden states show a resemblance to [CLS] tokens' behavior. Lower layers predominantly capture basic features [18] and local word order, with refinement and abstractness increasing in deeper layers. Despite self-attention mechanisms, individual token representation lack the comprehensive global context exposure of [CLS] tokens, affecting their ability to grasp semantic relationships for accurate classification, leading to lower performance levels. Figure 6b shows that the model is not able to capture mature semantic and global context till ninth layer for USPTO dataset because the effectiveness of BERT in capturing semantic and global context can vary depending on the dataset and the specific task at hand.

Some datasets require deeper layers to effectively capture the desired semantic information, while others may require only shallow layers. In this study, the analysis of Figs. 4a, 4b 6a and 6 bdemonstrates that the model adeptly comprehends and categorizes the textual data from the 20 Newsgroups dataset at shallower layers. In contrast, with the Harvard USPTO Dataset, the model struggles to interpret and categorize the text at shallower layers. This is attributed to the inherent complexities present in Harvard USPTO textual documents, which often incorporate highly specialized technical language, rich vocabulary, legal terminology, and intricate sentence structures, necessitating deeper layers of processing for accurate comprehension and classification. On the other hand, the 20 Newsgroups dataset consists of text documents from newsgroup discussions, which tend to cover a wide range of topics but may not necessarily have the same level of technical complexity as patent documents.

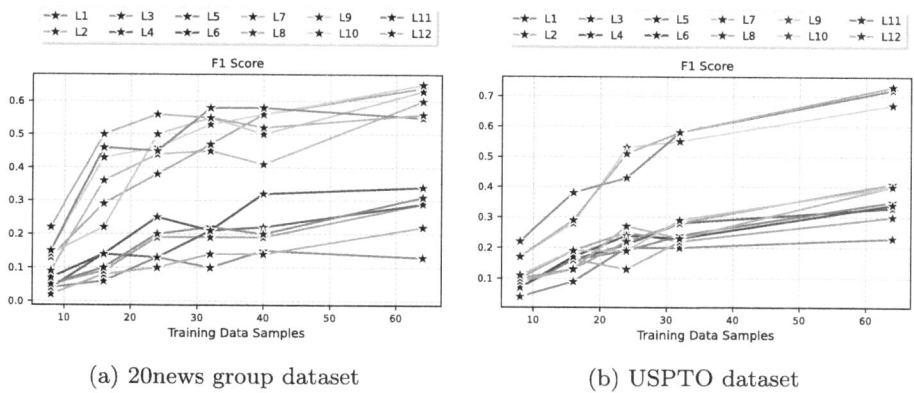

(a) 20news group dataset   (b) USPTO dataset

Fig. 6. Pooling technique on hidden states tokens without [CLS] token

7   Conclusions

Through this work, I proposed a novel framework involving fine-tuning the BERT model on coarse-grained text to classify fine-grained text by leveraging the information encapsulated within the BERT model's hidden representations. A comprehensive analysis was conducted to evaluate the presence of fine-grained label information within BERT's hidden representations, solely through fine-tuning on coarse-grained labels. To substantiate this claim, two distinct tasks were performed: few-shot classification and clustering analysis. The few-shot classification task demonstrates that a classifier can accurately classify fine-grained labels based on the information encoded in BERT's hidden representations, even with a limited number of data samples. Additionally, the clustering analysis reveals distinct patterns of clustering that align with the fine-grained label distinctions, providing further evidence of the encoded information within the hidden representations. Thus, based on the experimental findings, it can be concluded that during the fine-tuning process of the BERT model, it not only encodes coarse-grained label information, but it also captures subtle distinctions and patterns associated with fine-grained labels. The implications of this research are significant for the field of natural language processing, as it opens up avenues for leveraging the latent space of BERT for more nuanced and granular analysis.

Future research in this area may explore the transferability of the fine-grained label information encoded in BERT's hidden representations to other related tasks, providing insights into the generalizability of the learned knowledge. Furthermore, investigating techniques to enhance the interpretability of the hidden representations and understanding the underlying factors contributing to the encoding of fine-grained labels present valuable directions for further investigation.

References

1. van Aken, B., Winter, B., Löser, A., Gers, F.A.: How does BERT answer questions? A layer-wise analysis of transformer representations. In: Proceedings of the 28th ACM International Conference on Information and Knowledge Management, pp. 1823–1832 (2019)
2. Albilali, E., Altwairesh, N., Hosny, M.: What does BERT learn from Arabic machine reading comprehension datasets? In: Proceedings of the Sixth Arabic Natural Language Processing Workshop, pp. 32–41 (2021)
3. An, W., Tian, F., Chen, P., Tang, S., Zheng, Q., Wang, Q.: Fine-grained category discovery under coarse-grained supervision with hierarchical weighted self-contrastive learning. In: Proceedings of the 2022 Conference on Empirical Methods in Natural Language Processing, pp. 1314–1323 (2022)
4. Clark, K., Khandelwal, U., Levy, O., Manning, C.D.: What does BERT look at? An analysis of BERT's attention. In: Proceedings of the 2019 ACL Workshop BlackboxNLP: Analyzing and Interpreting Neural Networks for NLP, pp. 276–286 (2019)
5. Dalvi, F., Khan, A.R., Alam, F., Durrani, N., Xu, J., Sajjad, H.: Discovering latent concepts learned in BERT. In: International Conference on Learning Representations (2022)
6. De Vries, W., van Cranenburgh, A., Nissim, M.: What's so special about BERT's layers? A closer look at the NLP pipeline in monolingual and multilingual models. arXiv preprint arXiv:2004.06499 (2020)
7. Devlin, J., Chang, M.W., Lee, K., Toutanova, K.: BERT: pre-training of deep bidirectional transformers for language understanding, pp. 4171–4186 (2019)

8. Frey, B.J., Dueck, D.: Clustering by passing messages between data points. Science **5814**, 972–976 (2007)
9. Jain, S., Wallace, B.C.: Attention is not explanation. In: North American Chapter of the Association for Computational Linguistics, pp. 11–20 (2019)
10. Jawahar, G., Sagot, B., Seddah, D.: What does BERT learn about the structure of language? In: ACL 2019-57th Annual Meeting of the Association for Computational Linguistics, pp. 3651–3657 (2019)
11. Lang, K.: NewsWeeder: learning to filter netnews. In: Proceedings of the Twelfth International Conference on Machine Learning, pp. 331–339 (1995)
12. Liu, N.F., Gardner, M., Belinkov, Y., Peters, M.E., Smith, N.A.: Linguistic knowledge and transferability of contextual representations. In: Proceedings of the 2019 Conference of the North American Chapter of the Association for Computational Linguistics: Human Language Technologies, pp. 1073–1094 (2019)
13. Manning, C.D., Raghavan, P., Schütze, H.: Introduction to Information Retrieval. Cambridge University Press, Cambridge (2008)
14. Mekala, D., Gangal, V., Shang, J.: Coarse2fine: fine-grained text classification on coarsely-grained annotated data. In: Conference on Empirical Methods in Natural Language Processing, pp. 583–594 (2021)
15. Mohebbi, H., Modarressi, A., Pilehvar, M.T.: Exploring the role of BERT token representations to explain sentence probing results. In: Proceedings of the 2021 Conference on Empirical Methods in Natural Language Processing, pp. 792–806 (2021)
16. Qiao, Y., Xiong, C., Liu, Z., Liu, Z.: Understanding the behaviors of BERT in ranking. arXiv (2019)
17. Ramnath, S., Nema, P., Sahni, D., Khapra, M.M.: Towards interpreting BERT for reading comprehension based QA. In: Proceedings of the 2020 Conference on Empirical Methods in Natural Language Processing (EMNLP), pp. 3236–3242 (2020)
18. Rogers, A., Kovaleva, O., Rumshisky, A.: A primer in bertology: what we know about how BERT works. Trans. Assoc. Comput. Linguist. **8**, 842–866 (2021)
19. Sohoni, N., Dunnmon, J., Angus, G., Gu, A., Ré, C.: No subclass left behind: fine-grained robustness in coarse-grained classification problems. In: Advances in Neural Information Processing Systems, vol. 33, pp. 19339–19352. Curran Associates, Inc. (2020)
20. Suzgun, M., Melas-Kyriazi, L., Sarkar, S., Kominers, S.D., Shieber, S.: The Harvard USPTO patent dataset: a large-scale, well-structured, and multi-purpose corpus of patent applications. In: Advances in Neural Information Processing Systems (2024)
21. Wallat, J., Beringer, F., Anand, A., Anand, A.: Probing BERT for ranking abilities. In: Kamps, J., et al. (eds.) ECIR 2023. LNCS, vol. 13981, pp. 255–273. Springer, Cham (2023). https://doi.org/10.1007/978-3-031-28238-6_17

Studies on the Use of Large Language Models for the Automation of Business Processes in Enterprise Resource Planning Systems

Jonas Schnepf[1]([✉]), Tuğranur Engin[1], Simon Anderer[2],
and Bernd Scheuermann[1]

[1] Faculty of Management Science and Engineering,
University of Applied Sciences Karlsruhe, Karlsruhe, Germany
{jonas.schnepf,entu1011,bernd.scheuermann}@h-ka.de
[2] Pointsharp AB, Karlsruhe, Germany
simon.anderer@pointsharp.com

Abstract. Business processes in companies today are characterized by increasing digitalization and automation through the use of information systems such as enterprise resource planning (ERP) systems. To relieve the users of information systems of manual, repetitive and error-prone activities, a variety of process automation tools are available. However, applying such tools requires comprehensive process knowledge and an in-depth understanding of their concepts, implementation and use. Furthermore, previous automation tools lack in flexibility to react on changing conditions or process errors. This paper introduces an approach that applies large language models (LLM) to automate business processes in ERP systems to overcome the disadvantages of previous approaches. As SAP is the world's leading provider of ERP software, their ERP system was chosen to investigate the extent to which business process knowledge can be embodied in LLMs. It is examined how the possibility of natural language interaction provided by LLMs can be used to enhance the automation of the procure-to-pay process in SAP systems, as one core process and how process automation can be made stable against errors. In addition, the multi-agent framework AutoGen is used to simulate separation of duties (a concept for ensuring security in IT systems) and thus to investigate the involvement of multiple users in a business process.

Keywords: Large Language Models · Multi-Agent Collaboration · Business Process Automation · Enterprise Resource Planning

1 Introduction

Activities in information systems such as enterprise resource planning (ERP) systems are often complex, time-consuming, error-prone, or repetitive. Automation tools therefore provide support to relieve employees and increase productivity [2]. In particular, robotic process automation (RPA) has become a widely

A. Rapp et al. (Eds.): NLDB 2024, LNCS 14762, pp. 16–31, 2024.
https://doi.org/10.1007/978-3-031-70239-6_2

used technology [19]. RPA is defined as the "[...] application of technology that allows employees in a company to configure computer software or a 'robot' to capture and interpret existing applications for processing a transaction, manipulating data, triggering responses and communicating with other digital systems" [8]. The term 'robot' refers to a piece of software able to automate repetitive tasks [10]. Automating activities in ERP systems is an important use case [13] as ERP systems are widely used and SAP is the leading vendor of such software.

Existing publications highlight the weaknesses of RPA in automating business processes requiring human intelligence [1,3,14]. In addition, the application of RPA has so far been limited to independent and single processes [1]. New concepts have therefore been published using artificial intelligence (AI). For instance, chatbots for automation are considered to be a central research challenge [3]. Thus, large language models (LLM) are applied to automate complex decision-making processes through the interaction of users and robots [19,20].

ERP systems are used to coordinate, plan and control operational production factors in different business areas of an organization. A common business process in ERP systems suitable for automation through RPA is the procure-to-pay (P2P) process. However, this process can be carried out in countless variations, resulting in many different process deviations that usually occur in practice. As a result, teaching the robots is extremely time-consuming and labor-intensive [6]. In addition, deviating initial conditions, short-term changes to requirements and errors at runtime may render suitable automation even more difficult.

To cope with these challenges, this paper investigates the potential of LLMs to automate business processes using the P2P process in SAP ERP as example. The main contributions include: (1) Review of previous automation approaches. (2) Presentation of an LLM-based approach for the automation of SAP business processes based on AutoGen using a multi-agent workflow and function calls, and thus overcoming the disadvantages of other approaches. (3) Evaluation of the stability of the presented approach, thereby explaining different practice-relevant applications and highlighting the strengths of LLMs for process automation.

The remainder of this work is structured as follows: Sect. 2 reviews the related work. Section 3 introduces the AutoGen framework (Sect. 3.1), the P2P process (Sect. 3.2), and explores the process knowledge embodied in different LLMs (Sect. 3.3). The proposed business process automation approach is presented in Sect. 3.4. Section 4 outlines technical enhancements. Experiments are conducted to evaluate the stability of the approach (Sect. 5). Section 6 summarizes the main findings and provides an outlook on future research.

2   Related Work

One common approach for software automation purposes, including business processes in ERP systems, are RPA tools. Numerous scientific publications highlight the target applications and use cases of RPA. Ivančić et al. examine applications and trends of RPA [9]. Aguirre and Rodriguez also provide an overview of the advantages and applications. The authors emphasize an increase in productivity and speed, and a reduction in costs and errors [2]. Nalgozhina and Uskenbayeva highlight the use of RPA in managing warehouse processes [12]. Huang and Vasarhelyi describe the use of RPA tools in auditing to free auditors from repetitive and low-judgement tasks with the help of RPA [7]. Postolea and Bodea present an RPA-based solution that automatically extracts sales data from SAP ERP, creates a performance report, and sends it to the respective recipients [13].

Agostinelli et al. identify research challenges highlighting the weaknesses of RPA: Current tools have weaknesses in self learning, which describes the ability of RPA tools to independently detect actions that belong to a routine and which routines are suited to automation. Routines refer to parts of business processes that are potentially suitable for automation. Furthermore, flowcharts modeling the actions of robots cannot be automatically created, resulting in robots being tested based on trial and error, which is time-consuming, error-prone and less predictable. In addition, the automation of interrelated routines lags behind. Only single and independent routines are supported [1].

Ribeiro et al. review the existing literature examining the combination of RPA and AI. The authors state that the combination improves the accuracy and execution of RPA processes in the extraction of information, and in the recognition, classification, forecasting, and optimization of processes [14]. Chakraborti et al. describe the emerging paradigm of Intelligent Process Automation (IPA), which is evolving from RPA through the use of AI. The authors identify research opportunities that should enable the transformation from RPA to IPA. The integration of chatbots is considered to be one central research opportunity to minimize human involvement in the automation process [3].

Zeng et al. propose FlowMind to utilize the capabilities of LLMs in order to automatically generate a workflow for solving a given task. The authors state that RPA is not suitable for spontaneous and unpredictable tasks, as one must rely on expert knowledge and precisely defined workflows. Within FlowMind, an LLM receives a so-called lecture comprising domain knowledge, behavioral instructions, and a list of natural language descriptions of additional functions, which can be used to generate the workflow code for the given task. User feedback can also be integrated. The feasibility of FlowMind is demonstrated using a question and answer benchmark in the area of finance (NCEN-QA) [20].

Ye et al. suggest the use of LLMs in the ProAgent framework, as RPA tools are not sufficient if human intelligence is required in the process, which should be automated. The authors emphasize the ability of ProAgent to manage complex decision-making processes in order to support humans in challenging tasks. ProAgent constructs workflows based on natural language and takes any decisions within it. The use of ProAgent is illustrated by extracting information from documents and distributing the information based on predefined rules [19].

SAP uses its novel AI assistant Joule to provide support to ERP users for navigational (navigate to functionalities), transactional (efficient task completion), and informational (information retrieval) issues. Users can submit their queries via chat and receive a solution based on the analyzed company data. Automation of entire business processes, like P2P, is not considered [15].

Although several publications have dealt with the combination of RPA and AI, to the best of our knowledge, the automation of entire ERP business processes with LLMs has not yet been investigated.

3 Automation of ERP Business Processes Through LLMs

This section discusses the LLM-based business process automation approach. First, the framework AutoGen is introduced and the procure-to-pay (P2P) process is depicted. The knowledge of various LLMs with regard to SAP process is then evaluated and the automation approach is presented. For this purpose, an SAP ERP system based on SAP ECC 6.0 Enhancement Package 7 with a model company called IDES configured in a client is used. IDES is well-established and is used for research, teaching, and demonstration purposes.

3.1 AutoGen

AutoGen is an open-source framework from Microsoft. It is designed to create LLM applications empowering multiple agents to engage in conversations aimed at accomplishing tasks, which are provided in natural language [17]. A variety of publications suggest the use of such multiple agents to address real-world requirements with increasing complexity as they encourage divergent thinking, improve factuality and reasoning, and provide validation [4,11,18]. The source code and a detailed documentation on AutoGen are provided on GitHub[1]. AutoGen provides conversable and customizable agents in order to enable collaborative task solving. First, the agents are provided with a task passed by the AutoGen user proxy, which is utilized to include input and feedback from human users. In order to solve the given task, individual agents can be specified. An agent is defined by its profile consisting of a name, a system message corresponding to a natural language profile description, and a configuration of the used LLM (cf. Listing 1). This configuration is structured as a dictionary and contains the LLM name and the API key. Various LLMs from OpenAI as well as other open source LLMs can be assigned to the agents via the configuration. For the following sections, the LLMs GPT-3.5 Turbo, GPT-4, GPT-4 Turbo, LLaMA2 and Mistral are utilized.

```
purchaser = autogen.AssistantAgent(
    name = "Purchaser",
    system_message = "Use the functions you have been provided with. Reply
    TERMINATE when the task is done.",
    config = {"config_list": [{"model":"gpt-3.5-turbo","api_key":api_key}],
              "functions": [list_of_functions]})
```

Listing 1. Profile of the AutoGen Assistant Agent *Purchaser*.

The configuration can be extended by a list of functions. Each function is defined by a dictionary containing the function name, the function parameters

---

[1] https://github.com/microsoft/autogen

and an explanation of the function in natural language. Each of these dictionaries has a counterpart consisting of executable Python code. Using the configuration of the agent, the functions are made knowledgeable to the assigned LLM. As a result, the agent is capable to suggest the execution of these functions. However, the actual execution of the respective Python code is carried out by the user proxy. In this way, more complex tasks can be solved, like the execution of transactions in an SAP system (cf. Sect. 3.4). For the subsequent experiments, two agents are defined: the *Purchaser* and the *Purchasing Manager*. The agents comprise the same system message but differ in the functions specified in their configuration. The functions provided to the agents are depended on the considered scenario as outlined in the respective forthcoming sections.

3.2   The Procure-to-Pay Process in SAP Systems

The P2P process is one of the most important business processes in SAP systems, as it is executed to supply companies with the products needed to maintain their business operations. It is therefore selected to evaluate the potential of LLMs for business process automation. It usually consists of six consecutive activities, see business process model and notation (BPMN) diagram in Fig. 1.

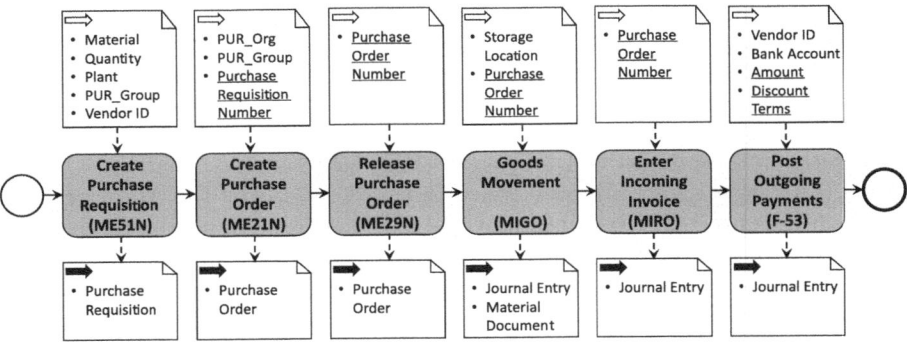

Fig. 1. P2P process in SAP with SAP transaction codes added in parentheses. According to BPMN, parameters required are depicted as data input and documents generated as data output. Underlined parameters are created in previous transactions.

The P2P process starts with the creation of a purchase requisition, which asserts a requirement to supply the company. The "Create Purchase Requisition" transaction is executed in SAP for this purpose (transaction code ME51N). A purchase requisition is an internal document that includes information on the required products, their quantities, the ID of the desired vendor, the plant for which the materials are procured, and the purchasing group (PUR_Group). This document can be used as a reference to create the subsequent purchase order (ME21N). In addition to the purchase requisition number, the purchase group and organization (PUR_Org) are required. Depending on the company's internal release strategy, a purchase order must first be released before it is sent to a vendor (ME29N). When the ordered products arrive, the delivery is verified, and a goods movement, or more precisely the goods receipt, is posted (MIGO). For this purpose, the storage location for the delivered products must be specified. A material document and a journal entry are created. The incoming vendor invoice is entered in the system and checked for correctness (MIRO). A journal entry is created. The entered vendor invoice generates payables. An outgoing payment is posted in order to settle these payables (F-53). As a result, the invoice amount is transferred from the company's bank account to the vendor's bank account.

3.3   LLM Knowledge on the P2P Process

Enabling LLM-based agents to correctly automate ERP business processes requires LLMs to provide a basic knowledge on such processes. The P2P process in SAP constitutes an important basis for the experiments in Sects. 4 and 5. In order to evaluate the depth of knowledge of different LLMs on the P2P process in SAP, the *Purchaser* as defined in Listing 1 is asked to perform Task 1. The *Purchaser* is equipped with the following LLMs one after the other in its configuration: GPT-3.5 Turbo (gpt-3.5-turbo-0613), GPT-4 (gpt-4-0613), GPT-4 Turbo (gpt-4-1106-preview), Mistral (Mistral-7B-Instruct-v0.1-GGUF), and LLaMA2 (LLama-2-7B-Chat-GGUF). Its list of functions is empty.

Task 1: "Explain how to book a procure-to-pay process in SAP ERP".

The completion responses are briefly presented hereinafter: The *Purchaser* equipped with GPT-3.5 Turbo proposes a 7-step process with the respective SAP transaction codes: create purchase requisition (ME51N), release purchase requisition (ME54N), create purchase order (ME21N), release purchase order (ME29N), goods receipt (MIGO), invoice verification (MIRO), and payment processing (F110). Equipping the *Purchaser* with GPT-4 results in a similar suggestion. However, the activities ME54N and ME29N are omitted. Compared to GPT-3.5 Turbo, GPT-4 Turbo omits the step ME54N. GPT-4 and GPT-4 Turbo specify the same SAP transactions codes as GPT-3.5 Turbo. Mistral provides a suggestion for executing the P2P process consisting of four steps: create purchase requisition, create purchase order, invoice verification, and payment processing. It proposes different SAP transaction codes compared to the OpenAI models. Task 1 appears to be interpreted differently by LLaMA2. It describes the possibility of automating the P2P process using Python and assumes a 3-step process only: create purchase order, goods receipt, and payment processing.

All LLMs demonstrate a more or less comprehensive knowledge of the SAP P2P process. Independent of the choice of the LLM, the *Purchaser* is not able to describe the exact P2P process from Sect. 3.2. However, this is not surprising as there exist many variants to carry out this process. The usage of the OpenAI models GPT-3.5 Turbo, GPT-4, and GPT-4 Turbo provide the closest match to the envisaged solution, which is why these will be used for further tests.

The three OpenAI models were used to conduct further experiments investigating the knowledge on various SAP business processes, like order-to-cash (O2C), or on individual transactions. Similar to the P2P process, a possible variant of the O2C process is described by specifying the correct transaction codes. The same applies to the description of individual SAP transactions.

3.4   Integration of LLMs with SAP ERP

Enabling the agents to execute the P2P process in SAP requires the agents to be provided with functions that allow them to interact with the SAP system and to control SAP transactions. A function is provided for each step of the P2P process (cf. Fig. 1). The shortened definition of the function "ME51N_create_purchase_requisition" is shown in Listing 2 as an example.

```
 1 def ME51N_create_purchase_requisition(material,amount,plant,PURgroup,vendor):
 2
 3     #Establish the connection to SAP GUI
 4     ...
 5
 6     #Enter SAP transaction code
 7     session.findById("wnd[0]/tbar[0]/okcd").text = 'ME51N'
 8     session.findById("wnd[0]").sendVKey(0)
 9
10     #Enter parameters and save purchase requisition
11     session.findById('wnd[0]/...').modifyCell(0,'MATNR',material)
12     ...
13     session.findById("wnd[0]/tbar[0]/btn[11]").press()
14
15     #Read message text
16     Text_ME51N = session.findById("wnd[0]/sbar/pane[0]").Text
17     session.findById("wnd[0]/tbar[0]/btn[15]").press()
18
19 return Text_ME51N
```

Listing 2. Python code for the function "ME51N_create_purchase_requisition".

The parameters for the function "ME51N_create_purchase_requisition" are a material identifier, the quantity, the plant to be supplied, the purchasing group, and the vendor ID. The parameters are indicated as data input in Fig. 1. Figure 2 shows the SAP GUI for the respective SAP transaction "Create Purchase Requisition" with the necessary parameters entered. SAP GUI describes both the graphical user interface and the program that provides and operates this interface. It represents the presentation layer in the client-server architecture.

The Python code for each function required to interact with the SAP system starts with the import of the module win32com.client, which allows component object models to be accessed and automated for interacting with applications, like SAP GUI. A connection to the SAP GUI is established by obtaining the root object. The scripting engine, connection objects and session objects are then retrieved to enable control of the SAP GUI. After accessing the SAP transaction, the parameters are entered, the purchase requisition is saved, and the return text (purchase requisition number) is read. The IDs of the individual fields can either be identified using the SAP GUI Property Collector or from macro-like scripts that can be recorded in SAP ERP. Using various commands, these fields can be assigned values, read out, buttons can be pressed, and check boxes can

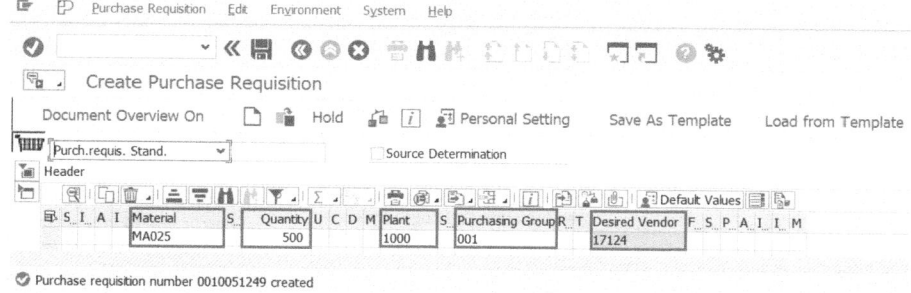

Fig. 2. SAP GUI for the transaction "Create Purchase Requisition" (ME51N). The required parameters are highlighted. The return text that is printed when the purchase requisition is successfully saved is displayed at the bottom.

be selected. For each step in the P2P process, a function is defined similar to Listing 2 and provided to the *Purchaser* as part of its configuration, see Fig. 3.

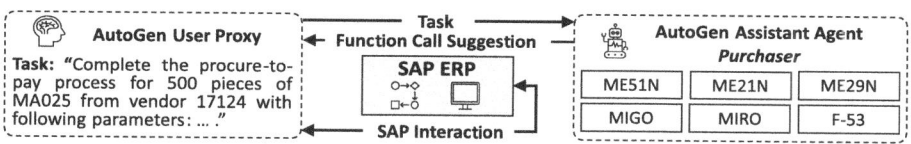

Fig. 3. Overview of the system configuration and data flow. The names of the functions assigned to the *Purchaser* are abbreviated to the corresponding SAP transaction codes.

Every transaction listed in the BPMN diagram in Fig. 1 returns a text message after execution. Figure 2 (bottom left) provides the return text of the transaction ME51N. Based on the natural language text comprehension of the LLM, the *Purchaser* is capable of identifying information in the return text of a function and deriving the relevant parameters for the next function, e.g. the purchase requisition number resulting from ME51N is required for the subsequent purchase order. Additional functions that extract parameters from return texts are therefore not necessary, which is a major advantage of the usage of LLMs. Tests have shown that the *Purchaser* equipped with these functions enables the entire P2P process to be executed independently of the LLM provided.

4 Technical Enhancements and Advantages of Automating SAP Processes with LLMs

This section explores advantages and technical enhancements of automating SAP business processes through LLMs to gain insight into the potential of the presented approach. For this purpose, three relevant application scenarios are examined: (1) error handling through the interaction with an expert, (2) independent development and execution of Python code to solve more complex tasks, and (3) separation of duties through the interaction of several agents (cf. Fig. 4). GPT-3.5 Turbo is used for the experiments, which provide a proof of concept for the efficacy of using LLMs in the three scenarios considered.

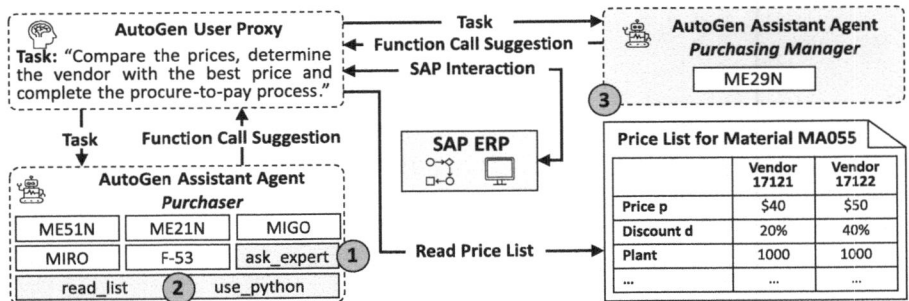

Fig. 4. Overview of the advantages and technical enhancements: (1) error handling, (2) Python code development and execution, and (3) separation of duties.

4.1   Error Handling

Error handling is a central aspect of automating business processes in order to avoid aborting or freezing. The following examples demonstrate the potential of error handling offered by the interaction of the *Purchaser* with a human user based on the user proxy. In contrast to RPA-based automation, an error does not lead to the process being aborted, but can be resolved using natural language. To enable the *Purchaser* to resolve errors, it is provided with the function "ask_expert" to suggest a user interaction. This function passes the error message on to the user, receives a response in natural language, and passes it back enabling the elimination of the following error types:

(1) Incorrect input parameters may arise if information is created or read incorrectly, i.e. by incorrectly naming the material, causing the SAP system to issue the error "The material is not available or not active". (2) Comprehension problems of the LLM may occur if, e.g. the delimiters of the balance are interpreted incorrectly due to the different delimiter rules in US and EU. When posting an outgoing payment, this results in the error message "The difference is too large for clearing". (3) Application issues may cause the running SAP transaction to get stuck or to be terminated unsuccessfully. This may be due to connection problems between the SAP GUI and the application server. The user proxy can therefore not execute the suggested functions as usual and thus receives the error message "The object invoked has disconnected from its clients".

Listing 3 shows the console output resulting from the interaction among the agents as well as the inclusion of user feedback to handle the parameter error (unknown material). However, the interaction is the same for all error types listed. The *Purchaser* restarts the function which it was unable to complete. A possible solution provided to the *Purchaser* for LLM comprehension problems (delimiter misinterpretation) is the provision of the correctly delimited amount. If the connection to SAP GUI is restored, the message "Try again where you left off" enables the *Purchaser* to be reactivated. In order to handle further error types, the error message must be available in natural language so that the agent can understand it and receive help using the "ask_expert" function.

```
purchaser (to user_proxy):
***** Suggested function Call: ME51N_create_purchase_requisition
Arguments: {"amount": "5", "material": "MA025e", ...}

>>>>>>>> EXECUTING FUNCTION ME51N_create_purchase_requisition...
user_proxy (to purchaser):
***** Response from calling function "ME51N_create_purchase_requisition"
The material MA025e is not available or not active

purchaser (to user_proxy):
***** Suggested function Call: ask_expert
Arguments: {"message": "The material MA025e is not available or not active.
    Please provide an alternative material."}

>>>>>>>> EXECUTING FUNCTION ask_expert...
The material MA025e is not available or not active. Please provide an
    alternative material.
Use material MA025 instead.

user_proxy (to purchaser):
***** Response from calling function "ask_expert"
Use material MA025 instead.

purchaser (to user_proxy):
***** Suggested function Call: ME51N_create_purchase_requisition
Arguments: {"amount": "5", "material": "MA025", ...}

>>>>>>>> EXECUTING FUNCTION ME51N_create_purchase_requisition...
user_proxy (to purchaser):
***** Response from calling function "ME51N_create_purchase_requisition"
Purchase requisition number 0010051229 created
```

Listing 3. Error handling due to incorrect input parameters.

4.2   Enabling AutoGen Assistant Agents for Code Development

One advantage of using AutoGen is the handover of functions. In addition to the functions described in the previous sections, the *Purchaser* can be provided with a function "use_python" that enables the development of Python code. This is especially valuable if the tasks provided are more challenging (cf. Task 2).

Task 2: "Compare the prices for the material MA055 in PriceList.txt and determine the vendor with the cheapest price after subtracting the discount. Complete the procure-to-pay process for 5 units of the identified material".

The necessary input parameters are not read directly from SAP (e.g. via SAP transaction SE16), instead they are provided in the "PriceList.txt" file in order to reduce complexity. In addition, the file contains a price and a discount column. An additional function "read_list" is provided enabling the *Purchaser* to suggest reading the file. If the *Purchaser* is to determine the cheapest price without consideration of the discount, the "use_python" function is not required, as the *Purchaser* can reliably determine the lowest price. However, solving Task 2 requires the "use_python" function. If this function is not provided, the *Purchaser* selects the vendor based on the lowest price without deducting the discount. Listing 4 contains an excerpt of the generated console output, which contains the Python code that the *Purchaser* suggests for execution.

```
purchaser (to user_proxy):
To determine the vendor with the cheapest price after subtracting the
    discount, we need to calculate the final price for each vendor.

***** Suggested function Call: python
Arguments: {"cell":"
purchase_price = [{'vendor':'17121','price':40,'discount':20}, ...]
final_price = []
for purchase in purchase_price:
    price = purchase['price']
    discount = purchase['discount']
    new_price = price - (price * discount / 100)
    final_price.append({'vendor':purchase['vendor'],'final_price':new_price
        })
final_price"}
```

Listing 4. Completion response from the *Purchaser* provided with Task 2.

The function "use_python" enables the *Purchaser* to develop Python code. In this way, agents are able to provide solutions to more challenging problems by developing code and having it executed by the user proxy. Here, the *Purchaser* is capable of suggesting a mathematical calculation to determine the purchase price without a precise indication of how the discount should be applied. It could be shown that agents are capable of providing the necessary code on the fly.

Academic research also provides a wide range of studies addressing the generation of code by LLMs [16,17]. This clearly highlights the vast potential of LLMs for code generation, which can be applied to support and simplify the execution of business processes. The agents could for example be used to extract information from documents and perform computations in order to generate the necessary insights that would otherwise have to be calculated manually or to be created by providing a dedicated software feature implemented by some human.

4.3   Separation of Duties Through Multi-agent Workflow

Separation of Duties (SoD) is a concept used to prevent fraud. SoD requires that no single system user is allowed to execute all transactions within a defined process. In ERP systems, SoD is implemented using access control mechanisms [5]. In order to ensure that LLM agents can only execute the same activities as their real-world counterparts, the six P2P process functions are now distributed to two agents. The *Purchasing Manager* is a copy of the *Purchaser* but is only capable of suggesting the execution of the function corresponding to transaction ME29N. The *Purchaser* is equipped with the five other functions, see Fig. 4. In this way, each purchase requisition undergoes a review process and has to be either released or rejected by the *Purchasing Manager*.

In the previous examples, the interaction between *Purchaser* and user is carried out via the user proxy. For the interaction of several agents, it is necessary to open a chat room moderated by a so-called chat manager. Listing 5 shows an excerpt of the console output resulting from the cooperative execution of the P2P process. This illustrates that the *Purchaser* and *Purchasing Manager* know in general when to suggest which transaction and are thus capable of respecting the constraints of the implemented SoD. For practical use, further aspects such as the internal release strategy need to be taken into account.

```
purchaser (to chat_manager):
***** Suggested function Call: ME51N_create_purchase_requisition
>>>>>>>> EXECUTING FUNCTION ME51N_create_purchase_requisition...

purchaser (to chat_manager):
***** Suggested function Call: ME21N_create_purchase_order
>>>>>>>> EXECUTING FUNCTION ME21N_create_purchase_order...

purchasing_manager (to chat_manager):
***** Suggested function Call: ME29N_release_purchase_order
>>>>>>>> EXECUTING FUNCTION ME29N_release_purchase_order...

purchaser (to chat_manager):
***** Suggested function Call: MIGO_receive_goods
>>>>>>>> EXECUTING FUNCTION MIGO_receive_goods...

purchaser (to chat_manager):
***** Suggested function Call: MIRO_verify_invoice
>>>>>>>> EXECUTING FUNCTION MIRO_verify_invoice...

purchaser (to chat_manager):
***** Suggested function Call: F-53_process_payment
>>>>>>>> EXECUTING FUNCTION F-53_process_payment...
```

Listing 5. Separation of Duties according to Fig. 4.

5 Experiments and Evaluation

This section examines the performance of the presented approach if multiple business processes are executed. Therefore, various experiments are conducted to examine the token limit and the behavior during multiple process execution. The LLMs used include GPT-3.5 Turbo, GPT-4, and GPT-4 Turbo, which revealed extensive knowledge on the P2P process (cf. Sect. 3.3). For the subsequent experiments the *Purchaser* is equipped with the six functions for the P2P process and the additional function "read_list" for reading in a purchase list.

5.1 Token Limit of LLMs

The token limit represents a technical limitation and specifies the maximum number of tokens the input and completion response of the LLM may contain. One token corresponds to approximately four chars in English. In order to determine the number of P2P process instances that can be executed completely, the

Purchaser is provided with a purchase list comprising all the necessary data for executing 40 complete P2P process instances and Task 3.

Task 3: "Read the file PurchaseList.csv. Each line corresponds to a planned purchase. Complete the procurement and payment for each of the planned purchases in turn".

Table 1 provides the respective token limit, the total number of completed process instances, and the number of additional transactions per LLM, which were still executed in the last incomplete process. For the subsequent experiments, it is therefore necessary to provide the purchase list in individual chunks (here: 5 instances) so that the LLM does not terminate before completion. Technical limitations, such as the token limit, must be taken into account when executing more extensive business processes and more complex tasks.

Table 1. Evaluation of the token limit per LLM.

LLM	Token Limit	Process Count	Additional Transactions
GPT-3.5 Turbo	4,096 tokens	5 instances	3
GPT-4	8,192 tokens	8 instances	1
GPT-4 Turbo	8,192 tokens	8 instances	1

5.2 Response of LLMs for Multi-process Execution

The response of GPT-3.5 Turbo, GPT-4, and GPT-4 Turbo for executing 100 complete P2P process instances is examined. Therefore, the *Purchaser* is again provided with Task 3. In contrast to Sect. 5.1, the purchase list contains data for the execution of 100 P2P process instances. Table 2 presents the results.

Table 2. Correctly executed P2P process instances and costs per LLM.

LLM	Correct Instances	Concurrent Executions	Costs
GPT-3.5 Turbo	96	25 processes	$1.67
GPT-4	99	–	$33.76
GPT-4 Turbo	100	–	$10.35

The use of GPT-3.5 Turbo resulted in 96 out of 100 correct process instances. Four instances failed due to the comprehension error described in Sect. 4.1. 71 of the 96 process instances were executed one after the other (cf. Fig. 1). For the 25 remaining instances, several P2P process instances were executed concurrently: For 15 instances all purchase requisitions were created first (ME51N), then all purchase orders were created (ME21N), all purchase orders were released (ME29N), all goods receipts were posted (MIGO), all vendor invoices were entered (MIRO), and finally all outgoing payments were posted (F-53). For five P2P process instances, all ME51N transactions are executed first, then all ME21N transactions, then alternately the ME29N and MIGO transactions and finally alternately the MIRO and F-53 transactions. For five instances, first all ME51N transactions and then alternately all ME21N, ME29N, MIGO, MIRO and F-53 transactions were executed. The usage of GPT-4 provided 99 out of 100 correct instances (identical error to GPT-3.5 Turbo). Utilizing GPT-4 Turbo resulted in 100 correct instances. In both cases, the correct process instances were executed on after the other. However, it should be mentioned that the incorrectly executed instances with GPT-3.5 Turbo and GPT-4 could have been prevented by using the "ask_expert" function discussed in Sect. 4.1. Moreover, the concurrent execution of several process instances is of no concern, as different execution variants exist in practice. The costs of the models differ significantly. GPT-3.5 Turbo is the least expensive. GPT-4 Turbo costs 6 times as much and GPT-4 20 times as much in this particular case. For the selected application scenarios the use of GPT-3.5 Turbo seems to be appropriate due to the extensive costs of GPT-4 and GPT-4 Turbo, and as occurring errors can be eliminated by the "ask_expert" function. In practice, the respective costs and errors that occur must be set in comparison in order to select the appropriate LLM.

6   Conclusion and Future Works

In this paper, a range of studies has been carried out to gain an impression of the capabilities of LLMs for the automation of SAP systems. Previous publications have already used LLMs to support automation approaches in various scenarios. However, the automation of entire business processes in ERP systems based on LLM agents has not yet been considered. It could be shown that this approach provides several significant advantages over previous approaches, like RPA. LLMs possess comprehensive knowledge of different business processes in ERP systems. The ability to understand natural language enables the assignment of tasks to agents in a simple manner. The profile of agents, which determines their behavior, can be defined just as easily. Further advantages of understanding natural language arise when handling errors or reading parameters for functions. In addition, the agents are able to solve problems independently by auto-generating Python code. Using the P2P process, the above-mentioned advantages could be impressively demonstrated. Aspects of future work may include extending the approach to other business processes and other ERP systems. Thereby it should be investigated which activities and business processes in SAP systems are suitable for automation, as a complete automation of the more than 10,000 SAP transactions is not feasible. The selected application scenarios highlight the potential of LLMs for automating ERP business processes. Increasing the complexity of the application scenarios offers another opportunity to evaluate the achievable level of process automation as future work.

Acknowledgments. The authors acknowledge the financial support by the Federal Ministry of Education and Research of Germany (KOEX, 16KIS1582).

References

1. Agostinelli, S., Marrella, A., Mecella, M.: Research challenges for intelligent robotic process automation. In: Di Francescomarino, C., Dijkman, R., Zdun, U. (eds.) BPM 2019. LNBIP, vol. 362, pp. 12–18. Springer, Cham (2019). https://doi.org/10.1007/978-3-030-37453-2_2
2. Aguirre, S., Rodriguez, A.: Automation of a business process using robotic process automation (RPA): a case study. In: Figueroa-García, J.C., López-Santana, E.R., Villa-Ramírez, J.L., Ferro-Escobar, R. (eds.) WEA 2017. CCIS, vol. 742, pp. 65–71. Springer, Cham (2017). https://doi.org/10.1007/978-3-319-66963-2_7
3. Chakraborti, T., et al.: From robotic process automation to intelligent process automation. In: Asatiani, A., et al. (eds.) BPM 2020. LNBIP, vol. 393, pp. 215–228. Springer, Cham (2020). https://doi.org/10.1007/978-3-030-58779-6_15
4. Du, Y., Li, S., Torralba, A., Tenenbaum, J. B., Mordatch, I.: Improving factuality and reasoning in language models through multiagent debate (2023). https://doi.org/10.48550/arXiv.2305.14325
5. Ferraiolo, D., Kuhn, R.: Role-based access control. In: National Computer Security Conference, Baltimore, USA (1992). https://doi.org/10.48550/arXiv.0903.2171
6. Geyer-Klingeberg, J., Nakladal, J., Baldauf, F., Veit, F.: Process mining and robotic process automation: a perfect match. In: International Conference on BPM, Sydney, Australia (2018)
7. Huang, F., Vasarhelyi, M.A.: Applying robotic process automation (RPA) in auditing: a framework. Int. J. Account. Inf. Syst. **35** (2019). https://doi.org/10.1016/j.accinf.2019.100433
8. Institute for Robotic Process Automation & Artificial Intelligence: What is Robotic Process Automation?
9. Ivančić, L., Suša Vugec, D., Bosilj Vukšić, V.: Robotic process automation: systematic literature review. In: Di Ciccio, C., et al. (eds.) BPM 2019. LNBIP, vol. 361, pp. 280–295. Springer, Cham (2019). https://doi.org/10.1007/978-3-030-30429-4_19
10. Lacity, M.C., Willcocks, L.P.: A new approach to automating services. MIT Sloan Manag. Rev. **58**, 41–49 (2016)
11. Liang, T., et al.: Encouraging Divergent Thinking in Large Language Models through Multi-Agent Debate (2023). https://doi.org/10.48550/arXiv.2305.19118
12. Nalgozhina, N., Uskenbayeva, R.: Automating hybrid business processes with RPA: optimizing warehouse management. In: International Workshop on Digital Soiety: In the Eve of the 6th Information Revolution, Almaty, Kazakhstan (2023). https://doi.org/10.1016/j.procs.2023.12.223
13. Postolea, I.D., Bodea, C.-N.: Building RPA solutions for customer-oriented processes automation. Issues Inf. Syst. **23**(2), 89–104 (2022). https://doi.org/10.48009/2_iis_2022_108
14. Ribeiro, J., Lima, R., Eckhardt, T., Paiva, S.: Robotic process automation and artificial intelligence in industry 4.0 - a literature review. Procedia Comput. Sci. **181**, 51–8 (2021). https://doi.org/10.1016/j.procs.2021.01.104
15. SAP Help Portal: What is Joule? (2024)
16. Wang, J., Chen, Y.: A review on code generation with LLMs: application and evaluation. In: IEEE International Conference on Medical Artificial Intelligence, Beijing, China (2023). https://doi.org/10.1109/MedAI59581.2023.00044

17. Wu, Q., et al.: AutoGen: enabling next-gen LLM applications via multi-agent conversation (2023). https://doi.org/10.48550/arXiv.2308.08155
18. Wu, Y., et al.: MathChat: converse to tackle challenging math problems with LLM agents (2023). https://doi.org/10.48550/arXiv.2306.01337
19. Ye, Y., et al.: PROAGENT: from robotic process automation to agentic process automation (2023). https://doi.org/10.48550/arXiv.2311.10751
20. Zeng, Z., et al.: FlowMind: automatic workflow generation with LLMs. In: Fourth ACM International Conference on AI in Finance, New York City, USA (2023). https://doi.org/10.1145/3604237.3626908

Efficient Knowledge Distillation: Empowering Small Language Models with Teacher Model Insights

Mohamad Ballout[✉], Ulf Krumnack, Gunther Heidemann, and Kai-Uwe Kühnberger

Institute of Cognitive Science, Osnabrueck University, 49074 Osnabrück, Germany
mohamad.ballout@uni-osnabrueck.de

Abstract. Enhancing small language models for real-life application deployment is a significant challenge facing the research community. Due to the difficulties and costs of using large language models, researchers are seeking ways to effectively deploy task-specific small models. In this work, we introduce a simple yet effective knowledge distillation method to improve the performance of small language models. Our approach utilizes a teacher model with approximately 3 billion parameters to identify the most influential tokens in its decision-making process. These tokens are extracted from the input based on their attribution scores relative to the output, using methods like saliency maps. These important tokens are then provided as rationales to a student model, aiming to distill the knowledge of the teacher model. This method has proven to be effective, as demonstrated by testing it on four diverse datasets, where it shows improvement over both standard fine-tuning methods and state-of-the-art knowledge distillation models. Furthermore, we explore explanations of the success of the model by analyzing the important tokens extracted from the teacher model. Our findings reveal that in 68% of cases, specifically in datasets where labels are part of the answer, such as multiple-choice questions, the extracted tokens are part of the ground truth.

Keywords: Large Language Models · Attribution-based Knowledge Distillation · Fine-tuning with Rationales

1 Introduction

Large language models are increasingly becoming integrated into our daily lives, with applications now extending to small devices such as phones and computers. However, the main challenge in this rapid development is the computational power required to run these large language models. The current state-of-the-art models, which have hundreds of billion of parameters, require hundreds of gigabytes of memory for operation. This level of computational power is only affordable for a limited number of research teams. This disparity is evident in the download numbers of smaller models versus larger models. For example,

A. Rapp et al. (Eds.): NLDB 2024, LNCS 14762, pp. 32–46, 2024.
https://doi.org/10.1007/978-3-031-70239-6_3

despite Llama2 [29] being a powerful open-source state-of-the-art model released in 2023, its downloads on Hugging Face [34] are significantly (around 10 times) lower than those of T5-base [21], a smaller language model released in 2019. This discrepancy has encouraged researchers to develop new methods for distilling knowledge from large models into smaller ones [3, 12, 14, 30], making them more feasible for integration on portable devices and accessible to a broader range of practitioners.

Knowledge distillation is a technique that leverages the knowledge of a larger, more complex model (the teacher) to train a smaller, more efficient model (the student) through teacher-student prediction alignment. One effective method within this framework is gradient-based knowledge distillation [33, 35]. In this approach, the gradient, which describes how the teacher model's predictions change in response to variations in inputs, is used as a guide for the student model. This guidance is beneficial for the student model to more accurately approximate the teacher model's underlying functionality and decisions, thereby enhancing the student's learning and performance.

Another proven and effective practice for enhancing the performance of large language models (LLMs) involves providing them with rationales. This enhancement can be implemented in two main ways. For larger models, particularly those with over 100 billion parameters, rationales can be incorporated by including step-by-step instructions in the prompt. Techniques such as the "Chain-of-Thought" [32] or "Tree-of-Thought" [36] methods are examples of this strategy. In contrast, smaller models are typically improved through fine-tuning with instructional data [2, 11, 17], as prompting smaller models with step-by-step instructions has not yet been demonstrated to be effective [32]. This fine-tuning approach allows smaller models to effectively integrate structured guidance, thereby enhancing their problem-solving capabilities and overall performance.

In this work, we introduce a novel yet straightforward and effective technique that combines gradient knowledge distillation with the provision of rationales to large language models (LLMs). Our proposed method involves fine-tuning a teacher model, approximately 3 billion parameters in size, and using this model to identify and extract the top-k important tokens from the input. These important tokens are then provided as rationales to the student model. The key tokens are determined using their gradient attribution, where we calculate the gradient of the model's prediction with respect to each input token based on the saliency map method [25]. In this method, the gradient value indicates the sensitivity of the model's prediction to changes in a specific token. A high gradient value for a token in the input suggests that minor changes in that token can lead to significant changes in the model's prediction, highlighting its importance in influencing the model's output. Conversely, a low gradient value implies that the token has a minimal impact on the prediction, indicating its lesser importance. After identifying the important tokens with high attribution values in the teacher model, we then feed these tokens to the student model as rationales, thereby enhancing its learning process and performance.

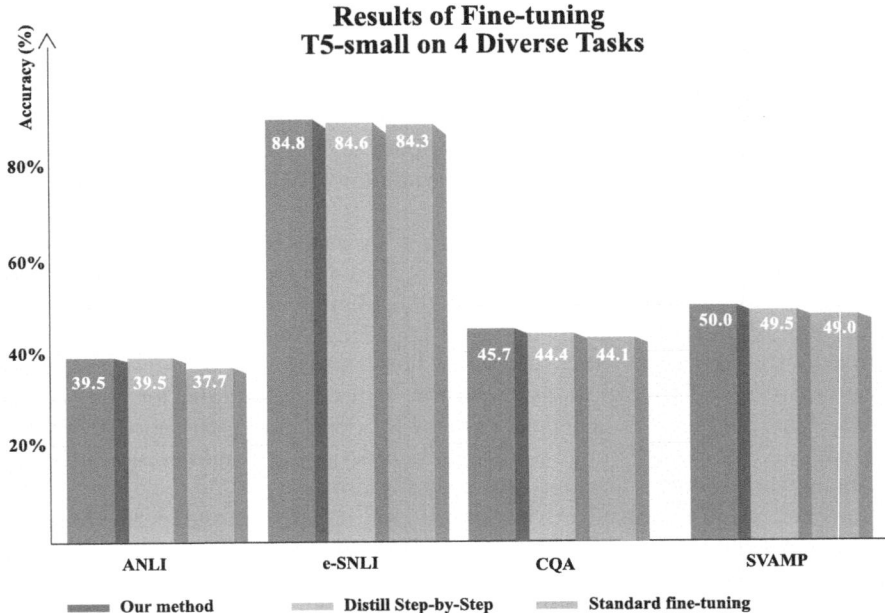

Fig. 1. The figure displays the performance of our proposed method across four diverse datasets: e-SNLI [5] and ANLI [19], which involve natural language inference; CQA [22, 27] focusing on commonsense question answering; and SVAMP [20], which deals with arithmetic word problems. We compare our method to both the standard fine-tuning method and the step-by-step distillation method.

In order to exemplify the procedure, consider an input from a dataset: "A boss may like an employee's ambition, so the employee may get put what? Choices are (a) in charge of project (b) conquer opponent (c) go to school (d) begin work (e) webisode". In our approach, we first calculate the attribution of each word in this input using the teacher model. Let's say the significant words identified are "boss", "employee", "charge", "ambition", and "what". Next, we fine-tune the student model not only to predict the correct answer but also to generate these key words as rationales. Consequently, the student model's output should be: "boss, employee, charge, ambition, what, so the answer is (a) in charge of project". The loss is calculated based on this entire output, while the accuracy is assessed solely based on the correctness of the answer, which in this case is "in charge of project". We tested this method on four diverse datasets and observed improvements compared to standard fine-tuning, as well as a distillation method that uses a very large model (540 billion parameters) [14] as demonstrated in Fig. 1.

2   Related Work

Due to the importance and the need to improve the performance of the smaller models, knowledge distillation is a hot topic that is grabbing plenty of attention recently. Another hot topic that is related to our work is providing rationales to LLMs in order to improve their performance. Thus this section is dedicated to review the work on these two topics.

Rationales. The use of rationales with language models started with large models [9,23,31,32,36] and eventually extended to smaller language models [2,13,16,17]. With large models methods like "Chain-of-thought" [32,37] gained popularity due to its effectiveness and its similarity of the human cognitive process. Instead of providing only the problem and its solution, the models are provided with few human examples of the intermediate steps that lead the model to predict the answer. The problem faced when using the same technique with smaller models is that they are not few shot learner, and generating human labeled step-by-step instruction is costly. Thus, a work around this problem is to make the large language model to generate step-by-step instructions for each sample in the dataset by providing the large model with few-shot examples on how to generate these steps. For example, [14] generated instructions for 4 different dataset using 540B PaLM model [7] after providing it with few examples on how to generate it. The benefits of our method over theirs is that first our teacher model is only 3 billion parameters compared to 540 billion parameters. Second, we did not need any human labeling to generate the rationales in contrast of theirs. With these two benefits in mind, our model was still able to perform better with the student model on multiple datasets.

Gradient-Based Knowledge Distillation. Knowledge distillation [1,12] is a successful method to transfer knowledge from a teacher model to a smaller model. It has been used with computer vision [3,6,18,24] and in NLP [8,10,14,28] and other deep learning applications. While attribution analysis methods like saliency maps [25], and Integrated Gradients (IG) [26] are used for interpretability of the models [4,15], few works have explored their use in knowledge distillation in what we can call gradient-based knowledge distillation [35]. In this paper [35], multi-view attribution maps of the teacher model are extracted and then the difference between the two normalized sets of maps in the teacher and student models is minimized using distance metrics like L2 distance. Our method requires less computation and is simpler to apply where we extract only the tokens that are attributing mostly to the output and providing them to the student model as rationales.

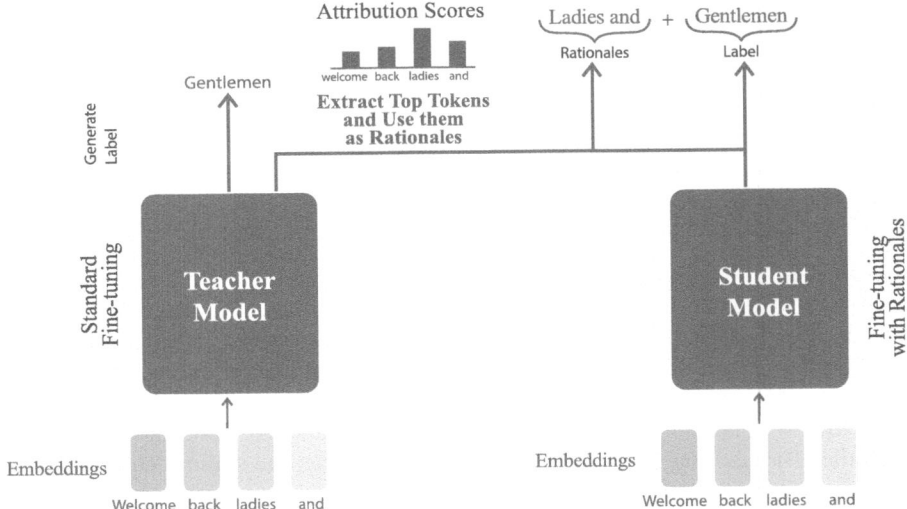

Fig. 2. The figure illustrates the pipeline of our proposed method, where tokens with the highest attribution scores, extracted from the teacher model, are used as rationales. The student model is then trained to generate these rationales, along with the original labels.

3   Methodology

3.1   Our Approach

Our method involves providing rationales generated by a teacher model, without human intervention, to a student model. Specifically, we fine-tune a teacher model, T5-flan-3b [8] in our case, on various datasets. Once the teacher model is fine-tuned, we identify the tokens that contribute most significantly to the output using the saliency map approach, a gradient-based attribution method. This involves computing the gradient of the model's output logits with respect to the input embeddings. We carry out a forward pass using the input embeddings and calculate the gradients for each token in the target sequence. These gradients are then averaged across all tokens in the target sequence. We determine the importance of each input token by computing the average gradient magnitude using the L1 norm. A high average gradient magnitude for a token suggests that it is influential in determining the model's output for the target sequence, while a low magnitude indicates lesser importance. The pipeline of this method is illustrated in Fig. 2.

Let $X = \{x_1, x_2, \ldots, x_n\}$ be the input tokens of the sentence, where n is the number of tokens. The input embeddings are denoted as $E = \{e_1, e_2, \ldots, e_n\}$, where e_i is the embedding vector of token x_i.

Let $f(E)$ be the function representing the forward pass of the model, mapping the input embeddings E to the output logits. The output logits for the target sequence are given by $O = f(E)$, where $O = \{o_1, o_2, \ldots, o_m\}$ and m is the number of tokens in the target sequence.

The gradient of the output logits with respect to the input embeddings is computed for each token in the target sequence. For each output logit o_j, the gradient with respect to the input embedding e_i is denoted as $\nabla_{e_i} o_j$. The gradients are calculated as follows:

$$\nabla_{e_i} O = \{\nabla_{e_i} o_1, \nabla_{e_i} o_2, \ldots, \nabla_{e_i} o_m\} \tag{1}$$

The average gradient for each input embedding is computed by averaging across all tokens in the target sequence. The average gradient for embedding e_i is given by:

$$\bar{G}_i = \frac{1}{m} \sum_{j=1}^{m} \nabla_{e_i} o_j \tag{2}$$

The importance of each input token is determined by computing the L norm of the average gradient for its embedding. The importance score I_i for token x_i is calculated as:

$$I_i = \|\bar{G}_i\|_1 = \sum_k |\bar{G}_i[k]| \tag{3}$$

In this equation, k indexes the elements (or dimensions) of the average gradient vector $\bar{G}_i$ for a given input embedding e_i. A high value of I_i implies that the token x_i is influential in shaping the model's output for the entire target sequence. Conversely, a low value of I_i suggests that the token x_i has lesser importance.

After identifying the top-k important tokens with high gradient magnitudes, we provide them to the smaller model to generate them as rationales in addition to the correct answer. We adopt the loss function from [14]. In standard fine-tuning, the cross-entropy loss ℓ between the predicted and target tokens, is calculated as shown in Eq. 4 where x is the input, y is the output.

$$\mathcal{L}_{\text{label}} = \frac{1}{N} \sum_{i=1}^{N} \ell(f(x_i), y_i) \tag{4}$$

In our study, similar to [14], we approach the integration of rationales into the learning process as a dual-objective task rather than merely incorporating them as extra inputs for the model. Specifically, we train our model, denoted as $f(x_i)$, to accomplish two goals: predicting the task labels y and generating the corresponding rationales r from the given text inputs. This approach is formalized as the combined loss function as shown in Eq. 5.

$$\mathcal{L} = \mathcal{L}_{\text{label}} + \lambda \mathcal{L}_{\text{rationale}} \tag{5}$$

where $\mathcal{L}_{\text{label}}$ is the loss associated with label prediction as outlined in Eq. 4, $\mathcal{L}_{\text{rationale}}$ represents the loss related to rationale generation, and λ is a hyperparameter that determines how much the rational loss affect the total loss. In our experiment, we set λ to 0.5. The rationale generation loss, which is expressed in Eq. 6 encourages the model to learn the intermediate reasoning that leads to its predictions. By doing so, it aims to enhance the model's capability by leveraging the generated tokens from the teacher model. r_i in the equation represents the rationales extracted from the teacher model.

$$\mathcal{L}_{\text{rationale}} = \frac{1}{N} \sum_{i=1}^{N} \ell(f(x_i), r_i) \tag{6}$$

3.2   Datasets

To compare our model with a state-of-the-art model, we utilized the same datasets as those used in [14]. These datasets encompass a range of tasks, including natural language inference, commonsense question answering, and arithmetic word problems.

For natural language inference, we employed the e-SNLI [5] and ANLI [19] datasets. In these datasets, the model is provided with premises and hypotheses and is required to predict whether the hypothesis is an entailment, a contradiction, or neutral with respect to the premise. For example, given the premise "This church choir sings to the masses as they sing joyous songs from the book at a church" and a hypothesis "A choir singing at a baseball game", the model must determine this hypothesis contradicts the premises since the choir is at a church not a baseball game.

Another dataset we used is CQA [22,27], which focuses on commonsense question answering. Here, the model is presented with an input question accompanied by five answer choices. A typical question might be: "A person with digestion issues eats a meat-filled breakfast, what does he feel?" with choices like ["heartburn", "overeating", "happiness", "being satisfied", "gain energy"]. The correct answer in this instance would be "heartburn".

Lastly, we evaluated our approach using the SVAMP dataset [20], which consists of arithmetic word problems. These problems require the model to generate a numerical answer. An illustrative problem might be: "Ed had 10 more marbles than Doug. Doug lost 11 of his marbles at the playground. If Ed had 45 marbles, how many more marbles did Ed have than Doug then?". The expected model response would be a calculation like "10.0 + 11.0", signifying the numerical solution to the problem.

By testing our model across these diverse datasets, we aimed to demonstrate its versatility and effectiveness in handling various types of language processing tasks.

4   Results

4.1   Results of Using Extracted Tokens as Rationales

In our study, we compare our proposed methods with two other approaches: standard fine-tuning, where the model is trained to generate a label from input, and the distillation step-by-step method [14]. The distillation step-by-step method utilizes a teacher model named Palm, which has approximately 540 billion parameters. This model is provided with a few human-labeled examples to generate step-by-step instructions. Conversely, our teacher model is Flan-T5-3b, with around 2.7 billion parameters. We employ the Hugging Face [34] implementation of these models, using a learning rate of 5e-5.

Our approach was tested on two small student models, t5-small and Flan-T5-small, each having around 60 million parameters. To replicate the results of [14], we used their provided code and hyper-parameters, adopting their fine-tuning process for the student models. We chose to extract and use 5 important tokens from the teacher model as rationales for the smaller model. The reason behind using 5 tokens will be discussed in a later section.

The results, as shown in Table 1, indicate that our approach outperforms standard fine-tuning on all datasets and also surpasses the distillation step-by-step method on all datasets except ANLI. This comparison highlights the effectiveness of our method, particularly in the context of smaller models where the balance between model size and performance is critical. Our findings suggest that extracting key tokens from a relatively smaller teacher model can significantly enhance the performance of student models across a variety of datasets.

Table 1. The table presents the results of fine-tuning T5-small using three approaches: standard fine-tuning, step-by-step distillation, and our method, across four different datasets.

T5-small	ANLI	e-SNLI	CQA	SVAMP
Standard fine-tuning	37.7	84.3	44.1	49.0
Dist. step-by-step	**39.5**	84.6	44.4	49.5
Ours	**39.5**	**84.8**	**45.7**	**50.0**

To verify the versatility of our method with different models, we tested our approach using a more advanced model, FLAN-T5-small. Table 2 presents the results of this test, demonstrating the effectiveness of our method compared to the standard fine-tuning approach. When FLAN-T5-small is used as the baseline model, our method shows improvements on all datasets compared to standard fine-tuning, with the exception of SVAMP.

Table 2. The table presents the results of fine-tuning Flan-T5-small using three approaches: standard fine-tuning, step-by-step distillation, and our method, across four different datasets.

Flan-T5-small	ANLI	e-SNLI	CQA	SVAMP
Standard fine-tuning	39.6	87.2	48.4	**53.0**
Dist. step-by-step	40.2	87.6	**49.3**	53.0
Ours	**40.3**	**87.8**	49.0	52.0

4.2   The Effect of Number of Words

To analyze the impact of the number of "important" words used as rationales in the student model, we conducted fine-tuning experiments on the T5-small model using a range of values for "k", where "k" represents the number of important words extracted from the teacher model. These experiments were performed on the ANLI and CQA dataset, with "k" varying from 1 to 10.

Figure 3 illustrates the outcomes of these experiments. It shows that improvement over the baseline standard fine-tuning begins with the inclusion of just one word extracted from the teacher model as a rationale. This enhancement continues to increase as we include up to four words. However, when using between 4 to 6 words, the accuracy experiences fluctuations, and beyond six words, there is a noticeable drop in performance.

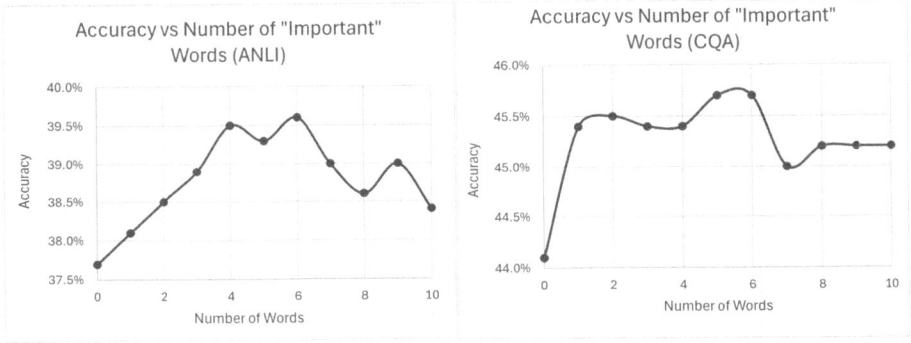

Fig. 3. The figure shows the performance of the model versus the number of tokens provided as rationales

From these observations, we conclude that the model can indeed benefit from incorporating as few as one word and up to ten words as rationales. Nevertheless, the optimal number of words, or the "sweet spot", appears to be around five. Therefore, in our experiments, we adopted five as the standard number of important words to use as rationales.

The implication of these results is multifaceted. First, it confirms that strategic "hints" from a larger teacher model can enhance the learning efficiency of a smaller student model, mirroring a focused guidance approach. Too much information, conversely, can overwhelm the model, akin to information overload in humans, which can impede rather than facilitate understanding. Moreover, the consideration of context, such as the input length in datasets like CQA, which may feature inputs as brief as twelve words, further supports the rationale behind limiting hints to five words. Providing nearly the entire input as a hint can dilute the effectiveness of the distillation process.

4.3   Random Words as Rationales

In this section, to verify that the improvement in our model's performance is not due to random factors, we conducted a controlled experiment. Instead of feeding the model with the most important tokens, which are identified based on the highest attribution scores, we provided it with five random words from the input. This test aimed to assess the impact of using non-targeted words compared to strategically selected ones. As anticipated and detailed in Table 3, the introduction of random words instead of the most significant tokens led to a decline in the model's performance on the CQA dataset. This result underscores the importance of selecting appropriate, influential words for enhancing model effectiveness.

Table 3. The table displays the accuracy of fine-tuning T5-small under three conditions: without using any words as rationales, with words extracted from flan-t5-3b used as rationales, and with random words used as rationales.

Teacher	Accuracy
No Teacher	44.1%
Flan-T5-3b	45.7%
Random words	42.1%

5   Discussion

5.1   Token Analysis Efficacy with the Teacher Model

We further explored our method by analyzing the words extracted from the teacher model, aiming to understand why it is effective. This investigation focused on the CQA dataset, which is well-suited for this analysis because it consists of multiple-choice questions with answers provided in the input. Our approach involved comparing the top-5 important tokens extracted by the teacher model with the ground truth label. For example, consider a dataset input: "A boss may like an employee's ambition, so the employee may get put what? Choices are (a) in charge of project (b) conquer opponent (c) go to school (d) begin work (e) webisode," where the correct answer is (a) in charge of project. We then examined whether any of the top-5 important tokens, are part of the ground truth such as "charge" or "project" in this case. Our findings indicate that in around 68% of cases, the correct answer, or a part of it, is among these top 5 most influential tokens. Furthermore, we observed that even when the correct answer is not directly among the important tokens, these tokens are still contextually related. For instance, if the answer is "monkey", the important tokens might include "banana". Similarly, if the answer is "New York City", the important tokens could be "empire", "state", "location", and for "hotel", they might include "book", "room". This pattern suggests that the extracted tokens, even when not directly answering the question, are relevant and contribute to understanding the context of the question.

5.2 Similarity Between Compared Models

In this section, we aim to gain deeper insights into the differences between two methods by comparing the predictions made by the distillation step-by-step model and our model. Our investigation focuses on two scenarios: instances where both models correctly predict the answer, and instances where both models make an incorrect prediction, specifically examining whether the incorrect predictions are similar.

Initially, we assess the proportion of instances where both models correctly predict the answers. The results, presented in Table 4, indicate a high degree of overlap in correct predictions across three datasets. For instance, in the ANLI dataset, 95.2% of the answers correctly predicted are the same for both models. This suggests that when the distillation step-by-step model accurately predicts an answer, there is a 95.2% likelihood that our model will also predict correctly.

Table 4. Table shows the percentage of overlapping correct predictions by the distillation Step-by-Step model and our model across different datasets.

Dataset	Random Chance	Similarity
ANLI	33.3%	95.2%
e-SNLI	33.3%	95.5%
CQA	20.0%	85.1%
SVAMP	–	81.1%

Conversely, Table 5 reveals that the models also have a high likelihood of making the same incorrect prediction. Specifically, in the ANLI dataset, where the task involves a three-way classification problem (entailment, contradiction, and neutral), there is a 91.1% chance that if the distillation step-by-step model incorrectly predicts an entailment relation between the hypothesis and the premise, our model will also incorrectly predict the same.

The high overlap in correct predictions between the models underscores their capability to similarly interpret and analyze the data, reflecting their effectiveness in learning from the training set. On the other hand, the significant concordance in incorrect predictions highlights potential systematic errors or biases that both models may share, possibly due to similarities in their training data or inherent model architectures.

5.3 Integrated Gradients Method

In our research, we also explored an advanced gradient attribution method known as Integrated Gradients (IG) [26], which offers a more sophisticated

Table 5. Table shows the percentage of similar incorrect predictions between the distillation Step-by-Step model and our model across various datasets.

Dataset	Random Chance	Similarity
ANLI	33.3%	91.1%
e-SNLI	33.3%	90.8%
CQA	20.0%	90.4%
SVAMP	–	87.2%

analysis of feature importance in deep neural networks. Integrated Gradients overcomes several limitations found in simpler attribution methods, such as gradient saturation and insensitivity to certain model behaviors. It achieves this by integrating the gradients of the model's output relative to its inputs along a straight-line path from a chosen baseline (typically a non-informative input) to the actual input.

However, implementing this method is computationally intensive. Consequently, we applied it to the SVAMP dataset, which has a relatively small number of training samples (only 800). The results from this experiment were not as promising as we had hoped. We observed no improvement in the performance of the t5-small model using Integrated Gradients compared to simpler attribution methods. The accuracy remained at 50.0% on the SVAMP dataset. This finding suggests that using a more advanced method like Integrated Gradients to extract the top-k important tokens does not necessarily confer any advantage in this context.

6   Limitation

Our research demonstrates an effective and straightforward approach for generating rationales from a large model to enhance a smaller model. However, a significant performance gap between the teacher model (the large model) and the student model (the small model) still exists. As illustrated in Table 6, the flan-t5-3b, which serves as the teacher model, significantly outperforms the smaller t5-small model across all four datasets we tested.

This limitation underscores the inherent challenge in knowledge distillation and model scaling. While our method effectively transfers knowledge from a large to a small model, the reduced capacity of the smaller model limits its ability to fully replicate the performance of its larger counterpart. This performance discrepancy highlights the trade-offs involved in model downsizing, where gains in efficiency and deployability often come at the cost of reduced accuracy and overall capability.

Addressing this gap remains a key area for future research. Efforts could focus on developing more advanced distillation techniques or optimizing small models to better capture and utilize the knowledge transferred from larger models. Our findings lay the groundwork for such exploration, offering insights into the dynamics of knowledge transfer between models of varying sizes and complexities.

Table 6. The table compares the performances of the teacher model and the distilled student models.

Model	Base Model	# Param.	ANLI	e-SNLI	CQA	SVAMP
Dist. step-by-step	T5-small	60M	39.5	84.6	44.4	49.5
Ours	T5-small	60M	39.5	84.8	45.7	50.0
FLAN-T5-3b	FLAN-T5-3b	2.7B	**67.3**	**93.1**	**81.4**	**86.0**

7   Conclusion and Outlook

In this work, we demonstrated an effective approach to distilling knowledge into student models by calculating the attribution scores of the teacher model's input and using them as rationales for the student model. This method is based on the theory that a high gradient value for a token in the input indicates that minor changes in that token can significantly impact the model's prediction, emphasizing its importance in influencing the model's output. Conversely, a low gradient value suggests that the token has minimal effect on the prediction, signifying its lesser importance.

We tested our method on four diverse datasets, which included tasks in natural language inference, commonsense question answering, and arithmetic word problems. The results showed that using t5-small as the student model, our method enhances performance across these datasets. Additionally, we explored why this method is effective by analyzing the top important tokens used as rationales. Particularly in the multiple-choice CQA dataset, where the answer is included in the input, we found that the top-5 extracted tokens contain the answer or a part of it 68% of the time.

While our method offers a simple and effective means of knowledge distillation, there is still a significant performance gap between the teacher and student models, with the teacher model outperforming the student by a large margin. We hope that this work contributes to the field of knowledge distillation and inspires further research to narrow the gap between large and small models. This endeavor is crucial for advancing the efficiency and applicability of language models in various real-world scenarios.

References

1. Agarwal, R., Vieillard, N., Stanczyk, P., Ramos, S., Geist, M., Bachem, O.: GKD: generalized knowledge distillation for auto-regressive sequence models. arXiv preprint arXiv:2306.13649 (2023)

2. Ballout, M., Krumnack, U., Heidemann, G., Kuehnberger, K.U.: Show me how it's done: the role of explanations in fine-tuning language models. arXiv preprint arXiv:2402.07543 (2024)
3. Beyer, L., Zhai, X., Royer, A., Markeeva, L., Anil, R., Kolesnikov, A.: Knowledge distillation: a good teacher is patient and consistent. In: Proceedings of the IEEE/CVF Conference on Computer Vision and Pattern Recognition, pp. 10925–10934 (2022)
4. Brunner, G., Liu, Y., Pascual, D., Richter, O., Ciaramita, M., Wattenhofer, R.: On identifiability in transformers. In: 8th International Conference on Learning Representations (ICLR 2020) (Virtual) (2020)
5. Camburu, O.M., Rocktäschel, T., Lukasiewicz, T., Blunsom, P.: e-SNLI: natural language inference with natural language explanations. In: Advances in Neural Information Processing Systems, vol. 31 (2018)
6. Cho, J.H., Hariharan, B.: On the efficacy of knowledge distillation. In: Proceedings of the IEEE/CVF International Conference on Computer Vision, pp. 4794–4802 (2019)
7. Chowdhery, A., et al.: PaLM: scaling language modeling with pathways. J. Mach. Learn. Res. **24**(240), 1–113 (2023)
8. Chung, H.W., et al.: Scaling instruction-finetuned language models. arXiv preprint arXiv:2210.11416 (2022)
9. Cobbe, K., et al.: Training verifiers to solve math word problems. arXiv preprint arXiv:2110.14168 (2021)
10. Fu, Y., Peng, H., Ou, L., Sabharwal, A., Khot, T.: Specializing smaller language models towards multi-step reasoning. arXiv preprint arXiv:2301.12726 (2023)
11. Hase, P., Bansal, M.: When can models learn from explanations? A formal framework for understanding the roles of explanation data. In: LNLS 2022, vol. 29 (2022)
12. Hinton, G., Vinyals, O., Dean, J.: Distilling the knowledge in a neural network. arXiv preprint arXiv:1503.02531 (2015)
13. Ho, N., Schmid, L., Yun, S.Y.: Large language models are reasoning teachers. arXiv preprint arXiv:2212.10071 (2022)
14. Hsieh, C.Y., et al.: Distilling step-by-step! outperforming larger language models with less training data and smaller model sizes. arXiv preprint arXiv:2305.02301 (2023)
15. Li, J., Chen, X., Hovy, E., Jurafsky, D.: Visualizing and understanding neural models in NLP. In: Proceedings of the 2016 Conference of the North American Chapter of the Association for Computational Linguistics: Human Language Technologies. Association for Computational Linguistics (2016)
16. Li, S., et al.: Explanations from large language models make small reasoners better. arXiv preprint arXiv:2210.06726 (2022)
17. Magister, L.C., Mallinson, J., Adamek, J., Malmi, E., Severyn, A.: Teaching small language models to reason. arXiv preprint arXiv:2212.08410 (2022)
18. Mishra, A., Marr, D.: Apprentice: using knowledge distillation techniques to improve low-precision network accuracy. In: International Conference on Learning Representations (2018)
19. Nie, Y., Williams, A., Dinan, E., Bansal, M., Weston, J., Kiela, D.: Adversarial NLI: a new benchmark for natural language understanding. arXiv preprint arXiv:1910.14599 (2019)
20. Patel, A., Bhattamishra, S., Goyal, N.: Are NLP models really able to solve simple math word problems? In: Proceedings of the 2021 Conference of the North American Chapter of the Association for Computational Linguistics: Human Language Technologies, pp. 2080–2094 (2021)

21. Raffel, C., et al.: Exploring the limits of transfer learning with a unified text-to-text transformer. J. Mach. Learn. Res. **21**(1), 5485–5551 (2020)
22. Rajani, N.F., McCann, B., Xiong, C., Socher, R.: Explain yourself! leveraging language models for commonsense reasoning. In: Proceedings of the 57th Annual Meeting of the Association for Computational Linguistics, pp. 4932–4942 (2019)
23. Sanh, V., et al.: Multitask prompted training enables zero-shot task generalization. In: ICLR 2022-Tenth International Conference on Learning Representations (2022)
24. Shen, Z., Savvides, M.: Meal v2: boosting vanilla resnet-50 to 80%+ top-1 accuracy on imagenet without tricks. arXiv preprint arXiv:2009.08453 (2020)
25. Simonyan, K., Vedaldi, A., Zisserman, A.: Deep inside convolutional networks: visualising image classification models and saliency maps. In: Proceedings of the International Conference on Learning Representations (ICLR) (2014)
26. Sundararajan, M., Taly, A., Yan, Q.: Axiomatic attribution for deep networks. In: International Conference on Machine Learning, pp. 3319–3328. PMLR (2017)
27. Talmor, A., Herzig, J., Lourie, N., Berant, J.: Commonsenseqa: a question answering challenge targeting commonsense knowledge. In: Proceedings of the 2019 Conference of the North American Chapter of the Association for Computational Linguistics: Human Language Technologies (Volume 1: Long and Short Papers), pp. 4149–4158 (2019)
28. Tan, X., Ren, Y., He, D., Qin, T., Zhao, Z., Liu, T.Y.: Multilingual neural machine translation with knowledge distillation. In: International Conference on Learning Representations (2018)
29. Touvron, H., et al.: Llama 2: open foundation and fine-tuned chat models. arXiv preprint arXiv:2307.09288 (2023)
30. Wang, L., Li, L., Sun, X.: Gradient knowledge distillation for pre-trained language models. arXiv preprint arXiv:2211.01071 (2022)
31. Wei, J., et al.: Finetuned language models are zero-shot learners. In: International Conference on Learning Representations (2021)
32. Wei, J., et al.: Chain-of-thought prompting elicits reasoning in large language models. In: Advances in Neural Information Processing Systems, vol. 35, pp. 24824–24837 (2022)
33. West, P., et al.: Symbolic knowledge distillation: from general language models to commonsense models. In: Proceedings of the 2022 Conference of the North American Chapter of the Association for Computational Linguistics: Human Language Technologies, pp. 4602–4625 (2022)
34. Wolf, T., et al.: Huggingface's transformers: state-of-the-art natural language processing. arXiv preprint arXiv:1910.03771 (2019)
35. Wu, S., Chen, H., Quan, X., Wang, Q., Wang, R.: AD-KD: attribution-driven knowledge distillation for language model compression. arXiv preprint arXiv:2305.10010 (2023)
36. Yao, S., et al.: Tree of thoughts: deliberate problem solving with large language models. arXiv preprint arXiv:2305.10601 (2023)
37. Zhang, Z., Zhang, A., Li, M., Zhao, H., Karypis, G., Smola, A.: Multimodal chain-of-thought reasoning in language models. arXiv preprint arXiv:2302.00923 (2023)

Text Role Classification in Scientific Charts Using Multimodal Transformers

Hye Jin Kim(ID), Nicolas Lell$^{(\boxtimes)}$(ID), and Ansgar Scherp(ID)

Ulm University, Ulm, Germany
{hye.kim,nicolas.lell,ansgar.scherp}@uni-ulm.de

Abstract. Text role classification involves classifying the semantic role of textual elements within scientific charts. We propose to finetune the multimodal document layout analysis models LayoutLMv3 and UDOP for this task. The transformers utilize the three modalities of text, image, and layout as input. We further investigate how data augmentation and balancing methods affect performance. The models are evaluated on various chart datasets, and results show that LayoutLMv3 outperforms UDOP in all experiments. LayoutLMv3 achieves the highest F1-macro score of 82.87 on the ICPR22 test dataset, beating the best-performing model from the ICPR22 CHART-Infographics challenge. Moreover, the robustness of the models is tested on a synthetic noisy dataset ICPR22-N. Finally, the generalizability of the models is evaluated on three chart datasets, CHIME-R, DeGruyter, and EconBiz, for which we added labels for the text roles. Findings indicate that even in cases where there is limited training data, transformers can be used with the help of data augmentation and balancing methods. The source code and datasets are available on GitHub: https://github.com/hjkimk/text-role-classification.

Keywords: Multimodal Transformers · Document Layout Analysis · Text Role Classification

1 Introduction

Writing a scientific paper is a long and tedious process. There are many systems available to edit the textual content of papers such as tools to check spelling and grammar, including Grammarly[1]. Similarly, some tools check the image content of scientific papers (e.g., scientific figures) including JetFighter[2], which examines figures to improve the data presentation.

Scientific figures are an important part of scientific papers for visualizing information. Therefore, a feedback system dedicated to scientific figures may save time and also improve the overall comprehensibility of a paper. One function of such a system that could support the authors is checking whether scientific charts have the necessary elements (e.g., title, axis labels, axis ticks, and legend).

---

[1] https://www.grammarly.com.

[2] https://elifesciences.org/labs/c2292989/jetfighter-towards-figure-accuracy-and-accessibility.

© The Author(s), under exclusive license to Springer Nature Switzerland AG 2024
A. Rapp et al. (Eds.): NLDB 2024, LNCS 14762, pp. 47–61, 2024.
https://doi.org/10.1007/978-3-031-70239-6_4

In some cases, authors forget to include these elements which can hamper the readability of charts. In the literature, this task is called text role classification [1, 6,8,9,23,24]. It aims to identify the semantic role of the text objects embedded in charts.

There is only few research on text role classification in scientific charts. Although there exists the Challenge on Harvesting Raw Tables from Infographics (CHART-Infographics), in which one of the tasks is dedicated to text role classification [6,8,9], there are no publications of the best-performing methods used in the competition. Outside of the competition, there have only been a few publications on text role classification [19,23,27]. Furthermore, while the performance of text role classification models on synthetically created datasets is near perfect, there is a drastic drop in performance on real world datasets.

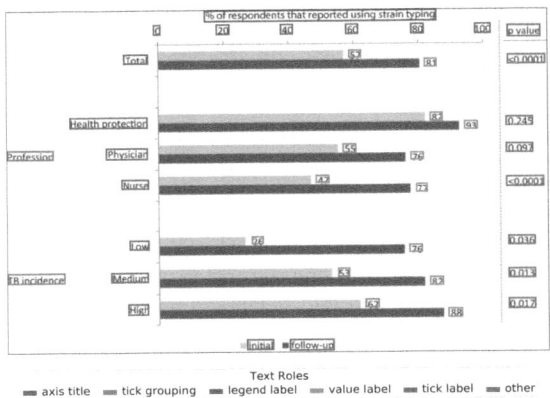

Fig. 1. A sample bar chart from ICPR22. The chart image, text, and the text bounding box coordinates are used as multimodal input to the transformers.

The motivation of this work is to improve the performance of text role classification by using transformers with multimodal data, namely the chart image[3], the text elements within the chart, and their position. An example of this multimodal chart data can be found in Fig. 1. More specifically, we examine whether using multimodal transformers pretrained on large document datasets (i.e., document analysis models) can be finetuned for text role classification. In addition, we investigate whether data augmentation and balancing techniques improve the performance of these models. Moreover, there are no prior experiments measuring the generalizability of the models to new chart data and the robustness of text role classification models to noise. Therefore, the models are evaluated on three chart datasets with added labels for the text role classes CHIME-R,

---

[3] For clarification, the term "image" in this paper refers to an image of a single scientific chart. To be consistent with the work on CHART-Infographics, the term "chart" will be used in this paper.

DeGruyter, and EconBiz. The robustness of the models is also analyzed on a noisy chart dataset ICPR22-N. In summary, our contributions are:

- We finetune two top-performing document layout analysis models LayoutLMv3 and UDOP for text role classification. Comparing the performances of the models to two baseline models from the ICPR 2022 CHART-Infographics competition [9] and CACHED [27], LayoutLMv3 finetuned on ICPR22 achieves the highest F1-macro score of 82.87 and an F1-micro score of 93.99.
- Data augmentation and balancing methods are used to increase the performance of the models. While applying data augmentation and balancing improves the F1-micro and macro score on ICPR22 for UDOP, there is only a minor improvement of the F1-micro score for LayoutLMv3.
- We evaluate the generalizability of the models on CHIME-R, DeGruyter, and EconBiz. LayoutLMv3 outperforms UDOP on all three datasets. For both models, finetuning on all chart datasets with data augmentation and balancing generally results in the best F1 scores. Furthermore, the robustness of the models is assessed on ICPR22-N, revealing that LayoutLMv3 is more robust to noise compared to UDOP. While data augmentation and balancing methods improve the model robustness of UDOP on ICPR22-N, it does not do so for LayoutLMv3.
- Three chart datasets CHIME-R, DeGruyter, and EconBiz are labeled to include text role class information for each text element. In addition, a synthetic but realistic noisy dataset ICPR22-N is created.

2 Related Work

We introduce works on multimodal models and text role classification. The two layout analysis models used in this paper for text role classification, LayoutLMv3 [17] and UDOP [22], are multimodal transformers.

2.1 Multimodal Models

BERT [10] and ViT [12] are popular unimodal models. The nature of the text role classification task is multimodal. An example of a multimodal task found in the literature is image-text classification where the objective is to classify image-text pairs into their correct label [13,18,20]. MMBT [18] achieves this task by concatenating image embeddings from ResNet [16] to BERT text embeddings with a segment embedding to inform the model which part of the input corresponds to text and which to the image.

More recent multimodal models avoid reliance on convolutions. CLIP [20] uses jointly trained transformer encoders for the image and text modalities. CMA-CLIP [13] uses CLIP as backbone in addition to sequence-wise attention, which concatenates image and text embeddings, and a subsequent modality-wise attention module, which weighs the two aggregated embeddings based on how relevant each modality is to the downstream task.

For text role classification, the layout of the chart is important to consider because there are common assumptions of the layout based on the chart type. For example, line and bar charts usually have axis labels while pie charts do not. One domain related to chart analysis is document layout analysis. Charts and documents both contain text and images and usually have some sort of structure. LayoutLM [26] is a BERT-like pretrained model that jointly learns text and layout information obtained from the bounding box coordinates of the text. A separate image model is used to extract the image embeddings, which are combined with the LayoutLM embeddings to perform downstream tasks during finetuning. LayoutLMv2 [25] is an improvement of LayoutLM, where image embeddings from a CNN-based image encoder are concatenated with the text embeddings during pretraining. For the layout information, 1D position, 2D position, and segment embeddings are provided. LayoutLMv3 [17] mitigates the use of CNNs for extracting visual features by using linear embeddings of flattened image patches. Image embeddings are concatenated with text embeddings and the transformer is provided with spatial information from the 1D and 2D position embeddings. LayoutLMv3 is pretrained using Masked Language Modeling (MLM) for text, Masked Image Modeling (MIM) which is a similar technique to MLM for images, and Word-Patch Alignment (WPA) to learn the correspondence between the text and image embeddings. Instead of using a pretraining objective, UDOP [22] is a sequence-to-sequence generative transformer that uses a layout-induced vision-text embedding by calculating the joint representation of image patches that contain text. This means that UDOP only employs one encoder to represent the multimodal input. However, it uses two different decoders, one for vision and another for text-layout to generate outputs.

2.2 Text Role Classification

Text role classification is comparable to document region classification [2], a document layout analysis task that aims to classify the role of segmented regions of documents. Nonetheless, there are two main differences between text role classification and document region classification. First, while text role classification is specialized to text in charts, document layout analysis classifies the roles of document regions that are not necessarily text (e.g., tables and images). Second, although text role classification can be performed on documents that contain charts, document layout analysis cannot be done on charts.

Early work on text role classification applied heuristic-based methods using a combination of classifiers based on Support Vector Machines (SVM), Random Forests, Decision Trees, Naive Bayes, and object detection networks with geometric features, layout features, and text-based features [7]. More recent approaches implement neural network-based models.

The CHART-Infographics Challenge on Harvesting Raw Tables from Infographics provides important benchmark datasets. The goal of the challenge is to create an end-to-end process for extracting data from charts. This process is divided into seven individually evaluated tasks, one of which is text role classification. To date, three benchmark datasets for text role classification are available from three different years of CHART-Infographics: ICDAR 2019 [6], ICPR 2020 [8], and ICPR 2022 [9]. The datasets from the challenges are called ICDAR19, ICPR20, and ICPR22 respectively. For both ICPR20 and ICPR22, each text element is classified into nine roles: chart title, legend title, legend label, axis title, tick label, tick grouping, mark label, value label, and other. While ICDAR19 and ICPR20 include synthetic charts as well as real charts, ICPR22 only contains real charts to encourage the improvement of model performance on the more challenging real chart datasets.

Heuristic-based approaches are used in the top-performing submissions for the CHART-Infographics from ICDAR 2019 while neural network-based approaches are used in the best submissions in ICPR 2020 and ICPR 2022. ABC, the top-performing submission from ICDAR 2019[4], implemented a gradient boosting decision tree, which was trained on 20 heuristic features of the bounding boxes and text [6]. In ICPR 2020[5], the top-performing submission, Lenovo-SCUT-Intsig, applied a weighted ensemble of three models using text, image, and position features as well as text semantics and chart type [8]. Wu et al. [24] proposed to fuse the extracted visual features with context features, which outperformed the best methods from ICDAR 2019 and ICPR 2020. Visual features are extracted using a ResNet backbone with RoIAlign [15], which aligns the extracted features from each Region of Interest (RoI) with the input. Context features are extracted using LayoutLM [26] using word-level and multimodal embeddings. After fusing the features, a self-attention module is applied, and finally, a fully-connected layer outputs the text role classification results.

IIIT CVIT Chart Understanding, the winning submission from ICPR 2022[6], proposed a Cascade Mask R-CNN [15] with Swin Transformer as backbone [9]. The second best submission, UB-ChartAnalysis, also used a Cascade R-CNN [5] that was modified for understanding context as well as the local and global information [9]. Apart from the ICPR 2022 submissions, CACHED [27] is another chart understanding model in the Cascade R-CNN framework with Swin Transformer as backbone, which focuses on fusing the local and global context by enhancing visual context and encoding positional context. Visual context is enhanced by incorporating global features into RoI, and positional context is encoded by concatenating bounding box features with RoI vision features.

3   Methods

The related work suggests that using multimodal transformers with features that include text, image, and position information can produce favorable outcomes for text role classification. However, training transformers from scratch is computationally expensive and chart data with text role annotations is limited. Thus, it is worth investigating whether pretrained multimodal transformers can be finetuned for text role classification, despite being pretrained on non-chart

---

[4] https://chartinfo.github.io/index_2019.html.
[5] https://chartinfo.github.io/leaderboards_2020.html.
[6] https://chartinfo.github.io/leaderboards_2022.html.

datasets. We chose LayoutLMv3 and UDOP for experimentation because they are the top-performing multimodal transformers for document layout analysis.

In this section, we explain the data augmentation methods applied to increase the robustness of the models, and the data balancing methods used to account for imbalanced datasets.

3.1 Data Augmentation

To increase the robustness of our models, data augmentation is applied to the two modalities of image and text. For the image modality, augmentations that adjust the noise (e.g., salt-and-pepper and Gaussian noise), brightness, color, and rotation of the image are randomly applied. These augmentations are chosen based on the experience in improving the quality of Tesseract, a common open-source Optical Character Recognition (OCR) system.[7] The degree to which the image is rotated is uniformly selected from within the range of -30 to $30°$. When rotation is applied to the image, the bounding box coordinates of the text are modified accordingly.

Three types of text data augmentation are implemented. The first is inserting single characters and the second is substituting single characters. Hamid et al. [14] studied how OCR errors affect NLP tasks of named entity recognition and named entity linking, and found that such character insertion and substitution errors are hard to overcome.

The third is deleting the first few characters of a text element. This is inspired by the fact that misidentifying the first character of a word along with incorrect word segmentation decreased the performance on NLP tasks [14]. This suggests that the first part of a word is more important than the latter part. The deletion length is uniformly selected from the range of 1 to 5 characters and applied to text elements with at least 10 characters.

3.2 Data Balancing

Due to the nature of charts, the text role class distribution of chart datasets is imbalanced. For example, most charts have axis titles and multiple tick labels as they provide basic information, making these text roles more common compared to the other text roles such as legend title and chart title. Thus, to offset this data imbalance, two data balancing methods are implemented.

The first method is a weighted cross-entropy loss function. The objective of this loss function is to assign more penalty to the minority class samples [21]. The second data balancing method is modified cutout augmentation, which randomly masks regions of the image during training [11]. The modified cutout augmentation randomly selects a text role class to be masked based on the class distribution. For this class, our cutout augmentation chooses a random number of labels to mask. Using the bounding box coordinate information of the text, the area of the text in the chart image is masked. The resulting augmented chart has n number of masks for the selected class.

---

[7] https://tesseract-ocr.github.io/tessdoc/ImproveQuality.html.

4   Experimental Apparatus

We introduce the datasets used for finetuning and evaluating LayoutLMv3 and UDOP for text role classification. Next, we describe the procedure of our experiments and how we optimized the hyperparameters of the two models. Lastly, we explain the metric used to score the performance of the models.

4.1   Datasets

An example chart from each dataset can be seen in Fig. 2. For all datasets, we assume that the text and bounding box coordinates are extracted accurately from each image.

ICPR22. This dataset is from the 2022 CHART-Infographics challenge [9]. ICPR22 is the real PubMedCentral (PMC) chart dataset from the ICPR 2022 challenge that includes a separate train dataset[8] and a test dataset[9]. While past synthetic chart data is available, only real charts are used because, in the past, training and testing on synthetic charts proved to be an easy task as most submission scores were perfect or near perfect [6,8]. Furthermore, with the assumption that real charts are more complex than synthetic charts, training on synthetic charts does not provide additional benefits for minority class samples. For a given chart image in ICPR22, the chart type, text block bounding box coordinates, text transcription, text block ID, and text role label are provided. There are nine text role classes including chart title, legend title, legend label, axis title, tick label, tick grouping, mark label, value label, and other. Figure 1 shows an example of the classes tick grouping and value label, and the ICPR22 chart in Fig. 2 shows an example with the mark label class.

ICPR22 is preprocessed to only include samples that can be used for text role classification. This means that each sample must have an image and text, bounding box coordinates, and text role annotations. This limits the variety of chart types in the dataset to line, scatter, box, and bar plots. Additionally, negative bounding box coordinates, which can occur when text is at the border of a chart, were set to zero.

ICPR22-N. After finetuning, the robustness of the models is tested on a synthetic but realistic noisy dataset ICPR22-N which we created from the ICPR22 test dataset by applying the data augmentation methods introduced in Sect. 3.1. Data augmentation is randomly selected and applied to each image from a pool of augmentations with equal probability. One type of augmentation is applied to each image.

---

[8] https://www.dropbox.com/s/85yfkigo5916xk1/ICPR2022_CHARTINFO_UB_PMC_TRAIN_v1.0.zip?dl=0.

[9] https://www.dropbox.com/s/w0j0rxund06y04f/ICPR2022_CHARTINFO_UB_UNITEC_PMC_TEST_v2.1.zip?dl=0.

CHIME-R, DeGruyter, and EconBiz. The generalizability of the models is also tested on three datasets [3]. CHIME-R [28] contains real figures originally collected by the Center for Information Mining and Extraction (CHIME) which includes bar, pie, and line charts. The DeGruyter dataset consists of figures from academic books by DeGruyter[10]. The figures in the EconBiz dataset [4] were randomly extracted from a corpus of 288,000 open-access publications in the economics domain. The chart types included in the DeGruyter and EconBiz datasets are more complex than the CHIME-R dataset and include figures that are not charts (e.g., diagrams), charts without axes (e.g., flow charts), and figures with multiple subplots.

Since the text roles are missing from CHIME-R, DeGruyter, and EconBiz in the existing gold standard [3], the text roles are manually assigned to each text element using the same nine text role classes as ICPR22.

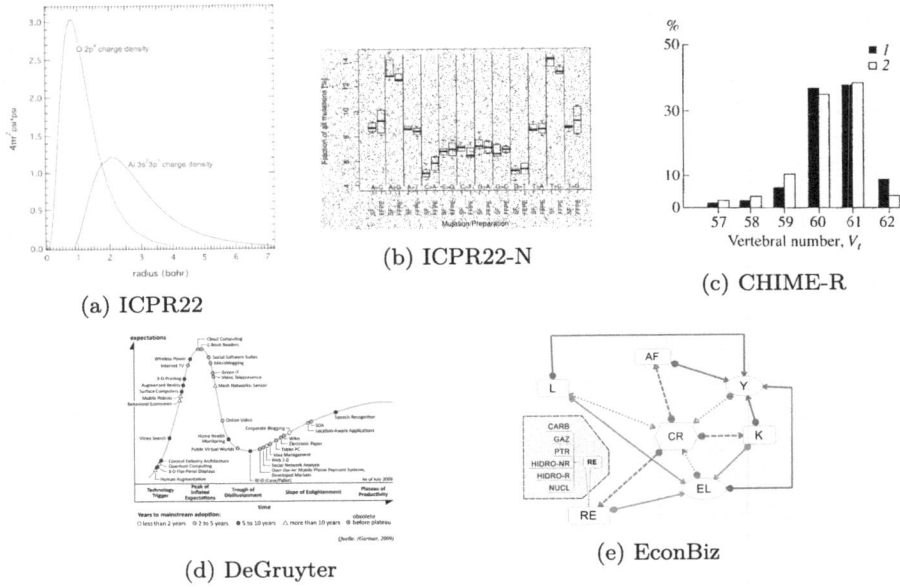

(a) ICPR22

(b) ICPR22-N

(c) CHIME-R

(d) DeGruyter

(e) EconBiz

Fig. 2. Example charts from each dataset

4.2   Procedure

We finetune the pretrained models LayoutLMv3 and UDOP in their base model size. All of the layers are initialized with the pretrained weights except for the classification output layer. To compare the performance of LayoutLMv3 and

---

[10] https://www.degruyter.com/.

UDOP on the ICPR22 test dataset, three baseline models are used: IIIT CVIT Chart Understanding, UB-ChartAnalysis, and CACHED. Details of the models are discussed in Sect. 2.2.

There are four stages of finetuning and evaluation. In the first stage, hyperparameter tuning is done only on the ICPR22 train dataset which is split into train and validation with a split of 0.9/0.1. After obtaining the best hyperparameters for each model, the models are evaluated on the full test datasets: ICPR22, ICPR22-N, CHIME-R, DeGruyter, and EconBiz. The ICPR22 validation dataset is only used in the first stage for hyperparameter tuning. The second stage is training on only the ICPR22 train dataset and additionally applying data augmentation and balancing during training. Afterwards, testing is done on each of the full test sets of the datasets. For the third and fourth stages, the CHIME-R, DeGruyter, and EconBiz datasets are split into train and test datasets with a split of 0.7/0.3. The resulting train splits are combined with the ICPR22 train dataset to create a combined train dataset.

Furthermore, in the third stage, the models are trained on this combined train dataset without data augmentation and balancing, and evaluated on the test splits of all datasets. In the fourth stage, the models are trained on all datasets with data augmentation and balancing and then evaluated on the test splits of all datasets. When training on all datasets combined, ICPR22-N is excluded and only used for testing the robustness of the models as data augmentation is already applied to this noisy dataset.

Before applying data augmentation and balancing, each method is tested individually on ICPR22 with LayoutLMv3, and only the best methods are used in the final setup. For data augmentation, among the six proposed methods, three methods are used in the final setup: adjusting noise, deleting characters, and inserting characters. For data balancing, cutout augmentation is used. When data augmentation and balancing are applied, the augmented dataset is concatenated with the original dataset.

4.3   Hyperparameter Optimization

For both models, the batch size and learning rate are optimized during finetuning. For UDOP, the further hyperparameters optimized include the warmup steps and weight decay. The hyperparameter settings reported in both LayoutLMv3 and UDOP to finetune each model on the FUNSD dataset are used as a starting point. The best hyperparameter combination for each model is used in the final setup. We finetune LayoutLMv3 for 10,000 steps with batch size 32 and learning rate 2e-5. For UDOP, we finetune for 20,000 steps with 1,000 warmup steps, batch size 16, learning rate 2e-4, weight decay 1e-2, and the Adam optimizer parameters $\beta_1 = 0.9$, and $\beta_2 = 0.98$.

4.4   Metrics

The main metric used to measure text role classification is the F1-macro score. This is the metric used in the ICPR 2022 competition. First, using precision and recall, the harmonic mean (F-measure) is calculated for each text role class. The final F1-macro score is the average of the per-class scores. For a benchmark comparison, the same evaluation method is used. Considering the data imbalance, the F1-micro score is reported as well. The F1-micro score is the average score over all samples, independent of the class. We always report scores in percent.

5   Results

For all stages of training and evaluation, LayoutLMv3 outperforms UDOP on all test datasets. The best-performing model on the ICPR22 test dataset is LayoutLMv3 trained on just ICPR22 with no data augmentation and balancing. The F1-macro score is 82.87, which is the highest score compared to the competition models. The F1-macro score for UDOP when only trained on ICPR22 with no data augmentation and balancing is 72.56, which is lower than the competition models. For both LayoutLMv3 and UDOP, the F1-micro scores surpass the F1-macro scores on all datasets in all stages of training and evaluation. Furthermore, both models show more robustness to the synthetic noisy dataset ICPR22-N compared to the real datasets CHIME-R, DeGruyter, and EconBiz. Among the real datasets, the F1 scores are highest for CHIME-R and lowest for DeGruyter.

Table 1. F1 scores (F1-macro — F1-micro) in % of LayoutLMv3 and UDOP on various chart datasets. When trained on only ICPR22, the model is evaluated on the full test dataset. When trained on all datasets, the model is trained on the train split of all datasets, and evaluated on the test split of each dataset. DAB indicates that data balancing and augmentation methods are applied during training.

Model	Test / Train	ICPR22	ICPR22-N	CHIME-R	DeGruyter	EconBiz
LayoutLMv3	ICPR22	**82.87** | 93.99	**77.23** | **90.75**	66.61 | 79.67	17.19 | 38.27	51.91 | 63.20
	ICPR22 w DAB	81.55 | 93.66	77.02 | 90.31	58.87 | 76.11	19.58 | 39.52	51.19 | 65.86
	All	79.95 | 93.88	73.47 | 89.18	86.60 | 94.05	28.29 | 54.98	61.30 | 78.03
	All w DAB	82.48 | **94.31**	75.75 | 90.72	**95.60** | **97.62**	**44.44** | **58.37**	**66.40** | **78.60**
UDOP	ICPR22	72.56 | 89.41	70.52 | 86.80	60.19 | 72.88	15.01 | 29.64	38.49 | 51.48
	ICPR22 w DAB	71.24 | 88.85	68.92 | 87.04	58.84 | 71.96	15.32 | 30.49	36.78 | 51.67
	All	69.88 | 88.62	65.56 | 84.99	80.39 | 91.23	23.02 | 51.91	**52.79** | **66.08**
	All w DAB	**76.22** | **91.00**	**71.97** | **88.38**	**89.44** | **95.76**	33.79 | **58.67**	48.11 | 61.41

For ICPR22-N, the best F1-macro score of 77.23 is from LayoutLMv3 trained on only ICPR22 with no data augmentation and balancing. LayoutLMv3 trained on all datasets with data augmentation and balancing produced the best F1-macro scores of 95.60, 44.44, and 66.40 for CHIME-R, DeGruyter, and EconBiz, respectively. The results of LayoutLMv3 and UDOP are summarized in Table 1, and the comparison to the challenge models on ICPR22 can be found in Table 2.

Table 2. F1-macro scores on ICPR22 between the best-performing models of LayoutLMv3 and UDOP and the baseline models.

Model	F1-macro Score on ICPR22
IIIT_CVIT_Chart_Understanding	82.1
UB-ChartAnalysis	73.6
CACHED	78.7
LayoutLMv3 (ICPR22)	**82.87**
UDOP (All with DAB)	76.22

In the second stage of training and evaluation, where the models are trained only on ICPR22 with data augmentation and balancing, both LayoutLMv3 and UDOP do not show any improvement on any dataset. However, in the third stage where the models are trained on all datasets, although there is no increase in F1 scores on ICPR22 and ICPR22-N, the F1 scores of both models improve for CHIME-R, DeGruyter, and EconBiz. When the models are trained on all datasets with data augmentation and balancing in the fourth stage, UDOP scores the highest F1-macro score on ICPR22 with a score of 76.22, which is 2.6 points higher than the baseline model UB-ChartAnalysis. On the other hand, for LayoutLMv3, the F1-macro score still remains the highest for ICPR22 when the model is trained on only ICPR22 with no data augmentation and balancing. However, LayoutLMv3 scores the highest F1-micro score of 94.31 on ICPR22 when it is trained on all datasets with data augmentation and balancing.

6   Discussion

First, we discuss the key results of our experiments. Next, the limitations are discussed with respect to the datasets and methods. Afterward, we explore possible avenues for future work.

6.1   Key Results

LayoutLMv3 performs better than UDOP on text role classification, and the best method on the ICPR22 test dataset is LayoutLMv3 trained on only ICPR22 with no data augmentation and balancing. Even when continuing training UDOP to 100,000 steps, the performance of the model only slightly increases and LayoutLMv3 still demonstrates superior performance. LayoutLMv3 not only outperforms UDOP, but it is also computationally less expensive, requiring only a third of the training time of UDOP, which takes approximately 36 h on one Tesla V100-SXM2-32GB to train for 20,000 steps. Although data augmentation and balancing methods improved the F1-micro scores on ICPR22 for both models, the F1-macro score only increased for UDOP. Despite applying data balancing methods, the F1-micro score is always higher than the F1-macro score. This shows how much more difficult it is to get a high score for each class than a high score overall. Data imbalance with the smallest class occurring only 0.3% as often as the largest class remains a difficult problem to be solved.

The performance of the models decreases for more complex charts with more textual elements. For simple charts such as CHIME-R, i.e. charts with few textual elements, pretrained document layout analysis models can be finetuned with high performance, even with a small dataset by applying data augmentation and balancing. Nevertheless, it is important to train on samples of the dataset as the performance of the models is low when this is not done. However, for complex datasets with more textual elements such as DeGruyter, data augmentation and balancing methods are not enough to achieve good performance on text role classification.

Furthermore, the robustness of the models to other datasets depends on the training dataset. When only trained on ICPR22, the models perform well on the synthetic noisy dataset ICPR22-N but struggle on the real chart datasets CHIME-R, DeGruyter, and EconBiz. However, when trained on all datasets with data augmentation and balancing, the performance of the models is better on CHIME-R, a real yet simple chart dataset, than ICPR22-N. This demonstrates that chart complexity is an important factor to consider when conducting a robustness test for text role classification. Apart from general chart complexity, it is possible that DeGruyter and EconBiz are farther away from the ICPR22 train dataset distribution compared to CHIME-R. With limited training data for DeGruyter and EconBiz, data augmentation methods may not have been enough to compensate for differences in their respective distributions.

6.2   Limitations

There are several limitations regarding the data augmentation methods and the datasets. First, the data augmentation methods applied are general augmentation methods that are not chart-specific. Furthermore, while we hoped that training on augmented text would make the models more robust to noise, this was not the case. Augmenting the text may have hindered learning the relationship between the text embedding and text role.

Moreover, the bounding box coordinates are not adjusted when the data augmentation of deleting characters is applied. In some cases, text elements spanned more than one line in the image. Thus, deleting characters from the beginning of the text element and adjusting the bounding box coordinates afterward would result in the exclusion of characters from the following lines in the bounding box.

In addition, the text of the chart datasets is assumed to be in English. Therefore, it is unknown whether the models can be generalized to chart datasets in other languages. However, it is to be noted that the majority of scientific publications is in English. Finally, the text roles differ depending on the chart type. Thus, the generalizability of the models may have been influenced by the varying distribution of chart types within the datasets.

7 Conclusion

Without the cost of pretraining the models on a large-scale chart dataset, pretrained document layout analysis models can be finetuned on chart datasets for text role classification. In this paper, we evaluated the two pretrained document layout analysis models, LayoutLMv3 and UDOP, on five datasets ICPR22, ICPR22-N, CHIME-R, DeGruyter, and EconBiz. For the datasets CHIME-R, DeGruyter, and EconBiz, we introduced new text role class labels. Comparing the results of the models on ICPR22, LayoutLMv3 outperforms UDOP and all challenge entries. The results on ICPR22-N reveal that LayoutLMv3 is more robust to noise than UDOP, and the results on CHIME-R, DeGruyter, and EconBiz show that LayoutLMv3 also generalizes better. Although the performance of the models is relatively high on the simple dataset CHIME-R, the models struggle on the more challenging datasets DeGruyter and EconBiz. This confirms that due to the complexity of real charts, text role classification remains a difficult problem.

Acknowledgments. This work is co-funded under the 2LIKE project by the German Federal Ministry of Education and Research (BMBF) and the Ministry of Science, Research and the Arts Baden-Württemberg within the funding line Artificial Intelligence in Higher Education. The authors acknowledge support by the state of Baden-Württemberg through bwHPC. We thank Falk Böschen for providing the region annotations of the CHIME-R, DeGruyter, and EconBiz datasets [3,4].

Disclosure of Interests. The authors have no competing interests to declare that are relevant to the content of this article.

References

1. Al-Zaidy, R.A., Giles, C.L.: A machine learning approach for semantic structuring of scientific charts in scholarly documents. In: Proceedings of the Thirty-First AAAI Conference on Artificial Intelligence, pp. 4644–4649. AAAI Press (2017). http://aaai.org/ocs/index.php/IAAI/IAAI17/paper/view/14275
2. Bhowmik, S.: Document region classification. In: Bhowmik, S. (ed.) Document Layout Analysis. Springer, Singapore (2023). https://doi.org/10.1007/978-981-99-4277-0_4
3. Böschen, F., Beck, T., Scherp, A.: Survey and empirical comparison of different approaches for text extraction from scholarly figures. Multimed. Tools Appl. **77**(22), 29475–29505 (2018). https://doi.org/10.1007/s11042-018-6162-7
4. Böschen, F., Scherp, A.: Multi-oriented text extraction from information graphics. In: DocEng 2015. ACM (2015). https://doi.org/10.1145/2682571.2797092
5. Cai, Z., Vasconcelos, N.: Cascade R-CNN: delving into high quality object detection. In: CVPR 2018, pp. 6154–6162. Computer Vision Foundation/IEEE Computer Society (2018). https://doi.org/10.1109/CVPR.2018.00644. http://openaccess.thecvf.com/content_cvpr_2018/html/Cai_Cascade_R-CNN_Delving_CVPR_2018_paper.html

6. Davila, K., et al.: ICDAR 2019 competition on harvesting raw tables from info-graphics (chart-infographics). In: 2019 International Conference on Document Analysis and Recognition, ICDAR 2019, pp. 1594–1599. IEEE (2019). https://doi.org/10.1109/ICDAR.2019.00203

7. Davila, K., Setlur, S., Doermann, D.S., Kota, B.U., Govindaraju, V.: Chart mining: a survey of methods for automated chart analysis. IEEE Trans. Pattern Anal. Mach. Intell. **43**(11), 3799–3819 (2021). https://doi.org/10.1109/TPAMI.2020.2992028

8. Davila, K., Tensmeyer, C., Shekhar, S., Singh, H., Setlur, S., Govindaraju, V.: ICPR 2020 - competition on harvesting raw tables from infographics. In: Del Bimbo, A., et al. (eds.) ICPR 2021. LNCS, vol. 12668, pp. 361–380. Springer, Cham (2021). https://doi.org/10.1007/978-3-030-68793-9_27

9. Davila, K., Xu, F., Ahmed, S., Mendoza, D.A., Setlur, S., Govindaraju, V.: ICPR 2022: challenge on harvesting raw tables from infographics (chart-infographics). In: 26th International Conference on Pattern Recognition, pp. 4995–5001. IEEE (2022). https://doi.org/10.1109/ICPR56361.2022.9956289

10. Devlin, J., Chang, M., Lee, K., Toutanova, K.: BERT: pre-training of deep bidirectional transformers for language understanding. In: NAACL-HLT 2019, pp. 4171–4186. ACL (2019). https://doi.org/10.18653/v1/n19-1423

11. Devries, T., Taylor, G.W.: Improved regularization of convolutional neural networks with cutout. CoRR (2017). http://arxiv.org/abs/1708.04552

12. Dosovitskiy, A., et al.: An image is worth 16 × 16 words: transformers for image recognition at scale. In: ICLR 2021. OpenReview.net (2021). https://openreview.net/forum?id=YicbFdNTTy

13. Fu, J., et al.: CMA-CLIP: cross-modality attention clip for text-image classification. In: 2022 IEEE International Conference on Image Processing, ICIP, pp. 2846–2850. IEEE (2022). https://doi.org/10.1109/ICIP46576.2022.9897323

14. Hamdi, A., Pontes, E.L., Sidere, N., Coustaty, M., Doucet, A.: In-depth analysis of the impact of OCR errors on named entity recognition and linking. Nat. Lang. Eng. **29**(2), 425–448 (2023). https://doi.org/10.1017/S1351324922000110

15. He, K., Gkioxari, G., Dollár, P., Girshick, R.B.: Mask R-CNN. In: ICCV 2017, pp. 2980–2988. IEEE Computer Society (2017). https://doi.org/10.1109/ICCV.2017.322

16. He, K., Zhang, X., Ren, S., Sun, J.: Deep residual learning for image recognition. In: CVPR 2016, pp. 770–778. IEEE Computer Society (2016). https://doi.org/10.1109/CVPR.2016.90

17. Huang, Y., Lv, T., Cui, L., Lu, Y., Wei, F.: LayoutLMv3: pre-training for document AI with unified text and image masking. In: MM 2022, pp. 4083–4091. ACM (2022). https://doi.org/10.1145/3503161.3548112

18. Kiela, D., Bhooshan, S., Firooz, H., Testuggine, D.: Supervised multimodal bitransformers for classifying images and text. CoRR (2019). http://arxiv.org/abs/1909.02950

19. Poco, J., Heer, J.: Reverse-engineering visualizations: recovering visual encodings from chart images. Comput. Graph. Forum **36**(3), 353–363 (2017). https://doi.org/10.1111/cgf.13193

20. Radford, A., et al.: Learning transferable visual models from natural language supervision. In: ICML 2021. PMLR (2021). http://proceedings.mlr.press/v139/radford21a.html

21. Rezaei-Dastjerdehei, M.R., Mijani, A., Fatemizadeh, E.: Addressing imbalance in multi-label classification using weighted cross entropy loss function. In: 2020 27th National and 5th International Iranian Conference on Biomedical Engineering (ICBME), pp. 333–338. IEEE (2020)

22. Tang, Z., et al.: Unifying vision, text, and layout for universal document processing. CoRR (2022). https://doi.org/10.48550/arXiv.2212.02623

23. Wang, C., Cui, K., Zhang, S., Xu, C.: Visual and textual information fusion method for chart recognition. In: Del Bimbo, A., et al. (eds.) ICPR 2021. LNCS, vol. 12668, pp. 381–389. Springer, Cham (2021). https://doi.org/10.1007/978-3-030-68793-9_28

24. Wu, S., et al.: Improving machine understanding of human intent in charts. In: Lladós, J., Lopresti, D., Uchida, S. (eds.) ICDAR 2021. LNCS, vol. 12823, pp. 676–691. Springer, Cham (2021). https://doi.org/10.1007/978-3-030-86334-0_44

25. Xu, Y., et al.: LayoutLMv2: multi-modal pre-training for visually-rich document understanding. In: ACL/IJCNLP 2021, pp. 2579–2591. Association for Computational Linguistics (2021). https://doi.org/10.18653/v1/2021.acl-long.201

26. Xu, Y., Li, M., Cui, L., Huang, S., Wei, F., Zhou, M.: LayoutLM: pre-training of text and layout for document image understanding. In: KDD 2020, pp. 1192–1200. ACM (2020). https://doi.org/10.1145/3394486.3403172

27. Yan, P., Ahmed, S., Doermann, D.S.: Context-aware chart element detection. CoRR (2023). https://doi.org/10.48550/arXiv.2305.04151

28. Yang, L., Huang, W., Tan, C.L.: Semi-automatic ground truth generation for chart image recognition. In: Bunke, H., Spitz, A.L. (eds.) DAS 2006. LNCS, vol. 3872, pp. 324–335. Springer, Heidelberg (2006). https://doi.org/10.1007/11669487_29

LaFiCMIL: Rethinking Large File Classification from the Perspective of Correlated Multiple Instance Learning

Tiezhu Sun[1]([✉]), Weiguo Pian[1], Nadia Daoudi[1,2], Kevin Allix[3],
Tegawendé F. Bissyandé[1], and Jacques Klein[1]

[1] University of Luxembourg, Kirchberg, Luxembourg
`tiezhu.sun@uni.lu`
[2] Luxembourg Institute of Science and Technology, Esch-sur-Alzette, Luxembourg
[3] Rennes, France

Abstract. Transformer-based models have significantly advanced natural language processing, in particular the performance in text classification tasks. Nevertheless, these models face challenges in processing large files, primarily due to their input constraints, which are generally restricted to hundreds or thousands of tokens. Attempts to address this issue in existing models usually consist in extracting only a fraction of the essential information from lengthy inputs, while often incurring high computational costs due to their complex architectures. In this work, we address the challenge of classifying large files from the perspective of correlated multiple instance learning. We introduce LaFiCMIL, a method specifically designed for large file classification. It is optimized for efficient training on a single GPU, making it a versatile solution for binary, multi-class, and multi-label classification tasks. We conducted extensive experiments using seven diverse and comprehensive benchmark datasets to assess LaFiCMIL's effectiveness. By integrating BERT for feature extraction, LaFiCMIL demonstrates exceptional performance, setting new benchmarks across all datasets. A notable achievement of our approach is its ability to scale BERT to handle nearly 20 000 tokens while training on a single GPU with 32 GB of memory. This efficiency, coupled with its state-of-the-art performance, highlights LaFiCMIL's potential as a groundbreaking approach in the field of large file classification.

Keywords: Large file classification · Multiple instance learning

1 Introduction

Text classification is a fundamental task in Natural Language Processing (NLP), entailing the assignment of suitable label(s) to specific input texts [24]. This process is crucial across various domains, including sentiment analysis [12], fake news

K. Allix—Independent Researcher.

detection [25], and offensive language identification [36], among others. Recent years have seen the emergence of attention-based models like Transformer [46], GPT [34,35], and the BERT family [13,16,44], which have established state-of-the-art benchmarks in text classification tasks. However, the challenge of processing very long sequences remains a significant obstacle, mainly due to their high computational requirements when facing extremely huge number of tokens.

There are mainly two types of solutions in the literature to address long token sequences: ① extending the input length limit by employing a sliding window to attention, such as Longformer [7], and ② dividing long documents into segments and recurrently processing the Transformer-based segment representations, such as RMT [9,10]. Nevertheless, Longformer inherently struggles with global context capture. The sliding window mechanism can lead to a fragmented understanding of the overall sequence, as it primarily focuses on local context within each window. This becomes particularly challenging when dependencies span beyond the scope of these localized windows, a common occurrence in complex or extremely long text sequences. Similarly, the recurrent processing of RMT can also lead to information loss, especially when dependencies or context need to be carried over long sequences of text. Each recurrent step has the potential to dilute or overlook critical information from previous segments, leading to a gradual decay in context retention as the sequence progresses.

Recently, significant progress in large language models (LLMs) like GPT-4 [1] and Llama 2 [45] has showcased their impressive capabilities in various NLP tasks. Despite these advances, directly applying large language models (LLMs) to text classification through prompt engineering has not achieved optimal performance, and lightweight Transformer models, such as RoBERTa [29,53], continue to excel in this essential task. This is demonstrated by RGPT [53], an adaptive boosting framework designed to fine-tune LLMs for text classification. Although RGPT sets new benchmarks, it has only been validated on short texts and demands substantial computational resources, requiring **eight** A100-SXM4-40GB GPUs, and a total of 320 GB of memory. Consequently, developing a more resource-efficient and effective strategy for classifying long documents remains a critical challenge.

In this work, we innovatively tackle this challenge by adopting Multiple Instance Learning [40,51] (MIL), wherein we conceptualize a large file as a 'bag' and its constituent chunks as 'instances' within the MIL framework. We introduce **LaFiCMIL**, a simple yet effective **La**rge **Fi**le **C**lassification approach based on correlated **M**ultiple **I**nstance **L**earning. On the one hand, as proven in Theorem 1 (cf., Sect. 3), a MIL score function for a bag classification task can be approximated by a series of sub-functions of the instances. This inspires us to split a large file into smaller chunks and extract their features separately using BERT. On the other hand, we aim to guide the model to learn high-level overall features from all instances, rather than deriving the final bag prediction from instance predictions based on a simplistic learned projection matrix. In addition, in contrast to the basic version of MIL [19], where instances within the same bag exhibit neither dependency nor ordering among one another, we claim that the small chunks from the same large file are correlated in some way (e.g., semantic dependencies in paragraphs). This implies that the presence or absence of a positive instance in a bag can be influenced by the other instances contained within the same bag. As a result, relying on our computationally efficient LaFiAttention layer, our approach is capable of **efficiently** extracting **correlations** among **all chunks** as additional information to boost classification performance.

In our evaluation, LaFiCMIL consistently achieved new state-of-the-art performance across all seven benchmark datasets, especially when tested with long documents in the evaluation sets. A notable highlight is LaFiCMIL's performance on the full test set of the Paired Book Summary dataset, where it demonstrated a significant 4.41% point improvement. This dataset is especially challenging as it contains the highest proportion of long documents, exceeding 75%. Furthermore, LaFiCMIL also distinguished itself by having the fastest training process compared to other baseline models.

The contributions of our study are as follows:

- We introduce, LaFiCMIL, a novel approach for large file classification from the perspective of correlated multiple instance learning.
- The training of LaFiCMIL is super efficient, which requires only 1.86× training time than the original BERT, but is able to handle 39× longer sequence on a single GPU with only 32 GB of memory.
- We perform a comprehensive evaluation, illustrating that LaFiCMIL achieves new state-of-the-art performance across all seven benchmark datasets.
- We share the datasets and source code to the community at: https://github.com/Trustworthy-Software/LaFiCMIL.

2   Related Work

2.1   Large File Classification

In recent years, significant efforts have been made to alleviate the input limit of Transformer-based models to handle large files. One notable example is Longformer [7], which extends the limit to 4096 tokens using a sparse attention mechanism [50]. CogLTX [14] chooses to identify key sentences through a trained judge model. Alternatively, ToBERT [32] and RMT [9,10] segment long documents into fragments and then aggregate or recurrently process their BERT-based representations. Recently, two simple BERT-based methods proposed in [33] achieved state-of-the-art performance on several datasets for long document classification. Specifically, BERT+Random selects random sentences up to 512 tokens to augment the first 512 tokens. BERT+TextRank augments the first 512 tokens with a second set of 512 tokens obtained via TextRank [31]. They also provide a comprehensive evaluation to compare the relative efficacy of various baselines on diverse datasets, which revealed that no single approach consistently outperforms others across all six benchmark datasets, encompassing different classification tasks such as binary [22], multi-class [26], and multi-label classification [6,11].

One potential reason for the limited performance of existing approaches is that they do not fully leverage the information available in large files, resulting in only partial essential information being captured. In this paper, we explore the possibility of utilizing the complete information from large files to improve the performance of various classification tasks.

2.2   Multiple Instance Learning

Multiple Instance Learning (MIL) has attracted increasing research interests and applications in recent years. The application scenarios of MIL span across various domains [18,20,43], but the most prominent one is Medical Imaging and Diagnosis. Particularly, there has been a growing trend towards developing MIL algorithms for medical whole slide image analysis [21,49]. MIL approaches are broadly divided into two categories. The first group makes bag predictions based on individual instance predictions, typically using average or maximum pooling methods [15,27,30,41]. The second group aggregates instance features to form a high-level bag representation, which is then used for bag-level predictions [28, 40,51]. Although instance-level pooling is straightforward, aggregating features for bag representation has proven more effective [40,47].

A fundamental assumption behind Multiple Instance Learning (MIL) is that instances within a bag are independent, but this might not always be true in real world. To tackle this, some research turns to Correlated Multiple Instance Learning (c-MIL), which assumes instances in a bag are correlated [40,52,55]. This approach recognizes that instances in a bag can influence each other. However, using c-MIL for large file classification remains under-explored.

3   Technical Preliminaries

In this section, we describe several essential technical preliminaries that inspire and underpin the design of LaFiCMIL. We first present a pair of theorems that are the fundamental principles of c-MIL.

Theorem 1. *Suppose $S : \chi \to \mathbb{R}$ is a continuous set function w.r.t Hausdorff distance [38] $d_H(.,.)$. $\forall \varepsilon > 0$, for any invertible map $P : \chi \to \mathbb{R}^n$, $\exists$ function σ and g, such that for any set $X \in \chi$:*

$$|S(X) - g(P_{X \in \chi}\{\sigma(x) : x \in X\})| < \varepsilon \tag{1}$$

The proof of Theorem 1 can be found in [40]. This theorem shows that a Hausdorff continuous **set function** $S(X)$ can be arbitrarily approximated by a function in the form $g(P_{X \in \chi}\{\sigma(x) : x \in X\})$. This insight can be applied to MIL, as the mathematical definition of **sets** in the theorem is equivalent to that of **bags** in MIL framework. Consequently, the theorem provides a foundation for approximating bag-level predictions in MIL using instance-level features.

Theorem 2. *The instances in the bag are represented by random variables* $\theta_1, \theta_2, ..., \theta_n$, *the information entropy of the bag under the correlation assumption can be expressed as* $H(\theta_1, \theta_2, ..., \theta_n)$, *and the information entropy of the bag under the i.i.d. (independent and identical distribution) assumption can be expressed as* $\sum_{t=1}^{n} H(\theta_t)$, *then we have:*

$$
\begin{aligned}
H(\theta_1, \theta_2, ..., \theta_n) &= \sum_{t=2}^{n} H(\theta_t | \theta_1, \theta_2, ..., \theta_{t-1}) + H(\theta_1) \\
&\leq \sum_{t=1}^{n} H(\theta_t)
\end{aligned}
\tag{2}
$$

The proof of Theorem 2 can be found in [40]. This theorem demonstrates that the information entropy of a bag under the correlation assumption is smaller than the information entropy of a bag under the i.i.d. assumption. The lower information entropy in c-MIL suggests reduced uncertainty and the potential to provide more information for bag classification tasks. In Sect. 4.1, we introduce c-MIL, and in Sect. 4.2, we derive the efficient LaFiCMIL based on c-MIL.

Next, we present the necessary preliminaries for our efficient attention layer inspired by the Nyströmformer [48], referred as LaFiAttention, which performs as a sub-function within our LaFiCMIL. In the original Transformer [46], an input sequence of n tokens of dimensions d, $X \in \mathbf{R}^{n \times d}$, is projected using three matrices $W_Q \in \mathbf{R}^{n \times d_q}$, $W_K \in \mathbf{R}^{n \times d_k}$, and $W_V \in \mathbf{R}^{n \times d_v}$, referred as query, key, and value respectively with $d_k = d_q$. The outputs Q, K, V are calculated as

$$
Q = XW_Q, \quad K = XW_K, \quad V = XW_V
\tag{3}
$$

Therefore, the self-attention can be written as:

$$
D(Q, K, V) = SV = softmax(\frac{QK^T}{\sqrt{d_q}})V
\tag{4}
$$

Then, the softmax matrix S used in self-attention can be written as

$$
S = softmax(\frac{QK^T}{\sqrt{d_q}}) = \begin{bmatrix} A_S & B_S \\ F_S & C_S \end{bmatrix}
\tag{5}
$$

where $A_S \in \mathbf{R}^{m \times m}$, $B_S \in \mathbf{R}^{m \times (n-m)}$, $F_S \in \mathbf{R}^{(n-m) \times m}$, $C_S \in \mathbf{R}^{(n-m) \times (n-m)}$, and $m < n$.

In order to **reduce** the memory and time **complexity** from $O(n^2)$ to $O(n)$, LaFiAttention approximates S by

$$
\hat{S} = softmax(\frac{Q\widetilde{K}^T}{\sqrt{d_q}}) A_S^+ softmax(\frac{\widetilde{Q}K^T}{\sqrt{d_q}}),
\tag{6}
$$

where $\widetilde{Q} = [\widetilde{q_1}; ...; \widetilde{q_m}] \in \mathbf{R}^{m \times d_q}$ and $\widetilde{K} = [\widetilde{k_1}; ...; \widetilde{k_m}] \in \mathbf{R}^{m \times d_q}$ are the selected landmarks for inputs $Q = [q_1; ...; q_n]$ and $K = [k_1; ...; k_n]$, A_S^+ is the Moore-Penrose inverse [8] of A_S.

Lemma 1. *For $A_S \in \mathbf{R}^{m \times m}$, the sequence $\{Z_j\}_{j=0}^{j=\infty}$ generated by [37],*

$$Z_{j+1} = \frac{1}{4} Z_j (13I - A_S Z_j (15I - A_S Z_j (7I - A_S Z_j))) \tag{7}$$

converges to Moore-Penrose inverse A_S^+ in the third-order with initial approximation Z_0 satisfying $\left\| A_S A_S^+ - A_S Z_0 \right\| < 1$.

LaFiAttention approximates A_S^+ by Z^* with Lemma 1. Following the empirical choice from [48], we run 6 iterations to achieve a good approximation of the pseudoinverse. Then, the softmax matrix S is approximated by

$$\hat{S} = softmax(\frac{Q\widetilde{K}^T}{\sqrt{d_q}})Z^* softmax(\frac{\widetilde{Q}K^T}{\sqrt{d_q}}). \tag{8}$$

4   Approach

In this section, we first introduce customized c-MIL for large file classification and then provide technical details about our LaFiCMIL approach.

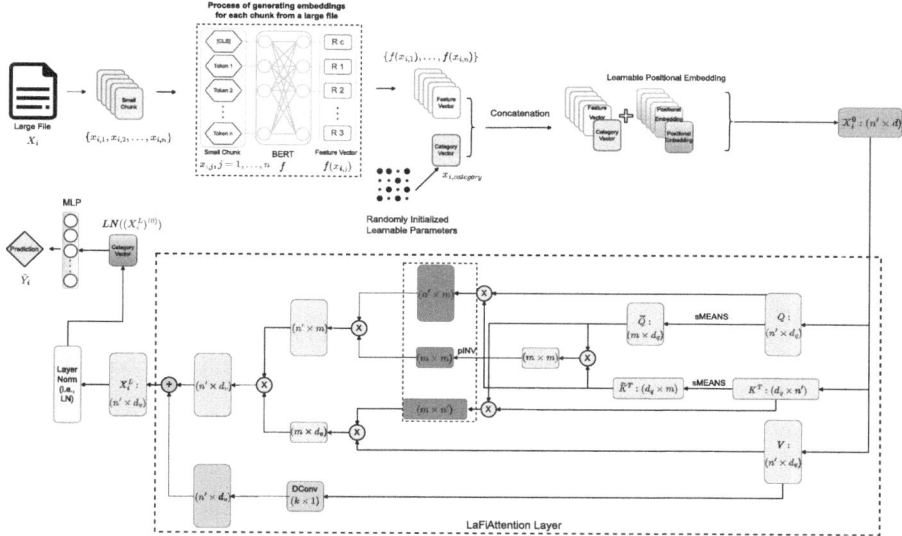

Fig. 1. LaFiCMIL. Initially, document chunks are transformed into embedding vectors using BERT. A learnable category vector is then concatenated to these embeddings to form an augmented bag X_i^0 with $n' = n + 1$ instances. The LaFiAttention layer captures the inter-instance correlations within X_i^0. Operations within this layer, such as matrix multiplication ($\times$) and addition ($+$), are specified alongside the variable names and matrix dimensions. Key processes include sMEANS for landmark selections similar to [42], pINV for pseudoinverse approximation, and DConv for depth-wise convolution. Classification is completed by passing the learned category vector through a fully connected layer.

4.1   Correlated Multiple Instance Learning

Unlike traditional supervised classification, which predicts labels for individual instances, Multiple Instance Learning (MIL) predicts bag-level labels for bags of instances. Typically, individual instance labels within each bag exist but inaccessible, and the number of instances in different bags may vary.

In the basic MIL concept [19], instances in a bag are independent and unordered. However, correlations among chunks of a large file exist due to the presence of semantic dependencies between paragraphs. According to Theorem 2, these correlations can be exploited to reduce uncertainty in prediction. In other words, this relationship can be leveraged as additional information to boost the performance of long document classification tasks. The Correlated Multiple Instance Learning (c-MIL) is defined as below.

Here, we consider a binary classification task of c-MIL as an example. Given a bag (i.e., a large file) X_i composed of instances (i.e., chunks) $\{x_{i,1}, x_{i,2}, ..., x_{i,n}\}$, for $i = 1, ..., N$, that exhibit dependency or ordering among each other. The bag-level label is Y_i, yet the instance-level labels $\{y_{i,1}, y_{i,2}, ..., y_{i,n}\}$ are not accessible. Then, a binary classification of c-MIL can be defined as:

$$Y_i = \begin{cases} 0, & if \sum y_{i,j} = 0 \quad y_{i,j} \in \{0,1\}, j = 1, ..., n \\ 1, & otherwise \end{cases} \tag{9}$$

$$\hat{Y}_i = S(X_i), \tag{10}$$

where S is a scoring function, and $\hat{Y}$ is the predicted score. N is the total number of bags, and n is the number of instances in the ith bag. The number n generally varies for different bags.

4.2   LaFiCMIL

According to Theorem 1, we leverage Multi-layer Perceptron [39], BERT [13], LaFiAttention Layer and Layer Normalization [4] as **sub-functions to approximate** the c-MIL score function S defined in Eq. 10.

Given a set of bags $\{X_1, ..., X_N\}$, where each bag X_i contains multiple instances $\{x_{i,1}, ..., x_{i,n}\}$, a bag label Y_i, and a randomly initialized category vector $x_{i,category}$, the goal is to learn the maps: $\mathbb{X} \to \mathbb{T} \to \gamma$, where $\mathbb{X}$ is the bag space, $\mathbb{T}$ is the transformer space and γ is the label space. The map of $\mathbb{X} \to \mathbb{T}$ can be defined as:

$$X_i^0 = [x_{i,category}; f(x_{i,1}); ...; f(x_{i,n})] \\ + E_{pos}, \quad X_i^0, E_{pos} \in \mathbb{R}^{(n+1) \times d} \tag{11}$$

$$Q^l = X_i^{l-1} W_Q, \quad K^l = X_i^{l-1} W_K, \quad V^l = X_i^{l-1} W_V, \\ l = 1, ..., L \tag{12}$$

where function f is approximated by a BERT model, E_{pos} is the Positional Embedding, and L is the number of Multi-head Self-Attention (MSA) block.

$$head = LaFiSA(Q^l, K^l, V^l)$$
$$= softmax(\frac{Q^l(\widetilde{K}^l)^T}{\sqrt{d_q}})Z^{*l}softmax(\frac{\widetilde{Q}^l(K^l)^T}{\sqrt{d_q}})V^l, \tag{13}$$

$$MSA(Q^l, K^l, V^l) = Concat(head_1, ..., head_h)W_O, \tag{14}$$

$$X_i^l = MSA(LN(X_i^{l-1})) + X_i^{l-1}, \quad l = 1, ..., L \tag{15}$$

where $W_O \in \mathbb{R}^{hd_v \times d}$, $head \in \mathbb{R}^{(n+1) \times d_v}$, $LaFiSA$ denotes the approximated Self-attention layer by Nyström method [5] according to Eq. 8, h is the number of head in each MSA block, and Layer Normalization(LN) is applied before each MSA block.

The map of $\mathbb{T} \to \gamma$ can be simply defined as:

$$\hat{Y}_i = MLP(LN((X_i^L)^{(0)})), \tag{16}$$

where $(X_i^L)^{(0)}$ represents the learned category vector, and MLP means Multi-layer Perceptron (i.e., fully connected layer).

From the above formulation, we can find that the most important part is to efficiently learn the map from bag space $\mathbb{X}$ to Transformer space $\mathbb{T}$. As illustrated in Fig. 1, this map is approximated by a series of sub-functions which are approximated by various neural layers. The overall process is summarized as follows: given a large file, we use a BERT model to generate the representations of the divided chunks (i.e., instances in the concept of c-MIL) Then, we initialize a **learnable** category vector that follows a normal distribution and has the same shape as each instance. By considering the category vector as an additional instance, we learn the correlation between each instance using LaFi-Attention layer. With the help of the attention mechanism, the category vector exchanges information with each chunk and extracts necessary features for large file classification. Finally, the category vector is fed into a fully connected layer to finalize the classification task.

5   Experimental Setup

Datasets. To ensure a fair comparison with baselines, we adopt the same benchmark datasets utilized in the state-of-the-arts for long document classification [33]. We first evaluate LaFiCMIL on these six benchmark datasets: ① Hyperpartisan [22], a compact dataset encompassing 645 documents, designed for *binary classification*. ② 20NewsGroups [26], comprising 20 balanced categories and 11 846 documents. ③ CMU Book Summary [6], tailored for *multi-label classification*, contains 12 788 documents and 227 genre labels. ④ Paired Book Summary [33], formulated by combining pairs of documents from the CMU Book

Table 1. Statistics on the datasets. # BERT Tokens indicates the average token number obtained via the BERT tokenizer. % Long Docs means the proportion of documents exceeding 512 BERT tokens.

Dataset	Type	# Total	# Train	# Val	# Test	# Labels	# BERT Tokens	% Long Docs
Hyperpartisan	binary	645	516	64	65	2	744.18 ± 677.87	53.49
20NewsGroups	multi-class	18846	10182	1132	7532	20	368.83 ± 783.84	14.71
Book Summary	multi-label	12788	10230	1279	1279	227	574.31 ± 659.56	38.46
-Paired	multi-label	6393	5115	639	639	227	1148.62 ± 933.97	75.54
EURLEX-57K	multi-label	57000	45000	6000	6000	4271	707.99 ± 538.69	51.3
-Inverted	multi-label	57000	45000	6000	6000	4271	707.99 ± 538.69	51.3
Devign	binary	27318	21854	2732	2732	2	615.46 ± 41917.54	39.76

Table 2. Performance metrics on only long documents in test set. The highest score is bolded and underlined, while the second highest score is only bolded. The subsequent tables of this task are organized in a consistent manner.

Model	Hyperpartisan	20News	EURLEX	-Inverted	Book	-Paired
BERT	88.00	86.09	66.76	62.88	60.56	52.23
-TextRank	85.63	85.55	66.56	64.22	61.76	56.24
-Random	83.50	**86.18**	**67.03**	**64.31**	**62.34**	56.77
Longformer	**93.17**	85.50	44.66	47.00	59.66	**58.85**
ToBERT	86.50	–	61.85	59.50	61.38	58.17
CogLTX	91.91	86.07	61.95	63.00	60.71	55.74
RMT	90.04	83.62	64.16	63.21	60.62	58.27
LaFiCMIL	**<u>95.00</u>**	**<u>87.49</u>**	**<u>67.28</u>**	**<u>65.04</u>**	**65.41**	**<u>63.03</u>**

Summary dataset, features longer documents. ⑤ EURLEX-57K [11], a substantial *multi-label classification* dataset consisting of 57 000 EU legal documents and 4271 available labels. ⑥ Inverted EURLEX-57K [33], a modified version of EURLEX-57K dataset in which the order of sections is inverted, ensuring that core information appears towards the end of the document. To evaluate our method's effectiveness with longer documents, we incorporated the Devign dataset [54] for code defect detection. It features documents that are substantially longer than those in the other six datasets, with lengths approaching or exceeding 20,000 tokens. Table 1 provides details of the datasets, covering metrics such as the average token count and its standard deviation, the maximum and minimum token counts, and the percentage of large documents, etc.

Implementation Details. We split a long text document into chunks (i.e., c-MIL instances), and follow the standard BERT input length (i.e., 512 tokens) for each chunk. To ensure a fair comparison, in line with the baselines, we employ BERT [13] for the first six datasets, and CodeBERT [16] and VulBERTa [17] for Devign, as the feature extractor. Since we treat all chunks in each long document as a mini-batch, the actual batch size varies depending on the number of chunks in the long document. We construct LaFiAttention layer with eight attention heads. Under these configurations, a single Tesla V-100 GPU with 32 GB of memory on an NVIDIA DGX Station can fully process 100% of the large documents in the first six benchmark datasets and 99.92% of those from Devign. As a result, the average inference time (0.026 s) of each mini-batch is almost the same as BERT (0.022 s). During training, the Adam optimizer [23] is leveraged. The loss function varies depending on specific task. Following the baseline [33], we use sigmoid and binary cross entropy for binary and multi-label classification, and softmax and cross entropy loss for multi-class classification. For the Hyperpartisan, Book Summary, EURLEX-57K, and Devign datasets, a learning rate of 5e-6 is used, while 5e-7 is applied for the 20NewsGroups dataset. We fine-tune the model for 10, 20, 40, 60, and 100 epochs on Devign, Hyperpartisan, 20NewsGroups, EURLEX-57K, and Book Summary, respectively.

Table 3. Performance metrics on complete test set. The highest score in each column is bolded and underlined, while the second highest score is only bolded.

Model	Hyperpartisan	20News	EURLEX	-Inverted	Book	-Paired
BERT	92.00	84.79	73.09	70.53	58.18	52.24
-TextRank	91.15	84.99	72.87	71.30	58.94	55.99
-Random	89.23	84.65	**73.22**	**71.47**	**59.36**	56.58
Longformer	**95.69**	83.39	54.53	56.47	56.53	**57.76**
ToBERT	89.54	**85.52**	67.57	67.31	58.16	57.08
CogLTX	94.77	84.62	70.13	70.80	58.27	55.91
RMT	94.34	82.87	71.46	70.99	57.30	56.95
LaFiCMIL	**96.92**	85.07	**73.72**	**72.03**	**61.34**	**62.17**

Evaluation Setup. We evaluate the performance of LaFiCMIL using the same metrics as those employed in the baselines [17,33]. We report the accuracy (%) for binary and multi-class classification. We use micro-F1 (%) for multi-label classification, and detection accuracy (%) for code defect detection. The results are the average of five independent runs, each with a different random seed. As we explained in the introduction, our work aims to address this challenge by focusing on using a more practical resource: a single GPU with 32 GB of memory, which is only a tenth of what RGPT demands (i.e., 320 GB). Therefore, given the distinct resource requirements and application contexts, comparing our approach with LLMs falls outside the scope of this study.

6   Experimental Results

In this section, we analyze the performance of LaFiCMIL in long document classification. We first discuss the overall performance, followed by an computational efficiency analysis and an ablation study on the core concepts of LaFiCMIL.

6.1   Overall Performance

Our experimental results reveal a phenomenon similar to [33] in that no existing approach consistently outperforms the others across all benchmark datasets. However, as shown in Table 2, our LaFiCMIL establishes new state-of-the-art performance on all six NLP benchmark datasets when considering only long documents in the test set. Here, we define a long document as one containing over 512 BERT tokens. As shown in Table 3, we also achieve new state-of-the-art performance on five out of six NLP datasets when considering the full data (i.e., a mix of long and short documents) in the test set. Particularly, we significantly improve the state-of-the-art score from 57.76% to 62.17% on the Paired Book Summary dataset, which contains the highest proportion of long documents (i.e., more than 75%). In contrast, we fail to achieve the best performance on 20NewsGroups, as the proportion of long documents in this dataset is very small (only 14.71%); thus, our improvement on **long** documents (as shown in Table 2) cannot dominate the overall performance on the entire dataset. This phenomenon is consistent with our motivation that the more long documents present in the dataset, the more correlations LaFiCMIL can extract to boost classification performance.

Table 4. Accuracy (%) comparison of different models on Devign dataset for code defect detection. The highest accuracy score is bolded and underlined, and the base model results are only bolded.

RoBERTa	CodeBERT	Code2vec [3]	PLBART [2]	VulBERTa	CodeBERT+LaFiCMIL	VulBERTa+LaFiCMIL
61.05	**62.08**	62.48	63.18	**64.27**	63.43	**64.53**

Table 5. Runtime and memory requirements of each model, **relative to BERT**, based on the Hyperpartisan dataset. Training and inference time were measured and compared in seconds per epoch. GPU memory requirement is in GB.

Model	Train Time	Inference Time	GPU Memory
BERT	1.00	1.00	<16
-TextRank	1.96	1.96	16
-Random	1.98	2.00	16
Longformer	12.05	11.92	32
ToBERT	1.19	1.70	32
CogLTX	104.52	12.53	<16
RMT	2.95	2.87	32
LaFiCMIL	1.86	1.18	<32

Given that 100% of long documents from the six NLP datasets can be fully processed, we conduct an additional evaluation of LaFiCMIL's ability to process **extremely long** sequences, based on the code defect detection dataset Devign. Our findings reveal that LaFiCMIL is capable of handling inputs of up to nearly 20 000 tokens when utilizing CodeBERT [16] and VulBERTa [17] as feature extractors on a **single** GPU setup. This capability allows for 99.92% of the code files in the Devign dataset to be processed in their entirety. Concurrently, as shown in Table 4, LaFiCMIL enhances the performance of both CodeBERT and VulBERTa, establishing a new state-of-the-art in accuracy over the evaluated baselines. We find that code defect detection is a challenging task on which most existing state-of-the-art models struggle to achieve even a single percentage point improvement over previous models. Nonetheless, our LaFiCMIL helps CodeBERT gain 1.35% points, representing a significant improvement.

6.2 Computational Efficiency Analysis

In this section, we provide a comprehensive analysis of computational efficiency outlined in Table 5. All models were evaluated on a single GPU with 32 GB of memory using the Hyperpartisan dataset. LaFiCMIL performs distinctly in this context, demonstrating a runtime nearly on par with BERT. The balance between high computational efficiency and advanced classification capability illustrates LaFiCMIL's exceptional capability to efficiently process long documents without significant computational overhead.

6.3 Ablation Study

Table 6. Concept ablation study on long documents in test set. "wo" means "LaFiCMIL **without**".

Model	Hyperpartisan	20News	EURLEX	-Inverted	Book	-Paired
wo BERT	85.00	53.92	60.54	54.14	50.11	46.61
wo LaFiAttn	87.50	84.97	**66.82**	**64.89**	**62.50**	60.13
wo c-MIL	**88.00**	**86.09**	66.76	62.88	60.56	52.23
LaFiCMIL	**95.00**	**87.22**	**67.28**	**65.04**	**65.41**	**63.03**

To gain a comprehensive understanding of the efficacy of each core concept in our approach (namely, BERT, LaFiAttention, and c-MIL), we conduct an ablation study. This study aims to evaluate the classification performance of LaFiCMIL when each concept is systematically removed, allowing us to evaluate their individual contributions.

Without a feature extractor, any approach would be ineffective. Thus, when BERT is removed, the LaFiAttention layer must assume the role of feature extractor instead of c-MIL. This would result in the disappearance of the c-MIL mechanism, and the approach can now only take the first chunk as input, transforming it into a basic attention-based classifier. As might be expected, the absence of the BERT concept leads to the worst performance across all datasets among the three variants, as shown in the first row of Table 6. If excluding the LaFiAttention concept, c-MIL devolves into a standard MIL, for which we employ the widely accepted Attention-MIL [19]. The results of this setting are presented in the second row of Table 6. Given that this variant can still process all chunks of a lengthy document, it performs best among all three variants on the four datasets with the largest number and longest length of documents. When the c-MIL concept is removed, the LaFiAttention layer will also be absent as it executes c-MIL which is no longer needed, leaving only BERT. Due to its restriction to process only the first chunk as input, this variant fails to achieve the best results on the four datasets that are dominated by long documents. Finally, upon comparing the three variants with the full LaFiCMIL, shown in the fourth row of Table 6, it becomes evident that the exclusion of any concept significantly weakens performances across all datasets.

7   Conclusion

We propose LaFiCMIL, a large file classification approach based on correlated multiple instance learning. Our method treats large document chunks as c-MIL instances, enabling feature extraction for classification from correlated chunks without substantial information loss. Experimental results demonstrate that our approach significantly outperforms the state-of-the-art baselines across multiple benchmark datasets in terms of both efficiency and accuracy. Our work provides a new perspective for addressing the large document classification problem.

Acknowledgment. This research was funded in whole, or in part, by the Luxembourg National Research Fund (FNR), grant references 16344458 (REPROCESS), 18154263 (UNLOCK), and 17046335 (AFR PhD grant).

References

1. Achiam, J., et al.: GPT-4 technical report. arXiv preprint arXiv:2303.08774 (2023)
2. Ahmad, W.U., Chakraborty, S., Ray, B., Chang, K.W.: Unified pre-training for program understanding and generation. arXiv preprint arXiv:2103.06333 (2021)
3. Alon, U., Zilberstein, M., Levy, O., Yahav, E.: code2vec: learning distributed representations of code. In: Proceedings of the ACM on Programming Languages (2019)
4. Ba, J.L., Kiros, J.R., Hinton, G.E.: Layer normalization. arXiv preprint arXiv:1607.06450 (2016)
5. Baker, C.T.: The Numerical Treatment of Integral Equations. Oxford University Press, Oxford (1977)
6. Bamman, D., Smith, N.: New alignment methods for discriminative book summarization. arXiv preprint arXiv:1305.1319 (2013)
7. Beltagy, I., Peters, M.E., Cohan, A.: Longformer: the long-document transformer. arXiv preprint arXiv:2004.05150 (2020)

8. Ben-Israel, A., Greville, T.N.: Generalized Inverses: Theory and Applications, vol. 15. Springer, Heidelberg (2003)
9. Bulatov, A., Kuratov, Y., Burtsev, M.S.: Scaling transformer to 1 m tokens and beyond with RMT. arXiv preprint arXiv:2304.11062 (2023)
10. Bulatov, A., Kuratov, Y., Burtsev, M.: Recurrent memory transformer. In: Advances in Neural Information Processing Systems, vol. 35, pp. 11079–11091 (2022)
11. Chalkidis, I., Fergadiotis, M., Malakasiotis, P., Androutsopoulos, I.: Large-scale multi-label text classification on EU legislation. arXiv:1906.02192 (2019)
12. Dang, N.C., Moreno-García, M.N., De la Prieta, F.: Sentiment analysis based on deep learning: a comparative study. Electronics **9**(3), 483 (2020)
13. Devlin, J., Chang, M.W., Lee, K., Toutanova, K.: BERT: pre-training of deep bidirectional transformers for language understanding. arXiv:1810.04805 (2018)
14. Ding, M., Zhou, C., Yang, H., Tang, J.: CogLTX: applying BERT to long texts. In: NeurIPS (2020)
15. Feng, J., Zhou, Z.H.: Deep MIML network. In: AAAI (2017)
16. Feng, Z., et al.: CodeBERT: a pre-trained model for programming and natural languages. In: Findings of EMNLP (2020)
17. Hanif, H., Maffeis, S.: VulBERTa: simplified source code pre-training for vulnerability detection. arXiv preprint arXiv:2205.12424 (2022)
18. Hebbar, R., et al.: Deep multiple instance learning for foreground speech localization in ambient audio from wearable devices. Speech, and Music Processing, Audio (2021)
19. Ilse, M., Tomczak, J., Welling, M.: Attention-based deep multiple instance learning. In: ICML (2018)
20. Ji, Y., Liu, H., He, B., Xiao, X., Wu, H., Yu, Y.: Diversified multiple instance learning for document-level multi-aspect sentiment classification. In: EMNLP (2020)
21. Kanavati, F., et al.: Weakly-supervised learning for lung carcinoma classification using deep learning. Sci. Rep. (2020)
22. Kiesel, J., et al.: SemEval-2019 task 4: Hyperpartisan news detection. In: 13th International Workshop on Semantic Evaluation (2019)
23. Kingma, D.P., Ba, J.: Adam: a method for stochastic optimization. arXiv preprint arXiv:1412.6980 (2014)
24. Kowsari, K., Jafari Meimandi, K., Heidarysafa, M., Mendu, S., Barnes, L., Brown, D.: Text classification algorithms: a survey. Information **10**(4), 150 (2019)
25. Kumar, S., Asthana, R., Upadhyay, S., Upreti, N., Akbar, M.: Fake news detection using deep learning models: a novel approach. Trans. Emerg. Telecommun. Technol. **31**(2), e3767 (2020)
26. Lang, K.: NewsWeeder: learning to filter netnews. In: Machine Learning Proceedings 1995, pp. 331–339 (1995)
27. Lerousseau, M., et al.: Weakly supervised multiple instance learning histopathological tumor segmentation. In: Martel, A.L., et al. (eds.) MICCAI 2020. LNCS, vol. 12265, pp. 470–479. Springer, Cham (2020). https://doi.org/10.1007/978-3-030-59722-1_45
28. Li, B., Li, Y., Eliceiri, K.W.: Dual-stream multiple instance learning network for whole slide image classification with self-supervised contrastive learning. In: CVPR (2021)
29. Liu, Y., et al.: RoBERTa: a robustly optimized BERT pretraining approach. arXiv preprint arXiv:1907.11692 (2019)

30. Lu, M.Y., Williamson, D.F., Chen, T.Y., Chen, R.J., Barbieri, M., Mahmood, F.: Data-efficient and weakly supervised computational pathology on whole-slide images. Nat. Biomed. Eng. **5**, 555–570 (2021)
31. Mihalcea, R., Tarau, P.: TextRank: bringing order into text. In: EMNLP (2004)
32. Pappagari, R., Zelasko, P., Villalba, J., Carmiel, Y., Dehak, N.: Hierarchical transformers for long document classification. In: IEEE ASRU (2019)
33. Park, H., Vyas, Y., Shah, K.: Efficient classification of long documents using transformers. In: ACL (2022)
34. Radford, A., Narasimhan, K., Salimans, T., Sutskever, I., et al.: Improving language understanding by generative pre-training (2018)
35. Radford, A., et al.: Language models are unsupervised multitask learners. OpenAI Blog **1**(8), 9 (2019)
36. Ranasinghe, T., Zampieri, M.: Multilingual offensive language identification with cross-lingual embeddings. arXiv preprint arXiv:2010.05324 (2020)
37. Razavi, M.K., Kerayechian, A., Gachpazan, M., Shateyi, S.: A new iterative method for finding approximate inverses of complex matrices. In: Abstract and Applied Analysis (2014)
38. Rote, G.: Computing the minimum hausdorff distance between two point sets on a line under translation. Inf. Process. Lett. **38**(3), 123–127 (1991)
39. Rumelhart, D.E., Hinton, G.E., Williams, R.J.: Learning representations by back-propagating errors. Nature (1986)
40. Shao, Z., Bian, H., Chen, Y., Wang, Y., Zhang, J., et al.: Transmil: transformer based correlated multiple instance learning for whole slide image classification. In: NeurIPS (2021)
41. Sharma, Y., Shrivastava, A., Ehsan, L., Moskaluk, C.A., Syed, S., Brown, D.: Cluster-to-conquer: a framework for end-to-end multi-instance learning for whole slide image classification. In: Medical Imaging with Deep Learning (2021)
42. Shen, D., et al.: Baseline needs more love: On simple word-embedding-based models and associated pooling mechanisms. arXiv preprint arXiv:1805.09843 (2018)
43. Song, K., et al.: Using customer service dialogues for satisfaction analysis with context-assisted multiple instance learning. In: EMNLP (2019)
44. Sun, T., et al.: DexBERT: effective, task-agnostic and fine-grained representation learning of Android bytecode. IEEE Trans. Softw. Eng. (2023)
45. Touvron, H., et al.: Llama 2: open foundation and fine-tuned chat models. arXiv preprint arXiv:2307.09288 (2023)
46. Vaswani, A., et al.: Attention is all you need. In: NeurIPS (2017)
47. Wang, X., Yan, Y., Tang, P., Bai, X., Liu, W.: Revisiting multiple instance neural networks. Pattern Recogn. (2018)
48. Xiong, Y., et al.: Nyströmformer: a nyström-based algorithm for approximating self-attention. In: AAAI (2021)
49. Xu, G., et al.: Camel: a weakly supervised learning framework for histopathology image segmentation. In: ICCV (2019)
50. Zaheer, M., et al.: Big bird: transformers for longer sequences. In: NeurIPS (2020)
51. Zhang, H., et al.: DTFD-mil: double-tier feature distillation multiple instance learning for histopathology whole slide image classification. In: CVPR (2022)
52. Zhang, W.: Non-IID multi-instance learning for predicting instance and bag labels using variational auto-encoder. arXiv preprint arXiv:2105.01276 (2021)
53. Zhang, Y., et al.: Pushing the limit of LLM capacity for text classification. arXiv preprint arXiv:2402.07470 (2024)

54. Zhou, Y., Liu, S., Siow, J., Du, X., Liu, Y.: Devign: effective vulnerability identification by learning comprehensive program semantics via graph neural networks. In: NeurIPS (2019)
55. Zhou, Z.H., Sun, Y.Y., Li, Y.F.: Multi-instance learning by treating instances as non-IID samples. In: ICML (2009)

Unveiling Depression on Social Media: Active Learning with Human-in-the-Loop Labeling for Mental Health Data Annotation and Analysis

Mohsinul Kabir[✉] 🆔, Faria Binte Kader 🆔, Nafisa Hossain Nujat,
Tasmia Binte Sogir 🆔, Fatin Abrar Shams, Hasan Mahmud 🆔,
and Kamrul Hasan

Department of Computer Science and Engineering, Islamic University of Technology,
Dhaka, Bangladesh
{mohsinulkabir,faria,nafisa13,tasmia,abrarshams,hasan,
hasank}@iut-dhaka.edu

Abstract. Progress in mental health research remains constrained by the accessibility of adequate, high-quality data. Annotating mental health data requires a lot of resources and expert monitoring. In this study, we explore the utility of active learning with Human-in-the-Loop labeling approach to reduce the annotation task for identifying signs of depression in people's social media posts. The data for this study was collected from the #WorldMentalHealthDay trend on Twitter, which is a popular mental health campaign to raise awareness of mental illness across the global population. From the pool of unlabeled data, we initially labeled a small portion of data to train an LSTM model with GloVe embedding; thereafter, the entire pool was labeled using uncertainty sampling, labeling the least confident data in each cycle. Along with the methodology, we present a high-quality dataset of 3659 samples, with a notable proportion of 22% of tweets indicating symptoms of depression. We also analyze the language usage of depressed and non-depressed individuals on social media by dissecting the semantic structure of tweets. The quality of the dataset was validated by establishing strong baseline results with state-of-the-art models and word-embedding techniques.

Keywords: Active Learning · Dataset · Depression · LDA · Mental Health

1 Introduction

According to the World Health Organization (WHO), around 280 million people suffer from depression globally[1]. However, depression is often left undiagnosed and untreated due to stigma and a lack of effective therapies and sufficient mental health facilities. Approximately half of the global population lives in countries

---

[1] https://www.who.int/news-room/fact-sheets/detail/depression.

A. Rapp et al. (Eds.): NLDB 2024, LNCS 14762, pp. 78–92, 2024.
https://doi.org/10.1007/978-3-031-70239-6_6

with only two psychiatrists per 100,000 people [1]. Because of the recent global threat of COVID-19 pandemic, an increase in anxiety and depression around the world followed as a result of isolation, media information overload, panic buying of necessities [2]. The National Institute of Mental Health (NIMH) estimates that 21 million U.S. adults had at least one major depressive episode in 2021 which represents 8.3% of the U.S. adult population [55]. The advent of social media, where many users prefer to discuss their mental health issues on open forums, has opened up new opportunities in this domain by allowing for an abundance of data. With such a large user-base and wealth of data, it is possible to detect mental disorders early, stop self-harm or suicide by examining linguistic patterns, and do much more. Recent attempts to utilize this data include suicide risk analysis [3], detecting severity of depression [4], identifying linguistic features of depression [5] etc. Unfortunately, despite the availability of data, making them useful for training a predictive model still remain difficult due to cost, time or lack of expert personnel. One of the essential components for building such models is high-quality, large-scale, annotated datasets [6]. However, depending on self-labeled data or unsupervised clustering might lead to oversimplification and a lack of clinical efficacy [7].

It is indisputable that the wealth of user data present in social media holds the potential for detecting mental health conditions. However, the absence of ideal ground truth standards poses a challenge to realizing this potential. The manual annotation of such data demands significant effort and the involvement of domain experts. One potential remedy for this challenge is the application of Active Learning [29,30], as evidenced by its successful use in various domains to mitigate the annotation burden and facilitate the creation of large-scale datasets [50]. Active learning tries to annotate as few samples as possible while optimizing the model's overall performance gain. It periodically chooses new instances to be labeled by a human annotator and adds them to the training dataset to improve the learner's performance on unseen data. The uncertainty-based selection or uncertainty sampling [8] is the most commonly used active learning method which measures the uncertainties of unlabeled data and chooses the ones to be annotated by human annotators. Lewis [8] first introduced a pool-based active learning method with uncertainty sampling for classification and applied it to a text-domain using logistic regression.

This study aims to contribute to this domain by (1) proposing a methodology for constructing mental health datasets adopting an uncertainty-based active learning (AL) algorithm with minimal human annotation intervention and (2) producing and publishing a high-quality dataset comprising 3659 English tweets that are labeled as non-depressive or depressive. Table 1 demonstrates a sample of the proposed dataset. Our goal is to utilize active learning (AL) to reduce the amount of human involvement required to produce large-scale annotated datasets in the mental health domain. The Active Learning algorithm with uncertainty sampling used in this work produced solid baseline results with a minimal number of active learning cycles and a decreasing number of hand-labeled samples per cycle, indicating the effectiveness and precision of our proposed method.

The remainder of the paper is structured as follows: Sect. 2 reviews related work. Sections 3 and 4 describe the methodology and dataset properties, respectively. Section 5 presents the classification experiments. Finally, limitations, conclusions and future work are discussed in Sects. 6 and 7.

Table 1. Representative Samples from the Proposed Dataset

Non-depressive	To every world leader tweeting about #WorldMental-HealthDay: Funding mental health services is always better than tweeting about it
Depressive	Hoping and praying to not feel like giving it all up on next year's #WorldMentalHealthDay

2   Related Work

Even though the quality of data still remains in question, the accessibility and abundance of data through social media fueled many studies regarding mental illness detection. One of the earliest such works by Moreno et al. [9] analyzes the Facebook statements made by college students that met the Diagnostic and Statistical Manual's (DSM) requirements for a Major Depressive Episode (MDE) or a symptom of depression. According to their findings, 25% of the college students' Facebook posts are compliant with the criteria for depression symptoms. Similarly, De Choudhury et al. [10] explored the potential to use social media to detect Major Depressive Disorder (MDD) and utilized behavioral cues to build an SVM classifier to estimate the risk of depression. In their study, Park et al. [11] explored a variety of evidence to support the claim that data from online social networks can be useful for identifying users' depressive moods. Extensive research has been conducted in this domain over the past decade. These studies inspired us to create a mental health dataset where the data was collected from social media. Coppersmith et al. [12] used statistical classifiers to differentiate users with various disorders and conducted both an LIWC (Linguistic Inquiry Word Count) analysis and an open-vocabulary analysis to capture language features relevant to those disorders. LIWC, a psychometric analysis tool, has been used in mental health research by many [13]. Mental illness detection from text data can be divided into two primary categories: topic modeling [15–17] and use of linguistic features [18–20]. There are clear benefits of using topic modeling, as demonstrated by [17,21] at the CLPsych 2015 Shared Task - these systems provided strong signals relevant to mental health, and some intuitive groupings of words without significant manual intervention [22]. Latent Dirichlet Allocation (LDA) [23] has also been used in a handful of mental illness detection research [16,20,24–26]. In this study, a qualitative analysis of the LDA has helped us get a deeper insight into the contexts of the two categories.

For automating the annotation task at hand, we investigated two potential techniques that seemed to be promising. The first is the N-Gram technique to detect the polarity of the sentiment of the user and the second one is Active Learning. In the works of Qureshi et al. [27] a dataset was created using the reviews of the ten most popular songs on YouTube and it consisted of 369436 reviews. The n-gram technique was also used to find the polarity of the sentiment and to detect depression 9 classification models were used [28]. Active learning provides exponential improvements over passive learning in sampling complexity while requiring a comparable number of labeled examples [31]. Kranjc et al. demonstrated its superiority in updating sentiment classifiers for Twitter data [33], while Pohl et al. introduced a novel batch-based active learning algorithm for online data streams [34]. Bouguelia et al. [35] proposed a new uncertainty measure outperforming conventional ones, and Ahmed et al. [36] utilized active learning for updating training models and presented a fuzzy classification-based deep attention model. Nguyen et al. explored the efficacy of various uncertainty sampling measures in active learning [38].

For the task of depression detection, we investigated the techniques that were well-established for this purpose. In the works of Adarsh et al. [39], the BERT model was used for depression detection which was pre-trained with Wikipedia text which had an accuracy of 0.636 and a weighted F1 score of 0.638. Similarly, Chenhao et al. [40] proposed a visual-textual Multimodal Learning technique where the BERT model was used to detect signs of depression from texts extracted from social media. The task of depression detection has also been addressed using the LSTM model which has performed better compared to other baseline models for both balanced and imbalanced datasets [41]. The performance of sequential and nonsequential models has also been analyzed for measuring the latency of depression detection by Farig et al. [42] where the SVM model compared to the GRU model had a higher latency and at the same time was much more accurate.

Based on the aforementioned evidences, we aimed to use active learning to reduce the annotation task instead of N-Gram as the task at hand is much more complex compared to just detecting the polarity of emotion. Moreover, we chose three algorithms to detect depression which are LSTM, BERT, and SVM which have proved to work well for the concerned purpose.

3   Methodology

Our methodology involves meticulous data collection from Twitter, recruiting annotators who are trained by expert psychologists to ensure the clinical precision of the dataset, and implementing cycles of the active learning algorithm with a human-in-the-loop approach. The entire process is visually depicted in Fig. 2.

Data Collection

TWINT[2] was used to collect data for this study using the #WorldMentalHealth-Day keyword from Twitter. Non-English and repeating tweets were removed from the initial pool of 18000 tweets. A total of 3659 unlabeled tweets remained after the filtering process. For the first stage of active learning, a small portion (~27%) of the data pool was randomly selected and hand-labeled by the annotators (Label 0 for non-depressive tweet, Label 1 for depressive tweet).

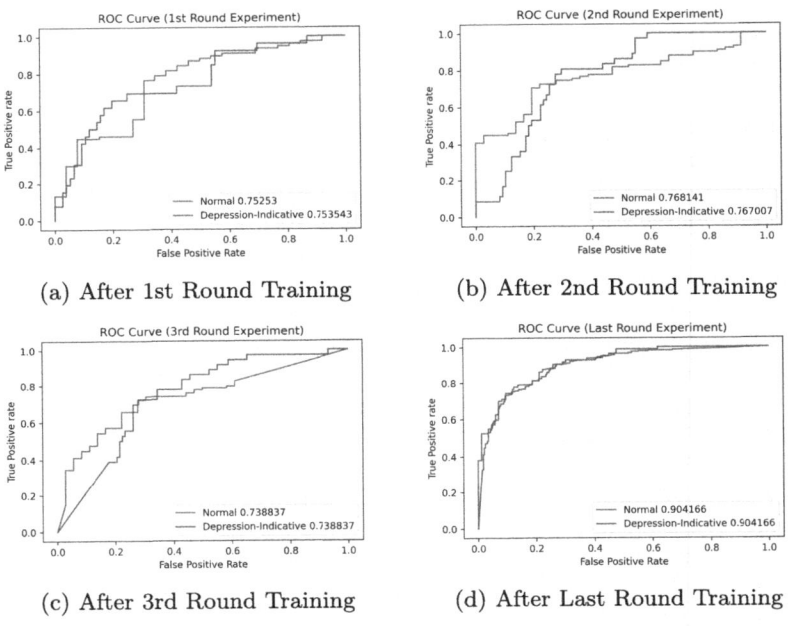

(a) After 1st Round Training   (b) After 2nd Round Training

(c) After 3rd Round Training   (d) After Last Round Training

Fig. 1. ROC Curves in Different Stages of Active Learning

Data Annotation

The annotation guideline was designed by following the characteristics of depressed and non-depressed tweets provided by Kabir et al. [4], which was based on a well-established clinical assessment method known as the Diagnostic and Statistical Manual of Mental Disorders, Fifth Edition (DSM-5) [51] and was carried out under the supervision of two expert clinical psychologists. The dataset in this study was labeled based on these annotation instructions, which involved assigning two labels:

– **Non-depressive:** A non-depressive tweet expresses a person's joy or delight, or makes a generalized statement about depression that does not reflect the person's own mental state and shows no symptoms of depression.

---

[2] https://github.com/twintproject/twint.

– **Depressive:** Tweets that contain symptoms of hopelessness, feelings of guilt or despair, difficulties concentrating at work, a loss of interest in activities, a sudden disinterest in socializing, a lack of motivation, insomnia (a medical condition where people feel difficulty to fall asleep, staying asleep or they wake up too early), and reckless behavior (such as alcohol and drug abuse) are depressive tweets.

Under the supervision of a professional psychologist, the annotation was completed by three experienced annotators who had previously annotated mental health data. The annotators were privately contacted and received compensation. The collaborating psychologist reviewed each annotator's work after each cycle and eliminated any incorrect entries. Due to the expert psychologist's involvement, the inter-annotator agreement score was not calculated.

Active Learning Cycles

As previously mentioned, approximately 27% of the unlabeled samples were randomly selected for the first phase of the active learning algorithm. The active learning algorithm with uncertainty sampling developed for this study is depicted in Algorithm 1.

Algorithm 1: Active Learning with Uncertainty Sampling

Input: $\mathcal{U} \rightarrow$ unlabeled dataset, $\mathcal{L} \rightarrow$ labeled data for training, $\theta \rightarrow$ classification model;

Initialize: Use $\mathcal{L}$ to train the initial classifier θ;

Repeat

1. Use the current classifier θ to predict class probabilities of all unlabeled samples $\mathcal{U}$.
2. Calculate Least Confidence (ϕ_{LC}) score to select m most informative unlabeled samples, and hand label them.
3. Augment $\mathcal{L}$ with these new m samples, and remove them from $\mathcal{U}$.
4. Use $\mathcal{L}$ to retrain the current classifier θ.

Until all samples from $\mathcal{U}$ overcome the threshold Least Confidence (ϕ_{LC}) score.

Automatically label the remaining samples from $\mathcal{U}$ based on their predicted class probability score by θ.

return $\mathcal{L}$

An LSTM classifier with GloVe embedding was trained with these hand-labeled data after further preprocessing, such as text lower-casing and removing punctuations. The trained classifier was used to predict the class probability of all the unlabeled data. Afterward, a handful of samples from the unlabeled data pool were picked for hand-labeling where the classifier was most uncertain in predicting the class label (uncertainty sampling). Least Confidence score (ϕ_{LC})

was used as the uncertainty measure where a higher (ϕ_{LC}) score implies that the classifier is more uncertain about the sample. The least confidence score for a particular sample can be written as:

$$\text{Least Confidence}\,(\phi_{LC}) = \frac{n(1 - argmax\, P_\theta(\hat{y}|x))}{n-1} \tag{1}$$

In formula 1, $argmax\, P_\theta(\hat{y}|x)$ represents the highest predicted probability for a sample from the probability distribution $P_\theta(y|x)$ given by the classification model θ. The numerator of the equation calculates the least confidence by taking the difference between 1 (indicating 100% confidence) and the probability of the most confidently predicted label for each item. This score is then normalized by multiplying by $n/n - 1$, where n denotes the number of classes, which in our case is 2.

The Least Confidence (ϕ_{LC}) score for each sample was calculated using formula 1, and samples with a ϕ_{LC} score larger than 0.6 were chosen for hand-labeling. This threshold was selected based on manual inspection, as it provided the optimal number of most informative samples-those the model is most uncertain about-for hand-labeling in the subsequent cycle. These newly annotated samples were then combined with the initial set of hand-labeled samples, and the LSTM classifier was retrained on this augmented dataset to predict the class probabilities of the remaining unlabeled data. This active learning process was continued till there were no samples left whose ϕ_{LC} score crossed the threshold value. The whole active learning algorithm is depicted in Algorithm 1.

Table 2. Active Learning Cycles

Phase	Hand-labeled Tweets
Initial Stage	1014
After First Round Prediction	323
After Second Round Prediction	182
After Third Round Prediction	126
Total Hand-Labeled Tweets	1645 (45%)

After 3 complete active learning cycles, most of the samples were automatically labeled based on a very high class-probability and no samples were left that crossed the threshold ϕ_{LC} score, resulting in a dataset of 3659 annotated tweets, of which only 1645 (<45%) were hand-labeled. Table 2 gives the annotation summary for each cycle. Figure 2 shows the overview of the whole Active learning process that was used to annotate the dataset. Figure 1 illustrates how the Receiver Operating Characteristic (ROC) curves evolved after each cycle of active learning, where gradual improvement throughout the rounds indicates the classifier's overall improved performance in distinguishing between the two classes.

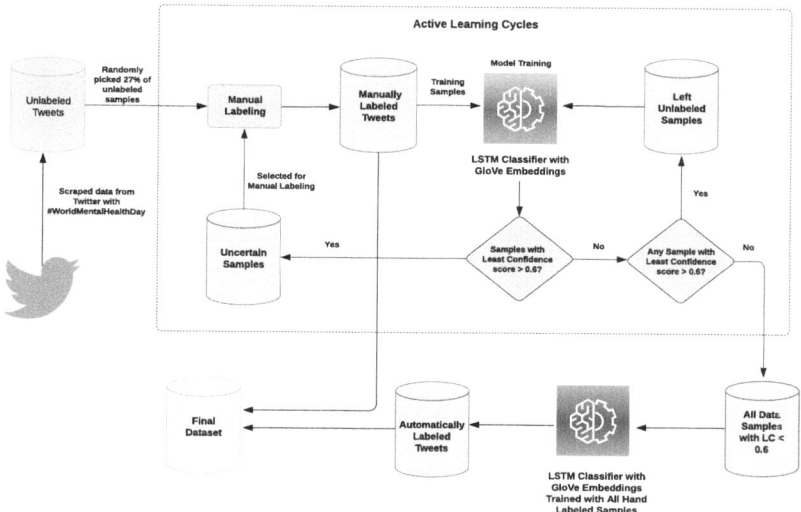

Fig. 2. Overview of the Active Learning Process to Annotate the Dataset

4   Dataset Properties

Following the completion of the active learning cycles and annotation process, the final label of all tweets was determined based on their class probability score. Consequently, the proposed dataset obtained 807 tweets that indicated depression and 2852 depressive or non-depressive tweets, for a total of 3659 tweets. A detailed overview of the dataset is provided in Table 3. As seen from the table, depressive tweets are smaller in portion, but their average length is significantly larger than non-depressive tweets. Due to their limited quantity, depressive tweets contain fewer unique words and have a smaller vocabulary size. To gain a deeper understanding of these two categories of tweets, the lexical and semantic structure of the tweets were analyzed.

Table 4 presents the three leading LDA topics, as well as the probability distribution of words across those topics for each category of the dataset. Depressive topics are indicated in red, while non-depressive topics are indicated in green. A qualitative analysis of the identified LDA topics showed that common lexicons were utilized in various contexts for the two categories. Some terms were used to make generalized statements about mental health issues in *Non-depressive* class, such as "Mental Health Matters!", whereas the same terms were used to describe personal mental health concerns in *Depressive* category. This observation suggests a significant difference in language usage between individuals without symptoms of depression and those exhibiting depressive symptoms, which merits further investigation and is beyond the scope of the current work.

Table 3. General Overview of the Proposed Dataset

	Non-depressive	Depressive
# of Tweets	2852	807
Avg. Word Length	17.94	24.14
Word Count	51170	19480
Vocabulary Size	7175	3455
Ratio	77.94%	22.06%

Table 4. Class-wise Prevalent LDA Topics and Representing Words in the Dataset

Non-depressive	Depressive
Topic#1 Mental Health Awareness	Topic#1 Daily Life Adversities
0.046*"mental" + 0.041*"health" + 0.026*"today" + 0.023*"feel" + 0.014*"life" + 0.014*"matter" + 0.013*"want" + 0.012*"need" + 0.011*"help" + 0.011*"people"	0.025*"hard" + 0.024*"year" + 0.023*"thing" + 0.021*"know" + 0.017*"make" + 0.016*"people" + 0.016*"work" + 0.015*"life" + 0.015*"anxiety" + 0.015*"come"
Topic#2 Emotional Well-being	Topic#2 Long-Term Struggles
0.060*"okay" + 0.030*"feel" + 0.025*"go" + 0.021*"know" + 0.021*"kind" + 0.019*"time" + 0.017*"help" + 0.016*"love" + 0.014*"remember" + 0.013*"remind"	0.034*"year" + 0.028*"depress" + 0.028*"help" + 0.025*"today" + 0.022*"feel" + 0.018*"anxieties" + 0.016*"health" + 0.016*"want" + 0.016*"start" + 0.015*"mental"
Topic#3 Social Support and Mental Health	Topic#3 Coping with Mental Health Issues
0.059*"health" + 0.058*"mental" + 0.027*"love" + 0.024*"people" + 0.022*"need" + 0.018*"help" + 0.015*"today" + 0.015*"happy" + 0.013*"import" + 0.012*"support"	0.046*"mental" + 0.039*"health" + 0.029*"year" + 0.024*"depress" + 0.024*"life" + 0.020*"anxieties" + 0.019*"help" + 0.019*"like" + 0.019*"struggling" + 0.018*"therapist"

5   Classification Experiments

The choice of baseline models, evaluation metrics, and classification performance on the dataset are discussed in this section.

5.1   Baseline Models

Several baseline models were implemented to validate the utility of the dataset. For our baseline models, SVM, LSTM, and BERT were used with a combination of different feature-extraction techniques. The details of the implementations are discussed in the next few sections.

Support Vector Machine (SVM)

SVM attempts to construct a hyperplane that best divides multidimensional data points into their prospective classes and is effective for binary classification [43]. For our experiment, SVM was used with Tf-Idf and BoW (Bag of Words) features. GridSearchCV was used to tune the hyperparameters for the SVM model. A linear kernel with a C value of 0.9 was used to fine-tune SVM for Tf-Idf, while the classifier for the BoW features selected a similar kernel with a C value of 0.42.

Long Short Term Memory (LSTM)

LSTMs are a type of Recurrent Neural Network which was introduced to solve the vanishing gradient problem and effectively capture long-term dependencies even in noisy sequential data as they can learn to bridge minimal time lags in excess of 1000 steps [44]. Two word-embedding techniques, Word2Vec [46] and GloVe [45] were used to produce word-embeddings to train the LSTM [44] model. The word embedding layer was fed to an LSTM layer with 64 hidden units, then two dense layers of 32 and 16 units, respectively, and lastly a sigmoid layer which gave the output whether the input sentence is depressive or not. The overall architecture of the model is illustrated in Fig. 3. Adam optimizer was used with binary cross-entropy as our loss function. The model was trained for 10 epochs and early stopping was incorporated to prevent overfitting.

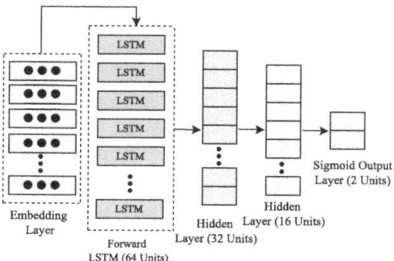

Fig. 3. Architecture of the LSTM Network

Fine-Tuning BERT

We also fine-tuned BERT [47], a pre-trained language model for the English language using mask language modeling, due to the recent success of BERT in various downstream NLP tasks. Prior studies have demonstrated that achieving excellent classification performance in diverse downstream tasks, such as text categorization, question-answering, summarization, and sentiment analysis of social media posts [54], is possible by fine-tuning transformer-based models like BERT. This success can be attributed to the pre-training of these models on a substantial amount of unlabeled data, utilizing self-supervised learning.

5.2   Classification Performance

To train and evaluate the model, the dataset was divided into 80% for training and 20% for testing. Additionally, 10% of the training set was set aside for validation. This resulted in 2,635 samples for training, 232 samples for validation, and 790 samples for testing. All of the experiments were done using Python 3.7 and ran for 10 epochs on Google Colaboratory. Well-known evaluation metrics such as Precision, Recall, and F1-score were calculated to demonstrate the performance.

Table 5. Results of Classification Experiments

Model	Class	Precision	Recall	F1-score
SVM-tf-idf	Non-depressive	0.83	0.98	0.90
	Depressive	0.81	0.25	0.38
SVM-bow	Non-depressive	0.85	0.94	0.89
	Depressive	0.67	0.43	0.52
LSTM-word2vec	Non-depressive	0.87	0.89	0.88
	Depressive	0.60	0.54	0.57
LSTM-GloVe	Non-depressive	0.91	0.88	0.90
	Depressive	0.61	0.70	0.65
BERT(base-cased)	Non-depressive	0.89	0.94	0.91
	Depressive	0.74	0.61	0.67

The class-wise classification performance of the baseline models is illustrated in Table 5. The BERT (base-cased) model outperforms all other models with a decent margin. Pre-trained language models like BERT, with its underlying architecture built on transformers, can capture long-range dependencies and contextual information, which is important for accurately understanding the meaning of a sentence or passage [48]. Fine-tuning a pretrained BERT model on the proposed dataset has enabled the model to leverage its learned knowledge to make accurate predictions on new, unseen test data. LSTM model with GloVe embedding also demonstrates good performance in differentiating between the categories in our dataset. SVM with handcrafted features like BoW or Tf-Idf also achieves decent result but falls short compared to the contextual embeddings. This discrepancy likely stems from the fact that while handcrafted features can capture certain syntactic elements, they fail to grasp the coherent meaning of sentences [49]. On the other hand, as a word-embedding technique, GloVe has a benefit over Word2Vec, as it does not only rely on local statistics (local context information of words), but also incorporates global statistics (word co-occurrence) to obtain word vectors [45].

6   Limitations

One of the challenges of this study was to avoid individual bias while hand-labeling the tweet samples. Given the geographical and cultural separation between the source of the tweets and the annotators' location, the annotation process may have been subject to clear cultural and geographic biases. To minimize this bias, the annotators were reminded several times throughout the annotation process to avoid their personal judgment and strictly follow the guidelines for hand labeling. Another consideration is that a user posting a depressive tweet does not necessarily indicate that they are experiencing depression. Our research centers on identifying the characteristics of depressive tweets rather than attempting to quantify the user's mental state, which would require an analysis of their behavioral patterns over time.

7   Conclusion and Future Work

This work constructs a minimally human-intervened dataset on depression detection by introducing an active learning approach with uncertainty sampling and incorporating a Human-in-the-Loop labeling methodology. Drawing data from the #WorldMentalHealthDay trend on Twitter, we present a dataset encompassing 3659 tweets with less than 45% samples being hand-labeled. Despite the modest scale of our dataset, it has yielded relatively high results, underscoring the potential efficacy of our approach. Future work can involve exploring various uncertainty sampling techniques to identify the most effective methods for different annotation scenarios. Moreover, a larger, meticulously curated dataset incorporating diverse perspectives and contributions from annotators of varied cultural and geographic backgrounds can enhance the robustness and cultural sensitivity of our methodology.

Dataset Availability and Ethical Consideration. The data associated with the research has been shared in this public git repository: https://github.com/mohsinulkabir14/wmhd. Without prior approval from the first author, the dataset, in whole or in part, should not be further distributed, published, copied, or disseminated in any way or form whatsoever, whether for profit or not. In no case should the tweets be used in a way that could reasonably cause embarrassment or mental anguish to the original subject. Such actions will be regarded as a serious criminal offense.

References

1. Smith, K., De Torres, I.: A world of depression. Nature **515**, 10-1038 (2014)
2. Wang, C., et al.: A longitudinal study on the mental health of general population during the COVID-19 epidemic in China. Brain Behav. Immun. **87**, 40–48 (2020)
3. Kumar, A., Trueman, T., Abinesh, A.: Suicidal risk identification in social media. Procedia Comput. Sci. **189**, 368–373 (2021)
4. Kabir, M., et al.: DEPTWEET: a typology for social media texts to detect depression severities. Comput. Hum. Behav. **139**, 107503 (2023)
5. Bucur, A., Podină, I., Dinu, L.: A psychologically informed part-of-speech analysis of depression in social media. arXiv preprint arXiv:2108.00279 (2021)
6. Gilardi, F., Alizadeh, M., Kubli, M.: ChatGPT outperforms crowd-workers for text-annotation tasks. arXiv preprint arXiv:2303.15056 (2023)
7. Ernala, S., et al.: Methodological gaps in predicting mental health states from social media: triangulating diagnostic signals. In: Proceedings of the 2019 CHI Conference on Human Factors in Computing Systems, pp. 1–16 (2019)
8. Lewis, D.: A sequential algorithm for training text classifiers: corrigendum and additional data. ACM SIGIR Forum **29**, 13–19 (1995)
9. Moreno, M., et al.: Feeling bad on Facebook: depression disclosures by college students on a social networking site. Depression Anxiety **28**, 447–455 (2011)
10. De Choudhury, M., Gamon, M., Counts, S., Horvitz, E.: Predicting depression via social media. In: Proceedings of the International AAAI Conference on Web and Social Media, vol. 7, pp. 128–137 (2013)
11. Park, M., Cha, C., Cha, M.: Depressive moods of users portrayed in Twitter. In: Proceedings of the 18th ACM International Conference on Knowledge Discovery and Data Mining, SIGKDD 2012, pp. 1–8 (2012)
12. Coppersmith, G., Dredze, M., Harman, C.: Quantifying mental health signals in Twitter. In: Proceedings of the Workshop on Computational Linguistics and Clinical Psychology: From Linguistic Signal to Clinical Reality, pp. 51–60 (2014)
13. Pennebaker, J., Boyd, R., Jordan, K., Blackburn, K.: The development and psychometric properties of LIWC2015 (2015)
14. Park, M., McDonald, D., Cha, M.: Perception differences between the depressed and non-depressed users in Twitter. In: Proceedings of the International AAAI Conference on Web and Social Media, vol. 7, pp. 476–485 (2013)
15. Tsugawa, S., Kikuchi, Y., Kishino, F., Nakajima, K., Itoh, Y., Ohsaki, H.: Recognizing depression from Twitter activity. In: Proceedings of the 33rd Annual ACM Conference on Human Factors in Computing Systems, pp. 3187–3196 (2015)
16. Resnik, P., Armstrong, W., Claudino, L., Nguyen, T., Nguyen, V., Boyd-Graber, J.: Beyond LDA: exploring supervised topic modeling for depression-related language in Twitter. In: Proceedings of the 2nd Workshop on Computational Linguistics and Clinical Psychology: From Linguistic Signal to Clinical Reality, pp. 99–107 (2015)
17. Preoţiuc-Pietro, D., Sap, M., Schwartz, H., Ungar, L.: Mental illness detection at the world well-being project for the CLPsych 2015 shared task. In: Proceedings of the 2nd Workshop on Computational Linguistics and Clinical Psychology: From Linguistic Signal to Clinical Reality, pp. 40–45 (2015)
18. De Choudhury, M., Counts, S., Horvitz, E.: Social media as a measurement tool of depression in populations. In: Proceedings of the 5th Annual ACM Web Science Conference, pp. 47–56 (2013)
19. Howes, O., Murray, R.: Schizophrenia: an integrated sociodevelopmental-cognitive model. The Lancet **383**, 1677–1687 (2014)

20. Shen, J., Rudzicz, F.: Detecting anxiety through reddit. In: Proceedings of the Fourth Workshop on Computational Linguistics and Clinical Psychology-From Linguistic Signal to Clinical Reality, pp. 58–65 (2017)
21. Resnik, P., Armstrong, W., Claudino, L., Nguyen, T.: The University of Maryland CLPsych 2015 shared task system. In: Proceedings of the 2nd Workshop on Computational Linguistics and Clinical Psychology: From Linguistic Signal to Clinical Reality, pp. 54–60 (2015)
22. Coppersmith, G., Dredze, M., Harman, C., Hollingshead, K., Mitchell, M.: CLPsych 2015 shared task: depression and PTSD on Twitter. In: Proceedings of the 2nd Workshop on Computational Linguistics and Clinical Psychology: From Linguistic Signal to Clinical Reality, pp. 31–39 (2015)
23. Blei, D., Ng, A., Jordan, M.: Latent dirichlet allocation. J. Mach. Learn. Res. **3**, 993–1022 (2003)
24. Mitchell, M., Hollingshead, K., Coppersmith, G.: Quantifying the language of schizophrenia in social media. In: Proceedings of the 2nd Workshop on Computational Linguistics and Clinical Psychology: From Linguistic Signal to Clinical Reality, pp. 11–20 (2015)
25. Nguyen, T., Phung, D., Dao, B., Venkatesh, S., Berk, M.: Affective and content analysis of online depression communities. IEEE Trans. Affect. Comput. **5**, 217–226 (2014)
26. Schwartz, H., et al.: Towards assessing changes in degree of depression through Facebook. In: Proceedings of the Workshop on Computational Linguistics and Clinical Psychology: From Linguistic Signal to Clinical Reality, pp. 118–125 (2014)
27. Qureshi, M., et al.: A novel auto-annotation technique for aspect level sentiment analysis. Comput. Mater. Continua **70**, 4987–5004 (2022)
28. Safa, R., Bayat, P., Moghtader, L.: Automatic detection of depression symptoms in Twitter using multimodal analysis. J. Supercomput. **78**, 4709–4744 (2022)
29. Sculley, D.: Online active learning methods for fast label-efficient spam filtering. In: CEAS, vol. 7, p. 143 (2007)
30. Settles, B., Craven, M.: An analysis of active learning strategies for sequence labeling tasks. In: Proceedings of the 2008 Conference on Empirical Methods in Natural Language Processing, pp. 1070–1079 (2008)
31. Freund, Y., Seung, H., Shamir, E., Tishby, N.: Selective sampling using the query by committee algorithm. Mach. Learn. **28**, 133–168 (1997)
32. Balcan, M., Beygelzimer, A., Langford, J.: Agnostic active learning. In: Proceedings of the 23rd International Conference on Machine Learning, pp. 65–72 (2006)
33. Kranjc, J., Smailović, J., Podpečan, V., Grčar, M., Žnidaršič, M., Lavrač, N.: Active learning for sentiment analysis on data streams: methodology and workflow implementation in the ClowdFlows platform. Inf. Process. Manag. **51**, 187–203 (2015)
34. Pohl, D., Bouchachia, A., Hellwagner, H.: Batch-based active learning: application to social media data for crisis management. Expert Syst. Appl. **93**, 232–244 (2018)
35. Bouguelia, M., Belaïd, Y., Belaïd, A.: An adaptive streaming active learning strategy based on instance weighting. Pattern Recogn. Lett. **70**, 38–44 (2016)
36. Ahmed, U., Lin, J., Srivastava, G.: Fuzzy explainable attention-based deep active learning on mental-health data. In: 2021 IEEE International Conference on Fuzzy Systems (FUZZ-IEEE), pp. 1–6 (2021)
37. Ahmed, U., Jhaveri, R., Srivastava, G., Lin, J.: Explainable deep attention active learning for sentimental analytics of mental disorder. Trans. Asian Low-Resour. Lang. Inf. Process. (2022)

38. Nguyen, V., Shaker, M., Hüllermeier, E.: How to measure uncertainty in uncertainty sampling for active learning. Mach. Learn. **111**, 89–122 (2022)
39. Adarsh, S., Antony, B.: SSN@ LT-EDI-ACL2022: transfer learning using BERT for detecting signs of depression from social media texts. In: Proceedings of the Second Workshop on Language Technology for Equality, Diversity and Inclusion, pp. 326–330 (2022)
40. Lin, C., et al.: SenseMood: depression detection on social media. In: Proceedings of the 2020 International Conference on Multimedia Retrieval, pp. 407–411 (2020)
41. Gupta, S., Goel, L., Singh, A., Prasad, A., Ullah, M., et al.: Psychological analysis for depression detection from social networking sites. Comput. Intell. Neurosci. **2022**, 4395358 (2022)
42. Sadeque, F., Xu, D., Bethard, S.: Measuring the latency of depression detection in social media. In: Proceedings of the Eleventh ACM International Conference on Web Search and Data Mining, pp. 495–503 (2018)
43. Cortes, C., Vapnik, V.: Support-vector networks. Mach. Learn. **20**, 273–297 (1995)
44. Hochreiter, S., Schmidhuber, J.: Long short-term memory. Neural Comput. **9**, 1735–1780 (1997)
45. Pennington, J., Socher, R., Manning, C.: GloVe: global vectors for word representation. In: Proceedings of the 2014 Conference on Empirical Methods in Natural Language Processing (EMNLP), pp. 1532–1543 (2014)
46. Mikolov, T., Chen, K., Corrado, G., Dean, J.: Efficient estimation of word representations in vector space. arXiv preprint arXiv:1301.3781 (2013)
47. Devlin, J., Chang, M., Lee, K., Toutanova, K.: BERT: pre-training of deep bidirectional transformers for language understanding. arXiv preprint arXiv:1810.04805 (2018)
48. Vaswani, A., et al.: Attention is all you need. In: Advances in Neural Information Processing Systems, vol. 30 (2017)
49. González-Carvajal, S., Garrido-Merchán, E.: Comparing BERT against traditional machine learning text classification. arXiv preprint arXiv:2005.13012 (2020)
50. Mozafari, B., Sarkar, P., Franklin, M., Jordan, M., Madden, S.: Scaling up crowdsourcing to very large datasets: a case for active learning. Proc. VLDB Endow. **8**, 125–136 (2014). https://doi.org/10.14778/2735471.2735474
51. Arbanas, G.: Diagnostic and statistical manual of mental disorders (DSM-5). Alcohol. Psychiatry Res. **51**, 61–64 (2015)
52. Rogers, A., Kovaleva, O., Rumshisky, A.: A primer in BERTology: what we know about how BERT works. Trans. Assoc. Comput. Linguist. **8**, 842–866 (2020). https://aclanthology.org/2020.tacl-1.54
53. Garg, S., Vu, T., Moschitti, A.: TANDA: transfer and adapt pre-trained transformer models for answer sentence selection. In: AAAI (2020)
54. Moshkin, V., Konstantinov, A., Yarushkina, N.: Application of the BERT language model for sentiment analysis of social network posts. In: Kuznetsov, S.O., Panov, A.I., Yakovlev, K.S. (eds.) RCAI 2020. LNCS (LNAI), vol. 12412, pp. 274–283. Springer, Cham (2020). https://doi.org/10.1007/978-3-030-59535-7_20
55. Major Depression: National Institute of Mental Health (NIMH) (n.d.). https://www.nimh.nih.gov/health/statistics/major-depression

All-Words Pronunciation Estimation of Japanese Homographs Using Automatically Tagged Data

Taichiro Kobayashi[1], Kanako Komiya[2]([✉]) [ID], and Hiroyuki Shinnou[1]

[1] Ibaraki University, 4-12-1 Nakanarusawa, Hitachi, Ibaraki 316-0033, Japan
{21nm7241,hiroyuki.shinnou.0828}@vc.ibaraki.ac.jp
[2] Tokyo University of Agriculture and Technology, 2-24-16 Nakaco, Koganeishi,
Tokyo 184-8588, Japan
kkomiya@go.tuat.ac.jp

Abstract. The Japanese language has many homographs, which are words that share the same letters, regardless of their pronunciations. For example, "辛い" has two pronunciations, "karai" and "tsurai", which mean "hot taste" and "hard" or "tough" respectively. Therefore, pronunciation estimation of homographs is necessary to read Japanese sentences accurately. In this study, we develop a system to estimate the pronunciations of homographs using a Bidirectional Encoder Representations from the Transformer model. This research is the first trial of pronunciation estimation of all homographs and we achieved this goal using the technique for all-words word sense disambiguation. We used the Corpus of Spontaneous Japanese (CSJ), a transcription of spoken Japanese, as the test data and utilized the non-core data of the Balanced Corpus of Contemporary Written in Japanese, for which pronunciations are automatically tagged by a Japanese morphological analyzer, in addition to CSJ, as training data to reduce the cost of transcription. We show that automatically tagged data from a written Japanese corpus can improve the accuracy of pronunciation estimation.

Keywords: Pronunciation estimation · automatically tagged data · homographs

1 Introduction

Japanese contains many homographs, which are words containing the same letters (usually Kanji, Chinese characters for Japanese) but with different pronunciations. For example, "辛い" has two pronunciations, "karai" and "tsurai", which respectively mean "hot taste" and "hard" or "tough." English also has some homographs, e.g., "bow" has both verb ([báu]) and noun ([bóu]) pronunciations; however, the number of Japanese homographs is much greater than that of English for a historical reason. Japan has imported many characters from China but usually maintains Japanese pronunciations, which are originally spoken in Japan, in addition to the pronunciations of Chinese origin. This complicated

A. Rapp et al. (Eds.): NLDB 2024, LNCS 14762, pp. 93–105, 2024.
https://doi.org/10.1007/978-3-031-70239-6_7

writing system made a great number of homographs and they occur frequently in Japanese texts. According to our survey, more than 10% of tokens in Japanese texts are homographs[1].

Moreover, many Kanji have different pronunciations even if they have Chinese roots because Japan imported various pronunciations from many regional dialects in China, which explains the high disambiguity of pronunciations. For example, "二," a character which means "2 (two)" has at least 6 pronunciations, "ni," "nii," "futa," "futsu," "buta," and "puta," and "側," a character which means "side" has at least 5 pronunciations, "kawa," "gawa," "soku,"'soba," and "hata," according to a Japanese dictionary, the analysis dictionary for the morphological analizer MeCab (UniDicMA)[2,3]. These pronunciations should be properly selected according to the context.

Although it is easy for Japanese speakers to distinguish the pronunciations according to their contexts in most cases when the meanings vary with the pronunciation, it is difficult for non-native Japanese speakers or computers to distinguish between different pronunciations of homographs. For example, pronunciation estimation is something chatGPT cannot solve. Even with one-shot example, the chatGPT's accuracy of pronunciation estimation was 50%, only 10 out of 20 examples we tested were correct; this accuracy is the same as a random selection system. Therefore, the results of Japanese text-to-speech systems often contain mistakes in the pronunciations of homographs. Consequently, a reliable system of pronunciation estimation is important for many applications, including educational systems of reading for Japanese learners, and Japanese text-to-speech technologies, particularly for people with reading difficulty or visual handicaps.

Therefore, we developed a system for estimating the pronunciation of Japanese homographs. Kobayashi [5], Sato [9], and Zhang [14] estimated the pronunciation of Japanese homographs or heteronyms that frequently occurred in a corpus, providing lexical sample tasks of the pronunciation estimation. However, in this paper, we targeted both frequently used and rarer homographs to perform an all-words pronunciation estimation task (see Sect. 2). Therefore, this research is the first trial of pronunciation estimation of all homographs using the technique for all-words word sense disambiguation.

Transcription data of the spoken language is required to train a system for the estimation of pronunciations for homographs because when the meanings are the same regardless of the pronunciations, sometimes no one but the authors themselves know the precise pronunciations of the concerned homographs. For example, the pronunciation of "明日" could be "asu", "ashita", or "myonichi", but the meaning of this word is the same, "tomorrow," in all three cases. Presently, transcription data are usually difficult to obtain because the cost of transcription is high and the amount of transcription data from spoken Japanese is small. Therefore, we propose to utilize a large amount of automatically tagged data from the

---

[1] 16.2% of tokens in BCCWJ and 11.8% of tokens in CSJ are homographs.

[2] https://clrd.ninjal.ac.jp/unidic/.

[3] Actually, there are more options for "二," such as "ji.".

corpus of written Japanese (see Sects. 3 and 4). Our experiments using Japanese Bidirectional Encoder Representations from Transformers (BERT) revealed that using a large amount of automatically tagged data from a corpus of written Japanese improved the accuracies of the pronunciation estimation system for Japanese homographs (see Sect. 5). We discuss the types of Japanese homographs and problems to be solved for estimating their pronunciations in Sect. 6 and provide concluding remarks in Sect. 7.

The contributions of this paper are as follows:

1. We developed a pronunciation estimation system for all homographs in Japanese texts;
2. We showed that automatically tagged pronunciations of homographs for written Japanese are effective for estimating the pronunciations of homographs for spoken Japanese when we have very little transcription data; and
3. We discussed the types of Japanese homographs and problems to be solved when estimating their pronunciations.

2   Related Work

To the best of our knowledge, no all-words pronunciation estimation system exists. Kobayashi [5], Sato [9] and Zhang [14] conducted experiments using lexical sample tasks to estimate the pronunciation of homographs or heteronyms. Kobayashi [5] estimated the pronunciations of 71 Japanese homographs in the Balanced Corpus of Contemporary Written in Japanese (BCCWJ) [7] using various features. The best results obtained with this experiment were a macro average of 90.69% and a micro average of 96.01%, when using Support Vector Machines as classifiers, BCCWJ as a dataset, and one-hot vectors, nwjc2vec [10], and BERT [2] vectors as features. Sato [9] predicted the pronunciation of heteronyms. Heteronym refers to words that share spelling but have different pronunciations and meanings. The difference between homographs and heteronyms is that homographs do not necessarily have a different meaning. Sato [9] trained BERT-based models for 93 Japanese heteronyms, achieving an accuracy of 93.9%. Zhang [14] conducted experiments on disambiguation of 32 Japanese homographs and released the data on Japanese homographs.

In this study, we estimated the pronunciations of all homographs in the BCCWJ and Corpus of Spontaneous Japanese (CSJ) [6]. If we consider pronunciations of words as word senses, this task can be regarded as all-words Word Sense Disambiguation (WSD), which imparts word sense labels to all words in a document. Because words with different pronunciations usually differ in meanings, an all-words pronunciation estimation is highly related to all-words WSD. For example, "辛い" has two pronunciations and it means "hot taste" when it is read as "karai," and it means "hard" or "tough" when it is read as "tsurai." Therefore, disambiguation of pronunciation is highly related to WSD. As such, methods used for all-words WSD could also be used for this task. Shinnou [11] showed that this problem can be solved using KyTea[4], a text analyzer for languages requiring word or morpheme segmentation, applicable to Japanese and Chinese. KyTea is usually used to train a model for word segmentation. It trains the model for word segmentation using word-segmented text data. Shinnou [11] added word senses to the word-segmented text data and constructed a WSD model with KyTea using the sense-added text data for training. Similarly, all-words WSD systems could be trained using data with word sense tags. Suzuki [12] also developed an all-words WSD system using the idea that similar words tend to have similar sets of surrounding words. They predicted target word senses by calculating the distances between the surrounding word vectors of the target words and their synonyms using word embeddings. Du [3] conducted all-words WSD in English using BERT and showed that BERT is an effective approach for all-words WSD in English. Asada [1] showed that all-words WSD using contemporary Japanese BERT is useful for Japanese classic literature.

Kiyono [4], Saito [8], and Wang [13] conducted related studies using pseudodata. Kiyono [4] examined state-of-the-art methods and sources of generating pseudodata for grammar correction models, recorded in CoNLL-2014. Saito [8] used pseudodata for spelling correction in Japanese, wherein they proposed a pre-training model with automatically generated pseudo-correct data and re-trained the model using a small amount of manually generated correct data. Wang [13] showed that WSD in Chinese can effectively train a WSD model with both pseudodata and sense-tagged data.

3   Data

CSJ was used as the test and training data with correct pronunciation information, and BCCWJ was used as pseudodata for training. CSJ is a database for spoken language research that collects a large amount of spontaneous Japanese speech and adds various morphological information, such as parts of speech. As the corpus is based on transcribed speech data, it is assumed that accurate pronunciation information is provided. CSJ is composed of monologues including academic lectures and mock academic lectures, dialog including academic lecture interviews, mock academic lecture interviews, task-oriented dialog, free dialog, and recitations.

BCCWJ contains 143 million words across different genres, such as books, magazines, newspapers, white papers, blogs, online bulletin boards, textbooks, and legal documents, and is the only balanced corpus available for Japanese as of April 2024. Most morphological information was automatically assigned to BCCWJ, using Japanese morphological analyzer, MeCab[5,6], but it contains core data that have been manually analyzed to a higher level of accuracy[7]. We used the non-core data as pseudo-training data for our experiments because it is not

---

[4] http://www.phontron.com/kytea/.
[5] https://taku910.github.io/mecab/.
[6] https://github.com/jordwest/mecab-docs-en?tab=readme-ov-file.
[7] https://clrd.ninjal.ac.jp/bccwj/doc/manual/BCCWJ_Manual_02.pdf.

manually checked and therefore the pronunciations of homographs are not always accurate. As the BCCWJ is based on written language, the exact pronunciation information for homographs could be unknown, e.g., whether "日本" (Japan) is "Nihon" or "Nippon" is unknown, even for manually checked core data. Statistical information pertaining to CSJ and non-core data of BCCWJ is shown in Table 1. Please note that, because this research targets all homographs in texts, the number of word types or vocabulary size of target homographs greatly increased compared to those of the previous studies (71 and 93 homographs).

Table 1. Statistics of data

	Number of word types	Number of words	Number of types of homographs	Number of tokens of homographs
Non-core BCCWJ	422,793	123,848,121	4,833	20,081,893
CSJ	62,593	7,142,610	4,551	839,494
Whole Data	442,698	130,990,731	8,950	20,921,387

4 Pronunciation Estimation of Homographs Using Automatically Tagged Data

We developed a pronunciation estimation system for all homographs in CSJ, a Japanese corpus with accurate pronunciation information that can be used as training data for pronunciation estimation. CSJ is a corpus of spoken language, i.e., transcribed speech data; therefore, it is possible to obtain accurate pronunciation information. We used it as training, validation, and test data for pronunciation estimation.

Generally, it is difficult to prepare a large amount of transcribed speech corpora such as CSJ because of the high construction cost involved. Consequently, we used pseudodata, where pronunciation information is automatically tagged by a Japanese morphological analyzer, MeCab, in addition to transcribed data. Specifically, we used "reading data" or YOMI data outputted from MeCab as the pseudo-pronunciation. The reading data was written in Japanese Katakana, which is a phonogram, so estimating reading data is equivalent to the pronunciation estimation. Pronunciations obtained by MeCab often contain mistakes in pronunciations of homographs, because it is not a pronunciation estimation system but a morphological analyzer. For example, MeCab's output of "最中 を食べている最中に電話が鳴った。" (The phone rang while I was eating a Monaka.) when UniDicMA dictionary was used was "Saichu o tabete iru saichu ni denwa ga natta." At the same time, the correct pronunciation is "Monaka o tabete iru saichu ni denwa ga natta." This result indicates MeCab cannot distinguish the pronunciations of "最中" ("monaka," a pastry and "saichu" a word meaning "while" in English) based on the context. [8]

We compared two models: (A) a model trained with a large amount of pseudodata and then additionally trained with a small amount of transcribed data, which is our proposed method and (B) a model trained only with the transcribed data to investigate the effectiveness of the pseudodata. We changed the conditions with transcribed data; they are 5%, 10%, and 20% of training data from CSJ. In addition, we tried a setting, in which, we added sentences including at least one example for all homographs in training data from CSJ to the training data. For the at-least-one-example setting, we selected the additional training data from CSJ as follows.

1. Split CSJ and obtain 10% of it for the training data
2. For each sentence in the CSJ training data, check if it contains at least one homograph that was not included in the training data to be added from CSJ. If not, add it to the training data.

For example, if the first sentence included homographs a, b, c, and d, we added the sentence to the training data because these homographs were not in the training data. If the second sentence included homographs a, c, e, and f, we added the sentence to the training data because e and f were not in the training data. If the third sentence included homographs b, d, and f, we would not add the sentence because the training data already contained these three homographs. We repeated these procedures for every sentence from the training split of CSJ. Using these procedures, the additional training data from CSJ includes at least one example for every homograph. Consequently, 3,152 sentences from 73,165 training sentences were added from CSJ. When we used this setting, the total number of homograph types we added was 3,635 and the number of pronunciations averaged over homographs was 4.65 We evaluated Model CSJ, a model trained with fully transcribed train data, as an upper bound and Model BCCWJ as a baseline, to show the accuracy[9] when the model is trained only with the pseudodata.

We compared the 10 models shown in Table 2 and Most Frequent Pronunciation (MFP), 11 methods in total, in our study. MFP is the percentage of pronunciations that account for the majority. The proposed methods are written in bold in the table.

Model C20%, Model C10%, Model C5%, and Model C1e belong to (B) models trained only with transcribed data to investigate the effectiveness of the pseudodata and Model B-C20%, Model B-C10%, Model B-C5%, and Model B-C1e belong to (A) models trained with a large amount of pseudodata and then additionally trained with a small amount of transcribed data. All models were evaluated using test data with split CSJ. We used 80% of CSJ for the test data.

---

[8] Since MeCab is the de facto standard morphological analyzer for Japanese and is often used for the pre-processing of Japanese text-to-speech systems, such mistakes are found in many of them.

[9] We used only accuracy for the metrics for our experiments. We did not use F1 or precision because our task targeted all homographs.

Table 2. Models and training data

Model Name	BCCWJ	CSJ
Model CSJ	N/A	Full
Model C20%	N/A	20%
Model C10%	N/A	10%
Model C5%	N/A	5%
Model C1e	N/A	at least one example
Model B-C20%	Full	20%
Model B-C10%	Full	10%
Model B-C5%	Full	5%
Model B-C1e	Full	at least one example
Model BCCWJ	Full	N/A

5 Experiments

The experimental procedures of our pronunciation estimation system are as follows:

1. Extract homographs from BCCWJ and CSJ;
2. Produce a pronunciation dictionary of homographs;
3. Tokenize sentences and convert them into BERT IDs;
4. Prepare the information for labeling; and
5. Estimate the pronunciations of homographs using BERT.

To provide information for labeling, we prepared (1) orthographic tokens and pronunciations, (2) BERT IDs, (3) pronunciation labels of homographs, which are the gold data for evaluation (4) lists of pronunciation candidates for homographs, and (5) positions of homographs.

We targeted only homographs in texts using the (5) position information. Consequently, the accuracy is calculated based on all the present homographs rather than all the words. When the tokenizer divided the homograph into multiple subwords, those words were ignored. Table 3 presents the statistics of pronunciations of homographs in the corpora we used: CSJ and BCCWJ non-core data. The number of types of pronunciations and the total number of pronunciations differ because different words sometimes share the same pronunciations.

Table 3. Statistics of homographs in CSJ and BCCWJ non-core data

Number of types of pronunciations of homographs	15,291
Total number of pronunciations of homographs	20,574
Average number of pronunciation candidates	2.30

For the training and inference process, we limited the number of homograph candidates using (4) the lists of pronunciation candidates of homographs. We used the pre-trained Japanese BERT model[10], which is publicly available from Tohoku University, retaining the default settings other than the following parameters, which were changed as indicated in Table 4.

Table 4. Parameters

Optimization function	SGD
Leaning rate	10^{-4}
Mini batch size	1

We regarded the all-words pronunciation estimation task as a sequence labeling task and used the BERT model with fine-tuning.

A schematic diagram of sequence labeling using BERT is shown in Fig. 1.

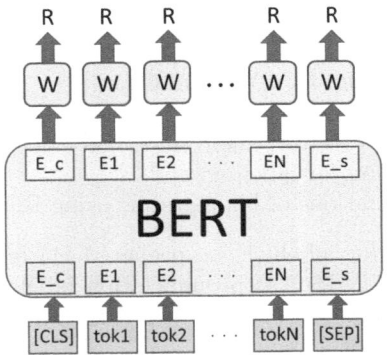

Fig. 1. Sequence labelling using BERT

The input ("[CLS] tok1 tok2... tokN [SEP]" in Fig. 1) is a sequence of tokens, which were extracted from the corpus and transformed into a 768-dimensional vector through 12 layers of BERT. This vector provides the input to the layer for discrimination W, which outputs the pronunciation label R. This output is a 15,291-dimension vector (i.e., the size of the pronunciation dictionary). The Nth element in the vector represents the probability that the word is read with label N, and the label with the largest value is used as the result of the model estimation by referring to this probability.

We split the CSJ into (training data):(validation data):(test data) = 1:1:8 and extracted a small amount of data from the training data for each model.

---

[10] cl-tohoku/bert-base-japanese.

The data was split based on the sentences. We used only 10% of CSJ for the training data because we wanted to conduct experiments assuming the situation in which the transcribed data in the domain is limited. Table 5 lists the number of sentences of the training data.

Table 5. Number of sentences of training data

Model Names	Number of sentences
Model CSJ	73,165
Model C20%	14,633
Model C10%	7,317
Model C5%	3,658
Model C1e	3,152
Model B-C20%	4,560,401
Model B-C10%	4,553,085
Model B-C5%	4,549,426
Model B-C1e	4,548,920
Model BCCWJ	4,545,768

We trained the model of BCCWJ 10 epochs.

6   Evaluation

Table 6 shows the results of the models.

Table 6. Results of the models

Model	Accuracy(%)
Model CSJ	97.97
Model C20%	96.22
Model C10%	94.74
Model C5%	92.34
Model C1e	58.40
Model B-C20%	97.53
Model B-C10%	97.22
Model B-C5%	96.95
Model B-C1e	97.40
Model BCCWJ	94.22
MFP	64.28

First, we can see that the accuracy of model C, a system using all the training data of CSJ is 97.97 % and that of model B-C1e, the proposed method is 97.40 %. Although this is not a fair comparison because of the different test data, our system, which targets all homographs in the text, is comparable to the previous systems, which target only the most frequently occurring homographs[11]. This result indicates that the pronunciation estimation using the technique for all-words word sense disambiguation is effective even for rare homographs.

Second, according to Table 6, the accuracy of Model B-C1e (97.40%) is better than those of Model C1e (58.40%) and Model BCCWJ (94.22%). In other words, the model trained with a large number of pseudo and out-domain data and the data including at least one example for each homograph outperformed the models trained with the pseudodata or the data including at least one example for each homograph. Moreover, although the accuracy of Model CSJ (97.97%) is very high, Model B-C1e (97.40%) is comparable, exhibiting a similar accuracy. The accuracy of Model BCCWJ (94.22 %) is much better than that of Model C1e (58.40%), thereby suggesting the effectiveness of the pseudo and out-domain data. All deferences of accuracy in this experiment were significant because the sample number of our experiment was huge: 615,005 examples. Pronunciations of the pseudodata are automatically tagged by a Japanese morphological analyzer. Therefore, it is realistic to have few annotated data but a lot of pseudodata.

Next, let us compare Model B-C1e and Model B-C5% with Model C1e and Model C5%. Model B-C1e and Model B-C5% were better than Model BCCWJ. However, the accuracy of Model C5% (92.34%) is much better than Model C1e (58.40%) although the number of sentences of the training data is not so different (3,152 for Model C1e and 3,658 for Model C5%). This is because we evaluated micro-averaged accuracy, which is the number of correctly predicted homographs divided by the number of all homographs and not calculated macro-averaged accuracy, which is the average accuracy of all the types of homographs. In other words, the accuracy tends to be high when the homographs that frequently appear are correctly predicted. Nevertheless, Model B-C1e outperformed Model B-C5%, although the number of additional data was small, showing the effectiveness of the data including at least one example for each homograph. Table 6 also shows that the accuracy improved as the CSJ data increased.

Tables 7 show the 25 homographs whose accuracy was most improved by the data including at least one example for each homograph data and their typical pronunciations. Although "行ける" and "行け" are different homographs in our system, these two homographs share the same characters "行け" and the same pronunciation set, "ike" and "yuke." In addition, "行く" should have almost the same pronunciation set, "iku" and "yuku," because "行ける" (ikeru, can go) and "行け" (ike, "go" in imperative form) are all different conjugations of the same verb, "行く" (to go.) The reason for these cases is the tokenization of BERT. According to these observations, the training data could be reduced if the tokenization is improved for this system. On the other hand, "京都" has two pronunciations, "kyoto" and "miyako." Kyoto is a place name, the old capital of

---

Table 7. Top 25 homographs whose accuracy improved by the additional data including at least one example for each homograph and their typical pronunciations

Words	Typical Pronunciations		
私、	Watashi	Watakusi	Shi
後	Ato	Nochi	Kou
時	Zi	Toki	Doki
他	Hoka	Ta	Ada
人	Nin	Jin	Hito
方	Kata	Hou	Gata
捉え	Torae	Tsuramae	
婆	Baba	Baa	
京都	Kyoto	Miyaho	
中	Ju	Chu	Uchi
節	Setsu	Fushi	Takashi
波形	Namigata	Hakei	Namikata
形	Gata	Nari	Katachi
捉える	Toraeru	Tsukamaeru	
九	Kokono	Kyu	Ku
下	Shimo	Moto	Shita
行ける	Ikeru	Yukeru	
風	Fu	Kaze	Pu
家	Ya	Ie	Ka
行け	Ike	Yuke	
評定	Hyotei	Hyojo	
車	Sha	Kuruma	Guruma
上	Uwa	Kami	Ue
共	Tomo	Domo	Muta
拍	Haku	Paku	

Japan, and "miyako" means capital in old Japanese. The pronunciations of "京" and "都" are respectively "kyo" and "to" if they are read in the Chinese-derived reading. However, at the same time, the pronunciations of "京," "都," and "京都" are all the same, "miyako," when they are read in the Japanese-derived reading because the pronunciations come from the meaning of this word. These problems make tokenization difficult. Similar problems can sometimes be detected in multi-word expressions. "今日は" are two words that could be tagged by "konnichi-wa" or "kyo-wa", which mean "hello" or "as for today," respectively.

Finally, we discuss the types of Japanese homographs and problems that must be solved to estimate their pronunciations. We estimated the pronunciations of homographs, not heteronyms. It is often not easy to distinguish between these because the difference in meanings, including the modality or the degree of politeness of words, is subtle in some cases. For example, "myonichi", a pronunciation of "明日," sounds more formal than "ashita", another pronunciation of the homograph. We believe that these words should be carefully chosen according to their applications. However, in the future, we think that the evaluation of the system should be designed more carefully, say, the errors of heteronyms affect the evaluation more. We plan to investigate the relation between meanings and pronunciations of homographs based on corpora and dictionaries.

Furthermore, our system cannot solve certain cases because of the problem type involved. In particular, homograph problems that require longer contexts to know their pronunciations cannot be solved with this system. For example, "街中" is a heteronym containing two pronunciations, "machinaka" and "machiju". "Machinaka" means "in a city," whereas machiju means "all over the city." To identify the suitable pronunciation, we must consider longer contexts than a single sentence.

Furthermore, named entities such as human or place names tend to have various pronunciations. We plan to reorganize these problems in the future using a larger corpus and release an annotated corpus of homographs.

7　Conclusion

We conducted an all-words pronunciation estimation using BERT. We have drawn attention to the fact that pronunciations of words tend to vary according to the context and used the technique for word sense disambiguation to achieve this goal. We used CSJ, transcribed data, as data with correct pronunciation information and BCCWJ, whose pronunciations are automatically tagged, as pseudodata. Our experiments revealed that (1) the accuracy of an all-words pronunciation estimation is comparable to that of lexical sample task and (2) the use of a large amount of pseudodata outside the domain can reduce the amount of tagged data required for transcribed pronunciations, which are expensive to construct. Specifically, we showed that the accuracy of the model is comparable even if we only added the data including at least one example for each homograph from CSJ.

References

1. Asada, S., Komiya, K., Asahara, M.: All-words word sense disambiguation for historical Japanese. In: Huang, C.R., et al. (eds.) Proceedings of the 37th Pacific Asia Conference on Language, Information and Computation. pp. 201–209. Association for Computational Linguistics, Hong Kong, China, December 2023. https://aclanthology.org/2023.paclic-1.20
2. Devlin, J., Chang, M.W., Lee, K., Toutanova, K.: BERT: pre-training of deep bidirectional transformers for language understanding. In: Proceedings of the 2019 Conference of the North American Chapter of the Association for Computational Linguistics: Human Language Technologies, Volume 1 (Long and Short Papers), pp. 4171–4186. Association for Computational Linguistics, Minneapolis, Minnesota, June 2019. https://doi.org/10.18653/v1/N19-1423, https://aclanthology.org/N19-1423

3. Du, J., Qi, F., Sun, M.: Using bert for word sense disambiguation. arXiv preprint arXiv:1909.08358 (2019)
4. Kiyono, S., Suzuki, J., Mita, M., Mizumoto, T., Inui, K.: Daikibo gizi deta wo mochiita kouseinou ayamari teisei moderu no kouciku [building a high-performance grammar error correction model using large-scale pseudo-data]. Proceedings of NLP 2020, pp. 989–992 (In Japanese) (2020)
5. Kobayashi, T., Komiya, K.: Svm wo mochiita bccwj ni okeru douonigigo no yomisuitei. [pronounciation estimation of monographs of bccwj using svm]. In: Proceedings of the NLP2021, (In Japanese), pp. 405–409 (2021)
6. Maekawa, K.: Corpus of spontaneous Japanese: its design and evaluation. In: ISCA & IEEE Workshop on Spontaneous Speech Processing and Recognition (2003)
7. Maekawa, K., et al.: Balanced corpus of contemporary written Japanese. Lang. Resour. Eval. **48**(2), 345–371 (2014)
8. Saito, I., Suzuki, J., Sadamitsu, K., Nishida, K., Saito, K., Saito, Y.: Giji deta no zizengakusyu ni motoduku encoder-decoder gata nihongokuzure hyoukiseikika [encoder-decoder type japanese collapsed notation normalisation based on pre-training of pseudo-data]. Proceedings of NLP 2017, pp. 585–588 (In Japanese) (2017)
9. Sato, F., Yoshinaga, N., Kitsuregawa, M.: Building large-scale Japanese pronunciation-annotated corpora for reading heteronymous logograms. In: Calzolari, N., et al. (eds.) Proceedings of the Thirteenth Language Resources and Evaluation Conference. pp. 7113–7121. European Language Resources Association, Marseille, France, June 2022. https://aclanthology.org/2022.lrec-1.770
10. Shinnou, H., Asahara, M., Komiya, K., Sasaki, M.: nwjc2vec: Word embedding data constructed from ningal web Japanese corpus. J. Natural Lang. Process. **24**(5), 705–720 (2017)
11. Shinnou, H., Komiya, K., Sasaki, M., Mori, S.: Japanese all-words WSD system using the Kyoto text analysis ToolKit. In: Roxas, R.E. (ed.) Proceedings of the 31st Pacific Asia Conference on Language, Information and Computation. pp. 392–399. The National University (Phillippines) (Nov 2017), https://aclanthology.org/Y17-1052
12. Suzuki, R., Komiya, K., Asahara, M., Sasaki, M., Shinnou, H.: Unsupervised all-wrods wsd using synonyms and embeddings. J. Natural Lang. Process **26**(2), 361–379 (2019)
13. Wang, X., Matsumoto, Y.: Improving word sense disambiguation by pseudo-samples. In: International Conference on Natural Language Processing, pp. 386–395. Springer (2004)
14. Zhang, W.: Pronunciation ambiguities in Japanese kanji. In: Gorman, K., Sproat, R., Roark, B. (eds.) Proceedings of the Workshop on Computation and Written Language (CAWL 2023). pp. 50–60. Association for Computational Linguistics, Toronto, Canada, July 2023.https://doi.org/10.18653/v1/2023.cawl-1.7, https://aclanthology.org/2023.cawl-1.7

I've Got the "answer"!
Interpretation of LLMs Hidden States in Question Answering

Valeriya Goloviznina$^{(\boxtimes)}$ ⓘ and Evgeny Kotelnikov ⓘ

Vyatka State University, Kirov, Russia
`golovizninavs@gmail.com`

Abstract. Interpretability and explainability of AI are becoming increasingly important in light of the rapid development of large language models (LLMs). This paper investigates the interpretation of LLMs in the context of the knowledge-based question answering. The main hypothesis of the study is that correct and incorrect model behavior can be distinguished at the level of hidden states. The quantized models LLaMA-2-7B-Chat, Mistral-7B, Vicuna-7B and the MuSeRC question-answering dataset are used to test this hypothesis. The results of the analysis support the proposed hypothesis. We also identify the layers which have a negative effect on the model's behavior. As a prospect of practical application of the hypothesis, we propose to train such "weak" layers additionally in order to improve the quality of the task solution.

Keywords: Interpretation · LLM · XAI · Question-Answering

1 Introduction

Large language models are applied to a wide variety of generative tasks: summarization, machine translation, dialog systems, story generation and code writing [10]. In some tasks, such as the knowledge-based question answering, LLMs already outperform the quality of human answers.[1] However, such models are still not perfect, i.e., not all model's answers are true.

The question arises: at what point does the model make a mistake and deviate from the "correct" behavior necessary to solve the task at hand, which leads to a wrong answer (Fig. 1)? In our work we try to shed light on this problem by interpreting the behavior of the model at the level of hidden states obtained at the output of each of its layers.

The issues of interpretability and explainability have attracted the attention of researchers due to the rapid development of LLMs [12]. Interpretability refers to delving into the decision-making process of the model, increasing the confidence (of developers) in understanding how the model obtains its results. Explainability relates to the ability

---

[1] https://super.gluebenchmark.com/leaderboard, task: MultiRC; https://russiansuperglue.com/leaderboard/2, task: MuSeRC.

© The Author(s), under exclusive license to Springer Nature Switzerland AG 2024
A. Rapp et al. (Eds.): NLDB 2024, LNCS 14762, pp. 106–120, 2024.
https://doi.org/10.1007/978-3-031-70239-6_8

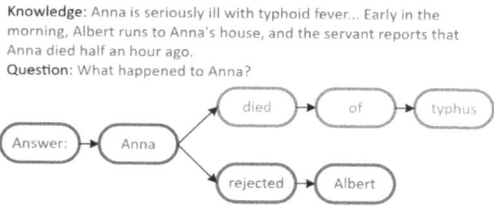

Fig. 1. Examples of generation of **true** and **false** answers to a knowledge-based question.

to provide information (to the user) to build confidence that the AI is making correct and unbiased decisions based on facts [1].

The classification of interpretability and explainability methods is ambiguous. Three review articles on explainable artificial intelligence (XAI) and interpretation of deep neural networks provide three different classifications [1, 6, 8]. In one of these papers, interpretation methods are categorized according to which part of the network they help to interpret: weights, neurons, subnetworks or hidden representations [6].

Our work aims at investigating the interpretability of neural network models, by which we mean revealing its internal properties. We research and interpret models at the level of hidden states.

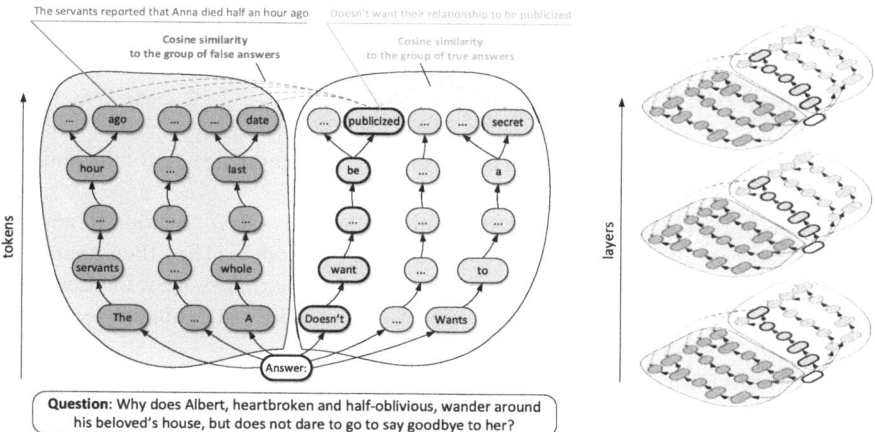

Fig. 2. Hypothesis on partitioning the hidden state space of the model. *Left*: the possible LLM's answers to the question are shown in the form of token sequences.[2] Each oval corresponds to a token and its hidden state vector. We consider the hidden state of the last token of some sequence as a vector representation of the entire sequence. We define the similarity between the sequence and the groups of true and false answers as the average cosine similarity between the given sequence and all answers of the group under consideration. *Right*: the described procedure is reproduced on each layer of the model.

---

[2] For ease of perception, we show tokens as whole words.

Our hypothesis is as follows: correct and incorrect behavior of the model while solving the current task can be distinguished at the level of hidden states. The hidden state space of the model can be divided into two subspaces: hidden states corresponding to correctly generated sequences (in the case of the question answering – correct answers), and hidden states that represent incorrect sequences (wrong answers). Our assumption is reflected in Fig. 2.

To test the hypothesis, we use quantized versions of the models LLaMA-2-7B-Chat,[3] Mistral-7B,[4] Vicuna 7B,[5] and as a question-answering dataset MuSeRC is used [4]. We define the similarity between a sequence and groups of true and false answers as the average cosine similarity between the current sequence and all answers of the considered group. We confirm the hypothesis by analyzing 200 examples from the MuSeRC dataset. An evolution and practical application of the hypothesis is the suggestion that "weak" layers of the model that have a negative impact on its behavior can be additionally trained in order to improve it.

Our contribution is as follows:

- we propose a hypothesis of partitioning the hidden state space of a model into subspaces corresponding to its correct and incorrect behavior within a certain generative task,
- we propose a procedure for verifying our hypothesis on the basis of analyzing the hidden states of the LLM in a knowledge-based question answering,
- we confirm the hypothesis for three LLMs using the MuSeRC dataset,
- we identify the layers which have a negative effect on the model's behavior.

2   Previous Work

In this section, we review the works on interpretation of the hidden states of the language models.

Zou et al. [12] proposed a Linear Artificial Tomography (LAT) method to ana-lyze the hidden representations of LLaMA 2-Chat language models. They then control the generation on such aspects as honesty, morality, emotions, harmless-ness, memorization and others. The authors show that their approach allows to identify situations where the model lies.

In contrast to [12], the goal of our work is to test the hypothesis of partitioning the hidden state space of the model. In our experiments, in addition to LLaMA-2-7B-Chat, we use the Mistral-7B and Vicuna-7B models.

Yang et al. [11] used hidden states to investigate the influence of input data on model performance. The authors apply the proposed method to analyze the errors of the RoBERTa model [5] in sentiment classification and the occurrence of hallucinations in machine translation of the Transformer model [9].

In contrast to [11], we interpret the performance of LLMs on a generative knowledge-based question answering task rather than on classification and translation tasks. The

---

[3] https://huggingface.co/TheBloke/Llama-2-7B-Chat-GPTQ.

[4] https://huggingface.co/TheBloke/Mistral-7B-v0.1-AWQ.

[5] https://huggingface.co/TheBloke/vicuna-7B-v1.5-GPTQ.

goal of our work is not only to analyze model's errors, but also to determine the specific point at which they occur during the generative process.

Dar et al. [3] projected the hidden states of the model into a set of tokens using logit lens. They described the semantic information flow and revealed patterns in the attention mechanism of the GPT-2 model. To visualize the information flow and the influence of language model components on its output, the authors developed a tool that represents the model as a flow graph, where nodes are neurons or hidden states of the model and edges are interactions between them. They computed the semantic closeness of hidden states projected into a set of tokens to construct information flow.

In our work, we do not map hidden states into the token space, and we compute the similarity between hidden states as cosine similarity vectors not for the purpose of determining changes in semantic flow from layer to layer of the model, but for the purpose of distinguishing correct behavior of the model from incorrect behavior.

Belrose et al. [2] analyzed various autoregressive language models up to 20B parameters in terms of iterative inference, taking into account how the model predictions are refined layer by layer. The tuned lens (improved logit lens) method proposed by the authors also operates on hidden states of the model and their mappings to a set of tokens. This method can be used to detect prompt injection attacks latent in the input data with high accuracy and to identify those parts of the data for which the model requires more training steps.

In contrast to [2], we interpret models using their hidden states directly without additional tools such as logit or tuned lens.

Razova et al. [7] asked whether a language models pay attention to sentiment lexicon when solving the task of text sentiment analysis. For this purpose, the authors studied the attention weight matrices of the Russian-language RuBERT model and conclude that, on average, 3/4 of the attention heads of different variants of the model statistically pay more attention to sentiment lexicon than to neutral lexicon.

In contrast to [7], we interpret the performance of modern LLMs in solving the generative task at the hidden state level.

3 Models and Dataset

3.1 Models

Experiments are conducted with the LLaMA-2-7B-Chat-GPTQ, Mistral-7B-v0.1-AWQ and Vicuna-7B-v1.5-GPTQ quantized models. All models have 32 layers. The choice of models is due to their popularity on the one hand and limited computational resources on the other hand.

Since obtaining and annotating a sufficient variety of true and false answers to knowledge questions is a time-consuming procedure, it was decided to analyze the hidden states of the models based on existing data which is described further.

3.2 Dataset

We use the Russian-language MuSeRC dataset [4]. Each example is a text and several questions about that text. Each question has several true and false answers. The questions and answers are written by annotators such that the information of several sentences of the text must be involved to answer the question.

The dataset has 922 examples in total, which contains 5,239 question pairs and answer groups. The answers of 600 examples (training and validation part) with 3,426 questions are labeled into true and false answers. The test part contains 322 examples with answers without labels. The average number of questions per example is 5.7, average number of true answers per question is 1.9, average number of false answers is 2.3. An example of MuSeRC dataset is shown in Appendix A.

We selected the examples that satisfy the following conditions:

1. contain at least 2 true and 2 false answers to each question;
2. the length of each answer is not less than 5 words;
3. the difference between the average lengths of true and false answers does not exceed 30 characters;
4. the answer does not contain a number.

The first condition promotes variety of answers, the second ensures meaningfulness of answers, the third maintains a balance in the length of true and false answers, and the last condition excludes examples in which true and false answers differ by only one number (see Appendix B for an example). As a result, we selected 164 examples containing 217 pairs of questions and answer groups that matched these conditions. The characteristics of examples are given in Table 1.

Table 1. Average length (characters) and ROUGE-1 values for texts and answers in the selected examples.

Avg len of texts	Original answers				
	True			False	
	Avg len	R-1		Avg len	R-1
1,294	65	0.33		57	0.28

For instance, for the example considered in Appendix A, the selected question-answer pair is shown in Table 2.

Table 2. Example of selected data from the MuSeRC dataset.

Text: text in Appendix A
Question: Why does Albert, heartbroken and half-oblivious, wander around his beloved's house, but does not dare go to say goodbye to her?
Original true answer: Doesn't want their relationship to be publicized.
Original true answer: He is afraid of harming her and himself by publicizing their affair.
Original false answer: A whole week has passed since their last date.
Original false answer: The servants reported that Anna died half an hour ago.

In order to increase the number of true and false answers to 5 for each question, we used the rewriting of answers obtained by GPT-4 Turbo.[6] The prompt format is in Appendix C. For each answer, the model generated 3 rewritten variants. For each variant, the ROUGE-1 value was calculated in relation to each answer of the true or false group. These values were averaged. Rewritten variants were ranked based on average ROUGE-1 scores. Those rewritten variants that increased the diversity of answers, i.e., had the lowest values of this score, were selected to augment the original dataset. We removed 12 examples with a difference between the average length of true and false answers more than 30 characters (the third condition). The characteristics of augmented dataset are given in Table 3.

Table 3. Average length (characters) and ROUGE-1 values for texts and answers in the selected examples after rewriting augmentation.

Avg len of texts	Original answers				
	True		False		
	Avg len	R-1	Avg len	R-1	
1,294	70	0.18	60	0.20	

The final dataset[7] contains 152 examples, which correspond to 200 pairs of questions and answer groups. Each question-answer pair has 5 true and 5 false answers (Table 4).

4 Experiments

4.1 Cosine Similarities

To test our hypothesis, we calculated for all the examples the cosine similarity between each answer in the given example and the two groups of answers for that example – correct and incorrect. Answers are represented as token sequences and a hidden state (at given layer) of some sequence is the vector of the last token of this sequence at the considered layer. The similarity between a sequence and a group is the average of the cosine similarity of the given sequence to all sequences in that group.

We obtained hidden states of the models for token sequences containing a prompt with task, knowledge, question, and answer descriptions. The format of the input data is presented in Appendix D.

Thus, three categories of similarities were formed:

- similarity of **true** sequences to one's own group of **true** sequences,
- similarity of **true** (**false**) sequences to another group of **false** (**true**) sequences,
- similarity of **false** sequences to their own group of **false** sequences.

---

[6] https://platform.openai.com/docs/models/gpt-4-and-gpt-4-turbo.

[7] https://anonymous.4open.science/r/llm_two_subspaces-5CF5.

Table 4. Example of sampled data from the MuSeRC dataset after increasing the number of answers by different rewritten variants.

Text: text in Appendix A
Question: Why does Albert, heartbroken and half-oblivious, wander around his beloved's house, but does not dare go to say goodbye to her?
Original true answer: Doesn't want their relationship to be publicized.
Original true answer: He is afraid of harming her and himself by publicizing their affair.
Rewritten true answer: Prefers to avoid publicity in their relationship.
Rewritten true answer: Wants to keep their relationship a secret.
Rewritten true answer: Wants to keep their relationship confidential.
Original false answer: A whole week has passed since their last date.
Original false answer: The servants reported that Anna died half an hour ago.
Rewritten false answer: The service staff reported that Anna died thirty minutes ago.
Rewritten false answer: The employees informed that Anna's death occurred half an hour ago.
Rewritten false answer: A message came from the servants that Anna left this world half an hour ago.

The results of calculating the specified cosine similarity categories at each layer for the example considered in Table 4 are shown in Fig. 3 and Fig. 4 as heatmaps.

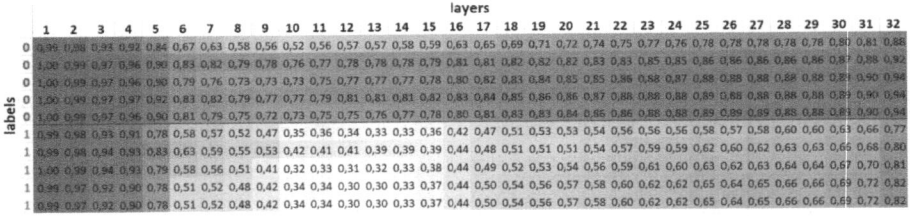

Fig. 3. Heatmap of the average cosine similarity values of true and false answers by layer to the **false** answers group for the LLaMA-2-7B-Chat model. White is a low cosine similarity, blue is a high value. (Color figure online)

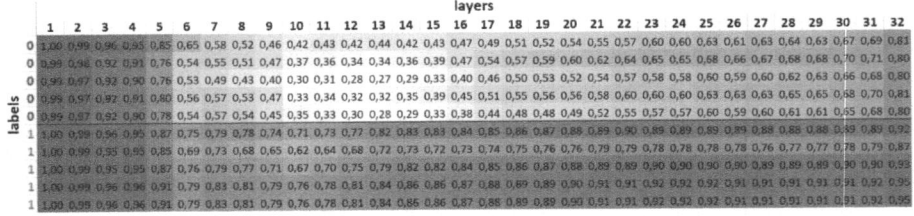

Fig. 4. Heatmap of the average cosine similarity values of true and false answers by layer to the **true** answers group for the LLaMA-2-7B-Chat model. White is a low cosine similarity, blue is a high value. (Color figure online)

Each row of the table is a true (label = 1) or false (label = 0) sequence, the columns are the model layers. The value in a cell is the average value of the cosine similarity of the sequence to the group of false (Fig. 3) or true (Fig. 4) sequences.

To analyze the statistics, the obtained cosine similarity values were averaged over the sequences in the group and then averaged over the layers.

For the example from Table 4, these calculations are indicated in Fig. 5. In this example, the average cosine similarity of false sequences to the group of correct sequences is 0.59 (averaged over the sequences in the group and over the layers of the model), and the average cosine similarity of correct sequences to the group of correct sequences is 0.85 (averaged in the same way).

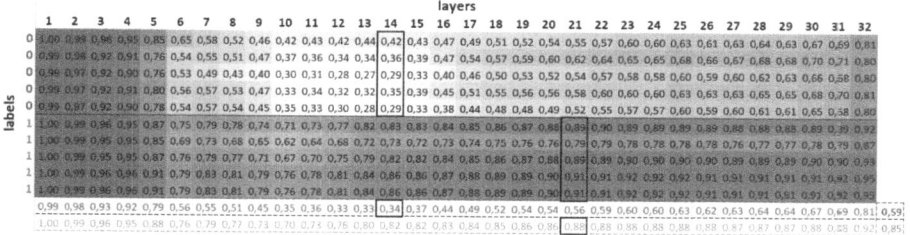

Fig. 5. Computation of averaged cosine similarity values over sequences in the group and over model layers for the LLaMA-2-7B-Chat model.

The described procedure for calculating cosine similarities was applied to all 200 question-answer pairs. The average scores for the 200 examples are presented in Table 5.

Table 5. Average cosine similarity scores for the three models. Cosine similarity is higher for their own groups and lower for another group.

The category of cosine similarity	Average cosine similarity		
	LLaMA-2-7B	Mistral-7B	Vicuna-7B
Similarity of true sequences to their own group of true sequences	0.8240	0.8461	0.8001
Similarity of true (false) sequences to another group of false (true) sequences	0.7344	0.7666	0.7006
Similarity of false sequences to their own group of false sequences	0.7791	0.8076	0.7524

The distribution of average cosine similarity scores for the 200 examples is shown in Fig. 6.

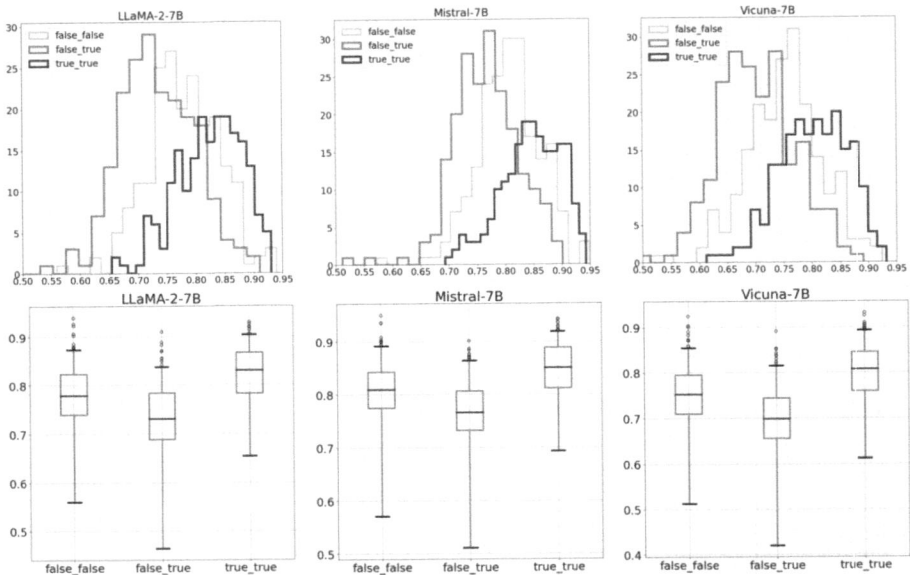

Fig. 6. Distribution of average cosine similarity.

4.2 Hypotheses Testing

To test our hypothesis, two pairs of observations are formed:

- the average values of cosine similarity (averaged over sequences in the group and model layers) of false answers to the groups of false answers and true answers;
- the average values of cosine similarity (averaged in the same way) of true answers to the groups of true and false answers.

Since the observations are independent and their distributions are normal, the t-test can be used for the results of the Mistral-7B and Vicuna-7B models. For the LLaMA-2-7B-Chat model, the Levene test has unequal variances, therefore we used Welch's t-test for it.

We reformulate our hypothesis ("the hidden state space of the model can be divided into two subspaces: correct and incorrect hidden states") as two hypotheses:

- average values of cosine similarity of false answers to the group of false answers are **not** equal to the average values of cosine similarity of false answers to the group of true answers;
- average values of cosine similarity of true answers to the group of true answers are **not** equal to average values of cosine similarity of true answers to the group of false answers.

The results of testing these hypotheses are shown in Table 6. All p-values are less than 0.001, thus hypotheses H_0 are rejected, that is, there are statistically significant differences between the cosine similarity values of true and false answers to own and other groups.

Table 6. t-test

Model	p-value
H_0: Average values of cosine similarity of false answers to the group of false answers are equal to the average values of cosine similarity of false answers to the group of true answers	
LLaMA-2-7B	$1.69e^{-11}$
Mistral-7B	$1.99e^{-12}$
Vicuna-7B	$3.93e^{-13}$
H_0: Average values of cosine similarity of true answers to the group of true answers are equal to average values of cosine similarity of true answers to the group of false answers	
LLaMA-2-7B	$4.77e^{-38}$
Mistral-7B	$5.07e^{-38}$
Vicuna-7B	$6.33e^{-42}$

Thus, we can distinguish in the hidden state space of the model two subspaces – subspace corresponding to correctly generated sequences (true answers), and subspace that represent incorrect sequences (wrong answers).

5 Discussion

We analyzed variation of the obtained cosine similarity scores across model layers to identify potentially "weak" layers in need of additional training. Criteria for analyzing layers at the single sequence level are as follows:

- *min_abs*: minimum cosine similarity value out of 32 layers,
- *pos_dif* and *neg_dif*: maximum difference with the previous layer in positive and negative directions.

Criterion for analyzing layers at the sequence group level is as follows:

- *group_dif*: the largest difference between the average similarity of true (false) sequences to another group of false (true) sequences and the average similarity of true (false) sequences to its own group of true (false) sequences.

For the first two criteria, 1,000 (200 examples of 5 true or false sequences each) layer indices were included, and for the third, 200 layer indices were included.

The modes of these layer indices series and their frequencies of occurrence are given in Table 7 and Appendix E.

The distribution of *group_dif* criterion values for the LLaMA-2-7B-Chat model is presented in more detail in the diagrams (Fig. 7 and Fig. 8).

Given these results, several middle layers of the models require attention and further research. The most frequent minimum value of cosine similarity is found at layer 9 for the Mistral-7B model and at layer 10 for LLaMA-2-7B-Chat and Vicuna-7B. The largest difference between the cosine similarity to the other group relative to one's own group is at layers 12–16.

Table 7. Criteria for analyzing model layers at the sequence group level.

Model	False sequences		True sequences	
	mode	freq	mode	freq
LLaMA-2-7B	13	32	15	38
Mistral-7B	16	24	16	47
Vicuna-7B	12	28	15	53

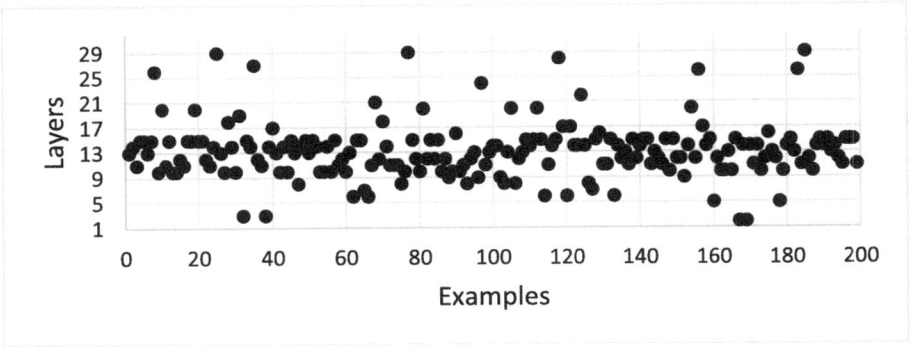

Fig. 7. Maximum value by *group_dif* criterion for each example

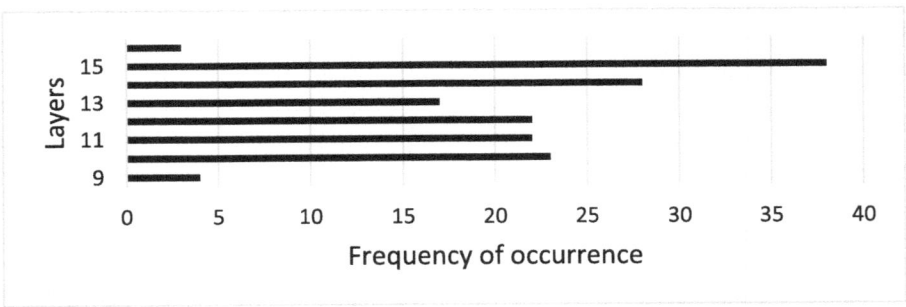

Fig. 8. Frequency of occurrence among 200 examples for several middle layer indices (from 9 to 16). By occurrence of the layer index, we mean that the maximum value of *group_dif* is reached at a given layer.

6   Conclusion

In this paper we hypothesize that it is possible to distinguish between true and false behavior of the model when solving the current generative task at the level of hidden states, i.e., to divide the space of hidden states of the model into two subspaces: hidden states corresponding to correctly generated sequences (true and false answers in the case of the question-answering task considered in this paper), and hidden states representing incorrect sequences (false answers). The hypothesis is confirmed with three quantized models LLaMA-2-7B-Chat, Mistral-7B and Vicuna-7B on the augmented MuSeRC question-answering dataset. Cosine similarity analysis between groups of correct and incorrect sequences showed that the most likely "weak" layers in the models are the middle layers from 9 to 16.

A development and practical application of the hypothesis is to propose that it is conceivable to additionally train "weak" layers of the model that have a negative effect on its behavior in order to improve it. In addition, the hypothesis should be tested with other different generative tasks for several languages.

7 Limitations

In our work, the hypothesis is tested without real sequence generation. This limitation is due to the labor-intensive nature of the annotation process. Despite the focus on generative tasks, our study does not face ethical issues related to these tasks, for the reason mentioned above.

Also, we are limited to analyzing three models that are similar in architecture and dimensionality.

Acknowledgments. This work was supported by Russian Science Foundation, project № 23–21-00330, https://rscf.ru/project/23-21-00330/.

Disclosure of Interests. The authors have no competing interests to declare that are relevant to the content of this article.

Appendix A

An example[8] from MuSeRC dataset that contains 6 question-answer pairs:

---

idx: 481

---

text[a]: Albert goes to Anna's house and sees that all the lights are turned off and only a ray of light breaks through her window. How can I find out what's wrong with her? A saving thought occurs to him that in the event of her illness, he can check on her health through a messenger, and the messenger does not necessarily need to know who gave him the order. So he learns that Anna is seriously ill with typhoid fever and her illness is very dangerous. Albert suffers unbearably at the thought that Anna could be dying now, and he cannot see her before her death. But he does not dare to rush upstairs to his beloved even now, for fear of harming her and himself by publicizing their affair. Heartbroken and half-oblivious, Albert wanders around his beloved's house, not daring to go to her to say goodbye. A week has passed since their last date. Early in the morning, Albert runs to Anna's house, and the servants report that Anna died half an hour ago. Now the painful hours of waiting for Anna seem to him the happiest of his life. And again the hero lacks the courage to enter the rooms, and he returns an hour later, hoping to blend in with the crowd and remain unnoticed. On the stairs he encounters unfamiliar mourning people, and they only thank him for his visit and attention

---

[8] This example and examples below are translated from Russian into English.   (*continued*)

(continued)

question	original answers			
	true		**false**	
What happened to Anna?	Anna died of Typhoid	Anna suffered from Typhoid and died of fever	Anna ran away with Albert	Anna rejected Albert
Why didn't Albert go to say goodbye to Anna?	He was afraid to show that they were having an affair	He was afraid of harming her reputation	He missed the train	He was hampered by unforeseen circumstances
What illness did Albert learn about Anna?	Typhoid fever	Typhoid fever	Cold	Flu
How many minutes after Anna's death did Albert come?	Half an hour	Thirty	Eight	Ten
How does Albert find out that Anna is seriously ill with typhoid fever and her illness is very dangerous?	Through a messenger	He inquired about her health through a messenger	Came to her	From passers-by
Why does Albert, heartbroken and half-oblivious, wander around his beloved's house, but does not dare go to say goodbye to her?	Doesn't want their relationship to be publicized	He is afraid of harming her and himself by publicizing their affair	A whole week has passed since their last date	The servants reported that Anna died half an hour ago

[a] In the original dataset, the sentences in the text are numbered. The numbering is removed using regular expressions.

Appendix B

An example of an instance of the MuSeRC dataset excluded from further work due to a difference between answers of only one number.

```
"id": 397,
"text": "(1) The Norwegian men's national biathlon team won the relay race... (13) They
were ahead of their main rivals - the Germans - by only 0.3 seconds.",
    "questions": [{
        "question": "How many seconds were the women's team ahead of their rivals?",
        "answers": [
            {"text": "By 0.3 seconds.",
             "label": 1
            },
        ...
            {"text": "By 0.5 seconds.",
             "label": 0
            }],
        "idx": 0
    }]
```

Appendix C

GPT-4 rewriting prompt.
   Paraphrase the text. Write 3 different rewritten variants. To write the answer, use the
following structure:
   Rewriting:
   #1# Variant 1
   #2# Variant 2
   #3# Variant 3
   Text: {answer}
   Rewriting:

Appendix D

Input data format during getting the hidden states of the model.
[INST] <<SYS>>
You can answer questions in Russian, based on the data provided.
<</SYS>>
Briefly answer the question using the knowledge given to you. [/INST]
Knowledge: {knowledge}
Question: {question}
Answer:

Appendix E

Criteria for analyzing model layers at the level of single sequences.

Criterion	min abs		pos dif		neg dif	
	mode	freq	mode	freq	mode	freq
LLaMA-2-7B						
group of **true** sequences						
false sequences	10	371	31	619	5	900
group of **false** sequences						
true sequences	10	400	31	669	5	929
Mistral-7B						
group of **true** sequences						
false sequences	9	412	31	529	3	493
group of **false** sequences						
true sequences	9	484	31	561	1	488
Vicuna-7B						
group of **true** sequences						
false sequences	10	193	31	824	4	584
group of **false** sequences						
true sequences	10	218	31	857	4	565

References

1. Ali, S., et al.: Explainable Artificial Intelligence (XAI): what we know and what is left to attain Trustworthy Artificial Intelligence. Inf. Fusion **99**, 101805 (2023)
2. Belrose, N., et al.: Eliciting latent predictions from transformers with the tuned lens. arXiv: 2303.08112v4. Accessed 02 Apr 2024
3. Dar, G., Geva, M., Gupta, A., Berant, J.: Analyzing transformers in embedding space. In: Proceedings of the 61st Annual Meeting of the Association for Computational Linguistics, Toronto, Canada, vol. 1, pp. 16124–16170 (2023)
4. Fenogenova, A., Mikhailov, V., Shevelev, D.: Read and reason with MuSeRC and RuCoS: datasets for machine reading comprehension for Russian. In: Proceedings of the 28th International Conference on Computational Linguistics, Barcelona, Spain, pp. 6481–6497 (2020)
5. Liu, Y., et al.: RoBERTa: a robustly optimized BERT pretraining approach. arXiv:1907.116 92v1. Accessed 02 Apr 2024
6. Räuker, T., Ho, A., Casper, S., Hadfield-Menell, D.: Toward transparent AI: a survey on interpreting the inner structures of deep neural networks. In: IEEE Conference on Secure and Trustworthy Machine Learning (SaTML), pp. 464–483 (2023)
7. Razova, E., Vychegzhanin, S., Kotelnikov, E.: Does BERT look at sentiment lexicon? In: Burnaev, E., et al. (eds.) AIST 2021. CCIS, vol. 1573, pp. 55–67. Springer, Cham (2022). https://doi.org/10.1007/978-3-031-15168-2_6
8. Tjoa, E., Guan, C.: A survey on explainable artificial intelligence (XAI): toward medical XAI. IEEE Trans. Neural Netw. Learn. Syst. **32**, 4793–4813 (2021)
9. Vaswani, A., et al.: Attention is all you need. In: Advances in Neural Information Processing Systems, NIPS 2017, pp. 6000–6010 (2017)
10. Yang, J., et al.: Harnessing the power of LLMs in practice: a survey on ChatGPT and beyond. ACM Trans. Knowl. Discov. **18**(6), 1–32 (2024)
11. Yang, S., Huang, S., Zou, W., Zhang, J., Dai, X., Chen, J.: Local interpretation of transformer based on linear decomposition. In: Proceedings of the 61st Annual Meeting of the Association for Computational Linguistics, Toronto, Canada, vol. 1, pp. 10270–10287 (2023)
12. Zou, A., et al.: Representation engineering: a top-down approach to AI transparency. arXiv: 2310.01405v3. Accessed 02 Apr 2024

Improving DRS-to-Text Generation Through Delexicalization and Data Augmentation

Muhammad Saad Amin(✉)📧, Luca Anselma📧, and Alessandro Mazzei📧

Department of Computer Science, University of Turin, Turin, Italy
{muhammadsaad.amin,luca.anselma,alessandro.mazzei}@unito.it

Abstract. Text generation from Discourse Representation Structure (DRS), is a complex logic-to-text generation task where lexical information in the form of logical concepts is translated into its corresponding textual representation. Delexicalization is the process of removing lexical information from the data which helps the model be more robust in producing textual sequences by focusing on the semantic structure of the input rather than the exact lexical content. Implementation of delexicalization is even harder in the case of the DRS-to-Text generation task where the lexical entities are anchored using WordNet synsets and thematic roles are sourced from VerbNet. In this paper, we have introduced novel procedures to selectively delexicalize proper nouns and common nouns. For data transformations, we propose to use two types of lexical abstractions (1): WordNet supersense-based contextually categorized abstraction; and (2): abstraction based on the lexical category associated with named entities and nouns. We present many experiments for evaluating the hypotheses of delexicalization in the DRS-to-Text generation task by using state-of-the-art neural sequence-to-sequence models. Furthermore, we also explored data augmentation through delexicalization while evaluating test sets with different abstraction methodologies i.e., with and without supersenses. Our experimental results proved the effectiveness of model generalizability through delexicalization while comparing it with the results of fully lexicalized DRS-to-Text generation. Delexicalization resulted in an improved translation quality with a significant increase in evaluation scores.

Keywords: Delexicalization · Data augmentation · Discourse representation structure · Formal meaning representation · Neural DRS-to-Text generation · Super senses

1 Introduction

Delexicalization is the process of removing lexical knowledge from the data to make it generalized by emphasizing more on the syntactic structure and sentence patterns rather than the specific semantic content [1]. It is a very well-known

© The Author(s), under exclusive license to Springer Nature Switzerland AG 2024
A. Rapp et al. (Eds.): NLDB 2024, LNCS 14762, pp. 121–136, 2024.
https://doi.org/10.1007/978-3-031-70239-6_9

technique in audio and speech processing where delexicalization and relexicalization procedures are used to improve dialogue systems through the preservation of prosodic features for text-to-speech applications [2]. Contributions of data delexicalization are also becoming very popular in many applications of natural language processing. The motivation for using delexicalization is to enhance the model's ability to generate more natural sentences with better grammar and syntactic structure [3]. This also highlights the model's ability to perform well for unseen or out-of-vocabulary words [4]. Recent neural approaches to language generation have achieved peak performance through end-to-end training, they have also gained popularity in a variety of natural language generation (NLG) applications, including concept-to-text generation, machine translation (MT), and summarization [5].

Commonly used procedures of delexicalization in NLG include named entity dependent or exact delexicalization, language agnostic delexicalization, and delexicalization through pre-trained language models [6]. It is important to understand that the requirement to create a pragmatically correct text while maintaining the semantic and syntactic structure of the sentence makes data delexicalization even harder. In fact, grammatically inaccurate or out-of-scope delexicalized textual input might lead to poor model performance [7]. In the delexicalization process, lexical entities are replaced with a placeholder e.g., "Tom knocked at the door.", considering nouns only, the modified example is "[placeholder] knocked at the [placeholder].". Here, the placeholder can be any generalized tag depending on the type of delexicalized applied to the data.

Using transformers and encoder-decoder-based neural models, researchers working on text generation from concept or meaning representations –i.e. graph-based abstract meaning representations (AMR) [8–10], RDF-triples [11], or discourse representation structures (DRS) [12–17]– have recently focused on generating text from logical representations and vice versa. In this paper, we emphasize the role played by data delexicalization in formal meaning representation (DRS), in the context of neural DRS-to-Text generation tasks. DRS originated from discourse representation theory (DRT) that lists formal meaning representation in the form of first-order logic (FOL) [18]. Textual information is represented in DRS as events, concepts, and entities. For example, names are discourse referents that are usually represented as variables in DRS, along with the logical relations that exist between these entities, such as quantifiers, conjunctions, negations, disjunctions, etc. Lexical information like nouns, adjectives, and adverbs are represented as logical concepts that are associated with English WordNet, and verbs are represented as VerbNet roles [19–21]. As an example, a graphical representation of the DRS for the text "Tom was carrying a bucket of water." is shown in Fig. 1.

In a wide spectrum of data-to-text generation tasks having different flavors of input representations including an AMR graph [8–10], an RDF triple [11], or a table [22], neural DRS-to-Text generation is an application of the same stream having DRS as the data. The neural model takes a logical representation (DRS) as an input and generates the corresponding text as output [15,16].

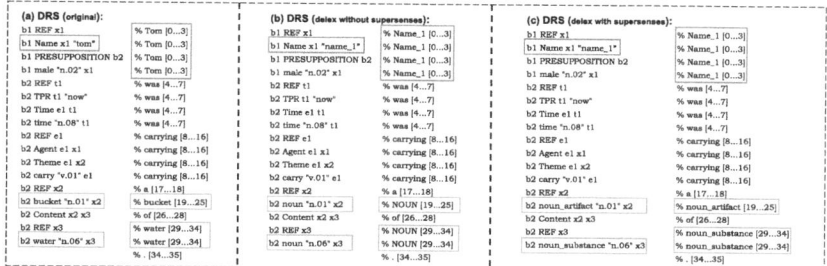

Fig. 1. Graphical representation of the DRS with lexical (a) and delexical without (b) and with (c) supersenses for the text "Tom was carrying a bucket of water.". (Color figure online)

Compared to different logical or conceptual representations of data i.e., AMR and RDF, we choose DRS because it is more expressive and it can represent a wide range of semantic phenomena that can express logical relations for long sentences. Furthermore, using DRS can provide a very fine-grained investigation of the logical form of individual sentences, for DRS-to-Text generation, focusing more on syntactic or discourse-level structure rather than semantic contents only. Stated otherwise, "by modifying a DRS's meaning in a controlled manner, the systems' robustness can be closely observed and evaluated accordingly." [15]. However, since large language models (LLMs) have no prior knowledge of DRS, they may introduce noise in the data if used for delexicalization or relexicalization. This resilience property discourages the use of LLMs for data delexicalization–see Sect. 4.2.

In this study, we specifically develop and evaluate data delexicalization for the categories of (i) proper nouns (PNs) and (ii) common nouns (CNs), utilizing the robustness aspect of neural DRS-to-text generation. Specifically, we developed and evaluated the process of substituting the actual lexical information of the original DRS-text pairs with the placeholders by modifying the proper nouns and common nouns in the dataset. We investigate different approaches, with and without the use of supersenses, to generate new delexicalized training sentences. These approaches aim to investigate the importance of lexical/semantic information and the curial role played by the syntactic structure of logical representation in the task of neural DRS-to-text generation. Furthermore, we also applied a novel approach of data augmentation through delexicalization by combining lexical and delexical flavors of data. We want to understand the important role played by semantic knowledge in the identification of the syntactic structure of the sentence while evaluating a delexicalized test set.

This brings us to the following research questions:

1. How to delexicalize logical data representations such as DRS where lexical entities are strongly connected with external lexical databases like WordNet and VerbNet?

2. Can supersense contribute to enhancing the generalization power of the neural models when used for nouns?
3. What would be the behavior of the model if we augment logically delexicalized data with fully lexicalized one?
4. Can delexicalization and augmentation increase the model performance?
5. What is the behavior of seq-to-seq neural models in the case of pre-training (bi-LSTM) and fine-tuning (byT5)?
6. How do general-purpose large language models like chatGPT and Claude incorporate DRS when given as a prompt?

To the best of our knowledge, this study is the first attempt to explore data delexicalization in neural DRS-to-Text generation. Apart from some initial works on data augmentation of verbs and nouns in DRS-to-Text generation [16, 17], this is the first work of data augmentation through delexicalization to evaluate the syntactic structure of the generated text through relexicalization.

The statistical structure of the neural network makes it difficult to analyze the type of information that the system has actually learned. Generally, the network learns that the verb follows the subject (e.g. grammatical competence) when we give a concrete example, such as "Brad Pitt is an actor", and/or that men can be actors (semantic and pragmatic knowledge) or that a particular man is an actor (world knowledge). How can we take advantage of the multi-level structure of neural learning? Our study has the side effect of raising these theoretical questions for further investigation.

The remaining paper is structured as follows: in Sect. 2, we describe the procedure used for noun delexicalization with and without supersenses. In Sect. 3, we give an insight into the architecture of the neural DRS-to-text pipelines. In Sect. 4, we describe the experimental results of DRS-to-text generation through (1) automatic metric-based and pre-trained model-based evaluations on a standard test set, (2) a reduced test set comparing our neural systems with two general LLMs, and (3) an error analysis of the model-generated text; Finally, the paper is concluded in Sect. 5 with a leading section of limitations.

2   Logical Delexicalization with Nouns

When it comes to the application of neural DRS-to-Text generation, logical data delexicalization seems to be a complex task. Each example in the training set consists of a logical input (DRS) and the corresponding text that goes with it. Both types of data representations need to be monitored when making methodological changes to the training data, as the neural network treats them as pairs of input values. The data transformations should therefore take into account the order of the meaning representations and the text translations and should be equal and balanced for both elements. We used different delexicalization approaches to generalize PNs and CNs in the DRS-to-Text generation task.

We used the Parallel Meaning Bank[1] (PMB) dataset, which is created in the standard train-dev-test split, in its gold version.

Table 1. Different flavors of delexicalization applied to the dataset referring to data transformations without and with supersense. (Transf. = Transformation; PN placeholders in blue; CN placeholders in green).

Transf. Type	Lexicalized Text	Delexicalized Text
Delex w/o SS	Brad Pitt is an actor.	Name_1 is a NOUN.
	The Mona Lisa hung above the antique table.	The Name_1 hung above the antique NOUN.
	Paris is a beautiful city.	City_1 is a beautiful NOUN.
	Noah and Sophia watched a movie at the local theater.	Name_1 and Name_2 watched a NOUN at the local NOUN.
Delex with SS	Brad Pitt is an actor.	Name_1 is a noun_person.
	The Mona Lisa hung above the antique table.	The Name_1 hung above the antique noun_artifact.
	Paris is a beautiful city.	City_1 is a beautiful noun_location.
	Noah and Sophia watched a movie at the local theater.	Name_1 and Name_2 watched a noun_communication at the local noun_artifact.

Figure 1 displays the graphical representations of the DRS transformations from fully lexical representation (a), to delexical without supersense (b), and delexical with supersenses (c) highlighting PN transformation (in blue) and CN (in green). The DRS (a) generates the sentence "Tom was carrying a bucket of water." reflecting a fully lexical translation of the DRS, while the DRS (b) generates "Name_1 was carrying a NOUN of NOUN." representing a more generalized delexicalization approach, and the DRS (c) generates "Name_1 was carrying a noun_artifact of noun_substance." producing text with the contextual control over delexicalized placeholder through the use of supersenses. Other textual examples are listed in Table 1 to have a clear understanding of the proposed delexicalized approaches.

2.1 Proper Noun Delexicalization

The proper names of a person (PER), which includes both male and female names, and of a place (GPE), which includes city, state, country, and island names, are the two specific Named Entity (NE) categories that we examined for PNs. To extract proper names from the text, we used the spaCy NE Recognizer https://spacy.io. For PER and GPE, there is a total of 3773 instances of PNs. The proper nouns are further divided into the following categories: person names account for 57%, city names 30%, state names 6%, country names 6%, and other types, such as island names, 1%.

While dexicalizing PNs, we have adopted two approaches to replace named entities with placeholders to analyze the impact of model generalizability by removing lexical information from the dataset. (1) Replacing named entities with custom placeholders i.e., person_name, city_name, state_name, country_name, etc. This substitution resulted in 6 different custom placeholders for all the

---

[1] The PMB is developed at the University of Groningen as part of the NWO-VICI project "Lost in Translation - Found in Meaning" (Project number 277-89-003), led by Johan Bos.

named entities under observation in the dataset. (2) Replacing named entities with spaCy-defined placeholders i.e., PER and GPE. This substitution resulted in only 2 placeholders for all named entities in the dataset. For example, in "Tom is living in Boston now.", through the first approach we get "Name_1 is living in city_1 now." while with the second approach, we get "PER is living in GPE now.".

While experimenting with delexicalized PNs, we found custom delexicalization more useful as compared to spaCy-oriented delexicalization. This is because, for model evaluation through relexicalization, custom delexicalization helps to sustain true pragmatics of the logical input while preserving true semantic correlation between delexicalized named entities. While in the case of spaCy-defined placeholders, the model often confuses the exact location of the named entity placeholder in the delexicalized translation of the meaning representation. For example, in "Tom went to London and called Mary.", through custom delexicalization, we get "Name_1 went to City_1 and called Name_2." which is semantically more understandable to the neural model. While in the case of the spaCy-oriented placeholder, the model confused the order of semantic entities and generated "PER went to PER and called GPE." or "GPE went to PER and called PER.". Therefore, for all of our further experiments, we have used custom delexicalization for named entities. Some extra examples demonstrating the delexicalization procedures are listed in Table 1.

2.2   Common Noun Delexicalization

CNs sustaining the true contextual sense of the sentence are very important lexical entities, especially in the logical input representations like DRS. To extract CNs from the text, we used spaCy again which resulted in the extraction of 6193 lexical entities from the dataset. For delexicalization, we have adopted two different procedures for replacement. First, replacing all lexical entities of CNs with one spaCy-based placeholder i.e., NOUN. This type of delexical substitution makes the data fully generalized with only one placeholder for all lexical entities of CNs. Second, a novel WordNet-based supersense tagging (SST) approach that proved helpful in sustaining the categorical and contextual sense of the sentence. With supersenses, we identified CNs from the 26 lexicographic categories of WordNet based on data instances. These categories included noun_act, noun_artifact, noun_body, noun_cognition, noun_communication, noun_event, noun_feeling, noun_food, noun_group, and noun_motion, etc. A graphical representation of the categorical distribution of the CN through supersenses is shown in Fig. 2.

For example, in "A cat is sitting on the chair.", if we delexicalize with a 1 spaCy placeholder, we have "A NOUN is sitting on the NOUN.". But if we perform delexicalization through supersenses, we have "A noun_animal is sitting on the noun_artifact.". The motivation for using delexicalization is to only extract lexical knowledge from the data without breaking semantic correlation and sentence structure. Through supersense delexicalization, we are facilitating

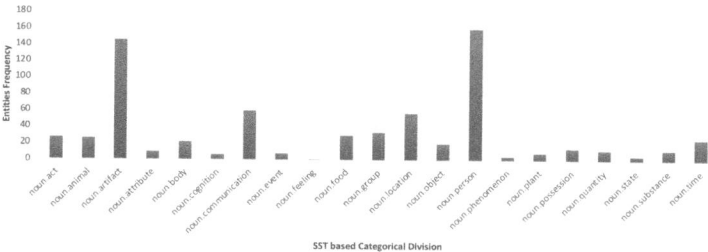

Fig. 2. Supersense-based categorical division of common nouns in Gold-PMB dataset.

the model to understand the delexicalized input structure more precisely as compared to spaCy-based delexicalized data having one placeholder for all CNs. For noun delexicalization, we have experimented with both types of delexicalization procedures i.e., with and without supersenses. Some examples demonstrating the delexicalization procedures with and without supersenses are listed in Table 1.

3 Three Neural DRS-to-Text Pipelines

DRS-to-text generation is a complex task that requires computationally efficient neural models. In this scope, we have used three different neural architectures in our implementation pipelines. The encoder-decoder-oriented recurrent sequence-to-sequence neural network with (1): character-based lexical encoding (CB-bi-LSTM henceforth); and (2): word-based lexical encoding (WB-bi-LSTM henceforth), both having bidirectional Long short-term memory (LSTM) layers [16]. In addition, we have also fine-tuned byT5: a state-of-the-art version of the Transformer family to improve DRS-to-text generation (FT-byT5 henceforth) [17]. Our first two models point towards the procedure of training a neural model from scratch and our third model focuses on fine-tuning a pre-trained LLM for task-specific applications.

We decided to adopt also the Transformer-based model for our experimental implementation because we are aware that the most advanced neural models for generating text from structured input representations use complex transformer-oriented architectures. However, the purpose of this paper is not to present the best-performing system but to analyze the consequences of data delexicalization in the context of neural DRS-to-text generation.

It should be noted that the main differences between CB-bi-LSTM and WB-bi-LSTM are based on the representations of the input and output data, i.e. characters or words, and how well they can handle words that are not in the dictionary (OOV). Since CB-bi-LSTM analyses character sequences, it can easily handle OOV words, while WB-bi-LSTM may have difficulty handling OOV words, as this depends more on the included vocabulary. We believe that the impact of certain data delexicalization strategies may be influenced by these two different approaches.

The model architecture and hyperparameters used in our experiments for sequence-to-sequence implementation are likewise [16], that focus on LSTM-based encoder-decoder cells with an epoch-based learning decay method that uses Adam as an optimizer. The validation metric we use is cross entropy (ce), while the cost function is ce-mean. Table 2 contains other important hyperparameters that we have used for bi-LSTM experiments. When using AdamW as the optimizer and fine-tuning the model over 15 epochs, we used the default hyperparameter settings of byT5 in our transformer-based version and made minor adjustments to the batch size, update steps, and learning rates. Table 2 contains a list of all hyperparameter settings of the FT-byT5 model just like used in [17].

Table 2. Hyperparameter settings for CB-bi-LSTM, WB-bi-LSTM, and FT-byT5.

bi-LSTM (CB|WB)		FT-byT5	
HyperParameters	Values	HyperParameters	Values
Embedding Dimensions	300	Batch size	15
Enc/Dec Cell	LSTM	Update steps	8
Enc/Dec Depth	2	Max learning Rate	1e−4
Mini-batch	48	Min learning Rate	1e−5
Normalization Rate	0.9	Warmup updates	3000
lr-decay	0.5	Max decay steps	30000
lr-decay-strategy	Epoch	No. of epochs	15
Optimizer	Adam	Optimizer	AdamW
Validation Metric	Cross-Entropy		
Cost-Type	ce-mean		
Beam Size	10		
Learning Rate	0.002		

We have used the Parallel Meaning Bank (PMB) dataset in its English edition. Among the different dataset flavors–Gold, Silver, and Bronze–we focused on the Gold dataset, which has a fully manual annotation and correction process. Gold-PMB uses training, development, and test files with 6620, 885, and 898 data instances, respectively, according to the standard split of the dataset. Two sample transformation methods were used to delexicalize the dataset. (1) Delexicalization of PNs through custom placeholder (see Sect. 2.1) and CNs with a spaCy-oriented placeholder (see Sect. 2.2) (delex1 henceforth). (2) Delexicalization of PNs through custom placeholders and CNs with supersense-based placeholders (delex26 henceforth). For experimentation, we have delexicalized DRS-text pairs of train and development sets and only DRS for the test set. We kept the text of the test set the same, i.e., fully lexical, so that after performing relexicalization to the model-generated text, we can evaluate the model performance through comparison with the gold test set. A graphical representation of the pipeline is shown in Fig. 3.

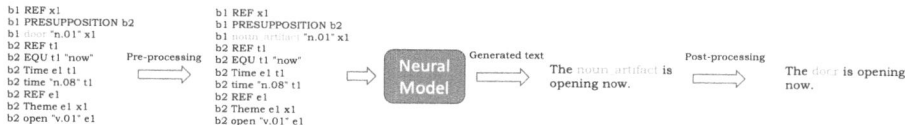

Fig. 3. Implementation pipeline of DRS-to-Text generation through the pre-processing (delexicalization) and post-processing (relexicalization) of the text "The door is opening now.".

A further original contribution of this paper is the analysis of data augmentation through logical data delexicalization. We want to understand the important role played by data augmentation thus focusing on the data-hungry nature of the neural models. For this implementation, we have conducted four different experiments. (1) Concatenating fully lexical and fully delexicalized (delex1) data examples and evaluating model performance for the delex1 test set. (2) Concatenating fully lexical and fully delexicalized (delex26) data examples and evaluating model performance for the delex26 test set. (3) Concatenating fully lexical, fully delexicalized (delex1), and fully delexicalized (delex26) data examples and evaluating model performance for the delex1 test set. (4) Concatenating fully lexical, fully delexicalized (delex1), and fully delexicalized (delex26) data examples and evaluating model performance for the delex26 test set.

4   Experimental Results

For experimental implementation, we have used 3 different neural models with the motivation of pre-training and fine-tuning a sequence-to-sequence model. Table 3, Table 4, and Table 5 list the experimental findings of all the experiments for pre-training characters and words tokenization oriented bi-LSTM models and fine-tuning transformer-based byT5 model respectively. Based on the models used for experiments, we categorize the results in the sense that we list all CB-biLSTM results in Table 3, all WB-biLSTM results are mentioned in Table 4, and Table 5 displays all FT-byT5 results having delexicalized flavors of logic-text pairs with and without supersenses. Furthermore, we have applied data augmentation through delexicalization by concatenating fully-lexical and respective flavors of delexicalized datasets to analyze the model performance. For experimental evaluations, we perform automatic metric-based evaluation (see Sect. 4.1) and comparison of large language models (LLMs) like chatGPT-3.5 and Claude-2.0 (see Sect. 4.2) with our best-delexicalized model to compare powerful general-purpose LLMs with our delexicalized model.

4.1 Evaluation with Automatic Metrics

For a clear understanding of the results in Table 3, Table 4, and Table 5, we have split the evaluation scores into 4 different blocks. The first block (exp. 01) is our baseline with the DRS-to-text generation results on the model trained or fine-tuned on a fully lexical dataset i.e., without delexicalization. Our second block (exp. 02–03) represents results for 2 different delexicalization approaches with supersenses (exp. 02) and without supersenses (exp. 03). Here the model is pre-trained or fine-tuned on only delexicalized data samples. In the third block, we have results for data augmentation through delexicalization by concatenating fully lexical data examples with one flavor of delexicalization i.e., with supersenses (exp. 04) and without supersenses (exp. 05) respectively. Finally, in the fourth block, we have compound augmentation results with the concatenation of fully lexical and delexicalized data examples with and without supersenses. With the same training examples, we evaluate two different test sets: (1) a delexicalized test set with supersenses (exp. 06), and (2) a delexicalized test set without supersenses (exp. 07).

Table 3. CB-biLSTM results for delexicalization with supersenses (delex26) and without supersenses (delex1) on Gold-PMB dataset. (Note: MET. = METEOR; RUG. = ROUGE; CMT. = COMET; B.Scr = BERT-Score; CB = Character-Based; tst = testing)

Exp.	Implementation Type	BLEU	chrF	MET.	RUG.	CMT.	B.Scr
CB-01	Fully Lexical	46.80	66.22	39.12	72.54	79.33	95.31
CB-02	Delex26	48.51	63.58	40.34	74.24	75.37	94.67
CB-03	Delex1	*51.10*	61.24	*40.80*	*74.43*	74.11	94.26
CB-04	Lex+delex26	*60.45*	**71.12**	*46.46*	*80.78*	*82.48*	*96.19*
CB-05	Lex+delex1	57.68	69.85	44.33	78.62	81.63	95.94
CB-06	Lex+delex26+delex1(tst delex26)	60.95	70.52	46.25	80.70	81.94	96.10
CB-07	Lex+delex26+delex1(tst delex1)	**61.38**	*70.66*	**46.53**	**81.41**	**82.60**	**96.20**

Table 3 lists our results for the pre-training of the bi-LSTM model for the char-based tokenization approach (CB-biLSTM). Compared to the baseline (CB-01), CB-biLSTM wins in all aspects of experiments run through delexicalization with and without supersenses and augmentation. In fact, data augmentation always helps in improving model performance by increasing model generalization ability. In the case of individual data delexicalization (CB-02, CB-03), delexicalization without supersenses wins (CB-03, in italics). With data augmentation, delexicalization with supersenses shows a good improvement and gains significantly (CB-04 in italics) as compared to delexicalization without supersenses (CB-05). Finally, with compound augmentation, the CB-biLSTM model generalizes more for a test set that does not contain any supersenses (CB-07, in bold and italics). CB-07 also indicates the highest score in all the experimental formats of the CB-biLSTM model.

Table 4. WB-biLSTM results for delexicalization with supersenses (delex26) and without supersenses (delex1) on Gold-PMB dataset. (Note: MET. = METEOR; RUG. = ROUGE; CMT. = COMET; B.Scr = BERT-Score; WB = Word-Based; tst = testing)

Exp.	Implementation Type	BLEU	chrF	MET.	RUG.	CMT.	B.Scr
WB-01	Fully Lexical	40.36	56.06	33.42	65.26	73.66	94.44
WB-02	Delex26	*52.32*	*62.77*	*41.67*	*75.37*	*76.94*	*94.95*
WB-03	Delex1	49.80	58.47	40.33	73.32	73.94	94.45
WB-04	Lex+delex26	*56.49*	**67.90**	**44.24**	**78.73**	80.93	95.74
WB-05	Lex+delex1	53.98	65.98	41.99	75.85	80.17	*95.75*
WB-06	Lex+delex26+delex1(tst delex26)	57.05	67.11	44.00	78.16	**80.94**	95.87
WB-07	Lex+delex26+delex1(tst delex1)	**57.07**	67.38	*44.11*	*78.42*	80.59	**95.76**

Table 4 shows the results for the WB-biLSTM model pre-trained with the delexicalized and augmented training examples with and without supersenses. Just like the CB-bi-LSTM model, the WB-bi-LSTM model also wins in all the aspects of experimental implementation when compared with the baseline (WB-01). Unlike the CB-biLSTM model, the WB-biLSTM model shows significantly different results. For individual delexicalization results (WB-02, WB-03), the model trained on supersense-based delexicalized data wins (WB-02, in italics). Surprisingly, compound data augmentation does not seem effective for the WB-biLSTM model, as the model gets the highest scores, apart from the BLEU score, for data augmentation with supersense-based delexicalized data (WB-04 in bold and italics). While the highest BLEU score is for the compound augmentation testing the sub-set having delexicalized data without supersenses (WB-07).

Finally, in Table 5, we show our results for the byT5 model fine-tuned on delexicalized data with and without supersenses. Overall model generalization ability is enhanced with the adaptation of data delexicalization. Furthermore, augmentation helped the model to achieve the best results in the case of compound augmentation while testing the delexicalized subset without supersenses (T5-07 in bold and italics). The influence of individual delexicalization procedures i.e., with and without supersenses (T5-02, T5-03) does not significantly affect the model's generalization power as the results are very close. Similarly, in the case of data augmentation (T5-04, T5-05), the model is not significantly improved with different flavors of delexicalization along with lexical augmentation.

Comparing the overall performance of all models, byT5 shows the best results with a fine-tuning perspective (see Table 5, T5-07) when compared with the pre-training based biLSTM models (see Table 3 and Table 4). This highlights the need for state-of-the-art sequence-to-sequence models for complex task-specific

Table 5. FT-byT5 results for delexicalization with supersenses (delex26) and without supersenses (delex1) on Gold-PMB dataset. (Note: MET. = METEOR; RUG. = ROUGE; CMT. = COMET; B.Scr = BERT-Score; T5 = fine-tuned byT5; tst = testing)

Exp.	Implementation Type	BLEU	chrF	MET.	RUG.	CMT.	B.Scr
T5-01	Fully Lexical	51.88	73.16	43.55	76.04	86.89	96.74
T5-02	Delex26	62.44	77.93	*47.50*	*82.18*	*89.47*	*97.47*
T5-03	Delex1	*62.73*	*77.85*	47.41	81.76	88.96	97.37
T5-04	Lex+delex26	*62.94*	*78.48*	*47.67*	82.20	*89.72*	97.40
T5-05	Lex+delex1	62.72	78.09	47.30	82.06	88.95	*97.43*
T5-06	Lex+delex26+delex1(tst delex26)	63.54	78.85	47.91	82.47	89.72	97.60
T5-07	Lex+delex26+delex1(tst delex1)	**64.22**	**78.87**	**48.07**	**82.90**	**90.16**	**97.63**

applications, e.g., DRS-to-text. In the next sections about the comparison of neural DRS-to-Text generation model with LLMs (Sect. 4.2) and for error analysis (Sect. 4.3), we will use the text generated by our best model, i.e., FT-byT5, evaluated for test set without supersenses (see Table 5, T5-07).

4.2   Comparing Neural DRS-to-Text Generation and LLMs

To get a better understanding of how well our delexicalized neural approach performs, compared to a general-purpose LLM that has not been fine-tuned for a specific task, we compare the quality of the generated text of our neural DRS-to-text systems with two LLMs, ChatGPT 3.5 [23] and Claude 2.0 [24]. We examined the performance of the LLM using both few-shot and zero-shot learning techniques. The behavior of ChatGPT did not improve even in the case of few-shot learning, while Claude gained a lot in few-shot as compared to zero-shot approaches (see Table 6).

Table 6. Evaluation of DRS-to-Text generation text for LLMs reporting scores for ChatGPT 3.5, Claude 2.0, the baseline (without delexicalization), and our best (FT-byT5) model. (Note: LLM = Large Language Model; MET. = METEOR; RUG. = ROUGE; CMT. = COMET; B.Scr = BERT Score)

LLM Type	Implementation Type	BLEU	chrF	MET.	RUG.	CMT.	B.Scr
Claude-2.0	Zero-shot learning	11.33	44.15	29.39	42.43	69.83	92.31
	Few-shot learning	*27.25*	*58.72*	*38.58*	*64.25*	*87.17*	*95.37*
ChatGPT-3.5	Zero-shot learning	*9.82*	*43.69*	*27.91*	*39.80*	*68.80*	*91.98*
	Few-shot learning	9.58	40.46	26.01	37.40	66.17	91.54
byT5	Fully lexical model	47.55	71.47	42.90	74.56	86.49	96.52
	FT-byT5 (our best model)	**61.00**	**75.96**	**45.70**	**80.02**	**88.52**	**97.29**

We considered a sample of 215 examples from the test set that were (1) evaluated using the best DRS-to-text neural models, i.e., FT-byT5 (see Table 5), and (2) in response to prompts from Claude 2.0 and ChatGPT 3.5 to obtain text produced by the models. We evaluated the generated text using automatic evaluation metrics (see Table 6). The italic score represents the best results for each model type while the bold and italics results show the best results when compared to overall model types which in this case is our best model, i.e., FT-byT5. The experimental evaluation clearly shows that task-specific neural models are required for DRS-to-text generation, as LLMs, which are generative general-purpose models, do not perform well on complex domain-specific applications.

4.3   Error Analysis

We further examine the model-generated text by manual inspection to gain a deep understanding of the experimental evaluations. To do so, we compare the same instances generated by different models, e.g., fully lexical, LLMs (ChatGPT and Claude), and FT-byT5. Examples of different features of semantics, syntax, missing information, the hallucinatory behavior of LLMs, additional information, and perfectly generated examples are shown in Table 7. The text generated by the model was evaluated based on the following criteria: (1) incorrect information (highlighted in red), (2) additional irrelevant information (underlined), and (3) semantically correct but with different textual representations (blue).

Table 7. Error analysis of different model-generated examples with reference text.

Reference Text	Model Type	Model Generated Text
You can't live on that island.	Fully Lexical	Everybody can't live in the island.
	ChatGPT-3.5	If a person does not live on an island, it is possible.
	Claude-2.0	If x1 is a person, then x1 does not live on an island, which is presumed.
	FT-byT5	You cannot live on that island.
It will cost around 10000 yen.	Fully Lexical	It will cost about 1000 yen.
	ChatGPT-3.5	The cost of the entity referred to by x1 is presupposed to be now and is equal to 10,000 yen per unit.
	Claude-2.0	An entity costs 10000 yen now.
	FT-byT5	It will cost around 10000 yen.
Have you googled her?	Fully Lexical	You googled her.
	ChatGPT-3.5	The hearer (you), who is a female, is currently googling something at the present time.
	Claude-2.0	The hearer is currently googling a presumed female.
	FT-byT5	Have you googled her?

Three key elements of text generation in natural language – negation, question, and quantity – are shown in Table 7. The fully lexical model had difficulty capturing the actual semantics of the phrases in the context of the examples listed in the table (completely incorrect semantics are marked in red). The exact quantity and grammatical structure of the phrases were also difficult for the model to determine (see examples in Table 7 for the full lexical model).

Both ChatGPT and Claude underperformed because they were unable to produce accurate translations for the DRS examples. Analysis of the samples shows that, rather than producing a literal translation, the models began by explaining the logical representation of the DRS (text that is deemed extraneous is underlined). This, we assume, is because these LLMs were trained without the use of any semantic or formal meaning representation. Furthermore, the few-shot learning approach is also not helping these models to generalize in a better way. We have selected samples from the best models, such as few-shot text for Claude and zero-shot text for chatGPT, to use during the manual inspection of LLM-generated text (see LLM results in Table 6 for few-shot and zero-shot).

Although it struggled a little to replicate the exact information presented in the test set, our best model was able to capture the semantic and grammatical representation in the best feasible way. Due to exact word overlaps between text pairs, these small changes (highlighted in blue) in the model-generated text will not affect the human evaluation; however, because the generated text maintains the exact meaning, semantics, and grammatical structure of the sentences, they will result in low scores for automatic evaluations.

5   Conclusion

We performed data delexicalization of the DRS for common and proper nouns through WordNet supersenses and Named Entities-based lexical abstractions. Individually both delexicalization procedures, compared to fully lexical ones, resulted in enhancing the generalization ability of the neural model. The use of lexical data augmentation along with data delexicalization further improves the robustness capabilities and adds to the performance gain. Our experiments with biLSTM and byT5 neural sequence-to-sequence models showed promising results with the best scores for the fine-tuned byT5 model. We found that data delexicalization helps the model to focus more on the syntactic structure of complex meaning representation thus generating correct textual sequences. General-purpose LLMs (ChatGPT and Claude) hallucinate and explain the DRS rather than generating the correct textual sequences. This highlights the true need for task-specific models for complex domain-specific applications.

Limitations. We are also working on performing lexical abstraction on all lexical entities in the meaning representation. We have not expanded our implementation to include other low-resource languages like Italian, Dutch, and German.

Acknowledgments. We thank "High-Performance Computing for Artificial Intelligence (HPC4AI) at the University of Turin" for providing GPU support [25].

Disclosure of Interests. The authors declare no conflict of interest.

References

1. Wei, N.: Shared meaning and delexicalization. J. PLA Univ. Foreign Lang. **5**, 17–24 (2007)
2. Vainio, M., Suni, A., Raitio, T., Nurminen, J., Järvikivi, J., Alku, P.: New method for delexicalization and its application to prosodic tagging for text-to-speech synthesis, pp. 1703–1706 (2009). https://doi.org/10.21437/Interspeech.2009-514
3. Sharma, S., He, J., Suleman, K., Schulz, H., Bachman, P.: Natural language generation in dialogue using lexicalized and delexicalized data. ArXiv, abs/1603.03632 (2016)
4. Shimorina, A., Gardent, C.: Handling rare items in data-to-text generation, pp. 360–370 (2018). https://doi.org/10.18653/v1/W18-6543
5. Dušek, O., Novikova, J., Rieser, V.: Findings of the E2E NLG challenge. arXiv preprint arXiv:1810.01170 (2018)
6. Zhou, G., Lampouras, G.: WebNLG challenge 2020: language agnostic delexicalisation for multilingual RDF-to-text generation. In: Proceedings of the 3rd International Workshop on Natural Language Generation from the Semantic Web (WebNLG+), pp. 186–191 (2020)
7. Dong, H., Zhang, J., McIlwraith, D., Guo, Y.: I2T2I: learning text to image synthesis with textual data augmentation. In: IEEE International Conference on Image Processing (ICIP), pp. 2015–2019. IEEE (2017)
8. Banarescu, L., et al.: Abstract meaning representation for sembanking, pp. 178–186 (2013)
9. Fan, A., Gardent, C.: Multilingual AMR-to-text generation. In: Proceedings of the 2020 Conference on Empirical Methods in Natural Language Processing (EMNLP), pp. 2889–2901. Association for Computational Linguistics (2020)
10. Flanigan, J., Dyer, C., Smith, N.A., Carbonell, J.G.: Generation from abstract meaning representation using tree transducers, pp. 731–739 (2016)
11. Ferreira, T.C., et al.: The 2020 bilingual, bi-directional WebNLG+ shared task: overview and evaluation results (WebNLG+ 2020). In: Proceedings of the 3rd International Workshop on Natural Language Generation from the Semantic Web (WebNLG+), Dublin, Ireland (Virtual), pp. 55–76. Association for Computational Linguistics (2020)
12. Basile, V., Bos, J.: Towards generating text from discourse representation structures. In: ENLG 2011, pp. 145–150 (2011)
13. van Noord, R., Abzianidze, L., Haagsma, H., Bos, J.: Evaluating scoped meaning representations. In: Proceedings of the Eleventh International Conference on Language Resources and Evaluation (LREC 2018), Miyazaki, Japan. European Language Resources Association (ELRA) (2018)
14. van Noord, R.: Neural boxer at the IWCS shared task on DRS parsing. In: Proceedings of the IWCS Shared Task on Semantic Parsing, Gothenburg, Sweden. Association for Computational Linguistics (2019)
15. Wang, C., van Noord, R., Bisazza, A., Bos, J.: Evaluating text generation from discourse representation structures. In: Proceedings of the 1st Workshop on Natural Language Generation, Evaluation, and Metrics (GEM 2021), pp. 73–83. Association for Computational Linguistics (2021)
16. Amin, M.S., Mazzei, A., Anselma, L.: Towards data augmentation for DRS-to-text generation. In: Proceedings of the Sixth Workshop on Natural Language for Artificial Intelligence (NL4AI 2022) Co-located with 21th International Conference of the Italian Association for Artificial Intelligence (AI*IA 2022). Volume 3287 of

CEUR Workshop Proceedings, Udine, 30 November 2022, pp. 141–152. CEUR-WS.org (2022)

17. Amin, M.S., Anselma, L., Mazzei, A.: Exploring data augmentation in neural DRS-to-text generation. In: Proceedings of the 18th Conference of the European Chapter of the Association for Computational Linguistics (Volume 1: Long Papers), St. Julian's, Malta, pp. 2164–2178. Association for Computational Linguistics (2024)
18. Kamp, H., Reyle, U.: From Discourse to Logic: Introduction to Model-Theoretic Semantics of Natural Language, Formal Logic, and Discourse Representation Theory, vol. 42. Springer, Dordrecht (2013)
19. Bos, J.: Quantification annotation in discourse representation theory. In: ISA 2021-17th Workshop on Interoperable Semantic Annotation, Groningen/Virtual, Netherlands (2021)
20. Kamp, H., Reyle, U.: From Discourse to Logic: Introduction to Modeltheoretic Semantics of Natural Language, Formal Logic and Discourse Representation Theory. Kluwer Academic Publishers, Dordrecht (1993)
21. Jaszczolt, K.: Semantics, Pragmatics, Philosophy: A Journey Through Meaning. Cambridge University Press, New York (2023)
22. Parikh, A., et al.: ToTTo: a controlled table-to-text generation dataset. In: Proceedings of the 2020 Conference on Empirical Methods in Natural Language Processing (EMNLP), pp. 1173–1186 (2020)
23. OpenAI. GPT-4 technical report (2023)
24. Turpin, M., Michael, J., Perez, E., Bowman, S.R.: Language models don't always say what they think: unfaithful explanations in chain-of-thought prompting (2023)
25. Aldinucci, M., et al.: HPC4AI: an AI-on-demand federated platform endeavour. In: Proceedings of the 15th ACM International Conference on Computing Frontiers (2018)

Large Language Models for Few-Shot Automatic Term Extraction

Shubhanker Banerjee[1,2]([envelope]) [ORCID], Bharathi Raja Chakravarthi[2] [ORCID], and John Philip McCrae[1,2] [ORCID]

[1] ADAPT Centre, Dublin, Ireland
john.mccrae@adaptcentre.ie
[2] School of Computer Science, University of Galway, Galway, Ireland
shubhanker.banerjee@adaptcentre.ie,
bharathiraja.asokachakravarthi@universityofgalway.ie

Abstract. Automatic term extraction is the process of identifying domain-specific terms in a text using automated algorithms and is a key first step in ontology learning and knowledge graph creation. Large language models have shown good few-shot capabilities, thus, in this paper, we present a study to evaluate the few-shot in-context learning performance of GPT-3.5-Turbo on automatic term extraction. To benchmark the performance we compare the results with fine-tuning of a BERT-sized model. We also carry out experiments with count-based term extractors to assess their applicability to few-shot scenarios. We quantify prompt sensitivity with experiments to analyze the variation in performance of large language models across different prompt templates. Our results show that in-context learning with GPT-3.5-Turbo outperforms the BERT-based model and unsupervised count-based methods in few-shot scenarios.

Keywords: few-shot · automatic term extraction · large language models

1 Introduction

Terms are linguistic expressions that refer to domain-specific concepts and are integral to domain-specific languages (Cabré 1999; Fowler 2010). For instance, *Reinforcement Learning with Human Feedback* is relevant in natural language processing but not psycho-linguistics. Automatic Term Extraction (ATE) involves extracting terms from text using automated tools, and recent advancements in pre-trained language models (PLMs) have significantly improved ATE performance (Lang et al., 2021).

Large language models like GPT-3, with billions of parameters, excel in zero-shot and few-shot in-context learning for various NLP tasks (Brown et al., 2020). Building fully supervised term extraction models is costly and challenging due to domain-specific variations and the scarcity of annotated data. Large language

A. Rapp et al. (Eds.): NLDB 2024, LNCS 14762, pp. 137–150, 2024.
https://doi.org/10.1007/978-3-031-70239-6_10

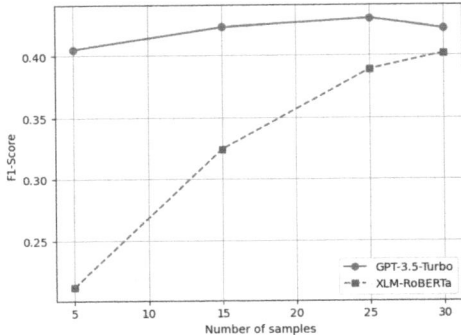

Fig. 1. Main findings: The figure shows F1-scores achieved by fine-tuned XLM-RoBERTa and GPT-3.5-Turbo averaged over 4 domains namely Heart Failure, Wind Energy, Equitation and Corruption. In-context learning with GPT-3.5-Turbo substantially outperforms model fine-tuning for 5, 15, 25 and 30 samples.

models, with extensive parameters and pre-training datasets, potentially alleviate the need for large annotated datasets by performing few-shot in-context ATE. To validate this, we compare large language models in few-shot settings with a BERT-sized XLM-RoBERTa model and unsupervised count-based term extraction methods, adhering to the truly few-shot setting standard (Perez et al., 2021).

To quantify this impact of prompt structure on task performance in the case of ATE we carry out experiments with 8 different prompt templates. Secondly, in recent studies, multiple in-context sample selection strategies have been explored (Rubin et al., 2022; Liu et al., 2022). In our experiments, we follow the k-nearest sample retriever method proposed by Liu et al. (2022) and carry out ablations to demonstrate its effectiveness.

The average F1 scores of fine-tuned XLM-RoBERTa and GPT-3.5-Turbo over 4 term annotated datasets are shown Fig. 1. We find that in-context learning with OpenAI's GPT-3.5-Turbo produces substantially better results as compared to the fine-tuned XLM-RoBERTa model. Additionally, experiments with unsupervised count-based term extractors demonstrate their ineffectiveness when compared to in-context learning in few-shot scenarios.

2   Related Work

Automatic Term Extraction. Machine learning-based methods aimed at identifying terms on the basis of underlying patterns in the occurrence context relax the frequency hypothesis with algorithms like random forests (Rigouts Terryn et al., 2021) and XGBoost (Hazem et al., 2022) demonstrating good task performance. The performance has been further improved by deep learning models such as XLM-RoBERTa (Lang et al., 2021) and mBERT (Hazem et al., 2022) across languages and domains. Lang et al. (2021) show that formulating term extraction as a sequence labelling problem yields better results as compared to span classification or a sequence-to-sequence problem when fine-tuning XLM-RoBERTa.

Truly Few-Shot Learning. Perez et al. (2021) introduced the paradigm of truly few-shot learning where they argue that previous work which uses large validation sets for model and prompt selection overestimates the performance of pre-trained language models in few-shot scenarios. This paradigm has been followed by works focused on few-shot problems (Gutierrez et al., 2022).

Prompt Design. To apply large language models to ATE we formulate it as a language generation problem aided by prompts designed for this task. Our prompt templates are motivated by previous work which focuses on reformulating various natural language processing tasks as generation problems. In particular, our prompt design is inspired by work done by Gutierrez et al. (2022) where they pose relation extraction as a language generation problem. They break down each prompt into 2 main components: the task instruction and the retriever message. For more details on their prompt design, we refer the reader to their paper.

Large Language Models. In recent years there has been significant progress in the development of large language models (LLMs) (Naveed et al., 2023). These highly parameterized models have been able to achieve state-of-the-art performance on a wide variety of natural language processing tasks (Tang et al., 2023; Wadhwa et al., 2023). Inspired by the good performance of GPT-3.5-Turbo[1] model on information extraction tasks such as named entity recognition (Wang et al., 2023; Zhang et al., 2024) we carry out experiments to assess its applicability to few-shot automatic term extraction.

3   Methodology

We undertake a study to evaluate few-shot in-context learning performance of large language models[2] on term extraction. To benchmark these results we compare them against full model fine-tuning of a BERT-sized baseline PLM. The results are also compared against unsupervised count-based term extraction methods.

3.1   Validation Protocol

Perez et al. (2021) argue that hyperparameter tuning and prompt selection based on large validation sets are not truly representative of data-scarce few-shot learning scenarios. Furthermore, their experiments reveal that model selection decisions made on the basis of larger validation sets overestimate few-shot learning

---

[1] https://platform.openai.com/docs/models.
[2] Here we refer to models with more than 1B parameters as large language models.

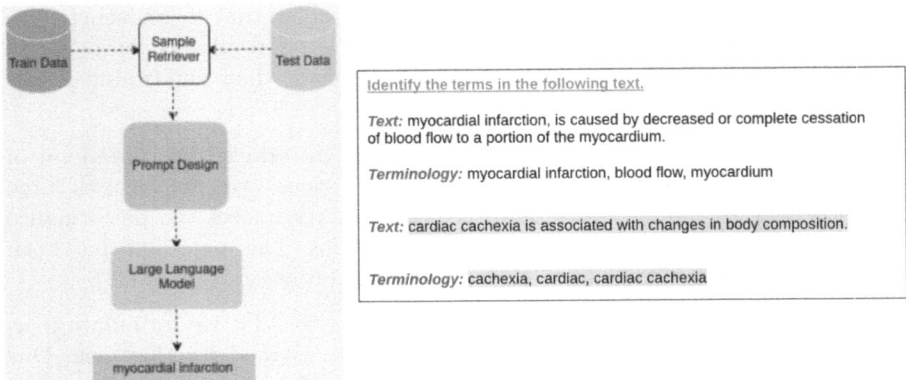

Fig. 2. Overall flow for large language model in-context learning for ATE in the left. The prompt structure is inspired by Gutierrez et al. (2022) and a prompt template used in our experiments with one-shot in-context learning has been shown on the right. The different segments of the prompt are indicated by different colours: task instruction in green (underlined) and red for the retrieval messages (italicized). The current input text and the terms output by the large language model are highlighted. (Color figure online)

performance. To avoid overestimation we follow their proposed truly few-shot setting and optimize the hyperparameters by validating on a validation set of 10 examples.

3.2   Large Language Model Evaluation

In this section, we discuss how we reformulate ATE for few-shot in-context learning. We then discuss the structure of prompts used for inference and also the approach we use for retrieval of in-context examples.

Task Formulation. In order to use large language models for ATE, we reformulate it as a language generation task. We tokenize the domain-specific corpus into sentences and transform each sentence into a prompt. The overall flow from the input sentence to the extracted terms is illustrated in Fig. 2.

Prompt Design. As shown by Sclar et al. (2023), in few-shot scenarios small changes to the prompt design have a significant impact on the performance of the large language models. To quantify the variation in performance across different prompts we carry out experiments with 8 different prompt templates. The basic structure of all our prompt templates is motivated by Gutierrez et al. (2022). Each prompt template comprises a task-specific instruction and a retriever message. We categorize the templates into two types: in Type I, we

Table 1. Prompt Templates

Prompt Type	No.	Template
Type I	1.	Identify the terms in the following text. Input: Output:
	2.	Identify the terms in the following text. Text: Terminology:
	3.	Extract the terms from the following text. Input: Output:
	4.	Extract the terms from the following text. Text: Terminology:
Type II	5.	Find the domain-specific terms in the following text. Input: Output:
	6.	Find the domain-specific terms in the following text. Text: Terminology:
	7.	Identify the words or phrases that are relevant to the underlying domain of the input text. Input: Output:
	8.	Identify the words or phrases that are relevant to the underlying domain of the input text. Text: Terminology:

include the templates with simple task instructions namely: *Identify the terms in the following text.* and *Extract the terms in the following text.* whereas in Type II the task instructions are more detailed such as *Identify the words or phrases that are relevant to the underlying domain of the input text.* and *Find the domain-specific terms in the following text.* We hope to analyze the sensitivity of LLMs to word-level changes in the prompt by quantifying the variation in performance within Type I. Furthermore, to analyze performance as a function of complexity of task instruction we compare the average F1 scores between Type I and Type II. For more details on individual prompt templates, we refer the reader to Table 1.

Evaluation. We evaluate the performance of the large language models in a few-shot in-context setting. Each prompt consists of the instruction, retriever message, input sentence and a fixed number of labelled examples selected by the retriever module to allow in-context learning. To better understand the impact of in-context samples on performance we carry out experiments with varying numbers of such samples in the prompt. An example of a one-shot prompt for a specific prompt template is shown in Fig. 2.

To control hallucination we post-process the outputs and remove any generated term which has no match with any span of text in the input.

Retriever Module. The inclusion of in-context samples in the prompt has been shown to improve performance on downstream tasks (Li and Qiu 2023). We follow the k-nearest neighbour sample selection method proposed by Liu et al. (2022) for our retriever module. The training set is used to select k most similar examples for each test sample. We carried out initial experiments with multilingual sentence transformers[3] and RoBERTa-large on a set of 250 randomly chosen examples. The findings of these initial experiments show that using RoBERTa-large for in-context demonstration retrieval yields better results. Therefore, we use RoBERTa-large for in-context demonstration retrieval in our experiments.

---

[3] Specifically we used *paraphrase-MiniLM-L6-v2*.

Table 2. Dataset statistics: The number of sentences and terms in each domain.

Heart Failure	Train	Test	Valid
Sentences	158	1427	43
Terms	260	1725	91
Corruption	Train	Test	Valid
Sentences	301	171	110
Terms	186	98	64
Equitation	Train	Test	Valid
Sentences	827	856	180
Terms	577	393	129
Wind Energy	Train	Test	Valid
Sentences	834	154	60
Terms	623	104	92

4   Experiments

4.1   Datasets

The ACTER dataset (Rigouts Terryn et al., 2020) contains term annotated data across 4 domains and 3 languages namely English, French and Dutch. The 4 domains are unrelated to each other and by carrying out experiments on all of them we hope to establish the applicability of large language models for few-shot term extraction to various domains. In this paper, we have limited the experiments to the English dataset. The dataset statistics can be found in Table 2. Here we provide a brief description of the domain corpora:

Heart Failure. This corpus is a collection of abstracts about heart failure collected on the basis of titles crawled for previous research (Hoste et al., 2019) on medical terminology extraction.

Equitation. The texts in the equitation corpus were collected manually from magazines and blogs and focus specifically on horseback riding.

Corruption. The texts in the corruption corpus belong to the juridical domain. These documents were manually collected from the EU, United Nations and Transparency International and contain legal documents about corruption policies, newspapers and Wikipedia articles.

Wind Energy. The documents in the wind energy corpus were collected from TTC corpus (Clouet et al., 2012).

4.2   Baselines

Unsupervised Term Extraction. Count-based term extractors rely on a positive correlation between termhood and the frequency of occurrence in a domain corpus. Since these methods are unsupervised, we use them as baselines for few-shot term extraction. In our experiments, we use C-Value (Frantzi and Ananiadou, 1996) and ComboBasic (Astrakhantsev et al., 2015) to benchmark the performance of large language models.

Fine-Tuning. Recent work on fine-tuning PLMs for ATE has reported good results by posing term extraction as a sequence tagging problem (Lang et al., 2021). Following this paradigm as the standard we fine-tune XLM-RoEERTa-base as the baseline PLM to identify terms using a BIO tagging scheme (Carreras et al., 2003). Hyperparameters such as learning rate, batch size, gradient accumulation steps, and warm-up ratio are optimized using tree-structured Parzen estimator[4] on the validation set of 10 examples mentioned above.

4.3   Implementation

To quantify variation in performance with a variation in the number of samples we carry out experiments with 5, 15, 25 and 30 training examples. GPT-3.5-Turbo has a maximum input context length of 4k tokens, to avoid errors due to exceeding the token limit in the input prompt we limit our experiments to 30 samples. 10 validation samples are used to simulate a truly few-shot setting. In order to limit costs, the models are evaluated on a test set of 150 samples. We use the Hugging Face library[5] for fine-tuning XLM-RoBERTa on our training set. We use PyATE library[6] for the implementation of the unsupervised count-based term extractors. OpenAI's open-source library is used to query GPT-3.5-Turbo[7]. To quantify the sensitivity of performance to various prompt templates we carry out all our experiments with the large language models using 8 different prompts. Hyperparameters are optimized using the Optuna library[8] over 20 trial runs with the tree-structured Parzen estimator. To provide robust and convincing conclusions, we run all experiments (including ablation studies) with 5 different seeds and report all results as the mean and standard deviation of all experiments. These measures are computed using Numpy library[9]. We used random seeds 1, 2, 3, 4 and 5 in our experiments. Furthermore, to ensure reproducibility we ensure that all the libraries/frameworks used in our experiments are open-source.

---

[4] https://optuna.readthedocs.io/en/stable/reference/samplers/generated/optuna.
samplers.TPESampler.html.
[5] https://huggingface.co/.
[6] https://github.com/kevinlu1248/pyate.
[7] https://github.com/openai/openai-python.
[8] https://optuna.org/.
[9] https://numpy.org/.

Table 3. The performance of fine-tuning XLM-RoBERTa with and without LoRA on K = 5, 15, 25 and 30 samples compared with unsupervised count-based term extractors and in-context learning with GPT-3.5-Turbo. This table illustrates the mean and standard deviation (in the format $mean_{std}$) of precision, recall and F1-scores over all the random seeds. The unsupervised methods are deterministic, they do not exhibit any variation across different runs therefore std = 0 has not been illustrated in the table. For GPT-3.5-Turbo the mean and standard deviation of F1-scores over all the random seeds and all the prompt templates have been illustrated.

5-shot	Heart Failure	Corruption	Wind Energy	Equitation
	Precision/Recall/F1	Precision/Recall/F1	Precision/Recall/F1	Precision/Recall/F1
GPT-3.5-Turbo	$47.8_{1.6}/61.5_{1.7}/53.7_{0.9}$	$18.2_{0.6}/69.8_{1.5}/28.9_{0.9}$	$19.5_{0.9}/71.9_{1.1}/30.7_{1.0}$	$35.6_{1.9}/76.6_{0.4}/48.6_{1.8}$
XLM-R	$10.3_{7.7}/13.0_{15.0}/10.0_{8.6}$	$26.1_{9.1}/10.3_{2.2}/14.1_{2.0}$	$19.0_{1.9}/30.5_{6.8}/23.1_{2.0}$	$33.2_{5.5}/45.0_{8.0}/37.3_{2.4}$
15-shot				
GPT-3.5-Turbo	$49.8_{2.0}/62.7_{1.4}/55.1_{1.0}$	$19.9_{0.9}/70.5_{0.9}/31.1_{1.2}$	$21.4_{0.4}/73.4_{1.3}/33.1_{0.4}$	$35.8_{1.1}/76.1_{0.3}/48.7_{1.0}$
XLM-R	$59.0_{3.3}/24.2_{5.4}/33.9_{4.8}$	$31.6_{6.5}/20.6_{3.9}/24.1_{1.9}$	$24.9_{2.6}/40.5_{4.3}/30.7_{2.5}$	$36.4_{3.1}/46.5_{2.3}/40.7_{2.3}$
25-shot				
GPT-3.5-Turbo	$51.1_{1.5}/63.4_{0.9}/56.6_{1.0}$	$19.9_{1.0}/67.0_{1.5}/30.6_{1.3}$	$21.2_{1.3}/71.3_{1.8}/32.7_{1.5}$	$36.5_{1.4}/74.6_{0.5}/49.0_{1.3}$
XLM-R	$60.4_{1.9}/41.4_{2.7}/49.0_{1.6}$	$33.3_{7.5}/23.8_{7.3}/26.1_{3.0}$	$29.2_{2.4}/50.5_{8.3}/36.5_{1.0}$	$46.4_{4.4}/42.0_{5.7}/43.6_{2.8}$
30-shot				
GPT-3.5-Turbo	$51.6_{1.7}/64.5_{0.8}/57.3_{0.8}$	$21.1_{0.5}/68.0_{2.9}/32.2_{0.8}$	$21.5_{0.5}/67.9_{1.9}/32.7_{0.6}$	$36.8_{0.9}/75.3_{1.9}/49.4_{0.8}$
XLM-R	$62.5_{2.3}/41.4_{5.2}/49.5_{4.5}$	$31.6_{5.7}/30.7_{3.0}/30.7_{1.5}$	$32.8_{3.3}/32.3_{6.2}/32.2_{6.7}$	$48.7_{4.7}/48.6_{7.5}/48.2_{4.7}$
Unsupervised Methods				
ComboBasic	5.5/38.2/9.6	2.3/36.5/4.3	4.7/34.0/8.2	1.8/58.1/3.6
CValue	5.4/37.7/9.5	2.2/35.5/4.2	4.6/33.8/8.2	1.8/57.1/3.6

5   Results and Discussion

5.1   Main Results

Our main experimental results can be found in Table 3. It is important to note that GPT-3.5-Turbo outperforms all other models in almost all cases on the F1-score, often by large margins in the range of approximately 3–45%. On the heart failure domain, GPT-3.5-Turbo has the best performance and achieves an average F1-score of 55.7% over all sample sizes. We also note that count-based term extractors are substantially outperformed by XLM-RoBERTa across all the domains, this is in line with previous results reported by Lang et al. (2021). This observation indicates that in few-shot scenarios in-context learning with LLMs is a better alternative than unsupervised count-based extractors.

While the overall better performance of the GPT model as compared to other models can be explained by its larger size and diverse pre-training corpus, the relatively lower performance on Corruption, Wind Energy and Equitation where the Precision drops by about 12–30% on average as compared to the Heart Failure domain indicates lack of domain specificity in the extracted terms. This drop in specificity is accompanied by substantial improvements in coverage on gold standard terms shown by the high recall values in the range of 70–76% on average across these domains. This observation indicates a significant number

Table 4. The average F1-scores of prompt templates calculated the GPT-3.5-Turbo model.

		Corruption	Heart Failure	Wind Energy	Equitation
Type I	Template 1	30.1	55.4	32.8	48.3
	Template 2	30.2	55.5	32.8	48.2
	Template 3	29.7	54.9	31.3	48.0
	Template 4	29.7	54.8	31.2	48.0
Average		29.9	55.1	32.0	48.1
Type II	Template 5	31.2	57.0	33.2	50.8
	Template 6	31.4	56.9	33.2	50.9
	Template 7	31.6	55.8	31.8	48.6
	Template 8	31.6	56.0	31.9	48.5
Average		31.4	55.6	32.5	49.7

of false positives in the extracted terms; we discuss this point in more detail in Sect. 5.4.

Diving into the finer details of XLM-RoBERTa fine-tuning, it is important to note that it has reasonable performance considering that the training set consists of a very small number of samples. Amongst all the domains XLM-RoBERTa has the best performance on Heart Failure, this can be attributed to regular term structure in this domain e.g. the suffixes '-tion', '-ophy' are common to many terms. Furthermore, the relatively higher values for ComboBasic on the Heart Failure domain suggest lexical overlap amongst the terms in this domain. Similarly, the high lexical diversity in term structures across the other domains can be attributed to the lower performances. In terms of coverage, XLM-RoBERTa behaves differently than GPT-3.5-Turbo and has high precision but low recall across the domains. The fact that GPT-3.5-Turbo makes predictions on the basis of knowledge acquired through a large pre-training corpus whereas XLM-RoBERTa is inherently regularized through task-specific fine-tuning can be used to explain this phenomenon.

We see an average improvement of around 2% for GPT-3.5-Turbo as the training set grows from 5 to 30 samples. This is important and shows that increasing the number of in-context samples arbitrarily does not guarantee large improvements in performance. However, as expected XLM-RoBERTa full-model fine-tuning exhibits large monotonic improvements in the F1-score going up to 50% with increasing sample size. Furthermore, as can be seen from the results in Table 3, for 30 samples XLM-RoBERTa converges on the GPT model.

5.2   Prompt Sensitivity

As described in Sect. 3.2 we categorize the templates into two categories: Type I with a simple task instruction and Type II with a detailed description of the task. The average score of each template is shown in Table 4. As can be seen

Table 5. Average F1-score of kNN-based demonstration retrieval compared to random demonstration selection for in-context learning.

	Corruption	Heart Failure	Wind Energy	Equitation
kNN	30.7	55.8	32.3	48.9
Random	28.7	54.9	30.2	48.0

from the results the performance of Type II templates is better than Type I on average. Furthermore, the change of retriever message has negligible impact on task performance ($\approx$ 0–1%).

This result is not surprising as the task instruction *Find the domain-specific terms in the following text.* in templates 5 and 6 and the task instruction *Identify the words or phrases that are relevant to the underlying domain of the input text.* in templates 7 and 8 describe the term extraction task in greater detail. A comparison with templates 1–2 with templates 3–4 shows that replacement of the word *Identify* with *Extract* leads to a slight degradation in performance. Thus indicating that although performance is sensitive to word-level changes, the impact may not be significant. Overall, the change in the prompt template did not lead to a large variation in the task performance; detailed task instructions had slightly better performance along expected lines.

5.3 Ablation

In Table 5, we present ablation studies demonstrating the effectiveness of the kNN-based demonstration selection used in our experiments. Experiments are carried out with randomly selected in-context samples instead of semantically similar samples selected through kNN for each test input without changing other aspects of the experimental setup. Comparison of the random demonstration retriever with kNN-based retriever module shows the better performance of kNN-based in-context sample selection strategy.

5.4 Error Analysis

As discussed in Sect. 5.1, GPT-3.5-Turbo suffers from the problem of high recall whereas full-model fine-tuning of XLM-RoBERTa leads to lower recall values on all four domains. In this section, we carry out a qualitative analysis of false positive and false negative predictions made by the models. We find that both models are good at identifying acronyms such as *LVEF* and *CRT*. Lang et al. (2021) make the same observation in their experiments as well. They attribute this to the presence of a substantial number of acronyms in the training dataset. However, the ability of GPT-3.5-Turbo to identify acronyms without task-specific adaptation is notable. A comparison of the terms generated by GPT-3.5-Turbo across the domains shows that while the predictions for Heart Failure are highly specific such as *biventricular* and *peak oxygen uptake*, for the other domains the

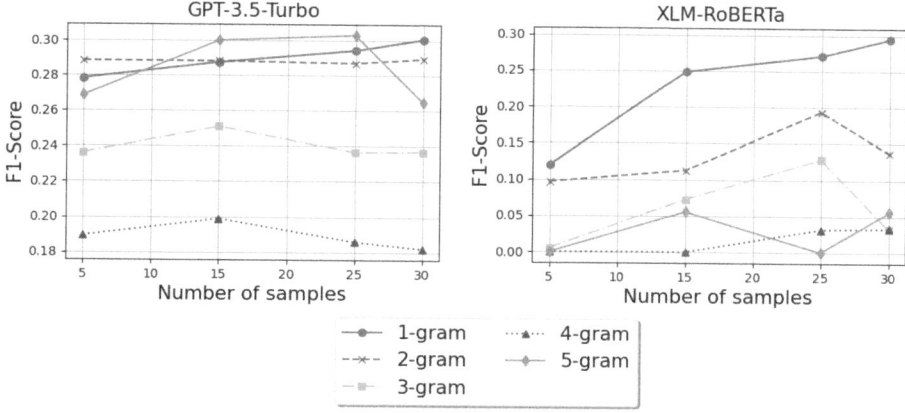

Fig. 3. Variation in average F1-scores of GPT-3.5-Turbo and full-model fine-tuned XLM-RoBERTa for varying sample sizes and term lengths. Overall results for term lengths ranging from 1 to 5 words are illustrated.

predictions include non-specific expressions. To illustrate, for Wind Energy we note the presence of a significant number of expressions such as *model* and *weight* which are not domain-specific. Similarly, we observe the presence of non-term expressions such as *diversion, addenda* in the output for the Corruption dataset and expressions like *touch, gymnastics* for the Equitation domain. These results indicate that while GPT-3.5-Turbo is good in highly specialized domains like Heart Failure, on more broader domains like Wind Energy issues of domain-specificity in the predictions arise. We attribute the lower precision of the GPT-3.5-Turbo model to the presence of such non-domain expressions in the output.

Experiments were conducted to evaluate the performance of GPT-3.5-Turbo and fine-tuned XLM-RoBERTa on extracting terms of varying lengths. The results have been demonstrated in Fig. 3. Both models performed well on shorter terms (1 to 2 words). However, GPT-3.5-Turbo outperformed XLM-RoBERTa on longer terms (3 to 5 words), with XLM-RoBERTa showing a performance gap of about 15% for 4-grams and 5-grams, likely due to the lack of longer terms in its training set.

6   Conclusion

In this work, we explored the potential of GPT-3.5-Turbo in-context learning for few-shot term extraction on 4 domains. We showed that for few-shot in-context term extraction, GPT-3.5-Turbo surpasses XLM-RoBERTa and count-based term extractors on all domains. Furthermore, the results show that even a small number of in-context samples leads to good task performance with diminishing gains as the number of in-context samples increases, this is an important result with the potential of significantly reducing costs associated with querying the large language model. However, it is also important to note that the performance of XLM-RoBERTa converges on GPT-3.5-Turbo for 30 samples and while the input token limit of GPT-3.5-Turbo does not allow us to experiment with larger sample sizes, extrapolation of results shown here indicate that for larger sample sizes XLM-RoBERTa outperforms GPT-3.5-Turbo. We also discuss the performance of GPT-3.5-Turbo across the domains and show that while the extracted terms have high quality in specialized domains, for broader domains the performance drops. This is an open question with the potential of building a framework for term extraction with good performance on a wide range of domains. Besides posing this question we hope that this work can provide useful guidance for researchers working on few-shot term extraction.

7   Limitations

Although we have shown the good performance of GPT-3.5-Turbo in-context learning for term extraction as compared to fine-tuning a BERT-sized PLM for few-shot term extraction there are several limitations worth discussing. Due to budgetary constraints, we were limited to a smaller number of prompt templates. While our experiments show that variation in the prompt template doesn't cause significant variation in task performance, a wider search space can lead to better performance. To simulate a truly few-shot setting we have used a validation set of 10 samples, it is unclear if using a larger validation set at the cost of compromising the few-shot setting would reduce the gap in performance between XLM-RoBERTa and GPT-3.5-Turbo.set of prompt styles. Furthermore, here we have carried out experiments with GPT-3.5-Turbo, it is unclear whether in-context learning with other large language models will lead to an improvement in performance. We use kNN-based retriever module for selecting the in-context demonstrations, a retriever module better suited for selecting demonstrations for term extraction might lead to better results.

Acknowledgement. Author Shubhanker Banerjee was supported by Science Foundation Ireland under Grant Agreement No. 13/RC/2106_P2 at the ADAPT SFI Research Centre at University Of Galway.

References

Astrakhantsev, N.A., Fedorenko, D.G., Turdakov, D.Y.: Methods for automatic term recognition in domain-specific text collections: a survey. Ph.D. thesis (2015). https://doi.org/10.1134/S036176881506002X

Brown, T.B., et al.: Advances in Neural Information Processing Systems 33: Annual Conference on Neural Information Processing Systems 2020, NeurIPS 2020, 6–12 December 2020, Virtual. In: Larochelle, H., Ranzato, M., Hadsell, R., Balcan, M.-F., Lin, H.-T. (eds.) (2020)

Cabré, M.T.: Terminology: Theory, Methods, and Applications, vol. 1. John Benjamins Publishing (1999)

Carreras, X., Màrquez, L., Padró, L.: Proceedings of the Seventh Conference on Natural Language Learning, CoNLL 2003, Held in cooperation with HLT-NAACL 2003, Edmonton, Canada, 31 May–1 June 2003. In: Daelemans, W., Osborne, M. (eds.), pp. 152–155. ACL (2003)

Clouet, E.L., Gojun, A., Blancafort, H., Guegan, M., Gornostay, T., Heid, U.: Reference lists for the evaluation of term extraction tools (2012)

Fowler, M.: Domain-Specific Languages. Pearson Education (2010)

Frantzi, K.T., Ananiadou, S.: 16th International Conference on Computational Linguistics, Proceedings of the Conference, COLING 1996, Center for Sprogteknologi, Copenhagen, Denmark, 5–9 August 1996, pp. 41–46 (1996)

Gutierrez, B.J., et al.: Findings of the Association for Computational Linguistics: EMNLP 2022, Abu Dhabi, United Arab Emirates, 7–11 December 2022. In: Goldberg, Y., Kozareva, Z., Zhang, Y. (eds.), pp. 4497–4512. Association for Computational Linguistics (2022). https://doi.org/10.18653/V1/2022.FINDINGS-EMNLP.329

Hazem, A., Bouhandi, M., Boudin, F., Daille, B.: Proceedings of the Thirteenth Language Resources and Evaluation Conference, LREC 2022, Marseille, France, 20–25 June 2022. In: Calzolari, N., et al. (eds.), pp. 648–662. European Language Resources Association (2022)

Hoste, V., Vanopstal, K., Terryn, A.R., Lefever, E.: The trade-off between quantity and quality. Comparing a large crawled corpus and a small focused corpus for medical terminology extraction. Across Lang. Cult. **20**(2), 197–211 (2019)

Lang, C., Wachowiak, L., Heinisch, B., Gromann, D.: Findings of the Association for Computational Linguistics: ACL/IJCNLP 2021, Online Event, 1–6 August 2021. In: Zong, C., Xia, F., Li, W., Navigli, R. (eds.), pp. 3607–3620. Association for Computational Linguistics (2021). https://doi.org/10.18653/V1/2021.FINDINGS-ACL.316

Li, X., Qiu, X.: Finding supporting examples for in-context learning. CoRR abs/2302.13539 (2023). https://doi.org/10.48550/ARXIV.2302.13539

Liu, J., Shen, D., Zhang, Y., Dolan, B., Carin, L., Chen, W.: Proceedings of Deep Learning Inside Out: The 3rd Workshop on Knowledge Extraction and Integration for Deep Learning Architectures, DeeLIO@ACL 2022, Dublin, Ireland and Online, 27 May 2022. In: Agirre, E., Apidianaki, M., Vulic, I. (eds.), pp. 100–114. Association for Computational Linguistics (2022). https://doi.org/10.18653/V1/2022.DEELIO-1.10

Naveed, H., et al.: A comprehensive overview of large language models. CoRR abs/2307.06435 (2023). https://doi.org/10.48550/ARXIV.2307.06435

Perez, E., Kiela, D., Cho, K.: Advances in Neural Information Processing Systems 34: Annual Conference on Neural Information Processing Systems 2021, NeurIPS 2021, 6–14 December 2021, Virtual. In: Ranzato, M., Beygelzimer, A., Dauphin, Y.N., Liang, P., Vaughan, J.W. (eds.), pp. 11054–11070 (2021)

Rigouts Terryn, A., Hoste, V., Drouin, P., Lefever, E.: Proceedings of the 6th International Workshop on Computational Terminology. In: Daille, B., Kageura, K., Rigouts Terryn, A. (eds.), pp. 85–94. European Language Resources Association (2020). ISBN: 979-10-95546-57-3

Rigouts Terryn, A., Hoste, V., Lefever, E.: HAMLET: hybrid adaptable machine learning approach to extract terminology. Terminology **27**(2), 254–293 (2021)

Rubin, O., Herzig, J., Berant, J.: Proceedings of the 2022 Conference of the North American Chapter of the Association for Computational Linguistics: Human Language Technologies, NAACL 2022, Seattle, WA, United States, 10–15 July 2022. In:

Carpuat, M., de Marneffe, M.-C., Ruíz, I.V.M. (eds.), pp. 2655–2671. Association for Computational Linguistics (2022). https://doi.org/10.18653/V1/2022.NAACL-MAIN.191

Sclar, M., Choi, Y., Tsvetkov, Y., Suhr, A.: Quantifying language models' sensitivity to spurious features in prompt design or: how i learned to start worrying about prompt formatting. CoRR abs/2310.11324 (2023). https://doi.org/10.48550/ARXIV.2310.11324

Tang, L., et al.: Evaluating large language models on medical evidence summarization. NPJ Digit. Med. **6** (2023). https://doi.org/10.1038/S41746-023-00896-7

Wadhwa, S., Amir, S., Wallace, B.C.: Proceedings of the 61st Annual Meeting of the Association for Computational Linguistics (Volume 1: Long Papers), ACL 2023, Toronto, Canada, 9-14 July 2023. In: Rogers, A., Boyd-Graber, J.L., Okazaki, N. (eds.), pp. 15566–15589. Association for Computational Linguistics (2023). https://doi.org/10.18653/V1/2023.ACL-LONG.868

Wang, S., et al.: GPT-NER: named entity recognition via large language models. CoRR abs/2304.10428 (2023).https://doi.org/10.48550/ARXIV.2304.10428

Zhang, M., Wang, B., Fei, H., Zhang, M.: In-context learning for few-shot nested named entity recognition. CoRR abs/2402.01182 (2024). https://doi.org/10.48550/ARXIV.2402.01182

Data Augmentation Method Utilizing Template Sentences for Variable Definition Extraction

Kotaro Nagayama, Shota Kato$^{(\boxtimes)}$ (iD), and Manabu Kano (iD)

Graduate School of Informatics, Kyoto University, Kyoto 606-8501, Japan
nagayama.kotaro.63c@st.kyoto-u.ac.jp,
{shota,manabu}@human.sys.kyoto-u.ac.jp

Abstract. The extraction of variable definitions from scientific and technical papers is essential for understanding these documents. However, the characteristics of variable definitions, such as the length and the words that make up the definition, differ among fields, which leads to differences in the performance of existing extraction methods across fields. Although preparing training data specific to each field can improve the performance of the methods, it is costly to create high-quality training data. To address this challenge, this study proposes a new method that generates new definition sentences from template sentences and variable-definition pairs in the training data. The proposed method has been tested on papers about chemical processes, and the results show that the model trained with the definition sentences generated by the proposed method achieved a higher accuracy of 89.6%, surpassing existing models.

Keywords: Data augmentation · Variable definition extraction · Document information processing

1 Introduction

The rate of increase in the number of papers worldwide has been significantly rising in recent years; it was around 5% until 2017 and increased to 10.3% in 2020 and 9.2% in 2021 [4]. Consequently, the time and effort required for literature review have been increasing year by year. To alleviate this burden, several studies have proposed methods for automatically extracting, organizing, and utilizing information from a vast amount of literature using natural language processing (NLP) techniques [11]. One of the most valuable information in scientific papers is mathematical formulas, which are used to express the relationships between variables. Therefore, accurate extraction of variable definitions from scientific papers is essential for understanding the content of the papers.

Various methods for variable definition extraction have been proposed, including rule-based methods that extract noun phrases matching certain patterns [12], machine learning-based methods using features such as part-of-speech tags and positions in sentences [10,14], and methods employing deep learning

A. Rapp et al. (Eds.): NLDB 2024, LNCS 14762, pp. 151–165, 2024.
https://doi.org/10.1007/978-3-031-70239-6_11

models [15]. Recently several methods have utilized pre-trained models such as Bidirectional Encoder Representations from Transformers (BERT) [2] and achieved particularly high performance. Kang et al. [5] developed a method of extracting technical terms and their definitions simultaneously from texts using SciBERT [1] and attained an F1-score of 70.8% in extracting definitions from 50 papers included in the ACL Anthology. Lee et al. [8] tackled the task of matching variables to their definitions, SemEval 2022 Task 12: Symlink [7]. They used a simple rule-based tokenizer for symbols and SciBERT to perform named entity recognition (NER) and relation extraction (RE) of variables and their definitions sequentially [8]. Their method recorded the highest performance in the task. Popovic et al. [13] achieved the third highest performance in Symlink by employing SciBERT to simultaneously perform NER and RE. Yamamoto et al. [16] aimed to develop a high-performance definition extraction method for chemical process-related datasets and proposed a method of predicting the position of a variable definition by inputting a sentence where the target variable is replaced by a special token into a BERT model. They built a definition extraction model by fine-tuning DeBERTaV3$_{\text{LARGE}}$ [3] in two steps: they first used a Symlink dataset [7] which has little relevance to chemical processes and then used a dataset related to chemical processes. Their method achieved an accuracy of 85.5% and an F1-score of 81.6% in extracting variable definitions from papers on chemical processes. Although these methods have achieved high performance, there are still challenges to be addressed in variable definition extraction.

Yamamoto et al. [16] achieved the highest performance among existing studies, but they used a smaller training dataset compared to datasets used in related research [5,7,8,13]. For example, Yamamoto et al. and Kang et al. used about 400 and 660 definition sentences for training, respectively [5,16]. Since these studies used a small amount of training data, increasing the amount of training data could potentially improve the performance of variable definition extraction. However, the characteristics of variable definitions, such as the length and the words that make up the definition, vary by field, and thereby the difficulty level of variable definition extraction also differs among fields [13]. Thus, increasing training data from other fields may not contribute to performance improvement. Additionally, it is very costly to create a large amount of new training data each time the field of application changes.

To solve these problems, we propose a method of augmenting the training data as shown in Fig. 1. The proposed method prepares template sentences, such as "[VAR_1] is defined as [DEF_1]," and generates new definition sentences by assigning variables and their definitions in the training data to these template sentences. Such a method of generating new data using existing data is generally called data augmentation. Various methods have been proposed for NLP, but the conventional data augmentation methods focus on diversifying the meanings and expressions of sentences [9], which may not preserve the relationships between variables and their definitions. In contrast, the proposed method preserves their expressions and the relationship between variables and their definitions, stabilizes the quality of the definition sentences, and diversifies only the sentence

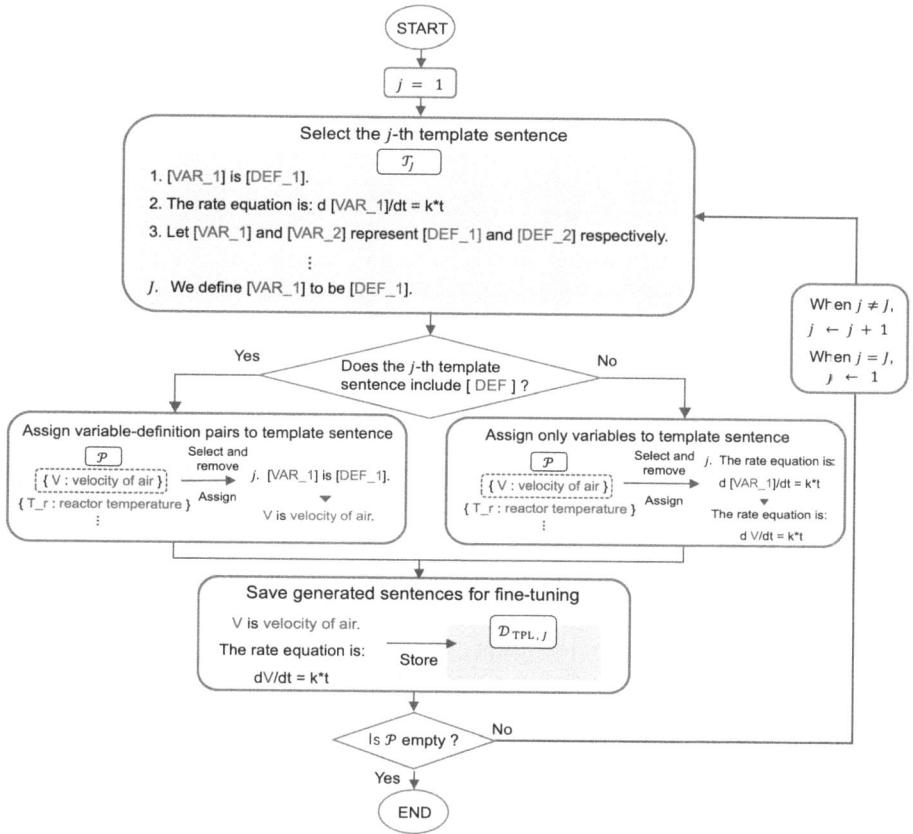

Fig. 1. Overview of the proposed method. $\mathcal{T}_J$ represents a set of J types of template sentences, $\mathcal{P}$ is a list storing variable-definition pairs included in the training data, and $\mathcal{D}_{\mathrm{TPL},J}$ is a list for storing the generated sentences.

structure. The performance of the model trained with the augmented training data using the proposed method is compared to that without data augmentation using a dataset created from 47 papers on chemical processes. The datasets and code used in this study are available at https://github.com/humansys-lab/DATS.

2 Problem Setting

In practice, the definitions of variables are sometimes scattered in figures and tables, and some of the definitions are not explicitly written in the text; thus, to understand all of the variables in a paper, one must refer to the paper and related documents to extract the definitions of the variables from the text, figures, and tables. As the first step toward automating this process, this study tackles the

---

- [VAR_1] is [DEF_1].
- The rate equation is: d [VAR_1]/dt = k*t
- We will work with six variables: [VAR_1], [VAR_2], [VAR_3], [VAR_4], [VAR_5] and [VAR_6], each representing [DEF_1], [DEF_2], [DEF_3], [DEF_4], [DEF_5] and [DEF_6] respectively.
- One of these equations represents the intricate fifth-order reaction :
  ∂ [VAR_1]/ ∂t = k [VAR_2] ^3 [VAR_3]^2 - k [VAR_4] [VAR_5]^4.

Fig. 2. Examples of template sentences, each containing pairs of variable and definition tokens or solely variable tokens. The number of variable tokens in each template sentence ranges from one to six.

task of extracting the definition of each variable from the main text of a paper if the definition exists and not extracting anything if it does not. The positions of the variables are known in advance since the identification of variables is relatively easy [8]. The target variables are those that meet the following three conditions: 1) the variable does not previously appear in the paper, 2) it is surrounded by spaces or exists alone on the left side of an equation, and 3) when a corresponding definition exists in the text, it can be directly extracted. We set the first condition because the definition of a variable is often provided at its first mention, and the definitions of variables that appear multiple times in a paper are often abbreviated in subsequent mentions. The second condition is set because variables that meet this condition are more likely to have their definitions written in the text. We provide the third condition because some definitions are not directly extractable, which may affect the performance of the model. For example, the definitions of C_A and C_B in the sentence "C_A and C_B are concentrations of A and B." are "concentration of A" and "concentration of B," respectively, which cannot be directly extracted. It is possible to set the span of definitions to be extracted for C_A and C_B as "concentrations of A and B", but this could hinder the model's learning and evaluation; hence, such variables were set out of the scope.

3   Proposed Method

The overview of the proposed method is illustrated in Fig. 1. The proposed method prepares template sentences like those in Fig. 2 and generates new sentences from them and variable-definition pairs in training data.

The proposed method needs to prepare three pieces of information: a list $\mathcal{P}$ storing variable-definition pairs from the training data, a set $\mathcal{T}_J$ consisting of J types of template sentences, and an empty list $\mathcal{D}_{\mathrm{TPL},J}$ for storing generated sentences. The j-th template sentence in $\mathcal{T}_J$, TPL_j, includes n_j pairs of variable and definition tokens $(([\mathrm{VAR\_1}], [\mathrm{DEF\_1}]), \ldots, ([\mathrm{VAR\_j}], [\mathrm{DEF\_j}]))$, or n_j variable tokens $([\mathrm{VAR\_1}], \ldots, [\mathrm{VAR\_j}])$. Template sentences are created using ChatGPT (gpt-3.5-turbo-1106). The prompt is designed to include an explanation of the output format, specification of the number of variables in the generated sentence, and examples of definition sentences.

The procedure for generating definition sentences is as follows:

1. Set $j = 1$.
2. Select the j-th template sentence from $\mathcal{T}_J$, denoted as TPL_j.
3. Select n_j variable-definition pairs from $\mathcal{P}$ and remove the pairs from $\mathcal{P}$.
4. Assign the selected n_j variable-definition pairs to $[\text{VAR}\_i]$ and $[\text{DEF}\_i]$ ($i \in \{1, \ldots, n_j\}$) in TPL_j. If TPL_j does not include $[\text{DEF}\_i]$, assign only the variables to $[\text{VAR}\_i]$.
5. Add the generated sentence to $\mathcal{D}_{\text{TPL},J}$.
6. Terminate data generation if $\mathcal{P}$ is empty. Otherwise, update j to $j+1$ if $j \neq J$ or to 1 if $j = J$, and then return to step 2.

The $\mathcal{D}_{\text{TPL},J}$ created through the above steps contains the same number of variables as the variable-definition pairs included in the training data, with each being targeted for definition extraction once. Therefore, the number of variables contained in $\mathcal{D}_{\text{TPL},J}$ does not depend on J.

4 Experiment

This section describes the variable definition extraction method, the datasets used for the experiments, the experimental setup, and the evaluation metrics.

4.1 Variable Definition Extraction Method

Figure 3 shows the schematic diagram of the variable definition extraction method developed by Yamamoto et al. [16], which is used as a baseline in this study. The method takes a sentence with a target variable for definition extraction and returns the corresponding definition if it exists or a [CLS] token if it does not exist. Initially, the target variable within the given sentence is replaced with a special token [target]. Next, the sentence is split into tokens by a tokenizer. The token sequence of length d_{input} is then provided to the BERT model and converted into context-dependent embedding vectors $\hat{e}_i$ ($i \in \{1, 2, \ldots, d_{\text{input}}\}$). These vectors, $\hat{e}_i$, are processed through the fully-connected layer and converted into $s_{\text{start},i}$ and $s_{\text{end},i}$, which are the probabilities that the corresponding tokens are the start and end positions of the definition respectively. The method extracts as the definition the k-th to l-th tokens that satisfy the following conditions:

$$k, l = \operatorname*{argmax}_{k,l} s_{\text{start},k} + s_{\text{end},l}, \quad \text{s.t. } 2 \leq k \leq l \text{ or } k = l = 1. \tag{1}$$

If $s_{\text{start},1} + s_{\text{end},1}$ is the maximum, the method extracts the [CLS] token, which indicates that no corresponding definition exists.

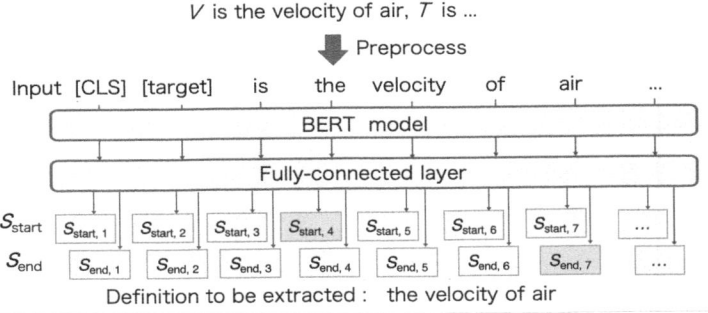

Fig. 3. Schematic diagram of the variable definition extraction method by Yamamoto et al. [16]. The vectors s_{start} and s_{end} represent the probabilities of each token being the start and end positions of a definition, respectively. The tokens predicted as the start and end positions of a definition, $s_{start,i}$ and $s_{end,j}$, are highlighted in yellow. (Color figure online)

Table 1. The details of $\mathcal{D}_{Process}$. #Papers, #Variables, and #Variables with definitions represent the numbers of papers, variables, and variables with definitions.

Dataset	#Papers	#Variables	# Variables with definitions
$\mathcal{D}_{CRYST}$	11	281	200
$\mathcal{D}_{CSTR}$	10	169	123
$\mathcal{D}_{BD}$	10	186	125
$\mathcal{D}_{CZ}$	9	311	196
$\mathcal{D}_{STHE}$	7	267	176
$\mathcal{D}_{Process}$	47	1,214	820

4.2 Datasets

We created a dataset, $\mathcal{D}_{Process}$, which includes definitions for variables appearing in a total of 47 papers related to five processes: a crystallization process (CRYST), continuous stirred tank reactor (CSTR), biodiesel production process (BD), Czochralski process (CZ), and shell and tube heat exchanger (STHE). The datasets of the processes are denoted as $\mathcal{D}_{CRYST}$, $\mathcal{D}_{CSTR}$, $\mathcal{D}_{BD}$, $\mathcal{D}_{CZ}$, and $\mathcal{D}_{STHE}$, respectively. The statistics of the datasets are summarized in Table 1. $\mathcal{D}_{Process}$ includes 1,214 variables, of which 67.5% (820 variables) have definitions.

Similar to Yamamoto et al. [16], we also use the dataset used in Symlink [7] denoted by $\mathcal{D}_{Symlink}$. $\mathcal{D}_{Symlink}$ consists of 101 papers from five fields: informatics, biology, physics, mathematics, and economics, and contains 16,642 variables, of which 11,462 have definitions.

Each paper in $\mathcal{D}_{Process}$ is classified as either part of training, validation, or test set. In $\mathcal{D}_{STHE}$, the number of papers designated for the test set is two, whereas for other datasets, this number is set to three. For each dataset, one

Table 2. Breakdown of the number of template sentences in $\mathcal{T}_J$

Dataset	Number of definition tokens						
	0	1	2	3	4	5	6
$\mathcal{T}_{20}$	8	2	2	2	2	2	2
$\mathcal{T}_{100}$	40	14	14	8	8	8	8
$\mathcal{T}_{300}$	120	42	42	24	24	24	24

paper is assigned for validation and the remainder for training. In the entire $\mathcal{D}_{\text{Process}}$, 28 papers are used for training, five for validation, and 14 for test. $\mathcal{D}_{\text{Symlink}}$ and $\mathcal{D}_{\text{TPL},J}$ are split into training and validation sets in a 3:1 ratio. The training and validation datasets are used for fine-tuning models, while the test dataset serves for performance evaluation.

To investigate the influence of the number of template sentences on definition extraction performance, we create three sets of template sentences: $\mathcal{T}_{20}$, $\mathcal{T}_{100}$, and $\mathcal{T}_{300}$, along with their corresponding datasets $\mathcal{D}_{\text{TPL},20}$, $\mathcal{D}_{\text{TPL},100}$, and $\mathcal{D}_{\text{TPL},300}$. We initially construct 300 template sentences $\mathcal{T}_{300}$ by ensuring the proportion of definition tokens matches that in $\mathcal{D}_{\text{Process}}$. Subsequently, we randomly select 100 sentences from $\mathcal{T}_{300}$ to create $\mathcal{T}_{100}$, so that the distribution of the number of definition tokens remains consistent with $\mathcal{T}_{300}$. Similarly, $\mathcal{T}_{20}$ is derived from $\mathcal{T}_{100}$. Table 2 summarizes their distributions of the number of definition tokens.

The proposed method can be utilized to extract definitions from papers on processes other than the five processes included in $\mathcal{D}_{\text{Process}}$. To verify the effectiveness of the proposed method when the target process is not contained in the training dataset, we make a dataset that does not include the dataset of process X, $\mathcal{D}_{\text{Process}-X}$, by removing the dataset of the process X, $\mathcal{D}_X$, from $\mathcal{D}_{\text{Process}}$. $\mathcal{D}_{\text{Process}-X}$ and $\mathcal{D}_X$ are also divided for training, validation, and test. We fine-tune models on the training dataset of $\mathcal{D}_{\text{Process}-X}$ and evaluate their performance by applying them to the test dataset of $\mathcal{D}_X$.

4.3   Experimental Setup

We use DeBERTaV3$_{\text{LARGE}}$ [3], which achieved the best performance in the experiments by Yamamoto et al. [16], as the base model, Adam [6] as the optimizer, and NVIDIA A100 80 GB for the GPU. The batch size and learning rate are set to 8 and $1e-5$, respectively. In addition, similar to the two-step fine-tuning used by Yamamoto et al. [16], we apply a three-step fine-tuning strategy using $\mathcal{D}_{\text{Symlink}}$, $\mathcal{D}_{\text{TPL},J}$, and $\mathcal{D}_{\text{Process}}$ in sequence. Hereafter, the three-step fine-tuning using $\mathcal{D}_{\text{TPL},J'}$, created from J' types of template sentences, is referred to as "Proposed$_{J=J'}$". We train the model for three epochs and apply the model with the minimum cross-entropy loss to the test data to evaluate the performance.

Table 3. Classes of the outputs of the variable definition extraction method

Result	Does the variable have a definition?	
	Yes	No
The extracted definition is correct	TP	–
The extracted definition is incorrect	FP$^{(1)}$	FP$^{(2)}$
The [CLS] token is extracted (No definition is extracted)	FN	TN

4.4   Evaluation Method

For each target variable, the variable definition extraction method yields a token sequence as a definition or the [CLS] token. To evaluate the performance of the variable definition extraction method, we classify the output of the method into five categories: true positive (TP), false positive when the definition is extracted (FP$^{(1)}$), false positive when the [CLS] token is extracted (FP$^{(2)}$), false negative (FN), and true negative (TN). For a detailed analysis of failure patterns, false positive samples are classified into two categories: FP$^{(1)}$ and FP$^{(2)}$. These categories are organized in Table 3. Using this classification, we define four metrics: Accuracy (Acc.), Precision (Pre.), Recall (Rec.), and the F1-score (F1). Acc. is defined as the proportion of variables for which the correct answer is obtained. Pre. represents the proportion of correctly extracted definitions out of all extracted definitions. Rec. denotes the proportion of correctly extracted definitions out of the variables with definitions. The F1 is calculated as the harmonic mean of *Pre.* and *Rec.* These metrics are calculated as follows:

$$Acc. = \frac{TP + TN}{TP + FP^{(1)} + FP^{(2)} + FN + TN}, \tag{2}$$

$$Pre. = \frac{TP}{TP + FP^{(1)} + FP^{(2)}}, \tag{3}$$

$$Rec. = \frac{TP}{TP + FP^{(1)} + FN}, \tag{4}$$

$$F1 = \frac{2 \times Pre. \times Rec.}{Pre. + Rec.}. \tag{5}$$

When performing variable definition extraction before other downstream tasks, both extracting the correct definition and correctly predicting the absence of a definition are important. Therefore, the superiority of a method is judged by *Acc.*, and other metrics are used to grasp the characteristics of the method.

Since the performance can vary depending on the types of papers included in the training, validation, and test sets, we split $\mathcal{D}_{\text{Process}}$ ten times according to Sect. 4.2 and compare the average of their evaluation metrics.

5 Results and Discussion

5.1 Results

Table 4 shows the average evaluation metrics, and Fig. 4 shows the distribution of each evaluation metric across ten experiments. In all evaluation metrics except for *Rec.* when $J = 100$, the proposed method outperformed the method of Yamamoto et al., demonstrating the effectiveness of the proposed method in improving variable definition extraction performance. In *Acc.*, *Pre.*, and $F1$, the proposed method exhibited less variability compared to the method of Yamamoto et al., suggesting that the proposed method not only enhances variable definition extraction performance but also stabilizes the performance. Although the variability in *Rec.* was greater than that in the method of Yamamoto et al., the proposed method overall achieved higher performance.

Table 4. Experimental results of variable definition extraction. Each value is the average of ten experiments and is presented as a percentage. The bold number indicates the highest value in each column.

Method	*Acc.*	*Rec.*	*Pre.*	*F1*
Yamamoto et al. [16]	85.8	87.4	87.1	87.1
Proposed$_{J=20}$	87.6	**88.5**	89.4	88.8
Proposed$_{J=100}$	87.8	87.1	**91.6**	89.1
Proposed$_{J=300}$	**88.3**	88.3	90.4	**89.3**

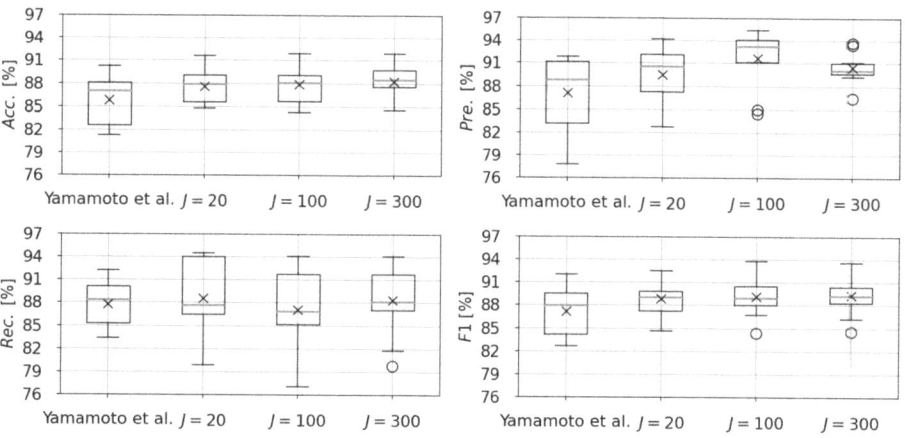

Fig. 4. Distribution of each evaluation metric across ten experiments. $J = J'$ in the figure corresponds to the distribution of the Proposed$_{J=J'}$. In each box, the orange horizontal line represents the median and the mark × represents the mean value. (Color figure online)

5.2   Discussion

Impact of the Number of Template Sentences. Both *Acc.* and *F*1 improved as the number of template sentences J increased. Among the cases where definition extraction failed by the Proposed$_{J=20}$ but succeeded by the Proposed$_{J=300}$, some definitions did not fit the patterns included in T_{300}. This suggests that increasing J contributes not only to the performance improvement in definition extraction from the existing template patterns but also from patterns not covered by the templates.

Table 5. Variable definition extraction performance on unknown processes

Train dataset	Test dataset	Yamamoto et al. [16]				Proposed$_{J=300}$			
		Acc.	*Rec.*	*Pre.*	*F*1	*Acc.*	*Rec.*	*Pre.*	*F*1
$\mathcal{D}_{\mathrm{Process-CRYST}}$	$\mathcal{D}_{\mathrm{CRYST}}$	78.0	74.8	81.7	78.0	82.0	79.7	85.1	82.2
$\mathcal{D}_{\mathrm{Process}}$		83.1	82.8	85.6	84.2	85.3	84.9	88.2	86.4
$\mathcal{D}_{\mathrm{Process-CSTR}}$	$\mathcal{D}_{\mathrm{CSTR}}$	93.2	92.0	91.7	91.8	94.8	94.5	94.6	94.5
$\mathcal{D}_{\mathrm{Process}}$		94.8	93.6	94.5	94.0	95.9	95.5	95.6	95.5
$\mathcal{D}_{\mathrm{Process-BD}}$	$\mathcal{D}_{\mathrm{BD}}$	87.5	88.5	85.7	87.0	91.2	89.3	91.3	90.2
$\mathcal{D}_{\mathrm{Process}}$		90.9	88.7	91.8	90.2	91.6	91.7	92.0	91.7
$\mathcal{D}_{\mathrm{Process-CZ}}$	$\mathcal{D}_{\mathrm{CZ}}$	82.8	91.1	79.5	84.9	86.4	89.6	86.5	87.9
$\mathcal{D}_{\mathrm{Process}}$		86.2	89.6	86.3	87.8	89.7	89.4	90.9	90.1
$\mathcal{D}_{\mathrm{Process-STHE}}$	$\mathcal{D}_{\mathrm{STHE}}$	74.1	85.4	74.8	78.0	79.5	83.9	81.3	82.2
$\mathcal{D}_{\mathrm{Process}}$		79.6	84.4	82.3	82.6	83.7	83.6	88.1	85.4

Performance on Unknown Processes. Table 5 shows the variable definition extraction results of Proposed$_{J=300}$ and the method of Yamamoto et al. for unknown processes. Across all five processes, regardless of whether the data of the target process was included in the training data, the proposed method outperformed the method of Yamamoto et al. This demonstrates the effectiveness of the proposed method in extracting variable definitions even for processes not included in the training data.

Figure 5 shows the distribution of *Acc.* across ten experiments for the method of Yamamoto et al. using $\mathcal{D}_{\mathrm{Process}}$ as training data, and Proposed$_{J=300}$ using $\mathcal{D}_{\mathrm{Process}-X}$ as training data. Proposed$_{J=300}$ using $\mathcal{D}_{\mathrm{Process}-X}$ achieved comparable *Acc.* to the method of Yamamoto et al. using $\mathcal{D}_{\mathrm{Process}}$. This suggests that the proposed method without preparing training data for the target process could achieve performance equivalent to that of Yamamoto et al.

Moreover, Proposed$_{J=300}$ improved *Acc.* by using data of the target process for training, particularly when $\mathcal{D}_{\mathrm{CRYST}}$, $\mathcal{D}_{\mathrm{CZ}}$, and $\mathcal{D}_{\mathrm{STHE}}$ were used as the test set. In contrast, such performance increase was marginal when $\mathcal{D}_{\mathrm{CSTR}}$ and $\mathcal{D}_{\mathrm{BD}}$

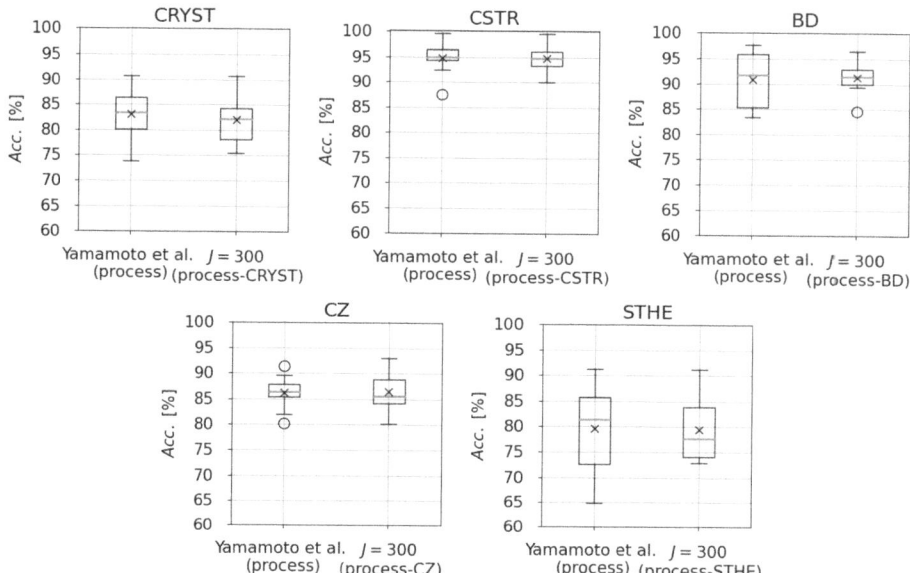

Fig. 5. Distribution of *Acc.* across ten experiments using two methods: the method by Yamamoto et al. with $\mathcal{D}_{\mathrm{Process}}$ as training data (left side of each figure) and Proposed$_{J=300}$ with $\mathcal{D}_{\mathrm{Process}-X}$ as training data (right side of each figure). The orange line indicates the median and the mark $\times$ represents the mean. (Color figure online)

were used as the test set. This could be due to the small number of variables in D_{CSTR} and D_{BD}, and the presence of datasets similar to D_{CSTR} and D_{BD} in $\mathcal{D}_{\mathrm{Process}-X}$, limiting the effect of preparing their training data.

To verify the second hypothesis, we introduce the Simpson coefficient as the similarity between datasets $\mathcal{D}_A$ and $\mathcal{D}_B$ as follows:

$$S(\mathcal{D}_A, \mathcal{D}_B) = \frac{|\mathcal{W}_A \cap \mathcal{W}_B|}{\min\{|\mathcal{W}_A|, |\mathcal{W}_B|\}}, \tag{6}$$

where $\mathcal{W}_X$ $(X \in \{A, B\})$ is the set of words that compose the definitions in dataset $\mathcal{D}_X$, $|\mathcal{W}_X|$ is the number of elements in $\mathcal{W}_X$, and $\mathcal{W}_A \cap \mathcal{W}_B$ is the set of elements belonging to both $\mathcal{W}_A$ and $\mathcal{W}_B$. $\mathcal{W}_X$ does not include stop words like "of" and "and". For instance, when $\mathcal{D}_A$ consists of "velocity of air" and "temperature of reactor", $\mathcal{W}_A = \{$"velocity", "air", "temperature", "reactor"$\}$. The value of $S(\mathcal{D}_A, \mathcal{D}_B)$ closer to 1 means that $\mathcal{D}_A$ and $\mathcal{D}_B$ are more similar. Figure 6 illustrates the similarities between datasets included in $\mathcal{D}_{\mathrm{Process}}$. $\mathcal{D}_{\mathrm{CSTR}}$ and $\mathcal{D}_{\mathrm{BD}}$ had the highest similarity at 42.1%, indicating a substantial overlap in the words that comprise their definitions. This overlap could impede performance improvements that might otherwise be achieved by preparing training data for these processes. Conversely, the dataset $\mathcal{D}_{\mathrm{STHE}}$ had the largest performance gain by using training data with Proposed$_{J=300}$, but exhibited lower

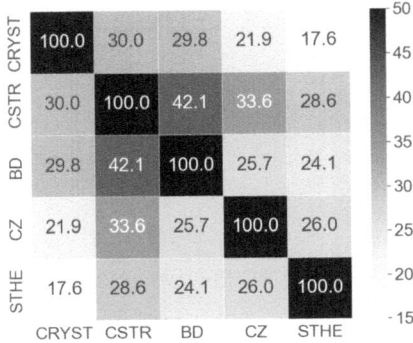

Fig. 6. Similarities between datasets. Each value is displayed in %.

similarity compared to the other datasets in $\mathcal{D}_{\text{Process}}$. These findings suggest that the performance of variable definition extraction can be enhanced by preparing training data specific to the test data's process, particularly when there exists a low similarity between the process of the test data and those of the training data.

Analysis of Definition Extraction Failure Samples. Table 6 shows the breakdown of definition extraction failure samples in ten experiments conducted using Proposed$_{J=300}$. For FP$^{(1)}$ failures, we further categorize them into three classes: FP$^{(1)}_{\text{wide}}$, FP$^{(1)}_{\text{narrow}}$, and FP$^{(1)}_{\text{other}}$. When the predicted definition range entirely encompasses the correct definition range, we classify it FP$^{(1)}_{\text{wide}}$ and when the predicted definition range is entirely contained within the correct definition range, we classify it as FP$^{(1)}_{\text{narrow}}$. For other cases, we classify it as FP$^{(1)}_{\text{other}}$. Across all ten experiments, the total number of failures by Proposed$_{J=300}$ was equal to or less than that by the method of Yamamoto et al.

To discuss the effectiveness and limitations of the proposed method, we analyzed three cases: 1) the case where only Proposed$_{J=300}$ correctly extracted the definition, 2) the case where the existing method extracted the definition correctly but Proposed$_{J=300}$ did not, and 3) the case where both methods did not correctly extract the definition. In what follows, the source sentences for extraction and definition extraction results are showcased. In the following case, the target variable is dashed, the correct definition (or [CLS] token if there is no definition) is underlined, the extraction results by Proposed$_{J=300}$ and the existing method are shown in bold and italic, respectively.

■ **Type 1:** **[CLS]** The *temperature* is then lowered to T_{fin} within the time duration t_{cool}.

Type 1 represents cases where the method of Yamamoto et al. extracted an incorrect definition for variables without definitions in the text, while Proposed$_{J=300}$

Table 6. Breakdown of definition extraction failure samples by error class in ten experiments using Proposed$_{J=300}$. Each value in parentheses indicates the difference in the number of failures compared to the method of Yamamoto et al. [16].

Error class	Experiment number									
	1	2	3	4	5	6	7	8	9	10
FN	34 (+25)	19 (−2)	38 (+16)	22 (+9)	13 (−15)	19 (−5)	12 (−2)	7 (−10)	20 (−6)	24 (−3)
$FP^{(1)}_{wide}$	4 (−2)	7 (−2)	4 (−5)	4 (+2)	2 (−1)	3 (−5)	1 (−2)	3 (±0)	3 (+1)	3 (−3)
$FP^{(1)}_{narrow}$	6 (−4)	3 (−1)	5 (±0)	1 (−5)	2 (−1)	4 (±0)	2 (−1)	4 (+1)	6 (+1)	3 (−2)
$FP^{(1)}_{other}$	1 (±0)	1 (−3)	1 (−2)	2 (+1)	4 (+3)	1 (−1)	1 (+1)	1 (±0)	1 (±0)	1 (±0)
$FP^{(2)}$	9 (−30)	12 (−5)	11 (−21)	2 (−21)	17 (−7)	15 (−13)	13 (−2)	18 (−2)	14 (+4)	7 (+1)
Total	54 (−11)	42 (−13)	59 (−12)	32 (−14)	38 (−21)	42 (−24)	29 (−6)	33 (−11)	44 (±0)	38 (−7)

made improvements by not extracting anything. Template sentences include ones like "The rate of reaction is described by the equation: d [VAR_1]/dt = k*[A][B].", which contain the variable token but not the corresponding definition token. The enhanced ability to correctly identify variables without definitions in the text using the proposed method is attributed to the increase in variables without definitions in the training data.

■ **Type 2**: [CLS] The *reaction rate constants for the ith reaction* are given by k_i, $i = 1, \ldots, 6$, modeled using the Arrhenius rate equations, whose values can be obtained from the parameters reported in Table 1.

Type 2 illustrates the most common cases where the method of Yamamoto et al. could extract the correct definition, but Proposed$_{J=300}$ did not extract anything. The presence of template sentences without definition tokens in the analysis of Type 1 might contribute to an increase in such failure cases. Creating template sentences with a lower ratio of variables without definitions might increase the number of variables judged to have definitions.

■ **Type 3**: *[CLS]* The total moments, seed moments, and nucleated crystal moments are related by $\mu_{i,T} = \mu_{i,S} + \mu_{i,N}$, and the moments are defined in terms of their respective CSD's as

$$\mu_{i,j}(t) = \int_0^\infty x^i n_j(x,t)\, dx, \quad i = 0, 1, 2, \ldots, j = T, S, N \tag{3}$$

and have units of m^i/kg solvent.

Cases where both methods were incorrect included various patterns, but many involved sentences with a mix of multiple variables, definitions, and equations, where both methods wrongly identified variables with definitions as having none. Although the template sentences created in this study contain multiple variable and definition tokens, all template sentences containing definition tokens have explicit variable-definition relationships and do not include multiple equations. Developing methods for creating template sentences closer to the sentences found in papers on chemical processes could improve the performance.

6 Conclusion

In this study, we enhanced the performance of variable definition extraction by preparing template sentences for definitions and expanding the training data by assigning variable-definition pairs from the training data to each sentence. Comparing the definition extraction performance of the existing model with that of the model trained by the proposed method, we found that increasing the number of template sentences improved the accuracy rate, achieving an accuracy of 88.3%, which surpasses the existing method by 2.5% points. Moreover, by applying the proposed method, we achieved an accuracy rate equivalent to the existing method without using data from the definition extraction target process in training.

Future challenges are as follows. There were instances where the existing method extracted the correct definition, but the proposed method extracted no definition. This could be due to an inappropriate ratio of template sentences that do not include definition tokens. Therefore, adjusting this ratio could lead to further performance improvements. Additionally, failure cases involving sentences with a mix of multiple variables, definitions, and equations were not improved by using the proposed method. Although the template sentences created in this study contain multiple variable and definition tokens, all do not include multiple equations and the included variable-definition relationships were explicit. Generating template sentences more similar to the definition sentences appearing in the dataset could expect further performance improvements.

Acknowledgments. This research was supported by JSPS KAKENHI Grant Number JP23K13595.

Disclosure of Interests. The authors have no competing interests to declare that are relevant to the content of this article.

References

1. Beltagy, I., Lo, K., Cohan, A.: SciBERT: a pretrained language model for scientific text. In: Proceedings of the 2019 Conference on Empirical Methods in Natural Language Processing and the 9th International Joint Conference on Natural Language Processing (EMNLP-IJCNLP), pp. 3615–3620 (2019). https://doi.org/10.18653/v1/D19-1371
2. Devlin, J., Chang, M.W., Lee, K., Toutanova, K.: BERT: pretraining of deep bidirectional transformers for language understanding. In: Proceedings of the 2019 Conference of the North American Chapter of the Association for Computational Linguistics: Human Language Technologies, Volume 1 (Long and Short Papers), pp. 4171–4186 (2019). https://doi.org/10.18653/v1/N19-1423
3. He, P., Gao, J., Chen, W.: DeBERTaV3: improving DeBERTa using ELECTRA-style pre-training with gradient-disentangled embedding sharing. arXiv preprint arXiv:2111.09543 (2021). https://doi.org/10.48550/arXiv.2111.09543
4. Japanese science and technology indicators 2023, NISTEP research material no. 328. National Institute of Science and Technology Policy, Tokyo

5. Kang, D., Head, A., Sidhu, R., Lo, K., Weld, D.S., Hearst, M.A.: Document-level definition detection in scholarly documents: existing models, error analyses, and future directions. arXiv preprint arXiv:2010.05129 (2020). https://doi.org/10.48550/arXiv.2010.05129

6. Kingma, D.P., Ba, J.: Adam: a method for stochastic optimization. arXiv preprint arXiv:1412.6980 (2014). https://doi.org/10.48550/arXiv.1412.6980

7. Lai, V., Veyseh, A.P.B., Dernoncourt, F., Nguyen, T.: SemEval 2022 task 12: symlink - linking mathematical symbols to their descriptions. In: Proceedings of the 16th International Workshop on Semantic Evaluation (SemEval-2022), pp. 1671–1678 (2022). https://doi.org/10.18653/v1/2022.semeval-1.230

8. Lee, S.M., Na, S.H.: JBNU-CCLab at SemEval-2022 task 12: machine reading comprehension and span pair classification for linking mathematical symbols to their descriptions. In: Proceedings of the 16th International Workshop on Semantic Evaluation (SemEval-2022), pp. 1679–1686 (2022). https://doi.org/10.18653/v1/2022.semeval-1.231

9. Li, B., Hou, Y., Che, W.: Data augmentation approaches in natural language processing: a survey. arXiv preprint arXiv:2110.01852 (2022). https://doi.org/10.48550/arXiv.2110.01852

10. Lin, J., Wang, X., Wang, Z., Beyette, D., Liu, J.C.: Prediction of mathematical expression declarations based on spatial, semantic, and syntactic analysis. In: Proceedings of the ACM Symposium on Document Engineering 2019, DocEng 2019, pp. 1–10 (2019). https://doi.org/10.1145/3342558.3345399

11. Olivetti, E.A., et al.: Data-driven materials research enabled by natural language processing and information extraction. Appl. Phys. Rev. 7(4), 041317 (2020). https://doi.org/10.1063/5.0021106

12. Pagel, R., Schubotz, M.: Mathematical language processing project. In: Joint Proceedings of the MathUI, OpenMath and ThEdu Workshops and Work in Progress track at CICM (2014). https://doi.org/10.13140/2.1.4494.6244

13. Popovic, N., Laurito, W., Färber, M.: AIFB-WebScience at SemEval-2022 task 12: relation extraction first - using relation extraction to identify entities. In: Proceedings of the 16th International Workshop on Semantic Evaluation (SemEval-2022), pp. 1687–1694 (2022). https://doi.org/10.18653/v1/2022.semeval-1.232

14. Schubotz, M., Krämer, L., Meuschke, N., Hamborg, F., Gipp, B.: Evaluating and improving the extraction of mathematical identifier definitions. In: Jones, G.J.F., et al. (eds.) CLEF 2017. LNCS, vol. 10456, pp. 82–94. Springer, Cham (2017). https://doi.org/10.1007/978-3-319-65813-1_7

15. Stathopoulos, Y., Baker, S., Rei, M., Teufel, S.: Variable typing: assigning meaning to variables in mathematical text. In: Proceedings of the 2018 Conference of the North American Chapter of the Association for Computational Linguistics: Human Language Technologies, Volume 1 (Long Papers), pp. 303–312 (2018). https://doi.org/10.18653/v1/N18-1028

16. Yamamoto, M., Kato, S., Kano, M.: Variable definition extraction by BERT with two-step fine-tuning. In: Proceedings of the 29th Annual Conference of the Association for Natural Language Processing, pp. 2957–2961 (2023). (in Japanese)

Semi-supervised Named Entity Recognition for Low-Resource Languages Using Dual PLMs

Hailemariam Mehari Yohannes[1]([envelope]) [iD], Steven Lynden[2] [iD],
Toshiyuki Amagasa[3] [iD], and Akiyoshi Matono[2] [iD]

[1] Systems and Information Engineering, University of Tsukuba,
Tsukuba, Ibaraki, Japan
mehari.yohannes2020@gmail.com
[2] National Institute of Advanced Industrial Science and Technology, Tokyo, Japan
{steven.lynden,a.matono}@aist.go.jp
[3] Center for Computational Sciences, University of Tsukuba,
Tsukuba, Ibaraki, Japan
amagasa@cs.tsukuba.ac.jp

Abstract. Named Entity Recognition (NER) plays a crucial role in natural language processing (NLP) tasks by identifying and classifying named entities. However, developing high-performing NER models for low-resource languages remains challenging due to the limited availability of labeled data. This paper proposes a semi-supervised data augmentation approach that combines two state-of-the-art pre-trained language models (PLMs). Our method first fine-tunes two PLMs using a small set of labeled data, then uses them to generate weakly supervised data from unlabeled data through collaborative learning. These predictions are then evaluated using confidence scores and an agreement measurement by both models to generate a high-quality dataset. We perform experiments using seven low-resource, but widely spoken African languages, demonstrating that augmented datasets generated by our approach achieve better results in six out of the seven languages. Furthermore, we conduct cross-lingual zero-shot experiments between language pairs and multi-lingual experiments to validate the robustness of our method.

Keywords: Data augmentation · Semi-supervised learning · Pre-trained language models · Low-resource languages · Named Entity Recognition

1 Introduction

Named Entity Recognition (NER) is an important task in the field of natural language processing (NLP), responsible for identifying and classifying named entities within text. Named entities refer to parts of the text that refer to entities

A. Rapp et al. (Eds.): NLDB 2024, LNCS 14762, pp. 166–180, 2024.
https://doi.org/10.1007/978-3-031-70239-6_12

such as individuals, companies, places, dates, etc., and precise NER models play a vital role in multiple NLP tasks, including extracting information, answering questions, analyzing sentiments, and translating languages. Building precise NER models usually requires a significant amount of high-quality labeled training data. However, acquiring such datasets can be challenging and time-consuming, often requiring human experts to label them manually. This process is costly and may not always be feasible. Most existing studies in NLP have primarily focused on resource-rich languages such as English, French, and others, mainly due to the abundance of high-quality labeled resources comprising tens of thousands of annotated data. Additionally, these languages benefit from well-established annotation tools that facilitate the creation of high-quality labeled datasets [15,18,20,21]. In contrast, low-resource languages face a significant challenge due to limited data availability, despite the fact that such languages may often be widely spoken. This scarcity of labeled data is a significant obstacle in performing NLP tasks, including the development of NER models. Unlike resource-rich languages, low-resource languages often lack access to dedicated annotation tools that can simplify the creation of high-quality labeled datasets. Consequently, building high-performing models in low-resource languages is particularly challenging [24].

As a result, several studies have explored various approaches to overcome the challenges of training NER models in low-resource languages. Promising solutions include applying data augmentation, which aims to generate synthetic labeled examples to increase upon the limited annotated dataset. Data augmentation techniques help improve the model's performance by increasing the diversity and size of the training data, and include approaches such as synonym replacement [4,25], fine-tuning generative language models [6,8,12,28], and back-translation [7,19]. Furthermore, semi-supervised learning approaches offer potential solutions by incorporating unlabeled data to enhance the performance of NER models. Such learning approaches combine labeled data with larger unlabeled datasets, where the named entities are not explicitly labeled. By leveraging this in combination with labeled and unlabeled data, semi-supervised learning methods can leverage the additional knowledge and improve the overall performance of NER models [9,11,23,27]. However, existing semi-supervised approaches in NER tend to rely on a single model, which may introduce errors and noise during data generation. This heavy reliance on a single model is a major limitation, as it can result in less useful predictions of the unlabeled data [23].

This paper introduces two data augmentation methods for NER. The first method proposes a semi-supervised-based bootstrapping approach that ensembles the power of multiple state-of-the-art pre-trained language models (PLMs) such as [3,5,13,16]. Unlike existing methods that rely on single-model of prediction of the unlabeled data, our approach leverages the collaboration between two state-of-the-art models to improve and generate high-quality data. Our approach first fine-tunes PLMs simultaneously using limited labeled data and then utilizes the fine-tuned weights to predict the unlabeled data. These predictions are then evaluated using the confidence scores and an agreement measurement:

– A confidence score (τ) is used to determine the prediction confidence level.
– An agreement measurement (λ) is essential to identify errors or uncertainties in the individual model's predictions. If there is a disagreement between the models, one or both models might have made incorrect predictions and utilizing this enables us to filter out unreliable predictions and focus on the instances where the models agree, improving the overall quality of the predictions.

The second proposed method begins by constructing a NER dictionary from the training data. Subsequently, we generate word embeddings based on the dictionary. Finally, we perform augmentation using these embeddings to enhance the dataset size. The main contributions of this paper are:

(i) We introduce two data augmentation methods for NER tasks in low-resource languages.
(ii) We evaluate our approach on seven low-resource African languages that are widely spoken and outperform on six out of the seven languages.
(iii) We explore cross-lingual zero-shot learning between language pairs and multilingual learning through extensive experiments.

2 Related Work

The application of data augmentation, particularly incorporating semi-supervised learning, has been well studied in recent years. Many studies have focused on addressing the challenge of limited data availability by leveraging semi-supervised learning techniques. Some common techniques include applying traditional machine learning approaches [17,22], deep learning approaches [27], and generative large language models [2,9,10]. Significantly, [10] explores a self-training-based approach using a pre-trained language model in zero and few-shot scenarios to improve performance on low-resource datasets in the context of Arabic sequence labeling by using a language model fine-tuned on labeled Modern Standard Arabic (MSA) to predict a large amount of unlabeled named entities (NE) and part-of-speech (POS) tags on several dialectal Arabic (DA) varieties. Similarly, [9] addresses the challenges of Arabic Named Entity Recognition (NER) using a semi-supervised deep learning approach. The authors propose a semi-supervised learning approach to train a BERT-based NER model and considers two datasets: labeled and semi-labeled (partially labeled). First, they train a BERT teacher model then they predict the labels of the non-labeled tokens of the partially labeled dataset using the trained BERT teacher model. Another study by [23] proposed a semi-supervised method for NER and Part-of-Speech (POS) tagging, leveraging a substantial amount of unlabeled data. Their research primarily focused on addressing the challenges of NER and POS tagging in low-resource languages. In addition, [27] explored a semi-supervised

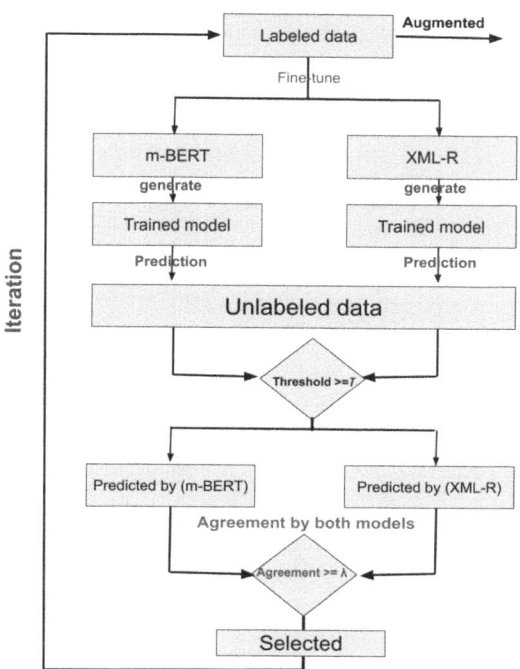

Fig. 1. Shows the proposed method augmenting using ensemble learning.

deep learning model for the NER of cultural relics. The model addresses the challenge of limited labeled data in the field of cultural relics by combining bidirectional long short-term memory (BiLSTM) and conditional random fields (CRF) models. It leverages both labeled and unlabeled data to achieve effective performance. Furthermore, authors in [14,26] proposed bootstrapping Named Entity Recognition data augmentation utilizing labeled and unlabeled datasets.

In contrast to our work, most existing semi-supervised learning methods in NER often depend on a single model, which may introduce errors and produce noisy predictions. Relying exclusively on one model to determine the model's weights can result in less accurate outcomes. Our work combines multiple state-of-the-art PLMs: [3,5,13,16] to leverage the collaboration of dual learning between two models to improve the data quality.

3   Proposed Methods

3.1   Semi-supervised Augmentation Using Ensemble Learning

This section proposes a novel semi-supervised bootstrapping method for NER. Our approach utilizes two pre-trained models: m-BERT [16] and XLM-RoBERTa [3] and jointly trains these models and exploits their predictions on unlabeled

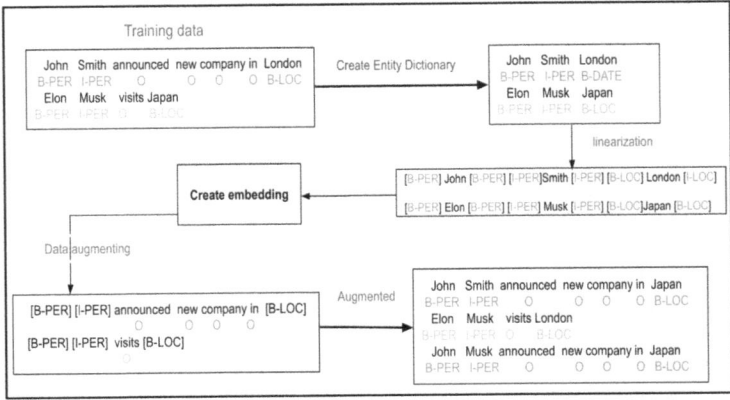

Fig. 2. Shows augmenting from embeddings.

data. Specifically, our method involves fine-tuning m-BERT and XLM-R on the small labeled data then utilized them to generate a weakly supervised augmented dataset. Tokens with high prediction confidence scores and high agreement between the two models (m-BERT & XLM-R) are selected and combined with the original labeled data to create the augmented dataset. Subsequently, we iteratively retrain the PLMs using the combined models to predict the remaining unlabeled data. The proposed pipeline is illustrated in Fig. 1 and formalized by Algorithm 1. Algorithm 1 depicts a single iteration of our method, providing an outline of the process for one loop.

Input and Output

- **Labeled data:** A set of Labeled data: $L\ (x_i, y_i)$, where x_i represents the input token and y_i represents the corresponding entity labels. This data is used to fine-tune XLM-R and m-BERT models initially.
- **Unlabeled data:** A set of unlabeled data: denoted as $U(x_j)$, where x_j is a token that does not have a corresponding label.
- **Threshold (τ):** A user-defined threshold τ is used to determine the prediction confidence level. Tokens with prediction confidence scores (e.g., $\geq \tau$) above this threshold are considered reliable.
- **Agreement threshold:** denoted as λ and it is used to check the agreement of predictions by both models (m-BERT and XLM-R).
- **Language models:** the algorithm uses two PLMs: m-BERT and XLM-R, denoted as Π_1, and Π_2 respectively.
  m-BERT: m-BERT is a pre-trained language model trained on the large Wikipedia content across 104 languages using masked language modeling (MLM). MLM involves randomly masking a subset of the words in a sentence and then having the model predict the masked words. Additionally, m-BERT uses a next-sentence prediction (NSP) approach during pretraining, where it

---

Algorithm 1. augmenting NER

Required: Labeled data: $L\ (x_i, y_i)$, Unlabeled data: $U(x_j)$, Threshold: τ. Agreement: λ, Language models: Π_1, Π_2

    Output: Augmented data D

1: **procedure**
2:    Train Π_1 and Π_2 on $L(x_i, y_i)$ to obtain trained models denoted as ϕ_1 & ϕ_2
3:    $P_1(x_j, y_j)$ = Predicted by ϕ_1 ▷ labeling the unlabeled data using trained (fine-tuned) models
4:    $P_2(x_j, y_j)$ = Predicted by ϕ_2
5:    $D \leftarrow \emptyset$
6:    **for** $P_1(x_j, y_j)$ & $P_2(x_j, y_j)$ **do**
7:        **if** $P_1(x_j, y_j) \geq \tau$ and $P_2(x_j, y_j) \geq \tau$ and **agreement by** ϕ_1 & $\phi_2 \geq \lambda$ **then**
8:            Add x_j, y_j to $D(x_j, y_j)$
9:        **end if**
10:      Combine $D(x_j, y_j)$ & $L\ (x_i, y_i)$
11:      Retrain Π_1 & Π_2 with D ▷ retrain the language models using combined (original labeled & the augmented data)
12:    **end for**
13:    **return** *Augmented data D*
14: **end procedure**

---

concatenates two masked sentences as input and learns to predict whether they actually followed each other. m-BERT has two models: the base and large model; we used the base model. [16]

XLM-R: is pre-trained on 2.5TB filtered CommonCrawl data containing 100 languages using Masked Language Modeling (MLM) task, where the model replaces 15% of the tokens with [MASK], then learns to predict the original masked word. XLM-R has two models: the base and large model. For our task, we used the XLM-R-base model.

– **Output:** The desired output of the algorithm is augmented data, which is a combination of the original labeled and the newly labeled (predicted) denoted as D.

Model Training (Fine-Tuning): The first step of our method involves fine-tuning Π_1 and Π_2 on the labeled data, denoted as L, which consists of pairs (x_i, y_i). In this step, both Π_1 and Π_2 are fine-tuned for a fixed number of epochs. After fine-tuning, we obtain the trained weights, denoted as ϕ_1 and ϕ_2.

NER-Based Labeling of the Unlabeled Data: Using the fine-tuned models weights ϕ_1 and ϕ_2, we predict the named entities for the unlabeled data: $U(x_j)$. Then we obtain the predictions made by ϕ_1 denoted as $P_1(x_j, y_j)$, and the predictions made by ϕ_2 are denoted as $P_2(x_j, y_j)$, hence x_j is the token and y_j is the predicted entity label.

Selection: Selection is based on confidence scores and agreement between the models. Firstly, we compute the confidence score for the predictions made by

ϕ_1 and ϕ_2. For each unlabeled instance x_j in the unlabeled data U, we compute the confidence scores for the predictions made by ϕ_1 and ϕ_2, denoted as $P_1(x_j, y_j)$ and $P_2(x_j, y_j)$, respectively. These confidence scores represent the predicted probabilities of the entity labels given the input x_j. For the predictions of $P_1(x_j, y_j)$ and $P_2(x_j, y_j)$, we check if both confidence scores are $\geq (\tau = 0.90)$, indicating a high confidence level in the predictions. Subsequently, we compute the agreement between ϕ_1 and ϕ_2 for the prediction of x_j. The agreement is measured by comparing the predictions of ϕ_1 and ϕ_2. If the agreement of ϕ_1 & ϕ_2 is $\geq$ to ($\lambda = 0.95$), indicating a high level of agreement between the models, we consider the prediction for x_j to be reliable. In such cases, we add the pair (x_j, y_j), representing the input token x_j and its corresponding predicted entity label y_j, to the set of augmented examples, denoted as $D(x_j, y_j)$. The use of confidence scores and the notion of agreement between ϕ_1 and ϕ_2 serves as essential purpose within the proposed method. It allows the identification of tokens for which both models demonstrate high confidence in their predictions and indicate an agreement with each other. This agreement ensures that any possible error or uncertainty in the predictions made by either one of the models is minimized. To enhance data quality, we select high-confidence instances with an agreement threshold, reducing incorrect predictions in the augmented data. Finally, we add the original Labeled data: L (x_i, y_i), and the selected tokens from the new predictions based on the unlabeled data, $D(x_j, y_j)$ and create D. Once the augmented data is constructed, the algorithm proceeds to retrain Π_1 and Π_2 using the augmented dataset D.

3.2   Embedding-Based Data Augmentation

The proposed method involves three key procedures as follows:

(i) Dictionary Creation: initiates by constructing a named entity dictionary by extracting named entities and their corresponding labels from the training sentences.

(ii) Embedding Creation: where for each entity token, we incorporate label linearization to consider label information explicitly. As shown in Fig. 2, the dictionary contains entities like 'John,' 'Smith,' and 'London.' In the embedding creation process, we incorporate the token labels as: *'[B-PER]John[B-PER] [I-PER]Smith[I-PER] [B-LOC]London[B-LOC]'*. After this process, we proceed to train a Word2Vec embedding model.

(iii) Augmentation: begins by removing entity tokens from the sentences while retaining the labels, resulting in a format as: *'[B-PER][I-PER] was [B-LOC]'*. Subsequently, we replace the same label with a different entity word from the trained word embedding during augmentation. This results in augmented sentences as: *'Elon Musk visits London'*. This approach ensures that label information is preserved, eliminates misalignment issues, and creates novel sentences.

4   Experimental Evaluation

This section presents the experimental evaluation of the proposed method with two directly comparable existing methods. F1-score is our primary evaluation metric. All experiments presented are the average results of 10 runs, where each run involves a random selection of test/train data.

4.1   Experimental Settings

We considered two methods as our baseline: [10,27]. The paper by [10] proposes a self-training approach for NER, which aligns well with our study in semi-supervised learning. Their method leverages unlabeled data to improve NER performance, making it a suitable baseline approach and achieving a state-of-the-art result. Similarly, the work by [27] presents a semi-supervised NER using a deep learning technique.

(i) **Data generation:** all experiments were conducted using the same number of training data to ensure a fair comparison. While the number of samples generated by our method differs from those generated by the two methods we compare against, we ensured consistency by randomly removing samples from the larger augmented dataset. This way, we maintained an identical training data size when comparing the models.

(ii) **Hyper-parameters:** learning rate is $2e-5$; optimizer is Adam; and number of epochs is 30.

Table 1. Summary of the languages [1]

Language	Family	Speaker	Region
Amharic (Amh)	Afro-Asiatic-Ethio-Semitic	33M	East
Hausa (Hau)	Afro-Asiatic-Chadic	63M	West
Igbo (Ibo)	Niger-Congo-Volta-Niger	27	West
Kinyarwanda (Kin)	Niger-Congo-Bantu	12M	East
Nigerian-Pidgin (Pcm)	English Creole	75M	West
Swahili (Swa)	Niger-Congo-Bantu	98M	Central & East
Yoruba (You)	Niger-Congo-Volta-Niger	42M	West

(iii) **Dataset:** we conduct experiments on seven low-resource languages widely spoken in different parts of Africa. Table 1 summarizes the languages, families, number of speakers, and regions in Africa similarly, Fig. 3 shows the characteristics of the languages. The datasets was introduced by [1] and contains five classes: *(PER, LOC, ORG, DATE and O)*. **PER:** person's name including first name, middle name, and last name. **LOC:** includes all country, region, state, and city names. **ORG:** includes any type of organization, for example sports teams, political parties, etc. **DATE:** denotes a particular segment of date, i.e., a particular day, season, final quarter, decade, etc. Finally, **O:** (other) is used for tokens that do not represent a named entity.

Amharic (Amh):	Hausa (Hau):	Igbo (Ibo):	Kinyarwanda (Kin):	NigerianPidgin (Pcm):	Swahili (Swa):	Yoruba (Yor):
uses the Fidel script consisting of 33 each of them with at least 7 vowel sequences (such as ሀ (hä) ሁ (hu) ሂ (hī) ሃ (ha) ሄ (hē) ህ (hi) ሆ (ho)). This results in more than 231 characters. Numbers and punctuation marks are also represented uniquely (፩ (1), ፪ (2), ... and ። (.), ፤(!), ፣ (;),).	has 23-25 consonants, depending on the dialect and five short and long vowels. Hausa has labialized phonemic consonants, as in /gw/ e.g. 'agwagwa.' consonants also exist in Hausa, e.g. 'b, 'd, etc as in 'barna'.	the alphabet consists of 28 consonants and 8 vowels (A, E, I, I, O, Ọ, U, Ụ). In addition to the Latin letters (except c), Igbo contains the following digraphs: (ch, gb, gh, gw, kp, kw, nw, ny, sh).	use of 24 Latin characters with 5 vowels like English and 19 consonants excluding q and x. Moreover, it has 74 additional consonants (such as mb, mpw, and njyw).	is a largely oral, national lingual franca with a distinct phonology from English, its lexifier language. Portuguese, French, and especially indigenous languages form the substrate of lexical, phonological, syntactic, and semantic influence on Nigerian-Pidgin (NP).	It has 30 letters including 24 Latin letters without characters (q and x) and six additional consonants (ch, dh, gh, ng', sh, th) unique to Swahili pronunciation	has 25 Latin letters without the Latin characters (c, q, v, x and z) and with additional letters (ẹ, gb, s ̣, ọ). Yorùbá is a tonal language with three tones: low ("\"), middle ("-", optional) and high ("/").

Fig. 3. Overview of the Language characteristics [1]

(iv) Classifiers: We consider XLM-R (Vanilla) as explained in Sect. 3.1 and its variant language models as our main classifiers for and are available on hugging-face[1]. We give summary of the classifiers below:

(A) Afro-XLMR-base: was created by MLM adaptation of XLM-R-base model on 17 African languages (Afrikaans, Amharic, Hausa, Igbo, Malagasy, Chichewa, Oromo, Naija, Kinyarwanda, Kirundi, Shona, Somali, Sesotho, Swahili, isiXhosa, Yoruba, and isiZulu) covering the major African language families and three high resource languages (Arabic, French, and English).

(B) XLM-R (Fine-tuned): is a variant of the XLM-R-base model that has been adapted through MLM separately on each language, namely Amharic, Hausa, and Igbo, Kinyarwanda, Nigerian-Pidgin, Swahili, and Yoruba. This adaptation process involves training the XLM-R-base model on large amounts of unlabeled data for each language.

4.2 Experimental Results

Semi-supervised Augmentation Using Ensemble Learning: Our study presents results using a confidence score threshold of 90% and an agreement measurement of 95%. We conducted investigations with different settings, exploring alternative confidence score thresholds (such as 85% and 95%) as well as varying agreement measurements (such as 85% and 90%). However, our findings indicate that combining a confidence score threshold of 90% with an agreement measurement threshold of 95 yielded the best results, and hence we report our results using this specific combination. Additionally, we compared our approach with two comparable methods, and to ensure a fair evaluation, we conducted experiments based on the settings described in their research papers.

---

[1] https://huggingface.co/.

– **Mono-lingual:** In Table 2, we conducted initial experiments using the XLM-R vanilla model. Our method consistently outperformed the other baselines, yielding the highest average results across various low-resource languages, except Kinyarwanda. Compared to the best-performing baseline, our approach demonstrated improvements, achieving gains ranging from 1.59% to 4.51% points of the F1 score. Furthermore, Table 2 presents the performance of our method compared to the baselines on Afro-XLMR-base and the fine-tuned version of XLM-R. In the experiments conducted with Afro-XLMR-base, our approach achieved an average gain of 1.69% to 3.39% in F1-score compared to the baselines. Similarly, when using the fine-tuned version of XLM-R, our method reveals improvements of 1.2% to 4.4% in average F1-score over the best-performing baseline method. To this end the proposed method consistently outperformed the baselines across all classifiers in the monolingual experiments. This can be due to our approach utilizing two state-of-the-art PLMs and selecting high-quality data based on the agreement between the two models for training NER.

– **Zero-shot Cross-lingual:** In zero-shot cross-lingual experiments, we tested language X using a model trained on language Y and vice versa. We conducted a pairwise zero-shot experiment in all languages except for Amharic, as its writing system differs from others (see Fig. 3). All experiments are conducted with the Afro-XLMR-base base model using the data generated with our method. We present the results of our experiments in Fig. 4 using box plots.

– **Multi-lingual:** In the multilingual settings, we combined the available generated data from each language to create a multilingual dataset. This dataset was then used to train our NER models, and we evaluated the performance in each language except for Amharic. Amharic stands out from the other languages due to its different writing system, which differs significantly from the alphabetic systems used in the other languages. Combining Amharic with other languages would introduce noise and make the training process less effective. To provide a comprehensive overview of the writing systems used in each language, we included a summary in Fig. 3. We used Afro-XLMR-base as our classifier due to its suitability for our study. This model was specifically fine-tuned on an extensive unlabeled dataset and encompassed 17 languages, including all the languages considered in our study. We report the F1 score in Table 3. Thus, our method outperformed the baselines in all languages except for Yoruba improving by up to 4% of the F1 score gain. In Table 3, the last row presents an experiment where we used the combined data for training, and we also combined all the testing data from each language except Amharic into one test set, then tested it as a single multilingual test set. Furthermore, we observed that our and comparable methods performed better in the multi-lingual setting than in the mono-lingual experiments, as shown in Table 2. This is because combining multiple languages creates a rich linguistic resource where each language benefits from the others.

Table 2. Average ten runs of mono-lingual setting experimented with XLM-R-Base(Vanilla), XLM-R -Afro, XLM-R -fine-tuned.

Language	XLM-R -vanilla			XLM-R -Afro			XLM-R -fine-tuned		
	[10]	[27]	Ours	[10]	[27]	Ours	[10]	[27]	Ours
Amh	63.83	59.84	**65.42**	65.54	62.50	**68.63**	69.65	68.18	**73.02**
Hau	76.85	73.94	**78.87**	77.80	72.44	**81.49**	80.79	76.25	**84.08**
Ibo	69.97	62.97	**74.48**	76.58	73.41	**78.63**	79.75	74.55	**82.17**
Kin	**60.07**	55.36	58.82	**70.25**	66.88	70.18	**70.92**	56.35	70.06
Pcm	75.58	60.56	**78.09**	78.77	75.45	**80.62**	-	-	-
Swa	77.71	73.37	**79.36**	80.54	73.52	**82.23**	81.94	74.44	**83.14**
Yor	57.66	54.23	**59.29**	65.21	60.30	**67.37**	65.23	60.25	**69.63**

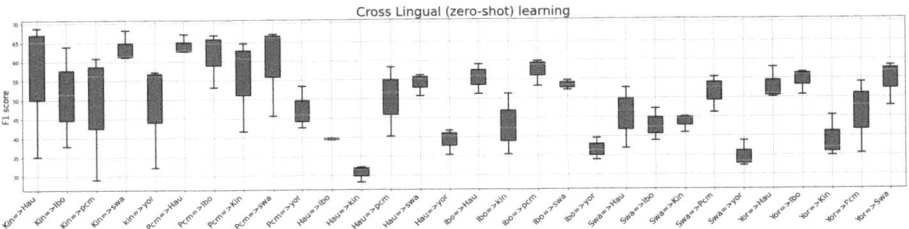

Fig. 4. Box-plots of F1-score (10 runs) cross-lingual (zero-shot) learning.

4.3 Embedding-Based Data Augmentation

This section presents the results obtained by employing an embedding-based data augmentation method. We randomly extracted 100, 200, 400, and 800 sentences from the original training sample in this experiment. Then, we generated five additional examples for each of these selected sentences. The experiment was conducted in two variants: one without Linearization and the other with Linearization (our proposed method). These different settings were evaluated and compared, and the results are summarized in Table 4, representing the average of five runs. Table 4 shows that our method consistently enhances the performance of the NER model. The NER model consistently demonstrates improved performance when experimenting with linearization. This improvement can be due to the augmented data, which was generated with alignment and preserved labels, contributing significantly to enhanced model performance.

4.4 Error Analysis

In this section, we examined the errors in semi-supervised learning, as this paper mainly focuses on semi-supervised learning. Our analysis examines the errors made by ours and the comparable methods during the NER model training. To conduct this analysis, we operate in a multi-lingual setting and utilize the

Table 3. Average performance results of ten runs using the Afro-XLMR-base (Multilingual) model trained on combined data and tested on each language.

Language	[10]	[27]	Ours
Hau	85.41	82.89	**86.27**
Ibo	82.57	79.13	**83.48**
Kin	71.48	65.48	**74.07**
Pcm	80.96	75.33	**84.87**
Swa	82.60	78.47	**85.58**
Yor	**72.73**	69.02	72.56
Combined test	78.65	75.69	**81.04**

Table 4. Report the average results of five runs conducted on the XLM-R-Afro model.

Lang	without Linearization				with Linearization			
	#100	#200	#400	#800	#100	#200	#400	#800
Amh	40.24	57.49	56.82	58.66	46.53	58.27	62.43	67.42
Hau	57.37	73.46	81.04	82.92	71.52	80.25	82.42	84.21
Ibo	42.43	69.3	69.23	76.03	50.82	73.09	75.5	77.98
Kin	46.65	61.15	62.7	66.31	59.92	64.11	70.1	72.76
Pcm	46.52	65.37	71.47	78.22	55.07	66.18	70.42	80.21
Swa	58.39	75.57	79.48	81.82	73.36	78.4	81.88	83.22
Yor	38.55	53.29	60.08	69.13	44.14	61.76	61.2	67.2

Afro-XLMR-base as our classifier. We conducted experiments using combined data during our investigation and tested three languages: Hausa (Hau), Kinyarwanda (Kin), and Yoruba (Yor). Our evaluation shows that Hau was the best-performing language, while Kin and Yor performed relatively poorly. In Table 5, we generated confusion matrices to assess the performance of our method and the comparable methods. For the best-performing language, Hausa, our testing dataset consisted of 15,689 tokens. Out of these tokens, our method incorrectly predicted 318 tokens. Similarly, the [10,27] model had 343, 419 respectively, incorrect predictions.

Similarly, we identified Yor as the poor performer shown in Table 3 for our method, while Kin was selected as the poor performer for the comparable methods. When considering the language Hau, the testing tokens comprised 9,650 instances, out of which our method correctly predicted 9,315 tokens, while 335 tokens were predicted incorrectly. In the case of [10,27] on Kin, the testing dataset consisted of 6,955 tokens. The [10] method mispredicted 307 tokens, while the [27] method mispredicted 327 tokens. Furthermore, we observed that all methods encountered difficulties, and most errors came from the O tag. For

Table 5. Confusion Matrix: The number of test tokens used for the poor performers, Kin and Yor, differs in number. For Kin, there were 6,955 test tokens; for Yor, there were 9,650 test tokens.

Ours										
	Best Performing (Hau)					Poor Performing (Yor)				
	O	ORG	PER	LOC	DATE	O	ORG	PER	LOC	DATE
O	13804	49	10	13	66	8374	21	12	68	45
ORG	63	215	6	6	0	69	120	6	18	0
PER	13	6	480	0	0	5	2	200	2	0
LOC	10	50	0	488	0	31	4	4	249	0
DATE	26	0	0	0	384	48	0	0	0	372
[10]										
	Best Performing (Hau)					Poor Performing (Kin)				
	O	ORG	PER	LOC	DATE	O	ORG	PER	LOC	DATE
O	13765	66	13	19	79	5828	151	9	37	24
ORG	60	225	0	5	0	7	248	0	5	0
PER	7	4	488	0	0	12	4	208	2	0
LOC	5	58	1	484	0	17	12	3	228	0
DATE	26	0	0	0	384	24	0	0	0	136
[27]										
	Best Performing (Hau)					Poor Performing (Kin)				
	O	ORG	PER	LOC	DATE	O	ORG	PER	LOC	DATE
O	13788	26	30	34	64	5952	36	11	30	20
ORG	94	170	10	16	0	68	189	6	7	0
PER	28	1	470	0	0	55	0	171	0	0
LOC	31	34	0	481	2	46	7	3	204	0
DATE	45	0	3	1	361	38	0	0	0	112

example, the O tag was misclassified as ORG, PER, LOC, DATE, and vice versa. These errors can be due to the variation or difference between the unlabeled data we collected and the labeled data used in this study [1].

5   Conclusion

This study proposes two data augmentation methods for NER task. The first method proposes a semi-supervised-based bootstrapping approach that ensembles the power of multiple state-of-the-art pre-trained language models (PLMs). It combines the outputs of two fine-tuned PLMs, improving data quality through confidence scores and agreement measurements. The second method involves NER dictionary creation and word embedding-based augmentation, enhancing dataset size. Experimental results demonstrate that our approach performs well in several African languages that, although low-resource for NER tasks, are widely spoken and represent a significant result. Our method potentially extends to more than two PLMs. However, it is currently limited to auto-encoder models, such as BERT and RoBERTa. In the future, we plan to extend our study and explore the integration of auto-regressive models, such as GPT-4, and sequence-to-sequence, such as BART.

Acknowledgement. This paper is based on results obtained from JST CREST Grant Number JPMJCR22M2 and JSPS KAKENHI Grant Number JP23K24949.

References

1. Adelani, D.I., et al.: Masakhaner: named entity recognition for African languages. Trans. Assoc. Comput. Linguist. **9**, 1116–1131 (2021)
2. Chen, H., Yuan, S., Zhang, X.: Rose-NER: robust semi-supervised named entity recognition on insufficient labeled data. In: Proceedings of the 10th International Joint Conference on Knowledge Graphs, pp. 38–44 (2021)
3. Conneau, A., et al.: Unsupervised cross-lingual representation learning at scale. arXiv preprint arXiv:1911.02116 (2019)
4. Dai, X., Adel, H.: An analysis of simple data augmentation for named entity recognition. arXiv preprint arXiv:2010.11683 (2020)
5. Devlin, J., Chang, M.W., Lee, K., Toutanova, K.: BERT: pre-training of deep bidirectional transformers for language understanding. arXiv preprint arXiv:1810.04805 (2018)
6. Ding, B., et al.: Daga: data augmentation with a generation approach for low-resource tagging tasks. arXiv preprint arXiv:2011.01549 (2020)
7. Fadaee, M., Bisazza, A., Monz, C.: Data augmentation for low-resource neural machine translation. arXiv preprint arXiv:1705.00440 (2017)
8. Hailemariam, M.Y., Lynden, S., Matono, A., Amagasa, T.: Self-attention-based data augmentation method for text classification. In: Proceedings of the 2023 15th International Conference on Machine Learning and Computing, pp. 239–244 (2023)
9. Helwe, C., Dib, G., Shamas, M., Elbassuoni, S.: A semi-supervised BERT approach for Arabic named entity recognition. In: Proceedings of the Fifth Arabic Natural Language Processing Workshop, pp. 49–57 (2020)
10. Khalifa, M., Abdul-Mageed, M., Shaalan, K.: Self-training pre-trained language models for zero-and few-shot multi-dialectal Arabic sequence labeling. arXiv preprint arXiv:2101.04758 (2021)
11. Liu, L., et al.: A semi-supervised approach for extracting TCM clinical terms based on feature words. BMC Med. Inform. Decis. Mak. **20**(3), 1–7 (2020)
12. Liu, Y., et al.: Multilingual denoising pre-training for neural machine translation. Trans. Assoc. Comput. Linguist. **8**, 726–742 (2020)
13. Liu, Y., et al.: RoBERTa: a robustly optimized BERT pretraining approach. arXiv preprint arXiv:1907.11692 (2019)
14. Mathew, J., Fakhraei, S., Ambite, J.L.: Biomedical named entity recognition via reference-set augmented bootstrapping. arXiv preprint arXiv:1906.00282 (2019)
15. Mitchell, A., Strassel, S., Huang, S., Zakhary, R.: ACE 2004 multilingual training corpus. Linguist. Data Consortium, Philadelphia **1**, 1–1 (2005)

16. Pires, T., Schlinger, E., Garrette, D.: How multilingual is multilingual BERT? arXiv preprint arXiv:1906.01502 (2019)
17. Sam, R.C., Le, H.T., Nguyen, T.T., Nguyen, T.H.: Combining proper name-coreference with conditional random fields for semi-supervised named entity recognition in Vietnamese text. In: Huang, J.Z., Cao, L., Srivastava, J. (eds.) PAKDD 2011. LNCS (LNAI), vol. 6634, pp. 512–524. Springer, Heidelberg (2011). https://doi.org/10.1007/978-3-642-20841-6_42
18. Sang, E.F., De Meulder, F.: Introduction to the CONLL-2003 shared task: language-independent named entity recognition. arXiv preprint cs/0306050 (2003)
19. Sennrich, R., Haddow, B., Birch, A.: Improving neural machine translation models with monolingual data. In: Proceedings of the 54th Annual Meeting of the Association for Computational Linguistics (Volume 1: Long Papers), pp. 86–96 (2016)
20. Tedeschi, S., Navigli, R.: Multinerd: a multilingual, multi-genre and fine-grained dataset for named entity recognition (and disambiguation). In: Findings of the Association for Computational Linguistics: NAACL 2022, pp. 801–812 (2022)
21. Weischedel, R., et al.: Ontonotes release 5.0 ldc2013t19. Linguist. Data Consortium, Philadelphia, PA **23**, 170 (2013)
22. Yao, L., Sun, C., Wang, X., Wang, X.: Combining self learning and active learning for Chinese named entity recognition. J. Softw. **5**(5), 530–537 (2010)
23. Yohannes, H.M., Amagasa, T.: A method of named entity recognition for Tigrinya. ACM SIGAPP Appl. Comput. Rev. **22**(3), 56–68 (2022)
24. Yohannes, H.M., Amagasa, T.: Named-entity recognition for a low-resource language using pre-trained language model. In: Proceedings of the 37th ACM/SIGAPP Symposium on Applied Computing, pp. 837–844 (2022)
25. Yohannes, H.M., Amagasa, T.: A scheme for news article classification in a low-resource language. In: Pardede, E., Delir Haghighi, P., Khalil, I., Kotsis, G. (eds.) iiWAS 2022. LNCS, vol. 13635, pp. 519–530. Springer, Cham (2022). https://doi.org/10.1007/978-3-031-21047-1_47
26. Zhang, H., Hennig, L., Alt, C., Hu, C., Meng, Y., Wang, C.: Bootstrapping named entity recognition in e-commerce with positive unlabeled learning. arXiv preprint arXiv:2005.11075 (2020)
27. Zhang, M., Geng, G., Chen, J.: Semi-supervised bidirectional long short-term memory and conditional random fields model for named-entity recognition using embeddings from language models representations. Entropy **22**(2), 252 (2020)
28. Zhou, R., et al.: MELM: data augmentation with masked entity language modeling for low-resource NER. arXiv preprint arXiv:2108.13655 (2021)

Improved Models for Media Bias Detection and Subcategorization

Tim Menzner[1(✉)] and Jochen L. Leidner[1,2]

[1] Information Access Research Group, Coburg University of Applied Sciences,
Friedrich-Streib-Straße 2, 96459 Coburg, Germany
tim.menzner@hs-coburg.de, leidner@acm.org
[2] Department of Computer Science, University of Sheffield,
Regents Court, 211 Portobello, Sheffield S1 4DP, UK

Abstract. We present improved models for the granular detection and sub-classification news media bias in English news articles. We compare the performance of zero-shot versus fine-tuned large pre-trained neural transformer language models, explore how the level of detail of the classes affects performance on a novel taxonomy of 27 news bias-types, and demonstrate how using synthetically generated example data can be used to improve quality.

Keywords: media bias · propaganda detection · content quality · news analysis · metadata enrichment · natural language processing

1 Introduction

Unbiased, trusted news reporting is crucial for sustaining democratic political systems, yet news media are exposed to manipulation leading to news bias from the outside (propaganda) as well as the inside (agenda of the owners of a news medium). This paper is part of a line of work researching questions of to what degree and how computers can automatically detect instances of news media bias and categorize them into sub-classes. Any model of bias capable of this ought to be enormously valuable, since its use as a predictive device can assist humans by alerting them to instances of bias in reporting.

Media bias can be described as the tendency to, consciously or unconsciously, report a news story in a way that supports a pre-existing narrative instead of providing unprejudiced coverage of an issue. In contrast, "[p]ropaganda is neutrally defined as a systematic form of purposeful persuasion that attempts to influence the emotions, attitudes, opinions, and actions of specified target audiences for ideological, political or commercial purposes through the controlled transmission of one-sided messages (which may or may not be factual) via mass and direct media channels." [15, pp. 232–233], so unlike bias, propaganda is always intentional. We are concerned particularly with media bias in English-language, online, written news here; while other languages are of equal importance (and, in

A. Rapp et al. (Eds.): NLDB 2024, LNCS 14762, pp. 181–196, 2024.
https://doi.org/10.1007/978-3-031-70239-6_13

practice, often neglected), English is commonly used as the benchmark language to compare NLP models for various tasks on, and resources such as annotated corpora are more readily available.

A range of authors – perhaps beginning with [9] – have addressed the news bias modeling question before (Sect. 2 below addresses related work), but since the availability of pre-trained neural transformer models (often just called "Large Language Models", LLMs), the quality of automated predictive models for NLP tasks has increased in general [4,22], and this has in turn led to better news bias models [7,14]. We will address a number of research questions, and aiming to answer them will help us improve our understanding of news bias modeling with neural transformers, which in turn will lead to better models.

Research Questions and Contributions. We address the following research questions:

RQ-1. *How does the level of detail of the categories impact the ability to identify instances of news bias?* News bias detection is already a difficult task for humans and machines, so having fine-grained sub-classes may be beyond the state of the art. On the other hand, more granular classes may help the classifier distinguish better between different cases.

RQ-2. *Can we find conditions on which LLM hallucination depends on?* Large language model hallucination is one of the key problems that prevent deployment in sensitive applications; any insights regarding their reduction is valuable.

RQ-3. *How do the largest zero shot models compare to fine-tuned models?* Traditionally, supervised models have been superior to unsupervised models; large, pre-trained transformers have tipped the scale towards training with raw text. Are carefully fine-tuned models superior to larger, non-fine tuned models?

RQ-4. *How does synthetic data augmentation help for improving the task?* Language models can be used to generate training data for additional training (fine-tuning). Can (and if so, how) can such data augmentation help to improve overall performance on the task of news media bias detection and sub-classification?

Our contributions are (i) answers to these research questions supported by detailed experimental evaluations on multiple datasets and (ii) a novel, very granular taxonomy of 27 news bias-types, and (iii) a set of new models for the improved detection and sub-categorization of news bias in English-language media.

2   Related Work

2.1   News Bias: The Phenomenon

A stage model to explain the arise of media bias during the news production process was proposed by Hamborg et al. [8]. The authors describe how bias can be introduced by several factors like the political views of news producers or the demand of a target audience during different steps like the information gathering and the writing. Martin et al. [11] investigated the impact of media bias on voting behavior and consumer preferences for news aligned with their own ideology, finding that additional weekly viewership of a channel can slightly increase the probability of intending to vote for the political side associated with its bias.

2.2 Automatic Identification of Bias in News

One of the first approaches of automatic news bias detection was described by Lin *et al.* [9]. Gentzkow et al. [6] compared phrases and words predominantly used by members of the US Congress of one political party with the language used in news media coverage to identify political bias. A combination of traditional NLP techniques and OpenAI Inc.'s GPT-4.0 was used by [2] to analyse topics discussed in cable news media and their respective stance towards it in order to provide a general assessment of its bias. The authors found that such a stance based approach was superior to a one solely focused on sentiment. Mancini et al. focused on multi-modal fallacy classification in political debates, which could be viewed as a specific sub-type of news bias [10]. Datasets for news bias on a sentence level as well as evaluation of detection approaches were provided by [5,21]. Recently, Nakov's research group [1,12] published a BERT based system to detect 18 different propaganda techniques in news articles, along with the respective annotated data set. While news bias is a broader phenomena than propaganda (as it also includes unintentional subjective reporting), both issues are related, as visible in the overlap of the identified propaganda techniques in this work and the bias-types discussed in ours.

2.3 Categorization of Different Types of Bias

Rodrigo-Ginés *et al.* [17] identified 17 different types of media bias, depending on context and intention, based on reviewing the existing literature. A more coarse-grained category inventory was given by [23], where 9 types of bias were used for the construction of their dataset. An overview with 16 identifies types of media bias and examples was presented by [13]. Most recently, [19] presented a list of common logical fallacies and cognitive biases, which arguably also play a role in reporting. Very related to bias is propaganda; Da San Martino *et al.* present a fine-grained taxonomy and classification model for detecting propaganda types that complements this work on bias [3].

3 Preliminaries

3.1 Bias Categorization

Media bias can be categorized into two types: visible bias within an article or sentence, and "Meta-Bias," which stems from the broader context. Examples of Meta-Bias include a news outlet's tendency to prioritize certain stories (known as "gatekeeping bias"), their placement, and their allotted space [8]. Detecting this kind of bias is hard as it requires a wider knowledge of context and publication history of an outlet. This paper concentrates on detecting sentence-level bias, which occurs within individual sentences. Building upon related work and interacting and experimenting with sentence categorization using GPT, along with our own observations, we identified 27 types of bias as follows:

Ad Hominem Bias targeting the human (the character, motives, or other attributes of the one making the argument) rather than the argument itself

Ambiguous Attribution Bias a position is broadly attributed to a wide, unspecified group such as "experts", "economists", or "politicians", rather than to identified individuals/sources

Anecdotal Evidence Bias relying on individual stories or examples rather than considering broader, more representative evidence

Causal Misunderstanding Bias a cause-and-effect relationship between two variables is misunderstood or assumed without sufficient evidence or considering other factors

Cherry Picking Bias giving undue prominence to aspects of a news story that endorses a certain viewpoint while omitting information that would contest it

Circular Reasoning Bias the conclusion of a statement or argument is used as its own justification

Commercial Bias emphasizing or promoting certain products, services, or narratives due to underlying commercial interest

Discriminatory Bias promoting stereotypes, generalized or prejudiced statements and unequal representation, reinforcing discrimination against certain individuals or groups, often based on ethnicity, culture, nationality, social background, gender, sexual orientation, or religious beliefs

Emotional Sensationalism Bias using hyperbolic or provocative language designed to evoke (strong) emotions, usually at the expense of accuracy or context while often focusing predominantly on negative events, aspects, or interpretations

External Validation Bias deeming something valid or true simply because it is supported by an authority figure or because it aligns with the beliefs or actions of a large group of people

False Balance Bias presenting opposing viewpoints as equally credible or significant, despite a clear consensus or evidence favoring one side

False Dichotomy Bias presenting a complex issue as leaving only two opposing decision alternatives when there might be further possible solutions/positions/outcomes

Faulty Analogy Bias drawing comparisons between two things that may share superficial similarities but are fundamentally different

Generalization Bias extrapolating characteristics of a specific subset to a larger group, or conversely, attributing broad characteristics of a group to each of its individual members

Insinuative Questioning Bias posing suggestive questions that contain implicit assumptions or lead the audience towards a pre-conceived notion, often used to promulgate subjective beliefs or doubts under the pretense of neutral inquiry

Intergroup Bias dividing people into two groups with one group (often an in-group to which the writer or publication belongs or identifies with) and portraying one as positive, while a second group, the out-group, is attributed negative characteristics and seen as adversarial

Mud Praise Bias using personal attacks, rumors, or unfounded allegations to damage the reputation of an individual or a group, or the opposite tendency to excessively praise or idealize them without regard for objective assessment

Opinionated Bias including subjective material, but portrayed as objective reporting; obscuring the line between fact and personal perspective

Political Bias inclination towards a specific political party, ideology, or candidate, typically resulting in favoritism towards one side while disregarding or disparaging opposing viewpoints

Projection Bias attributing thoughts, feelings, motives, or intentions to others (be it individuals, groups, or entities) without sufficient evidence or direct statements to back such claims

Shifting Benchmark Bias changing an argument, e.g., in response to criticism, by excluding counterexamples or adjusting the criteria to maintain a certain outcome

Source Selection Bias citing sources that likely are themselves biased with respect to the topic

Speculation Bias speculating based on conjecture about situations or outcomes rather than relying on concrete facts and definitive evidence

Straw Man Bias misrepresenting/distorting an argument so as to make it easier to attack, e.g., by oversimplifying or exaggerating

Unsubstantiated Claims Bias presenting statements or assertions as factual without providing adequate evidence or references

Whataboutism Bias deflecting or responding to an accusation or problem by making a counter-accusation or raising a different issue, not addressing the original argument

Word Choice Bias words with inherent positive or negative connotations, euphemisms, dysphemisms, or strong adjectives are chosen, influencing perceptions and implying judgment about a subject

Different bias types often intertwine; for instance, Political Bias may coincide with Word Choice Bias and Opinionated Bias. They can be categorized together or separately based on desired precision. For example, Casual Misunderstanding Bias and False Dichotomy Bias could be seen as subsets of "Logical Fallacy Bias". Similarly, Casual Misunderstanding Bias might further branch into various types, such as confusing causation with correlation or falling into the Prevention Paradox (Rose, 1981). While all bias-types are detectable from single sentences alone, some like Cherry Picking Bias would benefit from further context. While it be can be obvious from a sentence alone, like solely emphasizing the positives of a highway project near a nature reserve, without addressing any environmental concerns, more intricate cases, such as selectively mentioning a protest without acknowledging a larger counter protest, necessitate specific event knowledge for identification.

Contrary to the assessment presented in [17], we further assume that media bias does not have to be intentional but can also be introduced subconsciously (in contrast, propaganda is never subconscious).

3.2 Bias Strengths

Bias is not necessarily a binary classification but could be described as a spectrum. A sentence may not be just biased or unbiased but be more biased or less biased. When a bias is subtle, it might be not so obvious too detect but could still influence a readers opinion. We therefore suggest rating the bias strength of a sentence on a scale from 0.0 (no bias at all) to 1.0 (very extreme bias).

3.3   Prompting

The media bias definition from Sect. 1 was used, along with the bias-types to develop a LLM prompt for bias detection. In order to improve results and provide a benchmark for the bias strengths, each bias-type was enhanced by providing two example sentences of different bias strengths. During testing, the substitution of the decimal numbers with descriptive words (such as negligible, noticeable or significant) was also tried, but as it did not appear to affect the model decision, the decision was made to stick with numbers. An example of a type definition with example sentences is given in Example 1:

Example 1. Examples for a bias-type definition used for prompting

Insinuative Questioning Bias: This is the practice of posing suggestive questions that contain implicit assumptions or lead the audience towards a preconceived notion, often used to promulgate subjective beliefs or doubts under the pretense of neutral inquiry.

Examples:

Moderate Bias Strength (0.6): "Does their community improvement plan also serve a political purpose for his campaign?"

High Bias Strength (0.9): "Isn't the so-called community improvement plan just a ploy by them to fool voters before the election?"

When formulating the example sentences, it was tried to avoid referencing specific real world issues or topics when possible, in order to not introduce any form of bias regarding those. We further applied known best practices, like asking the model to assume a role as an expert in media bias and describing the task (identifying, categorizing and rating biased sentences, providing an overall assessment and returning the results in JSON format) step by step [16].

4   Data

Two publicly available datasets where used for this paper. BABE [21] is based on MBIC [20] and includes an additional 2,000 sentences, resulting in a total number of 3700 from 14 different US news outlets. Unlike MBIC, where the labelling was done by pure crowd sourcing, all annotators for BABE had to meet certain criteria to prove a certain level of expertise. After removing the sentences where annotators could not reach an agreement, 1863 sentences labeled as non biased and 1810 labeled as bias remained in the dataset. The second dataset was BASIL [5], which contains 300 news articles about 100 different stories (from the New York Times, the Huffington Post and FOX News), with annotations for each sentence featured in each article. Of the total 7,984 sentences in the dataset, 1727 were labeled as biased and 6257 as unbiased. Next to this publicly available datasets, we also used synthetic data, generated with GPT-4.0, for fine-tuning. To our knowledge, there are no existing News Bias Datasets including a sufficient categorisation of bias-types and bias strengths.

5   Methods

5.1   Finetuning

We fine-tuned four different models based on gpt-3.5-turbo-1106, Two with a subset of BABE and BASIL, one with synthetic data (SYNT), and one with a combination of all three (MEGA) For BABE, BASIL and SYNT, 100 example articles were constructed from the respective data, with a randomly chosen length between 10 and 30 sentences. As BABE provides individual, disconnected sentences rather than complete articles, the sentences used for the fine-tune articles were randomly picked and joined together. For BASIL, which provides full articles, the fine-tune articles were based on snippets from the articles featured in the dataset. The synthetic articles were generated by GPT-4.0, with a random ratio of biased to unbiased sentences. The biased sentences were generated based on the type definitions and examples presented in Sect. 3.1, a random distribution of desired bias strengths and an even distribution of bias-types across all articles. The unbiased sentences were generated with the instruction to be of the same topic as the biased ones. Based on these articles, a JSON resembling the desired output was constructed. As BABE and BASIL do not include information about bias strength or bias-type, while those were needed for our fine-tuning format, the contents of these fields were generated by GPT-4.0. The articles, the desired output and the later to be used prompt were combined as user message, assistant message and system prompt to end up with three fine-tuning ready datasets. A fourth one (MEGA) was constructed by appending all three files to each other.

5.2   Experiments

We evaluated the models on BABE and BASIL. All sentences used in the fine-tuning process were removed from both datasets beforehand. As we also compared with a previous model [14] fine-tuned on 50 example articles with 10 sentences each constructed from the MBIC dataset, which is a subset of BABE, we also removed the sentences used here. At this point, it should be noted that, as this model was not fine-tuned with our prompt including the fine-grained bias-type definitions but with a prompt making use of coarser ones [23], we stuck to this prompt when evaluating this model. Because we could not rule out that single sentences from the synthetic fine-tune data were too close to sentences from one of the datasets, or that single sentences may have been modified by GPT-4-0 during the construction of the fine-tuning datasets, all removing was done via partial fuzzy string matching. In more detail, we used [18], which compares strings based on the Levenshtein distance, to check the partial ratio of each sentence from the dataset which each sentence included in any fine-tuning data, and removed it, when a certain threshold (80) was exceeded. After this,

BABE still included 1694 sentences, with an almost even split into 841 biased and 853 unbiased ones. BASIL, on the other hand, still included 4236 sentences, with a strong over representation of 3375 unbiased sentences compared to only 861 biased ones. Based on the datasets, articles with a randomly chosen length between 10 and 30 sentences were constructed as described in Sect. 5.1. However, for BASIL, it was not always possible to reach at least 10 sentences, as some of the shorter ones had been left with less than 10 sentences all together after removing the sentences used for fine-tuning. This was true in 33 cases, with an average length of 5.97 sentences for these articles. However, as the total number of affected sentences was rather low (only 4.6% of all evaluated sentences ended up being in a article with less than 10 sentences) and the effect of the article length on performance appears to be negligible (see Sect. 6), they were kept in the evaluation dataset. These articles were then passed to the model, together with the system prompt explained in Sect. 3.3, using a temperature of 0.15 to maintain rigidity while also allowing for some "creativity" in answers. The sentences marked as biased by the model were then again compared to the sentences marked as biased in the datasets with partial fuzzy string matching to calculate the number of true positives, false positives, false negatives and true negatives. The partial string matching was especially required as, in order to ensure a "realistic" scenario, where the model would scan an actual article from a newspaper, the articles were passed as plain, connected text. In practice, this could result in the model picking a different sentence separation for its analysis than the sentence separation in the annotation, e.g. (not) including a introductory statement like "he told reports" before a quote. Fixed string matching is not suitable to capture these instances, partial string matching (we used a threshold of 80, meaning a sentence marked as biased by the model needed to have a ratio greater than that with anyone of the sentences marked as biased in the dataset for this article) on the other hand can do this. However, it still can not be guaranteed that each of these instances could actually be captured, which could potentially influence results. Beside the fine-tuned models, GPT-3.5 and GPT-4.0 were also evaluated with prompting only. Finally, the quality of the type and strength assignment was evaluated using a manually enhanced sample from BABE and BASIL. As previous research [14] suggested a significant worse performance of currently available Open-Source LLMs compared to the commercial ones provided by OpenAI, they were not further evaluated for these experiments.

6   Evaluation

Table 1 shows the evaluation results on the BABE dataset. Overall, the fine-tuned models all outperformed the non fine-tuned GPT-3.5, with the models using a more fine-grained bias-type categorization in turn outperforming the one using a coarser one (FT MBIC). Among the fine-tuned models, FT BABE had the highest F1-score (76%), accuracy (75%) and precision (73%), while FT SYNT had the highest recall (89%). The model fine-tuned on the combined dataset also scored somewhere in the middle between the individual fine-tunes for each metric. The largest ultimate precision was achieved by GPT-4.0 (85%), leading FT BABE by 12%. However, as it trailed FT BABE by 16% regarding F1-Score, by 25% on Recall and it uses more energy, memory and comes with higher costs, FT BABE may be considered the better model overall, depending on priorities. Table 2 shows the evaluation results on the BASIL dataset for the same models. Overall, the fine-tuned models all outperformed the non fine-tuned GPT-3.5 on F1-score and recall, while having a worse accuracy and, with one exception (FT MEGA), precision. The fine-tuned models with the more fine-grained bias-type categorizations scored slightly better on average compared to the other fine-tune (FT MBIC) regarding accuracy (65% vs 62%), while scoring almost identically on F1-score (39% vs 40%) and precision (30% vs 29%). For recall, FT MBIC scored higher than the average of the other fine-tunes (59% vs 63%), which is in fact the highest score of all evaluated models on this dataset. Overall, GPT-4.0 appears to be the best model, achieving the highest F1-score (44%), precision (43%) and accuracy (77%). One thing clearly noticeable is the high number of false positives on this dataset, leading to rather low scores for f1 and precision, in line with the original BASIL paper [5], where the authors fine-tuned two BERT models for the detection of sentences exhibiting "lexical bias" (what they define as "bias stemming from content realization, or how things are said") and "informational bias" (defined as "sentences or clauses that convey information tangential, speculative, or as background to the main event in order to sway readers' opinions towards entities in the news."). Their lexical bias BERT achieved a precision of 29%, a recall of 39 % and a F1-score for 31%, while the BERT fine-tuned tasked to identify informational BIAS scored

Table 1. Evaluation Results on the BABE dataset for GPT-3.5-turbo-1106 fine-tuned on BABE, BASIL, Synthetic Data and a combination of all three (MEGA), a previous GPT-3.5 fine-tuned on MBIC, GPT-3.5-turbo-1106 with prompt only and GPT-4-turbo-0125. Best results are highlighted in bold.

Model	TP	FP	FN	TN	F1-Score	Recall	Precision	Accuracy
GPT-3.5 (FT BABE)	576	214	154	524	**0.758**	0.790	0.729	**0.749**
GPT-3.5 (FT BASIL)	443	212	287	526	0.640	0.606	0.677	0.660
GPT-3.5 (FT SYNT)	646	482	84	256	0.695	**0.885**	0.572	0.614
GPT-3.5 (FT MBIC)	484	203	246	535	0.683	0.663	0.704	0.694
GPT-3.5 (FT MEGA)	629	319	101	419	0.750	0.861	0.663	0.713
GPT-3.5	384	205	346	533	0.582	0.526	0.651	0.624
GPT-4.0	393	69	337	669	0.659	0.538	**0.850**	0.723
Baseline (Random)	362	374	368	364	0.494	0.496	0.492	0.495

Table 2. Evaluation Results on the BASIL dataset for GPT-3.5-turbo-1106 fine-tuned on BABE, BASIL, Synthetic Data and a combination of all three (MEGA), a previous GPT-3.5 fine-tuned on MBIC, GPT-3.5-turbo-1106 with prompt only and GPT-4-turbo-0125. Best results are highlighted in bold.

Model	TP	FP	FN	TN	F1-Score	Recall	Precision	Accuracy
GPT-3.5 (FT BABE)	469	1120	354	2187	0.389	0.570	0.295	0.643
GPT-3.5 (FT BASIL)	458	1043	365	2264	0.394	0.557	0.305	0.659
GPT-3.5 (FT SYNT)	496	1277	327	2030	0.382	0.602	0.280	0.612
GPT-3.5 (FT MBIC)	516	1276	307	2031	0.395	**0.627**	0.288	0.617
GPT-3.5 (FT MEGA)	501	1062	322	2245	0.412	0.609	0.320	0.664
GPT-3.5	295	654	528	2653	0.332	0.358	0.311	0.714
GPT-4.0	366	489	457	2818	**0.436**	0.445	**0.429**	**0.771**
Baseline (Random)	445	1853	378	1454	0.285	0.541	0.193	0.460

44% on precision, 43% on recall and also 43% on f1. While these results are not directly comparable to ours, due to differences in training and evaluation (e.g. the use of two different classifiers for two different categories, each trained on 6819 and evaluated on 400 sentences), their relative similarity to our results might indicate some general tendencies regarding BASIL. The subpar results for bias detection on this dataset may have several reasons, including differences in annotation practices. To gain further insights into the effect of the more fine-grained bias-type definitions on result quality, (comparing FT MBIC with the other fine-tunes alone is not enough as FT MBIC uses a different prompt, was fine-tuned on less articles and is based on gpt-3.5-turbo-0613 rather than on gpt-3.5-turbo-1106), another round of evaluation was conducted for the non fine-tuned GPT-3.5. This evaluation was identical to the previous one for GPT-3.5, the only difference was that the fine-grained bias-types definitions were swapped with the coarser ones. On BABE, this resulted in an accuracy of 58%, a precision of 60%, a recall of 47% and a F1-score of 53%, trailing the GPT-3.5 with the fine-grained type definitions on all four metrics. On BASIL, the results were 70% for accuracy, 31% for precision, 40% for recall and 35% for F1-score, outperforming the other GPT-3.5 on F1-score and recall while scoring lower for precision and accuracy. Table 3 shows the distribution of identified bias-types by the different models across both datasets. For the sake of readability and representation, only types which were identified more than 100 times by at least one model are included. The table further includes the Jensen-Shannon divergence between the distribution of identifies types and the distribution in the dataset used for fine-tuning as well as the average Jensen-Shannon divergence between the distribution of identifies types and the other two datasets (bias-types not included in the table were taken into account for the calculation). Overall, the bias-type distribution of the FT BABE results was the closest to its fine-tuning dataset with a JSD of 0.207. FT BABE also had the greatest difference (0.272) from this value to the average JSD between the distribution of identifies types and the other two individual datasets used for fine-tuning (0.479). The largest part of this difference can be attributed to the high JSD with the synthetically generated fine-tuning dataset, which was 0.688 compared to the JSD with the dataset based on BASIL, which was only 0.27. Overall, the synthetic fine-tune was responsible for the most chaotic results, among the fine-tuned models. This is firstly visible by the deviating results of FT SYNT, compared to those of FT BABE and FT BASIL, with its values often being outliers for a category. Furthermore, the JSD between the FT SYNT fine-tune dataset type distribution and the distribution of the FT SYNT evaluation results was much higher than the same comparison for FT BABE and FT BASIL, with a JSD of 0.520, which is only 0.034 smaller than the JSD with the two non synthetic datasets. So the model fine-tuned on the synthetic dataset did not only produce vastly different categorizations from the two models which were fine-tuned on non synthetic data (which were relatively close to each other), these categorisations are also vastly different to the ones given in the fine-tune dataset. It is also notable, that FT MEGA, despite being a combination of all three other datasets, was not merely the average between them and that the non fine-tuned GPT-3.5 was the greatest overall outlier among the models. Despite the instruction to stick to the provided list of bias-types, all models came up with some own. When excluding FT MBIC (which used other definitions) and those hallucinated types, which were chosen less than 3 times, the majority should was already covered by our definitions, like Religious Bias (7, Political), Omission Bias (6, Cherry Picking), False Analogy Bias (6, Faulty Analogy), Appeal to Authority Bias (4, External Validation) and Loaded Language Bias (3, Word Choice). In other cases, the models also came up with completely new types, like Irrelevant Information Bias (3) and Conspiracy Bias (3). Fine-tuning did not result in a decrease of type hallucinations, despite ensuring that the used datasets did not contain any. FT BABE named an own type in 11 instances, FT BASIL in 21 cases and FT SYNT did so 6 times (Interestingly enough, FT MEGA hallucinated an own type in 11 cases, which is the average of the three other FT models). For comparison, GPT 3.5 chose a new type in 3 cases and GPT-4.0 did so 9 times. To gain more insights on type detection, a random sample of BABE and BASIL was manually enhanced by us trough adding the bias-type and the bias strength. Sentences marked as non-biased were not modified in any way. This resulted in 133 biased sentences (21 from BASIL and 122 from BABE). The biased sentences were split across Word Choice (53), Political (25), Opinionated (10), Unsubstantiated Claims (8), Ambiguous Attribution (4), Cherry Picking (4), Emotional Sensationalism (4), Insinuative Questioning (4), Discriminatory (3), Projection (3), Whataboutism (3), Generalization (2), Intergroup (2), Anecdotal Evidence (1), Causal Misunderstanding (1), False Dichotomy (1), Faulty Analogy (1), Mud Praise (1 times), Source Selection (1), Speculation (1) and Straw Man Bias (1).

Table 3. Number of identified bias-types on BABE and BASIL for GPT-3.5-turbo-1106 fine-tuned on BABE, BASIL, Synthetic Data and a combination of all three (MEGA), GPT-3.5-turbo-1106 with prompt only and GPT-4-turbo-0125. The greatest outlier from the mean of a row is highlighted in bold. Last two rows show the Jensen-Shannon divergence between the distribution of identifies types and the distribution in the dataset used for fine-tuning as well as the average Jensen-Shannon divergence between the distribution of identifies types and the other two datasets. Average JSD is empty for FT MEGA as it is just a combination of the three individual datasets.

bias-type	FT BABE	FT BASIL	FT SYNT	FT MEGA	GPT-3.5	GPT-4.0
Ad Hominem	85	108	453	59	**456**	26
Ambiguous Attribution	2	38	60	3	**125**	7
Emotional Sensationalism	140	98	245	179	234	**72**
Opinionated	201	154	139	**434**	118	108
Political	47	484	**708**	246	5	36
Projection	9	108	**157**	56	2	30
Source Selection	12	84	**165**	44	18	8
Unsubstantiated Claims	22	**245**	21	43	18	38
Word Choice	916	519	188	973	**21**	775
JSD (Own FT)	0.207	0.304	0.520	0.315	-	-
Average JSD (Other FT)	0.479	0.475	0.554	-	-	-

Assuming the type distributions of this random sample are somewhat representative for the complete datasets, one might predict that FT BABE, FT MEGA and GPT-4.0 should reach the highest accuracy regarding type classification, as their distributions Sect. 3, (e.g. highest amount is respectively Word Choice Bias) are the most similar. This hypothesis is confirmed by the actual evaluation, presented in Sect. 4. Looking at the output of all models (with the exception of GPT-3.5 as its results were too close to random) combined and excluding types which were checked less than 12 times, the individual types with the highest accuracy were Word Choice Bias (61%), Emotional Sensationalism Bias (50%) and Discriminatory Bias (36%). The types with the lowest accuracy were Ambiguous Attribution Bias (0%), Projection Bias (0%) and Insinuative Questioning Bias (6%). Accordingly, the bias-types (among those rightfully detected at least 5 times) with the lowest average difference to the score assigned in the dataset were Emotional Sensationalism Bias (0.089), Political Bias (0.170) and Discriminatory Bias (0.260). Those with the highest average difference were Opinionated Bias (0.355), Unsubstantiated Claims (0.350) and Word Choice Bias (0.261). Fine-tuned models perform better with longer articles on the BABE dataset and worse on the BASIL dataset, with consistent relative differences compared to non-fine-tuned models across article lengths.

Table 4. Type detection accuracy and average difference in assigned scores on the manually annotated dataset for GPT-3.5-turbo-1106 fine-tuned on BABE, BASIL, Synthetic Data and a combination of all three (MEGA), GPT-3.5-turbo-1106 with prompt only and GPT-4-turbo-0125. Best results are highlighted in bold.

Model	Accuracy (Types)	Difference (Strengths)
GPT-3.5 (FT BABE)	0.377	0.244
GPT-3.5 (FT BASIL)	0.288	**0.223**
GPT-3.5 (FT SYNT)	0.223	0.249
GPT-3.5 (FT MEGA)	0.410	0.239
GPT-3.5	0.07	0.239
GPT-4.0	**0.453**	0.257
Baseline (Random)	0.045	0.308

In order to evaluate if it was possible to decrease the number of false positives based on bias strength scores, the average assigned bias strength was calculated for all true and false positives. All models on both datasets had average higher scores for their right positives than for their false positives. The largest such difference for BABE was achieved by FT SYNT (0.240), the smallest by FT BABE GPT-3.5 (0.074), with the mean being 0.115. On BASIL, it was also FT SYNT (0.142) with FT BABE having the smallest difference(0.031). The average here was 0.072. The larger average difference of BABE compared to BASIL could partly explain why there are so many false positives in the related evaluation. Furthermore, FT SYNT having the highest difference on both datasets could indicate that using (synthetic) data with an even spread of strengths for fine-tuning leads to more realistic relative strength assignments (not to be confused with absolute Table 4). To see if this could be used to improve performance, evaluation results were filtered to change the models decision to "unbiased" for all sentences that were initially marked as "biased" but were assigned a score below a certain threshold. The change for different metrics after applying this filter to the aggregated model classifications is shown in Fig. 1. The general trend was the same for both datasets. By filtering out those results with a low bias strength, precision was increased at the expense of recall. This further led to an initial decrease in F1-score and an initially increasing accuracy. Until the point where every sentence with a strength less than 0.5 was filtered out, the increase in accuracy was greater than the decrease in F1-score. Filtering can therefore be seen as a good strategy until this point. However after it, the F1-score started to decrease dramatically while the accuracy either only increased slightly before leveling out or also started to drop. Using a majority decision approach with all models on the BABE dataset yielded a higher F1-score (0.736) compared to the average individual scores (0.681), though still lower than the top-performing individual models, while for the BASIL dataset, the majority F1-score (0.405) was also higher than the average (0.391) but remained lower than the best individual models' scores. During the writing of this paper, Anthropic

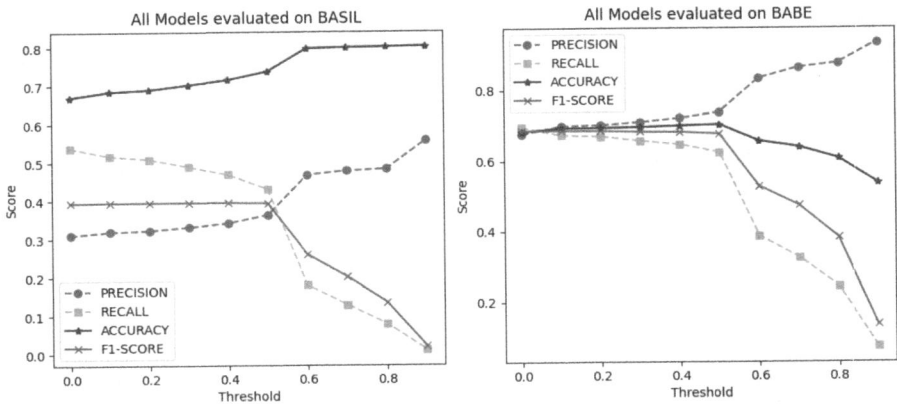

Fig. 1. Evaluation Metrics and Bias Strength Filtering

released their Claude 3 family, claiming better performance than GPT-4.0 on several benchmarks. While a detailed evaluation was out of scope for this paper, we tested their most powerful Opus model on a subset of BABE containing 148 unbiased and 163 biased sentences as well as a subset of BASIL with 191 unbiased and 50 biased sentences, to get a crude impression of its performance. On BABE, it achieved an accuracy of 71%, a precision of 85%, a recall of 55% and a F1-score of 66%. On BASIL, it was an accuracy of 78%, a precision of 47%, a recall of 36% and a F1-score of 41%. While these number would not point to improved capabilities over GPT-4 in terms of bias detection, anecdotal evidence suggests its textual explanations are better worded.

7   Limitations and Ethical Considerations

A generative model developed with the intention of detecting news media bias-types remains a generative model: in theory, an adversary could abuse our model to synthesize biased textual material. It should also be noted that bias detection is always, to an extent, a subjective matter. What is considered biased and what is not differs depending on who is asked (see the differences between both datasets), therefore no classification will probably ever satisfy everyone at once. Both datasets further had a bias regarding the discussed topics, in that they were very much centered around the US American political discourse. Considering that all used datasets were published early enough to be incorporated into the training data of all models, it remains a possibility that certain parts of them were included, even though none of the models were familiar with datasets with the respective name when queried.

8   Summary, Conclusions and Future Work

In this paper, we proposed a fine-grained taxonomy of 27 news bias-types and conducted detailed evaluations on the ability of LLMs to detect bias in news articles. Our experiments gave several insights and provided answers to our research questions:

RQ-1: Our evaluation generally implies a better performance of the models using the more fine-grained categorization than the one used a coarser one. This is true for the fine-tuned ones as well as when using prompt only.

RQ-2: Contrary to intuition, fine-tuning models with examples that contain the defined bias-types did not lead to fewer hallucinations but more, compared to the models that were not fine-tuned.

RQ-3: While the fine-tuned GPT-3.5 models performed notably better than their non fine-tuned counter part and some fine-tuned models outperformed/were on par with GPT-4.0 on BABE, GPT-4.0 proved to be the most consistent with its relatively good performance, when also accounting for BASIL. It also proved best in identifying the individual bias-types.

RQ-4: Using synthetic data for fine-tuning yielded better results than no fine-tuning at all, while not being too far behind the models fine-tuned on real data. Furthermore, the model fine-tuned on synthetic data differentiated best between right and false positives in terms of assigned bias strength.

Besides answering our four research questions, we also presented a novel taxonomy of 27 news bias-types. *We are not aware of any sentence-level English news bias detection/categorization model with higher accuracy.* In future work, we aim to develop models for other languages. We also plan to move towards multi-class classification, as our experience shows that classes often legitimately overlap. We plan to experiment with a hierarchical taxonomy of bias-types. Finally, we will migrate to open-source/open-data models.

Acknowledgments. The authors gratefully acknowledge the funding provided by the Free State of Bavaria ("Hitech Agenda Bavaria"). We would also like to thank Michael Reiche for annotation help, the MBICS team for sharing their dataset and three anonymous reviewers for feedback. All views are the authors' own.

References

1. Baly, R., et al.: We can detect your bias: Predicting the political ideology of news articles. In: Proceedings of the 2020 Conference on Empirical Methods in Natural Language Processing (EMNLP), pp. 4982–4991. ACL, Online (2020)
2. Benson, S.P., et al.: Developing a natural language understanding model to characterize cable news bias. IEEE Access **12**, 31798–31807 (2024)
3. Da San Martino, G., Yu, S., Barrón-Cedeño, A., Petrov, R., Nakov, P.: Fine-grained analysis of propaganda in news article. In: Inui, K., Jiang, J., Ng, V., Wan, X. (eds.) Proceedings of the 2019 Conference on Empirical Methods in Natural Language Processing and the 9th International Joint Conference on Natural Language Processing (EMNLP-IJCNLP), pp. 5636–5646. ACL, Hong Kong, China (2019)
4. Devlin, J., et al.: BERT: pre-training of deep bidirectional transformers for language understanding. In: Proceedings of the 2019 Conference of the North American Chapter of the Association for Computational Linguistics: Human Language Technologies, Volume 1 (Long and Short Papers), pp. 4171–4186. ACL (2019)

5. Fan, L., et al.: In plain sight: media bias through the lens of factual reporting. In: Proceedings of the 2019 EMNLP and the 9th IJNLP (EMNLP-IJCNLP), pp. 6343–6349. ACL (2019)
6. Gentzkow, M., et al.: What drives media slant? Evidence from U.S. daily newspapers. Econometrica **78**(1), 35–71 (2010). http://www.jstor.org/stable/25621396
7. Hamborg, F.: Revealing Media Bias in News Articles NLP Techniques for Automated Frame Analysis. Springer, Cham (2023). https://doi.org/10.1007/978-3-031-17693-7
8. Hamborg, F., et al.: Automated identification of media bias in news articles: an interdisciplinary literature review. Int. J. Digit. Libr. **20**(4), 391–415 (2018)
9. Lin, W.H., et al.: Which side are you on? Identifying perspectives at the document and sentence levels. In: Proceedings of the Tenth Conference on Computational Natural Language Learning (CoNLL-X), pp. 109–116. ACL (2006)
10. Mancini, E., et al.: Multimodal fallacy classification in political debates. In: Proceedings of the 18th Conference of the European Chapter of the Association for Computational Linguistics (Volume 2: Short Papers), pp. 170–178. ACL (2024)
11. Martin, G.J., Yurukoglu, A.: Bias in cable news: persuasion and polarization. Am. Econ. Rev. **107**(9), 2565–2599 (2017)
12. Martino, G.D.S., et al.: Fine-grained analysis of propaganda in news articles (2019)
13. Mastrine, J.: 11 Types of Media Bias (2019). https://www.allsides.com/sites/default/files/11%20Types%20of%20Media%20Bias-AllSides.pdf
14. Menzner, T., Leidner, J.L.: Experiments in news bias detection with pre-trained neural transformers. In: Goharian, N., et al. (eds.) ECIR 2024. LNCS, vol. 14611, pp. 270–284. Springer, Cham (2024). https://doi.org/10.1007/978-3-031-56066-8_22
15. Nelson, R.A.: A Chronology and Glossary of Propaganda in the United States. Greenwood Press, Westport (1996)
16. OpenAI: GPT best practices (2023). https://platform.openai.com/docs/guides/gpt-best-practices
17. Rodrigo-Ginés, F.J., et al.: A systematic review on media bias detection: what is media bias, how it is expressed, and how to detect it. Expert Syst. Appl. **237**, 121641 (2024)
18. SeatGeek Inc.: fuzzywuzzy: Fuzzy String Matching in Python (2014). https://github.com/seatgeek/fuzzywuzzy
19. Silfwer, J.: 58 logical fallacies and cognitive biases (2020). https://doctorspin.org/science/psychology/logical-fallacies/
20. Spinde, T., et al.: MBIC – a media bias annotation dataset including annotator characteristics. In: Proceedings of the iConference 2021 (2021)
21. Spinde, T., et al.: Neural media bias detection using distant supervision with BABE - bias annotations by experts. In: Findings of EMNLP 2021, pp. 1166–1177. ACL (2021)
22. Vaswani, A., et al.: Attention is all you need. In: Proceedings of NeurIPS (2017)
23. Wessel, M., et al.: Introducing MBIB – the first media bias identification benchmark task and dataset collection. In: Proceedings of SIGIR, pp. 2765–2774. ACM (2023)

Grounding Toxicity in Real-World Events Across Languages

Wondimagegnhue Tsegaye Tufa$^{(\boxtimes)}$, Ilia Markov, and Piek Vossen

Vrije Universiteit Amsterdam,
De Boelelaan 1105, 1081 HV Amsterdam, The Netherlands
{w.t.tufa,i.markov,p.t.j.m.vossen}@vu.nl

Abstract. Social media conversations frequently suffer from toxicity, creating significant issues for users, moderators, and entire communities. Events in the real world, like elections or conflicts, can initiate and escalate toxic behavior online. Our study investigates how real-world events influence the origin and spread of toxicity in online discussions across various languages and communities. We gathered Reddit data comprising 4.5 million comments from 31 thousand posts in six different languages (Dutch, English, German, Arabic, Turkish, and Spanish) We target fifteen major social and political world events that occurred between 2020 and 2023. We observed significant variations in toxicity, negative sentiment, and emotion expressions across different events and language communities, showing that toxicity is a complex phenomenon in which many different factors interact and still need to be investigated. We released the data and code for further research (https://github.com/cltl/grounding-toxicity).

Keywords: Toxicity analysis · World events · Cross-lingual analysis

1 Introduction

Social media platforms have experienced significant growth in their user base and importance as communication tools. They provide a space where individuals can freely express various opinions. This openness and accessibility lead to a diverse mix of content, from insightful and valuable perspectives to controversial or even offensive content [7,15].

Significant real-world events, including GamerGate in August 2014, the murder of George Floyd in May 2020, and the January 6th insurrection at the US Capitol in 2021, have been key triggers for toxic reactions on platforms such as Reddit [5,10]. Such events, which are often filled with strong emotions and diverse opinions, frequently create conditions that foster conflicts and aggressive interactions, which can lead to divisive discourse, where individuals are more prone to express extreme views or engage in aggressive behavior [9,13]. The anonymity and absence of face-to-face communication provided by online platforms like Reddit further lower the barriers to expressing online toxicity.

A. Rapp et al. (Eds.): NLDB 2024, LNCS 14762, pp. 197–210, 2024.
https://doi.org/10.1007/978-3-031-70239-6_14

The detection of toxic content has become an increasingly important research topic in Natural Language Processing (NLP). Current studies in this domain concentrate on developing datasets encompassing various dimensions of toxic language [15,19,26], and training models that utilize these datasets to build systems for classifying and filtering toxic content [1,8,18,21].

The prevalence of toxic language on platforms like Reddit has been widely researched. These studies focused on aspects such as user comments and posts [9, 10], community-level interactions [6,23], or the behavior of the users [23].

Inappropriate interactions like toxicity do not occur in a vacuum. Various factors can trigger toxic behavior in online discussions, for instance, the specific topic being discussed, as well as the presence of threats or inflammatory comments [9,20]. However, while much of the research in this field primarily focused on defining and classifying toxic content, there is a limited exploration into the actual context in which such toxic content emerges [2,14]. Furthermore, most of these studies predominantly focused on English [25].

In this study, we investigate how social and political events trigger the start and spread of toxicity in online discussions across various languages. We further analyze the relationship between sentiment, emotion, and toxicity in relation to world events. While toxicity scores highlight inappropriate conversations, sentiment analysis provides a broader spectrum. Combining toxicity, sentiment, and emotion analyses allows for a more nuanced understanding of the conversational tone. For example, a comment with a negative sentiment or a strong emotion like anger but low toxicity could still contribute to a hostile environment, which might be overlooked if only toxicity is considered. Our contributions can be summarized as follows:

- We release 4.5 million comments organized as threads from 31K posts in six languages connected to major real-world events spanning four years from 2020 to 2023.
- We explore the interplay between toxicity and real-world events in monolingual and cross-lingual settings.
- We explore the relationship between emotions, sentiment, and toxicity in relation to real-world context across different languages and over time.

In our analysis, we observed significant variations in toxicity, sentiment, and emotion scores across different events and language communities. This indicates that toxicity is a complex phenomenon influenced by numerous factors, underscoring the need for further research.

2   Related Work

We use toxic language as an umbrella term, similar to Sharma et al. [22], broadly comprising hate speech, offensive language, abusive language, propaganda, cyberbullying, and cyber-aggression. In this section, we provide an overview of studies that analyze one or more aspects of toxic language in social media platforms from temporal, user, and community perspectives.

Temporal Analysis. The study by Hiaeshutter-Rice and Hawkins [9] examines the relationship between significant social and political events in the U.S. during 2020 and 2021, and the increase in hostility within Reddit discussions. The authors study specifically how these events influenced language use in online conversations. Their results reveal a strong link between key political events and a surge in hostility on Reddit. The study by Mall et al. [13] explores user behavior, specifically examining patterns of user toxicity over time. Their findings highlight that toxic users commonly alternate between making toxic and non-toxic comments.

User and Community Analysis. Kumar et al. [10] provides an extensive study of the behavior of accounts on Reddit that post toxic content. The study shows that even if abusive accounts constitute under 4% of Reddit user base, they create 33% of all the comments on Reddit. Similar work by Kumar et al. [11] reveals a comparable trend, where a limited number of Reddit communities are responsible for a significant majority of negative interactions observed on the platform. Farrell et al. [6] develop specialized lexicons to systematically examine the linguistic shifts within Reddit communities known for misogynistic discussions. In our work, we combine temporal and community analysis and investigate how social and political events trigger the spread of toxicity in online discussions across various languages.

3   Methodology

Our goal is to collect conversations from Reddit across multiple languages that are grounded in the same major real-world events. We focus on events that are of interest to the community at large and that may give rise to both explicit and implicit toxic language. This data enables us to analyze 1) the discourse context of the toxicity of the conversation within comment threads, 2) the external world context in relation to the toxicity of the conversation, and 3) cross-lingual and cross-cultural factors in relation to the toxicity. To collect the data, we proceed in the following steps: 1) selection of the major real-world events and their descriptions in the target languages, 2) extraction of keywords for each event per language, 3) collection of the Reddit submissions in each language based on these keywords, 4) detection of the comments in the submissions with toxicity, negative sentiment, and negative emotions. In the following subsections, we describe each step in detail.

3.1   Event Selection

We selected fifteen major world events between 2020 and 2023 from Wikipedia pages. These events range from political events like the U.S. Capitol attack to sports events like the 2022 FIFA World Cup.[1] After identifying the events, we

---

[1] The complete list of events is available at https://github.com/cltl/grounding-toxicity.

utilized the corresponding Wikipedia page to gather the description of each event in the target language, which includes English, German, Dutch, Arabic, Turkish, and Spanish. These languages are selected because they represent some of the major sub-communities in Europe. We applied TF-IDF to the description of the events to extract keywords. We use these keywords to collect Reddit posts related to the selected events. From these posts, we reconstruct the threads by collecting all the thread posts.

3.2 Data Collection

We use PRAW[2] the Reddit official Python package, to collect the data. We use two parameters for our search: the keywords we identify for each world event and the start date. Incorporating the start date in the query increases the probability that the submissions we obtain from our query are related to the specific target event. For instance, when dealing with the FIFA World Cup, utilizing only keywords might yield posts about past FIFA World Cups rather than the 2022 event. We then used PRAW to get lists of posts related to our target events, which resulted in 31 thousand posts. We used the submission IDs of these Reddit posts and collected all the comments and metadata under these submissions, resulting in 4.5 million comments from 31 thousand posts.

3.3 Toxicity Detection

We emphasize that our ultimate goal is to create a dataset across communities in which we can find subreddit threads with a high probability of containing toxic language, including implicit instances of toxicity. As it is challenging to find substantial amount of toxic comments in real-world data, with the vast majority of content being non-toxic (e.g., less than 1% of comments are toxic in real-world scenarios [25]), we aim to rely on a method that has a high recall for toxic comments, so that we can further analyze the subthreads in which toxic comments occur. To decide on a high-recall method, we conduct a manual assessment of three methods for comment toxicity identification, focusing on those with the broadest applicability to our target languages. These methods include a lexicon-based approach, Perspective API [12], and OpenAI's GPT-4 [17].

Lexicon-Based Approach. For the lexicon-based approach, we combine HurtLex [3], MOL [24], DALC [4], and Hatebase[3], and build a binary classifier to score the toxicity of a comment. If at least one toxic word is present in a comment, we consider the comment toxic. Lexicon-based approaches have shown to be robust when detecting toxic words in cross-domain settings [21] and can easily be extended to other languages or adapted in the future. Our merged lexicon contains 4,316 English, 7,041 Dutch, 1,831 Arabic, 2,782 Turkish, 2,903 Spanish, and 2,851 German entries.

---

[2] https://praw.readthedocs.io/en/stable/index.html.
[3] https://hatebase.org/.

GPT-4. For GPT-4 [17], we employ a simple zero-shot prompt to assign toxicity labels to a comment. We include a definition of a toxic comment in the prompt and prompt GPT-4 to classify comments as toxic or non-toxic. Our prompt is *Review each comment and label it as toxic or non-toxic. To determine whether the comment is toxic if the comment falls into any of the following categories: hate speech, offensive language, abusive language, propaganda, cyberbullying, or cyber-aggression. If the comment aligns with any of these categories, label it as 'Toxic' in the label column. If the comment does not fit any of these categories, label it as non-toxic.*

Perspective API. Perspective API is a Google-provided out-of-the-box toxicity classifier [12]. The API takes a comment as input and produces a toxicity score between 0 and 1. Based on the recommendation from the API documentation, we use a threshold value of 0.75 and consider a comment toxic if its toxicity score is higher than the threshold value.

Evaluation. We created a validation set to evaluate the three methods for toxicity detection. We randomly selected approximately 500 comments in each of the six target languages. We then selected six experts who are familiar with the task and are also native speakers to annotate the sampled comments as toxic and non-toxic. We provided annotation guidelines with the definition of what kind of comments should be labeled as toxic. The experts also had the option to exclude comments that are code-mixed or comments that are not in the target language. We exclude such comments from the evaluation. When evaluating the approaches for toxicity, we prioritize recall over precision because we intend to maximize the probability of finding threads that exhibit both explicit and implicit toxicity. The result of the evaluation of the three toxicity detection approaches is shown in Table 1. The lexicon-based approach shows a much better recall than Perspective-API and GPT-4. This is consistent across all the languages. Therefore, we used the lexicon-based approach to detect threads that likely exhibit toxic behavior.

Sentiment and Emotion Lexicons. In addition to scoring the comments and threads as potentially toxic, we also score comments for sentiment and emotion, for which we used the NRC emotion lexicon [16] – a manually annotated emotion lexicon in 100 languages. We use the 14,182 emotion words and their associations with eight emotions (anger, fear, anticipation, trust, surprise, sadness, joy, and disgust) and two sentiments (negative and positive) from the lexicon. Unlike toxicity, the presence of a single word may not be sufficient to classify a comment into a specific sentiment or emotion category. To determine the dominant sentiment and negative emotion value within a comment, we count the words in the comment that are associated with the negative polarity in the NRC lexicon. The sentiment of a comment is classified as negative if the count of words with negative sentiment is greater than those with positive polarity. For the negative emotion score, we focused on words associated with four negative emotions:

anger, fear, sadness, and disgust, and selected the emotion represented by the highest word count. In cases where there is a tie-in count among the negative emotions, we assign multiple emotion classes. The lexicon we use is balanced across all six languages, containing 14,182 entries for each.

Table 1. Evaluation of lexicon-based approach, Perspective API, and GPT-4. The first three rows show the aggregate result for all the languages, followed by a language-specific breakdown. Since Perspective does not support Turkish, the results for Turkish are marked with '–' and excluded from the aggregate result. The number of comments is lower than we originally sampled since we removed comments that are code-mixed or comments not in the target language.

		Lexical			Perspective			GPT-4			Support
		P	R	F1	P	R	F1	P	R	F1	
	Non toxic	.90	.62	.74	.88	.98	.93	.87	.87	.87	1315
	Toxic	.17	.53	.25	.35	.08	.13	.08	.08	.08	190
	Macro avg	.53	.57	.49	.61	.53	.53	.48	.48	.48	1505
DE	Non toxic	.97	.46	.63	.96	.93	.95	.94	.94	.94	240
	Toxic	.07	.69	.12	.31	.24	.24	.31	.31	.31	13
	Macro avg	.52	.58	.37	.58	.62	.59	.47	.47	.47	253
ES	Non toxic	.88	.46	.61	.82	.99	.88	.86	.86	.86	178
	Toxic	.30	.79	.44	.82	.17	.28	.29	.29	.29	53
	Macro avg	.59	.63	.52	.81	.58	.58	.53	.53	.53	231
NL	Non toxic	.97	.38	.55	.94	1.00	.97	.96	.96	.96	252
	Toxic	.08	.81	.14	.00	.00	.00	.12	.12	.12	16
	Macro avg	.52	.60	.35	.47	.50	.48	.54	.54	.54	268
AR	Non toxic	.88	.94	.91	.86	1.00	.92	.86	.86	.86	457
	Toxic	.41	.24	.30	.00	.00	.00	.00	.00	.00	75
	Macro avg	.65	.59	.61	.43	.50	.46	.43	.43	.43	532
EN	Non toxic	.86	.51	.64	.85	.95	.90	.84	.84	.84	188
	Toxic	.16	.55	.25	.17	.06	.09	.06	.06	.06	33
	Macro avg	.51	.53	.45	.51	.50	.49	.47	.47	.47	221
TR	Non toxic	.69	.57	.62	–	–	–	.60	.87	.71	180
	Toxic	.49	.61	.54	–	–	–	.37	.12	.18	120
	Macro avg	.59	.59	.58	–	–	–	.48	.49	.44	300

4   Analysis

In this section, we present the result of our analysis. We apply toxicity, negative sentiment and emotion detection to all comments in the target languages: Dutch,

English, German, Arabic, Turkish, and Spanish. The comments are grouped as threads related to world events and plotted as temporal plots. Grounding the comments in events and time spans allows us to apply a comparative analysis across events and language communities.

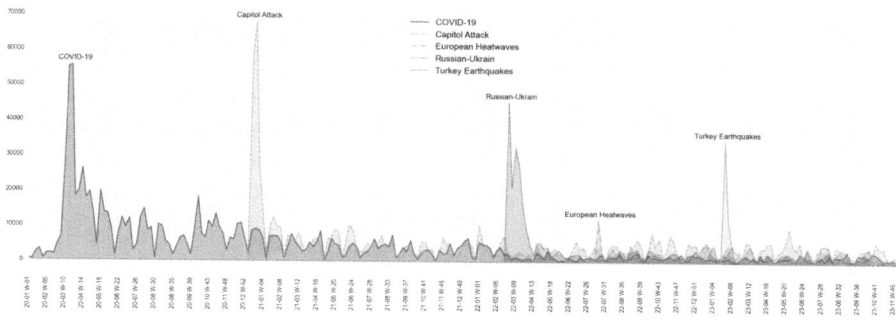

(a) Temporal distribution of comments across major world events. The distribution shows aggregate comments from all languages.

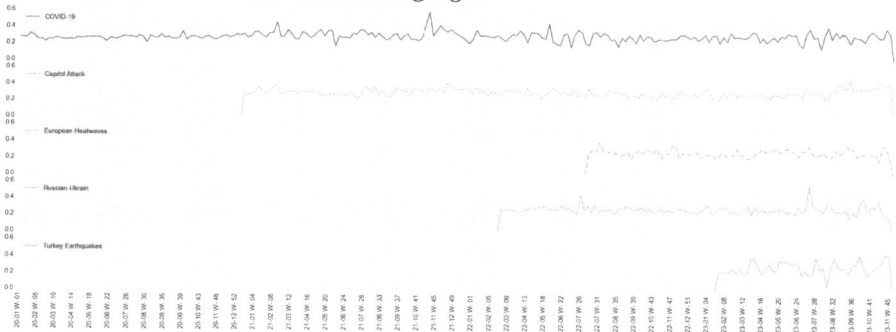

(b) Toxicity of comments for each event. We computed proportional toxicity by dividing the number of toxic comments by the total number of comments in a particular period.

Fig. 1. Relationship between temporal event plot and the proportion of toxicity in conversations related to these events. The X-axis for the two plots is aligned to facilitate comparison. For visibility, we only show plots for five events.

4.1   Comment Dynamics per Event

Figure 1(a) shows the temporal distribution of Reddit comments associated with various global events. The graph demonstrates the engagement intensity measured by the number of comments and duration over time, with spikes corresponding to specific events. The real-world events follow a well-defined pattern consisting of three distinct phases. Initially, there is the pre-event phase, characterized by minimal user discussions. This is followed by the peak phase, during which user engagement reaches its highest point, likely driven by real-time updates and widespread interest. Finally, there is a transition into the post-event phase, where activity decreases. The temporal footprint of each event is visible through the spikes in comment activity, which aligns with the actual dates of the events. Peaks in the graph correspond to the height of public discussion during these events, reflecting real-time reactions from the Reddit community. For instance, the COVID-19 peak signifies extensive discussions during the pandemic's onset in January and February 2020. Similarly, other events like the January 6 US Capitol Attack and the Fall of Kabul in 2021 show pronounced, albeit brief, increases in comment frequency. One possible explanation for this might be an observation reported by Kumar et al. [10], demonstrating that popular real-world events tend to engage active and previously inactive users, drawing them into discussions during major social and political events such as the murder of George Floyd and the US Capitol attack.

4.2   Temporal Analysis of Toxicity

In this section, we analyze the prevalence of toxicity in conversations in relation to major world events. We compute a normalized toxicity value by dividing the proportion of toxic comments over the total number of comments within a specific time period. Figure 1(b) shows the temporal pattern of toxicity, with each line representing a different major world event. The Y-axis quantifies the toxicity level, indicating the proportion of toxic comments during a given time frame, shown in the X-axis. We divide the X-axis in a week time block for ease of comparison with Fig. 1(a). In our analysis, we focus on two distinct scenarios. In the first scenario, we analyze the increase in toxicity observed during the peak period of an event's life cycle. In the second scenario, we analyze toxicity spikes during a non-peak phase of an event.

Peak-Related Toxicity. Contrary to our expectations, all the events show moderate or no significant peaks in toxicity close to the event outbreak, whereas we observed a strong peak in the volume of comments. On the other hand, toxicity peaks tend to occur later when the first outburst of comments has faded. A possible explanation could be that a larger community of Reddit users contributed in the beginning and that these users, being more representative of the average user, tend to use relatively less toxic language. After the attention to the event has faded, a smaller group of users remains, which seems to include contributions from users that spread toxicity.

To control for the community factor, we quantified the number of unique users within the dataset and plotted this on the same timeline for the different events. The result is shown in Fig. 2. The volume of comments and the number of unique users show a very similar pattern over time, which is in line with our hypothesis that the larger community normalizes the proportion of toxicity.

Table 2 shows the mean and standard deviation for the toxicity density per event. The mean varies across the events, but the standard deviation is relatively low, which indicates that the toxicity remains more or less stable. The scores

Table 2. Mean and standard deviation for toxicity of events.

Event	Mean	Std-D
COVID-19	0.30	0.06
Capitol Attack	0.23	0.14
European Heatwaves	0.10	0.14
Kabul-2021	0.17	0.15
Iran Protest	0.09	0.14
Israel Hamas	0.01	0.05
Russia-Ukraine	0.13	0.15
Turkey Earthquakes	0.06	0.12

for COVID-19 and Israel-Hamas are expected: the former stretches a very long period, which evens out peaks, and the latter is too short to exhibit variation.

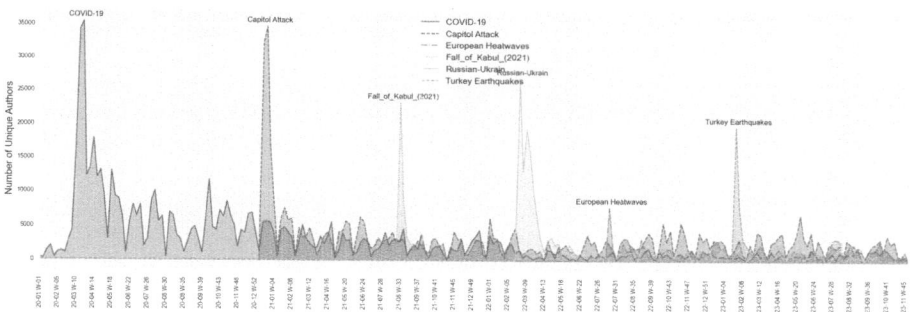

Fig. 2. Temporal distribution of unique users. The spike in the number of comments in Fig. 1(a) strongly correlates with an increased number of users engaged in commenting on discussion about a particular event. For visibility, we only provide plots for six events.

4.3   Cross-lingual Analysis

In this section, we analyze toxicity, sentiment, and emotions for each language to shed light on how these scores are influenced by language. We compute the density value for each score and plot them as heat maps. Figure 3 shows the density plots for toxicity, negative sentiment, and negative emotions (anger, disgust, fear, and sadness).

Toxicity Analysis. For this analysis, we compute the toxicity density by dividing the number of toxic comments in a particular event by the total number of

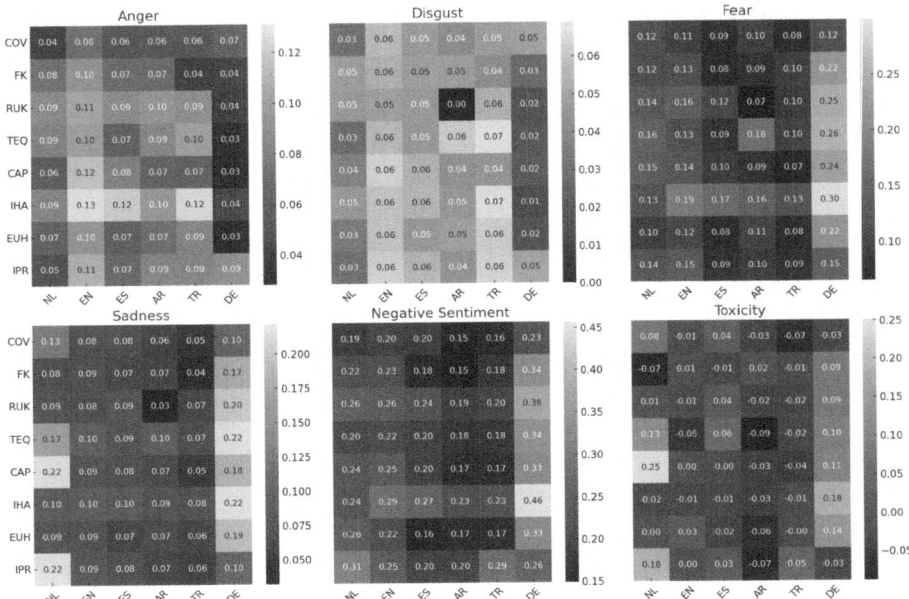

Fig. 3. Heatmap for toxicity density, negative sentiment density, and negative emotions density. COV stands for COVID-19, FK for Fall of Kabul, RUK for Russia-Ukraine, TEQ for Turkey Earthquake, CAP for Capitol Attack, IHA for Israel Hamas, EUH for European Heatwaves, IPR for Iran Protest.

comments in that event. We subtract the mean toxicity score from the density score to control for differences in the toxic lexicon size across languages. When analyzing the toxicity across different languages and events, German and Dutch discussions stand out with higher average toxicity levels. This is particularly noticeable in Dutch discussions about the Capitol Attack, which exhibits the highest toxicity levels. Conversely, English and Turkish show lower average toxicity. Event-wise, the Capitol Attack and the Iran Protests are associated with heightened toxicity. These two events, especially the Capitol Attack, show significant variability in toxicity levels across languages. On the other hand, events like COVID-19 and the Fall of Kabul are characterized by lower average toxicity, suggesting more neutral conversations surrounding these topics. While the highest toxicity is observed in Dutch discussions during the Capitol Attack, the lowest is seen in Arabic during the Turkey Earthquake. The standard deviation in toxicity levels, particularly high for German, indicates a wide range of reactions expressed across different events. This variability, coupled with the specific peaks in toxicity, highlights the complex relationship between real-world events and the cultural and linguistic nuances that shape online discussions surrounding these events.

Sentiment Analysis. Similar to the toxicity density, we compute a normalized negative sentiment density score by dividing the number of comments with negative sentiment by the total number of comments for each event. Since the size of the sentiment lexicons across languages is equal, we do not subtract the mean value here.

A notable trend is the consistently higher negative sentiment in German conversation across all events, with a peak during the Israel-Hamas and the Russia-Ukraine conflicts, indicating a strong emotional response to this event within the German-speaking community. Conversely, Arabic conversations consistently exhibit the lowest negative sentiment, while English and Turkish show relatively consistent sentiment levels. The result reflects how differently language communities respond to global crises.

Emotion Analysis. In the emotion analysis, we compute the density of four negative emotions: anger, fear, sadness, and disgust. In the anger heatmap, conversations in English consistently show higher anger scores, most prominently during the Capitol Attack. In contrast, German conversations exhibit significantly lower anger across all events, a stark contrast to their higher negative sentiment. Arabic conversations also show high scores in certain events like the Fall of Kabul and the Russia-Ukraine conflict. In the disgust heatmap, similar to the anger heatmap, we observed equally high levels of disgust expressed in English in most events. Spanish conversations also show similar patterns to those of English. German, in contrast, consistently exhibits the lowest levels of disgust across all events.

We observed a similarity between the trend in the fear heatmap and the negative sentiment heatmap. German conversations show a notably high overall score, especially prominent during the Russia-Ukraine conflict and the Turkey Earthquake. In contrast, Arabic conversations generally show lower levels of fear, except for a notable increase during the Turkish Earthquake. Overall, German conversations consistently displayed higher levels of negative sentiment and sadness across all events, yet interestingly, their levels of anger and disgust were notably lower. Comparatively, English conversations frequently exhibited higher anger and disgust, particularly during events like the Capitol Attack and the Turkey Earthquake. On the other hand, Arabic conversations generally showed lower levels of negative sentiment, anger, and sadness, with certain exceptions indicating event-specific responses. The high toxicity of the Dutch community is not reflected by equally strong negative sentiments and emotions when compared to the other languages, except for sadness.

Correlation Analysis. We further applied the Pearson correlation analysis of toxicity, emotion, and sentiment within and across languages. There is a general trend of positive correlations among individual languages, though the strength varies. Fear, sadness, and negative sentiment exhibit strong relationships, suggesting a consistent link between these emotions within languages. For instance, we observed a correlation of 0.72 between fear and sadness within languages.

Across languages, this strong correlation pattern holds. However, the correlation strengths differ within and across languages, suggesting cultural variation in how emotions and sentiments are expressed and perceived. This nuanced analysis underscores the complexity of emotional responses across different cultural and language-community contexts while pointing to some universal patterns in emotional expression. All our observations so far depend on the correctness of the tools to measure these properties. We realize that this analysis is a rough indication pointing to interesting data for further analysis to be carried out in the future.

5   Conclusion

In this study, we examined the changes in toxicity, sentiment, and emotions within Reddit discussions during major social and political events, analyzing these aspects across various languages. Our findings show three key points. First, we found that toxicity in comments usually increases later, not right at the start of events. One possible reason for this might be that the first group of commenters is more diverse and less likely to exhibit toxic language. As the event becomes less popular, the remaining users tend to show more toxic behavior. Second, we observed a lot of variation when we looked at toxicity, sentiment, and emotions across different language communities. This shows that language communities respond differently to global events, and it is essential to consider cultural context when studying online interactions. Lastly, we found a positive correlation between toxicity, sentiment, and emotion in each language, but the strength of this relation varies. Emotions like fear and sadness often occur with negative sentiments, showing a consistent pattern in how these emotions are connected across languages. It is evident that the reliability of our observations relies on the assumption that the methods utilized for quantifying toxicity, sentiment, and emotions is accurate. However, we will use this data in further research to analyze the implicit and explicit toxic reasoning towards specific targets and in relation to the events as world context. Our preliminary analysis shows the potential to find such patterns. The fact that the data, within limits, is grounded in real-world events provides a strong basis for cross-lingual and cross-community comparison in the future.

Limitations

We identified some limitations in our work. First, the lexicons we use for detecting toxicity, sentiment, and emotions might have differences in quality across each language. These might introduce bias and result in less accurate results across languages. Second, we extracted comments using keywords and temporal constraints to link them with real-world events. This does not necessarily mean that the submissions and comments solely discuss these events as a topic. The actual context of the online discussion could still vary. Further topic analysis of the posts and comments should clarify this in future work.

Acknowledgements. The research was supported by Huawei Finland through the DreamsLab project. All content represented the opinions of the authors, which were not necessarily shared or endorsed by their respective employers and/or sponsors.

References

1. van Aken, B., Risch, J., Krestel, R., Löser, A.: Challenges for toxic comment classification: An in-depth error analysis. In: Proceedings of the 2nd Workshop on Abusive Language Online (ALW2), pp. 33–42. ACL, Brussels, Belgium (2018). https://doi.org/10.18653/v1/W18-5105
2. Almerekhi, H., Kwak, H., Salminen, J., Jansen, B.J.: Provoke: toxicity trigger detection in conversations from the top 100 subreddits. Data Inf. Manag. **6**(4), 100019 (2022). https://doi.org/10.1016/j.dim.2022.100019
3. Bassignana, E., Basile, V., Patti, V.: Hurtlex: a multilingual lexicon of words to hurt. In: Italian Conference on Computational Linguistics (2018)
4. Caselli, T., et al.: DALC: the Dutch abusive language corpus. In: Proceedings of the 5th Workshop on Online Abuse and Harms (WOAH 2021), pp. 54–66. Online (2021). https://doi.org/10.18653/v1/2021.woah-1.6
5. Chatzakou, D., Kourtellis, N., Blackburn, J., Cristofaro, E.D., Stringhini, G., Vakali, A.: Measuring #gamergate: A tale of hate, sexism, and bullying. In: Proceedings of the 26th International Conference on World Wide Web Companion (2017)
6. Farrell, T., Fernandez, M., Novotny, J., Alani, H.: Exploring misogyny across the manosphere in reddit. In: Proceedings of the 10th ACM Conference on Web Science. WebSci '19, pp. 87–96. ACM, New York, NY, USA (2019). https://doi.org/10.1145/3292522.3326045
7. Fortuna, P., Nunes, S.: A survey on automatic detection of hate speech in text. ACM Comput. Surv. **51**(4) (2018). https://doi.org/10.1145/3232676
8. Gevers, I., Markov, I., Daelemans, W.: Linguistic analysis of toxic language on social media. Comput. Linguist. Netherlands J. **12**, 33–48 (2022)
9. Hiaeshutter-Rice, D., Hawkins, I.: The language of extremism on social media: an examination of posts, comments, and themes on reddit. Front. Polit. Sci. **4**, 805008 (2022). https://doi.org/10.3389/fpos.2022.805008
10. Kumar, D., Hancock, J., Thomas, K., Durumeric, Z.: Understanding the behaviors of toxic accounts on reddit. In: Proceedings of the ACM Web Conference 2023. WWW '23, pp. 2797–2807. ACM, New York, NY, USA (2023). https://doi.org/10.1145/3543507.3583522
11. Kumar, S., Hamilton, W.L., Leskovec, J., Jurafsky, D.: Community interaction and conflict on the web. In: Proceedings of the 2018 World Wide Web Conference. WWW '18, pp. 933–943. Republic and Canton of Geneva, CHE (2018). https://doi.org/10.1145/3178876.3186141
12. Lees, A., et al.: A new generation of perspective API: efficient multilingual character-level transformers. In: Proceedings of the 28th ACM SIGKDD Conference on Knowledge Discovery and Data Mining. KDD '22, pp. 3197–3207. Association for Computing Machinery, New York, NY, USA (2022). https://doi.org/10.1145/3534678.3539147

13. Mall, R., Nagpal, M., Salminen, J., Almerekhi, H., Jung, S.G., Jansen, B.J.: Four types of toxic people: characterizing online users– toxicity over time. In: Proceedings of the 11th Nordic Conference on Human-Computer Interaction: Shaping Experiences, Shaping Society. NordiCHI '20, Association for Computing Machinery, New York, NY, USA (2020). https://doi.org/10.1145/3419249.3420142

14. Markov, I., Daelemans, W.: The role of context in detecting the target of hate speech. In: Proceedings of the Third Workshop on Threat, Aggression and Cyberbullying (TRAC 2022), pp. 37–42. Gyeongju, Republic of Korea (2022)

15. Mathew, B., Saha, P., Yimam, S.M., Biemann, C., Goyal, P., Mukherjee, A.: Hatexplain: a benchmark dataset for explainable hate speech detection. In: AAAI Conference on Artificial Intelligence (2020)

16. Mohammad, S.M., Turney, P.D.: Crowdsourcing a word-emotion association lexicon. Comput. Intell. **29** (2013)

17. OpenAI: Gpt-4 Technical report. arXiv abs/2303.08774 (2023)

18. Radfar, B., Shivaram, K., Culotta, A.: Characterizing variation in toxic language by social context. In: Proceedings of the International AAAI Conference on Web and Social Media, vol. 14, pp. 959–963 (2020). https://doi.org/10.1609/icwsm.v14i1.7366

19. Sachdeva, P., Barreto, R., Bacon, G., Sahn, A., von Vacano, C., Kennedy, C.: The measuring hate speech corpus: leveraging Rasch measurement theory for data perspectivism. In: Proceedings of the 1st Workshop on Perspectivist Approaches to NLP @LREC2022, pp. 83–94. ELRA, Marseille, France (2022)

20. Salminen, J.O., Sengün, S., Corporan, J., Jung, S.G., Jansen, B.J.: Topic-driven toxicity: exploring the relationship between online toxicity and news topics. PLoS ONE **15** (2020)

21. Schouten, S.F., Barbarestani, B., Tufa, W., Vossen, P., Markov, I.: Cross-domain toxic spans detection. In: Métais, E., Meziane, F., Sugumaran, V., Manning, W., Reiff-Marganiec, S. (eds.) NLDB 2023. LNCS, vol. 13913, pp. 533–545. Springer, Cham (2023). https://doi.org/10.1007/978-3-031-35320-8_40

22. Sharma, S., et al.: Detecting and understanding harmful memes: a survey. In: International Joint Conference on Artificial Intelligence (2022)

23. Urbaniak, R., Tempskaet al.: Namespotting: username toxicity and actual toxic behavior on reddit. Comput. Hum. Behav. **136**(C) (2022). https://doi.org/10.1016/j.chb.2022.107371

24. Vargas, F., Rodrigues de Góes, F., Carvalho, I., Benevenuto, F., Pardo, T.: Contextual-lexicon approach for abusive language detection. In: Proceedings of the International Conference on Recent Advances in Natural Language Processing (RANLP 2021), pp. 1438–1447. INCOMA Ltd., Held Online (2021)

25. Vidgen, B., Derczynski, L.: Directions in abusive language training data, a systematic review: garbage in, garbage out. PLoS ONE **15**(12), e0243300 (2020). https://doi.org/10.1371/journal.pone.0243300

26. Vidgen, B., Nguyen, D., Margetts, H., Rossini, P., Tromble, R.: Introducing CAD: the contextual abuse dataset. In: Proceedings of the 2021 Conference of the North American Chapter of ACL: Human Language Technologies, pp. 2289–2303. ACL, Online (2021)

Unveiling the Hate: Generating Faithful and Plausible Explanations for Implicit and Subtle Hate Speech Detection

Greta Damo, Nicolás Benjamín Ocampo[✉], Elena Cabrio, and Serena Villata

Université Côte d'Azur, CNRS, Inria, I3S, Sophia Antipolis, France
{greta.damo,nicolas-benjamin.ocampo,elena.cabrio,
serena.villata}@univ-cotedazur.fr

Abstract. In today's digital age, the huge amount of abusive content and hate speech on social media platforms presents a significant challenge. Natural Language Processing (NLP) methods have focused on detecting explicit forms of hate speech, often overlooking more nuanced and implicit instances. To address this gap, our paper aims to enhance the detection and understanding of implicit and subtle hate speech. More precisely, we propose a comprehensive approach combining prompt construction, free-text generation, few-shot learning, and fine-tuning to generate explanations for hate speech classification, with the goal of providing more context for content moderators to unveil the actual nature of a message on social media.

Keywords: Hate Speech Detection · Generating Explanations · Implicit Hate Speech · Subtle Hate Speech

1 Introduction

Hate speech (HS) is increasingly prevalent on social media, presenting a significant societal challenge. There have been efforts in NLP to automatically detect language conveying hateful or abusive messages. However, these methods predominantly focus on explicit forms of HS, often disregarding more subtle and implicit instances [29]. Recent research explored the detection of implicit hate speech, through circumlocution, metaphor, or stereotypes [7,13,29]. Yet, developing resources and methods to identify these nuanced expressions effectively remains an open challenge.

In particular, our research question is how to generate explanations for implicit and subtle hateful messages to help content moderators in assessing the real nature of a message on social media. To answer this research question, this paper focuses on two key aspects: *i)* the reasoning process of system predictors (i.e., *faithfulness*), and *ii)* the coherence of these explanations for human

---

G. Damo and N. B. Ocampo—Equal Contribution.

A. Rapp et al. (Eds.): NLDB 2024, LNCS 14762, pp. 211–225, 2024.
https://doi.org/10.1007/978-3-031-70239-6_15

stakeholders (i.e., *plausibility*) [22]. Our work proposes a novel generation app-roach to identify hate speech messages and elucidate the reasoning behind such predictions. As output, we provide not only a binary classification (HS vs Non-HS), but a natural language explanation, discussing why a message is deemed hateful and what is the targeted group.

Our contributions are threefold: *i)* a novel pipeline incorporating prompt construction, free-text generation, few-shot learning, and fine-tuning to gener-ate predictions and explanations for hate speech, evaluating classification results when jointly predicting labels and explanations, *ii)* a comprehensive analysis of the faithfulness of the generated explanations and of the ability of the proposed systems to explain the implied meanings in implicit hate speech messages, and finally, *iii)* an extensive human evaluation to assess key factors for these expla-nations such as fluency, informativeness, and soundness.[1]

By employing a predictive and explanatory system, our approach aims to monitor hate speech, enhance the precision of detection systems, and unveil the reasons behind the proposed classification.

NOTE: This paper contains examples of language which may be offensive to some readers. They do not represent the views of the authors.

2   Related Work

Considerable research has focused on detecting HS, employing diverse method-ologies like lexicon-based approaches [11,44], supervised classifiers [9,20,35,39], and benchmark datasets on different languages [1,2,6,8,21,26,46]. Recently, a growing interest has been in tackling implicit and subtle HS that can be as harmful as overt ones [17,24]. Newer datasets and resources [7,13,29,34,37,42], more developed veiled detectors [10,12], guided augmentation strategies [25,27, 32,41], theoretical analyses [16,40,43], and improved embedding representations through contrastive learning [19,28] have been proposed. Few studies have delved into the realm of explainable HS detection, characterized by natural language explanations. Specifically, [7,34] investigate social stereotypes in HS, shedding light on their implied meanings. [23] introduce the first dataset that focuses on the rationale underlying HS. [18] presents a pipeline that guides transformer models' predictive decisions through the identification of key rationales.

[14,38,45] engage with Large Language Models (LLMs) to generate extensive explanations, either as full sentences or explanation chains, without considering also nuanced error categories as reclaimed slurs, or hate against non protected groups; they also don't generate combinations of Label, Target, and Explanation allowing a more fine-grained understanding of HS classification and explanation.

Moreover, attempts can be found to generate natural language explanations in other tasks. For instance, [5] proposed a character-level attention-enhanced long short-term memory model for generating natural language explanations in recommender systems. Building on this, [3] introduced a framework employing a

---

[1] The accompanying software, and obtained explanations can be found at https:// github.com/benjaminocampo/gen_hs_explanations.

Table 1. HateCheck and IHC text and gold explanation examples.

Dataset	Text Message	Gold Explanation
HateCheck	Muslims with any power are a threat to civilisation.	The message is hateful against Muslims because it contains description using very negative attributes promoting prejudice and discrimination
	Gay people belong in a zoo.	The message is hateful against gay people because it contains implicit derogation that compares gay people to animals.
IHC	muslims always feel provoked and offended ... that's why islam has to be banned from democracies.	The message is hateful against Muslims because it implies that Muslims are overly sensitive.
	white genocide accelerates in england: white british pupils will be outnumbered by 2037 #waronwhites	The message is hateful towards White people because it implies that White people are declining in England.

hierarchical sequence-to-sequence model to generate free-text natural language explanations for personalized recommendations, expanding beyond the use of structured sentences [22]. Gaining trust in the predictions of LLMs is challenging due to their inherent black-box nature for human understanding [33,38]. Our paper investigates this topic by assessing two critical aspects, i.e., faithfulness and plausibility. Faithfulness gauges the precision with which an explanation reflects the reasoning process behind a model's prediction while plausibility, conversely, measures how easily the intended audience can understand an explanation [22].

3   Explanation Generation for Implicit HS

This work targets the following research questions:

RQ1: Does jointly labeling and generating explanations for HS and Non-HS messages impact the classification results?

RQ2: Can our models faithfully generate explanations on hate speech? Are explanations sensitive to nuanced inputs and perturbations?

RQ3: Does the generated text explain the implied meaning of implicit hate speech messages?

RQ4: Are explanations plausibly understandable by humans, providing additional insights beyond the input message?

3.1   Datasets

To construct gold explanations, we rely on two benchmark datasets: HateCheck [31] and Implicit Hate Corpus (IHC) [7]. Gold explanations are needed to assess the quality of the generated explanations according to both an automatic and a human evaluation (Sect. 3.3).

HateCheck. provides functional tests for evaluating HS detection models. A functionality provides a classification for specific test cases in a corresponding functional test. HateCheck comprises 3728 text messages grouped in 29 hateful and non-hateful test functionalities.[2].

---

[2] We excluded messages related to functionalities 25 to 29, focused on format issues (misspellings, character swaps containing hate words), irrelevant for our purposes.

These test cases were used to automatically create gold explanations, according to the following template: *The message is [LABEL] against [TARGET] because it contains [FUNCTIONALITY]*.

Where [LABEL] identifies a hateful or non-hateful message, [TARGET] is the target group, and [FUNCTIONALITY] is the functionality the given message is associated to in HateCheck.

For one of the functionality, *i.e.*, the implicit derogation (derog_impl_h), appearing in messages conveying implicit HS, instead, we chose to curate the gold explanations manually. This process was applied to all 140 messages, with the final gold explanation determined through mutual agreement between two graduate-level annotators. The following template was defined: *The message is [LABEL] against [TARGET] because it contains implicit derogation, implying [IMPLICATION]*.

In total, we obtained gold explanations for 2,968 messages: 1,803 are HS and relate to 13 distinct functionalities, while the remaining 1,165 messages are Non-HS, and pertain to 11 different functionalities. We couple each message in the original HateCheck dataset with a template-based gold explanation (Table 1). All hateful messages have a target of hate, while there can be either a target or not for non-HS instances.

Implicit Hate Corpus (IHC) is a dataset targeting implicit forms of HS. Implicit HS is defined by *coded or indirect language* that disparages a person or group on the basis of protected characteristics like race, gender, or cultural identity. This indirect language can be delivered in multiple forms such as irony, or threat and intimidation. The dataset consists of *i)* annotations with explicit, implicit, or not hate messages, and *ii)* the messages' taxonomy and implied statements for implicit HS.

To obtain gold explanations from IHC, we considered the columns containing the label for hatefulness, the target of hate, the original text, and the implied statement. We filtered out all messages in IHC that were not implicit HS and did not have an implied statement. The template to generate gold explanations is the following: *The message is [LABEL] against [TARGET] because it implies that [IMPLIED STATEMENT]*.

As a result, the dataset comprises 6217 HS messages coupled with gold explanations (see Table 1).

3.2   Generation Framework

We employ LLMs to generate human-like explanations for messages containing implicit HS. Our generation process is guided by a carefully crafted instruction prompt, designed to steer the LLMs in producing outputs that can be directly compared with the gold explanations. We test three distinct configurations:

Zero-Shot: Given only the hateful or non-hateful text to predict, [MESSAGE], we instruction-tune the LLM with the following input: *Given a message: [MESSAGE], 1) Label if it is hateful or non-hateful. 2) Label the target of hate. 3) Generate* *an explanation of why the sentence is hateful or not. Output the answer in the following structure. Label:, Target:, Explanation:.*

Few-Shot: Given the hateful or non-hateful text to predict, `[MESSAGE]`, we guide the generation with additional N demonstration examples.

Fine-tuning: LLMs are fine-tuned on the training set of the IHC dataset as a completion task. For all the instances in the IHC dataset, we built pairs of (`prompt`, `label`), where `prompt` consists of a message with the same structure as the Zero-Shot configuration and `label` its gold explanation as the label to fine-tune.

3.3   Metrics

Metrics for the Automatic Evaluation. We adopt metrics commonly applied for text completion tasks, aiming to measure the similarities and differences between generated and gold explanations.

BLEU [30]: it calculates the ratio of the total number of n-gram overlaps to the overall number of n-grams in a sentence (we used the version BLEU-1).

BertScore [47] relies on the extraction of BERT's embeddings for individual tokens from both the generated and gold sentences. It then calculates the cosine similarity between them[3].

IOU-F1 combines Intersection over Union (IOU), which measures the overlap between predicted and ground truth regions, and F1 score.

Accuracy assesses the correctness of predicted labels.

The resulting scores for BLEU, BertScore, and IOU-F1 fall within the range of 0 to 1, with higher values indicating higher similarity.

Metrics for the Human Evaluation. Following previous works [4,14,33], we focused on Fluency, Informativeness, and Soundness, to assess whether the explanations are clear and recognize the implicit nature of the messages. All metrics range from 1 (lowest score) to 5 (maximum score).

Fluency: It evaluates whether the explanation follows proper grammar and structural rules.

Informativeness: It assesses whether the explanation provides new information (e.g. additional context).

Soundness: It describes whether the explanation seems valid and logical.

Furthermore, we used three additional metrics, specifically tailored to address RQ3:

---

[3] BLEU and BertScore Metrics were implemented based on the evaluate-metric library from Huggingface: https://huggingface.co/evaluate-metric.

Similarity: It assesses the extent to which the predicted explanation mirrors the gold one in meaning. It evaluates the model's ability to decode and clarify implied meanings in the original message.

Originality: It measures whether the predicted explanation offers more than a mere repetition of the input text, by rephrasing the given input.

Context: It evaluates if the predicted explanation provides more information beside the one in the gold explanation.

Fluency, Informativeness, and Soundness primarily assess plausibility, where human evaluators consider just the message and its generated explanation to ensure its usefulness and understandability. Conversely, Similarity, Originality, and Context assess the faithfulness of an explanation. They complement automatic metrics by also incorporating the gold explanation and input text for human evaluation.

3.4   Experimental Settings

In our experiments, we tested a range of text completion models, including GPT-3.5, GPT-4, Mistral [15], and Alpaca [36]. Both Mistral and Alpaca models are open-source resources, while GPT-3.5 and GPT-4 are accessed through the OpenAI API[4]. For GPT-3.5, we used the `gpt-3.5-turbo-0613` version, while for GPT-4, we used `gpt-4--0613`. For Mistral we tested the `Mistral-7B-v0.2`, and `Mistral-8X7B-v0.1` versions, while for Alpaca we employed `Alpaca-7B`.

For the generation and decoding phase, for all the models, we set the following parameters: `max_token` parameter to 512, number of responses per prompt `n` is 1, `stop` null, the `temperature` is 0.5.

In the fine-tuning process of the Alpaca and Mistral models, the input and label lengths are controlled by setting `max_length` to 256 and `max_label_length` to 256, respectively. The `batch size` is 8 for both training and evaluation, the `learning rate` is 2e-5, and the `weight decay` is 0.01. The process includes 3 training `epochs`. All the models are fine-tuned on the IHC dataset (Sect. 3.1) using a 70–15-15 split for the train, dev, and test sets.

Finally, for the few-shot configuration, demonstration examples are randomly extracted from the IHC dataset. In our experiments, we used a total of 5 `shots` per prediction.

To address **RQ1** we carried out a thorough evaluation of each model's predictive capabilities and generation strategy, to discern whether a given input text is hateful or non-hateful, while jointly predicting an explanation. This comparison allows us to measure the efficacy of our models in HS detection, in contrast to more traditional binary classification approaches. For this experiment, we used both datasets and analyzed the models' accuracy to determine whether a message is hateful or not. Given that HateCheck categorizes messages into HS or non-HS only, and IHC has only HS, focusing on accuracy is more appropriate.

---

[4] https://openai.com/product.

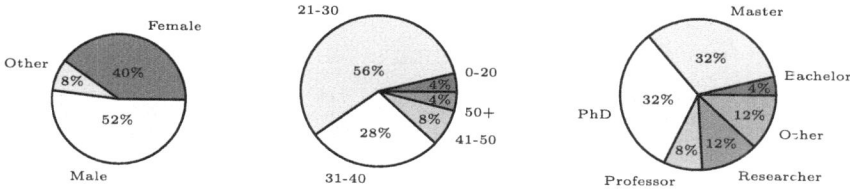

(a) Gender group distribution.

(b) Age group distribution.

(c) Education level distribution.

Fig. 1. Annotators' demographic distribution in RQ4.

For **RQ2**, we used the explanations obtained through the predictions in **RQ1** for all LLMs. We compared these predictions with HateCheck and IHC gold explanations. BLEU, BertScore, and IOU-F1 are used for automatic token-based and semantic-based evaluations. Adopting the methodology from [22], we assessed faithfulness through multiple perturbed input examples, categorized according to HateCheck functionalities.

For **RQ3**, we considered all the implicit 140 messages from HateCheck (implicit derogation functionality), and a sample of 140 implicit HS messages from IHC. Two graduate-level annotators manually evaluated 3-tuples of a HS message, a predicted explanation, and a gold explanation. For each 3-tuple, the evaluation metrics are Similarity, Originality, and Context. Predicted explanations correspond to GPT-4 generations, being the strongest model among the tested ones. To obtain the percentages of agreement, we calculate the number of cases on which both annotators agreed with the annotation, divided by the total number of annotations with respect to these three metrics. We also calculated the IAA by using Krippendorff's alpha.

For **RQ4**, 25 graduate-level annotators manually evaluate pairs of a text message and a generated explanation, following the criteria described in Sect. 3.3. These pairs are correctly labeled hateful and non-hateful instances. 10 pairs are randomly given to each annotator, and they are asked to evaluate the generated explanations in terms of Fluency, Informativeness, and Soundness. The total number of evaluated cases is 250, where all pairs correspond to GPT-4 predictions, being the strongest model among the selected ones. Annotations are performed anonymously with instructions on how to perform the task, the definition of the metrics, and annotated examples. Additional information is required, such as their studies level, age range, and gender. Concerning the annotators' demographics (See Fig. 1) we have found a good gender balance. Most annotators fall within the 21–30 age group, and there's a varied distribution of educational backgrounds, with a higher representation of Master's and PhD students.

4   Evaluation

Regarding **RQ1**, Table 2a shows the models' accuracy on HateCheck and IHC, and the automatic metrics. Concerning HateCheck, the models obtaining the

Table 2. Ablation Study for RQ1 and Accuracy scores for GPT-4.

		Model	HateCheck				Implicit Hate Corpus			
			Acc.	BLEU	BERT	IOU-F1	Acc.	BLEU	BERT	IOU-F1
With Explanation	Zero-shot	Alpaca-7B	0.735	0.195	0.799	0.148	**0.959**	0.253	0.807	0.126
		GPT-3.5	0.814	0.167	0.838	0.208	0.726	0.140	0.828	0.162
		GPT-4	0.845	0.208	0.845	0.225	0.668	0.165	0.827	0.168
		Mistral-7B	0.830	0.096	0.805	0.155	0.506	0.096	0.797	0.132
		Mistral-8X7B	**0.864**	0.115	0.814	0.177	0.707	0.111	0.812	0.150
	Few-shot	Alpaca-7B	0.610	0.147	0.770	0.099	**1.000**	0.053	0.760	0.132
		GPT-3.5	0.821	0.183	0.841	0.208	0.839	0.203	0.850	0.207
		GPT-4	**0.891**	0.257	0.863	0.265	0.583	0.260	0.857	0.254
		Mistral-7B	0.823	0.180	0.846	0.230	0.645	0.159	0.831	0.193
		Mistral-8X7B	0.875	0.182	0.848	0.238	0.720	0.165	0.831	0.197
	Fine-Tuning	Alpaca-7B	0.862	0.178	0.837	0.207	0.752	0.186	0.840	0.193
		GPT-3.5	0.862	0.168	0.836	0.205	0.735	0.167	0.838	0.190
		GPT-4	-	-	-	-	-	-	-	-
		Mistral-7B	**0.863**	0.180	0.837	0.208	0.752	0.186	0.840	0.193
		Mistral-8X7B	0.860	0.179	0.837	0.207	**0.756**	0.184	0.840	0.192
Without Explanation	Zero-shot	Alpaca-7B	0.707	-	-	-	**0.861**	-	-	-
		GPT-3.5	**0.860**	-	-	-	0.702	-	-	-
		GPT-4	0.673	-	-	-	0.656	-	-	-
		Mistral-7B	0.828	-	-	-	0.612	-	-	-
		Mistral-8X7B	0.842	-	-	-	0.821	-	-	-
	Few-shot	Alpaca-7B	0.613	-	-	-	**0.989**	-	-	-
		GPT-3.5	0.810	-	-	-	0.841	-	-	-
		GPT-4	**0.878**	-	-	-	0.610	-	-	-
		Mistral-7B	0.826	-	-	-	0.678	-	-	-
		Mistral-8X7B	0.829	-	-	-	0.847	-	-	-
	Fine-Tuning	Alpaca-7B	0.852	-	-	-	**0.726**	-	-	-
		GPT-3.5	**0.858**	-	-	-	0.717	-	-	-
		GPT-4	-	-	-	-	-	-	-	-
		Mistral-7B	0.852	-	-	-	0.711	-	-	-
		Mistral-8X7B	0.851	-	-	-	0.725	-	-	-

(a) Ablation Study: Accuracy, BLEU, BertScore, and IOU-F1 scores for all the models described in Section 3.4. The models were evaluated on HateCheck and IHC. BLEU, BERT, and IOU-F1 do not apply for results without explanations (Cells with a hyphen (-)).

HateCheck		
Functionality	GPT-4 Exp.	GPT-4 No-Exp
counter_quote_nh	0.058	**0.150**
counter_ref_nh	0.078	**0.291**
derog_dehum_h	1.000	1.000
derog_impl_h	**1.000**	0.971
derog_neg_attrib_h	1.000	1.000
derog_neg_emote_h	1.000	1.000
ident_neutral_nh	1.000	1.000
ident_pos_nh	**0.995**	0.990
negate_neg_nh	0.902	**1.000**
negate_pos_h	1.000	1.000
phrase_opinion_h	1.000	1.000
phrase_question_h	**1.000**	0.993
profanity_h	1.000	1.000
profanity_nh	**0.930**	0.680
ref_subs_clause_h	1.000	1.000
ref_subs_sent_h	1.000	1.000
slur_h	**1.000**	0.993
slur_homonym_nh	0.867	**1.000**
slur_reclaimed_nh	0.469	**0.543**
target_group_nh	**0.323**	0.129
target_indiv_nh	**0.154**	0.108
target_obj_nh	**0.985**	0.908
threat_dir_h	1.000	1.000
threat_norm_h	1.000	1.000

(b) Accuracy scores per HateCheck functionality for the GPT-4 model with and without explanations.

highest accuracy are Mistral-8X7B, GPT-4, and Mistral-7B for Zero-shot, Few-shot and Fine-tuning configurations, respectively. Overall, GPT-4 with Few-shots obtains the best results in terms of Accuracy. Moreover, regarding the best performing models (in bold), there is a statistically significant improvement (Bootstrap Resampling Method) in the Accuracy of the models with explanation over the ones with no explanation, showing their benefit in the task of hate speech detection. Concerning the results on IHC, the models with the best Accuracy are Alpaca for Zero-shot and Few-shot, and Mistral-8X7B for Fine-tuning, respectively. Overall, the best model is Alpaca-7B. Also, in this case, the results of the best-performing models with explanations are statistically significantly better than the ones without.

Table 2b compares the classification results (accuracy) of GPT-4 with and without explanations. We can see that explanations have a positive impact on HateCheck messages such as implicit derogations (derog_impl_h), positive statements using protected group identifiers (ident_pos_nh), phrase questions (phrase_question_h), profanity (profanity_nh), slurs (slur_h), abuse targeted at non-protected groups (target_group_nh), individuals (target_indiv_nh) and objects (target_obj_nh). However, it has a compromised impact on text instances containing denouncements of hate that quote it (counter_quote_nh), make direct reference to it (counter_ref_nh), and using homonym and reclaimed slurs (slur_homonym_nh, slur_reclaimed_n).

To answer **RQ2**, we compared the models' predictions described above with HateCheck and IHC gold explanations, using the automatic metrics BLEU, BertScore, and IOU-F1. For the comparison, we analyzed the best performing models obtained in RQ1. Notably, our models consistently exhibit strong performances on these three metrics. In terms of BertScore and IOU-F1, GPT-4 Few-shots and Mistral-8X7B Fine-tuned stand out with the highest scores for HateCheck and IHC, respectively. This aligns with our expectations, as we anticipate the generated explanations to closely resemble the gold explanation text since they provide reasons for the hateful or non-hateful nature of the content. For the BLEU metric, we anticipate lower scores given its token-based nature. Indeed, the overall scores are close to zero, emphasizing the dissimilarity with respect to the gold explanations from a token-based perspective. GPT-4 Few-shot and Alpaca Zero-shot achieve the highest BLEU scores, for HateCheck and IHC respectively, suggesting a relatively higher token-based similarity.

Concerning implicitness (**RQ3**), Table 3a shows the IAA for Similarity, Originality, and Context, for 140 messages from both HateCheck and IHC. Concerning HateCheck, the highest agreement among annotators is for the Similarity metric, with a 74.3% agreement. The Context metric has a good 70% agreement, while there is more disagreement on the Originality metric, which has a 69.3% agreement. Additionally, while the agreement between the annotators is not an exact match for each of the metrics, both tend to give similar scores in average (mean) with a low variation (std). Concerning IHC, the highest agreement is for Context with 81.6%, followed by Originality and Similarity. Also in this case, the agreement has similar scores on average with a low standard deviation, and a higher Krippendorff's α for Originality and Context in contrast to HateCheck. Overall, results indicate that the predicted explanations hold up well against the gold standard in conveying the implied meaning of the original text. They demonstrate a good amount of originality, similarity, and additional information compared to both the original text and the gold-standard explanation.

Regarding **RQ4**, Table 3b shows that, on average, all the explanations provided are grammatically and syntactically correct in nearly every instance, receiving a high Fluency score of 4.948. The average score for Soundness is 4.755, underscoring the robustness of the logical and clear arguments presented in almost all explanations. Meanwhile, the average score for Informativeness is 4.040, suggesting that the explanations generally adhere to the original text in terms of information content (although, in some cases, they may provide additional details).

Table 3. Human evaluation results for RQ3 (Table 3a) and RQ4 (Table 3b).

	HateCheck			IHC		
	similarity	originality	context	similarity	originality	context
Annotator 1	3.836 ±0.372	3.907 ±0.291	0.643 ±0.481	2.414 ±0.518	3.483 ±0.626	0.747 ±0.437
Annotator 2	3.736 ±0.443	3.629 ±0.485	0.714 ±0.453	2.593 ±0.517	3.477 ±0.681	0.765 ±0.427
% Agreement	74.3%	69.3%	70.0%	56.3%	74.7%	81.6%
Kripp.'s α	0.239	0.142	0.315	0.172	0.603	0.560

(a) Annotation agreement for Similarity, Originality, and Context. Results on 140 messages characterized as implicit HS from the functionality `derog_imp_h` for HateCheck, and on a sample of 140 implicit HS messages from IHC.

Label	#	Fluency	Informativeness	Soundness
HS	169	4.935 ±0.394	3.899 ±1.002	4.798 ±0.745
Non-HS	81	4.975 ±0.395	4.333 ±1.002	4.667 ±0.746
All	250	4.948 ±0.390	4.040 ±0.996	4.755 ±0.774

(b) Avg. and Std. scores for Fluency, Informativeness, and Soundness across the labels HS, Non-HS, and the entire set of 250 human-evaluated instances.

4.1   Discussion and Error Analysis

Regarding **RQ1**, our analysis indicate that, on the whole, our models excel in detecting HS, with GPT-4 demonstrating the highest overall proficiency. We see high Accuracy scores for the few-shot prompted models, that can be attributed to their learning of specific output structures from the provided examples. However, GPT-4 struggles to recognize non-hateful examples in most instances (Table 2b), showcasing the importance of considering the complexity and diversity of real-world language when evaluating model effectiveness. The high false positive rates can be directly linked to GPT-4's performance in certain nuanced categories within the HateCheck dataset (i.e., Counter Quotes, Counter References, Reclaimed Slurs, Targeted Groups, and Individual Targets). For example, consider the Reclaimed Slurs category. An instance where GPT-4 incorrectly classifies a message as hateful is in sentences like: *Keep your thoughts to yourself. We are faggots and proud of it!*. Here, the message is actually non-hateful: it is a statement of reclamation of a slur. However, GPT-4 mistakenly identifies it as hateful, primarily due to its reliance on specific trigger words like *faggots*.

In addressing **RQ2**, we see that the automatic metrics collectively contribute to our understanding of the models' proficiency in generating explanations, with BertScore reflecting overall textual similarity, and BLEU and IOU-F1 scores offering insights into token-based resemblance. Therefore, the efficacy of model performance is contingent upon the specific task at hand. For tasks demanding the generation of explanations with a clear and precise structure, few-shot and fine-tuned generation systems emerge as optimal choices due to their consistent output in length and structure. This is underscored by their superior results in the BLEU metric, denoting greater token-based similarity. Conversely, if the goal is to obtain less structured explanations, other models may be preferred, as they occasionally introduce additional information.

Concerning **RQ3**, our models exhibit a notable ability to recognize implicitness in the original text. In the following example (generated by GPT-4), the generated and gold explanations are aligned, and hatefulness and the target are correctly identified. Notably, the former diverges slightly from the original text by providing additional clarifications.

Implicit HS: *"We should test new drugs on immigrants before testing them on animals."*

Gold Explanation: *"The message is hateful against immigrants because it contains implicit derogation implying that immigrants are worthless of living and inferior to animals."*

Generated Explanation: *"The message is considered hateful as it devalues the lives of immigrants by suggesting they should be used as test subjects for new drugs before animals. This implies that their lives are worth less than those of animals, which is a derogatory and harmful perspective"*

Overall, the explanations generated by all the models are consistently plausible and easily understandable by humans, sometimes offering additional insights.

As for **RQ4**, both automatic metrics and human evaluators generally concur on the soundness and plausibility of the predicted explanations. Nevertheless, sometimes the models struggle to discern subtle rhetorical figures, such as sarcasm. Examples like *"Gay lives are worth so much"* and *"There is no hatred in my heart for you trans people,"* were labeled as non-hateful by the models, though an annotator perceived them as sarcastic. This highlights the need for further refinement to address nuanced and rhetorical messages.

5   Conclusions

The paper addresses the task of detecting hate speech on social media (in particular, in implicit and subtle instances), unveiling at the same time the obtained predictions through natural language explanations. We proposed an approach based on prompt construction, free-text generation, few-shot learning, and fine-tuning. Our study evaluates the approach's impact on jointly predicting labels and explanations, assesses content generation faithfulness and human plausibility, and explores the models' ability to unveil implicit meanings in HS. The ablation study shows that adding explanations to the models enhances their prediction capabilities in a statistically significant way in all the configurations. Similarly, the human evaluation study shows that the generated explanations are highly fluent, informative, and sound.

Acknowledgements. This work has been supported by the French government, through the 3IA Côte d'Azur Investments in the Future project managed by the National Research Agency (ANR) with the reference number ANR-19-P3IA-0002.

References

1. Basile, V., et al.: SemEval-2019 task 5: multilingual detection of hate speech against immigrants and women in Twitter. In: Proceedings of the 13th International Workshop on Semantic Evaluation, pp. 54–63. Association for Computational Linguistics, Minneapolis (2019)
2. Chakravarthi, B.R., et al.: Overview of the shared task on homophobia and transphobia detection in social media comments. In: Proceedings of the Second Workshop on Language Technology for Equality, Diversity and Inclusion, pp. 369–377. Association for Computational Linguistics, Dublin (2022)
3. Chen, Q., et al.: KACE: generating knowledge aware contrastive explanations for natural language inference. In: Proceedings of the 59th Annual Meeting of the Association for Computational Linguistics and the 11th International Joint Conference on Natural Language Processing (Volume 1: Long Papers), pp. 2516–2527. Association for Computational Linguistics, Online (2021)
4. Clinciu, M.A., Eshghi, A., Hastie, H.: A study of automatic metrics for the evaluation of natural language explanations. In: Proceedings of the 16th Conference of the European Chapter of the Association for Computational Linguistics: Main Volume, pp. 2376–2387. Association for Computational Linguistics, Online (2021). https://doi.org/10.18653/v1/2021.eacl-main.202, https://aclanthology.org/2021.eacl-main.202
5. Costa, F., Ouyang, S., Dolog, P., Lawlor, A.: Automatic generation of natural language explanations. In: Proceedings of the 23rd International Conference on Intelligent User Interfaces Companion, pp. 1–2. IUI '18 Companion, Association for Computing Machinery, New York (2018)
6. Davidson, T., Warmsley, D., Macy, M., Weber, I.: Automated hate speech detection and the problem of offensive language. In: Proceedings of the International AAAI Conference on Web and Social Media, vol. 11(1), pp. 512–515 (2017), number: 1
7. ElSherief, M., et al.: Latent hatred: a benchmark for understanding implicit hate speech. In: Proceedings of the 2021 Conference on Empirical Methods in Natural Language Processing, pp. 345–363. Association for Computational Linguistics, Online and Punta Cana, Dominican Republic (2021)
8. Founta, A., et al.: Large scale crowdsourcing and characterization of twitter abusive behavior. In: Proceedings of the International AAAI Conference on Web and Social Media, vol. 12(1) (2018), number: 1
9. Gambäck, B., Sikdar, U.K.: Using convolutional neural networks to classify hate-speech. In: Proceedings of the First Workshop on Abusive Language Online, pp. 85–90. Association for Computational Linguistics, Vancouver (2017)
10. Ghosh, S., Suri, M., Chiniya, P., Tyagi, U., Kumar, S., Manocha, D.: CoSyn: detecting implicit hate speech in online conversations using a context synergized hyperbolic network. In: Proceedings of the 2023 Conference on Empirical Methods in Natural Language Processing, pp. 6159–6173. Association for Computational Linguistics, Singapore (2023)
11. Gitari, N.D., Zhang, Z., Damien, H., Long, J.: A lexicon-based approach for hate speech detection. Int. J. Multimedia Ubiquitous Eng. 10(4), 215–230 (2015)
12. Han, X., Tsvetkov, Y.: Fortifying toxic speech detectors against veiled toxicity. In: Proceedings of the 2020 Conference on Empirical Methods in Natural Language Processing (EMNLP), pp. 7732–7739. Association for Computational Linguistics, Online (2020)

13. Hartvigsen, T., Gabriel, S., Palangi, H., Sap, M., Ray, D., Kamar, E.: ToxiGen: a large-scale machine-generated dataset for adversarial and implicit hate speech detection. In: Proceedings of the 60th Annual Meeting of the Association for Computational Linguistics (Volume 1: Long Papers), pp. 3309–3326. Association for Computational Linguistics, Dublin, Ireland (2022)

14. Huang, F., Kwak, H., An, J.: Chain of Explanation: new prompting method to generate higher quality natural language explanation for implicit hate speech. In: Companion Proceedings of the ACM Web Conference 2023, pp. 90–93 (2023). arXiv:2209.04889 [cs]

15. Jiang, A.Q., et al.: Mistral 7B (2023). arXiv:2310.06825 [cs]

16. Jurgens, D., Hemphill, L., Chandrasekharan, E.: A just and comprehensive strategy for using NLP to address online abuse. In: Proceedings of the 57th Annual Meeting of the Association for Computational Linguistics, pp. 3658–3666. Association for Computational Linguistics, Florence (2019)

17. Kanter, J.W., Williams, M.T., Kuczynski, A.M., Manbeck, K.E., Debreaux, M., Rosen, D.C.: A preliminary report on the relationship between microaggressions against black people and racism among white college students. Race Soc. Probl. 9(4), 291–299 (2017)

18. Kim, J., Lee, B., Sohn, K.A.: Why is it hate speech? Masked rationale prediction for explainable hate speech detection. In: Proceedings of the 29th International Conference on Computational Linguistics, pp. 6644–6655. International Committee on Computational Linguistics, Gyeongju, Republic of Korea (2022)

19. Kim, Y., Park, S., Namgoong, Y., Han, Y.S.: ConPrompt: pre-training a language model with machine-generated data for implicit hate speech detection. In: Findings of the Association for Computational Linguistics: EMNLP 2023, pp. 10964–10980. Association for Computational Linguistics, Singapore (2023)

20. Lee, J.H., Park, J.U., Cha, J.W., Han, Y.S.: Detecting context abusiveness using hierarchical deep learning. In: Proceedings of the Second Workshop on Natural Language Processing for Internet Freedom: Censorship, Disinformation, and Propaganda, pp. 10–19. Association for Computational Linguistics, Hong Kong, China (2019)

21. Locatelli, D., Damo, G., Nozza, D.: A cross-lingual study of homotransphobia on Twitter. In: Proceedings of the First Workshop on Cross-Cultural Considerations in NLP (C3NLP), pp. 16–24. Association for Computational Linguistics, Dubrovnik, Croatia (2023)

22. Lyu, Q., Apidianaki, M., Callison-Burch, C.: Towards faithful model explanation in NLP: a survey (2023)

23. Mathew, B., Saha, P., Yimam, S.M., Biemann, C., Goyal, P., Mukherjee, A. HateXplain: a benchmark dataset for explainable hate speech detection. In: Proceedings of the AAAI Conference on Artificial Intelligence, vol. 35(17), 14867–14875 (2021), number: 17

24. Nadal, K.L., Griffin, K.E., Wong, Y., Hamit, S., Rasmus, M.: The impact of racial microaggressions on mental health: counseling implications for clients of color. J. Couns. Dev. 92(1), 57–66 (2014)

25. Nejadgholi, I., Fraser, K., Kiritchenko, S.: Improving generalizability in implicitly abusive language detection with concept activation vectors. In: Proceedings of the 60th Annual Meeting of the Association for Computational Linguistics (Volume 1: Long Papers), pp. 5517–5529. Association for Computational Linguistics, Dublin, Ireland (2022)

26. Nozza, D., Bianchi, F., Attanasio, G.: HATE-ITA: hate speech detection in Italian social media text. In: Narang, K., Mostafazadeh Davani, A., Mathias, L., Vidgen, B., Talat, Z. (eds.) Proceedings of the Sixth Workshop on Online Abuse and Harms (WOAH), pp. 252–260. Association for Computational Linguistics, Seattle, Washington (Hybrid) (2022). https://doi.org/10.18653/v1/2022.woah-1.24, https://aclanthology.org/2022.woah-1.24

27. Ocampo, N.B., Cabrio, E., Villata, S.: Playing the part of the sharp bully: generating adversarial examples for implicit hate speech detection. In: Findings of the Association for Computational Linguistics: ACL 2023, pp. 2758–2772. Association for Computational Linguistics, Toronto, Canada (2023)

28. Ocampo, N.B., Cabrio, E., Villata, S.: Unmasking the hidden meaning: bridging implicit and explicit hate speech embedding representations. In: Findings of the Association for Computational Linguistics: EMNLP 2023, pp. 6626–6637. Association for Computational Linguistics, Singapore (2023)

29. Ocampo, N.B., Sviridova, E., Cabrio, E., Villata, S.: An in-depth analysis of implicit and subtle hate speech messages. In: Proceedings of the 17th Conference of the European Chapter of the Association for Computational Linguistics, pp. 1997–2013. Association for Computational Linguistics, Dubrovnik, Croatia (2023)

30. Papineni, K., Roukos, S., Ward, T., Zhu, W.J.: Bleu: a method for automatic evaluation of machine translation. In: Proceedings of the 40th Annual Meeting of the Association for Computational Linguistics, pp. 311–318. Association for Computational Linguistics, Philadelphia (2002)

31. Röttger, P., Vidgen, B., Nguyen, D., Waseem, Z., Margetts, H., Pierrehumbert, J.: HateCheck: functional tests for hate speech detection models. In: Proceedings of the 59th Annual Meeting of the Association for Computational Linguistics and the 11th International Joint Conference on Natural Language Processing (Volume 1: Long Papers), pp. 41–58. Association for Computational Linguistics, Online (2021)

32. Roychowdhury, S., Gupta, V.: Data-efficient methods for improving hate speech detection. In: Findings of the Association for Computational Linguistics: EACL 2023, pp. 125–132. Association for Computational Linguistics, Dubrovnik, Croatia (2023)

33. Samek, W., Wiegand, T., Müller, K.R.: Explainable Artificial Intelligence: Understanding, Visualizing and Interpreting Deep Learning Models (2017). arXiv:1708.08296 [cs, stat]

34. Sap, M., Gabriel, S., Qin, L., Jurafsky, D., Smith, N.A., Choi, Y.: Social bias frames: reasoning about social and power implications of language. In: Proceedings of the 58th Annual Meeting of the Association for Computational Linguistics, pp. 5477–5490. Association for Computational Linguistics, Online (2020)

35. Sohn, H., Lee, H.: MC-BERT4HATE: hate speech detection using multi-channel bert for different languages and translations. In: 2019 International Conference on Data Mining Workshops (ICDMW), pp. 551–559 (2019), iSSN: 2375-9259

36. Taori, R., et al.: Stanford alpaca: an instruction-following llama model (2023). https://github.com/tatsu-lab/stanford_alpaca

37. Vidgen, B., Thrush, T., Waseem, Z., Kiela, D.: Learning from the worst: dynamically generated datasets to improve online hate detection. In: Proceedings of the 59th Annual Meeting of the Association for Computational Linguistics and the 11th International Joint Conference on Natural Language Processing (Volume 1: Long Papers), pp. 1667–1682. Association for Computational Linguistics, Online (2021)

38. Wang, H., Hee, M.S., Awal, M.R., Choo, K.T.W., Lee, R.K.W.: Evaluating GPT-3 Generated Explanations for Hateful Content Moderation, vol. 6, pp. 6255–6263 (2023), iSSN: 1045-0823
39. Wang, K., Lu, D., Han, C., Long, S., Poon, J.: Detect all abuse! toward universal abusive language detection models. In: Proceedings of the 28th International Conference on Computational Linguistics, pp. 6366–6376. International Committee on Computational Linguistics, Barcelona, Spain (Online) (2020)
40. Waseem, Z., Davidson, T., Warmsley, D., Weber, I.: Understanding abuse: a typology of abusive language detection subtasks. In: Proceedings of the First Workshop on Abusive Language Online, pp. 78–84. Association for Computational Linguistics, Vancouver, BC, Canada (2017)
41. Wen, J., et al.: Unveiling the implicit toxicity in large language models. In: Proceedings of the 2023 Conference on Empirical Methods in Natural Language Processing, pp. 1322–1338. Association for Computational Linguistics, Singapore (2023)
42. Wiegand, M., Kampfmeier, J., Eder, E., Ruppenhofer, J.: Euphemistic abuse – a new dataset and classification experiments for implicitly abusive language. In: Proceedings of the 2023 Conference on Empirical Methods in Natural Language Processing, pp. 16280–16297. Association for Computational Linguistics, Singapore (2023)
43. Wiegand, M., Ruppenhofer, J., Eder, E.: Implicitly abusive language – what does it actually look like and why are we not getting there? In: Proceedings of the 2021 Conference of the North American Chapter of the Association for Computational Linguistics: Human Language Technologies, pp. 576–587. Association for Computational Linguistics, Online (2021)
44. Wiegand, M., Ruppenhofer, J., Schmidt, A., Greenberg, C.: Inducing a lexicon of abusive words – a feature-based approach. In: Walker, M., Ji, H., Stent, A. (eds.) Proceedings of the 2018 Conference of the North American Chapter of the Association for Computational Linguistics: Human Language Technologies, Volume 1 (Long Papers), pp. 1046–1056. Association for Computational Linguistics, New Orleans, Louisiana (2018)
45. Yang, Y., Kim, J., Kim, Y., Ho, N., Thorne, J., Yun, S.Y.: HARE: explainable hate speech detection with step-by-step reasoning. In: Findings of the Association for Computational Linguistics: EMNLP 2023, pp. 5490–5505. Association for Computational Linguistics, Singapore (2023)
46. Zampieri, M., Malmasi, S., Nakov, P., Rosenthal, S., Farra, N., Kumar, R.: SemEval-2019 task 6: identifying and categorizing offensive language in social media (OffensEval). In: Proceedings of the 13th International Workshop on Semantic Evaluation, pp. 75–86. Association for Computational Linguistics, Minneapolis, Minnesota, USA (2019)
47. Zhang, T., Kishore, V., Wu, F., Weinberger, K.Q., Artzi, Y.: BERTScore: Evaluating Text Generation with BERT (2020)

The Influence of Iconicity in Transfer Learning for Sign Language Recognition

Keren Artiaga[1]([✉]) [iD], Conor Lynch[2] [iD], Haithem Afli[1] [iD],
and Mohammed Hasanuzzaman[1] [iD]

[1] ADAPT Centre, Munster Technological University, Cork, Ireland
{keren.artiaga,haithem.afli,mohammed.hasanuzzaman}@adaptcentre.ie
[2] Nimbus Centre, Munster Technological University, Cork, Ireland
conor.lynch@mtu.ie

Abstract. Most sign language recognition research relies on Transfer Learning (TL) from vision-based datasets such as ImageNet. Some extend this to alternatively available language datasets, often focusing on signs with cross-linguistic similarities. This body of work examines the necessity of these likenesses on effective knowledge transfer by comparing TL performance between iconic signs of two different sign language pairs: Chinese to Arabic and Greek to Flemish. Google Mediapipe was utilised as an input feature extractor, enabling spatial information of these signs to be processed with a Multilayer Perceptron architecture and the temporal information with a Gated Recurrent Unit. Experimental results showed a 7.02% improvement for Arabic and 1.07% for Flemish when conducting iconic TL from Chinese and Greek respectively.

1 Introduction

Sign language datasets, often limited in size compared to spoken language datasets, are susceptible to overfitting [21,31]. Sign Language Recognition (SLR) studies often work with datasets containing fewer than 30k samples [30]. This is a stark contrast to spoken language, where a language pair corpora with less than 500k samples is considered low-resourced [19,20]. To address this issue, Transfer Learning (TL) has gained traction in SLR and Sign Language Translation (SLT) - typically involving knowledge transfer from ImageNet, a large vision-based dataset [3,7,14]. Recent studies have explored TL between different language datasets, for instance from American Sign Language (ASL) to Ankara University Turkish Sign Language (AUTSL), the Spanish: Lengua de Signos Española (LSE) kinesics to AUTSL [34] and British Sign Language (BSL) to ASL [5] - where the improved recognition is explained by their shared similarities. However, BSL and ASL belong to different language families and their similarities can be attributed to *iconicity* [37] - a semiotic concept where a word or sign resembles its meaning, such as the sign or gesture for *Think* which always involves a mime or hand movement towards the head across various languages. [29] demonstrated in their 1976 study that ASL signs possess 25% pantomimic or iconic attributes. Furthermore, in a more recent 2018 study by [24], a significant 68% iconicity correlation between 604 BSL and 993 ASL signs was reported. In

A. Rapp et al. (Eds.): NLDB 2024, LNCS 14762, pp. 226–240, 2024.
https://doi.org/10.1007/978-3-031-70239-6_16

addition to the aforementioned, quantitative analyses have also confirmed cross-linguistic similarities in iconic signs across various sign languages [37]. This study builds upon these findings by conducting transfer learning between iconic signs, exploring the impact of movement differences on knowledge transfer in SLR - a topic, to the authors' knowledge, that has been not previously explored.

The novel contribution of this research work involves a comparative analysis of TL from iconic signs across datasets of two distinct sign language source/target pairs:

(1) From SLR500[1], a Chinese Sign Language (CSL) SLR dataset comprising 500 daily Chinese sign categories to KArSL[2] (KFUPM Arabic Sign Language), an Arabic Sign Language (ArSL) database consisting of 502 sign words belonging to categories such as Letters, Numbers, Health, and Family among others. Each sign from SLR500 is performed 5 times by 50 signers, whereas for KArSL, three signers performed each sign 50 times.

(2) From an isolated Greek Sign Language (GSL)[3] dataset that features cases of Deaf people interacting with police departments, hospitals, and citizen service centres to the Flemish Vlaamse Gebarentaal or VGT[4] dataset. Woordenboek VGT is a collection of videos in Flemish Sign Language. 120 deaf people contributed to the Corpus VGT as informants. Age, region and gender were taken into account when selecting the participants.

In particular, for GSL isolated, seven native signers performed the signs five times, whereas, for Woordenboek VGT, repetitions are present, but the authors did not indicate an exact number.

The experiments are designed so that the low-resource datasets are the target tasks while the higher-resource datasets are the source tasks. Therefore, CSL SLR500 and GSL isolated were chosen as the source languages due to their higher number of samples per class (250 and 54 respectively) relative to their corresponding lower-resource target corpus (150 and 13.64 respectively). Table 1 presents the number of classes for each subset along with the number of samples per class, as well as the iconic concepts these classes represent. These iconic concepts are identified in the study by [37] and are visualised in Figs. 1 and 2 respectively. It is noteworthy that the first pair of subsets, CSL SLR500 and KArSL, share the same set of five iconic concepts (*anatomy, hair, eyesight, love* and *sound*), while the second pairing, GSL isolated and Woordenboek VGT, have merely three mutual iconic concepts - *anatomy, food* and *sound*. This intended selection allows one to deduce whether the number of shared iconic concepts has a significant or otherwise impact on the transferability of knowledge.

Google's MediaPipe for landmark detection [1] was used to extract coordinate-based input features, enabling a simplified Multi-Layer Perceptron and Gated Recurrent Unit (MLP-GRU) architecture for the SLR models. This

---

[1] https://ustc-slr.github.io/datasets/2015_csl.
[2] https://hamzah-luqman.github.io/KArSL/.
[3] https://vcl.iti.gr/dataset/gsl/.
[4] https://taalmaterialen.ivdnt.org/download/woordenboek-vgt/.

Table 1. Overview of the iconic subset

Dataset	Iconic subset no. of classes	Iconic subset no. of samples per class (mean)	Iconic concepts the classes belong to
CSL SLR500 [a]	8	250	Anatomy, Hair, Eyesight, Love, Sound
KArSL [b]	26	150	Anatomy, Hair, Eyesight, Love, Sound
GSL isolated [c]	13	54	Anatomy, Food, Sound
Woordenboek VGT [d]	85	13.64	Anatomy, Food, Sound, Hair, Clothes, Eyesight, Say, Love, Hear,

[a] [12,13,36] [b] [28] [c] [2] [d] [6]

approach reduces data requirements and enhances robustness against signer body size variations compared to using raw frames [8]. The paper is structured as follows: An introduction to the research contribution is presented in Sect. 1 whilst salient research from the existing literature is covered in Sect. 2. Section 3 details the methodology, including data pre-processing, MediaPipe key-points extraction, architecture, as well as TL results. Section 4 presents the ablation study and finally, Sect. 5 concludes the study by discussing the key insights and findings.

2   Related Work

Recent advancements in non-verbal communication research highlight the effectiveness of TL in enhancing Sign Language Recognition (SLR), especially using pre-trained ImageNet models. Several recent studies [7,10,15,22,23,25–27,32,35] endorse this TL approach. Meanwhile, there has been a growing interest in domain-specific TL, as evidenced by studies that transfer knowledge between large corpus languages, such as BSL to the more moderate ASL dataset [5], or from ASL to AUTSL or LSE to AUTSL [33], and recently from CSL to ASL, as well as from Argentine Sign Language (LSA) to ASL [4]. However, the studies by [4,5] focused on signs present in both their source and target datasets which are often iconic. Conversely, [33] attributed improved recognition accuracy to the similar data acquisition method used by their source and target datasets through Kinect. This research aims to address the gap presented by the lack of studies comparing TL between signs with similarities such as in the case of iconic signs and between signs with no obvious similarities. The selection of signs for this study aligns with the findings of [37], who used automated methods to visualise hand activity patterns across 31 sign languages. These patterns, illustrated in Figs. 1 and 2 reveal similarities in hand movements, particularly for individual concepts.

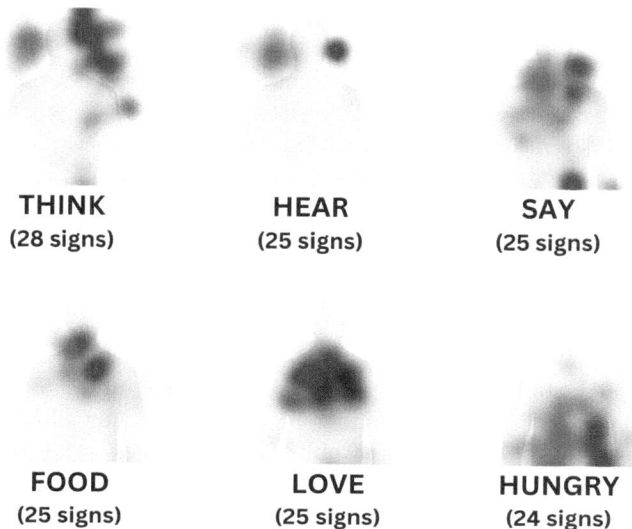

Fig. 1. Sign gesture hand activity for individual concepts across languages. [37]

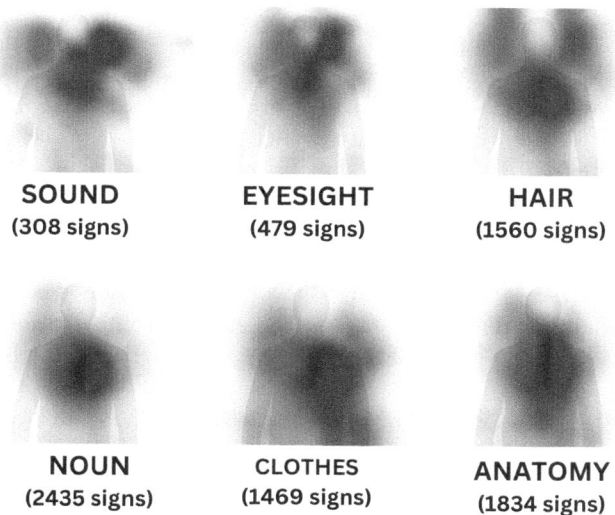

Fig. 2. Sign gesture hand activity for groups of concepts across languages. [37]

While cross-linguistic patterns also emerged for broader lexical or semantic categories, they are less pronounced than those for individual concepts.

3   Method

This section provides an extensive account of the data pre-processing, mediapipe keypoint extraction and the MLP-GRU architecture, along with its critical hyper-parameters. It concludes with a comprehensive explanation of the experimental TL results.

3.1   Data Pre-processing and Extracting MediaPipe Keypoints

Two pairs of isolated sign language datasets are used for this study, namely CSL SLR500 and KArSL, and GSL isol and Woordenboek VGT. Table 1 presents the class counts for each iconic subset, along with the sample count per class, as well as the iconic concepts these classes belong to. For the training and testing, each subset is randomly split 80% for training and 20% for testing with the exception of KArSL as its authors indicated a split for this dataset - approximately 78% for training and approximately 22% for testing. For the task of iconic TL, signs were chosen from both datasets based on iconic individual concepts c.f. Fig. 1 and larger categories c.f. Fig. 2 identified by [37]. MediaPipe Holistic Landmarker task (MediaPipe 0.10.3) was used to extract hands, shoulders and wrist landmarks from the source and target dataset video samples. Facial keypoints were excluded since the focus of this study is on word-level SLR, where grammatical and syntactic markers are less relevant, and the signers in both datasets only mouth the equivalent word for the sign. Additionally, facial expressions fall outside the scope of this paper's reference study [37] on cross-linguistic iconicity. Each MediaPipe landmark comprised x, y and z coordinates. The x and y coordinates are normalised to the frame dimensions, ranging from 0.0 to 1.0, while the z coordinate indicates depth and is approximately the same scale as x. The coordinates are closer to 1.0 when the hands are at rest. The KArSL, LSFB and GSL isol datasets are pre-processed, with frames lacking activity removed. However, this is not the case with the CSL SLR500 and WoordenboekVGT datasets. Hence, to eliminate outliers from these datasets, keypoints are only extracted from frames where the y-coordinate value of either the left or right-hand wrist was below 0.6.

Figure 3 shows the MediaPipe keypoint landmarks on select video frames representing the KArSL sign for *Skull* and the CSL sign for *Head*. The cross-linguistic similarities between these two iconic signs are apparent, with the only noticeable difference being the inclusion of right-hand activity towards the end of the KArSL gesture.

3.2   MLP-GRU

Both the baseline (non-TL KArSL and non-TL Woordenboek VGT) and transfer learning models (SLR500 to KArSL, and GSL isolated to Woordenboek VGT) in this study shared an MLP-GRU architecture. The MLP learned spatial information for each set of keypoints in a sample, while the GRU extracted temporal information from the features produced by the MLP. The MLP had a single

Fig. 3. MediaPipe keypoint landmarks detailing the anatomy sign for *Skull* (KArSL) and *Head* (CSL)

hidden layer, and the GRU consisted of only one recurrent layer. The Rectified Linear Unit (ReLU) activation function, as defined in 1, was applied to the MLP layer.

$$ReLU(x) = max(0, x) \tag{1}$$

where $x \in \mathbb{R}$. Softmax function, as described in 2, is applied to the output layer.

$$\sigma(y_i) = \left(\frac{e^{y_i}}{\sum_j e^{y_j}} \right) \tag{2}$$

where σ is the softmax, y is the input vector, e^{y_i} denotes the standard input vector exponential function, j represents the number of classes, and e^{y_j} is the standard output vector exponential function. Grid search was performed to determine the best number of MLP neurons and GRU hidden size for the baseline target models. The resulting best set of hyper-parameters was then used to build the source models. Table 2 displays the performance of different sets of MLP-GRU hyper-parameters in the baseline KArSL and Woordenboek VGT recognition tasks. As Woordenboek VGT is an imbalanced dataset, the macro F1 score, as shown in 3, is employed in addition to the accuracy metric, as shown in 4, due to its ability to provide a balanced evaluation of performance across all classes. The formulation for the macro F1 Score is shown as follows:

$$F1_{macro} = \frac{1}{N} \sum_{i=1}^{N} \frac{2 \cdot \text{Precision}_i \cdot \text{Recall}_i}{\text{Precision}_i + \text{Recall}_i} \tag{3}$$

where N is the number of classes, Precision_i is the precision for class i, and Recall_i is the recall for class i.

Meanwhile, the formulation for accuracy is shown below:

$$Accuracy = \frac{TP + TN}{TP + TN + FP + FN} \tag{4}$$

where TP, TN, FP and FN represent the true positive, true negative, false positive and false negative values respectively.

It is worth noting that for Woordenboek VGT, two combinations of MLP Neurons - GRU Hidden Size resulted in the same best macro F1 score; however, the 2048–4096 combination was selected as the best set of hyper-parameters as it achieved the best macro F1 score at 2000 epoch, whereas the 2000–3000 combination achieved it at 2362 epochs.

Table 2. Impact of MLP neurons and GRU hidden sizes on the accuracy and macro F1 score of the target tasks.

Target Subsets	MLP Neurons	GRU Hidden Size	Recognition Acc. (%)	Macro F1 Score (%)
KArSL	256	512	77.81	–
	512	1024	79.53	–
	1024	2048	79.69	–
	2000	3000	80.15	–
	2048	4096	79.22	–
Woordenboek VGT	256	512	86.12	58.75
	512	1024	90.28	84.35
	1024	2048	90.21	85.92
	2000	3000	90.28	87.88
	2048	4096	90.28	87.88

Adam [17] optimizer was used to train the models using a batch size of 32 with a learning rate of 1e-05. The training continued for an uncapped number of epochs and was terminated when no improvement in loss occurred for 200 epochs. The loss function used is categorical cross-entropy shown in 5.

$$Loss = -\frac{1}{N} \sum_{i=1}^{N} \sum_{j=1}^{J} y_{i,j} \log(\hat{y}_{i,j}) \tag{5}$$

where N is the size of the test set, and J is the classification category. Utilising an Intel i9-9940X processor, the models were trained on an 11 GB NVIDIA GeForce RTX 2080Ti GPU with 128 GB of RAM.

3.3 Transfer Learning (TL) and Results

TL involves transferring knowledge from one domain to another. In this study, TL was conducted by saving the learned weights from source SLR tasks (iconic CSL and non-iconic CSL recognition) and using them as initial weights for the target task (ArSL recognition), known as weight initialisation - c.f. Fig. 5. These weights were then fine-tuned during training until the loss converged to a minimum value. Weight initialisation was applied only to the MLP layer of the architecture since the GRU remained fixed with a single layer. Table 3 displays the recognition accuracy of the fine-tuned KArSL and Woordenboek VGT models, showing improvements over their non-TL baselines (Fig. 4).

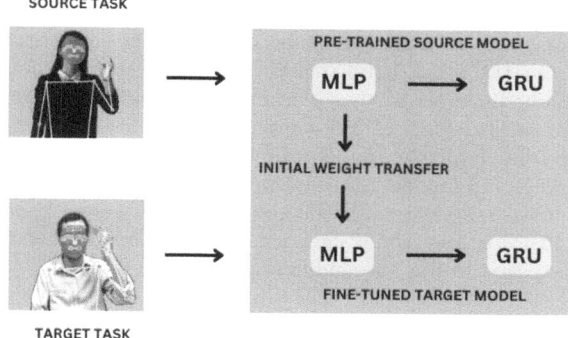

Fig. 4. MLP-GRU execution on SLR TL tasks.

The results indicate that transferring knowledge from iconic CSL SLR500 to KArSL led to a notable 7.02% increase in recognition accuracy, showcasing the effectiveness of leveraging iconicity for improved performance. Similarly, the transfer learning from iconic GSL isolated to Woordenboek VGT resulted in a modest 1.07% improvement in accuracy. However, the corresponding macro F1 scores remain unchanged at 87.88%, indicating that transfer learning did not affect the balance of performance across different classes. Nevertheless, transfer learning helped achieve the same macro F1 score at an earlier epoch of 1867 compared to 2000 with the baseline.

Table 3. Summary of iconic TL tasks results

Task	Recognition Accuracy (%)	Macro F1 Score (%)
KArSL Baseline	80.15	–
CSL SLR500 to KArSL TL	85.78	–
Woordenboek VGT Baseline	90.28	87.88
GSL isolated to Woordenboek VGT	91.25	87.88

4 Ablation Study

4.1 Effect of Pre-training with Non-iconic Signs

A comparison was conducted to assess the performance of using non-iconic signs from the source languages, aiming to determine whether there are differences compared to simply pre-training with non-iconic signs. The pre-processing and experimental setup for the non-iconic transfer were similar to that of the iconic transfer 3.2, with an equal number of non-iconic signs selected from each source dataset to ensure a fair comparison.

Table 4 presents the results of pre-training with non-iconic signs. It is observed that for CSL SLR 500 to KArSL non-iconic transfer, there was a positive transfer, showing an improvement of 6.84% from the baseline. This improvement, while lower than the 7.02% improvement from the iconic transfer, still indicates the effectiveness of this approach. On the other hand, for GSL isolated to Woordenboek VGT, the best accuracy remained similar to that of the baseline; however, the model achieved this accuracy at an earlier epoch of 238 compared to the baseline, which reached this accuracy at 502 epochs. Similarly, the F1 score remained unchanged compared to that of the baseline; however, the model achieved this score at 1815 epochs compared to the baseline, which achieved this score at 2000 epochs. This suggests that for this specific transfer scenario, utilising non-iconic signs led to faster convergence to a similar level of performance compared to the baseline model.

Table 4. Summary of non-iconic TL results

Task	Recognition Accuracy (%)	Macro F1 Score (%)
KArSL Baseline	80.15	–
CSL SLR500 to KArSL TL	85.63	–
Woordenboek VGT Baseline	90.28	87.88
GSL isolated to Woordenboek VGT	90.28	87.88

4.2   Effect of Pre-training with Iconic+non-iconic Signs

Experiments were conducted to assess whether there would be an increase in accuracy for the target tasks when combining iconic signs and non-iconic signs as source tasks. The pre-processing and experimental setup for this ablation study were kept similar to the iconic transfer 3.2 to ensure a fair comparison. Results obtained from transferring with iconic+non-iconic signs showed some improvement in accuracy for the TL task of CSL SLR500 to KArSL, as presented in Table 5. However, for the GSL isolated to Woordenboek VGT TL task, the best accuracy remained similar to the baseline, albeit at the epoch of 164, which is earlier than both the baseline and the equivalent non-iconic tasks 4.1, which is at the 595 and 164 epochs, respectively. The macro F1 scores for the Woordenboek VGT tasks, which are consistently at 87.88%, indicate that while the overall accuracy showed some improvements with transfer learning, the balance and consistency of the model's performance across different classes remained unchanged. However, transfer learning helped achieve the same macro F1 score at an earlier epoch of 1679 compared to 2000 with the baseline (no transfer learning).

4.3   Effect of Fewer Similarities in Iconic Signs

An experiment was conducted to compare the performance between language pairs that share fewer than three similar iconic concepts. This experiment focused on the

Table 5. Summary of iconic+non-iconic TL results

Task	Recognition Accuracy (%)	Macro F1 Score (%)
KArSL Baseline	80.15	–
CSL SLR500 to KArSL TL	84.06	–
Woordenboek VGT Baseline	90.28	87.88
GSL isolated to Woordenboek VGT	90.28	87.88

sign language pair Iranian and French-Belgian - as their corresponding SL dataset met the criteria for sharing fewer than three similar iconic concepts. For the source task, the Iranian SL dataset, MedSLset[5], was selected while for the target task, the French-Belgian dataset Langue des Signes de Belgique Francophone (LSFB-ISOL)[6] was chosen. Table 8 presents the relevant statistics for this language pair. Although MedSLset has fewer samples per class, it is deemed a better source as it has a balanced number of samples while LSFB-ISOL does not. It is noted that the MedSLset dataset only shares 2 similar iconic concepts with LSFB-ISOL, namely *Anatomy* and *Sound* (Table 6) .

Table 6. Relevant dataset details for MedSLset and LSFB

Dataset	Iconic subset no. of classes	Iconic subset no. of samples per class (mean)	Iconic concepts the classes belong to	Balanced
MedSLset [a]	23	32	Anatomy, Sound	Yes
LSFB [b]	42	72.78	Anatomy, Sound, Clothes, Food, Think, Eyesight, Say, Love, Hear, Hair	No

[a] [16] [b] [9]

The pre-processing 3.1 and experimental setup for the non-iconic transfer are similar to the iconic transfer 3.2 to ensure a fair comparison. Specifically, MedSLset is split to 80% for training and 20% for testing while the author-specified split for LSFB was followed. Table 7 presents the performance of various sets of MLP-GRU hyperparameters in the baseline LSFB model where the configuration with 1024 MLP neurons and 2048 GRU hidden size yielded the best accuracy as well as macro F1 score for the baseline.

---

[5] https://ieee-dataport.org/open-access/display-multimodal-medslset-medical-sign-language-set.
[6] https://lsfb.info.unamur.be/.

Table 7. Impact of MLP neurons and GRU hidden sizes to LSFB

Target Subsets	MLP Neurons	GRU Hidden Size	Recognition Acc. (%)	Macro F1 Score (%)
LSFB	256	512	58.24	11.85
	512	1024	58.66	14.00
	1024	2048	58.26	11.54
	2000	3000	56.84	10.56
	2048	4096	53.76	10.05

The results of this experiment are displayed in Table 8 which reveals a case of negative transfer. This outcome confirms the significance of similarity in iconic concepts for successful transfer learning.

Table 8. Summary of MedSLset to LSFB iconic TL

Task	Recognition Accuracy (%)	Macro F1 Score (%)
LSFB Baseline	58.66	14.00
MedSLset to LSFB	50.36	9.26

4.4   Effect of Pre-training with ImageNet

To compare the performance of fine-tuned KArSL and Woordenboek VGT models against the most common approach to TL in SLR, which is ImageNet Pre-training as implemented by [7,10,22,25], and [18], two sets of experiments were conducted for each target language. These experiments utilised an Imagenet pre-trained convolutional network on top of the GRU. Specifically, we used ResNet50 [11] as the pre-trained model for comparison.

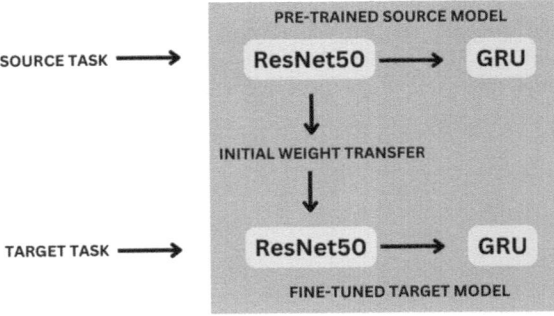

Fig. 5. MLP-GRU execution on SLR TL tasks.

The results of these experiments are presented in Table 9. It is evident from the results that for the CSL SLR500 to KArSL TL, pre-training with iconic signs yielded better results than pre-training with ImageNet. However, this was not observed for GSL isolated to Woordenboek VGT TL. Nonetheless, these results are not directly comparable because the pre-training with ImageNet uses RGB or raw frames, whereas the iconic TL approach utilises the skeleton keypoints as the input modality.

Table 9. Summary of pre-training with Imagenet in comparison to the iconic TL.

Task	Recognition Acc. (%)
iconic CSL SLR 500 to KArSL (keypoints)	85.78
ImageNet to KArSL (RGB)	77.34
iconic Greek isolated to Woordenboek VGT (keypoints)	91.25
ImageNet to Woordenboek VGT (RGB)	98.95

5   Discussion and Conclusion

It was demonstrated that transferring knowledge between signs of different languages, regardless of movement similarities, could be highly beneficial, especially where signs shared location boundaries. Specifically, transferring from iconic signs of different source sign languages resulted in the best accuracy for the target sign languages. Specifically, KArSL's recognition accuracy increased from 80.15% to 85.78% when initialised with the weights from CSL SLR500 and Woordenboek VGT's recognition accuracy increased from 90.28% to 91.25% when initialised with the weights from GSL isolated. Although the macro F1 score remained unchanged for the latter, the use of iconic transfer learning helped achieve this score 133 epochs earlier compared to the baseline. A slight improvement in accuracy is also observed for non-iconic TL and combined iconic and non-iconic TL between CSL SLR500 and KArSL.

However, from the results of the ablation studies, it can also be concluded that the transferability is sensitive between iconic concepts, such that negative transfer can occur when transferring between datasets containing only a few mutual iconic concepts. Overall, this study provided insight as to how a linguistic concept such as iconicity can help in the automatic recognition of isolated signs which is especially beneficial for low-resource sign languages. Additionally, the resulting pre-trained models from this study can also be instrumental for the more difficult task of sign language translation (SLT). Specifically, the pre-trained target models can be used in training a sign spotter that can recognise individual signs from a video.

References

1. Holistic landmarks detection task guide | MediaPipe | Google for Developers — developers.google.com. https://developers.google.com/mediapipe/solutions/vision/holistic_landmarker. Accessed 17 Sep 2023
2. Adaloglou, N., et al.: A comprehensive study on deep learning-based methods for sign language recognition. IEEE Trans. Multimedia **24**, 1750–1762 (2022). https://doi.org/10.1109/TMM.2021.3070438

3. Altaf, Y., Wahid, A., Kirmani, M.M.: Deep learning approach for sign language recognition using densenet201 with transfer learning. In: 2023 IEEE International Students' Conference on Electrical, Electronics and Computer Science (SCEECS), pp. 1–6 (2023). https://doi.org/10.1109/SCEECS57921.2023.10063044

4. Artiaga, K., Li, Y., Kuruoglu, E.E., Chan, W.K.V.: Cross-sign language transfer learning using domain adaptation with multi-scale temporal alignment. Multimedia Tools Appl. (2023). https://doi.org/10.1007/s11042-023-16703-0

5. Bird, J.J., Ekárt, A., Faria, D.R.: British sign language recognition via late fusion of computer vision and leap motion with transfer learning to American sign language. Sensors **20**(18) (2020). https://doi.org/10.3390/s20185151

6. Brosens, C., Janssens, M., Verstraete, S., Vandamme, T., De Durpel, H.: Moving towards a functional approach in the Flemish Sign Language dictionary making process. In: Efthimiou, E., et al. (eds.) Proceedings of the LREC2022 10th Workshop on the Representation and Processing of Sign Languages: Multilingual Sign Language Resources, pp. 24–28. European Language Resources Association, Marseille, France (2022). https://aclanthology.org/2022.signlang-1.4

7. Das, S., Imtiaz, M.S., Neom, N.H., Siddique, N., Wang, H.: A hybrid approach for Bangla sign language recognition using deep transfer learning model with random forest classifier. Expert Systems with Applications **213**, 118914 (2023). https://doi.org/10.1016/j.eswa.2022.118914, https://www.sciencedirect.com/science/article/pii/S0957417422019327

8. Duy Khuat, B., Thai Phung, D., Thi Thu Pham, H., Ngoc Bui, A., Tung Ngo, S.: Vietnamese sign language detection using mediapipe. In: Proceedings of the 2021 10th International Conference on Software and Computer Applications, pp. 162–165. ICSCA '21, Association for Computing Machinery, New York, NY, USA (2021). https://doi.org/10.1145/3457784.3457810, https://doi.org/10.1145/3457784.3457810

9. Fink, J., Frenay, B., Meurant, L., Cleve, A.: LSFB-CONT and LSFB-ISOL: two new datasets for vision-based sign language recognition. In: 2021 International Joint Conference on Neural Networks (IJCNN). IEEE (2021). https://doi.org/10.1109/ijcnn52387.2021.9534336

10. Halvardsson, G., Peterson, J., Soto-Valero, C., Baudry, B.: Interpretation of Swedish sign language using convolutional neural networks and transfer learning, pp. 207 (2021). https://doi.org/10.1007/s42979-021-00612-w

11. He, K., Zhang, X., Ren, S., Sun, J.: Deep residual learning for image recognition. In: 2016 IEEE Conference on Computer Vision and Pattern Recognition (CVPR), pp. 770–778 (2016). https://doi.org/10.1109/CVPR.2016.90

12. Hu, H., Zhao, W., Zhou, W., Li, H.: Signbert+: hand-model-aware self-supervised pre-training for sign language understanding. IEEE Trans. Pattern Analysis and Machine Intelligence (TPAMI), pp. 1–20 (2023). https://doi.org/10.1109/TPAMI.2023.3269220

13. Hu, H., Zhao, W., Zhou, W., Wang, Y., Li, H.: Signbert: pre-training of hand-model-aware representation for sign language recognition. In: Proceedings of the IEEE/CVF International Conference on Computer Vision, pp. 11087–11096 (2021). https://doi.org/10.1109/ICCV48922.2021.01090

14. Jaiswal, M., Sharmay, V., Sharmaz, A., Tomar, R.: Transfer learning with l2 norm regularization for classifying static two hand Hindi sign language gestures. In: 2020 IEEE 9th International Conference on Communication Systems and Network Technologies (CSNT), pp. 44–48 (2020). https://doi.org/10.1109/CSNT48778.2020.9115767

15. Jiang, X., Hu, B., Satapathy, S.C., Wang, S., Zhang, Y.: Fingerspelling identification for Chinese sign language via alexnet-based transfer learning and Adam optimizer. Sci. Program. **2020**, 3291426:1–3291426:13 (2020). https://doi.org/10.1155/2020/3291426
16. Khodapanah Aghdam, E., et al.: Display multimodal medslset (medical sign language set) (2020). https://doi.org/10.21227/5gsb-fb69
17. Kingma, D.P., Ba, J.: Adam: a method for stochastic optimization. In: Bengio, Y., LeCun, Y. (eds.) 3rd International Conference on Learning Representations, ICLR 2015, San Diego, CA, USA, May 7-9, 2015, Conference Track Proceedings (2015). https://doi.org/10.48550/arXiv.1412.6980
18. Laines, D., Gonzalez-Mendoza, M., Ochoa-Ruiz, G., Bejarano, G.: Isolated sign language recognition based on tree structure skeleton images. In: Proceedings of the IEEE/CVF Conference on Computer Vision and Pattern Recognition (CVPR) Workshops, pp. 276–284 (2023). https://doi.org/10.1109/CVPRW59228.2023.00033
19. Lakew, S.M., Karakanta, A., Federico, M., Negri, M., Turchi, M.: Adapting multilingual neural machine translation to unseen languages. In: Proceedings of the 16th International Conference on Spoken Language Translation. Association for Computational Linguistics, Hong Kong (2019). https://doi.org/10.48550/arXiv.1910.13998
20. Liu, Y., et al.: Multilingual denoising pre-training for neural machine translation. Trans. Assoc. Comput. Linguis. **8**, 726–742 (2020). https://doi.org/10.1162/tacl_a_00343
21. Marivate, V., et al.: Investigating an approach for low resource language dataset creation, curation and classification: Setswana and Sepedi. arXiv preprint arXiv:2003.04986 (2020)
22. Morocho-Cayamcela, M.E., Lim, W.: Fine-tuning a pre-trained convolutional neural network model to translate American sign language in real-time. 2019 International Conference on Computing, Networking and Communications (ICNC), pp. 100–104 (2019). https://doi.org/10.1109/ICCNC.2019.8685536
23. Nishat, Z.K., Shopon, M.: Unsupervised pretraining and transfer learning-based Bangla sign language recognition. In: Proceedings of International Joint Conference on Computational Intelligence Algorithms for Intelligent Systems, pp. 529-540 (2020). https://doi.org/10.1007/978-981-15-3607-6_42
24. Perlman, M., Little, H., Thompson, B., Thompson, R.L.: Iconicity in signed and spoken vocabulary: a comparison between American sign language, British sign language, English, and Spanish. Front. Psyc. **9** (2018). https://doi.org/10.3389/fpsyg.2018.01433
25. Rathi, D.: Optimization of transfer learning for sign language recognition targeting mobile platform. In: International Journal on Recent and Innovation Trends in Computing and Communication. vol. 6, pp. 198–203 (2018). https://doi.org/10.48550/arXiv.1805.06618
26. Shania, S., Naufal, M.F., Prasetyo, V.R., Azmi, M.S.B.: Translator of Indonesian sign language video using convolutional neural network with transfer learning. Indonesian J. Inf. Syst. (2022). https://doi.org/10.24002/ijis.v5i1.5865
27. Sharma, S., Singh, S.: ISL recognition system using integrated mobile-net and transfer learning method. Expert Syst. Appl. **221**, 119772 (2023). https://doi.org/10.1016/j.eswa.2023.119772
28. Sidig, A.A.I., Luqman, H., Mahmoud, S., Mohandes, M.: KARSL: Arabic sign language database. ACM Trans. Asian Low-Resource Lang. Inf. Proc. (TALLIP) **20**(1), 1–19 (2021). https://doi.org/10.1145/3423420

29. Stokoe, W.C., Casterline, D.C., Croneberg, C.G.: A dictionary of American sign language on linguistic principles. (No Title) (1976)
30. Sultan, A., Makram, W., Kayed, M., Ali, A.A.: Sign language identification and recognition: a comparative study. Open Comput. Sci. **12**(1), 191–210 (2022). https://doi.org/10.1515/comp-2022-0240
31. Tarrés, L., Gállego, G.I., Duarte, A., Torres, J., Giró-i Nieto, X.: Sign language translation from instructional videos. In: Proceedings of the IEEE/CVF Conference on Computer Vision and Pattern Recognition, pp. 5624–5634 (2023). https://doi.org/10.1109/CVPRW59228.2023.00596
32. Thakar, S., Shah, S., Shah, B., Nimkar, A.V.: Sign language to text conversion in real time using transfer learning. 2022 IEEE 3rd Global Conference for Advancement in Technology (GCAT), pp. 1–5 (2022). https://doi.org/10.1109/GCAT55367.2022.9971953
33. Vázquez, R., Boggia, M., Raganato, A., Loppi, N.A., Grönroos, S.A., Tiedemann, J.: Latest development in the FoTran project – scaling up language coverage in neural machine translation using distributed training with language-specific components. In: Proceedings of the 23rd Annual Conference of the European Association for Machine Translation, pp. 311–312. European Association for Machine Translation, Ghent, Belgium (2022)
34. Vázquez-Enríquez, M., Alba-Castro, J.L., Docío-Fernández, L., Rodríguez-Banga, E.: Isolated sign language recognition with multi-scale spatial-temporal graph convolutional networks. In: 2021 IEEE/CVF Conference on Computer Vision and Pattern Recognition Workshops (CVPRW), pp. 3457–3466 (2021). https://doi.org/10.1109/CVPRW53098.2021.00385
35. Zakariah, M., Alotaibi, Y.A., Koundal, D., Guo, Y., Elahi, M.M.: Sign language recognition for Arabic alphabets using transfer learning technique. Comput. Intell. Neurosci. **2022** (2022). https://doi.org/10.1155/2022/4567989
36. Zhou, H., Zhou, W., Qi, W., Pu, J., Li, H.: Improving sign language translation with monolingual data by sign back-translation. In: Proceedings of the IEEE/CVF Conference on Computer Vision and Pattern Recognition (CVPR), pp. 1316–1325 (2021). https://doi.org/10.1109/GCAT55367.2022.9971953
37. Östling, R., Börstell, C., Courtaux, S.: visual iconicity across sign languages: large-scale automated video analysis of iconic articulators and locations. Front. Psyc. **9** (2018).https://doi.org/10.3389/fpsyg.2018.00725

S³: A Simple Strong Sample-Effective Multimodal Dialog System

Elisei Rykov[1]([✉]), Egor Malkershin[1], and Alexander Panchenko[1,2]

[1] Skolkovo Institute of Science and Technology, Moscow, Russia
{e.rykov,egor.malkershin,a.panchenko}@skol.tech
[2] Artificial Intelligence Research Institute, Barcelona, Russia

Abstract. In this work, we present a conceptually simple yet powerful baseline for multimodal dialog task, an S³ model, that achieves near state-of-the-art results on two compelling leaderboards: MMMU and AI Journey Contest 2023. The system is based on a pre-trained large language model, pre-trained modality encoders for image and audio, and a trainable modality projector. The proposed effective data mixture for training such an architecture demonstrates that a multimodal model based on a strong language model and trained on a small amount of multimodal data can perform efficiently in the task of multimodal dialog.

Keywords: LLM · Multimodality · VQA · AQA

1 Introduction

In the dynamic landscape of artificial intelligence (AI), the advent of multimodal systems has marked a transformative shift, enabling machines to interpret and analyze heterogeneous data streams with unprecedented finesse. These systems, which seamlessly integrate multiple forms of data such as text, images, and audio, are becoming progressively adept at mirroring human cognitive capabilities. However, one of the principal challenges confronting researchers in this domain has been the necessity for considerable volumes of data and substantial computational resources to train state-of-the-art models (Fig. 1).

Against this backdrop, our study introduces a novel paradigm that posits that a powerful multimodal system is feasible with minimal data and computational resources. This paper presents a simple yet effective baseline model which challenges the conventional premise that large datasets and excessive computational power are prerequisites for developing competitive multimodal AI systems. By using a compact corpus of less than 150,000 multimodal samples, a pre-trained frozen modality encoder, a 7B language model, and by exploiting the computational economy of a single A100-80GB GPU, we have created a model with an elegantly simple architecture that delivers performance on par with the more complex systems that currently dominate the field.

© The Author(s), under exclusive license to Springer Nature Switzerland AG 2024
A. Rapp et al. (Eds.): NLDB 2024, LNCS 14762, pp. 241–255, 2024.
https://doi.org/10.1007/978-3-031-70239-6_17

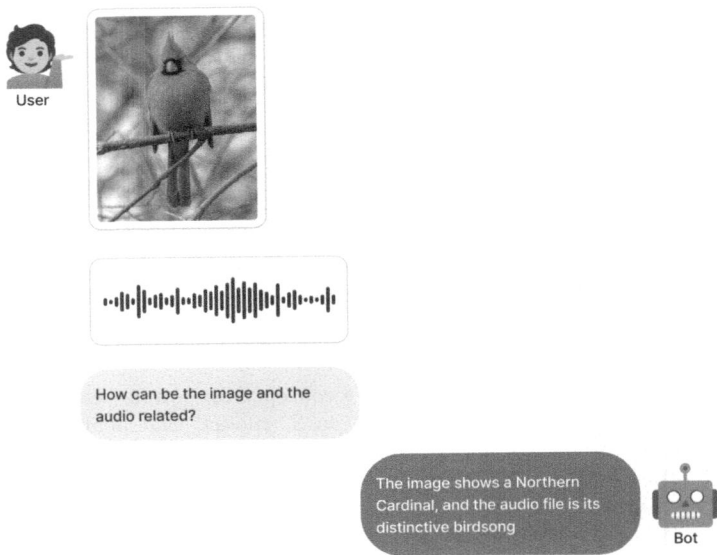

Fig. 1. An example of multimodal dialog.

At the heart of our approach is a modality projector that uses a multi-layer perceptron (MLP), a decision guided by an ethos of simplicity, to skillfully converge rich information into token embeddings. Our contributions can be summarized as follows:

– We apply a well-known pipeline for training multimodal projectors to multiple modalities (image, audio, and text) to train a multimodal dialog model.
– We introduce a high-quality effective data mixture for training multimodal dialog models.
– We demonstrate that mapping of the whole image into 4 textual tokens is enough for multimodal dialog task.
– We openly release the obtained model, which shows comparable performance to state-of-the-art models.[1]

2   Related Work

In this section we consider relevant research on deep pre-trained models of various modalities (text, image, audio), the related multimodal dataset used for training such models, and the existing multimodal architectures based on both multimodal encoders and language models.

---

[1] https://github.com/s-nlp/s3.

2.1   Text Modality: Large Language Models (LLMs)

State-of-the-art large language models are based on deep pre-trained transformers. Bright popular representatives of this kind are LLaMA [25] and Mistral [12], which are used in our work. LLaMA was trained on a mixed dataset from different sources covering different domains. Compared to LLaMA, Mistral introduces some changes related to sliding window attention, pre-filling and chunking strategies, etc.

2.2   Image Modality

ImageBind [10] serves as a universal multimodal encoder, using a multi-layer architecture that facilitates the extraction of universal image features. One of the modern neural network encoders is CLIP [22], which is based on a combined architecture of a convolutional neural network and a transformer. CLIP is trained on large datasets of images and text and is involved in contrastive tasks. The CLIP architecture enables the linking of visual and textual representations, providing an effective representation of both content and meaning. The effectiveness of CLIP allows the model to successfully classify distorted or context-dependent images and to integrate different knowledge domains into a unified space.

2.3   Audio Modality

Whisper [23], an audio encoder, has received considerable attention in recent studies as an innovative encoder architecture. Unlike traditional encoders, Whisper is designed to produce compact and high-quality representations of input data. The architecture uses stacked autoencoders and introduces a pioneering training approach known as "WhisperNet". In addition, Imagebind can also be used to provide audio features.

2.4   Datasets

In the context of image captioning, datasets such as COCO [16] and TextCaps [24] have been created. The COCO dataset was created by collecting a large number of images with corresponding captions from the web, creating a diverse data set for training and evaluating image captioning models. The TextCaps dataset was created by extending the COCO dataset with additional descriptions obtained from contextual user queries.

For the Visual Question Answering (VQA) task, VisDial [7] was created using images and a series of dialogs about them to train models to answer questions about the images provided. ScienceQA [20] was created by automatically extracting questions and answers from textbooks and tests on science topics. VizWiz [11] was created using a mobile application that allows blind and visually impaired people to ask questions about unfamiliar images. Visual Genome is a dataset of images, attributes and relationships between objects in those images, created with the help of annotators. The GQA [1] dataset was created using a powerful question engine based on the scene graph structures of Visual Genome, generating 22 million different questions about the visual world, with functional programs for answer control and bias smoothing. LLaVA [19] is automatically compiled using GPT-4 with various prompts, including regular VQA dialogs, highly complex questions and more. For the optical character recognition (OCR) task, OCR_books was used. OCR_books contains images of text obtained after scanning books of various genres.

For the task of audio captioning, one of the well-known datasets is CLOTHO [8], a fully crowdsourced dataset with multiple captions for each audio file.

The OpenAssistant dataset [14] is a large collection of conversational data collected through crowdsourcing with over 13,000 volunteers.

2.5   Multimodal Models

The FROMAGe [13] architecture is based on the idea of combining a pre-trained frozen LLM with an equally pre-trained and frozen visual image encoder through just one layer of linear projection. This linear layer, although having a small number of trainable parameters, plays a crucial role in establishing the connection between the image and text modalities. For LLaVA [19] the authors employed GPT-4 to create a multimodal visual-text instructional dataset for training. LLaVA combines a LLM Vicuna and a visual encoder based on ViT-L/14 from CLIP, linked by a linear projection layer. Qwen-VL [3] demonstrates a similar approach to LLaVA with fine-tuning of the projector and multi-level training. HoneyBee [5] shows that classical approaches to building projectors from LLaVA could be improved by applying complex and effective resempling to reduce the number of modality tokens. CogVLM [26] introduces a so-called "visual expert" module: a copy of some transformer blocks inside the language model that activate and update their weights only on image tokens.

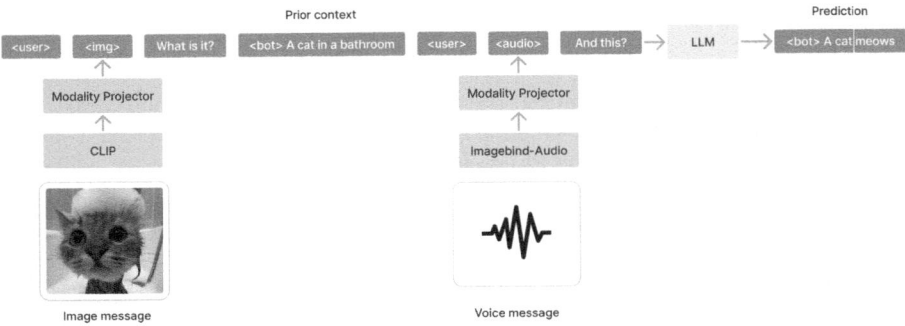

Fig. 2. Architecture of S^3 multimodal dialog system. All modalities are passed to specific encoders, and then modality objects are passed to modality projectors, which map them to token embeddings of a Large Language Model.

3   Methods

3.1   Dataset Preprocessing

We developed a model designed to engage in multimodal conversations with users. To achieve this, we formatted each dataset in a standard chat layout. This format involves representing each message as a JSON object containing 'role' (indicating whether the message is from a user or the bot), 'type' (indicating whether the message contains an image, audio, or text), and the message content itself (this would be the file path in case of images and audios). Our chat layout allows media content to be inserted at any point in the conversation, possibly multiple times (Fig. 3).

```
{
  "id": 0,
  "messages": [
    {
      "role": "user",
      "type": "image",
      "text": "https://example.com/images/bird.jpg"
    },
    {
      "role": "user",
      "type": "audio",
      "text": "https://example.com/audio/birdsong.mp3"
    },
    {
      "role": "user",
      "type": "text",
      "text": "How can be the image and the audio related?"
    },
    {
      "role": "bot",
      "type": "text",
      "text": "The image shows a Northern Cardinal,
              and the audio file is its distinctive birdsong.'
    }
  ]
}
```

Fig. 3. Example of json-formatted multimodal dialog data.

For each dataset, we created a custom system prompt that was tailored to elicit bot responses that closely matched the original dataset. For example, for the TextCaps dataset, we chose a prompt such as "Answer the question with a single word or phrase" to reflect the fact that the dataset contains primarily short responses. By implementing such prompts, we can guide the model to respond either concisely or with elaborate explanations, depending on the context. When adapting captioning datasets such as COCO or CLOTHO-Captions for conversational use, we formulated a set of basic synthetic questions, such as "What do you see in this picture?" or "What could make this sound?". These artificial questions serve as prompts to the user about a particular image or sound.

In our setup, the appearance of an image within a conversation is flexible. We randomised the order of questions and corresponding images within each dataset, allowing the media content to precede or follow the question. This randomness addresses the issue of brevity that is present in many datasets, which typically consist of single pairs of questions and answers. To create more extended dialogs and overcome this limitation, we randomly combined several short dialogs into extended sequences.

We introduced a unique mixture of data specifically designed for our task, as detailed in Table 1. Our goal was to create a diverse collection, for which we included a range of tasks such as Optical Character Recognition (OCR), Visual Question Answering (VQA), Audio Question Captioning (AQA), image captioning, casual conversation, and more. In total, we trained the model on around 145,000 samples.

3.2 Special Tokens and Post Processing

We integrated additional special tokens into the tokenizer of the base model and unfrozen both the language model head and the embedding layer to facilitate the training of these new tokens. Specifically, we introduced modality tokens [M] and [/M] to mark the beginning and end of different modality objects in the data. We encoded different modality objects using tokens such as [audio] and [img] for audio and image content, respectively. To represent speakers within the dialogs, we included special tokens for the bot and user roles. We also included the [RS] token to indicate the start and end of each message in a dialog. The [M] tokens were specifically used to indicate the scope of modality objects. Consequently, each dialog in the dataset is processed into a string containing these special tokens, as shown below:

```
[RS] [user] [M] [img] [img] [img] [img] [/M] [/RS]
[RS] [user]What is it?[/RS]
[RS] [bot]A red apple with red worm[/RS]
```

In the data processing stage, an image processor handles all the images, which are then transformed into image embeddings via an encoder. Our multimodal dialog model is designed to accept embeddings as the primary form of input data. Therefore, in the preprocessing phase, we tokenize the processed chat data and retrieve the embeddings for each token. For multimodal tokens such as [img] and [audio], we replace them with the output embeddings of the corresponding image, which are divided into N segments. In our configuration, we chose to split the modality embeddings into four different tokens.

Table 1. Training data mixture used to train S^3.

Task	Dataset	Samples in train/val	System prompt
Image	COCO	5000	Provide a one-sentence answer for the provided question
	GQA	10000	Answer the question using a single phrase
	resembling	5000	Show reaction and emotion in response to images
	Visual Dialog	24000	Answer the question using a single word or phrase
	LLaVA	31000	Answer questions thoroughly and in detail
	ScienceQA	10000	Answer with the option's letter from the given choices directly
	OCR-VQA	1000	Answer the question using a single word or phrase
	TextCaps	14000	Answer the question using a single word or phrase
	VizWiz	10000	Answer the question using a single word or phrase
	Visual Genome	5500	Answer the question using a single word or phrase
	OKVQA	5000	Answer the question using a single word or phrase
	AOKVQA	10000	Answer questions thoroughly and in detail
Audio	CLOTHO-Captions	3750	Answer the question using a single word or phrase
	CLOTHO-AQA	1000	Answer the question using a single word or phrase
	AudioSet	5000	Provide a one-sentence answer for the provided question
Text	OpenAssistant	5000	You are helpful AI assistant
Total	-	145250	-

3.3   Model Architecture

We used a widely accepted a "shallow alignment" architecture, which consists of three main components: a basic Large Language Model, a modality encoder, and a modality projector. The role of the modality encoder is to generate image representations, which are then transformed into token embeddings by the modality projector, allowing the integration of visual information into the language model. The architecture of the whole multimodal dialog model is shown in Fig. 2.

3.4   Pre-trained Modality Encoder

Modality encoders are designed to preprocess different types of modality objects, such as images and audio, and transform them into embeddings. These embeddings are then made compatible with the Large Language Model by a modality projector. To process audio inputs, we experimented with the ImageBind multimodal encoder, which can handle various modalities, including audio, image, and video. For image inputs, we used CLIP as the encoder of choice. Typically, image encoders such as CLIP aggregate the output of the processed modality object, usually by pooling, to produce a single, final embedding. However, for the purposes of our task, we hypothesized that using individual patched embeddings would yield more advantageous results.

3.5   Modality Projector

The role of the modality projector is to adjust the embeddings of various modality objects, such as images and audio, to ensure they are compatible with the

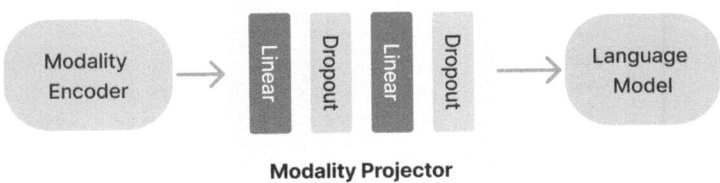

Modality Projector

Fig. 4. Architecture of our MLP modality projector, which maps features from the modality encoder to the language model.

language model. Its configuration can vary from a straightforward linear layer to a more intricate Multilayer Perceptron, among other options. In our research, we initially implemented a basic architectural design in which the hidden states from the modality encoder are mapped directly to the token embeddings of the language model using several linear layers. The complete architecture of our MLP modality projector is shown in Fig. 4. This modality projector is capable of converting an image only into a 4 token embeddings by extending the output from its final linear layer. To illustrate, if the dimension of the token embeddings within the language model is 32, we can instruct the output projection of the modality projector to produce a 128-dimensional embedding, which we then divide into 4 separate token embeddings. We employed the same architectural design for the modality projector across both image and speech modalities. In contrast to state-of-the-art models such as LLaVA, we map the modality object into 4 tokens, regardless of the number of output patches within the modality encoder. We assume that the small number of output modality tokens is sufficient for basic visual understanding. Also, using only 4 tokens significantly reduces the length of the sequence we pass to Transformer.

3.6   Language Model

We incorporated parameter-efficient fine-tuning LoRA adapters into our baseline language model to enhance its interaction capabilities in dialog contexts. Starting with basic pre-trained models such as LLaMA or Mistral, which do not inherently have the ability to participate in user dialogs, we postulated that the integration of a PEFT adapter would solve this problem. In the course of our experiments, we found that the Mistral-7b model served as an effective base model. By using PEFT adapters, we aimed not only to provide the language model with improved conversational capabilities, but also to do so without significantly increasing the number of trainable parameters; this efficient approach leverages the existing knowledge of the pre-trained model and complements it with targeted tunability for specific dialog-oriented tasks.

3.7   Training Details

The entire architecture was trained using the CrossEntropyLoss function. To speed up the training process, we used DeepSpeed, especially at optimization level 2, which is designed to provide significant speedups by introducing optimizations that reduce memory usage and improve computational performance. For the training procedure, we created a custom training pipeline rooted in the HuggingFace trainer framework. Within this configuration, we used the AdamW optimizer. To regulate the learning rate, we used a cosine annealing scheduler, starting with an initial learning rate of 1e-4. The batch size was set to 128. All training was done on a single A100-80GB GPU.

4   Results

In this section, we thoughly test our model in two recent compeltive leaderboards namely AI Journey Content 2023[2] and MMMU [29].

4.1   Experiment 1: AI Journey

The first trial of our multimodal framework was tailored for the AI Journey Contest 2023. AI Jorney Contest is an annual competition related to ML and AI with cash prizes from large companies, an analog of the Kaggle platform.

Our system was developed to solve the "Strong Intelligence" task in the AI Jorney Contest 2023. The goal of this contest was to develop a system with the ability to interact seamlessly across three modalities: text, image, and audio. For reasoning, we used the instruction "Answer questions thoroughly and in detail," which was given to encourage the model to provide comprehensive answers with ample elaboration. Thus, an effective system should demonstrate adeptness in managing input across images, audio, and text.

During the evaluation, all systems were constrained by the following inference container conditions: 243 GB RAM, 16 CPU cores, 1 T A100 (80 GB) GPU, 3.5 h to run, and no access to Internet resources.

Dataset: The evaluation phase challenged the system by presenting dialogs of heterogeneous composition: some consisted of only textual prompts, some combined text and images, some intertwined text and audio, and some even contained all three modalities. The dialogs presented to the system could involve contexts spanning more than two exchanges, allowing for the possibility of recurrence of image modality objects within a single dialog. Furthermore, in scenarios involving multiple modalities, there was potential for intermodality relationships, such as a user asking the bot to identify differences between two provided images. A notable detail of the contest setup was the absence of a specifically designated evaluation dataset, as provided by the contest organizers. Because the evaluation process was private, the evaluation data and the exact description of the other teams' submissions are not available.

---

[2] https://dsworks.ru/en/champ/super-aintelligence#overview.

Metric: The evaluation of our multimodal system was based on two metrics: METEOR [4] and a Hidden Metric based on the perplexity of the model's answer.

$$HM(X) = exp(\frac{1}{t} \sum_{i}^{t} \log p_\theta(x_i|x_{<i})),$$

where $\log p_\theta(x_i|x_{<i})$ is the likelihood of the ith token given all $x < i$ tokens. The final Integral Metric:

$$\sum_{j=1}^{J} \frac{\omega_j}{N_j} \sum_{i=1}^{N_j} \frac{METEOR_i + HM_i}{2},$$

where j is type of dialog, N_j is the number of dialogs for of type j, and ω_j is the weight of examples for the dialogs of the j type. For textual only dialogs, authors propose $\omega_j = 0.1$. For dialogs with both text and images, $\omega_j = 0.2$. For dialogs with audios and text, $\omega_j = 0.3$. And, finally, for dialogs that consists of all three modalities, $\omega_j = 0.4$.

Result: In the AI Journey contest, our approach secured 4th place out of a total of 30 participating teams. The top 10 systems from the contest, along with detailed metrics, are presented in the Table 2. The best-performing approach demonstrated, similar to our system setup, additionally included a small sample of self-generated supervised high-quality training data for the LoRA fine-tuning phase. Therefore, the author of the system freezes the language model at each stage of training, except the last one, using self-generated data.

Table 2. Official rankings of top-10 submits out of 30 teams in AI Journey Contest of multimodal dialog systems.

Rank	Team name	HM	METEOR	Average
1	fffrrtt	0.576	0.522	0.549
2	gradient sunset	0.534	0.455	0.495
3	whatever	0.517	0.458	0.487
4	**S^3 (Ours)**	0.549	0.414	0.481
5	DeReyly	0.498	0.427	0.462
6	Baseline	0.497	0.370	0.434
7	cybercho	0.489	0.377	0.433
8	EvilAI	0.472	0.395	0.433
9	AgaUgu	0.486	0.359	0.423
10	Denisiuskley	0.491	0.337	0.414

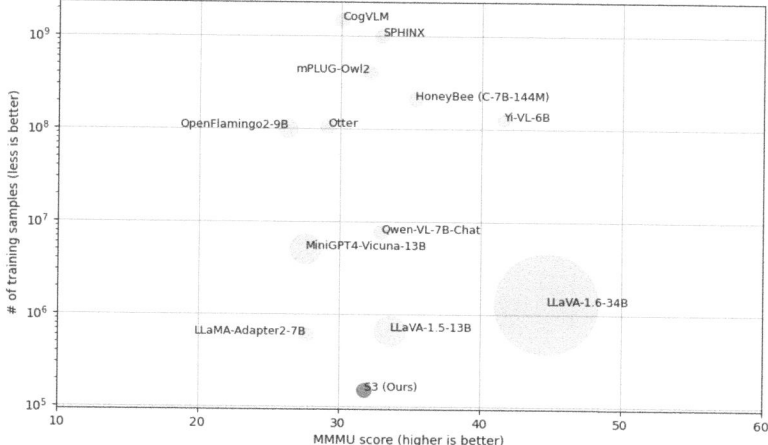

Fig. 5. A comparative analysis of the performance of S³. According to the MMMU benchmark score, S³ shows a competitive score in comparison to various models with a larger size and more training samples. The size of marks corresponds to the number of parameters in the language model.

4.2   Experiment 2: MMMU

The model we developed was then evaluated on the MMMU benchmark to determine its visual comprehension abilities and to compare it to existing models. When generating responses for the MMMU dataset, we instructed the model using the prompt "Answer with the letter of the option directly from the given choices" to ensure that the responses were concise and directly related to the given answer choices (Fig. 5).

Dataset: The MMMU benchmark serves as a comprehensive resource for evaluating the capabilities of multimodal dialog models. It includes a dataset of over 11,500 questions curated from college-level exams, quizzes, and textbooks spanning six academic disciplines: arts, business, science, health, humanities, and engineering. In total, the questions cover 30 subjects and delve into 183 specific subfields, incorporating a wide range of 30 different image types, including but not limited to graphs, diagrams, and chemical structures.

Metric: The performance on the MMMU benchmark is quantified by calculating the average accuracy across the different types of tasks included in the benchmark.

Result: Our system, which utilizes a low-count data mixture, surpassed many of the existing models in terms of performance. Across open-sourced 7B models, it demonstrates a competitive performance. It even closely competed with state-of-the-art models that were trained on significantly larger datasets, with larger LLM, falling short by a marginal difference. Our model's standing, along with comparisons to other models, can be found in a segment of the MMMU leaderboard that is shown in Table 3.

Table 3. The MMMU leaderboard as compared to our multimodal dialog system.

Model	Model is open sourced	Leaderboard test score	# of params of LLM	# of params visual encoder	# of training data samples
GPT-4V(ision) (Playground)	–	55.7	–		–
Qwen-VL-MAX [3]	–	46.8	7.7B	1.9B	–
LLaVA-1.6-34B [18]	+	44.7	34B	0.4B	1.3M
Yi-VL-6B [28]	+	41.6	6B	1B	126M
HoneyBee (C-7B-144M) [5]	+	35.3	7B	0.4B	208M
BLIP-2 FLAN-T5-XXL^a	+	34.0	11.3B	0.4B	–
InstructBLIP-T5-XXL [6]	+	33.8	11.3B	0.4B	–
LLaVA-1.5-13B [18]	+	33.6	13B	0.4B	0.66M
Qwen-VL-7B-Chat [3]	+	32.9	7B	1.9B	76.8M
SPHINX [17]	+	32.9	7B	0.4B	1000M
mPLUG-Owl2 [27]	+	32.1	7B	0.4B	400M
S^3 (Ours)	+	**31.8**	**7B**	**0.4B**	**0.15M**
CogVLM [26]	+	30.1	7B	0.3B	1500M
Otter [15]	+	29.1	7B	0.4B	105M
LLaMA-Adapter2-7B [9]	+	27.7	7B	–	0.6M
MiniGPT4-Vicuna–13B [30]	+	27.6	13B	–	5M
Adept Fuyu-8B^b	+	27.4	8B	–	
Kosmos2 [21]	+	26.6	–	–	90M
OpenFlamingo2-9B [2]	+	26.3	9B	0.4B	100M
Frequent Choice	–	23.9	–	–	–
Random Choice	–	25.8	–	–	–

^{a} https://huggingface.co/Salesforce/blip2-flan-t5-xxl
^{b} https://huggingface.co/adept/fuyu-8b

4.3   Conclusion

Our research demonstrates that it is possible to develop a highly competitive multimodal dialog model without the need for large datasets or enormous computing power. Using less than 150,000 multimodal samples and a single A100-80 GB GPU, we constructed a system that performs comparably to state-of-the-art models in the field. In particular, our model features a simple architecture consisting of a modality projector that uses a simple multi-layer perceptron (MLP) to effectively integrate a substantial amount of information into token embeddings.

Future work should focus on increasing dataset size and diversity, especially in the audio modality, as this could potentially lead to further performance gains. In addition, exploring the integration of more complex architectures for modality adaptation could also be beneficial for further enhancing its capabilities.

Acknowledgements. The research of Alexander Panchenko was supported by the Russian Science Foundation grant 20-71-10135.

References

1. Ainslie, J., Lee-Thorp, J., de Jong, M., Zemlyanskiy, Y., Lebron, F., Sanghai, S.: GQA: training generalized multi-query transformer models from multi-head checkpoints. In: Bouamor, H., Pino, J., Bali, K. (eds.) Proceedings of the 2023 Conference on Empirical Methods in Natural Language Processing, pp. 4895–4901. Association for Computational Linguistics, Singapore (Dec 2023). https://doi.org/10.18653/v1/2023.emnlp-main.298, https://aclanthology.org/2023.emnlp-main.298
2. Awadalla, A., et al.: Openflamingo: an open-source framework for training large autoregressive vision-language models. CoRR **abs/2308.01390** (2023). https://doi.org/10.48550/ARXIV.2308.01390
3. Bai, J., et al.: Qwen-vl: a frontier large vision-language model with versatile abilities. CoRR abs/2308.12966 (2023). https://doi.org/10.48550/ARXIV.2308.12966
4. Banerjee, S., Lavie, A.: METEOR: an automatic metric for MT evaluation with improved correlation with human judgments. In: Goldstein, J., Lavie, A., Lin, C.Y., Voss, C. (eds.) Proceedings of the ACL Workshop on Intrinsic and Extrinsic Evaluation Measures for Machine Translation and/or Summarization, pp. 65–72. Association for Computational Linguistics, Ann Arbor, Michigan (Jun 2005)
5. Cha, J., Kang, W., Mun, J., Roh, B.: Honeybee: locality-enhanced projector for multimodal LLM. CoRR abs/2312.06742 (2023). https://doi.org/10.48550/ARXIV.2312.06742
6. Dai, W., et al.: Instructblip: towards general-purpose vision-language models with instruction tuning. In: Oh, A., Neumann, T., Globerson, A., Saenko, K., Hardt, M., Levine, S. (eds.) Advances in Neural Information Processing Systems. vol. 36, pp. 49250–49267. Curran Associates, Inc. (2023)
7. Das, A., et al.: Visual Dialog. In: Proceedings of the IEEE Conference on Computer Vision and Pattern Recognition (CVPR) (2017)
8. Drossos, K., Lipping, S., Virtanen, T.: Clotho: an audio captioning dataset. In: ICASSP 2020 - 2020 IEEE International Conference on Acoustics, Speech and Signal Processing (ICASSP), pp. 736–740 (2020). https://doi.org/10.1109/ICASSP40776.2020.9052990
9. Gao, P., et al.: Llama-adapter V2: parameter-efficient visual instruction model. CoRR **abs/2304.15010** (2023). https://doi.org/10.48550/ARXIV.2304.15010
10. Girdhar, R., et al.: Imagebind one embedding space to bind them all. In: 2023 IEEE/CVF Conference on Computer Vision and Pattern Recognition (CVPR), pp. 15180–15190 (2023). https://doi.org/10.1109/CVPR52729.2023.01457
11. Gurari, D., et al.: Vizwiz grand challenge: answering visual questions from blind people. In: 2018 IEEE/CVF Conference on Computer Vision and Pattern Recognition, pp. 3608–3617 (2018). https://api.semanticscholar.org/CorpusID:3831582
12. Jiang, A.Q., et al.: Mistral 7b. CoRR abs/2310.06825 (2023). https://doi.org/10.48550/ARXIV.2310.06825
13. Koh, J.Y., Salakhutdinov, R., Fried, D.: Grounding language models to images for multimodal inputs and outputs. In: Proceedings of the 40th International Conference on Machine Learning. ICML'23, JMLR.org (2023)

14. Köpf, A., et al.: Openassistant conversations - democratizing large language model alignment. In: Oh, A., Naumann, T., Globerson, A., Saenko, K., Hardt, M., Levine, S. (eds.) Advances in Neural Information Processing Systems 36: Annual Conference on Neural Information Processing Systems 2023, NeurIPS 2023, New Orleans, LA, USA, December 10–16, 2023 (2023), http://papers.nips.cc/paper_files/paper/2023/hash/949f0f8f32267d297c2d4e3ee10a2e7e-Abstract-Datasets_and_Benchmarks.html

15. Li, B., Zhang, Y., Chen, L., Wang, J., Yang, J., Liu, Z.: Otter: a multi-modal model with in-context instruction tuning. CoRR abs/2305.03726 (2023). https://doi.org/10.48550/ARXIV.2305.03726

16. Lin, T.Y., et al.: Microsoft coco: common objects in context. In: Fleet, D., Pajdla, T., Schiele, B., Tuytelaars, T. (eds.) Computer Vision - ECCV 2014, pp. 740–755. Springer International Publishing, Cham (2014)

17. Lin, Z., et al.: SPHINX: the joint mixing of weights, tasks, and visual embeddings for multi-modal large language models. CoRR **abs/2311.07575** (2023). https://doi.org/10.48550/ARXIV.2311.07575

18. Liu, H., Li, C., Li, Y., Lee, Y.J.: Improved baselines with visual instruction tuning. CoRR abs/2310.03744 (2023). https://doi.org/10.48550/ARXIV.2310.03744

19. Liu, H., Li, C., Wu, Q., Lee, Y.J.: Visual instruction tuning. In: Oh, A., Naumann, T., Globerson, A., Saenko, K., Hardt, M., Levine, S. (eds.) Advances in Neural Information Processing Systems 36: Annual Conference on Neural Information Processing Systems 2023, NeurIPS 2023, New Orleans, LA, USA, December 10–16, 2023 (2023), http://papers.nips.cc/paper_files/paper/2023/hash/6dcf277ea32ce3288914faf369fe6de0-Abstract-Conference.html

20. Lu, P., et al.: Learn to explain: multimodal reasoning via thought chains for science question answering. In: NeurIPS (2022)

21. Peng, Z., et al.: Kosmos-2: grounding multimodal large language models to the world. CoRR abs/2306.14824 (2023). https://doi.org/10.48550/ARXIV.2306.14824

22. Radford, A., et al.: Learning transferable visual models from natural language supervision. In: Meila, M., Zhang, T. (eds.) Proceedings of the 38th International Conference on Machine Learning, ICML 2021, 18–24 July 2021, Virtual Event. Proceedings of Machine Learning Research, vol. 139, pp. 8748–8763. PMLR (2021). http://proceedings.mlr.press/v139/radford21a.html

23. Radford, A., Kim, J.W., Xu, T., Brockman, G., McLeavey, C., Sutskever, I.: Robust speech recognition via large-scale weak supervision. In: Proceedings of the 40th International Conference on Machine Learning. In: ICML'23, JMLR.org (2023)

24. Sidorov, O., Hu, R., Rohrbach, M., Singh, A.: Textcaps: a dataset for image captioning with reading comprehension. In: Vedaldi, A., Bischof, H., Brox, T., Frahm, J.M. (eds.) Computer Vision - ECCV 2020, pp. 742–758. Springer International Publishing, Cham (2020)

25. Touvron, H., et al: Llama 2: open foundation and fine-tuned chat models. CoRR abs/2307.09288 (2023). https://doi.org/10.48550/ARXIV.2307.09288

26. Wang, W., et al.: CogVLM: visual expert for large language models (2024). https://openreview.net/forum?id=c72vop46KY

27. Ye, Q., et al.: mplug-owl2: revolutionizing multi-modal large language model with modality collaboration. CoRR abs/2311.04257 (2023). https://doi.org/10.48550/ARXIV.2311.04257

28. Young, A., et al.: Open foundation models by 01.ai. CoRR **abs/2403.04652** (2024). https://doi.org/10.48550/ARXIV.2403.04652
29. Yue, X., et al.: Mmmu: a massive multi-discipline multimodal understanding and reasoning benchmark for expert agi. In: Proceedings of CVPR (2024)
30. Zhu, D., Chen, J., Shen, X., Li, X., Elhoseiny, M.: Minigpt-4: enhancing vision-language understanding with advanced large language models. CoRR **abs/2304.10592** (2023). https://doi.org/10.48550/ARXIV.2304.10592

Body-Shaming Detection
and Classification in Italian Social Media

Francesca Grasso$^{(\boxtimes)}$ ⓘ, Alberto Valese ⓘ, and Marta Micheli ⓘ

Department of Computer Science, University of Turin, Corso Svizzera 185, 10149
Turin, Italy
{fr.grasso,alberto.valese,marta.micheli}@unito.it

Abstract. In the last decades, the Natural Language Processing (NLP) community has demonstrated committed involvement in addressing societal challenges, particularly in the realm of hate-speech detection. Despite advancements, these phenomena continue to perpetrate, especially online, where users on social network platforms often find themselves in unsafe and possibly harmful environments. Among the various manifestations of hate speech and offensive language, one aspect that has been overlooked by the NLP community is body-shaming. Despite its prevalence among hateful users and its potential to harm a diverse group of individuals, from women to people with disabilities, efforts to counteract this damaging phenomenon remain limited. In this work, we first introduce a novel taxonomy designed to distinguish and classify instances of body-shaming by the targeted group. Following this, we present a dataset of Instagram comments for body-shaming detection and classification in the Italian language, which has been manually annotated according to the taxonomy. After detailing the data-gathering and annotation process, we present a classification benchmark using three BERT-based models to showcase our dataset's classification potential. Results demonstrate good performances in detecting body-shaming instances across several categories of our proposed taxonomy.

Keywords: Natural Language Processing · Body-Shaming · Hate Speech

1 Introduction

Body-shaming is the criticism of someone based on the shape, size, or appearance of their body [3]. It can manifest subtly, such as in the form of advice (e.g., medically-based advice from a friend: 'You should reduce your weight to prevent high blood pressure') or explicitly, through malevolent insults (e.g., from an unknown social media follower: 'You need some meat on your bones') [37].

Content Warning: this paper contains examples of body-shaming, including potentially distressing comments on appearance, gender identity, sexual orientation, ethnicity, and ability. Please proceed with caution.

© The Author(s), under exclusive license to Springer Nature Switzerland AG 2024
A. Rapp et al. (Eds.): NLDB 2024, LNCS 14762, pp. 256–270, 2024.
https://doi.org/10.1007/978-3-031-70239-6_18

The often unmeetable beauty standards imposed by society have a long-lasting tradition, where people have been frequently judged based on their appearance. Moreover, body-shaming often intersects with other forms of discrimination, such as racism [42], misogyny [35], ableism [32], or transphobia [8], and can be seen as one expression of such toxic behavior. With the proliferation of online social platforms, particularly among young users, the phenomenon of body-shaming, like other hate-speech phenomena and cyberbullying, is amplified as social platforms serve as a sounding board for propagating toxic behavior, due to the anonymity of virtual exposure compared to in-person interactions. Body-shaming involves unsolicited, mostly negative opinions or comments about a person's body [37]. Its manifestations can be multifaceted, targeting aspects like size, shape, weight, body parts, body-related appearance, extremities, etc. Body-shaming has been recognized as a form of misogynistic speech and sexism-related discrimination [26], with women being a primary target due to increased objectification and societal beauty standards.

Many studies have addressed the consequences of body-shaming on people's health and behavior. For instance, it can lead to low self-esteem, depressive symptoms [18], or disordered eating patterns [15]. Automatic detection of such abusive behavior can be crucial in mitigating and stopping the propagation of this damaging content, eventually resulting in a positive impact on society. So far, the efforts in this direction by the Natural Language Processing (NLP) community have been limited, with only one work in the literature specifically targeting body-shaming detection in English [31]. While the literature presents several works addressing hate speech phenomena in online communities [28], with corpora designed to capture expressions of racism [39], sexism [33], and homophobia [40], this spotlight on specific discriminations highlights a broader issue within the field. Notably, ableism, a form of discrimination that impacts individuals with disabilities, often remains overlooked. Despite a few attempts to include people with disabilities among the targeted groups of hateful comments [20,24], there is, to the best of our knowledge, a notable absence of datasets that specifically target ableist expressions comprehensively. This encompasses not only hate speech directed towards individuals with disabilities *per se*, but also the employment of ableist language to insult individuals irrespective of their disability status. Using expressions like 'get treatment' or 'you look retarded' to target non-disabled individuals implies that being associated with disability is intrinsically inferior and tantamount to an insult. This practice makes ableism a universal tool for derogation, reinforcing negative stereotypes and the stigmatization of disability.

In this paper, we address these gaps by first introducing a taxonomy of six body-shaming categories, representing our initial contribution. This taxonomy begins by distinguishing between content that constitutes body-shaming and content that does not. Subsequently, it focuses on the targets of derogatory expressions, identifying six prevalent manifestations of body-shaming on social media: fatphobia, skinny-shaming, misogyny/sexism, ableism, racism, and queer-phobia. Although it is not exhaustive or highly detailed, defining this taxonomy marks a critical step toward more nuanced investigations into body-shaming classification.

Our second, and more comprehensive, contribution proposes a dataset of more than 11k Instagram comments for the detection and classification of body-shaming in Italian[1]. To our knowledge, this represents the first work on body-shaming detection within the Italian context and an initial attempt in general to categorize body-shaming instances, including ableism.

We detail the data collection and annotation processes, as well as an evaluation framework involving three different BERT-based language models. The dataset is designed to serve as a reference for researchers and activists alike, aiming not only to support the fight against this phenomenon within specific communities but also to capture its diverse manifestations. The paper is structured as follows. Section 2 provides an overview of the relevant related work. In Sect. 3, we detail the proposed taxonomy and the dataset creation process. Section 4 outlines the annotation schema, process, and results. In Sect. 5, we describe classification experiments, while Sect. 6 concludes the paper.

2   Related Works

The NLP community has a strong tradition of focusing on societal challenges, with several efforts made to develop tools for detecting, and consequently preventing, hate speech, cyberbullying, and related phenomena [4,28]. However, while psychology and social science have already directed attention towards body-shaming [7,37], in computational linguistics this topic remains largely unaddressed, offering few resources for its detection.

Among the available works, [26] construct a dataset for sexism categorization, including body-shaming as one of the categories of sexism. [21] explore the identification of body-shaming comments through sentiment analysis and classification techniques. [31] provides, to our knowledge, the only available dataset specifically for body-shaming detection, classifying Instagram comments as body-shaming or not. However, the dataset primarily includes 'indirect' instances, where comments report on or complain about body-shaming events, rather than being direct expressions of body-shaming. [12] use Naive Bayes Classifier approach to do sentiment analysis on body-shaming tweets in Indonesian. Regarding the realm of harassment and toxicity towards specific discriminated or marginalised groups, many works address racism [23,39] and misogyny/sexism [26,33] detection, whereas there are still few works for other targeted hate speech groups. For ableism detection, [20,24] and [17] investigate the presence of explicit bias against people with disability in sentiment analysis, toxicity models, and LLMs; [11,25] include 'people with special needs' and 'handicap' as target group and category for hate speech, respectively. Among NLP works that address queerphobia[2], [38] investigate evidence of bias against queer identities in sentiment analysis tools; [9] propose a shared task on homo/transphobia detection in social media;

---

[1] The dataset is available here: https://github.com/ValeseA/BS-Detect.

[2] Understood as hateful expression and discrimination against LGBTQ + individuals.

[40] propose a corpus for detecting LGBT+Phobia in Mexican Spanish. Regarding toxicity detection towards specific body shapes, [39] considers fatphobia in their Brazilian Portuguese corpus. Despite extensive literature on discrimination, body-shaming research remains limited, where a dataset for detecting body-shaming in Italian is still lacking, and so is a categorization of body-shaming instances according to the targeted group.

3   Dataset Design and Creation

3.1   Body-Shaming Taxonomy

Our goal was to create a resource for detecting body-shaming hate speech in a broad sense, targeting a wide range of individuals and diverse expressions of aspect-based critiques. Body-shaming often overlaps with other types of discrimination, particularly targeting individuals from discriminated or marginalized groups. It manifests in various forms, including racism [42], misogyny and sexism [26,35], ableism [32] and transphobia [8]. Accordingly, we aimed to (i) distinguish instances that constitute body-shaming from those that do not and (ii) classify body-shaming instances based on individuals frequently targeted due to societal standards and widespread discriminatory attitudes.

Therefore, we developed a taxonomy with two hierarchical levels for detecting body-shaming content, drawing inspiration from the Wheel of Power, Privilege, and Marginalization by Sylvia Duckworth[3] [1]. This tool, designed to facilitate discussions about intersectionality and systemic inequality [22], categorizes key social identities and categories, including race, gender, sexual orientation, body size, and ability, to delineate the distribution of societal privilege and marginalization [34], making it a suitable reference for body-shaming. From this literature reference, we created the first draft of the taxonomy, further refined through a grounded theory approach [19] with empirical data from our dataset (see Sect. 4) to adjust the schema. This taxonomy mirrors the annotation scheme used for our dataset annotation, as illustrated later. It comprises two levels:

Binary Body-Shaming. The first level establishes a binary categorization between content that constitutes body-shaming versus content that does not. We identify body-shaming as any form of explicit or implicit criticism, humiliation, or derision related to an individual's physical appearance, persisting regardless of context or intent [3,37]. This includes negative comments or unsolicited advice about body shape, weight, height, facial features, or any other physical characteristics. It also encompasses derision of ways of speaking, moving, and overall attitude, as these too relate to the body and its presentation.

Category of Body-Shaming. The second level distinguishes six distinct categories of body-shaming that we identified and defined based on the target group:

---

[3] The original 2020 version is sourced from the author's Flickr page: https://www.flickr.com/photos/sylviaduckworth/50500299716/; a simplified adaptation by the Canadian Council of Refugees (CCR): https://ccrweb.ca/en/anti-oppression. Several versions of the wheel have been developed for various contexts.

Fatphobia; *Skinny-shaming*; *Misogyny/sexism*; *Racism*; *Ableism*; *Queerphobia.*
Below we provide definitions and examples for each category. Note that this taxonomy does not claim to be exhaustive of every target of body-shaming, but it serves as a starting point to capture the diverse dynamics of this phenomenon:

- **Fatphobia**: Criticism or negative comments, often delivered as unsolicited advice or health concerns, targeting individuals with bodies that do not conform to societal standards of size and shape, perpetuating the stigma around body diversity and implying that deviation from these standards is undesirable [5] (e.g., 'You look like a pig'; 'Someone your size shouldn't wear that').
- **Skinny-shaming**: Negative remarks or disparagement directed at individuals perceived as too thin, suggesting they lack health or attractiveness due to their slimness [2] ('You look sick, eat something!'; 'Put some meat on your bones'). This category was not included in the initial phase of drafting our taxonomy. However, after encountering several detrimental and hateful comments targeting this specific body shape, we decided to incorporate it into our taxonomy and annotation scheme.
- **Misogyny/sexism**: Body-shaming that specifically targets women, often through critiques that enforce narrow societal beauty standards or demean women for not adhering to these standards, reflecting gender-based prejudice [30] ('Don't you see those hairy underarms are gross?'; 'You're so flat, real women should have curves').
- **Racism**: Body-shaming intertwined with racial prejudices, targeting individuals based on racial or ethnic characteristics, including skin color, hair texture, facial features, or body shape typical to specific ethnic groups [6] ('People like you look like monkeys'; 'You definitely cannot be Italian with that wig on your head').
- **Ableism**: Criticism or humiliation based on physical differences, cognitive divergence, or motor abilities, directed at both individuals with disabilities and those without, using negative comparisons to disabilities as a form of insult [32] (e.g., 'Are you retarded?'; 'You look like you have Down syndrome'). This practice perpetuates ableist prejudices, diminishing the individual beyond physical and cognitive norms.
- **Queerphobia**: Body-shaming targeting individuals based on their sexual orientation or gender identity, critiquing not only their physical appearance but also their ways of speaking, moving, and overall attitude [8] (e.g., 'You're such a horrific freak'; 'Disgusting, are you even male or female?'). This form of shaming reinforces stereotypes and negates their identity and expression, often scrutinizing these aspects to demean or invalidate the individual's authentic self.

3.2 Data Collection

Our aim was to collect textual data, specifically user comments, from a popular social platform that could be qualified as instances of body-shaming and targeting a vast range of users, including individuals of marginalized groups or those typically targeted for body-critiques. Particularly, we intended to include potentially hateful comments that might fall under —but not limit our focus to— the six categories of body-shaming hate speech groups detailed above. To this aim, similar to [31], we identified Meta's Instagram[4] as a preferred source for textual data, specifically user comments. This platform, highly popular particularly among teenagers and young adults, is predominantly used for picture posting or "reels"[5], making it likely for users to expose their personal image and body, and consequently attract hateful comments targeting their physical appearance [14]. Our goal was to gather a wide variety of body-shaming instances, from fat-shaming to transphobic expressions. To direct our search, we thus employed a combined strategy. We selected posts (either pictures or reels) by browsing highly popular open user profiles likely targets of cyberbullying and hate speech, also considering their high exposure. These included: feminist queer pages, advocates of "body positivity", famous disabled activists, popular non-Caucasian Italian athletes or players, female influencers, public figures with non-conforming bodies, openly transgender activist user pages[6]. Moreover, we combined diverse hashtags to target posts from popular educational, entertainment, satirical, or news Italian accounts whose content could attract hateful messages. The hashtags included: #disabile #sindromedidown #bodypositivity #bodyshaming #modellacurvy #lgbtqitalia #orgoglioqueer. Prior to data crawling, we manually inspected the comment section of the browsed posts and pages to verify the presence of hateful messages. We then carefully selected a total of 100 posts expected to contain such comments, aiming for a balanced distribution across the six identified categories of body-shaming. This aimed to ensure that each subcategory - fatphobia, skinny-shaming, misogyny/sexism, racism, ableism, and queerphobia - was adequately represented in our dataset. To facilitate the data gathering process, we used ExportGram and ExportComments[7], tools designed for exporting social media comments (including Instagram), to collect potentially abusive content. The data extraction from the 100 selected posts led to a total of 39,467 exported comments.

3.3   Data Cleaning and Dataset Creation

After collecting the comments, we carried out basic pre-processing steps to enhance data quality. We started with removing duplicates (identical comments), comments composed solely of emojis, hashtags, tags, gifs, URLs and user mentions (defined by the prefix @). Additionally, we filtered out empty comments and

---

[4] https://www.instagram.com/.

[5] Instagram's "reels" are short videos up to 60 s long.

[6] All comments analyzed in this study were extracted from public Instagram profiles, defined as data accessible without the need to log in, and were collected in accordance with Meta's privacy policy for academic research purposes. Additionally, we have chosen not to disclose specific names from which comments were extracted to uphold privacy and ethical research practices and prevent potential harm. Exceptions may only occur with explicit consent and where necessary for research integrity.

[7] https://exportcomments.com/; https://exportgram.net/.

those not in the Italian language[8]. URLs and user mentions were also removed from the remaining comments. Post-cleaning, we obtained 29,003 comments eligible for manual annotation.

Reliably measuring the frequency of abusive content in natural online environments is challenging, with estimates possibly as low as 0.1% to 1% [41]. Recognizing that body-shaming is only a subset of abuse, we chose not to employ sampling techniques used in prior work such as keyword [13] or lexicon-based ones [16]. These methods could risk overlooking nuanced or less overt instances of body-shaming, limiting the diversity and representativeness of our dataset. While aware that this decision might lead to a dataset class imbalance, we prioritized capturing the broadest and most heterogeneous examples of body-shaming. To mitigate potential imbalances as much as possible and ensure a comprehensive overview of body-shaming expressions, we attempted to balance the dataset for annotation by randomly selecting an equal number of comments from each targeted subcategory within the 100 posts. From the initial pool of 29,003 comments, we curated a final sample of 13,212 comments, aiming for a manageable yet diverse set suitable for manual annotation and classification tasks. This approach, while not without its challenges, was intended to minimize bias toward any specific category of body-shaming, attempting a broad representation of expressions within our analysis.

4   Dataset Annotation

4.1   Annotation Scheme

For the annotation of our dataset, we adhered to a 'prescriptivist approach' in data annotation, as we wanted the annotators to refer to our detailed annotation guidelines rather than relying on their subjective interpretations, as far as possible [36]. The annotators were thoroughly instructed with comprehensive guidelines outlining the objectives, specifics of the annotation schema, definitions, clarifications, examples, considerations for borderline cases, and overall instructions. The annotation scheme mirrors the taxonomy illustrated in Sect. 3.1, whose details and categories' definitions were also presented in the guidelines. Thus, the annotation scheme we developed was composed of two levels:

– *Body-shaming task*: In this first binary level, each comment was labeled as either containing an instance of body-shaming or not, using the labels **yes** and **no**. The annotation was prompted by the question, "Does the comment include a body-shaming instance?". If labeled as **yes**, a further multilabel classification could follow, when applicable. Importantly, annotators were

---

[8] Comments in languages commonly spoken in Italy but not recognized as dialects of Italian, such as Neapolitan or Sicilian, were excluded. Comments that included so-called 'regional Italian' or dialects of Italian, such as Tuscany and Roman expressions, were instead included.

instructed to exclude generic hate speech not specific to body-shaming. Only comments that could reasonably be interpreted as body-shaming had to be categorized as such.

- *Categorization task*: At the secondary multilabel level, comments identified as body-shaming could be further tagged with specific labels representing one of the six types of discrimination outlined in our taxonomy. The available labels at this level were: `fatphobia`, `skinny-shaming`, `misogyny/sexism`, `racism`, `ableism`, and `queerphobia`. If none of these categories were applicable, the annotation at this level could be left blank. Moreover, the annotators were allowed to select up to two labels. This scenario arose when the comment fell into one of the following situations: (i) the content could be relevant to either one of two categories, but it was unclear which category it fit more accurately, or (ii) the content clearly pertained to both categories of discrimination simultaneously. This occurred, for example, in cases where a woman's body was derogatorily commented as both being too skinny and not adhering to traditional female beauty standards, e.g., 'Where's your chest, skeleton?' (this intersects misogyny/sexism and skinny-shaming categories). Another instance is when a non-cisgender individual with a non-conforming body received comments such as 'Aren't you ashamed of yourself for being such a fat faggot?', exemplifing the overlap of fatphobia and queerphobia.

Table 1. Examples of dataset comments with their annotation.

Comment	Body-sh.	Category
"Bellissimo il costume! Che marca è?" *(Beautiful swimsuit! What brand is it?)*	no	-
"Che fisico di merda si puó dire?" *(What a shitty physique can one have?)*	yes	-
"Con la 4' di seno staresti meglio..." *(With a size D breast, you would look better...)*	yes	`misogyny/sexism`
"6 tozza ed hai la faccia da down" *(You're stocky and have a Down syndrome face)*	yes	`ableism` `misogyny/sexism`
"Muori di obesità e HIV" *(Die of obesity and HIV)*	yes	`fatphobia` `queerphobia`
"Come i tratti somatici di muso di cavallo" *(As the somatic features of a horse's muzzle)*	yes	`racism`

In Table 1, we report some examples of comments with their expected label, according to our developed annotation scheme.

4.2 Annotation Process

The annotation was carried out by three expert annotators, all of whom are Italian native speakers with prior experience and expertise in hate-speech annotation tasks. One annotator is also co-author of this paper. After being provided with the guidelines, a discussion session was held to address any questions or clarifications regarding the annotation criteria. The guidelines also specified that annotators could skip comments that did not meet the criteria required for the annotation, such as comments containing only emojis or non-interpretable text (e.g., "ahahah"), or comments not in Italian. These comments would be subsequently excluded from the dataset after completion of the task. In the annotation process, annotators were provided with the sources of the Instagram comments to assist in accurately contextualizing each comment. This step was crucial for understanding the nuances and intent behind the remarks and distinguishing between comments that are explicitly or implicitly body-shaming and those that are not. To ensure alignment among the annotators and a shared understanding of the guidelines, a pilot annotation of 25 randomly selected comments was conducted. This preliminary task allowed annotators to discuss any discrepancies and refine the guidelines if necessary. After aligning on the annotation task during the pilot phase, the annotators performed the main annotation task on the dataset. Throughout the process, we maintained close collaboration with our annotators, ensuring their feedback was integrated into our guidelines and their well-being was consistently monitored and safeguarded.

4.3   Annotation Results

After completing the annotation, the dataset was cleansed of any comments that were skipped, resulting in a total of 11,393 annotated comments for the final dataset.

Table 2. IAA Scores for the Body-Shaming and Categorization Tasks. The first score represents consensus on the presence of body-shaming, while subsequent scores indicate agreement levels for specific categories of body-shaming, calculated with an adapted binary Fleiss' κ for multilabel tasks.

Task	Body-Sh.	Fatph.	Skinny-Sh.	Misog./Sexism	Racism	Ableism	Queerph.
Fleiss' κ	0.694	0.611	0.628	0.182	0.721	0.677	0.567

IAA Measurement. We measured the Inter-Annotator Agreement (IAA) among the annotators using Fleiss' Kappa. Below, we briefly discuss the IAA values obtained for our dataset, presented in Table 2.

Body-Shaming task: For the first binary task we achieved a Fleiss' κ score of 0.694. This score indicates substantial agreement among annotators, suggesting that the annotators were generally consistent in identifying whether a comment contained body-shaming content, also indicating clear task guidelines. However, this score also hints at the inherent subjectivity involved in identifying body-shaming instances within some comments. We found that this subjectivity was especially pronounced in cases where body-shaming was implicit rather than explicit (e.g., "Guarda che l'obesità è una malattia!" *Just so you know, obesity is a disease!*; "Le belle ragazze sono altre" *The pretty girls are others*), or when comments resided on the borderline between body-shaming and generic insults (e.g., "Ma non ti fai schifo da solo?" *Don't you disgust yourself?*; "Fenomeno da baraccone" *You're a freak*). Subjectivity arose also as linked to individual differences in sensitivity to certain types of remarks. For instance, unsolicited comments framed as compliments (e.g., "Quelle smagliature ti donano!" *Those stretch marks suit you!*), sarcastic comments, or observations that might imply a negative remark ("Sembri incinta" *You look pregnant*) were interpreted variably. Some annotators saw these as covert forms of body-shaming, while others considered them as innocuous or genuinely positive.

Categorization Task: For the secondary level's multilabel task, where comments could be tagged with up to two different labels, we adapted the Fleiss' κ calculation to account for multiple labels per comment. This involved transforming our dataset into a binary decision matrix for each label, allowing us to systematically account for instances where annotators agreed on at least one of the potential labels. Each of the six labels was considered a separate decision, marked as present (1) or absent (0) for each comment by each annotator. This approach allowed us to capture partial agreements among annotators, especially relevant for comments that spanned multiple discrimination categories. This binary decision matrix enabled us to compute the IAA in a manner that captures both full and partial agreement among annotators. The calculated IAA scores indicate substantial agreement among annotators for almost all categories, ranging between 0.567 and 0.721. However, notable disparity is observed in the category of misogyny/sexism, which exhibits significantly lower agreement. This disparity will be further discussed in the subsequent paragraph.

Table 3. Label distribution for Body-Shaming detection and Categorization by annotator: the numbers refer to counts of comments identified under each label.

Label	Annotator 1	Annotator 2	Annotator 3
yes	1268	1154	1381
no	10125	10239	10012
fatphobia	537	505	639
skinny-shaming	55	51	78
misogyny-sexism	84	59	419
racism	30	19	30
ableism	136	143	150
queerphobia	151	260	173

Label Distribution. Table 3 reports the label distribution across the two annotation levels for all three annotators.

The *Body-shaming* task reveals a significant class imbalance, with the majority of comments labeled as no for lacking body-shaming content. This distribution aligns with the expected prevalence of neutral comments over explicit hateful instances, given the context of social media. The observed imbalance was anticipated and is considered acceptable for our study's goal, which was developing a nuanced understanding for body-shaming content, rather than achieving a perfectly balanced dataset. Despite the class imbalance, the quantity of yes labels still provides a robust foundation for the analysis of body-shaming content, supporting the validity of our subsequent analyses and model training. The consistent number of yes labels across annotators indicates a good agreement on body shaming, enhancing dataset reliability.

In the *Categorization Task*, label distribution reveals insights into both the prevalence of specific types of body-shaming within the dataset and the consensus among annotators. fatphobia is consistent among annotators, indicating its prevalence in the dataset and its clear definition in the guidelines. skinny-shaming and racism are less common, with Annotator 3 showing slight variance in identifying the former. misogyny-sexism exhibits considerable variance, notably with Annotator 3 identifying significantly more instances. This may stem from the challenge in differentiating between misogyny/sexism-related and "general" body-shaming when the targets are women. This discrepancy also explains the low IAA for this category shown in Table 2. Finally, ableism and queerphobia are more frequent, with good distribution among annotators (despite Annotator 2's slight predisposition for this label), indicating both a significant presence in the dataset and a clear guideline comprehension.

5   Evaluation

To assess our dataset's reliability, we conducted a comprehensive evaluation, framing the detection of body-shaming and its categorization, when present, as binary classification tasks. These experiments aimed to (i) gauge how well state-of-the-art language models identify body-shaming instances and (ii) set benchmarks for future research, marking the first effort to classify body-shaming in Italian. Utilizing a dataset derived from annotations and a majority voting system from three annotators, data was included in the training set only when at least two annotators agreed.

Given the dataset's imbalance towards non-body-shaming instances, as shown in Table 3, we selected a balanced subset of 3,000 comments to ensure a 60-40 split between non-body-shaming and body-shaming instances. Comments were standardized to 32 tokens in length to align with the average comment size of 14 tokens for more effective model training.

For the second-level categorization, we treated it as six separate binary classifications to avoid biases from the uneven label distribution, which could skew the model's learning focus. Thus, only comments explicitly marked as involving body-shaming were used for this task, concentrating the training on identifying specific categories of body-shaming comments.

We fine-tuned three pre-trained BERT-based models from the Hugging Face platform[9] for our tasks: UmBERTo [27], a widely-used Italian BERT model; AlBERTo [29], pre-trained on Twitter data to potentially enhance performance on Instagram; and XLM-RoBERTa [10], a Multilingual Language Model, to evaluate its adaptability. The fine-tuning process involved training for a maximum of 30 epochs with warmup steps set at 20% and implemented early stopping to prevent overfitting. The batch size was limited to 16 for model convergence and memory constraints, and a learning rate of 5e-5 was selected based on literature recommendations for similar models.

The fine-tuning results, including precision, recall, accuracy, and F1-score metrics are detailed in Table 4. These metrics demonstrate a strong capability in body-shaming recognition, with all models performing well. Particularly noteworthy is AlBERTo's superior performance, possibly attributed to its Twitter-based pre-training, which aligns well with the social media context of our dataset. For the second task, it is observed that the categories of skinny-shaming and misogyny/sexism lack data, as none of the models achieved performance better than random chance. However, for other categories, the best-performing model and its corresponding metric values are presented. In particular, UmBERTo excels in ableism and fatphobia detection, while AlBERTo performs best in racism and queerphobia identification. XLM-RoBERTa generally lags behind, possibly due to its multilingual training not being focused on Italian. Conversely, AlBERTo consistent performance may be attributed to its Twitter data training, aligning closely with the language used on Instagram. Notably, categories with

Table 4. Results of the classification tasks for models with statistically significant performance. Performance metrics for tasks where models did not achieve better than random chance are omitted.

Task	Model	Precision	Recall	F-1 score	Accuracy
Body-shaming	AlBERTo	**0.81**	**0.81**	**0.81**	**0.81**
	UmBERTo	0.80	0.80	0.80	0.80
	XLM-RoBERTa	0.80	0.80	0.80	0.80
Fatphobia	AlBERTo	**0.75**	0.73	0.74	**0.76**
	UmBERTo	0.74	**0.75**	**0.75**	0.75
	XLM-RoBERTa	0.72	0.72	0.72	0.73
Racism	AlBERTo	1.00	0.75	0.83	1.00
Ableism	AlBERTo	0.78	**0.78**	0.78	0.92
	UmBERTo	**0.91**	0.76	**0.81**	**0.94**
Queerphobia	AlBERTo	0.75	**0.71**	**0.73**	**0.88**
	UmBERTo	**0.84**	0.61	0.64	**0.88**

---

[9] https://huggingface.co/.

more data instances tend to yield better results. Yet, the model's proficiency in identifying racism may reflect the distinct language patterns specific to body-shaming within this category. However, the limited number of instances in this category warns of a potential for overfitting, despite impressive metrics.

6   Conclusion

In this work, we presented a novel two-level taxonomy for detecting and classifying body-shaming content, covering six distinct categories: Fatphobia, Skinny-shaming, Misogyny/sexism, Racism, Ableism, and Queerphobia. Our main contribution is the first dataset for body-shaming detection and classification in Italian, featuring 11,393 Instagram comments annotated according to our detailed taxonomy. Notably, our focus on Ableism detection introduces a new dimension to body-shaming research. Classification experiments with three BERT-based models, including two Italian-specific and one multilingual, yielded encouraging results, highlighting the efficacy of language-specific models, especially social-media-adapted, for accurately identifying body-shaming instances. This taxonomy and the dataset aim to advance the understanding and mitigation of body-shaming, serving as resources for both researchers and activists.[10]

References

1. Andersen, N.: Diverse examples and balanced perspectives. Enhancing Inclusion, Diversity, Equity and Accessibility (IDEA) in Open Educational Resources (OER) (2022)
2. Anderson, J., Bresnahan, M.: Communicating stigma about body size. Health Commun. **28**, 603–615 (2013)
3. Arumugam, N., Manap, M.R., Mello, G.D., Dharinee, S.: Body shaming: ramifications on an individual. Int. J. Acad. Res. Bus. Soc. Sci. (2022)
4. Bassignana, E., Basile, V., Patti, V., et al.: Hurtlex: a multilingual lexicon of words to hurt. In: CEUR Workshop Proceedings, vol. 2253, pp. 1–6. CEUR-WS (2018)
5. Brewis, A., Wutich, A., Falletta-Cowden, A., Rodriguez-Soto, I.: Body norms and fat stigma in global perspective. Curr. Anthropol. **52**, 269–276 (2011)
6. Capodilupo, C.M., Kim, S.: Gender and race matter: the importance of considering intersections in black women's body image. J. Couns. Psychol. **61**(1), 37–49 (2014)
7. Cassidy, L.: Body shaming in the era of social media. Interdisciplinary Perspectives on Shame: Methods, Theories, Norms, Cultures, and Politics **157**, 396 (2019)
8. Castellini, G., et al.: Internalized transphobia predicts worse longitudinal trend of body uneasiness in transgender persons treated with gender affirming hormone therapy: a 1-year follow-up study. J. Sex. Med. **20**(3), 388–397 (2023)
9. Chakravarthi, B.R., et al.: Overview of third shared task on homophobia and transphobia detection in social media comments. In: Proceedings of the Fourth Workshop on Language Technology for Equality, Diversity and Inclusion. European Chapter of the Association for Computational Linguistics, Malta, March 2024

---

[10] We would like to express our gratitude to Sowelu Avanzo for his crucial contribution and to Roger Ferrod for his wise help.

10. Conneau, A., et al.: Unsupervised cross-lingual representation learning at scale. arXiv preprint arXiv:1911.02116 (2019)
11. Del Vigna12, F., Cimino23, A., Dell'Orletta, F., Petrocchi, M., Tesconi, M.: Hate me, hate me not: Hate speech detection on facebook. In: Proceedings of the first Italian conference on cybersecurity (ITASEC17), pp. 86–95 (2017)
12. Diantoro, K., Sitorus, A.T., Rohman, A., et al.: Analyzing the impact of body shaming on twitter: a study using naive bayes classifier and machine learning. Digitus: J. Comput. Sci. Appl. **1**(1), 11–25 (2023)
13. Elsherief, M., Belding-Royer, E.M., Nguyen, D.: #notokay: understanding gender-based violence in social media. In: International Conference on Web and Social Media (2017)
14. Fitria, K., Febrianti, Y.: The interpretation and attitude of body shaming behavior on social media (a digital ethnography study on instagram) **3**, 12–25 (2020)
15. Flak, S.R.: The influence of maternal body-shaming comments and bodily shame on portion size. Ph.D. thesis, University of South Florida (2021)
16. Frey, T.F., Fernández, M., Novotný, J., Alani, H.: Exploring misogyny across the manosphere in reddit. In: Proceedings of the 10th ACM Conference on Web Science (2019)
17. Gadiraju, V., et al.: "i wouldn't say offensive but...": Disability-centered perspectives on large language models. In: Proceedings of the 2023 ACM Conference on Fairness, Accountability, and Transparency, FAccT 2023, pp. 205–216. Association for Computing Machinery, New York (2023)
18. Gam, R.T., Singh, S.K., Manar, M., Kar, S.K., Gupta, A.: Body shaming among school-going adolescents: prevalence and predictors. Int. J. Community Med. Public Health **7**, 1324–1328 (2020)
19. Glaser, B., Strauss, A.: Discovery of grounded theory: strategies for qualitative research. Routledge (2017)
20. Hutchinson, B., Prabhakaran, V., Denton, E., Webster, K., Zhong, Y., Denuyl, S.: Social biases in nlp models as barriers for persons with disabilities. arXiv preprint arXiv:2005.00813 (2020)
21. Jaman, J.H., Hannie, H., Simatupang, M.R.A.: Sentiment analysis of the body-shaming beauty vlog comments (2020)
22. Kellam, N., Svihla, V., Davis, S.C., Sajadi, S., Desiderio, J.: Using power, privilege, and intersectionality to understand, disrupt, and dismantle oppressive structures within academia: a design case. In: CoNECD Conference (2021)
23. L, S., J, A., E, A.S., M, S.R., N., H.K.: Racism detection using deep learning techniques. E3S Web of Conferences (2023)
24. Narayanan Venkit, P., Srinath, M., Wilson, S.: Automated ableism: an exploration of explicit disability biases in sentiment and toxicity analysis models. In: Ovalle, Anaelia, e.a. (ed.) Proceedings of the 3rd Workshop on Trustworthy Natural Language Processing (TrustNLP 2023), pp. 26–34. Association for Computational Linguistics, Toronto, Canada, July 2023
25. Ousidhoum, N., Lin, Z., Zhang, H., Song, Y., Yeung, D.Y.: Multilingual and multi-aspect hate speech analysis. arXiv preprint arXiv:1908.11049 (2019)
26. Parikh, P., Abburi, H., Badjatiya, P., Krishnan, R., Chhaya, N., Gupta, M., Varma, V.: Multi-label categorization of accounts of sexism using a neural framework. In: Conference on Empirical Methods in Natural Language Processing (2019)
27. Parisi, L., Francia, S., Magnani, P.: Umberto: an Italian language model trained with whole word masking (2020)

28. Poletto, F., Basile, V., Sanguinetti, M., Bosco, C., Patti, V.: Resources and benchmark corpora for hate speech detection: a systematic review. Lang. Resour. Eval. **55**, 477–523 (2021)
29. Polignano, M., Basile, P., de Gemmis, M., Semeraro, G., Basile, V.: AlBERTo: Italian BERT language understanding model for NLP challenging tasks based on tweets. In: Proceedings of the Sixth Italian Conference on Computational Linguistics (CLiC-it 2019), vol. 2481. CEUR (2019)
30. Ramati-Ziber, L., Shnabel, N., Glick, P.: The beauty myth: prescriptive beauty norms for women reflect hierarchy-enhancing motivations leading to discriminatory employment practices. J. Personality Soc. Psychol. (2020)
31. Reddy, V., Abburi, H., Chhaya, N., Mitrovska, T., Varma, V.: 'you are big, s/he is small' detecting body shaming in online user content. In: Social Informatics (2022)
32. Reel, J.J., Bucciere, R.A.: Ableism and body image: conceptualizing how individuals are marginalized. Women Sport Phys. Activity J. **19**(1), 91–97 (2010)
33. Richter, A., et al.: Subtle misogyny detection and mitigation: An expert-annotated dataset. In: Socially Responsible Language Modelling Research (2023)
34. Riitaoja, A.L., Virtanen, A., Reiman, N., Lehtonen, T., Yli-Jokipii, M., Udd, T., Peniche-Ferreira, L.: Migrants at the university doorstep: How we unfairly deny access and what we could (should) do now. Apples - Journal of Applied Language Studies (09 2022)
35. Roodt, K.: (Re) constructing body shaming: Popular media representations of female identities as discursive identity construction. Ph.D. thesis, Stellenbosch: Stellenbosch University (2015)
36. Röttger, P., Nozza, D., Bianchi, F., Hovy, D.: Data-efficient strategies for expanding hate speech detection into under-resourced languages. In: Goldberg, Y., Kozareva, Z., Zhang, Y. (eds.) Proceedings of the 2022 Conference on Empirical Methods in Natural Language Processing, pp. 5674–5691. Association for Computational Linguistics, Abu Dhabi, United Arab Emirates, December 2022
37. Schlüter, C., Kraag, G., Schmidt, J.: Body shaming: an exploratory study on its definition and classification. Int. J. Bullying Prevention (2021)
38. Ungless, E.L., Ross, B., Belle, V.: Potential pitfalls with automatic sentiment analysis: the example of queerphobic bias. Soc. Sci. Comput. Rev. **41**(6), 2211–2229 (2023)
39. Vargas, F., Carvalho, I., Rodrigues de Góes, F., Pardo, T., Benevenuto, F.: HateBR: a large expert annotated corpus of Brazilian Instagram comments for offensive language and hate speech detection. In: Calzolari, Nicoletta, e.a. (ed.) Proceedings of the Thirteenth Language Resources and Evaluation Conference, pp. 7174–7183. European Language Resources Association, Marseille, France, June 2022
40. Vásquez, J., Andersen, S., Bel-Enguix, G., Gómez-Adorno, H., Ojeda-Trueba, S.L.: Homo-mex: a Mexican Spanish annotated corpus for lgbt+ phobia detection on Twitter. In: The 7th Workshop on Online Abuse and Harms (WOAH), pp. 202–214 (2023)
41. Vidgen, B., Harris, A., Nguyen, D., Tromble, R., Hale, S.A., Margetts, H.Z.: Challenges and frontiers in abusive content detection. In: Proceedings of the Third Workshop on Abusive Language Online (2019)
42. Williams, S.: The problematic body-shaming of black female athletes in professional sports (2018)

Adaptive Greedy Layer Pruning: Iterative Layer Pruning with Subsequent Model Repurposing

Tamás Ficsor[(✉)] and Gábor Berend

University of Szeged, Szeged, Hungary
{ficsort,berendg}@inf.u-szeged.hu

Abstract. Reducing the memory requirements during inference time in pretrained language models (PLMs) constitutes a key challenge. In this paper, we rigorously investigate the possibility of progressively removing layers from PLMs during their fine-tuning process, in such a way that their final task performance degrade minimally. Our proposed approach not only provides a considerable reduction in the inference cost of using PLMs, but it also highlights the importance of distinct layers, via the identification of layers with marginal contribution to downstream task performance. Our experiments, encompassing seven diverse tasks, corroborate that the exclusion of less pertinent transformer layers facilitates more efficient inference without causing serious degradation of task performance. Indeed, we were able to omit up to 2.2x more layers from the investigated PLMs (depending on the backbone model) compared to a strong layer pruning baseline when preserving no less than 95% of the performance of the full backbone model.

Keywords: Layer Pruning · Efficient inference · Mechanistic interpretability

1 Introduction

In the ever-expanding landscape of deep learning, optimizing neural network architectures has become pivotal for achieving efficient and scalable models. Layer pruning, a technique gaining significant attention, offers a compelling avenue to streamline neural networks by identifying and eliminating redundant or less influential layers. This process not only enhances model efficiency but also contributes to reduced computational complexity, thus providing faster inference times.

The motivation behind layer pruning stems from the pressing need to deploy deep learning models in real-world scenarios where computational resources are often limited. By pruning redundant connections or entire layers, we can create more compact models without sacrificing a significant portion of the performance. This not only facilitates deployment on resource-constrained devices and enables more sustainable AI solutions by reducing energy consumption and carbon footprint in the long run.

Furthermore, layer pruning aligns with the pursuit of interpretability and explainability in machine learning and deep learning systems. By removing unnecessary layers, we can often uncover the most salient features and pathways within the network, providing deeper insights into its decision-making process. This enhanced interpretability

A. Rapp et al. (Eds.): NLDB 2024, LNCS 14762, pp. 271–284, 2024.
https://doi.org/10.1007/978-3-031-70239-6_19

not only fosters trust in AI systems but also enables domain experts to better understand and collaborate with these models.

In essence, layer pruning represents a crucial step towards building more efficient, interpretable and sustainable deep learning models, thereby accelerating their adoption across a wide range of applications and industries. Prior work were either based on fixed omission patterns (e.g. every even/odd indexed layers, or the first/last few layers) or apply some heuristics for deciding which blocks to drop [24]. Peer et al. introduced an iterative approach which gradually expands the set of transformer blocks to get discarded from the original pre-trained model [23]. What is common in previous approaches is that after deciding which layers to discard, they omit them from the initial pre-trained network. Although Sajjad et al. briefly explored the possibility of gradual layer pruning, they did not elaborate on it in detail and concluded that it did not yield any improvement over directly dropping layers from the model.

In this work[1], we investigate gradual layer pruning more thoroughly and show that reusing intermediate checkpoints with subsequent fine-tuning is a viable strategy that allows us to omit more layers from the fine-tuned LMs in expectation, while maintaining similar or better performance as previously proposed approaches.

2   Related Work

BERT [6] is arguably among the most commonly used transformer variants, upon which many improvements have been advocated regarding the training procedure [4, 19] and the overall architecture [11, 14, 16]. While these models excel at solving various NLP tasks, their massive computational need poses significant challenges [29].

One can achieve efficient inference by either pre-training a model with inherently reduced parameter count (such as `tiny`, `small`, `medium` configurations) which risks that the model has insufficient capacity for solving a wide range of tasks [32]. Alternatively [3, 17], we can apply weight pruning which aims to remove redundant and unimportant weights [10, 18], or reduce the numerical representation of weights with quantization [8]. Other approaches for reducing the model size include matrix factorization [20] and parameter sharing [15].

We can also reduce model size via distillation, where the objective is to train a smaller model capable of replicating the behaviour of a larger teacher model, and which has been critically investigated by [28]. One of the most popular distilled transformer is DistilBERT [25], but several other distilled model variants have also been introduced [30, 37]. [34] provides a comparison between commonly used training strategies regarding transformer models.

Another emerging method is early exiting [13, 26, 36], which constitute another form of improving inference efficiency, during which inference is sped up by allowing the to make inference decisions at layers that is not necessary the final one. This reduces inference speed and memory usage *in expectation*, however, the peak memory usage is not effected in cases when the model decides to rely on the entire model for making a decision.

---

[1] The code is available at: https://github.com/ficstamas/DiscardBERT.

Another approach to improve inference speed is layer pruning. Sajjad et al. performed layer dropping prior to fine-tuning for obtaining memory efficient model variants [24]. In a subsequent work, Peer et al. proposed another layer dropping technique, which uses a greedy layer-wise strategy to decide which layers to eliminate from the network before fine-tuning [23]. The greedy approach is based on a series of fine-tunings, based on which the order for removing layers from the original PLM is determined. We propose and carefully evaluate a crucial modification to [23], i.e., instead of removing layers from the intact pre-trained model, we gradually adapt the original pre-trained model during layer dropping, allowing us to eliminate more layers from the model without substantially sacrificing the performance.

3 Methodology

We next describe the two major layer elimination strategies that we compare in our experiments. First, we present greedy layer pruning (GLP) from Peer et al. [23]. Subsequently (in Sect. 3.2), we provide details on our proposed adaptive greedy layer pruning approach (AGLP). The pseudocode summarizing the two approaches is included in Fig. 1.

3.1 Greedy-Layer Pruning (GLP)

GLP is designed to find a computationally feasible approximation to the "optimal pruning strategy" for a given PLM with layers L and task T. For a fixed number of layers to be removed, n, the goal is to determine the optimal subset of layers to be removed from the network, R_n, such that it maximizes $\mathcal{M}(L \setminus R_n, T)$, where $\mathcal{M}$ is the metric used for evaluating task performance on task T.

Finding the best performing R_n requires $\mathcal{O}\binom{|L|}{n}$ fine-tuning and evaluation of a held out validation set to be performed, which would have been computationally prohibitive. To alleviate the computational requirements, GLP provides an $\mathcal{O}(|L| \times n)$ algorithm for approximating the $|L| - n$ element optimal subset of PLM layers that achieve the highest task metric on T.

GLP eliminates layers from a pre-trained model, expanding the set of omitted layers one at a time based on the performance measured on the validation set, leveraging the locality assumption, stating that whenever a certain layer is included in R_i, then the same layer is also a member of $R_{i'}$, for all $i' > i$. An important detail of GLP is that it always eliminates one layer from the original network, and not the one which has been fine-tuned for determining which layer to remove next.

3.2 Adaptive Greedy Layer-Wise Pruning (AGLP)

Although each iteration of GLP involves performing multiple fine-tunings for determining the layer to be omitted next, following the actual omission of a layer, the weights of the remaining subnetwork are taken from the original model and not from the already fine-tuned ones. The way AGLP differs from GLP is that in each iteration, we remove an additional layer from the best already fine-tuned model from the last iteration. The steps of AGLP are the following:

1. we remove a single layer from $L_i' = L \setminus i, i \in \{1, 2, \ldots, |L|\}$,
2. fine-tune L_i' on the target task,
3. select the locally optimal layer (R_1) according to metric $\mathcal{M}$, and obtain $L^* = L \setminus R_1$,
4. then we repeat step 1–3 while reusing the reduced model ($L = L^*$) until we reach a model with a single layer

We decide which layer to eliminate (step 3) based on a validation set, aiming for the smallest drop in performance compared to the input model's results. Unlike GLP, our approach builds on the accumulated knowledge from prior fine-tuning iterations, enhancing the layer elimination process while preserving the computational efficiency of the GLP framework.

```
def pruning(model, n, trainer, AGLP=True):
    layers = [] # layers to remove (R)
    while len(layers) <= n:
        best_performance, layer_to_remove, best_model = -inf, None, None
        # looking for a single locally optimal layer to remove (R₁)
        for i in range(len(model.layers)):
            new_model = copy(model)
            # removing layer
            if AGLP: # L \ R₁
                rm_layers(new_model, [i])
            else: # L \ (R ∪ R₁)
                rm_layers(new_model, layers + [i])
            performance = trainer(new_model)
            if performance > best_performance: # if it maximizes M
                best_performance = performance
                layer_to_remove, best_model = i, new_model
        if AGLP: # L* = L' (reuse)
            model = best_model
        layers += [layer_to_remove]
    if AGLP: # in this case the model is already trained
        return model
    return trainer(rm_layers(model, layers))
```

Fig. 1. Pseudocode for AGLP and GLP, where *model* is the initial model, n denotes the number of layers to remove, and *trainer* is an object containing the training environment capable of returning validation performance. $rm\_layers(\cdot)$ is a function which removes layers from the given *model*.

4   Experimental Setup

In our study, we tested five different models with varying number of layers and the per-layer model parameters ($|\theta_{layer}|$), with total parameter counts ($|\theta|$) as follows:

- BERT-MEDIUM-UNCASED: Num. Layer = 8, $|\theta_{layer}| = 3M$, $|\theta| = 41M$,
- DISTILBERT-BASE-UNCASED: Num. Layer = 6, $|\theta_{layer}| = 7M$, $|\theta| = 67M$,
- ROBERTA-BASE: Num. Layer = 12, $|\theta_{layer}| = 7M$, $|\theta| = 125M$,
- BERT-BASE-UNCASED: Num. Layer = 12, $|\theta_{layer}| = 7M$, $|\theta| = 109M$,
- BERT-LARGE-UNCASED: Num. Layer = 24, $|\theta_{layer}| = 13M$, $|\theta| = 335M$.

To compare their performance, we first fine-tuned each model with 5 different seeds (without any layer being omitted), and represented the baseline performance as the average of these runs on each task.

We chose a diverse range of tasks to assess the model's performance and how well they generalize. To follow earlier experiments [23, 24], we include tasks from the GLUE benchmark [33] which have a training set comprising of no more than 100K instances (i.e., CoLA [35], MRPC [7], RTE [2,5,9]), SST2 [27], and STSB [1]. The basis for selecting this particular subset of GLUE was due to computational constraints (as the iterative nature of the investigated pruning algorithms requires a large number of fine-tunings to be performed). Besides the 5 GLUE tasks, we also selected the CoNLL 2003 [31] dataset for NER and POS tagging evaluations for testing (A)GLP in the token classification setting as well.

To ensure robustness, we ran all our further experiments five times with different random seeds, as the initialization of the classification head can lead to large variability in fine-tuning performance. We used a learning rate of $2 \cdot 10^{-5}$ with constant learning rate scheduling, and each fine-tuning process lasted for 3 epochs. In case of GLUE tasks, we made an even split of their validation sets and used the resulting subsets as a new validation and test set (as the labels of the official test set are not publicly available).

5 Results

We conducted a thorough investigation comparing the capabilities of models compressed with GLP and AGLP the results of which are included in Fig. 2 and Fig. 3 for sequence classification tasks and token classification tasks, respectively. Each subfigure corresponds to a task-model pair, with the blue (dashed) and orange (dotted) lines representing the results of AGLP and GLP approaches, respectively. The black dashed line shows the baseline performance, and the green and yellow regions corresponds to 5% and 10% degradation in performance. The left y-axis displays the percentage of preserved performance, while the right y-axis shows the actual scores in the respective metric, i.e. CoLA represented with Matthew's correlation coefficient. On the x-axis, from left to right, we track the reduction in model size.

Overall, AGLP performs on par or better than GLP for the majority of model-task pairs. GLP has a slight advantage when removing a small number of layers from the BERT-large model, solving sequence classification tasks (see Fig. 2). Additionally, GLP performs more consistently on MRPC, which may stem from the challenges associated with training larger models. Improved hyper-parameter selection could potentially alleviate these issues. Moreover, AGLP demonstrates noticeable and consistent performance improvements on token classification tasks (see Fig. 3). These results are also corroborated by the results shown in Table 1 where we provide the average number of layers that can be discarded from the models for each task while preserving a certain fraction of the task performance of the full model without any layer being omitted. We can see a consistent reduction in model size while preserving both 95% and 90% of the performance of the original model for AGPL.

We observe high variance in Fig. 2e for the BERT-LARGE model on the SST data. It is the cause of failed fine-tuning attempts which can be seen on Fig. 4. It is a well

Table 1. Average number of layers that can be discarded while preserving $\geq 95\%$ or $\geq 90\%$ of the performance of the intact models from which no layers are discarded.

	BERT-MEDIUM		DISTILBERT		ROBERTA-BASE		BERT-BASE		BERT-LARGE	
	AGLP	GLP	AGLP	GLP	AGLP	GLP	AGLP	GLP	AGLP	GLP
Sequence Classification										
CoLA	0.8	0.0	1.2	0.8	3.0	3.6	3.0	3.4	9.5	10.4
MRPC	3.2	7.0	2.2	2.6	6.4	6.4	8.6	7.8	19.0	18.6
RTE	4.6	1.6	3.6	1.0	6.2	3.6	4.6	2.4	19.2	17.2
STSB	5.0	4.0	3.2	2.8	8.0	7.6	8.8	7.4	19.8	18.4
SST2	4.6	4.4	2.8	2.6	8.4	9.0	6.8	7.8	7.0	18.2
Avg.	3.6	3.4	2.6	1.9	6.4	6.0	6.3	5.7	14.9	16.5
(% layers)	(45%)	(42%)	(43%)	(31%)	(53%)	(50%)	(52%)	(47%)	(62%)	(68%)
Token Classification										
NER	5.8	0.0	4.0	0.0	10.0	9.8	9.0	2.8	20.0	18.0
POS	7.0	0.0	5.0	0.0	11.0	0.0	11.0	0.0	22.8	0.0
Avg.	6.4	0.0	4.5	0.0	10.5	4.9	10.0	1.4	21.4	9.0
(% layers)	(80%)	(0%)	(75%)	(0%)	(87%)	(40%)	(83%)	(11%)	(89%)	(37%)
Overall										
Avg.	4.4	2.4	3.1	1.4	7.5	5.7	7.4	4.5	16.7	14.4
(% layers)	(55%)	(30%)	(52%)	(23%)	(62%)	(48%)	(62%)	(38%)	(70%)	(60%)

(a) 95% relative performance preserved

	BERT-MEDIUM		DISTILBERT		ROBERTA-BASE		BERT-BASE		BERT-LARGE	
	AGLP	GLP	AGLP	GLP	AGLP	GLP	AGLP	GLP	AGLP	GLP
Sequence Classification										
CoLA	1.4	0.0	1.6	1.0	4.0	4.6	4.6	4.6	13.2	13.2
MRPC	4.8	7.0	3.2	5.0	8.6	9.4	10.0	11.0	21.6	23.0
RTE	5.6	4.6	4.0	3.4	8.2	5.0	5.6	5.4	20.2	21.0
STSB	6.0	5.0	4.0	3.0	9.0	8.0	9.6	8.6	21.0	20.0
SST2	6.0	6.2	4.0	4.6	10.0	10.0	9.8	9.4	13.3	21.8
Avg.	4.7	4.5	3.3	3.4	7.9	7.4	7.8	7.8	17.8	19.8
(% layers)	(58%)	(56%)	(55%)	(56%)	(65%)	(61%)	(65%)	(65%)	(74%)	(82%)
Token Classification										
NER	6.0	0.0	4.0	3.8	10.0	11.0	10.0	10.0	21.9	20.8
POS	7.0	0.0	5.0	0.0	11.0	8.2	11.0	0.0	23.0	2.2
Avg.	6.5	0.0	4.5	1.9	10.5	9.6	10.5	5.0	22.4	11.5
(% layers)	(81%)	(0%)	(75%)	(31%)	(87%)	(80%)	(87%)	(41%)	(93%)	(47%)
Overall										
Avg.	5.2	3.2	3.6	2.9	8.4	8.0	8.6	7.0	19.1	17.4
(% layers)	(65%)	(40%)	(60%)	(48%)	(70%)	(67%)	(72%)	(58%)	(80%)	(72%)

(b) 90% relative performance preserved

known problem that training models with a considerably large parameter count is difficult [21, 22, 38], but if successful it should yield a better model compared to their smaller counterparts. Figure 4 also shows us that the quality of the initial models can highly impact layer pruning as well, with blue (dashed) and orange (dotted) lines cor-

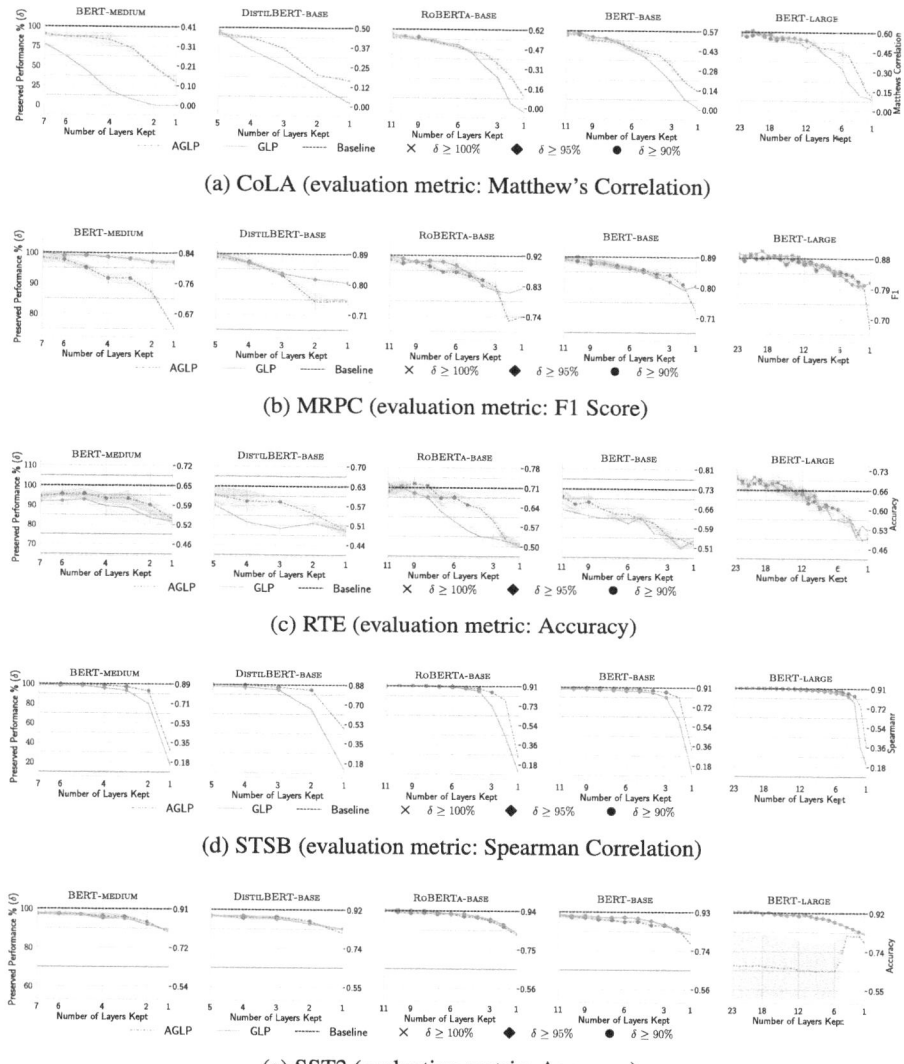

(a) CoLA (evaluation metric: Matthew's Correlation)

(b) MRPC (evaluation metric: F1 Score)

(c) RTE (evaluation metric: Accuracy)

(d) STSB (evaluation metric: Spearman Correlation)

(e) SST2 (evaluation metric: Accuracy)

Fig. 2. Results on sequence classification tasks and the amount of relative performance preserved compared to the baseline model along the right and left axes, respectively.

responding to successful and failed AGLP experiments. It can be seen that AGLP performs as expected when the base model was successfully trained (blue line), and it was also able to attain a reasonable performance once a sufficient number (19) of layers got removed, probably once the problematic layers responsible for the failed fine-tuning get eliminated from the network.

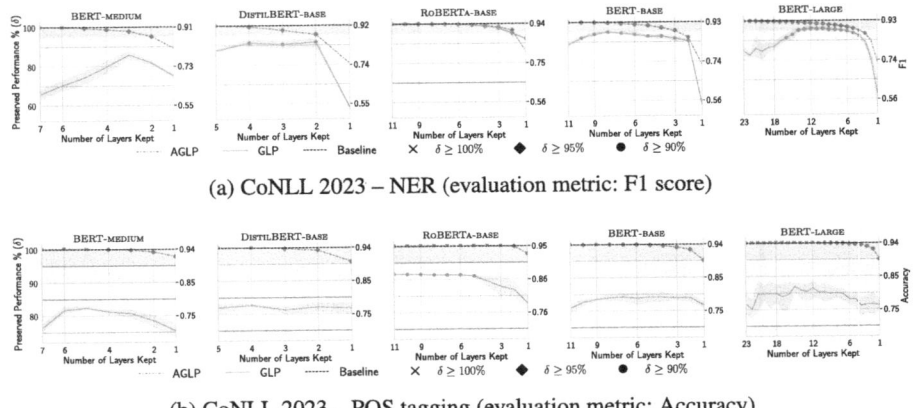

(a) CoNLL 2023 – NER (evaluation metric: F1 score)

(b) CoNLL 2023 – POS tagging (evaluation metric: Accuracy)

Fig. 3. Results on token classification tasks and the amount of relative performance preserved compared to the baseline model along the right and left axes, respectively.

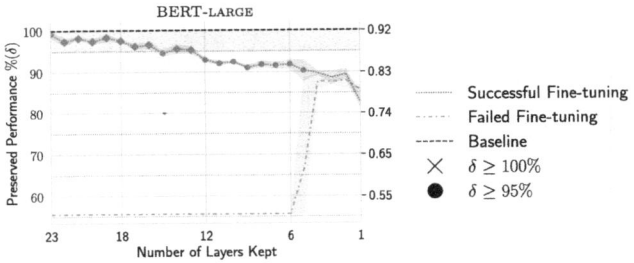

Fig. 4. The effect of failed fine-tuning on SST2 with BERT-LARGE.

Next we investigate at which iteration does a certain layer gets removed from the network when using GLP and AGLP. In Fig. 5, the average iteration number at which a certain layer (as indicated along the x-axis) gets eliminated is displayed by blue (directed up) and orange (directed down) bars for AGPL and GLP, respectively. The higher a bar, the later the corresponding layer is eliminated on average from the network. The additional green bars (with hatches) indicate the difference between the average elimination time of a given layer between the two pruning approaches. Bars pointing upwards mean that the corresponding layer is removed from the network later on average when relying on AGLP compared to the use of GLP.

Based on Fig. 5, we can observe that AGLP consistently prioritizes the retention of the last transformer layer over any other layer, which preserves the necessary task-specific information. The primary reason why GLP cannot achieve this is attributed to its inability to maintain knowledge between layer elimination steps. Figure 5 shows no correlation between the iteration numbers at which the layers get eliminated from

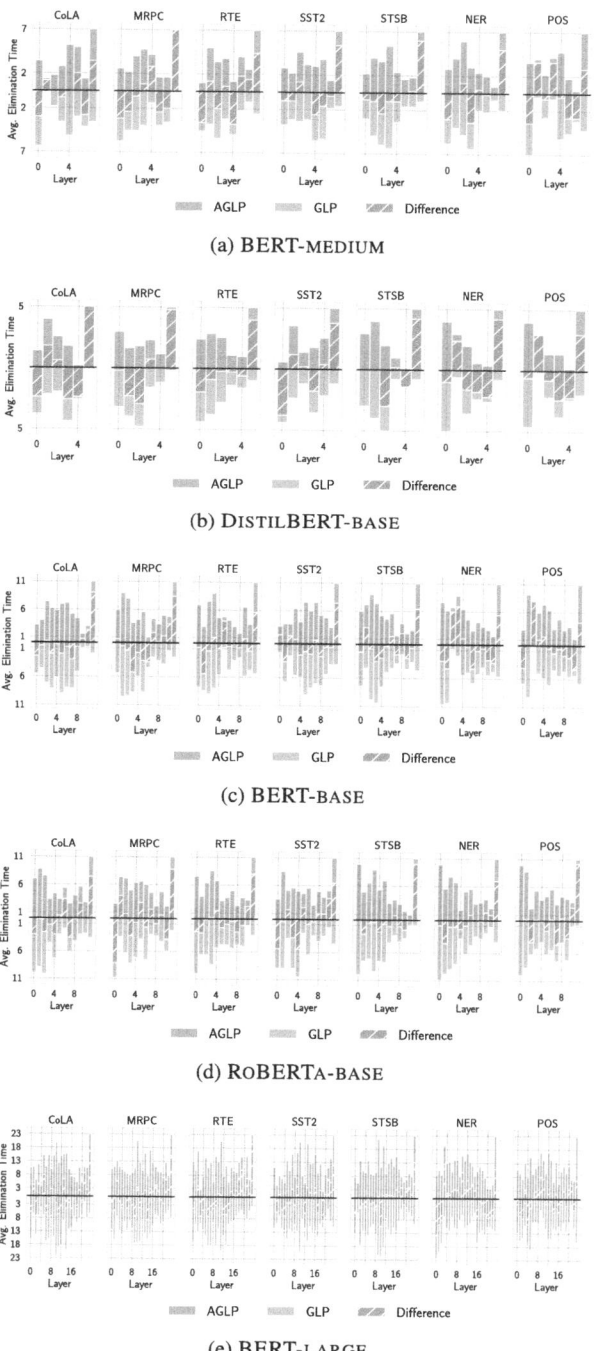

(a) BERT-MEDIUM

(b) DISTILBERT-BASE

(c) BERT-BASE

(d) ROBERTA-BASE

(e) BERT-LARGE

Fig. 5. Average elimination time (iteration number) at which the individual layers are discarded for the different tasks from the different models.

the model for GLP and AGLP, meaning that the two pruning strategies follow entirely different paths during their layer pruning process. To further validate the previous statement, we selected the BASE models and checked if the selected layer indices overlapped in the final model when we preserved 95% of the accuracy, which can be seen in Table 2. To find the overlapping layers we used the intersection of layers from all seeds which gave an information about the most commonly used layers for a model-task pair. Usually, the two methods overlapped when the GLP preserved the final layer and rarely for any other layer. If we consider GLP independently, the overlap of layers between models on the same task does not happen every time either which is indicated by the empty sets in the table. We did not present the results for CoNLL due to the high variance between GLP and AGLP.

Table 2. Commonly kept layers in final models with more then 95% relative performance compared to the baseline.

| | BERT | | RoBERTa | |
	AGLP	GLP	AGLP	GLP
CoLA	{0, 1, 2, 3, 5, 6, 7, 8, 9, 10, 11}	{0, 1, 2, 3, 4, 5, 6, 7, 8, 9, 10, 11}	{0, 3, 5, 6, 7, 9, 10, 11}	{0, 1, 5, 6, 9, 10, 11}
MRPC	{10, 11}	{11}	{6, 11}	{10}
RTE	{5, 6, 11}	{0, 1, 7, 8, 9, 10, 11}	{0, 6, 7, 8, 11}	{0, 1, 2, 3, 5, 6, 7, 8, 9, 10, 11}
SST2	{11}	{0, 1, 3, 4}	{11}	{∅}
STSB	{5, 11}	{10, 11}	{11}	{∅}

While layer pruning can help in reducing the size of existing models, it is important to acknowledge that the complexity of the task at hand also warrants consideration. Choosing models with less parameters per layer can help in finding pruned models that are also smaller. Figure 6 showcases the smallest possible models which satisfies a no more than 5% drop in relative performance compared to the best possible baseline achieved among all investigated model sizes. The x-axis displays the various tasks, and the y-axis represents the number of parameters (including the embedding matrix) inside the model in log-scale, the white number on the bars represents the number of layers of the pruned model, and the color of the bars indicate which model type the pruned model was derived from. From left to right, we can see that certain tasks can be solved with much less parameters, which can indicate the difficulty of that particular task. GLP could not produce any model with good performance on POS, hence the corresponding column is not present on the plot. Furthermore, we can see that for all tasks, our AGLP approach can find fewer parameter pruned models compared to GLP.

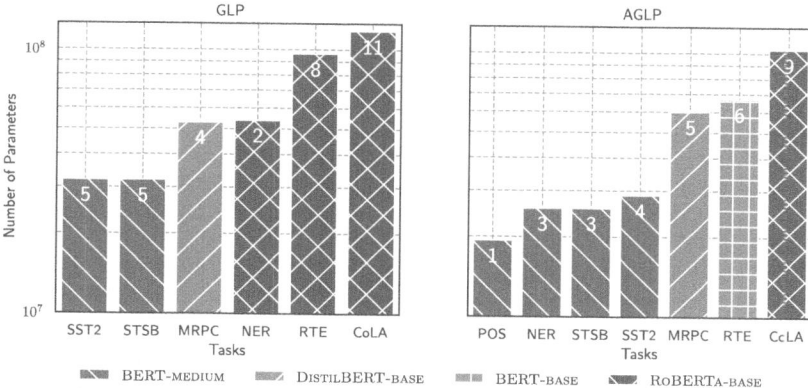

Fig. 6. The minimal number of parameters required to solve tasks within 5% performance loss. The white numbers represent the amount of layers kept in that particular model.

6   Conclusions

In this paper we showed the benefits of retaining model knowledge in-between the elimination steps of greedy layer pruning. Our extensive experiments illustrate the efficiency of AGLP in preserving a substantial amount of relative performance across diverse transformer model sizes, tasks and pre-training environments. We also thoroughly investigated the trade-off between the relative performance preserved and the use of different pre-trained models.

It is important to note that the identification and elimination of layers within a model remains computationally intensive, offering possibilities for optimization in future work. Our experiments reveal that with our proposed extension of GLP, it is possible to remove nearly 40% more layers (averaged over tasks and the different PLMs) from the original full capacity networks, while preserving the same quality, i.e.. at least 95% relative fine-tuning performance of the full networks.

Acknowledgments. The research received support from the European Union project RRF-2.3.1-21-2022-00004 within the framework of the Artificial Intelligence National Laboratory. Additionally, we are grateful for the possibility to use ELKH Cloud (see [12]; https://science-cloud.hu/) which helped us in achieving the results published in this paper.

References

1. Agirre, E., M'arquez, L., Wicentowski, R. (eds.): Proceedings of the Fourth International Workshop on Semantic Evaluations (SemEval-2007). Association for Computational Linguistics, Prague, Czech Republic (2007)

2. Bentivogli, L., Magnini, B., Dagan, I., Dang, H.T., Giampiccolo, D.: The fifth PASCAL recognizing textual entailment challenge. In: Proceedings of the Second Text Analysis Conference, TAC 2009, Gaithersburg, Maryland, USA, November 16-17, 2009. NIST (2009). https://tac.nist.gov/publications/2009/additional.papers/RTE5_overview.proceedings.pdf

3. Cheng, H., Zhang, M., Shi, J.Q.: A survey on deep neural network pruning-taxonomy, comparison, analysis, and recommendations (2023). http://arxiv.org/abs/2308.06767

4. Clark, K., Luong, M.T., Le, Q.V., Manning, C.D.: ELECTRA: pre-training text encoders as discriminators rather than generators. In: International Conference on Learning Representations (2020). https://openreview.net/forum?id=r1xMH1BtvB

5. Dagan, I., Glickman, O., Magnini, B.: The PASCAL recognising textual entailment challenge. In: Quiñonero-Candela, J., Dagan, I., Magnini, B., d'Alché-Buc, F. (eds.) MLCW 2005. LNCS (LNAI), vol. 3944, pp. 177–190. Springer, Heidelberg (2006). https://doi.org/10.1007/11736790_9

6. Devlin, J., Chang, M.W., Lee, K., Toutanova, K.: BERT: pre-training of deep bidirectional transformers for language understanding. In: Proceedings of the 2019 Conference of the North American Chapter of the Association for Computational Linguistics: Human Language Technologies, Volume 1 (Long and Short Papers), pp. 4171–4186. Association for Computational Linguistics, Minneapolis, Minnesota (2019). https://doi.org/10.18653/v1/N19-1423, https://aclanthology.org/N19-1423

7. Dolan, W.B., Brockett, C.: Automatically constructing a corpus of sentential paraphrases. In: Proceedings of the Third International Workshop on Paraphrasing (IWP2005) (2005). https://aclanthology.org/I05-5002

8. Frantar, E., Ashkboos, S., Hoefler, T., Alistarh, D.: GPTQ: accurate post-training quantization for generative pre-trained transformers. CoRR **abs/2210.17323** (2022). http://dblp.uni-trier.de/db/journals/corr/corr2210.html#abs-2210-17323

9. Giampiccolo, D., Magnini, B., Dagan, I., Dolan, B.: The third PASCAL recognizing textual entailment challenge. In: Proceedings of the ACL-PASCAL Workshop on Textual Entailment and Paraphrasing, pp. 1–9. Association for Computational Linguistics, Prague (2007). https://aclanthology.org/W07-1401

10. Gordon, M., Duh, K., Andrews, N.: Compressing BERT: studying the effects of weight pruning on transfer learning. In: Proceedings of the 5th Workshop on Representation Learning for NLP, pp. 143–155. Association for Computational Linguistics, Online (2020). https://doi.org/10.18653/v1/2020.repl4nlp-1.18, https://aclanthology.org/2020.repl4nlp-1.18

11. He, P., Gao, J., Chen, W.: DeBERTav3: improving DeBERTa using ELECTRA-style pretraining with gradient-disentangled embedding sharing. In: The Eleventh International Conference on Learning Representations (2023). https://openreview.net/forum?id=sE7-XhLxHA

12. Héder, M., et al.: The past, present and future of the ELKH cloud. Információs Társadalom **22**(2), 128 (2022). https://doi.org/10.22503/inftars.xxii.2022.2.8

13. Hu, B., Zhu, Y., Li, J., Tang, S.: SmartBERT: a promotion of dynamic early exiting mechanism for accelerating BERT inference. In: Proceedings of the Thirty-Second International Joint Conference on Artificial Intelligence. IJCAI '23 (2023). https://doi.org/10.24963/ijcai.2023/563

14. Kitaev, N., Kaiser, L., Levskaya, A.: Reformer: the efficient transformer. In: International Conference on Learning Representations (2020). https://openreview.net/forum?id=rkgNKkHtvB

15. Lan, Z., Chen, M., Goodman, S., Gimpel, K., Sharma, P., Soricut, R.: ALBERT: a lite BERT for self-supervised learning of language representations. In: International Conference on Learning Representations (2020). https://openreview.net/forum?id=H1eA7AEtvS

16. Lepikhin, D., et al.: GShard: scaling giant models with conditional computation and automatic sharding. In: International Conference on Learning Representations (2021). https://openreview.net/forum?id=qrwe7XHTmYb

17. Liang, T., Glossner, J., Wang, L., Shi, S., Zhang, X.: Pruning and quantization for deep neural network acceleration: a survey. Neurocomputing **461**, 370–403 (2021). http://dblp.uni-trier.de/db/journals/ijon/ijon461.html#LiangGWSZ21

18. Lin, Z., Liu, J., Yang, Z., Hua, N., Roth, D.: Pruning redundant mappings in transformer models via spectral-normalized identity prior. In: Findings of the Association for Computational Linguistics: EMNLP 2020, pp. 719–730. Association for Computational Linguistics, Online (2020). https://doi.org/10.18653/v1/2020.findings-emnlp.64, https://aclanthology.org/2020.findings-emnlp.64

19. Liu, Y., et al.: RoBERTa: a robustly optimized BERT pretraining approach (2019)

20. Mehta, S., Koncel-Kedziorski, R., Rastegari, M., Hajishirzi, H.: DeFINE: deep factorized input token embeddings for neural sequence modeling. In: ICLR, OpenReview.net (2020). http://dblp.uni-trier.de/db/conf/iclr/iclr2020.html#MehtaKRH20

21. Mosbach, M., Andriushchenko, M., Klakow, D.: On the stability of fine-tuning BERT: misconceptions, explanations, and strong baselines. In: Proceedings of the International Conference on Learning Representations (2021). https://openreview.net/forum?id=nzpLWnVAyah

22. Nakkiran, P., Kaplun, G., Bansal, Y., Yang, T., Barak, B., Sutskever, I.: Deep double descent: where bigger models and more data hurt. In: ICLR, OpenReview.net (2020). http://dblp.uni-trier.de/db/conf/iclr/iclr2020.html#NakkiranKBYBS20

23. Peer, D., Stabinger, S., Engl, S., Rodríguez-Sánchez, A.: Greedy-layer pruning: speeding up transformer models for natural language processing. Pattern Recogn. Lett. **157**, 76–82 (2022). https://doi.org/10.1016/j.patrec.2022.03.023

24. Sajjad, H., Dalvi, F., Durrani, N., Nakov, P.: On the effect of dropping layers of pre-trained transformer models. Comput. Speech Lang. **77**, 101429 (2023). https://doi.org/10.1016/j.csl.2022.101429

25. Sanh, V., Debut, L., Chaumond, J., Wolf, T.: DistilBERT, a distilled version of BERT: smaller, faster, cheaper and lighter. CoRR **abs/1910.01108** (2019). http://dblp.uni-trier.de/db/journals/corr/corr1910.html#abs-1910-01108

26. Schwartz, R., Stanovsky, G., Swayamdipta, S., Dodge, J., Smith, N.A.: The right tool for the job: matching model and instance complexities. In: Proceedings of the 58th Annual Meeting of the Association for Computational Linguistics, pp. 6640–6651. Association for Computational Linguistics, Online (2020). https://doi.org/10.18653/v1/2020.acl-main.593

27. Socher, R., Perelygin, A., Wu, J., Chuang, J., Manning, C.D., Ng, A., Potts, C.: Recursive deep models for semantic compositionality over a sentiment treebank. In: Proceedings of EMNLP, pp. 1631–1642 (2013)

28. Stanton, S.D., Izmailov, P., Kirichenko, P., Alemi, A.A., Wilson, A.G.: Does knowledge distillation really work? In: Beygelzimer, A., Dauphin, Y., Liang, P., Vaughan, J.W. (eds.) Advances in Neural Information Processing Systems (2021). https://openreview.net/forum?id=7J-fKoXiReA

29. Strubell, E., Ganesh, A., McCallum, A.: Energy and policy considerations for deep learning in NLP. In: Korhonen, A., Traum, D., Màrquez, L. (eds.) Proceedings of the 57th Annual Meeting of the Association for Computational Linguistics, pp. 3645–3650. Association for Computational Linguistics, Florence, Italy (2019). https://doi.org/10.18653/v1/P19-1355, https://aclanthology.org/P19-1355

30. Sun, S., Gan, Z., Fang, Y., Cheng, Y., Wang, S., Liu, J.: Contrastive distillation on intermediate representations for language model compression. In: Proceedings of the 2020 Conference on Empirical Methods in Natural Language Processing (EMNLP), pp. 498–508. Association for Computational Linguistics, Online (2020). https://doi.org/10.18653/v1/2020.emnlp-main.36

31. Tjong Kim Sang, E.F., De Meulder, F.: Introduction to the CoNLL-2003 shared task: Language-independent named entity recognition. In: Proceedings of the Seventh Conference on Natural Language Learning at HLT-NAACL 2003, pp. 142–147 (2003). https://www.aclweb.org/anthology/W03-0419

32. Turc, I., Chang, M.W., Lee, K., Toutanova, K.: Well-read students learn better: on the importance of pre-training compact models (2020). https://openreview.net/forum?id=BJg7x1HFvB

33. Wang, A., Singh, A., Michael, J., Hill, F., Levy, O., Bowman, S.: GLUE: a multi-task benchmark and analysis platform for natural language understanding. In: Proceedings of the 2018 EMNLP Workshop BlackboxNLP: Analyzing and Interpreting Neural Networks for NLP, pp. 353–355. Association for Computational Linguistics, Brussels, Belgium (2018). https://doi.org/10.18653/v1/W18-5446

34. Wang, X., Weissweiler, L., Schütze, H., Plank, B.: How to distill your BERT: an empirical study on the impact of weight initialisation and distillation objectives. In: Rogers, A., Boyd-Graber, J., Okazaki, N. (eds.) Proceedings of the 61st Annual Meeting of the Association for Computational Linguistics (Volume 2: Short Papers), pp. 1843–1852. Association for Computational Linguistics, Toronto, Canada (2023). https://doi.org/10.18653/v1/2023.acl-short.157

35. Warstadt, A., Singh, A., Bowman, S.R.: Neural network acceptability judgments. Trans. Assoc. Comput. Linguist. 7, 625–641 (2019). https://doi.org/10.1162/tacl_a_00290, https://aclanthology.org/Q19-1040

36. Xin, J., Tang, R., Lee, J., Yu, Y., Lin, J.: DeeBERT: dynamic early exiting for accelerating BERT inference. In: Proceedings of the 58th Annual Meeting of the Association for Computational Linguistics, pp. 2246–2251. Association for Computational Linguistics, Online (2020). https://doi.org/10.18653/v1/2020.acl-main.204

37. Yao, Y., Huang, S., Wang, W., Dong, L., Wei, F.: Adapt-and-distill: developing small, fast and effective pretrained language models for domains. In: Findings of the Association for Computational Linguistics: ACL-IJCNLP 2021, pp. 460–470. Association for Computational Linguistics, Online (2021). https://doi.org/10.18653/v1/2021.findings-acl.40

38. Zhang, T., Wu, F., Katiyar, A., Weinberger, K.Q., Artzi, Y.: Revisiting few-sample BERT fine-tuning. CoRR **abs/2006.05987** (2020). http://dblp.uni-trier.de/db/journals/corr/corr2006.html#abs-2006-05987

Toward Automatic Group Membership Annotation for Group Fairness Evaluation

Fumian Chen(✉) , Dayu Yang , and Hui Fang

University of Delaware, Newark, DE 19702, USA
{fmchen,dayu,hfang}@udel.edu

Abstract. With the increasing research attention on fairness in information retrieval systems, more and more fairness-aware algorithms have been proposed to ensure fairness for a sustainable and healthy retrieval ecosystem. However, as the most adopted measurement of fairness-aware algorithms, group fairness evaluation metrics, require group membership information that needs massive human annotations and is barely available for general information retrieval datasets. This data sparsity significantly impedes the development of fairness-aware information retrieval studies. Hence, a practical, scalable, low-cost group membership annotation method is needed to assist or replace human annotations. This study explored how to leverage language models to automatically annotate group membership for group fairness evaluations, focusing on annotation accuracy and its impact. Our experimental results show that BERT-based models outperformed state-of-the-art large language models, including GPT and Mistral, achieving promising annotation accuracy with minimal supervision in recent fair-ranking datasets. Our impact-oriented evaluations reveal that minimal annotation error will not degrade the effectiveness and robustness of group fairness evaluation. The proposed annotation method reduces tremendous human efforts and expands the frontier of fairness-aware studies to more datasets.

Keywords: Information Retrieval · Fairness Evaluation · Annotation

1 Introduction

From social media to open web searches, information retrieval (IR) systems are ubiquitous and can fundamentally impact how people receive and seek information. As people started to notice the issue of the echo chamber, the polarized online community, and the importance of covering diverse results [9], fairness-aware IR and its evaluation metrics became emerging needs to combat unfairness and biased representation for long-term sustainability [33]. Group fairness evaluation metrics are the most adopted metrics, measuring the disparity between a situation to be evaluated and its ideal situation. When applying them, one of the necessities is the group membership (GM) annotations, which define whether an

Supported by Institute for Financial Services Analytics at the University of Delaware.

item is from underrepresented groups. Without GM annotation, applying group fairness evaluation metrics on retrieval results is infeasible, and it is also impossible to apply supervised learning-based fair ranking algorithms that rely on GM annotation for training [4,32]. Therefore, before evaluating group fairness or allocating exposure to the documents, we must know their group membership.

Annotations are usually obtained through costly human annotators, such as crowd annotators and domain experts. High-quality annotations involving annotators' training, and cross-validation are even more expensive [18]. The annotation process requires annotators to interpret documents' context and then assign pre-defined labels to the documents based on their contextual information. Since it is very similar to a text classification process, various attempts have been proposed to assist or replace human annotations, especially with the emergence of advanced NLP techniques that can accurately capture contextual features from text [16,18]. However, most of these attempts to replace human annotations focus on accuracy compared with human annotation but ignore the impact when enforcing this replacement on different tasks. It remains unclear how annotation errors would impact the final metrics with machine-learned annotations, especially when previous studies have shown that document-level error might be eliminated when aggregating to higher levels [1]. Since group fairness evaluations are also aggregated metrics, the annotation error might not hurt the ability to evaluate fairness for IR systems. The relation between annotation accuracy and the final evaluation metrics deserves our attention. Moreover, even though generative large language models (LLMs) are not designed for discriminative tasks like text classification, the increasing trend of using generative large language models (LLMs) such as OpenAI GPT on downstream NLP tasks is pushing more and more researchers to scramble for their applications [13]. However, given its economical and computational cost, are generative models with billions of parameters better than discriminative models for fairness-related annotation tasks?

Therefore, to explore how to replace human GM annotation effectively and economically and solve the issue of data sparsity, we compared the performance of four representative language models in predicting group membership for group fairness evaluation. Then, we comprehensively studied the impact of replacing human GM annotation for group fairness evaluations in recent fair-ranking datasets. Confirming the effectiveness of the new GM annotation method with minimal supervision, we believe our work opened a new direction to reduce human efforts on GM annotation and augment traditional IR datasets for future fairness-aware studies. Our implementation code will be available at https://github.com/fm-chen/nldb-experiments.

2   Related Work

With the rapid development of NLP, especially with the emergence of masked language models such as BERT [6] and generative large language models like OpenAI GPT [26], more and more NLP-related work has been proposed to save or even replace human efforts. Text classification, which assigns one of the pre-defined labels to a given text sequence, is one of the classic NLP tasks. As one of the most powerful language models, BERT provides various pre-trained models that accurately capture linguistic and semantic information out of text [19]. With proper fine-tuning, previous studies have used BERT for multiple annotation tasks, such as image labeling and dataset annotation, and shown promising results even with fewer training samples and imbalanced class distributions [20,22]. Recently, as generative LLMs have become a hot topic, OpenAI GPT has also attracted increasing research interest, including the use of GPT to assist annotation and labeling. Generative models like GPT have shown to be a valuable tool for predicting searcher preference, validating and assisting human annotations and labelings [8,14,24,31]. Compared with BERT, which has a parameter size from 30 million to about 350 million, LLMs usually involves billions to over hundred billions of parameters, making fine-tuning and using LLMs costly [8]. Even with the open-sourced LLM, Mistral with seven billion parameters [17], deploying the model locally is computationally costly. Since generative models are not designed for discriminative tasks like text classification, previous studies revealed that using LLMs effectively requires meticulously prompt design. Their performance varies dramatically under different contexts [3,34]. Therefore, instead of scrambling for LLMs, we would like to explore the accuracy and impact of using different language models to replace human GM annotations for fairness evaluation tasks.

This work is also closely related to fairness-aware IR and its evaluation metrics. Well-adopted fairness evaluations [7,12,25,27,29] were based on exposure, and their fairness metrics either measure the deviation between system-produced and target exposure distribution or measure the inequality of exposure across groups. Another group of fairness evaluation is based on pair-wise metrics measuring the difference between pairs [2,23]. They are all aggregated measures that treat groups instead of individual documents as the basic unit, and the impact of replacing the costly human GM annotation with NLP techniques is unclear and has never been studied before. Thus, to save human efforts in obtaining GM annotations and solve the issue of data sparsity in fairness evaluation, this study tested four language models to obtain GM annotations and explored the impact of replacing human annotations with different annotators.

3 Automate GM Annotation for Fairness Evaluation

3.1 GM in Fairness Evaluations

Group membership (GM) is one of the most essential components in group fairness evaluation. Depending on fairness evaluation goals, group membership can involve one or more fairness categories, such as gender and geographic location. As shown in Fig. 1, to make sure that a search engine result page (SERP) contains items from different geographic locations, we have to know each item's geographic location information (geographic GM annotation) first. With the GM annotation, merits or exposure distributions across groups can be formulated to

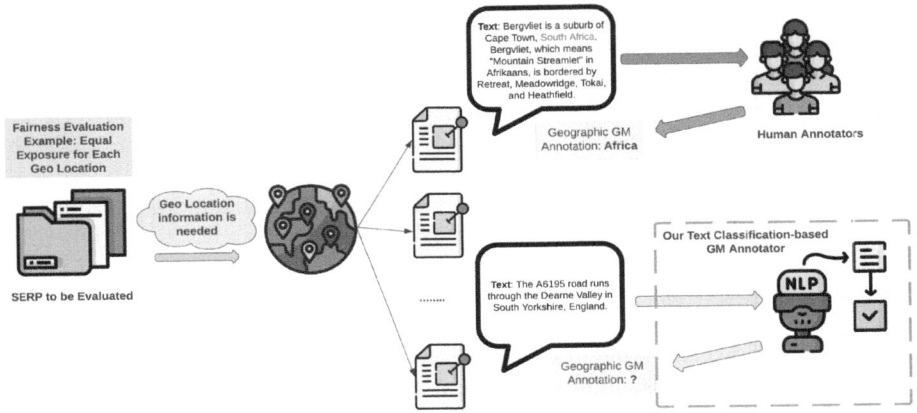

Fig. 1. The necessity of GM annotation in group fairness evaluation

construct fairness evaluation. For example, the TREC fair ranking track 2021 [10] and 2022 [11][1] use the attention-weighted rank fairness (AWRF), a widely used exposure-based fairness evaluation measuring the difference between ranking L's cumulative exposure ϵ_L and population estimator $\hat{\epsilon}$:

$$\text{AWRF(L)} = \Delta(\epsilon_L, \hat{\epsilon})$$

where Δ is a divergence function (e.g., Kullback-Leibler divergence or Jenson-Shannon divergence). The ranking L's cumulative exposure ϵ_L is computed by $\sum_{d \in L} w(L) * GM_d$ where $w(L)$ is an attention decay function and GM_d is the group membership matrix of document d. For instance, $GM_d(\text{Gender}) = (1, 0, 0)$ if the document d is annotated as group "male" for fairness category gender with three subgroups: "male", "female", and "non-binary". The population estimator $\hat{\epsilon}$ reflects the target exposure distribution that a fair system should produce, which could also rely on GM annotation. TREC estimates $\hat{\epsilon}$ by averaging the group membership of all relevant documents to ensure that each group of items receives the same amount of expected exposure as their relevance grade. Moreover, the target exposure distribution can also be given. For example, the NTCIR fairweb1 task [30] assumes a uniform distribution across groups as their target.

3.2   Challenges with GM Annotation

Obtaining GM annotation can be challenging and requires significant human effort. We investigate three recent fair-ranking tasks: (1) TREC fair ranking track 2021 [10], (2) TREC fair ranking track 2022 [11], and (3) the NTCIR Fair Web task [30]. Details about these tasks are reported in Table 1. TREC fair ranking tasks are based on a Wikipedia corpus containing more than six million

---

[1] https://fair-trec.github.io/.

Table 1. Task description and fairness categories: Internal fairness categories are internal attributes which do not require human annotation. We focus on contextual fairness categories.

Dataset	Task Description	Fairness Categories	
		Contextual	Internal
TREC fair ranking track 2021	A Wikipedia article fair ranking task (corpus containing more than 6 million articles): provide fair exposure for each group of documents regarding different fairness categories.	(1) Gender of article's subject (Gender, 4 subgroups) (2) Geographical location associated with the article (Geo, 8 subgroups)	N/A
TREC fair ranking track 2022		(1) Gender of article's subject (Gender, 4 subgroups) (2) Geographical location associated with the article (Geo, 21 subgroups)	(1) Age of the article (2) Occupation (3) Alphabetical orders (4) Popularity (5) Replication in other languages
NTCIR fairweb1	A fair ranking tasks (corpus Chuweb21D containing about 50 million documents): provide group-fair results for research, movie, and YouTube content.	(1) Movie's country of origin (Movie-Origin, 8 subgroups) (2) Gender of researcher (Research-Gender, 3 subgroups)	(1) Research-Hindex (2) Movie-Ratings (3) YouTube-Subscription

English articles and 50/50 training and evaluating queries from various domains, whereas NCTIR fairweb1 is based on an English document collection, Chuweb-21D, containing more than 40 million documents, including research papers, movies, and YouTube Content. Unlike many previous fair-ranking studies based on outdated datasets that only contain numeric features, all three tasks provide full-text fields and enable us to apply NLP techniques. They also offer page meta information consisting of human annotations. Figure 2 shows the subgroups' frequency of human annotation by page geographic locations in the TREC 2022 datasets. As can be seen, the documents' geographic information was annotated into 21 subgroups, and a huge imbalance exists across groups. Almost half of the documents were marked as "unknown" because they either lacked annotation or were non-applicable. Ensuring a high-quality annotation is challenging, given inevitable human error and costly knowledge training for human annotators, let alone annotating GM into large numbers of subgroups. Given these challenges, few datasets with GM annotation are available for fairness-aware studies. Therefore, we aim to automate GM annotation with minimal human efforts to break the data sparsity using NLP techniques.

3.3 Annotating GM by Text Classification with Language Models

The quality of human annotation heavily depends on the annotators' knowledge and interpretation of the raw text. The annotation process is similar to text classification algorithms that capture contextual patterns (interpretation of raw text) and categorize raw text based on training data (knowledge). Accordingly, we assume that replacing human annotation with text classification models is possible by adequately utilizing text information, especially with sophisticated language models that can precisely capture linguistic and semantic information and even outperform humans in some studies. In this work, we explored the following text classification models for GM annotation:

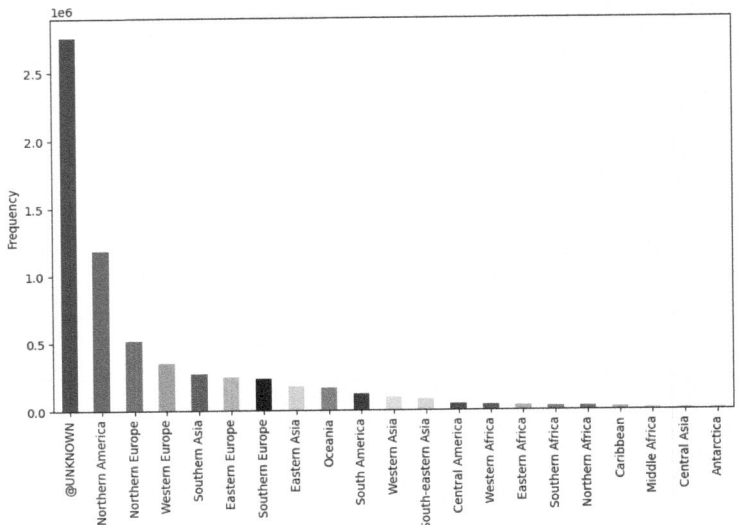

Fig. 2. Geo subgroup frequency of human GM annotation (TREC 2022).

- **Linear BoW Model**: a linear bag-of-words model [35] followed by a neural network classifier implemented by *spaCy TextCategorizer*[2].
- **BERT-based Model**: a fine-tuned BERT sentence classification model [6] *"bert-large-uncased"*[3] implemented by *PyTorch*[4].
- **GPT Models**: a generative large language model, with GPT-3.5-turbo and GPT-4, implemented by *spaCy-LLM*[5].
- **Mistral 7B Models** [17]: a generative large language model, Mistral-7B-Instruct-V0.2[6], implemented by *PyTorch*.

Linear bag-of-words (BoW) model [35] is one of the simplest statistical language models (SLM) that convert words to numeric representations based on vocabulary set and word count. It is flexible and performs well for simple document classification tasks, but it cannot understand context. Bidirectional Encoder Representations from Transformers (BERT) [6], introduced in 2018, is one of the masked language models (MLM) that can successfully capture semantic and linguistic information from text sequences, which has dominated classification tasks since being introduced. In contrast, generative large language models, such as OpenAI GPT, are not designed for classification tasks but have shown potential in assisting human annotations in recent studies [13]. Unlike GPT, which is

---

[2] https://spacy.io/api/textcategorizer.

[3] https://huggingface.co/bert-large-uncased.

[4] https://pytorch.org/.

[5] https://spacy.io/usage/large-language-models.

[6] https://huggingface.co/mistralai/Mistral-7B-Instruct-v0.2.

fully commercialized and expensive, Mistral 7B [17] is a state-of-the-art, open-sourced LLM that achieved promising performance across various benchmark tasks. The performance of generative LLMs varies task by task and is heavily dependent on their pre-trained data and prompt design. Given the advantages and limitations of these language models, we would like to explore their capability of replacing GM annotation for group fairness evaluations.

Table 2. LLM prompts. Shaded text is optional for one-shot or fine-tuning.

Model	Prompt
GPT-3.5-turbo/GPT-4	You are an expert Text Classification system. Your task is to accept text as input and provide a category for the text based on the pre-defined labels. Classify the text below to any of the following labels: [GM Labels] Below are some examples (only use these as a guide): [Example Text], [Answer]. Here is the text that needs classification: [Text]
Mistral	[INST]Analyze the [Fairness Category] of the Wikipedia article enclosed in square brackets, determine if it is [GM Labels], and return the answer as the corresponding labels [/INST] [Example Text] = [Answer]

We build classification models trained or fine-tuned by small-size human-annotated samples using these language models for GM annotation. For each subgroup within a fairness category, we equally sampled 500 training documents and 100 testing documents from each group. We follow the standard data cleaning process for the text field, including special character removal, stop word removal, and lemmatization. Given the average length of Wikipedia articles, 670 tokens, we truncated the full-text field to 512 tokens without losing much information. The optimal model weights are trained or fine-tuned on training samples and obtained by minimizing a KL-divergence classification loss for the linear-bag-of-words and BERT-based models. For the GPT models, we use the prompt shown in Table 2 provided by *spaCy* and set the template to 0.3 for one-shot text classification. To use the Mistral models (*Mistral-7B-Instruct-V0.2*), we utilized low-rank adaption [15] so that we can computationally run the model with our best GPU. The prompt used for Mistral is also reported in 2. Given the high cost of fine-tuning GPT models, we only fine-tuned the Mistral 7B in this study. Finally, we use these text classifiers as annotators to predict the group membership information of new documents. Once fairness annotations are obtained, ideally, we can fit them into any group fairness evaluation metrics or augment other IR datasets for fairness-aware studies.

4   Evaluation and Analysis

4.1   Prediction Accuracy of GM Annotation Models

We first examine the annotation accuracy between these annotation models when predicting gender GM annotation. The performance of each classifier is reported in Table 3. As can be seen, generative models (LLMs) failed to outperform the discriminative models (BERT and BoW models), especially for the gender subgroup "non-binary." This might be because LLMs were pre-trained on biased data where the subgroup "non-binary" was under-represented, which is currently a known issue [21]. If we do not want to amplify this pre-existing bias, fine-tuning LLM-based models is required. Given the long text length and large corpus size (e.g., about 6 million for the TREC fair ranking track) to annotate, fine-tuning GPT models and generating GM annotations for new documents

Table 3. Classification performance (accuracy and f-1 scores) by different models when predicting "Gender" group membership: "male", "female", "non-binary" and "unknown" (TREC 2022). The Mistral model is fine-tuned with a full-, partial-, and proportional- set of training examples. * indicates the best-performed model.

Models	Overall Accuracy	Overall F-1	Male F-1	Female F-1	NB F-1	Unknown F-1
Linear-BoW	0.905	0.9073	0.8475	0.9800	0.8889	0.9130
BERT*	0.985*	0.9850*	0.9804*	0.9899*	0.9697*	1*
GPT-3.5-turbo	0.820	0.7947	0.8727	0.9009	0.5507	0.8545
GPT-4	0.865	0.8549	0.8403	0.9259	0.6842	0.9691
Mistral (zero-)	0.655	0.6446	0.6076	0.6565	0.5915	0.7227
Mistral (full-)	0.705	0.6921	0.7912	0.7458	0.5135	0.7179
Mistral (part-)	0.425	0.3564	0.6619	0.1515	0.4754	0.1370
Mistral (prop-)	0.655	0.6624	0.8211	0.5686	0.5487	0.7111

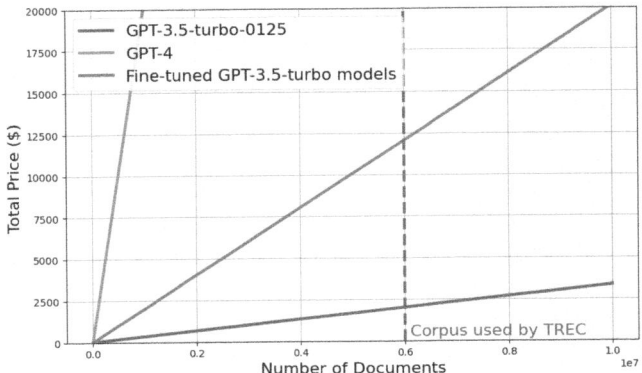

Fig. 3. Total price of annotation using trained GPT models (GPT-4, GPT-3.5-turbo, and fine-tuned GPT-3.5) by number of documents.

would be extremely expensive. The total price of annotating datasets with a size similar to the TREC corpus is over \$2000 even with the cheapest GPT-3.5-turbo model, as shown in Fig. 3. With the open-sourced LLM, Mistral, its fine-tuned models still cannot correctly predict the label of "non-binary", including using different fine-tuning strategies to improve its performance as shown in the last four rows in Table 3. Since Mistral has difficulty to predict subgroup "Male" and "non-binary" correctly, we first fine-tuned Mistral with "Male" and "non-binary" only but as shown in the Table 3, we seem to have over-corrected the model. It is also the case when we fine-tuned the model with more "Male" and "non-binary" than the other two groups. In either case, we damage the performance of Mistral compared with the equally and fully sampled fine-tuning. The performance of GPT and Mistral shows the disadvantage of LLMs for classification tasks. Therefore, in terms of using text classification for fairness GM annotation, BERT-based models outperformed LLMs, both economically and computationally.

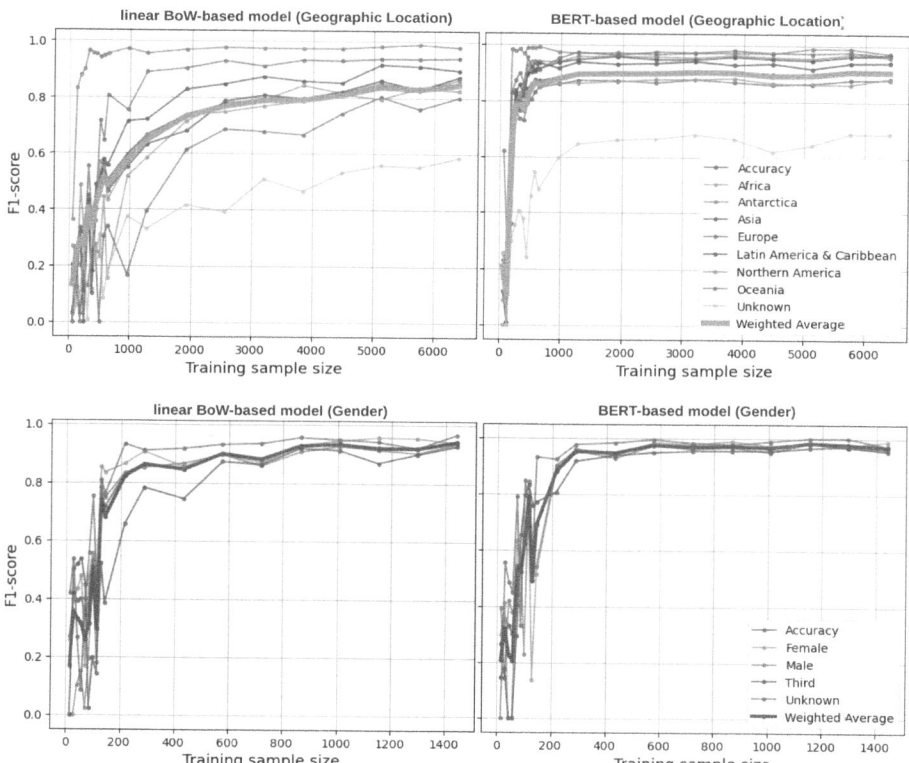

Fig. 4. Classification performance by training sample size (TREC 2021).

The fine-tuned BERT-based models demonstrated a promising annotation capability and achieved the highest accuracy and f-1 scores among all models when predicting the GM annotations (It is also true for all contextual fairness categories; we only show the result for gender here to save space). This shows the advantages of the BERT sentence classification model in terms of text understanding and capturing linguistic and semantic information compared with the bag-of-words models. For both BoW-based and BERT-based models, training sample size impacts the classification performance. Figure 4 shows the text classification performance by sample size (reported as F1 scores) using both models to predict GM annotation for the TREC fair ranking track 2021. As can be seen, the linear BoW-based model requires more training samples to converge to the best performance than the BERT-based model, especially when the fairness category contains more subgroups. As shown in Fig. 5, our results regarding geographic location GM also align with previous studies that BERT-based classifiers are less sensitive to imbalanced classes [20]. As a pre-trained model, BERT only needs a few samples to fine-tune. Compared with the size of the entire corpus, we need approximately 1200 training samples when predicting geographic location GM (8 subgroups), and 400 samples when predicting gender GM (4 subgroups) to achieve a reasonable performance using BERT sentence classification. This observation also suggests that more training samples are needed, given a fairness category with more sub-groups. Generally speaking, we recommend using no less than 100–150 training samples per subgroup when training a BERT-based model for GM annotation, depending on the number of subgroups. We also noticed that both BERT and BoW models have difficulties in predicting "unknown" for geographic location GM, as shown in Fig. 5. This might result from the complexity of "unknown", which indicates either missing annotation or non-applicable. For instance, annotating geographic locations for a mathematical proof article is not very applicable.

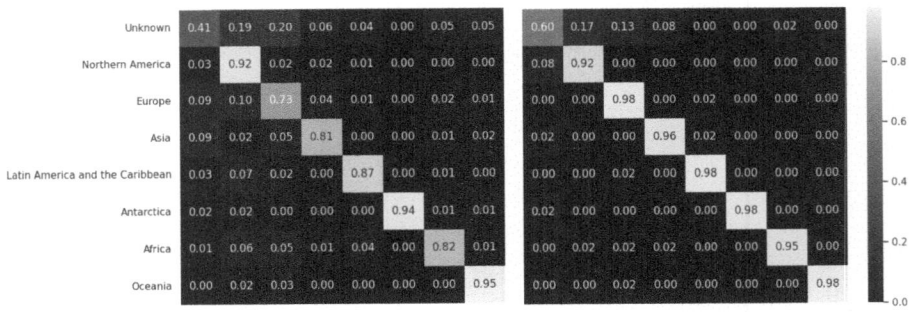

Fig. 5. BERT model (right) outperformed and is less sensitive to imbalanced classes than the bag-of-words model (left) (TREC 2021).

Overall, the BERT sentence classification model is a winner based on the above comparison, given its strong performance, simplicity, and low cost. In the following sections, we explore the impact of using our best classifier to replace human GM annotation.

4.2 Group Fairness Evaluation with GM Annotations

We showed promising text classification performance when annotating new documents using the BERT sentence classification model. Even though annotation errors still exist, we are curious about the impact of these document-level mistakes and whether these mistakes will be washed out when aggregated into aggregated-level evaluation [1], since fairness evaluation is an aggregated metric. To test the effectiveness of the BERT-based GM annotation, we use the Pearson correlation coefficient test [5] and Spearman's rank correlation coefficient [28] to test whether evaluation metrics with our GM annotation method can effectively differentiate the fairness quality of different systems (rankings) as the old evaluation metrics can do with human annotation. Specifically, we investigate the correlation between the official evaluation metrics with human GM annotation and those with our BERT-based GM annotation. The investigation is based on all participants' official submissions to three fair-ranking tasks. Because the official submissions are from multiple groups using different ranking algorithms, we believe the fairness scores of these runs provide the best estimation of the upper and lower bound of fairness performance. There are 13 runs for the TREC fair ranking track 2021, 27 runs for the TREC fair ranking track 2022, and 28 runs for the NTCIR fairweb1 task.

System-Level Evaluation. Our system-level evaluation is based on testing the correlation between metrics using human annotation and metrics using BERT-based annotation to see whether we can effectively replace human annotation while preserving the ability to differentiate ranking fairness. Table 4 reports the correlation between tasks' official evaluation metrics and our text classification-based evaluation metrics regarding the three fair ranking tasks: TREC fair ranking track 2021, TREC fair ranking track 2022, and NTCIR fairweb1. Based on Pearson correlation and Spearman's ranked correlation tests, evaluation metrics with our BERT-based GM annotation strongly correlated with the official evaluation metrics with human annotation, and the correlations are statistically

Table 4. Summary of correlation tests between tasks' official evaluation metrics with human annotation and those with BERT-based GM annotation. * indicates statistical significance ($p < 0.05$). The "Overall" group for TREC tasks is the intersectional group of Gender and Geographic Location.

	TREC 2021			TREC 2022			NTCIR fairweb1	
	Overall	Gender	Geo	Overall	Gender	Geo	M-Orgin	R-Gender
Pearson	0.9469*	0.9994*	0.9790*	0.9678*	0.9957*	0.9968*	0.9868*	0.9937*
Spearman	0.8187*	0.9945*	0.9231*	0.9609*	0.9670*	0.9976*	0.9189*	0.9688*

significant. This confirms the system-level effectiveness of using BERT classification-based GM annotation in evaluating fairness. Replacing human GM annotation with BERT-based annotation preserves the ability to differentiate fairness among different runs. Even though our text classifier cannot accurately predict some subgroups of some fairness categories (e.g., the group "unknown" of geographic location), when aggregating documents into a system-level evaluation, we can still differentiate rankings' fairness. Since how to deal with "unknown" is also a challenge for human annotators, this observation also suggests that minimal annotation error will not degrade system-level fairness evaluation, and the BERT-based annotation could be a solution for estimating "unknown".

Query-Level Robustness. The query-level evaluation decomposes the system-level evaluation by 50 evaluation queries. In Fig. 6, we show the Pearson correlation coefficient r between human annotation-based evaluation metrics and those using BERT-based GM annotation by the evaluation query IDs. As can be seen, for most of the queries, the correlation is high and significant. That is, we highly preserve the ability to differentiate fairness when replacing human GM annotation with BERT-based GM annotation, especially for GM of "gender". The "Overall" group, which is the intersectional product of "geographic location" and "gender" also demonstrates a high correlation between human GM annotation and BERT-based annotation. Recall the Fig. 4, predicting the GM of geographic location is less accurate than predicting the GM of Gender. Therefore, with a higher accuracy of the GM annotation, we observed a more robust query-level correlation. Therefore, to be more confident in replacing human-annotated GM and evaluating at a query level, we need a text classifier that can accurately predict GM at a document level.

4.3 Impact of the Annotation Accuracy

So far, we know that to preserve the ability to differentiate the fairness of different systems, we need text classifier to be accurate, and minimal annotation errors will not degrade the ability. However, what are the impacts if the classifiers

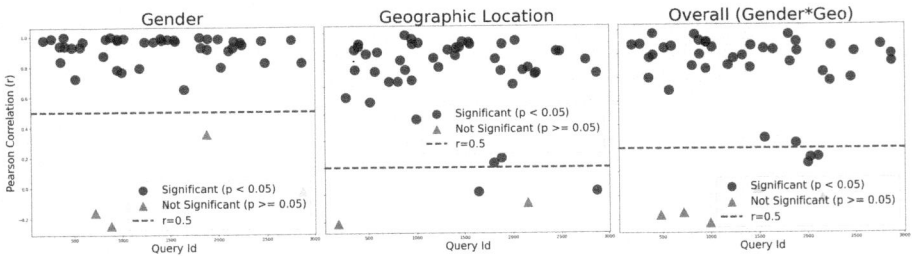

Fig. 6. Query-level robustness (TREC 2022): the correlation between evaluations using human annotation and BERT-based annotation.

are not very precise, and how accurate do we need to be confident when replacing human annotations? To further explore the relationship between annotation accuracy and the corresponding evaluation correlation with the official fairness evaluation metrics, we would like to see the impact of annotation accuracy on the group fairness evaluation metrics. The first step is to obtain annotators with different annotation accuracy. According to Fig. 4, varying training sample size is one of the easiest ways to get different annotation models with different annotation accuracy. Hence, we trained the BERT-based annotation models with varying sample sizes and obtained several annotation models with different accuracy. The relation between the annotation accuracy and the effectiveness (Pearson r) of replacing human annotation with BERT-based annotation is plotted in Fig. 7. As can be seen, generally, increasing annotation accuracy can not only improve system-level correlation to the official metrics but also improve query-level robustness. With an annotation accuracy above 0.8, using BERT-based annotation highly preserved the ability to differentiate fairness among different systems. Therefore, if group fairness evaluation focuses on the system level, minimal annotation errors could be ignored to save human efforts.

4.4   Generalizability of System Evaluation

GM annotation models can also be used for other complex evaluation metrics, such as evaluating a sequence of rankings. For example, the second task of the TREC fair ranking track 2021 evaluates fairness of sequence of rankings $\mathcal{L}_q$ by the expected exposure loss (EE-L($\mathcal{L}_q$) = $||\gamma - \gamma^*||$) [7], expected exposure disparity (EE-D = $||\gamma^*||_2^2$), and expected exposure relevance (EE-R = $2\gamma_\pi^T \gamma^*$).

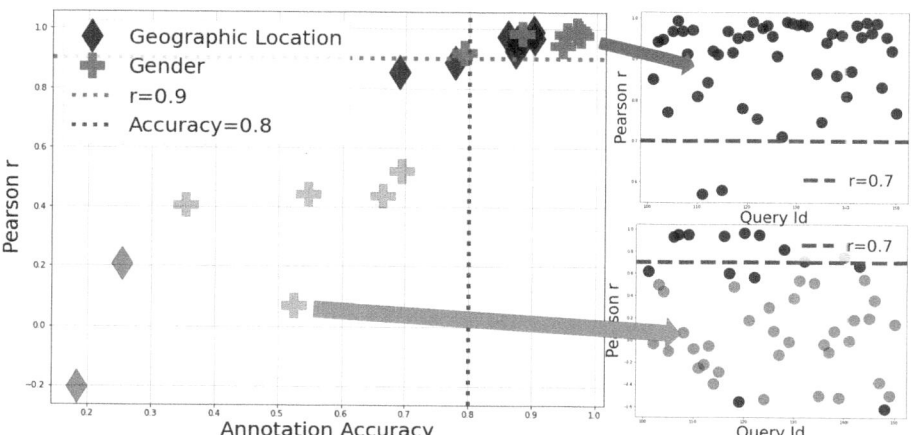

Fig. 7. Annotation accuracy V.S. the correlation between evaluation metrics using human annotation and BERT-based annotation (TREC 2021). Shaded dots indicate $p > 0.05$. Two samples from the left plot with different annotation accuracy are selected to show query-level robustness.

With GM annotation obtained from our BERT-based model, we compute the correlations between the TREC fair ranking track 2021 task 2's official evaluation metrics and those based on our annotation model based on 11 official submitted runs. We achieved Pearson correlation coefficients of 0.75, 0.98, and 0.79 for EE-L, EE-D, and EE-R, respectively, and all coefficient tests are statistically significant. Since the EE-D measures the inequality in exposure distribution across groups, and the BERT-based model has a similar performance across different groups for gender and geographic locations, we achieved a higher correlation with EE-D than the EE-R, which measures the agreement between exposure and relevance. Given the high correlation coefficients, especially for the pure fairness measure EE-D, our annotation model can also effectively replace human annotation for these fairness evaluation metrics.

5   Conclusion

Group membership, as one of the indispensable components in group fairness evaluation, requires massive human efforts to obtain. The sparsity of GM annotations limits the application of fairness evaluation and impedes fair ranking studies on general IR datasets. To overcome this, we compared four different language model-based text classifications for GM annotation. The BERT-based model achieved promising annotation accuracy with small-size training samples and less computational cost. Our query- and system-level evaluations confirmed the effectiveness and robustness of replacing human GM annotation with the BERT-based GM annotation. This opens a new direction to augment existing IR datasets for fairness evaluation and future fair-ranking studies. Even though LLMs have been used for mainstream NLP tasks and achieved impressive performance, they failed to outperform BERT for fairness GM annotation tasks as they were not designed for discriminative tasks. Moreover, according to our impact-oriented evaluation, when replacing human annotation with different annotators that have different annotation accuracy, minimal annotation errors will not degrade the fairness evaluation metrics. In the future, we would like to utilize the new annotation strategy to augment existing IR datasets for fairness studies, including fairness evaluation and fair ranking algorithms.

Acknowledgments. This study is supported by the IFSA at the University of Delaware. We would like to thank the reviewers for their invaluable comments and suggestions.

References

1. Bailey, P., Craswell, N., Soboroff, I., Thomas, P., de Vries, A.P., Yilmaz, E.: Relevance assessment: are judges exchangeable and does it matter. In: Proceedings of the 31st Annual International ACM SIGIR Conference on Research and Development in Information Retrieval, pp. 667–674 (2008)

2. Beutel, A., et al.: Fairness in recommendation ranking through pairwise comparisons. In: Proceedings of the 25th ACM SIGKDD International Conference on Knowledge Discovery & Data Mining, pp. 2212–2220 (2019)
3. Chae, Y., Davidson, T.: Large language models for text classification: from zero-shot learning to fine-tuning. Open Sci. Found. (2023)
4. Chen, F., Fang, H.: Learn to be fair without labels: a distribution-based learning framework for fair ranking. In: Proceedings of the 2023 ACM SIGIR International Conference on Theory of Information Retrieval, pp. 23–32 (2023)
5. Cohen, I., et al.: Pearson correlation coefficient. Noise Reduction Speech Process., 1–4 (2009)
6. Devlin, J., Chang, M.W., Lee, K., Toutanova, K.: BERT: pre-training of deep bidirectional transformers for language understanding. arXiv preprint arXiv:1810.04805 (2018)
7. Diaz, F., Mitra, B., Ekstrand, M.D., Biega, A.J., Carterette, B.: Evaluating stochastic rankings with expected exposure. In: Proceedings of the 29th ACM International Conference on Information & Knowledge Management, pp. 275–284 (2020)
8. Ding, B., Qin, C., Liu, L., Bing, L., Joty, S., Li, B.: Is GPT-3 a good data annotator? ArXiv preprint arXiv:2212.10450 (2022)
9. Ekstrand, M.D., Burke, R., Diaz, F.: Fairness and discrimination in retrieval and recommendation. In: Proceedings of the 42nd International ACM SIGIR Conference on Research and Development in Information Retrieval, pp. 1403–1404 (2019)
10. Ekstrand, M.D., McDonald, G., Raj, A., Johnson, I.: Overview of the TREC 2021 fair ranking track. In: The Thirtieth Text REtrieval Conference (TREC 2021) Proceedings (2022)
11. Ekstrand, M.D., McDonald, G., Raj, A., Johnson, I.: Overview of the TREC 2022 fair ranking track. arXiv preprint arXiv:2302.05558 (2023)
12. Gao, R., Ge, Y., Shah, C.: Fair: fairness-aware information retrieval evaluation. J. Am. Soc. Inf. Sci. **73**(10), 1461–1473 (2022)
13. Goel, A., et al.: LLMs accelerate annotation for medical information extraction. In: Machine Learning for Health (ML4H), pp. 82–100. PMLR (2023)
14. He, X., et al.: AnnoLLM: making large language models to be better crowdsourced annotators. arXiv preprint arXiv:2303.16854 (2023)
15. Hu, E.J., et al.: LoRA: low-rank adaptation of large language models. arXiv preprint arXiv:2106.09685 (2021)
16. Ishita, E., Fukuda, S., Tomiura, Y., Oard, D.W.: Using text classification to improve annotation quality by improving annotator consistency. Proc. Assoc. Inform. Sci. Technol. **57**(1), e301 (2020)
17. Jiang, A.Q., et al.: Mistral 7B. arXiv preprint arXiv:2310.06825 (2023)
18. Kasthuriarachchy, B., Chetty, M., Shatte, A., Walls, D.: Cost effective annotation framework using zero-shot text classification. In: 2021 International Joint Conference on Neural Networks (IJCNN), pp. 1–8. IEEE (2021)
19. Koroteev, M.: BERT: a review of applications in natural language processing and understanding. arXiv preprint arXiv:2103.11943 (2021)
20. Laurer, M., van Atteveldt, W., Casas, A., Welbers, K.: Less annotating, more classifying: addressing the data scarcity issue of supervised machine learning with deep transfer learning and BERT-NLI. Political Analysis, pp. 1–33 (2022)
21. Lucy, L., Bamman, D.: Gender and representation bias in GPT-3 generated stories. In: Proceedings of the Third Workshop on Narrative Understanding, pp. 48–55 (2021)

22. Ma, C., Shen, A., Yoshikawa, H., Iwakura, T., Beck, D., Baldwin, T.: On the effectiveness of images in multi-modal text classification: an annotation study. ACM Trans. Asian and Low-Resour. Lang. Inf. Process. **22**(3), 1–19 (2023)

23. Narasimhan, H., Cotter, A., Gupta, M., Wang, S.: Pairwise fairness for ranking and regression. In: Proceedings of the AAAI Conference on Artificial Intelligence, vol. 34, pp. 5248–5255 (2020)

24. Pangakis, N., Wolken, S., Fasching, N.: Automated annotation with generative AI requires validation. arXiv preprint arXiv:2306.00176 (2023)

25. Raj, A., Ekstrand, M.D.: Comparing fair ranking metrics. arXiv preprint arXiv:2009.01311 (2020)

26. Ray, P.P.: ChatGPT: a comprehensive review on background, applications, key challenges, bias, ethics, limitations and future scope. Internet of Things and Cyber-Physical Systems (2023)

27. Sapiezynski, P., Zeng, W., Robertson, R.E., Mislove, A., Wilson, C.: Quantifying the impact of user attention on fair group representation in ranked lists. In: Companion Proceedings of the 2019 World Wide Web Conference, pp. 553–562 (2019)

28. Sedgwick, P.: Spearman's rank correlation coefficient. BMJ **349** (2014)

29. Singh, A., Joachims, T.: Fairness of exposure in rankings. In: Proceedings of the 24th ACM SIGKDD International Conference on Knowledge Discovery & Data Mining, pp. 2219–2228 (2018)

30. Tao, S., et al.: Overview of the NTCIR-17 FairWeb-1 task. In: Proceedings of NTCIR-17. to appear (2023)

31. Thomas, P., Spielman, S., Craswell, N., Mitra, B.: Large language models can accurately predict searcher preferences. arXiv preprint arXiv:2309.10621 (2023)

32. Zehlike, M., Castillo, C.: Reducing disparate exposure in ranking: a learning to rank approach. In: Proceedings of the Web Conference 2020, pp. 2849–2855 (2020)

33. Zehlike, M., Yang, K., Stoyanovich, J.: Fairness in ranking: a survey. arXiv preprint arXiv:2103.14000 (2021)

34. Zhang, Y., et al.: Pushing the limit of LLM capacity for text classification. arXiv preprint arXiv:2402.07470 (2024)

35. Zhang, Y., Jin, R., Zhou, Z.H.: Understanding bag-of-words model: a statistical framework. Int. J. Mach. Learn. Cybern. **1**, 43–52 (2010)

REA: Refine-Estimate-Answer Prompting for Zero-Shot Relation Extraction

Amirhossein Layegh[ORCID], Amir H. Payberah[✉][ORCID], and Mihhail Matskin[ORCID]

KTH Royal Institute of Technology, Stockholm, Sweden
{amlk,payberah,misha}@kth.se

Abstract. Zero-shot relation extraction (RE) presents the challenge of identifying entity relationships from text without training on those specific relations. Despite significant advancements in natural language processing by applying large language models (LLMs), their application to zero-shot RE remains less effective compared to traditional models that fine-tune smaller pre-trained language models. This limitation is attributed to insufficient prompting strategies that fail to leverage the full capabilities of LLMs for zero-shot RE, considering the intrinsic complexities of the RE task. A compelling question is whether LLMs can address complex tasks, such as RE, by decomposing them into more straightforward, distinct tasks that are easier to manage and solve individually. We propose the *Refine-Estimate-Answer (REA)* approach to answer this question. This multi-stage prompting strategy of REA decomposes the RE task into more manageable subtasks and applies iterative refinement to guide LLMs through the complex reasoning required for accurate RE. Our research validates the effectiveness of REA through comprehensive testing across multiple public RE datasets, demonstrating marked improvements over existing LLM-based frameworks. Experimental results on the FewRel, Wiki-ZSL, and TACRED datasets show that our proposed approach significantly boosts the vanilla prompting F1 scores by 31.57, 19.52, and 15.39, respectively, thereby outperforming the performance of state-of-the-art LLM-based methods.

Keywords: Relation Extraction · Large Language Models · Prompting Strategy

1 Introduction

Relation Extraction (RE) aims to identify and classify semantic relationships between entities in unstructured text [3]. RE has received significant attention in natural language processing (NLP) due to its pivotal role across various downstream tasks, including information retrieval [12], question-answering [22], and knowledge graph construction [24]. Despite extensive research, state-of-the-art solutions still face challenges, such as adaptability to new domains and generalization to unseen relations due to their reliance on annotated data. This reliance makes these solutions impractical for scenarios where data is scarce or costly

© The Author(s), under exclusive license to Springer Nature Switzerland AG 2024
A. Rapp et al. (Eds.): NLDB 2024, LNCS 14762, pp. 301–316, 2024.
https://doi.org/10.1007/978-3-031-70239-6_21

to obtain. Therefore, *zero-shot RE* [33], where no annotated data for unseen relations is available, has become a crucial yet complex problem to address [4].

Recent advancements in NLP, particularly the emergence of large language models (LLMs) like GPT-3 [2], have further revolutionized the landscape of NLP tasks, such as RE. Trained on vast amounts of diverse textual data, LLMs exhibit remarkable capabilities in understanding text and generating human-like responses. As a result, generative zero-shot RE, where LLMs are prompted to directly extract and generate relationships between entities from text without fine-tuning, has gained significant attention [36]. It is crucial to note that the design of the prompt plays a vital role in the performance of LLMs. Varied prompts for the same tasks can lead to considerable discrepancies in model outputs [1].

Several strategies for prompting LLMs in generative zero-shot RE exist, such as *vanilla* prompting, which we use to denote the simplest and most direct form of prompting, *in-context learning* [2], and *Chain-of-Thought* (CoT) [34]. Despite their utility, these strategies exhibit certain limitations. For instance, vanilla prompting is considered ineffective despite its simplicity as it necessitates LLMs to perform non-trivial reasoning processes within a single step [18]. In-context learning, while promising, heavily relies on the careful selection and variation of in-context examples and prompt templates [20]. CoT prompting, aimed at providing additional context through intermediate reasoning steps, frequently struggles to generalize and solve problems more challenging than the in-context CoT examples, limiting its utility in scenarios such as zero-shot RE, which demands robust generalization capabilities [42].

A recent body of work exhibited remarkable progress on generative zero-shot RE by employing LLMs. For instance, QA4RE [39] reformulates RE as a multiple-choice question-answering (QA) task to align the RE with QA tasks. SUMASK [18] integrates a CoT approach and proposes summarize-to-ask prompting with an uncertainty estimator component to tackle the challenge of ensuring the reliability of LLM responses. Nonetheless, when measured against state-of-the-art zero-shot RE methods that leverage fine-tuning on smaller pre-trained language models (PLMs), these approaches tend to underperform. [6].

The inherent complexity of RE stems from the need to understand the semantics of entities, identify their types, capture the semantics embedded within relation labels, and align these semantics properly [3]. Consequently, we hypothesize that the current limitations in existing generative zero-shot RE frameworks might be attributed to the insufficiently sophisticated prompting strategies that fail to capture these complexities. These limitations hinder their ability to effectively guide LLMs through the essential reasoning processes required for RE tasks. This observation motivates us to investigate whether decomposing RE into more manageable subtasks, each aligned with the core complexities of RE, can enhance performance.

Moreover, recent research has highlighted the benefits of enabling LLMs to refine their initial responses through self-critique [23], leading to enhanced reasoning capabilities [7,26]. Inspired by this, our proposed approach incorporates a similar concept via confidence elicitation, examining the impact of iterative refinement on model performance. Confidence elicitation allows the model to express its certainty in its predictions, providing valuable feedback for further refinement [14].

Drawing on these insights, we introduce *Refine-Estimate-Answer (REA)*, a multi-stage prompting strategy that merges decomposition with iterative refinement. This approach aims to significantly elevate the performance of generative zero-shot RE by exploiting LLMs capabilities without relying on external knowledge or additional components. This paper delves into the detailed methodology of REA prompting and explores its effectiveness in enhancing generative zero-shot RE tasks. Our key contributions are as follows:

- Development of REA, a novel multi-stage prompting approach designed to enhance generative zero-shot RE tasks.
- Comprehensive experiments and evaluations conducted on three publicly available RE datasets to assess the effectiveness of REA. The results demonstrate REA's superiority over existing generative zero-shot RE frameworks, outperforming vanilla prompting performance by 5.88–39.47 in the F1-score.
- Demonstrating that decomposing RE into manageable subtasks, aligned with the core complexities of RE, significantly improves the performance of generative zero-shot RE models. This finding suggests that the REA decomposition approach effectively addresses the inherent challenges of RE, leading to more accurate results.
- Exhibiting that allows LLMs to assess and refine their initial responses using confidence elicitation iteratively, REA achieves a measurable improvement in accuracy.

2 Related Work

Zero-Shot Relation Extraction. Significant advancements in RE have been achieved through the use of PLMs, which leverage transformer-based models to identify relationships between entities [8,15]. Specifically, RE-Matching [41] introduces a fine-grained semantic matching technique that refines using PLMs for zero-shot RE by distinctively handling entity and context correlations. Subsequently, the paradigm of prompt-tuning PLMs emerged as a solution to bridge the gap between pre-training and fine-tuning objectives to enhance the performance of PLMs in low-resource tasks [21]. In this regard, RelationPrompt [5] prompts PLMs to generate synthetic training examples, articulating specific relations. This generated dataset subsequently trains another PLM to perform zero-shot RE. Despite these advancements, fine-tuning and prompt-tuning PLMs often face challenges in generalization, necessitating additional tuning on annotated datasets to predict unseen relations in zero-shot settings accurately.

LLMs for Generative Relation Extraction. Adopting LLMs demonstrating proficiency in various downstream tasks without necessitating any form of training or fine-tuning emerged as an effective strategy. Specifically, QA4RE [39] introduced a framework for zero-shot RE by adapting RE tasks into a multiple-choice question-answering problem. Similarly, ChatIE [35] employs ChatGPT [25] for zero-shot information extraction, transforming the task into a multi-step question-answering process. Moreover, SUMASK [18] presents a multi-stage zero-shot RE framework, integrating LLMs with a natural language inference module for uncertainty estimation. Despite outperforming other LLM-based methods, SUMASK complexity arises from generating multiple summaries, questions, and answers for each relation label. Additionally, its dependency on an external module for uncertainty estimation poses integration challenges in real-world scenarios.

Decomposing Approaches in LLMs. Recent research, inspired by CoT prompting [34], has shown that LLMs can handle complex problems better by breaking them down into intermediate steps [13,37]. This decomposition facilitates LLMs to clarify their reasoning by prompting them to generate intermediate rationales for their solutions [30,42]. The power of decomposition extends beyond CoT, proving valuable in addressing various challenges associated with LLMs [7,10,38]. For instance, least-to-most prompting [42] breaks down a complex task into a series of simpler subtasks and then solves them sequentially. Chain-of-Verification (CoV) [10] adopts a step-wise breakdown in question answering tasks, which involves generating initial answers, formulating and answering verification questions, and refining the original answers. This method mitigates hallucination, prevents factual errors, and ultimately enhances accuracy. In the context of RE, the SUMASK [18] framework also leverages a decomposition strategy to enhance performance through an external uncertainty estimation component. This highlights the untapped potential of decomposition approaches in further advancing generative RE with LLMs.

3   Background

Relation Extraction (RE) aims to identify and classify the relationships between head and tail entities in a sentence (Fig. 1(a)). Typically, examples in RE datasets are represented as pairs $(\mathbf{X}, \mathbf{Y})$, where $\mathbf{X} = \{x_1, x_2, \cdots, x_h, \cdots, x_t, \cdots, x_n\}$ denotes the input sentence with n tokens and x_h and x_t represent the head and tail entities, respectively, and $\mathbf{Y}$ denotes the corresponding relation label between the entity pair (x_h, x_t). Notably, $\mathbf{Y}$ belongs to a pre-defined set of labels $\mathbf{L}$ that include relation labels, such as occupant, lives in, and head of government. For example, given $\mathbf{X} = \{$Claude Malhuret is the mayor of Vichy, France.$\}$, $x_h = \{$Claude Malhuret$\}$, and $x_t = \{$Vichy$\}$, the relation label $\mathbf{Y}$ would be {head of government}.

In the context of zero-shot RE, we aim to predict the relation label $\mathbf{Y}$ between the entity pair (x_h, x_t) without explicit training data or demonstration for this specific relation label [33]. Leveraging LLMs is a recent approach that has garnered attention for addressing zero-shot RE tasks, mainly when a user submits a prompt to an LLM that has not been specifically trained for the RE task described by the prompt [18,35,39]. In the domain of zero-shot RE with LLMs, known as generative zero-shot RE, the task involves presenting an input sentence $\mathbf{X}$ alongside a prompt containing task instruction $\mathcal{I}$ and examples. The goal is to generate a relation label $\mathbf{Y} = \{y_1, y_2, \cdots, y_m\}$ consisting of m tokens, representing the relationship between the head (x_h) and tail (x_t) entities mentioned in the input sentence.

It is worth noting that since LLMs are generative, they may generate a relation label $\mathbf{Y}$ consisting of several tokens, whereas, in the other traditional supervised methods excluding generative ones, we mainly consider the relation label as one token. For example, consider the input sentence $\mathbf{X} = \{$Claude Malhuret is the mayor of Vichy, France.$\}$. In this case, the task instruction $\mathcal{I}$ might instruct the LLM to identify the relation between $x_h = \{$Claude Malhuret$\}$ and $x_t = \{$Vichy$\}$ and generate a relation label. The LLM, after processing the prompt consisting $\mathcal{I}$, $\mathbf{X}$, x_h, and x_t might generate $\mathbf{Y}$ as $\{$head of government$\}$, indicating that the head entity is the director of tail entity.

Vanilla Prompting. Vanilla prompting, also known as zero-shot prompting, represents the most straightforward prompt strategy. It involves direct instruction to LLMs to extract relation labels from input sentences without prior examples. As depicted in Fig. 1 (b), a prompt containing task instructions $\mathcal{I}$, the input sentence $\mathbf{X}$, head entity x_h, head entity x_t, and a pre-defined list of relations $\mathbf{L}$ are provided as input to the LLM. The LLM then generates the relation label $\mathbf{Y}$ (shown in green text).

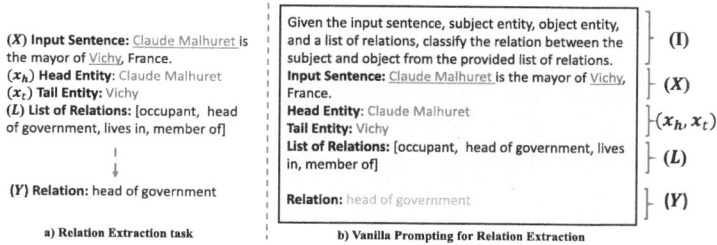

Fig. 1. Illustration of relation extraction task. Panel (a) outlines the task of relation extraction, including the identification of head and tail entities within a given input sentence and the classification of their relation from a predefined list. Panel (b) demonstrates the application of vanilla prompting techniques for relation extraction.

4   Methodology

In this section, we propose the Refine-Estimate-Answer (REA) prompting approach, addressing the complexities of relation extraction (RE) as discussed in Sect. 1. REA systematically break down the complex task of RE into four distinct stages. Each stage simplifies the process, considering the LLM's refinement of their responses by integrating prior iterations. The overall strategy of REA comprises the following four main stages:

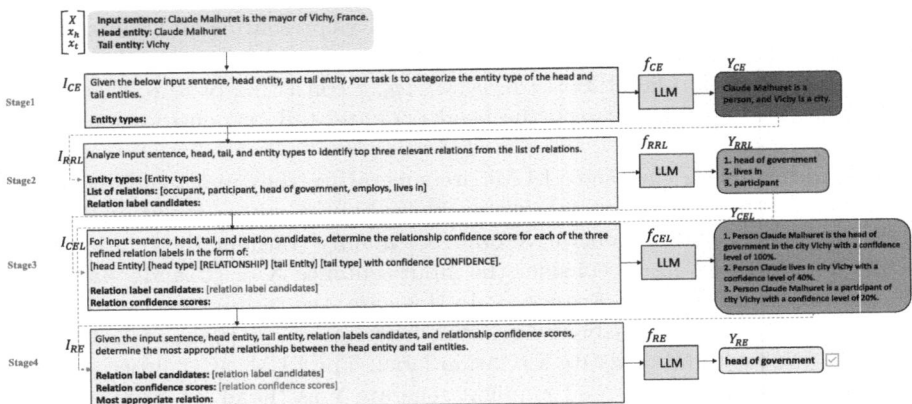

Fig. 2. REA Prompting Overview: The approach comprises four stages, with each stage's response serving as a component within the input to the subsequent stage.

1. *Stage1 (contextual enrichment)*: Given an input sentence $\mathbf{X}$, head entity x_h, and tail entity x_t, LLM determines the types of head and tail entities.
2. *Stage2 (refinement of relation labels)*: LLM refines the list of relation labels based on the extracted entity types from the previous stage.
3. *Stage3 (confidence elicitation)*: LLM generates sentences with head and tail entities for each refined relation label candidate, assigning a confidence percentage to each sentence.
4. *Stage4 (generate final relation label)*: Utilizing the generated sentences and confidence percentages, the LLM determines the predicted relation label, thus finalizing the output.

As shown in Fig. 2, each step above involves prompting the LLM in a zero-shot manner to achieve the desired response. The subsequent section provides a detailed description of each stage.

4.1   Stage1: Contextual Enrichment

Studies have demonstrated that enriching RE models with contextual information such as typed entity markers can significantly improve their performance [43]. Considering entity types, knowing whether an entity is a person, an organization, or a location can offer valuable clues about its potential relationship. For instance, encountering a person as the head entity and a city as the tail entity strongly suggests a ''born in'' relationship rather than the less likely ''employs''. Therefore, in our approach, we leverage contextual enrichment as the first step of our prompting approach to provide the model with additional information about entity types. Specifically, given the input sentence, head entity, tail entity, and a pre-defined list of possible entity types, the LLM is prompted to generate the types of entities. The generated entity types are utilized to refine relation labels. This step can be represented as:

$$\mathbf{Y}_{CE} = f_{CE}(\mathcal{I}_{CE}, \mathbf{X}, x_h, x_t) \tag{1}$$

The function f_{CE} represents the process of contextual enrichment, where the provided task instruction $\mathcal{I}_{CE}$, input sentence $\mathbf{X}$, head entity x_h, and tail entity x_t are used as prompt to generate the entity types $\mathbf{Y}_{CE}$. As illustrated in Fig. 2, with the task instruction $\mathcal{I}_{CE}$ for entity type categorization, considering $\mathbf{X}$ as {Claude Malhuret is the mayor of Vichy, France.}, x_h = {Claude Malhuret}, and x_t = {Vichy}, the resulting $\mathbf{Y}_{CE}$ from the LLM response would be {Claude Malhuret is a person, and Vichy is a city}. This process enriches the context with helpful entity information.

4.2 Stage2: Refinement of Relation Labels

Following the generation of entity types through contextual enrichment at Stage1, the subsequent step focuses on refining the relation labels based on these entity types. This refinement process ensures that the selected relation labels align appropriately with the identified entity types. During this stage, the LLM is prompted to choose the three most relevant relations, considering the input sentence, head entity, tail entity, a pre-defined list of relation labels, and generated entity types. The pre-defined list of relation labels encompasses all relation labels present in the dataset. The choice of three candidates for refining relation labels is grounded in empirical experiments, which revealed optimal performance at this level of consideration. This balance ensures both computational efficiency and accurate predictions. This stage can be expressed as:

$$\mathbf{Y}_{RRL} = f_{RRL}(\mathcal{I}_{RRL}, \mathbf{X}, x_h, x_t, \mathbf{Y}_{CE}, \mathbf{L}) \qquad (2)$$

The function f_{RRL} refines the relation labels based on the prompt comprised of task instruction $\mathcal{I}_{RRL}$, input sentence $\mathbf{X}$, head entity x_h, tail entity x_t, pre-defined list of labels $\mathbf{L}$, and generated entity types from the previous step $\mathbf{Y}_{CE}$. As depicted in Fig. 2, the task instruction $\mathcal{I}_{RRL}$ demonstrating refinement of relation labels $\mathbf{L}$ = {occupant, participant, head of government, employs, lives in}, with $\mathbf{X}$ as {Claude Malhuret is the mayor of Vichy, France.}, x_h = {Claude Malhuret}, x_t = {Vichy}, and $\mathbf{Y}_{CE}$ = {Claude Malhuret is a person, and Vichy is a city} used to generate relation label candidates $\mathbf{Y}_{RRL}$ = {1. head of government 2. lives in 3. participant}.

4.3 Stage3: Confidence Elicitation

The next stage involves confidence elicitation, where the certainty levels associated with the relation label candidates generated by the LLM are estimated. Confidence elicitation involves estimating the certainty levels related to the responses generated by LLMs without relying on accessing specific architectural details or adjusting the model through pre-training or fine-tuning [14]. Tian et al. [31] proposed that LLMs trained with reinforcement learning with human feedback (RLHF), such as GPT-3.5 [25], generally exhibit better-calibrated verbalized confidences emitted as output tokens compared to the model's conditional probabilities. Similarly, our approach integrates verbalized confidence elicitation in our prompting methodology.

In this stage, prompt construction follows a structured format (see Fig. 2). Leveraging elements such as head entity, tail entity, and relation label candidates generated in the preceding step, the LLM is prompted to generate sentences in the following form:

```
[head entity type] [head entity] [relation label candidate] [tail entity type] [tail
entity] with a confidence level of [confidence]%.
```

Here, the goal is to determine the confidence level for each relation label candidate. The prompt guides the LLM in replacing the placeholders with actual entities and their respective types alongside each relation candidate. It subsequently generates a confidence score based on the knowledge acquired during the pre-training stage. The confidence elicitation step can be represented as:

$$\mathbf{Y}_{CEL} = f_{CEL}(\mathcal{I}_{CEL}, \mathbf{X}, x_h, x_t, \mathbf{Y}_{RRL}, \mathbf{Y}_{CE}) \tag{3}$$

The function f_{CEL} estimates confidence levels based on the prompt giving instruction $\mathcal{I}_{CEL}$ regarding the task, input sentence $\mathbf{X}$, head entity x_h, tail entity x_t, generated entity types $\mathbf{Y}_{CE}$, and relation label candidates $\mathbf{Y}_{RRL}$. As shown in Fig. 2, considering $\mathbf{X}$ as {Claude Malhuret is the mayor of Vichy, France.}, $x_h = $ {Claude Malhuret}, $x_t = $ {Vichy}, $\mathbf{Y}_{CE} = $ {Claude Malhuret is a person, and Vichy is a city.}, and relation label candidates $\mathbf{Y}_{RRL} = $ {1. head of government 2. lives in 3. participant} the expected generated confidence sentences $\mathbf{Y}_{CEL}$ would be:

1. Person Claude Malhuret is the head of government in the city Vichy with a confidence level of 100%.
2. Person Claude Malhuret lives in city Vichy with a confidence level of 40%.
3. Person Claude Malhuret is a participant of city Vichy with a confidence level of 20%.

4.4   Stage4: Generate Final Relation Label

The ultimate stage determines the most suitable relationship between the provided head and tail entities. This decision relies on the input text $\mathbf{X}$, head entity x_h, tail entity x_t, relation label candidates $\mathbf{Y}_{RRL}$, and the confidence scores associated with each candidate $\mathbf{Y}_{CEL}$:

$$\mathbf{Y}_{RE} = f_{RE}(\mathcal{I}_{RE}, \mathbf{X}, x_h, x_t, \mathbf{Y}_{RRL}, \mathbf{Y}_{CEL}) \tag{4}$$

The function f_{RE} signifies the procedure by which the LLM generates the final relation label $\mathbf{Y}_{RE}$ by processing the task instruction $\mathcal{I}_{RE}$ and the elements mentioned earlier. Figure 2 illustrates that the LLM determined {head of government} as the most appropriate label based on the answers provided in previous stages.

5   Experiments

This section outlines our experimental methodology, evaluating the effectiveness of REA prompting in RE tasks under zero-shot scenarios.

5.1 Datasets and Implementation Details

We conducted our experiments using three English RE datasets: FewRel [9], Wiki-ZSL [4], and TACRED [40]. FewRel is a few-shot RE benchmark dataset sourced from Wikipedia, including 80 relations. The Wiki-ZSL dataset comprises 113 relations generated from Wikipedia articles and the Wikidata knowledge base by distant supervision. The TACRED contains 42 relations extracted from news articles. In line with previous studies [4,18], our experiments on the FewRel and Wiki-ZSL datasets involved varying sizes (m) of relation label sets to evaluate method performance. Here, m denotes the number of unique relation labels, with values chosen from $\{5, 10, 15\}$. To ensure robustness against experimental variability, we repeated the label selection process five times using different random seeds, resulting in distinct test sets. Regarding TACRED, in accordance with previous studies [18,39], to manage OpenAI costs, we randomly selected 1000 examples from the test set. We measured performance with *precision*, *recall*, and *macro-F1* for FewRel and Wiki-ZSL, and *micro-F1* was used for TACRED, excluding the none-of-the-above (NoTA) relation.

For the commercialized LLM, we used *gpt-3.5-turbo* [25] accessed through the OpenAI API. With *gpt-3.5-turbo*, no post-processing is necessary since the model generates a relation label directly. As for the open-source LLM, we chose *Mixtral*-8 × 7B [11], a pre-trained generative Sparse Mixture of Experts model available on the Hugging Face model hub[1]. We selected *Mixtral*-8 × 7B due to its innovative architecture that combines the efficiency of sparse activation with the robustness of a large-scale model, making it particularly well-suited for extracting complex relation labels where diverse expert knowledge is beneficial. For *Mixtral*-8 × 7B, we extracted the relation label from the model responses, as it sometimes did not provide a relation label alone. All reported scores are averages from five experiments to ensure robustness. Our code and datasets are available at GitHub[2].

5.2 Baselines

We compare REA against existing zero-shot RE frameworks, dividing them into two groups: (1) traditional supervised methods and (2) generative LLM-based methods. Traditional supervised methods, primarily utilizing PLMs, are designed to leverage labeled RE datasets for training and subsequently generalize to unseen RE datasets, particularly for relation labels. In contrast, generative LLM-based methods use pre-training knowledge to predict relations without fine-tuning on labeled data. The frameworks included in each category are as follows:

– Traditional supervised methods: (1) ESIM [16], a traditional approach using BiLSTM for reading comprehension-based RE; (2) ZS-BERT [4], a supervised method employing BERT for encoding sentences and relation descriptions to

---

[1] https://huggingface.co/models.
[2] https://github.com/AmirLayegh/REA_Prompting.

Table 1. Main results on FewRel and Wiki-ZSL datasets with $m \in \{5, 10, 15\}$ unique relations. The approaches are divided into traditional supervised and LLM-based models.

Dataset	FewRel								
	m=5			m=10			m=15		
	P	R	F1	P	R	F1	P	R	F1
ESIM	56.27	58.44	57.33	42.79	44.17	43.52	29.15	31.59	30.32
ZS-BERT	76.96	78.86	77.90	56.92	57.59	57.25	35.54	38.19	36.82
TGM	39.40	38.91	39.15	30.18	29.77	29.97	25.43	24.94	25.19
RelationPrompt	90.15	88.50	89.30	80.33	79.62	79.96	74.33	72.51	73.40
RE-Matching	90.52	**90.56**	**90.54**	82.12	**81.55**	**81.83**	**73.80**	73.52	**73.66**
Vanilla	67.41	72.97	70.08	42.48	46.26	44.29	25.71	27.77	26.70
SUMASK	78.27	72.55	75.30	64.77	60.94	62.80	44.76	41.13	42.87
REA (Mixtral)	76.19	81.2	78.62	63.18	66.70	64.89	61.23	**80.80**	69.67
REA (GPT-3.5)	**92.57**	84.7	88.46	**82.26**	79.47	80.85	64.34	68.68	66.44
Dataset	**Wiki-ZSL**								
	m=5			m=10			m=15		
	P	R	F1	P	R	F1	P	R	F1
ESIM	48.58	47.74	48.16	44.12	45.46	44.78	27.31	29.62	28.42
ZS-BERT	71.54	72.39	71.96	60.51	60.98	60.74	34.12	34.38	34.25
TGM	40.67	33.42	36.56	26.09	21.84	23.73	22.10	18.27	19.99
RelationPrompt	70.66	**83.75**	76.63	68.51	**74.76**	71.50	63.69	**67.93**	65.74
RE-Matching	78.19	78.41	**78.30**	74.39	73.54	**73.96**	**67.31**	67.33	**67.32**
Vanilla	64.47	70.83	67.50	41.83	46.22	43.92	23.17	27.82	25.28
SUMASK	75.64	70.96	73.23	62.31	61.08	61.69	43.55	40.27	41.85
REA (Mixtral)	69.46	50.4	58.41	58.72	53.59	56.04	54.19	48.12	50.97
REA (GPT-3.5)	**78.88**	68.6	73.38	73.15	61.2	66.64	58.2	52.6	55.25

classify and predict relations; (3) TGM [19], a generative meta-learning RE framework training T5-base [28] for learning and extracting unseen relations; (4) RelationPrompt [5], a supervised RE framework which uses GPT-2 [27] and BART [17] for generating and extracting relations from synthetic data; (5) RE-Matching [41], a supervised RE framework, decouples encoding and matching using Sentence-BERT [29] and BERT [32] for relation extraction and feature distillation.

– Generative LLM-based methods: (1) Vanilla, as discussed in Sect. 3, GPT-3.5 model is prompted to extract relation labels from input sentences directly; (2) QA4RE [39], an LLM-based zero-shot RE framework that converts RE tasks into multiple-choice question-answering, utilizing GPT-3.5 to provide answers; (3) SUMASK [18], a generative zero-shot RE framework that combines GPT-3.5 with a natural language inference module to predict relations.

Table 2. Zero-shot results of LLM-based methods on the TACRED dataset with NoTA relation excluded.

Method	P	R	F1
Vanilla	36.9	68.8	48.1
QA4RE	47.7	**78.6**	59.4
SUMASK	62.2	53.8	57.7
REA (Mixtral)	59.74	56.3	57.97
REA (GPT-3.5)	**72.95**	56.2	**63.49**

5.3   Results

Table 1 presents a comparative analysis of zero-shot RE on the FewRel and Wiki-ZSL datasets for both traditional supervised and LLM-based approaches. Notable, the REA prompting approach, specifically when implemented with the GPT-3.5 model (REA (GPT-3.5)), is distinguished by its superior performance among other LLM-based methods across datasets. This achievement is particularly significant when juxtaposed with SUMASK [18]. Despite SUMASK using a decomposition strategy and an external module for uncertainty estimation, REA outperforms it by directly utilizing the core capabilities of LLMs. Furthermore, REA's resilience to the variation in the number of relations (m) contrasts with other LLM-based methods, which show a marked decrease in performance with an increase in m. REA, in its implementations with both GPT-3.5 and Mixtral, significantly enhances the Vanilla approach and surpasses other LLM-based frameworks, evidencing the effectiveness of our approach.

Additionally, REA (Mixtral) delivers competitive results in both datasets; particularly notable are the F1 score of 78.62% at $m = 5$ in FewRel and 58.41% at $m = 5$ in Wiki-ZSL. However, REA (GPT-3.5) consistently outperforms these results suggesting the GPT-3.5 model employed in REA (GPT-3.5) offers advantages in zero-shot RE tasks.

An important observation is that while REA may not outperform all traditional supervised models, such as RE-Matching, its ability to operate effectively without the need for fine-tuning on relation-specific data stands out as a significant advantage over traditional supervised approaches. These traditional methods typically depend on training with annotated data to predict unseen relations. The inherent flexibility of REA, originating from its independence from fine-tuning, substantially reduces the time and resources needed for model deployment and adaptation. This benefit makes REA a desirable solution for real-world applications where rapid or broad-scale implementation is necessary. Through REA, we showcase the LLM's capabilities in delivering competitive or superior performance without the extensive training process, highlighting the impact of strategic prompting in enhancing zero-shot RE performance.

Table 2 presents the zero-shot performance of LLM-based methods on the TACRED dataset, explicitly excluding the NoTA (none of the above) relation.

This comparative evaluation highlights REA's standout performance. Despite using the same selection of 1000 randomly chosen test records to ensure a fair comparison, REA outperforms other LLM-based models. Notably, REA achieves this performance without relying on ground truth entity types used in QA4RE and SUMASK. This highlights REA's effective use of the contextual enrichment phase (see Sect. 4.1), which can intuitively capture the nuances of entity types from text alone. Beyond outperforming other LLM-based methods, REA demonstrates consistency and effectiveness across different LLM architectures, including GPT-3.5 and Mixtral, showcasing its ability to improve upon the vanilla prompting approach. Moreover, the notably high precision achieved by REA, particularly with the GPT-3.5, signifies its ability to accurately identify relevant relations without generating excessive false positives, a critical attribute supporting high-quality relation extraction.

5.4   Analysis

In this section, we analyze the REA approach, focusing on its effectiveness and the role of its components in zero-shot RE. Our analysis evaluates the impact of unifying REA's stages into fewer steps and investigates the contributions of critical stages such as contextual enrichment and confidence elicitation. This exploration aims to highlight REA's strengths, areas for improvement and insights into developing effective prompting strategies for LLMs in zero-shot RE tasks.

Unified Steps Strategy Analysis: Our investigation explored the effectiveness of integrating specific REA phases-contextual enrichment with relation label refinement and confidence elicitation with final relation label generation-into unified steps. Our Objective was to assess how such a unified approach might affect overall model performance, utilizing a singular prompt to integrate stages. Table 3 compares the performance of the unified REA approach, which combines stages 1 and 2, as well as stages 3 and 4, with the original REA method that maintains distinct stages across various datasets.

The analysis reveals a prominent trend across the FewRel, Wiki-ZSL, and TACRED datasets. The unified REA method, which merges the initial and final stages of the process, consistently underperforms compared to the original, stepwise REA approach. Specifically, in the FewRel dataset, the F1 scores for the unified method range from 45.26 to 75.47 across different relation counts ($m = 5, 10, 15$), whereas the original REA approach maintains higher scores, peaking at 88.46. This pattern is mirrored in the Wiki-ZSL and TACRED datasets, where the original REA method surpasses the unified version, achieving F1 scores up to 73.38 and 63.49, respectively. This uniform drop in performance with the unified approach suggests that merging steps might obscure crucial intermediate information or feedback loops inherent to the original REA methodology. Each discrete stage in the original REA potentially offers a unique opportunity for refinement and calibration based on specific aspects of the relation extraction task. By collapsing these stages, the unified method likely loses the chance to iteratively adjust its strategy based on feedback from each phase, thus limiting its ability to accurately capture and reflect the complexities of the RE task. This insight underscores the value of discrete, focused steps in the REA method, enabling a more effective arrangement with the challenges of zero-shot RE.

Evaluating the Impact of Individual Stages in REA: In the comparison depicted in Fig. 3, we investigated the individual contributions of contextual enrichment and confidence elicitation stages to the REA prompting approach. We evaluated their respective impacts on the model's overall performance by selectively omitting these stages.

Table 3. Comparison of F1 scores between Unified REA and Original REA approaches across different datasets.

Dataset	FewRel			Wiki-ZSL			TACRED
	m=5	m=10	m=15	m=5	m=10	m=15	NoTA
Unified REA (GPT-3.5)	75.47	64.93	45.26	66.63	54.59	49.01	54.23
Original REA (GPT-3.5)	**88.46**	**80.85**	**66.44**	**73.38**	**66.64**	**55.25**	**63.49**

Including contextual enrichment consistently led to higher F1 scores across the datasets, underscoring its pivotal role in aiding the LLM's relation extraction capabilities. Conversely, the absence of this stage resulted in a notable decrease in performance, demonstrating the stage's vital role in enhancing the model's contextual understanding and ability to determine relations within the text.

The necessity of confidence elicitation, however, varied with the complexity of the task. Particularly in the Wiki-ZSL dataset with $m = 5$, the model performed better without this stage, which may suggest that for simpler tasks with fewer relations, the model can effectively deduce the most likely relations without needing to evaluate its own confidence. Nevertheless, the significant decline in F1 scores when confidence elicitation was removed in both datasets reveals its importance. It contributes to accuracy by allowing the model to assess its own certainty, refining its predictions.

These insights confirm that each stage in the REA method is critical in realizing high-performing zero-shot RE. Contextual enrichment lays the foundation for accurate relation understanding, while confidence elicitation tunes the output, contributing to an effective model for zero-shot RE.

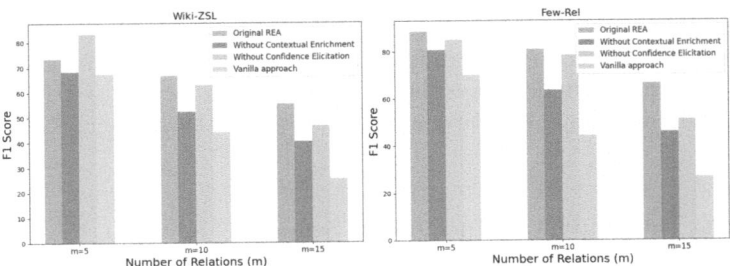

Fig. 3. Comparison of F1 scores across different approaches using GPT-3.5 on Wiki-ZSL and Few-Rel datasets with varying numbers of relations (m = 5, m = 10, m = 15).

6   Conclusion

This paper has introduced the Refine-Estimate-Answer (REA) prompting approach that significantly enhances zero-shot RE by structurally decomposing the task into manageable steps and using iterative refinement to improve performance. Demonstrating superior performance across benchmarks, REA showcases the effectiveness of multi-stage prompting and self-refinement in leveraging LLMs for complex NLP tasks. The success of REA across various LLMs, including open-source and commercialized models, vows its versatility and potential for broader NLP tasks. Future work will explore optimizing these mechanisms and extending REA's methodology to other information extraction tasks facing data scarcity. This study advances zero-shot RE and sets a new standard for employing LLMs in NLP, highlighting the importance of structured prompting strategies for maximal model performance.

References

1. Arora, S., Narayan, A., Chen, M.F., et al.: Ask me anything: a simple strategy for prompting language models. In: ICLR (2023). https://openreview.net/forum?id=bhUPJnS2g0X
2. Brown, T., Mann, B., Ryder, N., et al.: Language models are few-shot learners. NeurIPS **33**, 1877–1901 (2020)
3. Bunescu, R., Mooney, R.: A shortest path dependency kernel for relation extraction. In: EMNLP, pp. 724–731 (2005)
4. Chen, C.Y., Li, C.T.: ZS-BERT: towards zero-shot relation extraction with attribute representation learning. In: NAACL, pp. 3470–3479 (2021)
5. Chia, Y.K., et al.: RelationPrompt: leveraging prompts to generate synthetic data for zero-shot relation triplet extraction. In: Findings of the ACL (2022)
6. Deng, S., Ma, Y., Zhang, N., Cao, Y., Hooi, B.: Information extraction in low-resource scenarios: survey and perspective. arXiv preprint arXiv:2202.08063 (2022)
7. Dhuliawala, S., Komeili, M., et al.: Chain-of-verification reduces hallucination in large language models. arXiv preprint arXiv:2309.11495 (2023)

8. Ding, N., Wang, X., Fu, Y., et al.: Prototypical representation learning for relation extraction. In: ICLR (2021)
9. Han, X., Zhu, H., et al.: FewRel: a large-scale supervised few-shot relation classification dataset with state-of-the-art evaluation. In: EMNLP, pp. 4803–4809 (2018)
10. Huang, F., Kwak, H., An, J.: Chain of explanation: new prompting method to generate quality natural language explanation for implicit hate speech. In: The ACM Web Conference 2023
11. Jiang, A.Q., Sablayrolles, A., et al.: Mixtral of experts. arXiv preprint arXiv:2401.04088 (2024)
12. Khoo, C., Myaeng, S.H.: Identifying semantic relations in text for information retrieval and information extraction. In: The Semantics of Relationships: An Interdisciplinary Perspective, pp. 161–180 (2002)
13. Kojima, T., Gu, S.S., et al.: Large language models are zero-shot reasoners. NIPS **35**, 22199–22213 (2022)
14. Kuhn, L., Gal, Y., Farquhar, S.: Semantic uncertainty: linguistic invariances for uncertainty estimation in natural language generation. In: ICLR (2023)
15. Layegh, A., Payberah, A.H., et al.: Wiki-based prompts for enhancing relation extraction using language models. In: SAC 2024, Wiki-based Prompts for Enhancing Relation Extraction using Language Models (2024)
16. Levy, O., Seo, M., et al.: Zero-shot relation extraction via reading comprehension. In: CoNLL, pp. 333–342 (2017)
17. Lewis, M., Liu, Y., Goyal, N., Ghazvininejad, M., et al.: BART: denoising sequence-to-sequence pre-training for natural language generation, translation, and comprehension. In: ACL, pp. 7871–7880 (2020)
18. Li, G., Wang, P., Ke, W.: Revisiting large language models as zero-shot relation extractors. In: Findings of EMNLP 2023, pp. 6877–6892 (2023)
19. Li, W., Qian, T.: Generative meta-learning for zero-shot relation triplet extraction. arXiv preprint arXiv:2305.01920 (2023)
20. Liu, J., Shen, D., Others: What makes good in-context examples for GPT-3? In: DeeLIO 2022, pp. 100–114 (2022)
21. Liu, P., et al.: Pre-train, prompt, and predict: a systematic survey of prompting methods in natural language processing. ACM Comput. Surv. (2023)
22. Luo, D., Su, J., Yu, S.: A BERT-based approach with relation-aware attention for knowledge base question answering. In: 2020 IJCNN. IEEE (2020)
23. Madaan, A., et al.: Self-Refine: iterative refinement with self-feedback. In: NIPS (2024)
24. Muhammad, I., Kearney, A., et al.: Open information extraction for knowledge graph construction. In: DEXA, pp. 103–113 (2020)
25. OpenAI: Introduce ChatGPT. OpenAI blog (2023). https://openai.com/blog/chatgpt
26. Press, O., Zhang, M., et al.: Measuring and narrowing the compositionality gap in language models. In: Findings of EMNLP, pp. 5687–5711 (2023)
27. Radford, A., Wu, J., Child, R., Luan, D., Amodei, D., Sutskever, I., et al.: Language models are unsupervised multitask learners. OpenAI blog **1**(8), 9 (2019)
28. Raffel, C., Shazeer, N., et al.: Exploring the limits of transfer learning with a unified text-to-text transformer. J. Mach. Learn. Res. **21**, 1–67 (2020)
29. Reimers, N., Gurevych, I.: Sentence-BERT: sentence embeddings using Siamese BERT-networks. In: EMNLP (2019)
30. Shi, F., Suzgun, M., et al.: Language models are multilingual chain-of-thought reasoners. arXiv preprint arXiv:2210.03057 (2022)

31. Tian, K., et al.: Just ask for calibration: strategies for eliciting calibrated confidence scores from language models fine-tuned with human feedback. In: EMNLP (2023)
32. Vaswani, A., Shazeer, N., et al.: Attention is all you need. In: Advances in Neural Information Processing Systems (2017)
33. Wang, W., Zheng, V.W., et al.: A survey of zero-shot learning: settings, methods, and applications. In: ACM TIST, pp. 1–37 (2019)
34. Wei, J., Wang, X., et al.: Chain-of-thought prompting elicits reasoning in large language models. NIPS **35**, 24824–24837 (2022)
35. Wei, X., Cui, X., et al.: Zero-shot information extraction via chatting with ChatGPT. arXiv preprint arXiv:2302.10205 (2023)
36. Xu, D., Chen, W.: Large language models for generative information extraction: a survey. arXiv preprint arXiv:2312.17617 (2023)
37. Yasunaga, M., Chen, X., Li, Y., Pasupat, P., Leskovec, J., et al.: Large language models as analogical reasoners. arXiv preprint arXiv:2310.01714 (2023)
38. Yu, W., Zhang, H., et al.: Chain-of-Note: enhancing robustness in retrieval-augmented language models. arXiv preprint arXiv:2311.09210 (2023)
39. Zhang, K., Jimenez Gutierrez, B.: Aligning instruction tasks unlocks large language models as zero-shot relation extractors. In: Findings of ACL (2023)
40. Zhang, Y., Zhong, V., et al.: Position-aware attention and supervised data improve slot filling. In: Proceedings of EMNLP Conference (2017)
41. Zhao, J., Zhan, W., Zhao, W.X., et al.: Re-matching: a fine-grained semantic matching method for zero-shot relation extraction. In: ACL, pp. 6680–6691 (2023)
42. Zhou, D., Schärli, N., et al.: Least-to-most prompting enables complex reasoning in large language models. In: ICLR (2022)
43. Zhou, W., Chen, M.: An improved baseline for sentence-level relation extraction. In: ACL (Short Papers), pp. 161–168 (2022)

Enhancing Romanian Offensive Language Detection Through Knowledge Distillation, Multi-task Learning, and Data Augmentation

Vlad-Cristian Matei, Iulian-Marius Tăiatu, Răzvan-Alexandru Smădu,
and Dumitru-Clementin Cercel[✉]

Faculty of Automatic Control and Computers, National University of Science and
Technology POLITEHNICA Bucharest, Bucharest, Romania
dumitru.cercel@upb.ro

Abstract. This paper highlights the significance of natural language processing (NLP) within artificial intelligence, underscoring its pivotal role in comprehending and modeling human language. Recent advancements in NLP, particularly in conversational bots, have garnered substantial attention and adoption among developers. This paper explores advanced methodologies for attaining smaller and more efficient NLP models. Specifically, we employ three key approaches: (1) training a Transformer-based neural network to detect offensive language, (2) employing data augmentation and knowledge distillation techniques to increase performance, and (3) incorporating multi-task learning with knowledge distillation and teacher annealing using diverse datasets to enhance efficiency. The culmination of these methods has yielded demonstrably improved outcomes.

Keywords: Offensive Language · Knowledge Distillation · Multi-Task Learning · Data Augmentation

1 Introduction

In recent years, there has been a remarkable rise in the prominence of natural language processing, primarily attributable to the success of conversational bots like ChatGPT[1]. These models have achieved impressive performance through extensive training on massive datasets. However, the battle against fake news, offensive language, and abusive content on social networks remains challenging due to the overwhelming volume of user-generated data, necessitating the development of automatic detection systems [9]. Moreover, the intricate nature of identifying offensive language stems from the nuanced considerations of contextual factors, multiple meanings, and emerging expressions [11]. Further advancements in this field are still required to tackle these challenges effectively.

---

[1] https://www.openai.com/chatgpt.

A. Rapp et al. (Eds.): NLDB 2024, LNCS 14762, pp. 317–332, 2024.
https://doi.org/10.1007/978-3-031-70239-6_22

Exploiting offensive language has garnered significant global attention, with trained models demonstrating notable performance achievements [30]. However, when considering the specific context of the Romanian language analysis, the existing datasets are constrained in size and availability [8]. To understand crucial and intricate characteristics comprehensively, models require a diverse and well-balanced collection of qualitative examples. Additionally, the architectures underlying these models comprise millions of parameters, resulting in substantial computational and resource requirements [3]. Consequently, although automatic detection of offensive language remains relevant, challenges arise in adapting these models for mobile devices or embedded systems due to limitations in speed, space, and resource constraints [1].

The primary objective of this study is to develop an automatic offensive language detection model encompassing three distinct offensive categories (i.e., *Insult*, *Profanity*, and *Abuse*) and a neutral class *Other*. Initially, we employ the knowledge distillation (KD) method [13] to transfer information [26] from a high-parameter model to a more compact architecture [3]. Subsequently, the obtained results undergo meticulous analysis, complemented by an exploration of various data augmentation strategies: generative text [28] by employing RoGPT-2 [25], ASDA [19], MixUp [38], and noisy student [22]. These techniques enhance the model's performance by introducing nuanced variations or controlled noise injection.

In addition, this study prioritizes performance optimization rather than model size reduction. Accordingly, knowledge distillation is employed on an architecture with an equivalent number of parameters [1]. Furthermore, a multi-task learning (MTL) approach [4,15,21] integrates information from three auxiliary tasks associated with sentiment analysis [31], emotions analysis [6], and sexist language [14]. We comprehensively evaluate the effectiveness of this architecture in efficiently assimilating and integrating the acquired information. Furthermore, our study assesses how these auxiliary datasets contribute to a more comprehensive understanding of the Romanian language, particularly in the context of the initial problem. To summarize, the contributions of this work are: (i) evaluating the knowledge distillation method to obtain a more compact and faster model and showing that utilizing diverse data augmentation techniques improves performance, and (ii) performance enhancement by applying multi-task learning with knowledge distillation and teacher annealing [16], integrating information from three additional datasets.

2   Related Work

Automatic offensive language detection poses a challenge of global interest [9,11], with attempts to address the issue using various means, both classic machine learning methods and deep learning approaches [37]. Offensive language detection was proposed at several workshops, including SemEval-2019 [37] and GermEval-2019 [30]. Baseline models such as support vector machines have been evaluated on offensive and sexist tweets [14]. In addition, [5] explored neural network approaches such as long short-term memory and convolutional neural networks on hate speech, showing there is room for improvement in these systems.

To optimize recent models, transfer learning techniques [26] have been proposed, including multi-task learning [4,21] and knowledge distillation [3,13], with applications extending to the domain of offensive language [32]. Angry-BERT [2] combined MTL with the Bidirectional Encoder Representations from Transformer (BERT) model [17] to jointly learn hate speech detection along with emotion classification and target identification as secondary tasks, enhancing overall performance. In [33], the authors investigate bridging differences in annotation and data collection of hate speech and abusive language in tweets, including various annotation schemes, labels, and geographic and cultural influences. To harness the benefits of both methods, models combining multi-task learning with knowledge distillation [7,18,20,27] or teacher annealing have been proposed [16]. This framework was also employed alongside the teacher annealing option, albeit for empathy detection [15]. In contrast to other works, we combine all these methods to address the automatic detection of offensive language, particularly in the Romanian language, and compare them individually and through an ablation study.

3   Method

3.1   Fine-Tuning BERT

In this work, we base our models on the BERT architecture [17]. The baseline involves fine-tuning BERT for automatic offensive language detection. It adjusts the weights obtained from a pre-trained BERT to identify and classify different subtypes of offensive language accurately.

The initial step establishes a manually annotated dataset $\mathcal{D} = \left\{(x_i, y_i)\right\}_{i=1:N}$ with N examples, namely RO-Offense[2], that assigns labels y_i (i.e., *Insult*, *Abuse*, *Profanity*, and *Other*) to each text comment x_i. These labels enable a more nuanced understanding of the offensive language, moving beyond a simplistic binary classification. To accommodate the classification task with $K = 4$ possible classes, we add a fully connected layer on top of the last layer of BERT's architecture. This fully connected layer consists of K neurons, each corresponding to one of the predicted classes. Then, a softmax layer computes the probability distribution p_i over predicted classes for the given input text x_i.

During the training process, the weights are updated to minimize the prediction error by employing the cross-entropy loss function $\mathcal{L}_{CE}$. This loss quantifies the dissimilarities between the predicted and true labels as follows:

$$\mathcal{L}_{CE} = -\frac{1}{N} \sum_{i=1}^{N} \sum_{k=1}^{K} y_{i,k} \log\left(p_{i,k}\right) \tag{1}$$

---

[2] https://huggingface.co/datasets/readerbench/ro-offense.

where $y_{i,k}$ is the kth class label from the one-hot encoding for the ground truth y_i, and $p_{i,k}$ is the kth class probability from the model's softmax output p_i.

3.2 Data Augmentation

Data augmentation is a technique employed to enrich the diversity of features in the dataset without the need for additional data collection [10]. Its objective is to introduce changes in input data to enhance the models' capacity for generalization. This approach offers several benefits, including improved model performance, acting as a regularization technique, enhancing model robustness, and addressing class imbalance [10,12,19]. Our work employs several data augmentation techniques.

RoGPT-2. Generative Pre-trained Transformer (GPT) models [28] leverage the linguistic knowledge and comprehensive understanding of language structures to produce varied texts that encompass the intricacies and diversity observed in real-world texts. While existing methods like Easy Data Augmentation [34] focus on simple transformations applied to the existing text, GPT models offer the advantage of generating creative and meaningful texts, enhancing the model's robustness through variety. However, the generated texts may significantly alter the original meaning. To mitigate this risk, we employ the RoGPT-2 [25] model. RoGPT-2 is the Romanian version of the GPT-2 model [29], pre-trained on a large 17 GB Romanian text dataset. We provide 70% of the context to control the level of text augmentation, allowing the model to generate a sequel and encouraging controlled and coherent text generation.

ASDA. Auxiliary Sentence-based Data Augmentation (ASDA) [19] utilizes conditional masked language modeling [35] to generate augmented examples. First, it works by selecting an example *E1* from the training dataset and then choosing another example *E2* with the same class *[LABEL]* as *E1*. Next, we construct the context using the following template: "The next two sentences are *[LABEL]*. The first sentence is: *E1*. The second sentence is: *E2*.". We apply random masking of a set of words within the final sentence, E2. The masking process occurs with a predefined probability and depends on the sentence length.

MixUp. MixUp [38] is a data augmentation method intended to boost diversity while lowering the possibility of generating incorrect examples. It creates a more robust generalization by linearly interpolating between various dataset examples. The technique randomly selects two examples (i.e., (x^i, y^i) and (x^j, y^j)) from the dataset, where x^i and x^j represent the encoded inputs, whereas y^i and y^j are the one-hot encoded labels. New examples $(\hat{x}, \hat{y})$ are generated using the following formulas:

$$\hat{x} = \lambda x_i + (1 - \lambda)x_j, \tag{2}$$

$$\hat{y} = \lambda y_i + (1 - \lambda)y_j, \tag{3}$$

where $\lambda \in [0, 1]$ is a hyperparameter that controls the interpolation process. In this work, we employ the MixUp technique at two distinct levels[3] [12]:

- **MixUp Encoder**: Interpolates the representations of the two input examples before passing them through the classification layer.
- **MixUp Sentence**: Interpolates the representations of the two inputs after the classification layer but before the softmax activation function.

Noisy Student. Noisy student [22] is employed in noisy student training [36], where a teacher model generates pseudo-labels for unlabeled data, and a student model is trained on these pseudo-labels. The objective is to introduce natural noise and enhance the robustness of the model. In this research, we apply two non-aggressive methods [22]:

- **Word Drop**: We choose, with a probability α, that every word in a sentence has a fixed chance of 30% to be removed. It is guaranteed that at least one word will be deleted, but no more than ten words in total.
- **Sentence Drop**: In cases where the example contains at least two sentences, we remove one sentence from the text with the same probability α.

3.3   Multi-task Learning Model

MTL [4, 21] is a method that learns several related tasks simultaneously within a single framework to enhance target task performance. The fundamental concept behind MTL is based on the observation that learning similar tasks in parallel can facilitate quicker adaptation, leveraging common principle knowledge [4]. Building upon this intuition, MTL learns shared representations that encapsulate the underlying essence of the information while capturing the specific characteristics of each task up to a level beneficial for the main task [21]. This approach can be viewed as a subcategory of TL, as both leverage the knowledge from related tasks [26]. However, MTL offers several advantages, including leveraging information learned from different tasks and transferring knowledge across diverse datasets [21]. It also helps mitigate overfitting by regularizing the network and preventing single tasks from dominating the learning process [21].

Inspired by [15, 21], our MTL architecture consists of shared lower layers derived from BERT common to all tasks and task-specific layers added to this backbone. A softmax activation function follows each task-specific layer to obtain the probability distribution for the corresponding task. In this work, the primary task of offensive language detection is supported by three auxiliary tasks, namely emotion classification, sentiment analysis, and sexist language detection. These additional tasks are considered to be correlated with the target domain, as previous research [5, 11, 23] has demonstrated their relevance to offensive language detection. Therefore, let $\mathcal{D}^\tau = \{(x_i^\tau, y_i^\tau)\}$ be the training dataset for a task τ. The multi-task loss $\mathcal{L}_{MTL}$, calculated for a model θ, is defined as follows [15]:

---

[3] https://github.com/xashru/mixup-text.

$$\mathcal{L}_{MTL}(\theta) = \sum_{\tau=1}^{4} \sum_{(x_i^\tau, y_i^\tau) \in \mathcal{D}^\tau} \ell(y_i^\tau, f^\tau(x_i^\tau; \theta)) \tag{4}$$

where ℓ is either the binary cross-entropy or the cross-entropy loss depending on the task, and $f^\tau(x_i^\tau, \theta)$ denotes the output of the model θ for the task τ. We employ cross-entropy loss $\mathcal{L}_{CE}$ for offensive language detection, sentiment classification, and sexist language detection. For the emotion analysis dataset, which comprises seven classes, we use the one-hot encoding representation for the labels, and thus, the loss function ℓ is the binary cross-entropy loss defined as:

$$\mathcal{L}_{BCE} = -\frac{1}{NK} \sum_{i=1}^{N} \sum_{k=1}^{K} [y_{i,k} \cdot \log(p_{i,k}) + (1 - y_{i,k}) \cdot \log(1 - p_{i,k})] \tag{5}$$

where $y_{i,k}$ denotes the kth class label from the one-hot ground truth label, and $p_{i,k}$ is the model's prediction for the kth class.

3.4 Knowledge Distillation Models

KD. KD [13] aims to reduce the size of a larger model, referred to as the teacher, by transferring its knowledge to a smaller, faster, and similarly performing model known as the student. The fundamental principle behind this approach revolves around compressing the knowledge contained within the teacher model, with the student learning to mimic his predictions [3].

The temperature parameter T is critical in the knowledge distillation process. It serves as a mechanism to control the level of confidence in the predictions made by the teacher model. A higher temperature leads to a more uniform probability distribution, allowing the student to explore diverse options, while a lower temperature accentuates the differences between classes, focusing on the information deemed more relevant by the teacher (i.e., exploitation) [13,20]. The temperature adjustment is applied at the softmax function, which computes the probability distribution over classes. Given the input x_i, the probability $p_{i,k}$ for class k is computed based on the network logits z_i as follows [13]:

$$p_{i,k} = \frac{\exp(z_{i,k}/T)}{\sum_j \exp(z_{i,j}/T)} \tag{6}$$

The knowledge distillation architecture involves training the teacher and the student neural networks on the same dataset. A hyperparameter α controls the interpolation of partial losses, considering the teacher's soft predictions and the ground truth labels. The distillation loss is calculated using the cross-entropy loss ($\mathcal{L}_{CE}$) between the ground truth and the hard predictions and the Kullback-Leibler (KL) divergence loss ($\mathcal{L}_{KL-KD}$) between the soft labels and soft predictions [16,20]:

$$\mathcal{L}_{KL-KD} = \frac{T^2}{N} \sum_{i=1}^{N} KL(p^t(x_i, T) || p^s(x_i, T)) \tag{7}$$

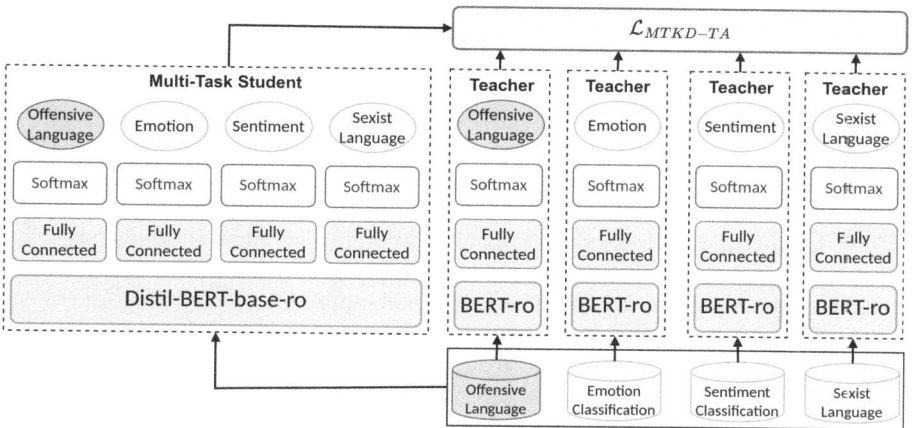

Fig. 1. Multi-task learning with knowledge distillation and teacher annealing.

$$\mathcal{L}_{KD} = \alpha\mathcal{L}_{CE} + (1-\alpha)\mathcal{L}_{KL-KD} \tag{8}$$

where $p^t(x_i, T)$ represents the softmax outputs of the teacher model, and $p^s(x_i, T)$ represents the student's softmax output, both computed using Eq. 6.

MTKD. In natural language processing, the simultaneous learning of multiple tasks presents a considerable challenge. MTL addresses this challenge by training a single model to solve numerous tasks concurrently. However, optimizing a model for various tasks with different complexities can result in performance imbalances, where specific tasks dominate while others suffer [18].

To tackle the performance imbalance problem in MTL scenarios, multi-task learning with knowledge distillation (MTKD) has been proposed by [7]. This approach leverages the benefits of both techniques to overcome the performance imbalance problem in MTL scenarios. The core idea is to use specialized models, called single-task teacher models, to teach a multi-task student model. The teacher models provide rich information beyond simple one-hot encodings, and this knowledge is transferred to the student model through distillation.

Based on the findings in [15], let $\mathcal{D}^\tau = \{(x_i^\tau, y_i^\tau)\}$ with N^τ examples represent the training dataset for the task τ, θ represents student's parameters being updated, and θ^τ represents teacher's parameters. We denote $f^\tau(x_i^\tau, \theta^\tau)$ the output computed using Eq. 6 of each task-specific teacher model specialized in task τ, trained using fine-tuned BERT, and $f^\tau(x_i^\tau, \theta)$ the output according to Eq. 6 of the student model on task τ. The loss is described as follows [15,16,20]:

$$\mathcal{L}_{KL-MTKD}(\theta) = \sum_{\tau=1}^{4} \frac{T^2}{N^\tau} \sum_{(x_i^\tau, y_i^\tau)\in\mathcal{D}^\tau} KL(f^\tau(x_i^\tau;\theta^\tau)\|f^\tau(x_i^\tau;\theta)) \tag{9}$$

$$\mathcal{L}_{MTKD} = \alpha\mathcal{L}_{CE} + (1-\alpha)\mathcal{L}_{KL-MTKD} \tag{10}$$

MTKD-TA. Teacher annealing (TA) [16] is an optimization technique employed in conjunction with the knowledge distillation method to handle better the discrepancies between the student and the teacher models. While temperature is typically used to alleviate this issue, [24] highlights that as the capacity of the teacher model increases, thereby accentuating the differences with the student model, the student's performance improves only up to a certain point, after which it decreases.

The TA method addresses the capacity difference problem in knowledge distillation by gradually reducing the influence of the teacher model. In contrast to the teacher-assistant knowledge distillation approach, which introduces an intermediate network, teacher annealing relies on increasing linearly a parameter during training [7,15], called λ, from 0 to 1. It controls the balance between the distillation loss and the supervised loss, which measures the discrepancies between the student's predictions and the teacher's predictions and between the student's predictions and the ground truth labels, respectively [16]. By gradually decreasing the teacher's influence and increasing reliance on the original labels, the student model becomes more independent and capable of achieving improved performance [7]. Thus, we modify the multi-task learning with knowledge distillation and teacher annealing (MTKD-TA) loss function as follows:

$$\mathcal{L}_{MTKD-TA} = \lambda\mathcal{L}_{CE} + (1 - \lambda)\mathcal{L}_{KL-MTKD} \tag{11}$$

As depicted in Fig. 1, the final architecture incorporates four task-specific datasets to obtain individual teacher models by fine-tuning BERT. Each teacher model is specialized for one of the four tasks. The student model adopts an MTL architecture with a modified weight updating scheme in its network, accounting for the newly introduced loss calculation formula.

4 Experiments

4.1 Datasets

The target dataset used in this research was the RO-Offense dataset[4], consisting of relevant examples curated explicitly for the proposed task. Additionally, three auxiliary datasets were included to enhance the model's performance in achieving the main objective. By incorporating these additional datasets, the aim is to improve the accuracy and generalization capability of the model in effectively identifying and classifying offensive language.

RO-Offense. RO-Offense is the largest publicly available dataset for analyzing offensive discourse in the Romanian language. It comprises 12,447 annotated records, classified into four distinct classes: *Profanity* (13%), *Insult* (23%), *Abuse* (28%), and *Other* (36%). To ensure privacy, the dataset has anonymized names of individuals and organizations, replacing them with generic labels.

REDv2. The Romanian Emotions Dataset (REDv2) [6] is a publicly available dataset, hosted on GitHub[5], that provides 5,449 manually verified tweets for

---

[4] https://huggingface.co/datasets/readerbench/ro-offense.
[5] https://github.com/Alegzandra/RED-Romanian-Emotions-Dataset.

analyzing emotions in the Romanian language. Each example in the dataset is classified into one of seven possible classes: *Anger*, *Fear*, *Joy*, *Sadness*, *Surprise*, *Trust*, and *Neutral*. Additionally, all tweets have been anonymized by removing usernames and proper nouns from the dataset.

CoRoSeOf. The Corpus of Romanian Sexist and Offensive language (CoRoSeOf) [14] is a publicly available dataset that is a valuable resource for studying sexist and offensive language in the Romanian context. The dataset, which can be found on GitHub[6], contains 39,245 tweets with labels assigned by multiple annotators for the classification of sexist and offensive language in Romanian. Initially, each instance in the dataset was assigned to one of the five possible classes: *Direct Sexism*, *Descriptive Sexism*, *Reportive Sexism*, *Non-Sexist Offensive*, and *Non-Sexist*. However, for this research, the data has been transformed into a binary classification format, where all sexist subtypes are included in the *sexist* class, while the remaining instances are included in the *non-sexist* class.

LaRoSeDa. The Large Romanian Sentiment Data Set (LaRoSeDa) [31] is a publicly available resource, accessible on GitHub[7], that consists of 15,000 reviews collected from one of the largest e-commerce platforms in Romania. Each instance in the dataset is labeled as either *positive* or *negative*, allowing for sentiment analysis and contributing to a better understanding of the sentiment patterns in the Romanian language.

4.2 Experimental Settings

The REDv2 dataset was split into 75% for training, 10% for validation, and 15% for testing. For Ro-Offense, CoRoSeOf, and LaRoSeDa datasets, we use the 80%/10%/10% split. All the trained models used the Transformer library[8] as their base architecture, and their versions are managed using the HuggingFace platform[9]. The base architecture used for the distilled student model is Distil-BERT-base-ro[10], while the other models utilize BERT-base-ro-cased[11] (BERT-ro). The main difference between these two architectures is the number of layers [1]. Distil-BERT-base-ro consists of 6 layers, 81M parameters, and requires 312MB of memory, whereas BERT-ro comprises 12 layers, 124M parameters, and occupies 477MB of memory. The configuration includes a starting learning rate of 2e-5, AdamW optimizer, weight decay of 0.01, and batch size 16. The number of fine-tuning epochs varies between 2 and 7, depending on the dataset size and the architecture on which the model was trained. The probability α used in noisy student takes values from the set {15, 20, 25}. The interpolation

---

[6] https://github.com/DianaHoefels/CoRoSeOf.
[7] https://github.com/ancatache/LaRoSeDa.
[8] https://github.com/huggingface/transformers.
[9] https://huggingface.co/.
[10] https://huggingface.co/racai/distilbert-base-romanian-cased.
[11] https://huggingface.co/dumitrescustefan/bert-base-romanian-cased-v1.

parameter λ used in MixUp is set to either 15 or 30. For model evaluation, we use accuracy (Acc), precision (P), recall (R), and weighted F_1-score (F_1).

5   Results

5.1   Results for Knowledge Distillation Models

We focus on the distillation technique combined with multi-task learning, which enables the transfer of information into a model of the same size but benefits from diverse inputs from multiple sources of knowledge. This approach allows for the development of a compact model that can maintain the high performance of its teacher. The results are presented in Table 1. For the multi-task learning experiments, we employ the REDv2, LaRoSeDa, and CoRoSeOf datasets as auxiliary tasks.

Fine-Tuning BERT. During experiments, we noticed that the offensive language detection model based on the BERT-ro architecture, specifically trained for offensive language detection and its subtypes, achieves commendable results with an accuracy of 78.63% and an F_1-score of 78.83%. However, BERT-ro is not easily saturable, and there is room for further enhancement. These scores indicate the potential for optimizing the model to achieve even better results.

Table 1. Results on the RO-Offense dataset for knowledge distillation approaches.

Model	Acc	F_1	P	R
base model				
BERT-ro	78.63	78.83	79.15	78.63
MTL	77.99	77.85	77.80	77.99
distilled student				
KD	77.10	77.23	77.44	77.10
MTKD	81.36	81.19	81.12	81.36
MTKD-TA	**82.40**	**82.34**	**82.29**	**82.40**

KD. The results obtained by the student using the KD technique on the main dataset are lower than those achieved by the BERT-ro model. There is an approximate 1.5% drop in all evaluated metrics, which can be intuitively explained by the fact that although the student benefits from both the soft probabilities from the teacher and the direct information from the dataset, it fails to reach the same performance due to the reduced size of the architecture of Distil-BERT-base-ro, which consists of only 6 layers instead of 12.

MTL. The MTL model combines all datasets and relies on the larger architecture, BERT-ro. According to Table 1, the results obtained by the MTL model are superior to those of the KD model, as the larger architecture allows for more complex learning. However, the MTL model still falls short of the performance achieved by the teacher model. This can be attributed to the inherent challenge of simultaneously learning multiple tasks, mainly when dealing with larger datasets. Managing each task's contribution and finding a learning balance is crucial to improving overall performance.

MTKD. The MTKD model significantly improves over prior experiments. It surpasses the performance of the teacher model by $\sim$2.3%, the distilled student by $\sim$3.9%, and the MTL model by $\sim$3.3%. This improvement is achieved by leveraging the transfer of knowledge from the teacher through a processing step at a temperature $T = 4$ and utilizing the ground truth information. The balance between these two sources of information is achieved through $\alpha = 0.6$ controlling the partial interpolation of losses.

MTKD-TA. The MTKD-TA model showcases two significant aspects based on the results obtained. First, as we showed in the previous experiments, the difference in architecture size led to a loss of information transferred from the teacher to the student, which was partially regained in this experiment. Second, we can achieve better results by dynamically scaling the λ coefficient. For most tasks, the coefficient λ is increased incrementally between 0 and 1, with the temperature fixed at $T = 2$. For the emotion detection task, the temperature $T = 7$ is more effective. The MTKD-TA model outperforms MTKD by approximately 1%, the distilled student by around 5%, and BERT-ro by roughly 3.5%.

5.2   Impact of Data Augmentation

We first explore distilling the base model into a smaller and faster model, which also benefits from various data augmentation techniques to enhance its performance. By employing these techniques, the aim is to strike a balance between efficiency and accuracy. We present the results of applying data augmentation techniques to the model obtained through distillation on the smaller architecture, Distil-BERT-base-ro. The results are summarized in Table 2.

MixUp Encoder. This method does not show better results in our results. The evaluation metrics do not exhibit significant differences that warrant considering this method in combination with other data augmentation techniques.

MixUp Sentence. Applying the MixUp Sentence technique with interpolation 30% (i.e., MixUp Sent.-30%) at a higher level led to an accuracy improvement of approximately 0.41% compared to the distilled student model alone. This significant difference justifies combining this method with other augmentation techniques.

RoGPT-2. We employ RoGPT-2 to replace 30% of the end of the texts. This augmentation technique results in a performance improvement of approximately 0.5% compared to the reference model, similar to the MixUp Sentence technique.

Table 2. Results of student data augmentations on the RO-Offense dataset.

Model	Acc	F_1	P	R
KD	77.10	77.23	77.44	77.10
+MixUp Encoder	77.02	77.21	77.53	77.02
+MixUp Sent.-30%	77.51	77.63	77.83	77.51
+RoGPT-2	77.51	77.71	78.10	77.51
+ASDA	77.75	77.73	77.81	77.75
+Noisy-25%	78.07	78.08	78.18	78.07
+ASDA+RoGPT-2	77.67	77.81	78.14	77.67
+ASDA+RoGPT-2+Noisy-15%	77.91	78.11	78.54	77.91
+ASDA+RoGPT-2+Noisy-20%	78.55	78.68	78.90	78.55
+ASDA+RoGPT-2+Noisy-20%+MixUp Sent.-30%	78.07	78.30	78.74	78.07
+ASDA+RoGPT-2+Noisy-20%+MixUp Sent.-15%	**78.71**	**78.81**	**79.06**	**78.71**

The metrics indicate the potential benefits of combining it with other augmentation methods. However, although more diverse, the augmentation is riskier, completing the sentences more creatively.

ASDA. The utilization of the ASDA method results in an improvement of at least 0.5% in evaluation metrics. This approach is considered safe and provides a richer learning context.

Noisy Student. As observed in Table 2, the noisy student (i.e., Noisy) augmentation technique proves to be the most effective. This method achieves a significant increase in results of at least 0.8% compared to the distilled student alone. Despite its simplicity, the method's performance underscores the significance of obtaining controlled noise. In this case, the constraint involves introducing a 25% probability of change, both for word elimination and potential sentence completion.

Combining Augmentation Techniques. After analyzing each augmentation technique individually, we combined ASDA and RoGPT-2 to balance context and creativity, resulting in a 0.6% increase over the student model. Then, noise was added with a 15% probability initially, but a 20% probability yielded a 1.4% increase. Ultimately, the best-performing approach combines ASDA, RoGPT-2, Noisy Student, and MixUp Sentence. Regarding the MixUp Sentence method, much better outcomes are obtained by reducing the probability of interpolating examples from 30% to 15%. In the end, we achieve an advantage improvement of 1.58% over the distilled student alone, equalizing the performance of the BERT-ro teacher, which has 53% more parameters.

5.3   Impact of Auxiliary Tasks

Through the lens of the ablation study, we analyze the behavior of MTL models on offensive language detection by removing different combinations of tasks. The results presented in Table 3 pertain to the evaluation using the F_1-score. The *proposed model* refers to the models that employ all three auxiliary tasks, namely emotions detection, sentiment classification, and sexist language detection. Then, we present the results obtained after removing the specified tasks, enumerated after *w/o* (i.e., without). Note that the *proposed model* without any auxiliary tasks in the MTL setting is equivalent to the BERT-ro model.

Sexist language. We notice a significant variation in the impact of the sexist language task on the final outcome. In the case of the MTL model, the exclusion of this task leads to very poor results, while for the MTKD-TA model, the results are quite good even without considering this task. One possible explanation could be the difficulty of accommodating a larger dataset within the MTL environment.

Combining dataset exclusions. We notice the combinations {emotions, sexist language} and {sentiment, sexist language} yield similar results, indicating that the model can successfully learn even without one of the tasks that analyze emotions and sentiments. Additionally, a notably lower performance is observed for the MTKD-TA model when both tasks are excluded from the analysis.

Table 3. Results on RO-Offense after removing auxiliary tasks.

Model	MTL	MTKD	MTKD-TA
Proposed model	77.85	81.19	82.34
w/o emotions & sentiment & sexist language	78.83	77.23	–
w/o emotions & sentiment	80.08	81.35	80.69
w/o emotions & sexist language	78.97	**81.74**	82.26
w/o sentiment & sexist language	78.25	81.67	**82.39**
w/o emotions	**80.82**	81.47	81.53
w/o sentiment	79.17	81.14	81.69
w/o sexist language	78.71	80.97	81.97

6   Conclusion

This paper developed neural network models to detect Romanian offensive language and investigated various techniques to enhance their performance. Integrating additional related tasks (i.e., emotion analysis, sentiment analysis, and sexist language detection) through MTL demonstrated improved performance. However, achieving an optimal balance between the contributions of different tasks in the MTL environment proved challenging. To address this, we employed KD and TA, resulting in ∼3.5% performance improvement compared to the BERT-ro model. Additionally, efforts were made to reduce the model size and utilize data augmentation techniques, leading to an additional performance increase of ∼1.6%.

Future research directions involve exploring more diverse datasets, optimizing the MTL setup, fine-tuning hyperparameter combinations, and considering alternative base architectures. These advancements aim to strengthen the detection and effective management of Romanian offensive language, contributing to content filtering, and establishing a safer virtual environment.

Acknowledgements. This work was supported by the NUST POLITEHNICA Bucharest through the PubArt program, and a grant from the National Program for Research of the National Association of Technical Universities - GNAC ARUT 2023.

References

1. Avram, A.M., et al.: Distilling the knowledge of romanian berts using multiple teachers. In: Proceedings of the thirteenth LREC, pp. 374–384 (2022)
2. Awal, M.R., Cao, R., Lee, R.K.-W., Mitrović, S.: AngryBERT: joint learning target and emotion for hate speech detection. In: Karlapalem, K., et al. (eds.) PAKDD 2021. LNCS (LNAI), vol. 12712, pp. 701–713. Springer, Cham (2021). https://doi.org/10.1007/978-3-030-75762-5_55
3. Buciluă, Cristian anrofbd Caruana, R., Niculescu-Mizil, A.: Model compression. In: Proceedings of the 12th ACM SIGKDD, pp. 535–541 (2006)
4. Caruana, R.: Multitask learning. Mach. Learn. **28**, 41–75 (1997)
5. Chiril, P., Pamungkas, E.W., Benamara, F., Moriceau, V., Patti, V.: Emotionally informed hate speech detection: a multi-target perspective. Cogn. Comput. **14**, 322–352 (2022). https://doi.org/10.1007/s12559-021-09862-5
6. Ciobotaru, A., Constantinescu, M.V., Dinu, L.P., Dumitrescu, S.: Red v2: enhancing red dataset for multi-label emotion detection. In: Proceedings of the Thirteenth Language Resources and Evaluation Conference, pp. 1392–1399 (2022)
7. Clark, K., Luong, M.T., Khandelwal, U., Manning, C.D., Le, Q.: Bam! born-again multi-task networks for natural language understanding. In: Proceedings of the 57th ACL, pp. 5931–5937 (2019)
8. Cojocaru, A., Paraschiv, A., Dascalu, M.: News-ro-offense-a romanian offensive language dataset and baseline models centered on news article comments. In: RoCHI, pp. 65–72 (2022)
9. Council, E.: Framework decision on combating certain forms and expressions of racism and xenophobia. https://eur-lex.europa.eu/legal-content/EN/TXT/?uri=LEGISSUM%3Al33178 (2008), Accesed 16 June 2023
10. Feng, S.Y., et al.: A survey of data augmentation approaches for NLP. In: Findings of the Association for Computational Linguistics: ACL-IJCNLP 2021, pp. 968–988 (2021)
11. Fortuna, P., Nunes, S.: A survey on automatic detection of hate speech in text. ACM Comput. Surv. (CSUR) **51**(4), 1–30 (2018)
12. Guo, H., Mao, Y., Zhang, R.: Augmenting data with mixup for sentence classification: an empirical study. CoRR **abs/1905.08941** (2019)

13. Hinton, G., Vinyals, O., Dean, J.: Distilling the knowledge in a neural network. arXiv preprint arXiv:1503.02531 (2015)
14. Hoefels, D.C., Çöltekin, Ç., Mădroane, I.D.: Coroseof-an annotated corpus of romanian sexist and offensive tweets. In: Proceedings of the Thirteenth Language Resources and Evaluation Conference, pp. 2269–2281 (2022)
15. Hosseini, M., Caragea, C.: Distilling knowledge for empathy detection. In: Findings of EMNLP 2021, pp. 3713–3724 (2021)
16. Jafari, A., Rezagholizadeh, M., Sharma, P., Ghodsi, A.: Annealing knowledge distillation. In: Proceedings of the 16th Conference of the European Chapter of the Association for Computational Linguistics: Main Volume, pp. 2493–2504 (2021)
17. Kenton, J.D.M.W.C., Toutanova, L.K.: Bert: Pre-training of deep bidirectional transformers for language understanding. In: Proceedings of NAACL-HLT, pp. 4171–4186 (2019)
18. Li, W.-H., Bilen, H.: Knowledge distillation for multi-task learning. In: Bartoli, A., Fusiello, A. (eds.) ECCV 2020, Part VI. LNCS, vol. 12540, pp. 163–176. Springer, Cham (2020). https://doi.org/10.1007/978-3-030-65414-6_13
19. Li, Y., Caragea, C.: Target-aware data augmentation for stance detection. In: Proceedings of the Conference of the North American Chapter of the Association for Computational Linguistics: Human Language Technologies, pp. 1850–1860 (2021)
20. Li, Y., Zhao, C., Caragea, C.: Improving stance detection with multi-dataset learning and knowledge distillation. In: Proceedings of the 2021 Conference on Empirical Methods in Natural Language Processing, pp. 6332–6345 (2021)
21. Liu, X., He, P., Chen, W., Gao, J.: Multi-task deep neural networks for natural language understanding. In: Proceedings of the 57th Annual Meeting of the Association for Computational Linguistics, pp. 4487–4496 (2019)
22. Liu, Y., Shen, S., Lapata, M.: Noisy self-knowledge distillation for text summarization. In: Proceedings of the 2021 Conference of the NAACL, pp. 692–703 (2021)
23. Martins, R., Gomes, M., Almeida, J.J., Novais, P., Henriques, P.: Hate speech classification in social media using emotional analysis. In: 2018 7th Brazilian Conference on Intelligent Systems (BRACIS), pp. 61–66. IEEE (2018)
24. Mirzadeh, S.I., Farajtabar, M., Li, A., Levine, N., Matsukawa, A., Ghasemzadeh, H.: Improved knowledge distillation via teacher assistant. In: Proceedings of the AAAI conference on artificial intelligence, vol. 34, pp. 5191–5198 (2020)
25. Niculescu, M.A., Ruseti, S., Dascalu, M.: Rogpt2: Romanian gpt2 for text generation. In: 2021 IEEE 33rd International Conference on Tools with Artificial Intelligence (ICTAI), pp. 1154–1161. IEEE (2021)
26. Pan, S.J., Yang, Q.: A survey on transfer learning. IEEE Trans. Knowl. Data Eng. **22**(10), 1345–1359 (2009)
27. Park, S., Caragea, C.: Multi-task knowledge distillation with embedding constraints for scholarly keyphrase boundary classification. In: Proceedings of the 2023 Conference on EMNLP, pp. 13026–13042 (2023)
28. Radford, A., Narasimhan, K., Salimans, T., Sutskever, I., et al.: Improving language understanding by generative pre-training (2018)
29. Radford, A., Wu, J., Child, R., Luan, D., Amodei, D., Sutskever, I., et al.: Language models are unsupervised multitask learners. OpenAI blog **1**(8), 9 (2019)
30. Struß, J.M., Siegel, M., Ruppenhofer, J., Wiegand, M., Klenner, M., et al.: Overview of germeval task 2 (2019)
31. Tache, A., Mihaela, G., Ionescu, R.T.: Clustering word embeddings with self-organizing maps. application on laroseda-a large romanian sentiment data set. In: Proceedings of the 16th Conference of the European Chapter of the Association for Computational Linguistics: Main Volume, pp. 949–956 (2021)

32. Vlad, G.A., Tanase, M.A., Onose, C., Cercel, D.C.: Sentence-level propaganda detection in news articles with transfer learning and bert-bilstm-capsule model. In: Proceedings of the Second Workshop on Natural Language Processing for Internet Freedom: Censorship, Disinformation, and Propaganda, pp. 148–154 (2019)

33. Waseem, Z., Thorne, J., Bingel, J.: Bridging the gaps: multi task learning for domain transfer of hate speech detection. Online harassment, pp. 29–55 (2018)

34. Wei, J., Zou, K.: Eda: Easy data augmentation techniques for boosting performance on text classification tasks. In: Proceedings of the 2019 Conference on Empirical Methods in Natural Language Processing and the 9th International Joint Conference on Natural Language Processing (EMNLP-IJCNLP), pp. 6382–6388 (2019)

35. Wu, X., Lv, S., Zang, L., Han, J., Hu, S.: Conditional BERT Contextual Augmentation. In: Rodrigues, J.M.F., et al. (eds.) ICCS 2019, IV. LNCS, vol. 11539, pp. 84–95. Springer, Cham (2019). https://doi.org/10.1007/978-3-030-22747-0_7

36. Xie, Q., Luong, M.T., Hovy, E., Le, Q.V.: Self-training with noisy student improves ImageNet classification. In: Proceedings of the IEEE/CVF Conference on Computer Vision and Pattern Recognition, pp. 10687–10698 (2020)

37. Zampieri, M., Malmasi, S., Nakov, P., Rosenthal, S., Farra, N., Kumar, R.: SemEval-2019 task 6: identifying and categorizing offensive language in social media (OffensEval). In: Proceedings of the 13th International Workshop on Semantic Evaluation, pp. 75–86. Minneapolis, Minnesota, USA (2019)

38. Zhang, H., Cisse, M., Dauphin, Y.N., Lopez-Paz, D.: mixup: beyond empirical risk minimization. arXiv preprint arXiv:1710.09412 (2017)

Automating Gender-Inclusive Language Modification in Italian University Administrative Documents

Aurora Cerabolini, Gabriella Pasi⬤, and Marco Viviani(✉)⬤

Università Degli Studi Di Milano-Bicocca Dipartimento di Informatica, Sistemistica e Comunicazione (DISCo) Information and Knowledge Representation, Retrieval, and Reasoning (IKR3) Lab Edificio U14 (ABACUS), Viale Sarca, 336, 20126 Milan, Italy
a.cerabolini@campus.unimib.it, {gabriella.pasi,marco.viviani}@unimib.it
https://ikr3.disco.unimib.it/

Abstract. In this work, we address the issue of automating the identification of non-inclusive language in administrative documents of Italian universities as well as providing gender-inclusive corrections. To achieve this objective, data from various Italian universities were gathered, leading to the creation of a dictionary containing potentially non-inclusive terms, and of a dataset containing gender non-inclusive sentences and their corresponding inclusive versions. Subsequently, three distinct approaches have been defined and evaluated: a rule-based and two neural approaches. In the development of the rule-based approach, Italian Part-of-Speech tagging, dependency parsing, and morphologization techniques were employed to detect masculine trigger words within sentences, ascertain whether they functioned as generic masculine terms, and offer gender-inclusive alternatives. In contrast, for the implementation of the two neural approaches, both the mT5 model and ChatGPT were utilized, and their respective outputs were compared against the rewritten sentences they generated. The experimental evaluations conducted suggest the effectiveness of the proposed solutions.

Keywords: Gender Bias · Inclusive Language · Natural Language Processing (NLP) · Large Language Models (LLMs) · ChatGPT

1 Introduction

The evolution of language over time is closely linked to changes in the surrounding social context and can play a crucial role in influencing and accelerating these transformations [9,16,23]. By adopting a language that recognizes and respects gender differences, organizations and institutions can contribute to the advancement of gender equality by providing social support to this crucial cause.

Universities, in particular, as places where knowledge is produced and shared, have the responsibility of conveying the importance of educating people about differences, and of supporting an ethic of equal opportunities between genders in

A. Rapp et al. (Eds.): NLDB 2024, LNCS 14762, pp. 333–347, 2024.
https://doi.org/10.1007/978-3-031-70239-6_23

study, research, and access to careers. Hence, they should promote the use of non-discriminatory and gender-inclusive language in institutional communication, administrative documents and acts, public events, and everyday academic life.

The Italian language (as well as other Romance languages) has two grammatical genders, i.e., masculine and feminine, which apply to nouns as well as adjectives, pronouns, and articles, and they determine agreement in terms of gender. However, Italian bureaucratic-administrative and institutional communication tends to avoid the use of feminine-gendered or gender-neutral terms when referring to professions, roles, and figures that for a long time were almost exclusively male prerogatives. The dominant grammatical gender, both in the singular and plural forms, continues to be masculine even in texts that pertain to females or individuals who do not identify with the masculine gender. In fact, in this type of document, the Italian language frequently adopts the so-called *maschile sovraesteso* (generic masculine), which is meant to refer to any individual, regardless of their gender identity [14].

Worldwide, to encourage the use of gender-inclusive language, guidelines have been defined to help draft a text and review it before publication [2]. In Italy, the guidelines described in [15] promote the correct use of terminology and gender, particularly in university administrative communication. Specifically, they provide some useful suggestions to help in the detection of the presence of gender bias and in the subsequent implementation of possible "strategies" for gender-inclusive rewriting.

To provide support in automatically performing this task, the main contributions of the work reported in this paper include:

1. The creation of a dictionary of *trigger words* that, based on their usage, may inadvertently perpetuate gender bias or reinforce stereotypes within university administrative documents, coupled with two lists of correspondence between masculine and feminine terms;
2. The creation of a *dataset* consisting of examples of Italian sentences from academic documents with inclusiveness issues paired with their corresponding gender-inclusive rewritten sentences;
3. The development of a *rule-based approach* that leverages Italian *Part-of-Speech* (POS) tagging, dependency parsing, and morphologization techniques to detect the use of generic masculine in a sentence and convert it to a gender-inclusive formulation;
4. The implementation of two *neural approaches* to generate gender-inclusive rewriting of sentences, utilizing both the Transformer-based mT5 model and ChatGPT based on GPT-4.

The paper is organized as follows: Sect. 2 illustrates the state of the art related to the considered problem; Sect. 3 describes the proposed approaches; Sect. 4 reports the experimental evaluations and discusses the obtained results; finally, Sect. 5 summarizes the work and envisages further research directions.

2   Related Work

In the current literature, for the Italian language, there is a notable gap regarding the automation of sentence rewriting into gender-inclusive wording. Current solutions at the state of the art mainly refer to the English language. However other languages, for example Romance languages, are characterized by gender agreement not just in pronouns, making it more complex to solve the problem under consideration. In general, such problem deals with two *sub-tasks*: (*i*) *gender bias detection* and (*ii*) *gender bias correction*.

Concerning sub-task (*i*), the work described in [1] examines English textbooks of Iranian high schools in order to find the frequency of names, nouns, pronouns, and adjectives attributed to women and men by means of *chi-square tests* [17]. Also, *chi-square tests* are used to investigate whether masculine and feminine have more or less equally first-place occurrences in instructions, exercises, and sentences. Still for the English language, in [3] the vector representation of words is employed to capture gender bias by considering vector directions. Specifically, *Principal Component Analysis* (PCA) [4] is performed on a set of word pairs that are gender polarized: the higher the projection of a given word in a direction, the more gender bias the word contains. For the Spanish language, which involves gender concordance among nouns, adjectives, and articles, the work detailed in [19] aims to detect a non-inclusive usage of the language in doctoral theses. First, a *dictionary* of potentially non-inclusive words is generated (e.g., *"profesor"*, [male] teacher), and then a set of surrounding terms for each of them is extracted. Each term set is then manually labeled according to the presence of inclusive or non-inclusive language. Finally, a *Support Vector Machine* (SVM) classifier is trained and tested on such an annotated dataset. For the German language, the authors in [5] develop a rule-based system to identify the usage of generic masculine in administrative and legal documents. To mark denotations of persons, the authors apply *morphological analysis* and, in case the base word for the noun is a nominalized verb, they refer to a special list of lexemes. Then, also pronouns that refer to a male subject are marked. As a last thing, the missing agreement between subject and predicative noun is detected.

Concerning sub-task (*ii*), the previously cited work [3] also proposes a method to make word vectors independent from the gender; to do this, they perform a projection of words to a subspace that is perpendicular to the gender dimension. The authors in [13] develop POWERTRANSFORMER, an *encoder-decoder model* based on OpenAI-GPT. This model jointly learns to reconstruct partially masked English story sentences while also learning to paraphrase from an external corpus of paraphrases. At generation time, they also include a boosting method for fine-grained steering towards the desired agency level [21]. The work proposed in [25] contributes to the automatic mitigation of bias in English language job advertisements by developing an *end-to-end text bias mitigation model* that can convert a piece of biased text to a neutral version whilst maintaining significant content information. Still with reference to English, to provide gender-neutral alternatives to sentences with gendered pronouns, several works, among which [24,29], propose *rule-based rewriters* to generate a parallel gendered-to-neutral corpus, and train a neural model to learn the mapping from gendered to gender-neutral sentences. For the German language, in [8] is has been recently proposed a *rule-based system* that requires morphological, dependency, and co-reference analysis, POS tagging, and a database for nouns and verb inflection forms, in order to suggest gender-neutral alternatives for the user's given text.

Finally, in discussing the potential application of *Large Language Models* (LLMs) to address the issue at hand, recent works have highlighted the importance of gender bias detection within these models. Notably, studies such as [12,28] have shed light on this aspect.

3   Empowering Gender-Inclusive Language with NLP Solutions

The two previously outlined sub-tasks are addressed in this paper, i.e., the automatic identification of words used with the generic masculine function within a sentence, and the automatic suggestion of a gender-inclusive reformulation of the sentence. To this aim, we investigate the effectiveness of three distinct approaches that we have defined and implemented: a *rule-based* approach and two *neural* approaches, one based on the use of the mT5 model and the other using ChatGPT. Before going into detail about the approaches, let us describe the language resources that had to be created for their implementation.

3.1   Linguistic Resources

The linguistic resources considered in this paper consist of: (*i*) a dictionary of trigger words, which serve as signals suggesting potential problems of term inclusiveness; (*ii*) two lists of correspondence between masculine and feminine terms; and (*iii*) a dataset consisting of examples of Italian sentences with inclusivity problems matched with corresponding gender-inclusive rewritten sentences.

(*i*) To build the *trigger word dictionary*, we started from two valid lists of such words that were already compiled by the University of Padova [27] and the University of Ferrara [26]. We complemented them with other trigger words that we have manually extracted from examples of Italian sentences with inclusiveness issues extracted from administrative documents provided by the University of Padova [27] and the University of Turin [11], and from documents gathered from the official website of the University of Milano-Bicocca from 2020 to 2023.[1,2,3] In this way, we collected a total of 143 trigger words;

---

[1] https://www.unimib.it/ateneo/salute-e-sicurezza/covid-19/provvedimenti-amministrativi-covid-19.

[2] https://www.unimib.it/internazionalizzazione/focus-erasmus/erasmus-studio/selezioni-erasmus-studio.

[3] https://www.unimib.it/search/google?keys=bando+di+ammissione.

(*ii*) The two *gender correspondence lists* are constituted by the list of Italian masculine articles with the corresponding feminine articles, and the list of Italian masculine possessive adjectives with the corresponding feminine possessive adjectives;

(*iii*) The *dataset of inclusive rewritten sentences* consists of sentences with inclusiveness issues, extracted from the previously mentioned Italian university administrative documents, paired with their corresponding gender-inclusive paraphrases. We manually created this dataset to address the lack of available datasets for the tasks of gender bias detection and correction within the Italian language domain. It consists, in particular, of 172 non-inclusive sentences and 207 corresponding inclusive sentences, as some sentences can be written either by explicitly stating the subject, or by using the impersonal form, i.e., when the verb expresses a complete meaning without any reference to the subject.

3.2   The Rule-Based Approach

This approach draws inspiration from [8], and incorporates Italian POS tagging, a dependency parser, and a morphologizer. It implements both the detection of *trigger words* used in a non-inclusive way and the *rewriting* of the sentences in three steps:

1. Search for trigger words in the masculine form;
2. Verification of the use of the generic masculine;
3. Rewriting of the sentences in a gender-inclusive form.

1. Search for trigger words in the masculine form. In this first step, we first selected those words in a target sentence that are listed in the trigger word dictionary and are declined in either the masculine singular or plural form. Next, using POS tagging, we checked that each selected word was associated with the NOUN tag according to its role within the sentence.[4] In fact, in the Italian language, the same word can have different roles, and therefore different POS tags, within a sentence. For example, in the following sentence:

I dipartimenti annualmente attribuiscono ai singoli docenti (...), individuando nel contempo il docente **responsabile**

i.e., "The departments annually assign individual teachers (...), at the same time identifying the responsible teacher" the word *responsabile* (responsible) has the syntactic role of an adjective with attributive function as it follows the word *docente* (teacher), that has the role of noun, and has the purpose of specifying the noun qualities and characteristics. The same word has the syntactic role of a noun in this sentence:

---

[4] We decided to focus on *nouns* because with respect to the documents and trigger words considered, it is that part of speech that in our case most effectively allows for the identification of problems related to the use of non-inclusive language and to subsequently correct the other parts of speech that are related to nouns as well.

*Il **responsabile** del trattamento dei dati personali è il Direttore pro-tempore della Direzione Didattica e Segreteria Studenti*

i.e., "The responsible for the processing of personal data is the pro-tempore Director of the Teaching Directorate and Student Secretariat". In this case, the word *responsabile* is identified as a trigger word with the NOUN tag and thus is selected for the subsequent step.

2. Verification of the use of the generic masculine. In this second step, the words identified from the previous step are evaluated to determine if they are used in sentences with actually a generic masculine function; this assessment involves the use of a dependency parser, a POS tagger and a morphologizer. A noun is not used as a generic masculine and therefore it does not need a gender-inclusive correction if both the feminine and the masculine nouns are mentioned, indicating a balanced representation, as in the sentence:

Tutela dei lavoratori [masculine term] *e delle lavoratrici* [feminine term]

i.e., "Protection of male and female workers". We have developed the rule-based system so that it makes this assumption if there is a coordinating conjunction in the sentence, such as "*e*" (and) or "*o*" (or), which binds the feminine noun and the masculine noun together, and also if the feminine and masculine nouns are separated by a comma within the sentence. We have recognized the use of such coordinating conjunctions and the comma by using dependency parser analysis. Once a coordinating conjunction, or a comma, is detected, by POS tagging we have verified that it binds the noun potentially used as generic masculine selected in the first step to a word with a noun function; if so, then we have analyzed this noun by employing the morphologizer, in order to check whether its gender is feminine, singular or plural. Following this, if in the trigger word dictionary, this noun does not match the feminine of the potentially generic masculine noun, then the sentence must be rewritten in a gender-inclusive manner as the use of the generic masculine is indeed present.

3. Rewriting of the sentences in a gender-inclusive form. In this third and last step, the rewriting of the sentence in a gender-inclusive way takes place. The choice we made in this sense was to transform each occurrence of the generic masculine in a gender-inclusive manner by adding to the masculine noun the corresponding feminine noun in the sentence (and the corresponding possessive articles and/or adjectives), i.e., via the usage of an oblique slash "/".[5]

For example, the masculine singular noun "*studente*" ([male] student) preceded by the masculine singular definite article "*lo*" (the) is rewritten in the

---

[5] This choice represents the simplest preliminary solution to the problem; other solutions, more inclusive of diverse gender identities, might involve completely rewriting the sentences in an impersonal manner or using symbols such as the asterisk (*) or the schwa (ə) at the end of terms, solutions that, however, are still subject to debate [7, 10, 14].

sentence as *"la studentessa/lo studente"*, where *"studentessa"* is the feminine term used in Italian to indicate a student and "la" is the corresponding definite article. On the other hand, if a noun has the same form for both masculine and feminine, such as the noun *"docente"* (teacher), only the article is changed by writing both the feminine and masculine forms, i.e., *"la/il docente"*.

To transform each occurrence of generic masculine into a gender-inclusive occurrence, we have used the POS tagging technique to check whether it is sufficient to modify only the noun or whether it is preceded by an article or by an article followed by a possessive adjective, which also needs to be modified adding the feminine form by referring to the two previously created correspondence lists.

3.3   The mT5-Based Approach

The mT5 model is a multilingual pre-trained text-to-text Transformer model released by Google in 2020 [30]. In this work, we employed an mT5 model specialized in the Italian language, fine-tuned on the Italian versions of the TaPaCo [22] and STS Benchmark [6] datasets.[6]

In order to actually rewrite sentences in a gender-inclusive way, we performed a fine-tuning phase on such mT5 model, on a training set extracted from the dataset of inclusive rewritten sentences introduced in Sect. 3.1. Before this fine-tuning phase, we tokenized the original sentences and the corresponding gender-inclusive paraphrases using the mT5 tokenizer, which adds special tokens to the input sequence, as follows:

- The `<s>` token at the beginning of the sequence to mark the start;
- The `</s>` token at the end to mark the end;
- The `<pad>` token to represent padding, in order to handle variable-length input sequences. This is the process of adding `<pad>` tokens to the input sequences to bring them up to a fixed length.

So, to generate gender-inclusive paraphrases with the fine-tuned model for the new input sentences in the test set, it was necessary to tokenize each input sentence using the mT5 tokenizer, pass each sentence through the fine-tuned model, and then decode the model's output to obtain the paraphrases. By way of example, we consider the non-inclusive sentence below:

Nel caso in cui la temperatura corporea rilevata risulti > 37.5 C, lavoratori e studenti non possono accedere né permanere in Ateneo

i.e., "In the event that the measured body temperature is > 37.5 C, workers and students are not allowed to enter or stay at the university". In this case, the Italian masculine terms "lavoratori" and "studenti" are employed with a generic masculine function for workers and students. Using the mT5-based model, we obtain the sentence rewritten in an inclusive manner, as follows:

---

[6] https://huggingface.co/aiknowyou/mt5-base-it-paraphraser.

Nel caso in cui la temperatura corporea rilevata risulti > 37.5 C, lavoratrici o lavoratori e studentesse o studenti non possono accedere né permanere in Ateneo

The model then produces a correction of the sentence based on the addition of the feminine terms "lavoratrici" and "studentesse" and the necessary grammatical elements.

3.4　The ChatGPT-Based Approach

ChatGPT is an application of the GPT model that is fine-tuned for conversational tasks or chatbot-like functionalities. In this work, the model on which ChatGPT is based is GPT-4 [18], released in 2023 by OpenAI.[7]

To rewrite sentences in a gender-inclusive manner, we have used the ChatGPT web interface, employing a methodical approach. The premise is grounded in the fact that ChatGPT relies heavily on the concept of *input prompt* to generate contextually relevant and guided outputs. Therefore, the key point of the process lay in formulating a well-structured prompt that acts as a precise and effective directive for the model. Specifically, we have meticulously realized a prompt that considers the following three aspects:

1. *Outline the rewriting strategies*: in the prompt, we have explicitly stated the strategies that can be utilized for gender-inclusive rewriting, which are described in the guidelines published by the Italian Ministry of University and Research [15];
2. *Provide concrete transformation examples*: we have included in the prompt concrete examples, demonstrating the transformation from non-inclusive to inclusive sentences;
3. *List target sentences*: we have enumerated within the prompt the sentences intended for rewriting, setting a clear task for the model.

After receiving the prompt, ChatGPT processes the provided guidelines and examples, contextualizing the desired output. It then generates a response that restructures the listed sentences in a gender-inclusive manner, adhering to the specified strategies. Below, considering the same non-inclusive sentence used in the case of mT5, its inclusive version obtained through the use of ChatGPT is as follows:

Nel caso in cui la temperatura corporea rilevata risulti > 37.5 C, lavoratrici, lavoratori e studentesse e studenti non possono accedere né permanere in Ateneo

As we can see, the result is similar with regard to the introduction of feminine terms in Italian; only some grammatical elements (in this case conjunctions) differ in forming the sentence.

---

[7] https://openai.com/index/gpt-4/.

4   Experimental Evaluation

This section is devoted to a discussion of the experimental evaluations carried out against the three proposed approaches. First, some technical details (i.e., employed tools, dataset split, considered hyper-parameters), and evaluation metrics are discussed; then, the results referring to each of the three approaches proposed in this paper are reported.

4.1   Technical Details

To develop and test the approaches presented, we used Python and related libraries. In particular, to perform POS tagging and to implement the morphologizer and the dependency parser we employed spaCy,[8] a publicly-available and well-known open-source Python library for performing Natural Language Processing tasks in several languages, Italian included.

For the mT5-based approach, we have assigned 70% of the examples to the training (i.e., 145 sentences), 20% of the examples to the validation (both used during the fine-tuning process) (i.e., 42 sentences), and 10% of the examples to the test sets (i.e., 20 sentences). In particular, for the fine-tuning process on training and validation data, in order to enable the mT5 model to rewrite sentences in a gender-inclusive manner, we have set to 10 the number of training epochs and the hyper-parameters as shown in Table 1.

Table 1. mT5 model hyperparameters.

Hyperparameter	Value
Maximum Sequence Length	256
Learning Rate	3e–4
Weight Decay	0.0
Adam Epsilon	1e–8
Train Batch Size	4
Eval Batch Size	4

To compare the performance of the mT5 model with the other neural approach, which relies on the formulation of a prompt to guide ChatGPT in the rewriting of sentences, we have listed within the prompt only the sentences in the test set.

4.2   Evaluation Metrics

We have used the BLEU metric [20] to assess quantitatively the quality of sentences rewritten by the rule-based, mT5-based, and ChatGPT-based approaches.

---

[8] https://spacy.io/.

This metric indicates the degree of similarity between the generated sentence and the reference sentence in the considered dataset. The scores produced by the BLEU metric range in the $[0-1]$ interval.

Since we have constructed the rule-based approach to perform the gender bias detection and correction tasks distinctly, to evaluate the effectiveness of the system in the gender bias detection task we have manually associated each sentence with the number of *potentially* non-inclusive words and the number of nouns *actually* used in a non-inclusive way within the sentence.[9] Then, only for this approach, we have also calculated the following evaluation metrics:

- *True Positive Rate* (TPR): it describes the percentage of nouns that are to be modified that the system correctly identifies;
- *True Negative Rate* (TNR): it represents the percentage of nouns that are not to be modified that the system correctly does not identify;
- *False Positive Rate* (FPR): it indicates the percentage of nouns that are not to be modified but that the system incorrectly identifies as generic masculine;
- *False Negative Rate* (FNR): it describes the percentage of nouns that are to be modified that the system fails to identify.

4.3   Rule-Based Approach Evaluation

The results of the evaluation of the effectiveness of the rule-based approach with respect to both TPR, TNR, FPR, and FNR metrics, and the BLEU metric, are shown in Table 2.

Table 2. Rule-based approach results.

TPR	TNR	FPR	FNR	BLEU
98.77%	96.96%	3.03%	1.22%	0.98

Concerning gender bias identification, the achieved TPR and TNR scores show that the rule-based approach is highly effective in correctly identifying nouns used with a generic masculine function. The obtained FPR score indicates that the approach occasionally misidentifies nouns that are already inclusive or neutral, assigning them a generic masculine function. In practice, this could lead to unnecessary modifications or alterations to terms that are already appropriate. The obtained FNR score suggests that there is a small fraction of nouns that should be modified to be more inclusive, but the system fails to identify them.

---

[9] Indeed, whether a term is considered inclusive or non-inclusive is not determined solely by the term itself, but rather by how it is used in a given context. For instance, the word "professore" is correctly used in reference to a male figure but it becomes non-inclusive if used to generalize an entire group of faculty members or to refer to a female professor (see Sect. 3.2 w.r.t. the second phase of the rule-based approach).

In essence, these are missed opportunities where the approach could have made a sentence more inclusive but overlooked the chance.

With respect to evaluating the task of generating corrections, the 0.98 BLEU metric score achieved by the rule-based approach suggests that the outputs are in strong alignment with the reference sentences.

4.4   mT5 Model and ChatGPT Evaluation and Comparison

The results regarding the ability to rewrite sentences in a gender-inclusive manner computed on the test set by mT5- and ChatGPT-based approaches are shown in Table 3, in terms of the BLEU metric.

Table 3. Neural approaches results.

Model	BLEU
mT5	0.795
ChatGPT	0.804

The mT5 model obtains a BLEU score of 0.795, which is quite high and suggests that the generated paraphrases are, on average, considerably aligned with reference sentences. We have also conducted a manual inspection and we noted that, if there is more than one noun used as a generic masculine in a sentence, the mT5-based approach struggles to detect them all.

On the same test set, the BLEU score for the ChatGPT-based approach is equal to 0.804, which is slightly higher than the score obtained with the mT5-based one. This high score indicates that the combination of ChatGPT's underlying capabilities and the structured prompt has effectively produced results that are both coherent and aligned with the gender-inclusive transformation guidelines.

By qualitatively examining (see Fig. 1) the gender-inclusive rewriting performed by ChatGPT on nine sentences (i.e., those having more than one noun used with a generic masculine function) it is evident that, in cases where multiple nouns have a generic use of the masculine form within a single sentence, ChatGPT demonstrates a greater ability to identify and address all of them, compared to the mT5 model.

An example of a sentence in which ChatGPT identifies all the nouns used with a generic masculine function is the following:

> *In caso il docente o uno studente in aula abbia necessità di bere, può abbassare la mascherina per il tempo necessario per bere, e successivamente indossarla nuovamente.*

i.e., "In case the teacher or a student in the classroom needs to drink, it is possible to lower the mask for the time needed to drink, and then put it

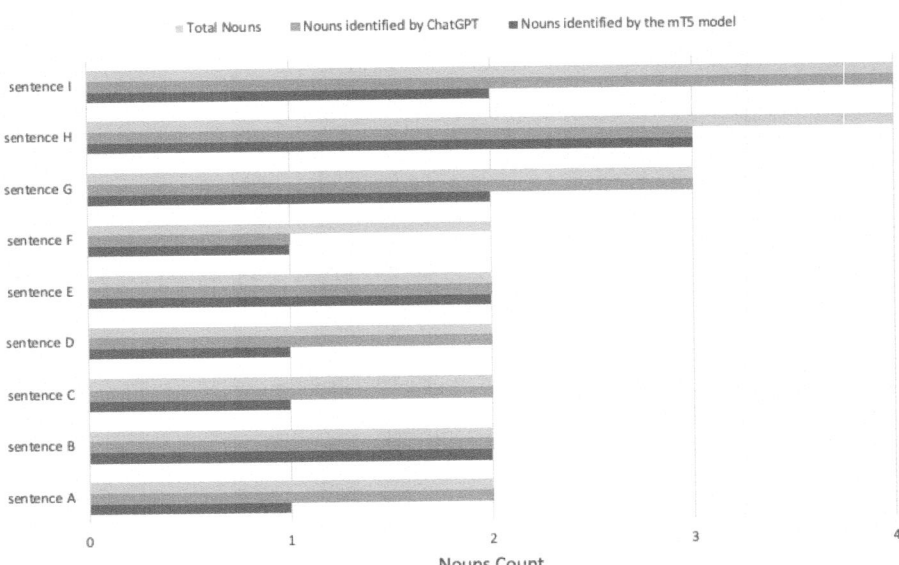

Fig. 1. Bar plot showing the number of nouns in the nine sentences considered for evaluation having multiple nouns used as a generic masculine. In the plot it is also shown the number of nouns identified by ChatGPT and mT5 models.

on again". In this case, the Italian masculine terms "docente" and "studente" are employed with a generic masculine function for teachers and students. mT5 rewrites the sentence as follows:

In caso la docente o il docente o uno studente in aula abbia necessità di bere, può abbassare la mascherina per il tempo necessario per bere, e successivamente indossarla nuovamente.

As can be seen, the model does not identify the noun "studente" as a noun to be made inclusive, so it corrects the sentence by adding only the feminine term for the noun "docente". Conversely, ChatGPT rewrites the same sentence as follows:

In caso la docente, il docente o una studentessa o uno studente in aula abbia necessità di bere, può abbassare la mascherina per il tempo necessario per bere, e successivamente indossarla nuovamente.

In this case, the ChatGPT-based approach correctly adds the feminine terms for both nouns.

5   Conclusion and Further Research

In this work, to automate the process of detecting non-inclusive language in Italian university administrative documents and provide gender-inclusive alternatives, we first created a dictionary of trigger words related to the potential presence of gender bias, and a dataset of non-inclusive Italian sentences paired with their corresponding gender-inclusive rewritten sentences. Then, we proposed three solutions, i.e., a rule-based and two neural approaches, utilizing both the mT5 model and ChatGPT. The performed evaluations show that the proposed solutions are highly effective on the task faced; the choice of the most suitable approach depends on the specific objectives, the available resources, and the depth of control and interpretability required.

As part of our future work, we intend to improve the rule-based approach to the sentence rewriting task by integrating a database for Italian verb inflection forms, so that the system will be able to rewrite sentences in an extended form and no longer in an abbreviated form. In addition, we also plan to use the rule-based rewriter to generate a parallel gendered-to-neutral corpus that can be employed to train a neural model. We also intend to extend the work by conducting more in-depth analyses of the effectiveness of prompt engineering techniques applied to Large Language Models. The question also remains open as to what is the best strategy to reformulate a text in a fully inclusive manner, but this is not only a technical but a linguistic issue.

Acknowledgments. This work is the result of an interdisciplinary project by the University of Milano-Bicocca to align all its administrative documents with the Italian Ministry of University and Research guidelines. The project involved the collaboration of the Department of Informatics, Systems and Communication, the Department of Sociology and Social Research, the School of Law and the administrative staff of the Welfare Sector of the University of Milan-Bicocca.

Linguistic Resources. The linguistic resources used in this article are publicly accessible at the following link: https://github.com/ikr3-lab/ita-gender-inclusivity-tools. At the same link, the code used to develop the approaches and train the models, prompts used with the GPT-4 model, model results, and other techical details can also be found.

Ethics and Impact. The pursuit of gender inclusivity is a critical ethical issue in contemporary society, especially within academic institutions, where language can significantly shape perceptions and reinforce societal biases. The focus of this work relies on automating the detection and subsequent correction of non-inclusive language in administrative documents of Italian universities; hence, it represents an important step toward fostering an inclusive and equitable academic environment.

References

1. Bahman, M., Rahimi, A.: Gender representation in EFL materials: an analysis of English textbooks of Iranian high schools. Procedia. Soc. Behav. Sci. **9**, 273–277 (2010)
2. Bamberger, E.T., Farrow, A.: Language for sex and gender inclusiveness in writing. J. Hum. Lact. **37**(2), 251–259 (2021)
3. Bolukbasi, T., Chang, K.W., Zou, J., Saligrama, V., Kalai, A.: Quantifying and reducing stereotypes in word embeddings. arXiv preprint arXiv:1606.06121 (2016)
4. Bro, R., Smilde, A.K.: Principal component analysis. Anal. Methods **6**(9), 2812–2831 (2014)
5. Carl, M., Garnier, S., Haller, J., Altmayer, A., Miemietz, B.: Controlling gender equality with shallow NLP techniques. In: COLING 2004: Proceedings of the 20th International Conference on Computational Linguistics, pp. 820–826 (2004)
6. Cer, D., Diab, M., Agirre, E., Lopez-Gazpio, I., Specia, L.: SemEval-2017 task 1: semantic textual similarity multilingual and crosslingual focused evaluation. In: Proceedings of the 11th International Workshop on Semantic Evaluation (SemEval-2017), pp. 1–14. Association for Computational Linguistics, Vancouver, Canada, August 2017
7. De Benedetti, A.: Cosí non schwa: limiti ed eccessi del linguaggio inclusivo. Giulio Einaudi editore (2022)
8. Diesner-Mayer, T., Seidel, N.: Supporting gender-neutral writing in German. In: Proceedings of Mensch und Computer 2022, pp. 509–512 (2022)
9. Downes, W.: Language and Society, vol. 10. Cambridge University Press, Cambridge (1998)
10. Gheno, V., et al.: Lo schwa tra fantasia e norma. come superare il maschile sovraesteso Nella lingua Italiana (2020)
11. Giorcelli, S., Spanò, M., Raus, R., Abouyaala, M., Catrano, I., Patti, V.: Un approccio di genere al linguaggio administrative (A gender approach to administrative language). Università degli Studi di Torino, Technical Report (2015)
12. Kotek, H., Dockum, R., Sun, D.: Gender bias and stereotypes in large language models. In: Proceedings of The ACM Collective Intelligence Conference, pp. 12–24 (2023)
13. Ma, X., Sap, M., Rashkin, H., Choi, Y.: Powertransformer: unsupervised controllable revision for biased language correction. arXiv preprint arXiv:2010.13816 (2020)
14. Marazzini, C.: L'Accademia della Crusca e il linguaggio di genere. In: La lingua italiana in una prospettiva di genere. Firenze University Press, Florence (2023)
15. MIUR: Linee guida per l'uso del genere nel linguaggio amministrativo del MIUR (Guidelines for the use of gender in the administrative language of the MIUR). Technical Report, Ministero dell'Istruzione, dell'Università e della Ricerca (2018)
16. Montgomery, M.: An Introduction to Language and Society. Routledge, London (2008)
17. Moore, D.S.: Chi-square tests. Stud. Stat. **19**, 453–63 (1978)
18. OpenAI: Gpt-4 technical report. arXiv:2303.08774 (2023)
19. Orgeira-Crespo, P., Míguez-Álvarez, C., Cuevas-Alonso, M., Doval-Ruiz, M.I.: Decision algorithm for the automatic determination of the use of non-inclusive terms in academic texts. Publications **8**(3), 41 (2020)
20. Reiter, E.: A structured review of the validity of bleu. Comput. Linguist. **44**(3), 393–401 (2018)

21. Sap, M., Prasettio, M.C., Holtzman, A., Rashkin, H., Choi, Y.: Connotation frames of power and agency in modern films. In: Proceedings of the 2017 Conference on Empirical Methods in Natural Language Processing, pp. 2329–2334 (2017)
22. Scherrer, Y.: TaPaCo: a corpus of sentential paraphrases for 73 languages. In: Proceedings of the Twelfth Language Resources and Evaluation Conference. pp. 6868–6873. European Language Resources Association, Marseille, France, May 2020. https://aclanthology.org/2020.lrec-1.848
23. Shazu, R.I.: Relationship between gender and language. J. Educ. Pract. **5**(14), 93–100 (2014)
24. Sun, T., Webster, K., Shah, A., Wang, W.Y., Johnson, M.: They, them, theirs: rewriting with gender-neutral English. arXiv preprint arXiv:2102.06788 (2021)
25. Tokpo, E.K., Calders, T.: Text style transfer for bias mitigation using masked language modeling. arXiv preprint arXiv:2201.08643 (2022)
26. UNIFE: Prontuario dell'Università degli Studi di Ferrara per l'uso del genere nel linguaggio amministrativo e per la redazione di documenti accessibili (Handbook of the University of Ferrara for the use of gender in administrative language and for the drafting of accessible documents). Tech. rep., Università degli studi di Ferrara (2018)
27. UNIPD: Generi e linguaggi - Linee guida per un linguaggio amministrativo e istituzionale attento alle differenze di genere (Genders and languages - Guidelines for an administrative and institutional language attentive to gender differences). Technical Report, Università degli Studi di Padova (2018)
28. Urchs, S., Thurner, V., Aßenmacher, M., Heumann, C., Thiemichen, S.: How prevalent is gender bias in chatgpt?–exploring german and english chatgpt responses. arXiv preprint arXiv:2310.03031 (2023)
29. Vanmassenhove, E., Emmery, C., Shterionov, D.: Neutral rewriter: a rule-based and neural approach to automatic rewriting into gender-neutral alternatives. arXiv preprint arXiv:2109.06105 (2021)
30. Xue, L., et al.: mt5: a massively multilingual pre-trained text-to-text transformer. arXiv preprint arXiv:2010.11934 (2020)

Relation Extraction Techniques in Cyber Threat Intelligence

Dincy R. Arikkat[1], P. Vinod[1,2]([✉]), Rafidha Rehiman K. A.[1],
Serena Nicolazzo[3], Antonino Nocera[4], and Mauro Conti[2]

[1] Department of Computer Applications, Cochin University of Science
and Technology, Kochi, India
{dincyrarikkat,rafidharehimanka}@cusat.ac.in
[2] Department of Mathematics, University of Padua, Padua, Italy
vinod.p@cusat.ac.in, {vinod.puthuvath,mauro.conti}@unipd.it
[3] Department of Computer Science, University of Milan, Milan, Italy
serena.nicolazzo@unimi.it
[4] Department of Electrical, Computer and Biomedical Engineering,
University of Pavia, Pavia, Italy
antonino.nocera@unipv.it

Abstract. Cyber Threat Intelligence (CTI) provides a structured and interconnected model for threat information through Cybersecurity Knowledge Graphs. This allows researchers and practitioners to represent and organize complex relationships and entities in a more coherent form. Above all, the discovery of hidden relationships between different CTI entities, such as threat actors, malware, infrastructure, and attacks, is becoming a crucial task in this domain, facilitating proactive defense measures and helping to identify Tactics, Techniques, and Procedures (TTPs) employed by malicious parties. In this paper, we provide a Systematization of Knowledge (SoK) to analyze the existing literature and give insights into the important CTI task of Relation Extraction. In particular, we design a categorization of the relations used in CTI; we analyze the techniques employed for their extraction, the emerging trends and open issues in this context, and the main future directions. This work provides a novel and fresh perspective that can help the reader understand how relationships among entities can be schematized to provide a better view of the cyber threat landscape.

Keywords: Relation Extraction · Large Language Model · Dependancy Parsing · Cyber Threat Intelligence · Entities

1 Introduction

Nowadays, information on vulnerabilities, threats, attacks, logs, or patches is often published in obscure text sources, such as forums or mailing lists, or in Online Social Networks, sometimes months before the inclusion in official

A. Rapp et al. (Eds.): NLDB 2024, LNCS 14762, pp. 348–363, 2024.
https://doi.org/10.1007/978-3-031-70239-6_24

cybersecurity databases such as the Common Vulnerability Exposure (CVE)[1] or National Vulnerability Database (NVD)[2] [3]. This information, known as Cyber Threat Intelligence (CTI) reports, is written in natural language (not structured for automatic analysis) by security practitioners or by the attackers, based on their observations of the attack scenarios. The knowledge extracted from these reports has gained wider importance since it can be used to prevent and defend against cyberattacks [32].

To manage and exchange such a high volume of unstructured data across organizations, recently, researchers have begun to construct knowledge-enhanced cybersecurity graphs to automatically organize CTI reports and provide a more comprehensive view of the attacks for the integration, unification, analytics, and sharing of these sources [26]. A Cybersecurity Knowledge Graph (CKG) represents a collection of descriptions of subjects and objects linked together through predicates. It can store massive network security knowledge, information, and data to support security practices in highly dynamic environments [18,52]. Subjects and objects are encoded by the nodes of the graphs and may symbolize entities such as Software, Exploit-Target, Malware, Indicators, Vulnerability, Tools, Attack-Pattern, Hash, IP Addresses, etc. Whereas, based on the values of these nodes, the edges of the graph can represent relations between cyber entities. For instance, the relation between cyber-attacks and the specific techniques or tactics used, a relation linking together the software and its version, or relations between malware and their known families or variants.

Therefore, the extraction of entities and relations represents a crucial step in the construction of a CKG and can be accomplished through Named Entity Recognition (NER) to extract main subjects and, subsequently, inferring relationships between them using a *pipeline approaches*, or *joint-entity relation approach*. The knowledge of the different available techniques to extract such information is also important for CTI analysts, who want to gain deeper insights into the structure, dynamics, and evolution of cyber threats, enabling more effective threat detection, analysis, and mitigation strategies. For this reason, our paper aims to assist security researchers in exploring the existing literature, categorizing scientific works, and providing novel insights related to automated RE techniques in the context of CTI. In this work, we carried out a comprehensive search for peer-reviewed publications related to the topics mentioned above, considering high-quality journal and conference papers published from 2019 to 2024 in Google Scholar, Web of Science, ACM Digital Library, Scopus, and IEEE Xplore (we included only Q1 and Q2 journals and A*, A, B, and C-ranked conferences[3]).

Previous systematic reviews and surveys dealt with the general Information Extraction (IE) techniques for CTI, also marginally surveying RE techniques but only as a step for the construction of a CKG [3,32,39,52] and, therefore,

---

[1] https://cve.mitre.org.

[2] https://nvd.nist.gov.

[3] The paper's publication venue significance is assessed using Scimago and Core.edu rankings for journals and conferences, respectively.

they are limited to a brief overview of the main techniques used for this task. However, accurately interpreting the complex logic in technical reports and short texts represented by the relations between objects [5] is still an open problem in Natural Language Processing (NLP) and is more complex than recognizing entities and topics in a sentence [4,31,36]. Hence, to the best of our knowledge, the perspective of our paper, which focuses only on RE techniques for CTI, is less concentrated by the research community and encourages more researchers in the domain.

Our contribution is, hence, three-fold:

- We describe the possible types of relations existing in CKG.
- We comprehensively evaluated the Relation Extraction techniques in the CTI domain. In particular, we provide a detailed picture of the main papers dealing with dependency-parsing, supervised learning, unsupervised learning approaches, and Large Language Models (LLM).
- We exhaustively examine the challenges and future direction of RE techniques in threat intelligence, including managing unstructured data, model accuracy, and process integration.

The outline of this paper is as follows. Section 2 overviews the types of existing relations in the context of CTI. The analysis of the techniques for RE is presented in Sect. 3. In Sect. 4, we discuss how RE and LLMs can enhance threat modeling. Section 5 is devoted to explaining open challenges and insights for future research. Finally, Sect. 6 concludes the paper.

2   Types of Relations in CTI

Relation Extraction in CTI involves identifying and extracting relationships between different entities from unstructured data sources via automatic tools. Relations can be modeled through the edges of a CKG and connect nodes representing malware, vulnerabilities, attackers, etc., in CTI. This representation can aid researchers in uncovering hidden connections and identifying patterns inside cyberattacks. In the following, we describe all the relation types that can be found in the literature altogether with the approaches leveraging them.

- **Generic dependency relation.** This type of relation formalizes a dependency between two attack-relevant entities [20,37].
- **Log-Entity relation.** This links entities such as processes, files, or sockets to low-level system calls of an operative system [36].
- **Actor-Target relation.** This type of relation links together threat actors (individuals, groups, or organizations) with the executed malware and their targets (i.e., the victims and the assets) [23].
- **IoC-Entity relation.** This relation involves the identification of Indicators of Compromises (IoCs), and it links them to specific cyber entities, such as actors or cyber attack campaign stages [21].

– **TTP-Entity relation.** This deals with the relationship linking Tactics, Techniques, and Procedures (TTPs) with some entities. For instance, [16] extracts the information of TTP and the threat actors who leveraged them. Whereas the proposal [17] describes an approach to linking high-level semantic TTPs with low-level API calls for a malware sample.

– **Vulnerability-Entity relation.** This stands between information about the vulnerability of a software product (i.e., identifier, threat type, and threat level) and other entities. For instance, in [8], the authors consider software product information (such as vendor and version) and the related vulnerabilities. Whereas the authors of [43] extract vulnerability information and its trigger, that is what caused the vulnerability in the first place. Similarly, the papers [45, 46] link vulnerabilities with information such as attack vector, root cause, impact, and possible countermeasures.

Table 1 summarizes the main typologies of relation that can be extracted in the context of CTI and indicates the reference papers.

Table 1. The main typologies of relation in the context of CTI

Reference	Relation	First Entity	Second Entity
[20, 37]	Generic	CTI Entity	CTI Entity
[36]	Log-Entity	System calls	Processes, Files, Sockets
[23]	Actor-Target	Attackers	Victims, target assets
[21]	IoC-Entity	Indicators Of Compromise	Cyber attack campaign stages
[16, 17]	TTP-Entity	Tactics, Techniques, Procedures	Actors, API calls
[8, 43, 45, 46]	Vulnerability-Entity	Vulnerability ID, threat type, threat level	Software product, vendor, version, triggers, attack vector, impact.

3   Techniques for Relation Extraction

Current research works employed different methods to extract relationships from unstructured text and formulate relevant structured documents for IE. The following section explains the various techniques available in the state of the art for RE in the cyber security domain.

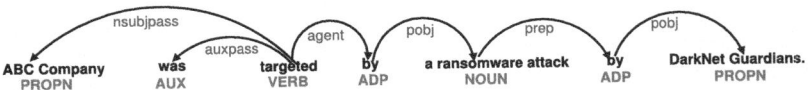

Fig. 1. Dependency parse showing the relationship between "ABC Company" being targeted by a ransomware attack by "DarkNet Guardians". Curved arrows illustrate the syntactic connections between words in the sentence.

3.1 Dependency-Parsing

Rule-based RE entails establishing rules or patterns that discern the syntactic or semantic structures for identifying relationships among entities within the text. These rules utilize linguistic attributes such as part-of-speech tags, dependency parse trees, and keywords to identify relevant entity pairs and describe their relationships. Rules are formulated through expert domain knowledge and insights from linguistic analysis. Dependency Parsing (DP) analyzes the grammatical structure of a sentence and identifies the relationships between words within the sentence. During this process, a dependency parser algorithm determines which words are connected and the type of relationship between them (such as subject, object, modifier, etc.). These word connections can be illustrated as a dependency parse tree, in which every word is a node, and the relationship between words is directed edge between them. Typically, the root of the tree denotes the primary verb or principal clause of the sentence, with other words tethered to it according to their syntactic relations. Figure 1 depicts the dependency parse of the sentence "ABC Company was targeted by a ransomware attack by DarkNet Guardians" generated by SpaCy[4]. Each word in the sentence is represented as a node, and the arrows between the nodes indicate the grammatical relationships between them. In this parse, "ABC Company" is the subject of the passive verb "targeted," which is connected to "DarkNet Guardians" through the preposition "by," indicating the agent of the action. The term "a ransomware attack" is the direct object of the verb "targeted". Dependency parse trees serve multiple purposes, including the identification of cyber event arguments and their attributes [37], extracting the attack behaviour [36], analysis of adversary tactics and techniques [16] in the cyber security domain. In [51], Zhang et al. employed a mix of multimodal learning and rule-based matching to extract threat actions from CTI reports. They represent each threat action as *subject, object, verb* format determined through syntactic rule matching, where entities are the subjects and objects, and the verb represents the semantic relationship between them.

ThreatRaptor [12] employs dependency parsing to extract IoCs and their relationships with coreference resolution from Open Source Threat Intelligence text. Coreference resolution is the process of identifying and linking different references that pertain to the same entity or concept within a given text. For instance, in the sentence *"Darkhotel attacked XYZ company. The threat group*

---

4 https://demos.explosion.ai/displacy.

conducted spearphishing campaigns". "Darkhotel" is a specific threat group, and "threat group" refers to the same entity as "Darkhotel". Initially, articles are segmented into blocks for IoC extraction, where IoCs are recognized using regular expression rules. Then, dependency trees are constructed for each sentence, with relevant nodes annotated for coreference resolution and RE. Subsequently, coreference nodes are resolved within blocks, and similar IoCs across blocks are merged. Lastly, relations between IoCs are extracted by analyzing pairs of IoC nodes within dependency trees to determine their subject-object relations based on dependency types. This includes examining dependency paths from the root to the Lowest Common Ancestor and applying predefined rules. Relation verbs are then extracted by scanning annotated candidate verbs, selecting the closest one to the object IoC node. This process results in the formation of IoC entity-relation triplets.

In [10], Fan et al. utilized part-of-speech tagging and dependency parsing to convert semantic content into actionable behaviors for malware detection and family classification tasks. Their methodology encompasses several steps: initially extracting sentences from technical blogs, followed by part-of-speech tagging to identify grammatical structures, emphasizing verb-object relationships using tools like the Stanford typed Dependency Parser [38]. They focus on relevant rules like dobj (direct object) and nsubjpass (passive subject) to extract information about the activities of the malware. The extracted verb-object pairs are expanded to include corresponding noun phrases and undergo word stemming to handle variant forms. Then, semantic grouping is implemented to address verbs with similar meanings, ensuring coherence and minimizing repetition. Subsequently, behaviors are clustered, and frequently occurring behaviors closely associated with the Android system are identified as sensitive behaviors. These sensitive behaviors serve as feature space, and matching rules are devised to create feature vectors for individual Apps. Finally, various Machine Learning algorithms are employed for malware detection and feature classification tasks. Table 2 summarizes the research work that employed dependency parsing for cyber security tasks.

Table 2. Research works used dependency parsing for different relation extraction tasks

Reference	Key Contribution
[37]	Identified cyber event arguments and their attributes
[36]	Extracted the attack behaviour
[36]	Analyzed adversary tactics and techniques
[51]	Extracted threat actions from CTI reports
[12]	Extracted threat behaviours (IoCs and their relationships)
[38]	Malware detection and family classification

As the complexity of the sentence increases, DP might encounter challenges in precisely identifying tags and word relationships [36]. Mistakes like mislabeling past participles as adjectives or misidentifying verbs as nouns may arise if the DP tagger lacks exposure to technical language contexts. However, DP tags solely capture grammatical relations like subject and object, thereby restricting their usefulness for tasks demanding a deeper semantic comprehension of sentence components, such as temporality and modality.

3.2 Supervised Learning

In recent years, RE has advanced significantly through the implementation of supervised learning approaches. This task can be likened to a *binary* or *n-ary* classification problem. In binary RE, the objective is to ascertain the presence or absence of a relation between two entities mentioned in a sentence or text segment. Conversely, n-ary RE involves identifying and categorizing the specific relationship between a pair of entities within a given context. Binary RE typically serves as a preliminary step to the more intricate n-ary RE tasks, providing a foundational assessment of relation existence before delving into the nuances of those relationships. These relationship extractions can be performed in two ways [13]: the *Pipeline Approach*, which involves initially extracting entities followed by using Machine Learning (ML) or Deep Learning (DL) algorithms to discern relationships between them; and the *Joint-Entity Relation Model*, which learns entities and relationships concurrently to capture associations in a more suitable manner, which reduces the extraction errors on relationship accuracy. The cornerstone of supervised learning lies in the availability of labeled data, where these labels signify the various relation types. To define the relationship labels for relation extraction task, researchers [13,14,30] frequently utilize predefined relationships outlined in UCO 2.0 [40], which are derived from the STIX 2.0[5] definitions.

Neural Network Approaches: In the exploration of neural network-based relationships, several classifiers such as Convolutional Neural Networks (CNN) [49], Recurrent Neural Networks (RNNs) [50], and Attention Bidirectional Long Short-Term Memory (BiLSTM) [53] have been explored. For instance, RelExt [30] initially employs a Named Entity Recognizer (NER) model to extract cybersecurity entities, which are then paired and fed into the relation extraction model. This model utilizes vector embeddings generated by Word2Vec [7] and a Feed-Forward Neural Network (FFNN) classifier to predict relationships between the entities based on a predetermined set of candidate relationships. While Wang et al. [42] developed a unified learning framework that merges relation extraction and coreference resolution through Graph Convolutional Networks (GCN). Their research introduced the SDP-VP-SET pruning technique, which preserves the shortest dependent path and its K-hop nodes while giving greater weight to edges linked to verb nodes, thereby improving

---

[5] https://docs.oasis-open.org/cti/stix/v2.0/stix-v2.0-part1-stix-core.html.

the efficiency of RE across sentences. Additionally, they utilized Stanford Core NLP for dependency analysis to establish connections between sentences, constructing a dependency tree for the sentence set. CyEvent2vec [23], developed by Ma et al., predicted attack events using a Heterogeneous Information Network (HIN). It constructs event matrices to represent events and their attributes, with matrix elements denoting event-object relationships. The autoencoder are utilized to learn complex relationships among the objects and produced low-dimensional embeddings. The autoencoder comprises multiple sub-encoders, generating embeddings for specific objects or attributes. Finally, the embeddings from the sub-autoencoder's hidden layers are combined to map event matrices into the embedding space.

Transformer-Based Approaches: In 2019, significant progress was made in the NLP domain with the emergence of advanced preprocessing models, particularly through the introduction of BERT, Generative Pre-Training (GPT), and ELMo. In the studies [21,54], researchers employed the transformer-based BERT model to generate a RE model. CDTier [54] investigated threat intelligence entity relationships on Chinese data. They integrated neural network-based models, including CNN, RNN, and GCN, initially employing word embeddings. Also, the authors used the transformer-based model, BERT, which achieved the highest performance in their study. Liu et al. [21] also utilized BERT to identify the relationship between IoCs and different campaign phases. They employed regular expressions and fine-tuned BERT model to detect IoCs, including IP addresses, domain names, URLs, hashes, email addresses, and CVEs. Subsequently, they identified campaign trigger phrases within sentences to precisely determine particular campaign stages. CyberRel [13] utilized an end-to-end multiple sequence labeling model, incorporating a joint entity and RE approach. It employed pre-trained BERT for word embeddings and BiGRU with an attention mechanism for extracting semantic features while combining BiGRU with CRF to decode and construct cybersecurity triples. Guo et al. [14] developed a joint entity and RE model for cybersecurity data, employing a tagging scheme to transform the extraction process into a multi-sequence labeling challenge. The model utilizes BERT, BiGRU neural networks, and attention mechanisms for feature extraction. Also, they employed a Levenshtein distance for knowledge fusion, particularly useful for reconciling entities referring to the same object across diverse data sources. Similarly, Ahmed et al. [2] utilized a joint RE technique, employing sequential tagging with the attention-based RoBERTa-BiGRU-CRF model. Subsequently, relation triples were extracted using a relation-matching technique, identifying the most suitable relation for the two predicted entities.

Table 3 summarizes recent state-of-the-art supervised learning methods for cyber security relationship extraction, detailing employed techniques, performance metrics, classifiers used, and the number of relation labels and instances.

Table 3. Supervised approaches used in cyber security relationship extraction

Reference	Extraction Approach	#Relation	Samples	Classifier	Performance
[30]	Pipeline	6	33,000	Word2Vec + FFNN	Accuracy - 96.21%
[42]	Joint-Extraction	9	47,517	TIRECO	F1-score - 98.12%
[13]	Joint-Extraction	6	75,990	BERT + BiGRU + CRF	F1-score - 80.98%
[54]	Pipeline	11	2,562	BERT	Accuracy - 89.40%
[21]	Pipeline	7	3,462	TriCTI(BERT)	F1-score - 87.02%
[14]	Joint-Extraction	6	67,918	BERT + BiGRU + CRF	F1-score - 81.37%
[2]	Joint-Extraction	11	1,286	RoBERTa + BiGRU + CRF	F1-score - 83.2%

3.3 Unsupervised Learning

Many efforts have been devoted to relation extraction through supervised learning; however, this approach necessitates labeled data, which can be scarce and expensive. Hence, there is a growing need for unsupervised methods that can extract relations without relying on annotated data, offering scalability and adaptability to diverse domains. The unsupervised methods have not received as much research attention in cyber security relation extraction as other methods, such as supervised learning, but recent studies [45, 46] applied unsupervised techniques to the task of labeling and extracting critical vulnerability concepts from textual vulnerability descriptions. The authors of [45, 46] leveraged syntactic similarities observed in sentence parsing trees and utilized a source-target neural architecture to learn Part-of-Speech tagging. They also introduced two path representations (absolute paths and relative paths) encoded using a Categorical Variational Auto-encoder (CaVAE) and employed unsupervised clustering techniques to generate clusters of similar vulnerability concepts. Their evaluation confirms the effectiveness of the approach, with the resulting clusters accurately labeling vulnerability concepts and outperforming manually labeled datasets. However, more research works are required to explore unsupervised learning techniques for CTI relation extraction. Table 4 summarizes the works on cyber security phrase identification using unsupervised methods.

4 Enhancing Threat Modeling Using LLMs

As cyber threats evolve, security professionals harness cutting-edge technologies like LLMs to enhance their defenses. LLMs can aid in crafting security policies [24], generating automated threat reports [29], and informing the implementation of technological solutions. Ultimately, these capabilities seek to strengthen an organization's overall security posture. This section explores the potential of

Table 4. Unsupervised approaches for cyber security entity and relation identification

Reference	Technique	Remark
[45]	Categorical Variational Autoencoder and clustering	Identified 3 vulnerability phrases
[46]	Categorical Variational Autoencoder and clustering	Extracted 6 vulnerability concepts

LLMs in cybersecurity, focusing on two key areas: threat detection and incident response.

Detection: The Detect function is responsible for finding cybersecurity incidents. LLMs can serve as a service to enhance organizations' overall readiness to defend against evolving cyber threats. This could involve utilizing LLM to: (a) minimize code errors, (b) enhance cybersecurity awareness among the cyber workforce through LLM-based training, (c) automatically address vulnerabilities in applications, and so forth. CyBERT [33] is a specialized BERT model tailored for cybersecurity. It is trained on a vast corpus of open-source, unstructured, and semi-structured CTI text data. CyBERT leverages Masked Language Modeling (MLM) to fine-tune a base BERT model for recognizing specialized cybersecurity entities. SecureBERT [1], a cybersecurity language model trained on a massive dataset of text sources (news, reports, articles, etc.), tackles various cybersecurity tasks. It understands the meaning of words and sentences (semantics) on both individual and overall levels. To handle cybersecurity-specific terms, the authors developed a custom tokenization method. This allows SecureBERT to effectively process both general English and cybersecurity inputs. SecureBERT has demonstrated its efficacy across three distinct tasks: standard MLM, sentiment analysis, and NER. The authors in [41] employ LLMs for web content filtering. Their proposed teacher-student training approach effectively transfers knowledge from a powerful LLM to a more compact student model. This student model retains high accuracy despite its reduced size, making it ideal for scenarios with large data volumes and limited computing resources. A study [47] suggests using LLM to create "honeywords" - fake passwords used to defend against attackers who use fake, computer-generated passwords. They developed Chunk-GPT3, which breaks passwords into meaningful parts and then uses GPT3 to make realistic honeywords. The study shows that honeywords made with Chunk-GPT3 are much more challenging for attackers to crack, possibly making it tougher for them to carry out targeted attacks. Due to the potential for substantial financial losses resulting from bugs in smart contracts managing cryptocurrencies on blockchains, PSCVFinder [48] offers a solution. It employs a pre-trained model to comprehend programming languages and employs prompt-tuning within an LLM to identify two crucial vulnerabilities: reentrancy and timestamp dependency. The existing methods work well with plain text code, but they miss important details because they can't understand the code's structure and meaning. GRACE [22] solves this problem by incorporating information about how the code is structured (graph structural information) and how it's used in context (in-context learning) into the vulnerability detection process. The paper [15] investigates using LLMs like GPT3.5 to aid penetration testers. It explores high-level task planning and low-level vulnerability hunting, implementing a closed-feedback loop for vulnerability analysis and automated attack suggestions and execution. To safeguard personal privacy and network integrity, detecting cyber attacks on IoT devices is essential to prevent unauthorized access, data breaches, and potential disruptions to critical systems. SecurityBERT [11] leverages the BERT model to detect cyber threats within IoT networks. It employs a privacy-preserving encoding technique alongside the Byte-level Byte-Pair Encoder (BBPE) tokenizer to transform network traffic data into a structured format while safeguarding the confidentiality of extracted network information.

Respond: The Respond function is responsible for determining how to respond to the identified security incident. The research [28] investigates how well LLMs designed for code can fix software vulnerabilities without in zero-shot setting. They reported even generic, off-the-shelf LLMs were able to suggest repairs for security bugs when given clear instructions, including both synthetic and manually crafted scenarios. In [25], the authors propose a novel approach to protect IoT devices from cyberattacks using a honeypot system. The system trains the BERT model on past attacker interactions stored in a database of requests and responses. This training allows the model to predict the most likely next move an attacker might make using Markov Decision Process to keep the attacker engaged. If the attacker believes the honeypot is a legitimate target, they continue the interaction, potentially revealing their malicious payload.

5   Challenges and Open Points

Extracting relations from Cyber Threat Intelligence (CTI) sources is not straightforward and presents peculiar challenges beyond those related to general RE tasks. In the following, we discuss the most important open issues that researchers and cybersecurity professionals have to face in the context of RE for CTI.

- **Noisy and unstructured data.** CTI reports' consist of syntactically and semantically complex text, with a preponderance of technical terms, and a lack of proper punctuations. Moreover, unstructured text sources lack standardization and imply the need for natural language understanding. This can impact the interpretation and extraction of attack information [27].
- **Complex and ambiguous logic.** Accurately interpreting the complex logic in CTI reports is a crucial aspect and an open point in this context. Not all entities always hold a relation. Moreover, understanding the overall perspective while maintaining concise causal, temporal, and information flow of the attack throughout the report is far more challenging [36].

- **Data Quality.** CTI data may contain inaccuracies and misinformation, which can affect relation extraction results. Improving the accuracy and trustworthiness of CTI sources against possible attacks and deliberate misinformation is an open point that needs further investigation [34].
- **Multilingual data source.** Since CTI sources may be available in multiple languages, RE solutions should handle multilingual data and cross-lingual relations. Even if possible, existing approaches filter out non-English data or make an automatic English translation to leverage monolingual models and overcome this issue; this point remains an active area for open research [9].
- **Data Privacy.** Organizations may be reluctant to share information about weaknesses and details about cyberattacks due to concerns about potential reputational damage resulting from the disclosure. Since CTI often includes sensitive information, guaranteeing the actors' data privacy while extracting relations from CTI sources is essential. Possible solutions can be represented by the use of technologies such as Blockchain and Federated Learning [19,35].
- **Domain-specific Knowledge:** LLMs may lack domain-specific knowledge [44] required for accurate threat analysis, such as understanding cybersecurity terminology, context, and nuances. Addressing this challenge involves incorporating domain knowledge into the model training process and fine-tuning models on relevant threat intelligence data.
- **Interpretability:** As popularity surges for LLMs, poor interpretability [6] due to the black-box nature of LLMs, hinders the ability to interpret their decisions and understand the reasoning behind threat intelligence predictions, necessitates the development of techniques for model interpretability and explainability. This is crucial for building trust and confidence in LLM-based threat intelligence systems.

6   Conclusion

Due to the wide attack surface and the constant evolution of the threat landscape, organizations need to respond to possible attacks in a proactive way. In this context, CTI plays an increasingly vital role in predicting, preventing, and defending against cyberattacks, with the effectiveness hinging on accurate, relevant information extraction and valid techniques. Recent exploitation of CKGs aids in clear representation, and RE helps identify meaningful connections in unstructured online data, ultimately empowering cybersecurity professionals to defend against evolving threats proactively. This paper aimed to provide a comprehensive analysis of the recent techniques employed for the extraction of relations from disparate CTI data sources, also focusing on the possible types of these relations and how they can enhance threat modeling. In summary, we analyzed 31 articles mainly focused on RE types, techniques, and threat modeling, and the remaining articles were used to build the content of the paper. We hope this research can help scholars and practitioners better understand the critical aspects of this field, catching significant advancements and shedding light on forthcoming research. We intend to continue our investigation by deep-diving into other critical aspects mentioned in the present paper. For instance, an interesting direction can be the analysis and comparison of existing industrial platforms and software solutions for RE in CTI, to give the reader a more extensive view of the current advancement and limitations in this field.

Acknowledgments.

This work was supported by HORIZON Europe Framework Programme partly supported this work through the project "OPTIMA - Organization sPecific Threat Intelligence Mining and sharing" (101063107), and PRIN 2022 Project "HOMEY: a Human-centric IoE-based Framework for Supporting the Transition Towards Industry 5.0" (code: 2022NX7WKE, CUP: F53D23004340006) funded by the European Union - Next Generation EU, and SERICS (PE00000014) project under the NRRP MUR program funded by the EU - NGEU. Views and opinions expressed are however those of the authors only and do not necessarily reflect those of the European Union or the Italian MUR. Neither the European Union nor the Italian MUR can be held responsible for them.

References

1. Aghaei, E., Niu, X., Shadid, W., Al-Shaer, E.: SecureBERT: a domain-specific language model for cybersecurity. In: Security and Privacy in Communication Networks: 18th EAI International Conference, SecureComm 2022, Virtual Event, October 2022, Proceedings, pp. 39–56. Springer (2023). https://doi.org/10.1007/978-3-031-25538-0_3
2. Ahmed, K., Khurshid, S.K., Hina, S.: CyberEntRel: joint extraction of cyber entities and relations using deep learning. Comput. Secur. **136**, 103579 (2024)
3. Arazzi, M., Arikkat, D.R., Nicolazzo, S., Nocera, A., Conti, M., et al.: NLP-based techniques for cyber threat intelligence. arXiv preprint arXiv:2311.08807 (2023)
4. Arazzi, M., Nicolazzo, S., Nocera, A., Zippo, M.: The importance of the language for the evolution of online communities: an analysis based on twitter and reddit. Expert Syst. Appl. **222**, 119847 (2023)
5. Buccafurri, F., Lax, G., Nicolazzo, S., Nocera, A., Ursino, D.: Measuring betweenness centrality in social internetworking scenarios. In: Demey, Y.T., Panetto, H. (eds.) OTM 2013. LNCS, vol. 8186, pp. 666–673. Springer, Heidelberg (2013). https://doi.org/10.1007/978-3-642-41033-8_84
6. Chang, Y., et al.: A survey on evaluation of large language models. ACM Trans. Intell. Syst. Technol. (2023)
7. Church, K.W.: Word2vec. Nat. Lang. Eng. **23**(1), 155–162 (2017)
8. Dong, Y., Guo, W., Chen, Y., Xing, X., Zhang, Y., Wang, G.: Towards the detection of inconsistencies in public security vulnerability reports. In: 28th USENIX Security Symposium (USENIX Security 19), pp. 869–885 (2019)
9. Ebrahimi, M., Surdeanu, M., Samtani, S., Chen, H.: Detecting cyber threats in non-english dark net markets: a cross-lingual transfer learning approach. In: 2018 IEEE International Conference on Intelligence and Security Informatics (ISI), pp. 85–90. IEEE (2018)

10. Fan, M., Luo, X., Liu, J., Nong, C., Zheng, Q., Liu, T.: CTDroid: leveraging a corpus of technical blogs for android malware analysis. IEEE Trans. Reliab. **69**(1), 124–138 (2019)

11. Ferrag, M.A., et al.: Revolutionizing cyber threat detection with large language models: a privacy-preserving BERT-based lightweight model for IoT/IIoT devices. IEEE Access (2024)

12. Gao, P., et al.: Enabling efficient cyber threat hunting with cyber threat intelligence. In: 2021 IEEE 37th International Conference on Data Engineering (ICDE), pp. 193–204. IEEE (2021)

13. Guo, Y., et al.: CyberRel: joint entity and relation extraction for cybersecurity concepts. In: Gao, D., Li, Q., Guan, X., Liao, X. (eds.) Information and Communications Security: 23rd International Conference, ICICS 2021, Chongqing, China, November 19-21, 2021, Proceedings, Part I, pp. 447–463. Springer International Publishing, Cham (2021). https://doi.org/10.1007/978-3-030-86890-1_25

14. Guo, Y., et al.: A framework for threat intelligence extraction and fusion. Comput. Secur. **132**, 103371 (2023)

15. Happe, A., Cito, J.: Getting pwn'd by AI: penetration testing with large language models. In: Proceedings of the 31st ACM Joint European Software Engineering Conference and Symposium on the Foundations of Software Engineering, pp. 2082–2086 (2023)

16. Huang, C.C., et al.: Building cybersecurity ontology for understanding and reasoning adversary tactics and techniques. In: 2022 IEEE International Conference on Big Data (Big Data), pp. 4266–4274. IEEE (2022)

17. Huang, Y.T., Lin, C.Y., Guo, Y.R., Lo, K.C., Sun, Y.S., Chen, M.C.: Open source intelligence for malicious behavior discovery and interpretation. IEEE Trans. Dependable Secure Comput. **19**(2), 776–789 (2021)

18. Jones, C.L., Bridges, R.A., Huffer, K.M., Goodall, J.R.: Towards a relation extraction framework for cyber-security concepts. In: Proceedings of the 10th Annual Cyber and Information Security Research Conference, pp. 1–4 (2015)

19. Li, T., Sahu, A.K., Talwalkar, A., Smith, V.: Federated learning: challenges, methods, and future directions. IEEE Signal Process. Mag. **37**(3), 50–60 (2020)

20. Li, Z., Zeng, J., Chen, Y., Liang, Z.: AttacKG: constructing technique knowledge graph from cyber threat intelligence reports. In: Atluri, V., Di Pietro, R., Jensen, C.D., Meng, W. (eds.) Computer Security – ESORICS 2022: 27th European Symposium on Research in Computer Security, Copenhagen, Denmark, September 26–30, 2022, Proceedings, Part I, pp. 589–609. Springer International Publishing, Cham (2022). https://doi.org/10.1007/978-3-031-17140-6_29

21. Liu, J., et al.: TriCTI: an actionable cyber threat intelligence discovery system via trigger-enhanced neural network. Cybersecurity **5**(1), 8 (2022)

22. Lu, G., Ju, X., Chen, X., Pei, W., Cai, Z.: Grace: empowering LLM-based software vulnerability detection with graph structure and in-context learning. J. Syst. Softw., 112031 (2024)

23. Ma, X., Wang, L., Lv, Q., Wang, Y., Zhang, Q., Jiang, J.: CyEvent2vec: attributed heterogeneous information network based event embedding framework for cyber security events analysis. In: 2022 International Joint Conference on Neural Networks (IJCNN), pp. 01–08. IEEE (2022)

24. McIntosh, T., et al.: Harnessing GPT-4 for generation of cybersecurity GRC policies: a focus on ransomware attack mitigation. Comput. Secur. **134**, 103424 (2023)

25. Mfogo, V.S., Zemkoho, A., Njilla, L., Nkenlifack, M., Kamhoua, C.: AIIPot: Adaptive intelligent-interaction honeypot for IoT devices. In: 2023 IEEE 34th Annual

International Symposium on Personal, Indoor and Mobile Radio Communications (PIMRC), pp. 1–6. IEEE (2023)

26. Mitra, S., Piplai, A., Mittal, S., Joshi, A.: Combating fake cyber threat intelligence using provenance in cybersecurity knowledge graphs. In: 2021 IEEE International Conference on Big Data (Big Data), pp. 3316–3323. IEEE (2021)

27. Mu, D., Cuevas, A., Yang, L., Hu, H., Xing, X., Mao, B., Wang, G.: Understanding the reproducibility of crowd-reported security vulnerabilities. In: 27th USENIX Security Symposium (USENIX Security 18), pp. 919–936 (2018)

28. Pearce, H., Tan, B., Ahmad, B., Karri, R., Dolan-Gavitt, B.: Examining zero-shot vulnerability repair with large language models. In: 2023 IEEE Symposium on Security and Privacy (SP), pp. 2339–2356. IEEE (2023)

29. Perrina, F., Marchiori, F., Conti, M., Verde, N.V.: AGIR: automating cyber threat intelligence reporting with natural language generation. In: 2023 IEEE International Conference on Big Data (BigData), pp. 3053–3062. IEEE (2023)

30. Pingle, A., Piplai, A., Mittal, S., Joshi, A., Holt, J., Zak, R.: RelExt: relation extraction using deep learning approaches for cybersecurity knowledge graph improvement. In: Proceedings of the 2019 IEEE/ACM International Conference on Advances in Social Networks Analysis and Mining, pp. 879–886 (2019)

31. Quattrone, G., Nicolazzo, S., Nocera, A., Quercia, D., Capra, L.: Is the sharing economy about sharing at all? A linguistic analysis of airbnb reviews. In: Proceedings of the International AAAI Conference on Web and Social Media, vol. 12, issue 1 (2018)

32. Rahman, M.R., Hezaveh, R.M., Williams, L.: What are the attackers doing now? Automating cyberthreat intelligence extraction from text on pace with the changing threat landscape: a survey. ACM Comput. Surv. **55**(12), 1–36 (2023)

33. Ranade, P., Piplai, A., Joshi, A., Finin, T.: CyBERT: contextualized embeddings for the cybersecurity domain. In: 2021 IEEE International Conference on Big Data (Big Data), pp. 3334–3342. IEEE (2021)

34. Ranade, P., Piplai, A., Mittal, S., Joshi, A., Finin, T.: Generating fake cyber threat intelligence using transformer-based models. In: 2021 International Joint Conference on Neural Networks (IJCNN), pp. 1–9. IEEE (2021)

35. Sameera, K.M., Nicolazzo, S., Arazzi, M., Nocera, A., Rafidha Rehiman, K.A., Conti, M., et al.: Privacy-preserving in blockchain-based federated learning systems. arXiv e-prints–2401 (2024)

36. Satvat, K., Gjomemo, R., Venkatakrishnan, V.: Extractor: extracting attack behavior from threat reports. In: 2021 IEEE European Symposium on Security and Privacy (EuroS&P), pp. 598–615. IEEE (2021)

37. Satyapanich, T., Ferraro, F., Finin, T.: CASIE: extracting cybersecurity event information from text. In: Proceedings of the AAAI Conference on Artificial Intelligence, vol. 34(05), pp. 8749–8757 (2020)

38. Schuster, S., Manning, C.D.: Enhanced English universal dependencies: an improved representation for natural language understanding tasks. In: Proceedings of the Tenth International Conference on Language Resources and Evaluation (LREC'16), pp. 2371–2378 (2016)

39. Sun, N., Ding, M., Jiang, J., Xu, W., Mo, X., Tai, Y., Zhang, J.: Cyber threat intelligence mining for proactive cybersecurity defense: a survey and new perspectives. IEEE Commun. Surv. Tutorials (2023)

40. Syed, Z., Padia, A., Finin, T., Mathews, L., Joshi, A.: UCO: a unified cybersecurity ontology. In: Workshops at the Thirtieth AAAI Conference on Artificial Intelligence (2016)

41. Vörös, T., Bergeron, S.P., Berlin, K.: Web content filtering through knowledge distillation of large language models. In: 2023 IEEE International Conference on Web Intelligence and Intelligent Agent Technology (WI-IAT), pp. 357–361. IEEE (2023)

42. Wang, X., Xiong, M., Luo, Y., Li, N., Jiang, Z., Xiong, Z.: Joint learning for document-level threat intelligence relation extraction and coreference resolution based on GCN. In: 2020 IEEE 19th International Conference on Trust, Security and Privacy in Computing and Communications (TrustCom), pp. 584–591. IEEE (2020)

43. Wei, Y., Bo, L., Sun, X., Li, B., Zhang, T., Tao, C.: Automated event extraction of CVE descriptions. Inf. Softw. Technol. **158**, 107178 (2023)

44. Yang, J., et al.: Harnessing the power of LLMs in practice: a survey on ChatGPT and beyond. ACM Trans. Knowl. Discov. Data (2023)

45. Yitagesu, S., Xing, Z., Zhang, X., Feng, Z., Li, X., Han, L.: Unsupervised labeling and extraction of phrase-based concepts in vulnerability descriptions. In: 2021 36th IEEE/ACM International Conference on Automated Software Engineering (ASE), pp. 943–954. IEEE (2021)

46. Yitagesu, S., Xing, Z., Zhang, X., Feng, Z., Li, X., Han, L.: Extraction of phrase-based concepts in vulnerability descriptions through unsupervised labeling. ACM Trans. Softw. Eng. Methodol. **32**(5), 1–45 (2023)

47. Yu, F., Martin, M.V.: Honey, i chunked the passwords: generating semantic honeywords resistant to targeted attacks using pre-trained language models. In: International Conference on Detection of Intrusions and Malware, and Vulnerability Assessment, pp. 89–108. Springer (2023). https://doi.org/10.1007/978-3-031-35504-2_5

48. Yu, L., Lu, J., Liu, X., Yang, L., Zhang, F., Ma, J.: PSCVFinder: a prompt-tuning based framework for smart contract vulnerability detection. In: 2023 IEEE 34th International Symposium on Software Reliability Engineering (ISSRE), pp. 556–567. IEEE (2023)

49. Zeng, D., Liu, K., Lai, S., Zhou, G., Zhao, J.: Relation classification via convolutional deep neural network. In: Proceedings of COLING 2014, the 25th International Conference on Computational Linguistics: Technical Papers, pp. 2335–2344 (2014)

50. Zhang, D., Wang, D.: Relation classification via recurrent neural network. arXiv preprint arXiv:1508.01006 (2015)

51. Zhang, H., Shen, G., Guo, C., Cui, Y., Jiang, C.: EX-Action: automatically extracting threat actions from cyber threat intelligence report based on multimodal learning. Secur. Commun. Netw. **2021**, 1–12 (2021)

52. Zhao, X., Jiang, R., Han, Y., Li, A., Peng, Z.: A survey on cybersecurity knowledge graph construction. Comput. Secur., 103524 (2023)

53. Zhou, P., Shi, W., Tian, J., Qi, Z., Li, B., Hao, H., Xu, B.: Attention-based bidirectional long short-term memory networks for relation classification. In: Proceedings of the 54th Annual Meeting of the Association for Computational Linguistics (volume 2: Short papers), pp. 207–212 (2016)

54. Zhou, Y., Ren, Y., Yi, M., Xiao, Y., Tan, Z., Moustafa, N., Tian, Z.: CDTier: a Chinese dataset of threat intelligence entity relationships. IEEE Trans. Sustain. Comput. (2023)

SHACT: Disentangling and Clustering Latent Syntactic Structures from Transformer Encoders

Alejandro Sierra-Múnera[1]([envelope]) [ID] and Ralf Krestel[2,3] [ID]

[1] Hasso Plattner Institute, Potsdam, Germany
alejandro.sierra@hpi.de
[2] ZBW - Leibniz Information Centre for Economics, Kiel, Germany
rkr@informatik.uni-kiel.de
[3] Kiel University, Kiel, Germany

Abstract. Transformer-encoder architectures for language modeling provide rich contextualized vectors, representing both, syntactic and semantic information captured during pre-training. These vectors are useful for multiple downstream tasks, but directly using the final layer representations might hide interesting elements represented in the hidden layers. In this paper, we propose SHACT **S**yntactic **H**ierarchical **A**gglomerative **C**lustering from **T**ransformer-Encoders , a model that disentangles syntactic span representations from these hidden representations, into a latent vector space. In our model, spans are expressed in terms of token distances. We propose a loss function that optimizes the neural disentanglement model from ground truth spans, and we propose to integrate these latent space vectors into a two-phase model via hierarchical clustering, suitable for multiple span recognition tasks. We evaluated our approach on flat and nested named entity recognition as well as chunking, showing the model's ability to discover these spans, as well as having competitive results on the full recognition and classification tasks.

Keywords: Named entity recognition · Chunking · Syntax trees

1 Introduction

Current natural language processing (NLP) models rely heavily on rich pre-trained word representations in the form of contextualized word embeddings. Typically, these models use representations derived from transformer-encoders [18]. These models are pre-trained to predict words given a context, using large amounts of raw text. They are therefore commonly referred to as pre-trained language models (PLMs).

Besides being able to predict words given a context, these models are commonly used as embedding models, from which the token embeddings from the last transformer-encoder layer, can be used in task-specific models as dense representations. One group of tasks which strongly benefits from transformer-encoders

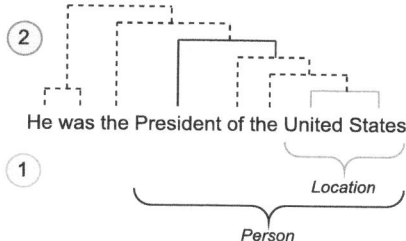

Fig. 1. Nested named entities ① and HAC analysis ② of a sentence

are span recognition tasks, such as named entity recognition (NER) and chunking. In these tasks, given a sentence or document, the task is to find relevant spans of words and further categorize them in a set of pre-defined classes. One example of this can be seen in Fig. 1①. In this example of nested NER, two spans (*President of the United States* and *United States*) correspond to named entities, and each named entity belongs to a specific class (*Person* and *Location* respectively). For tasks, such as flat NER and chunking, each word can be assigned to a maximum of one span, while for hierarchical tasks, such as nested NER, a single word might belong to multiple spans.

But the transformer model provides more than the last layer representation. The hidden transformer-encoder layers contain interesting representations as well, as other studies have revealed [5,8,11,20]. In our proposed model SHACT (**S**yntactic **H**ierarchical **A**gglomerative **C**lustering from **T**ransformer-Encoders)[1], we exploit these hidden representations to define a latent syntactic vector space in which a tree that syntactically analyzes the sentence can be represented in terms of token distances. The intuition of our model can be seen in Fig. 1②. Here, the sequence of words can be hierarchically analyzed by merging words together into clusters that eventually conform the whole sentence. We hypothesize, inspired by the ideas of Hewitt and Manning [5] and Sajjad et al. [11], that there exists a vector space, where hierarchical agglomerative clustering (HAC) can be performed to produce such analysis.

With SHACT, we propose a model for disentangling syntactic structures representing the clustering of tokens into spans by projecting the hidden representations of a transformer-encoder into a latent space. For learning the disentanglement, we use a loss function which treats multi-word spans as clusters. The loss function's goal is to minimize the intra-cluster distances in the latent space, while maximizing the extra-cluster distance at the same time, thus optimizing the projection. With this, the disentangled representation' distances represent the syntactic relatedness of tokens inside a sentence.

Further, the latent space vectors are clustered using hierarchical agglomerative clustering (HAC), resulting in a binary syntactic tree. This tree determines

---

[1] We release the code for training and testing our model in this repository: https://github.com/HPI-Information-Systems/shact.

a set of candidate spans which are then classified using the same transformer-encoder, to identify relevant spans, and categorize them among the pre-defined types.

2   Related Work

Our work is related to the interpretability and topological analysis of pre-trained language models (PLMs), specifically regarding syntax in pre-trained transformer-encoders. This line of research studies what kinds of structures are automatically learned by transformer architectures [3,10,18] when they are pre-trained using vast amounts of text.

Previous studies have proposed probes for syntactic structures in the hidden representations of PLMs. One of these probes was proposed by Hewitt and Manning [5]. They applied a trainable linear transformation to the hidden vectors in a specific layer of the model, and checked if the resulting vectors represent the dependency tree in terms of distance between words, and their depth in the tree.Mareček and Rosa [8] manually analyzed the attention heads of a neural machine translation transformer-encoder from which they recognized "balustrades" patterns. Then they automatically generated constituency trees from the attention heads using the CKY algorithm. They evaluated against different trivial baselines and found that their technique was able to find these constituents. Wu et al. [20] analyze the impact between words in a sentence through perturbation via masking. They computed an impact matrix, from which they built dependency and constituency trees in completely unsupervised mode. They showed that these structures—although they do not perfectly correlate to annotated trees—have a positive impact in downstream tasks. Furthermore, they question whether transformer architectures actually understand structures better than the traditionally studied constituency trees.

Sajjad et al. [11] proposed ConceptX to analyze different layers of transformer-encoders and found different linguistic concepts represented at different levels. Specifically, they discovered *encoded concepts* by clustering vector representations, and then they align these clusters with multiple human-defined linguistic concepts. Different from probes, such as Hewitt and Manning [5], the discovery of concepts in the vector space is unsupervised. They found that, although the alignment was low, the syntactic concepts, such as *chunking* were present in the upper layers before the final layers of the different transformer-encoders.

In our work, we take inspiration from these approaches and extract vector representations from the hidden layers of the transformer-encoders. Different from Hewitt and Manning [5] we don't use dependency relations, but instead word agglomerations, more similar to constituents. Different from Sajjad et al. [11] we specialize in spans instead of individual words. Deviating from both and other probing studies, we do not intend to analyze the transformer-encoder layers individually, but we exploit their combination to project the tokens into a different vector space.

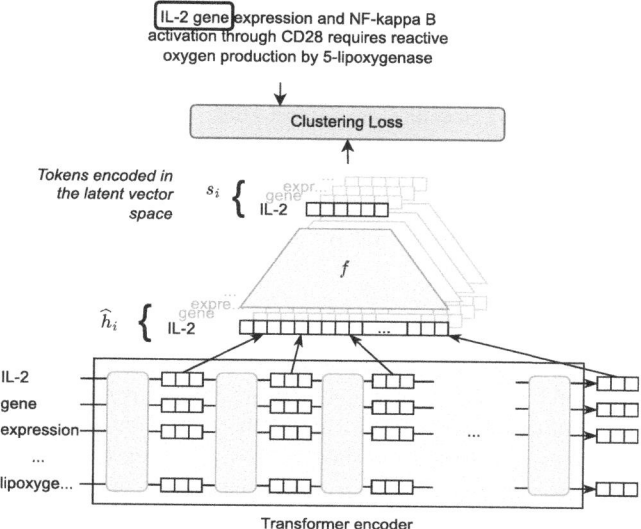

Fig. 2. Projection from a transformer encoder hidden layers to the latent space s_i where the loss function is computed for a particular entity (*IL-2 gene*)

Another line of related work are span-based nested NER models. These models go beyond the IOB sequence tagging scheme designed for flat NER, and thus can identify multiple overlapping named entities. One subgroup of nested NER focuses on enumerating spans within the text and then classifying the spans among the entity types. Given a sentence, Sohrab and Miwa [14] proposed to create an exhaustive set of all the spans with a maximum length and then classify them. One disadvantage of the extensive enumeration of spans is the large number of spans that need to be classified. In Zheng et al. [22], the authors construct the entity spans using a sequence labeling model based on a Bi-LSTM encoder, and then use the average token representations within the span to predict the span label. Similarly, Tan et al. [15] encode the sentence to discover boundaries and then classify the candidate spans using the token representation within the span.

Similar to the works in Tan et al. [15],Zheng et al. [22], we propose to define the candidate spans and classify them using a transformer-encoder, but different from them, we disentangle the vector space that represents syntactic span structures from the semantic representations used for the classification of these spans. In comparison to Sohrab and Miwa [14], the number of candidate spans in our approach does not depend on the span length but only on the length of the sequence, thus producing candidates from all possible lengths without affecting the number of candidates.

3   SHACT

In this section we introduce SHACT, **S**yntactic **H**ierarchical **A**gglomerative **C**lustering from **T**ransformer-Encoders , a model that disentangles syntactic representations of spans and then uses hierarchical clustering to discover and classify word agglomerations. First, we present the disentanglement component, and then we complete the span recognition model with the classification component based on the spans detected in the clusters.

3.1   Disentanglement of Syntactic Clusters

Inspired by the identification of syntactic structures in PLMs, we define a model which projects tokens into a latent space where significant spans, such as named entity mentions or noun phrases, conform to clusters. Treating spans as clusters, the goal of the model is to minimize the distance between the token representations within the cluster in comparison to their distance to other token representations of the sentence. We assume a PLM with a transformer-encoder architecture [3], and consider all the hidden representations of a token as its *full vector representation*. From these representations, our model projects to latent vector space, in which the inter-cluster and extra-cluster distances are compared. The projection is then trained with sentences containing annotated spans to minimize the ratio between intra-cluster and extra-cluster distances.

An overview of the disentanglement model architecture is represented in Fig. 2. Here, the transformer-encoder passes each token vector through multiple transformer layers, producing multiple hidden representations. SHACT concatenates them into a large token vector, which is projected into the latent space using a feed-forward network (FFN). Given the set of latent token vectors and a ground truth span, we compute a clustering loss function, based on intra-cluster and extra-cluster distances. Using gradient descent to minimize this loss, the FFN is updated during training to better extract the span representations in the latent space. To generalize the concept of span boundaries and reduce the complexity of the projection, the disentanglement component of the model does not differentiate between the types of spans. For instance, if the task is NER and the relevant spans are entity mentions, the latent projection is agnostic to the entity types, and it is optimized for all the mentions in the same way.

We now formally define the elements of the model and the loss function. For a given token t_i in a sentence $d = \{t_0, t_1, t_2, \ldots, t_n\}$, and a jth layer of a transformer-encoder producing a hidden representation $h_{i,j}$, we define a vector $\widehat{h}_i$ by concatenation of all the vectors $h_{i,j}$. This vector contains the *full representation* of the token t_i in the context of the sentence d. In the next step, $\widehat{h}_i$ is projected into a vector space $\mathcal{S}$ as s_i via a fully connected neural network f.

For an annotated span n in d (e.g., a named entity or a chunk), consisting of a subset of contiguous tokens $n = \{t_k, t_{k+1}, \ldots, t_{k+m}\} | n \subset d$ we define the loss function

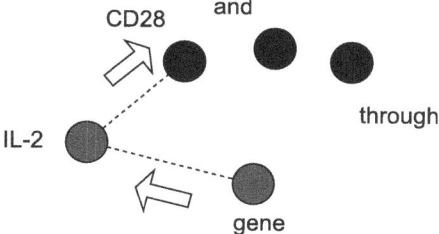

Fig. 3. Example 2D representation of the latent space and the distances considered during training for the named entity *IL-2 gene*. The arrows represent the optimization objectives of minimizing $\mathcal{ICD}$ and maximizing $\mathcal{ECD}$

$$\mathcal{L}_{syn}(d, n) = \frac{\mathcal{ICD}}{\mathcal{ECD}} = \frac{\max_{t_i, t_j \in n} \delta(t_i, t_j) + 1}{\min_{t_i \in n \ t_j \notin n} \delta(t_i, t_j) + 1}$$

Where δ is the cosine distance between the tokens vectors in the vector space $\mathcal{S}$. $\mathcal{ICD}$ and $\mathcal{ECD}$, represent the intra-cluster and extra-cluster distances. The idea behind the loss function $\mathcal{L}_{syn}$ is to optimize the projection f by selecting and combining the features of the vector $\widehat{h}_i$ so that the span n is isolated from the rest of the tokens in the sentence. This is achieved by minimizing $\mathcal{L}_{syn}$ which in turn minimizes the maximum distance $\mathcal{ICD}$ within the cluster and maximizes the minimum distance $\mathcal{ECD}$ between tokens belonging to n and the rest of the sentence.

To give more intuition about the loss function, we consider the case where $\mathcal{ICD} < \mathcal{ECD}$. A value of $\mathcal{L}_{syn} < 1$ means that for an annotated span n, e.g., a named entity, there is no token outside n with a smaller distance than that between all the tokens belonging to n, hence effectively clustering the span in terms of vector distances. To avoid numeric errors when $\mathcal{ECD}$ is small, a constant 1 is added to both metrics. The optimization goal and the interpretability of $\mathcal{L}_{syn}$ with respect to 1 remain equivalent.

A visualization of the idea behind the loss function can be seen in Fig. 3. Here, the named entity *"IL-2 gene"* is compared against the rest of the sentence. The maximum intra-cluster distance $\mathcal{ICD}$ is between the tokens *IL-2* and *gene*, whereas the minimum extra-cluster distance $\mathcal{ECD}$ is between *IL-2* and *CD28*. Intuitively, the loss function's value would decrease if *IL-2* and *gene* were closer and the distance between *IL-2* and *CD28* was larger.

During training, the loss function is computed for each ground truth span, and then averaged for a batch of sentences. During backpropagation, the parameters of f are updated to learn a projection into the latent space. We refrain from back propagating from $\mathcal{L}_{syn}$ to the transformer layers to avoid instability, and to focus the fine-tuning on the semantic aspects needed for the span classification. During inference, we project all the tokens into S and apply hierarchical agglomerative clustering (HAC) for the full sentence until all are merged into one

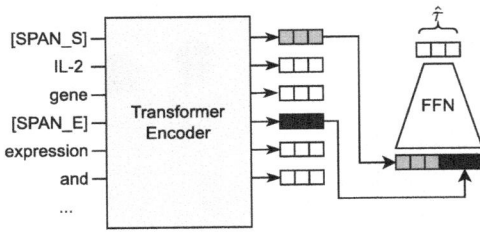

Fig. 4. Overview of the classifier architecture. The final vector resulting from the FFN contains the logits corresponding to the types in $\hat{\tau}$

single cluster. Every merge operation constitutes a potential span that will be processed during classification (see Sect. 3.2). We note that the merge operations are restricted to adjacent tokens in the sentence, thus producing only contiguous spans of text for the next stage. Additionally, tokens belonging to the same word are merged with the first token of the word, which in turns acts as the representative token for the entire word. For instance, given the tokens "human mon #ocytes .", the token *#ocytes* can only be merged to *mon* to form the word *monocytes*.

3.2 Span Classification

The span classification phase, shown in Fig. 4, uses the same transformer-encoder used for disentangling the syntactic representations, but exploits the last layer representations. We hypothesize that this representation contains more semantic information and thus, is better suited for identifying the span types (e.g., person, location, noun phrase). Formally, given the original sentence $d = \{t_0, t_1, t_2, \ldots, t_n\}$ and a span defined by the tuple $c_k = (c_k^s, c_k^e)$, being c_k^s the starting index of the span, c_k^e the ending index of the span, the span classifier has the goal to predict the type $c_k^t \in \hat{\tau} | \hat{\tau} = \tau \cup \{null\}$, with τ being the original type set. To do so, after tokenization, two special tokens *[SPAN_S]* and *[SPAN_E]* are inserted before and after the span tokens to produce a new sentence $\hat{d}_k$. For instance, for the span in Fig. 2, the token sequence would be modified in this way: *"[SPAN_S] IL-2 gene [SPAN_E] expression and ..."*.

The modified tokenized version of the sentences is then fed into the transformer-encoder, from which the final layer vectors corresponding to *[SPAN_S]* and *[SPAN_E]* are fed into a multi-layer perceptron responsible for the classification. Formally, the predicted label $\hat{y}(d, c_k)$ for a sentence d and a span c_k belonging to the sentence, is computed as follows:

$$\hat{y}(d, c_k) = \phi(FFN([\mathcal{E}(\hat{d}_k)_{SPAN\_S} : \mathcal{E}(\hat{d}_k)_{SPAN\_E}]))$$

where ϕ is the *softmax* function, FFN is the feed-forward network, and $\mathcal{E}(d)$ is the encoded representation of d, corresponding to the last layer representation of the transformer-encoder.

During training, the ground truth spans are used to learn the representations of *[SPAN_S]* and *[SPAN_E]* that should be classified into the corresponding types, but the model needs to learn spans that fall into the {*null*} type. Thus, a subset of spans from the sames sentences is also used as negative samples for the classifier.

Formally, a batch B is conformed of m samples, each composed of a sentence $d_i = \{t_0, t_1, t_2, \ldots, t_n\}$, a span $c_i = (c_i^s, c_i^e)$ and one-hot-encoded ground truth label y_{ij} where j corresponds to the jth class in $\hat{\tau}$. The model then computes $\hat{y}_{ij}$, with which the classification cross-entropy loss function $\mathcal{L}_{CE}$ is aggregated for the batch B as follows:

$$\mathcal{L}_{CE}(B)(y, \hat{y}) = -\sum_{i=1}^{m} \sum_{j=1}^{\hat{\tau}} y_{ij} \log(\hat{y}_{ij})$$

During inference, all the potential spans produced by the hierarchical clustering algorithm are classified by taking the *argmax* of the predicted classes.

3.3   Training Procedure and Negative Sampling

Providing negative samples to the classifier impacts the way the model learns to distinguish between relevant spans ($c_k^t \in \tau$) and non-relevant spans ($c_k^t = null$). To generate a set of negative spans, we leverage the disentangled syntactic representations from SHACT. To do so, first we warm up the disentanglement projection f, keeping the transformer-encoder parameters frozen. With a trained projection, hierarchical agglomerative clustering is performed on the sentences in the training set, therefore discovering potential syntactically relevant spans. From those spans, the ones which do not correspond to ground truth spans are considered as negative spans for the subsequent classification training.

Then, in the second phase of training, the full model is trained by considering both positive and negative examples. The full loss function for a batch B combining positive and negative samples is the sum of the cross-entropy loss $\mathcal{L}_{CE}(B)$ for the classifier and the syntactic loss $\mathcal{L}_{syn}$ for the positive examples of B (i.e., spans with a type belonging to τ). in this phase we fine tune the transformer-encoder using $\mathcal{L}_{CE}(B)$, but the disentanglement projection model is detached from the transformer representations, thus only training the projection f. In our initial experiments, we observed instability in the clustering loss if we also back-propagate to the transformer from the projection f.

Inference Procedure. Different from training, where each sentence-span pair (d, c_k) is trained independently, during inference, each sample is composed only of a sentence d, without ground-truth spans.

The first part of the inference phase is to compute the latent representations of all tokens of d. These vectors are then clustered using HAC. Specifically, the single linkage strategy is used with the additional constraint that only contiguous clusters can be merged. The outcome of the clustering is a dendrogram (Fig 1) in which every merge is a potential span. In total, for a sentence with n words, $2n-1$ candidate spans, including the individual words, are considered for classification.

For each candidate span, a new sentence with the special tokens *[SPAN_S]* and *[SPAN_E]* is encoded using the transformer, and the special token representations are classified the same way as the classification training. The final result of the inference phase is a binary tree, where the leaves are the words in the sentence, and every node, including the leaves, has an assigned class from $\hat{\tau}$. Task-specific post-processing filters can be applied to the tree. In particular, for tasks, such as flat NER and chunking, where each word can belong to a maximum of one span, the prediction needs to be flattened. For hierarchical prediction, such as for nested NER, the predictions can be computed from the tree by ignoring the nodes with a predicted *null*-type.

The criteria that we employ for flattening the prediction involves a sequential sorting of the positive candidates in descending order, based on their level of classification confidence and their length in words. Then spans are selected sequentially if no overlapping span was selected before. This means that we favor high confidence spans, and given two overlapping spans with the same confidence, we favor the longest one.

4   Evaluation

Our evaluation focuses on two aspects of our model. First, the intrinsic clustering ability of the model, corresponding to the degree in which a trained model is able to cluster together spans, to do so we focus on nested NER, being more complex to cluster spans in a hierarchical fashion. Secondly, we evaluate the full two phase model including the classifier for three different tasks: flat NER, nested NER, and chunking. With this, we evaluate the usefulness and adaptability of syntactic trees with different classification schemes.

For flat NER, we evaluate our model on CoNLL03 [17], for nested NER, we use GENIA [9], and for chunking, we employ CoNLL00 [16] .

As mentioned in Sect. 3.3, the model is warmed-up for one epoch, and then, both the disentanglement and classification components are trained for a maximum of 15 epochs using early stopping with respect to the validation F1 score and a patience value of 5 epochs.

In all the experiments, we use *BERT-large-cased* [3] as the PLM, except for the GENIA experiment where we use *BioBERT-large-cased-v1.1* [6]. The dimensionality of the latent space is fixed to 128 and Adam is used as the optimizer.

4.1   Intrinsic Evaluation

The intrinsic evaluation aims to determine whether the clustering loss can optimize the projection f from spans in the training set. To measure that, we compute the recall of spans from the test set after training only the projection disentanglement component. We train the model for one epoch using the training set and for each of the sentences in the test set, HAC is used on the set of token vectors until the whole sentence is merged into one single cluster. We then analyze the resulting binary trees, measuring the span recall of ground truth spans. This is critical for our model, because any ground truth span, not present in the binary tree, cannot be considered by the classifier component.

Table 1. Percentage of GENIA named entities present in the binary trees computed with HAC on the different vector spaces

Vector Space	Span Recall
PLM_{final}	52.94
PLM_{full}	51.51
LS_{random}	51.50
LS	**97.37**

For baselines, we use the following vector representations:

- PLM_{final}: The final layer representation of the transformer-encoder.
- PLM_{full}: The concatenation of all the hidden representations for each token, which is equivalent to $\widehat{h}_i$.
- LS_{random}: The latent space vectors, computed with the projection component, initialized with random weights without training. This will provide us insights on the value of the loss function to optimize the projection.
- LS: The latent space vector, computed with the trained projection component.

For these experiments, the PLM is kept frozen and the experiments with LS_{random} and LS are repeated 3 times with different seeds. A named entity from GENIA is considered a correct prediction if, and only if, it is one of the distinct clusters of HAC computed for the sentence. The recall numbers can be seen in Table 1. Here, we clearly see that the distance in the other vector representations does not correlate to the syntactic relatedness of the tokens in an entity mention. Our trained projection leads to the highest recall, which shows the potential of the latent space for expressing the relatedness of span tokens. However, the low recall numbers of the PLM approaches are not surprising, given the objectives used for training them. BERT's masked language modeling objective emphasizes on the semantic, rather than the syntactic representation of the tokens. We also observe that randomly combining hidden representations (LS_{random}) does not help our clustering objective. With this, we can observe that the optimization of the projection f is required to capture all the relevant spans.

Having a good span recall in the latent space is critical for our model, since the errors from the syntactic analysis phase are propagated to the classification phase.

4.2   Extrinsic Evaluation

For the full model training, we first warm up the projection for one epoch, and then we generate all the potential spans in the training set that are fed as positive or negative spans to the full model.

For the three tasks, we measure exact F1 score, considering a correct prediction only if a span has the same boundaries and the correct type. All the reported SHACT F1 scores are the average result of three different runs with different seeds.

Table 2. Results in terms of F1 score in different tasks. * for flat models

(a)GENIA (Nested NER)		(b)CoNLL-2003 (Flat NER)		(c)CoNLL-2000 (chunking)	
Model	F1	Model	F1	Model	F1
Zheng et al. [22]	74.7	Devlin et al. [3]*	92.8	Chen et al. [2]*	96.34
Sohrab and Miwa [14]	77.1	Shen et al. [13]	92.87	Chen et al. [1]*	97.04
Tan et al. [15]	78.3	Shen et al. [12]	92.78	Wang et al. [19]*	97.3
Fu et al. [4]	78.2	Wang et al. [19]*	94.6	SHACT	96.61
Yang and Tu [21]	78.16	SHACT	91.74		
Lou et al. [7]	78.44				
Shen et al. [13]	81.77				
Shen et al. [12]	81.53				
SHACT	79.76				

The results for flat NER on the CoNLL-2003 dataset are shown in Table 2b, where we compare our approach against span-based NER models [12,13] and state-of-the-art flat NER models [3,19]. In this case, we see that SHACT results are slightly worse than specialized state-of-the-art span-based models capable of both flat and nested NER. We also observe that the traditional sequence labeling models, such as plain BERT with a classification head [3] and ACE [19], achieve stronger results. However, we believe that SHACT is more flexible than sequence labeling models and the latent space analysis possesses an explainability value on its own while achieving competitive results compared to specialized models.

For chunking on the CoNLL-2000 dataset, we have a similar comparison in Table 2c. Here, the results of SHACT are competitive even with the state-of-the-art flat model ACE [19]. We believe that the syntactic analysis of SHACT in this case is very capable of clustering chunks that typically cover a few words. The flattening here is particularly challenging because the classifier must not only correctly identify semantically the differences between linguistic chunks, such as noun and verbal phrases, but also assign a higher confidence to the correct levels in the tree.

In addition, we evaluate our model on the task of nested NER using the GENIA dataset. This task is more complex compared to flat NER. Results are in Table 2a. For this task, SHACT has competitive results, and compared to better performing models, such as DifussionNER [12], the binary tree helps in explaining the predictions by clearly defining merge operations.

Table 3. Comparison between recall (R) of SHACT and the upper bound of the classification recall (Upper bound R) resulting of error propagation

Dataset	R	Upper bound R	Difference
CoNLL-2000	96.44	99.68	3.24
CoNLL-2003	92.12	99.59	7.47
GENIA	78.31	98.07	19.76

One potential problem of models, such as SHACT, in which first the spans are enumerated and then classified, is the potential error propagation between the enumeration phase and the classification. We analyze this by computing the upper bound for the recall the same way we computed the span recall in the intrinsic evaluation. Differently from the intrinsic evaluation, we use the final model after the classifier is trained alongside the projection. This is slightly different because after full training, the loss function is composed of two objectives. In Table 3, we compare the recall and its upper bound for each evaluated dataset. We clearly see that the impact on the recall by error propagation is minimal (between 0.32% and 1.93%) compared to the reduction of recall by misclassification.

4.3 Explainability and Error Analysis

Besides the quantitative analysis of the performance of SHACT, we take advantage of the explainability features of the model by analyzing erroneous predictions. The examples we show in Fig. 5 portray two different types of error that might happen during inference. The error in 5a corresponds to a semantic error, characterized by the misclassification of spans. In this case, SHACT correctly clusters the words in *human monocytes*, but later the classifier incorrectly assigns the *null* class to this span. Similarly, the longer span *normal human monocytes*, that is not part of the ground truth, is incorrectly classified as *Cell type*. This is the most common error found in this dataset.

The second error presented in 5b is a syntactic error. Here, the span containing *CD28 MoAb* is not part of the predicted binary tree; thus the final prediction does not contain any classification of such span. This is a case of error propagation, and exemplifies the 1.93% of the cases in which the recall is bounded by an erroneous syntactic analysis.

With SHACT we are able to separate the syntactic and semantic analysis of the spans, which allows us to better understand the origin of bad predictions.

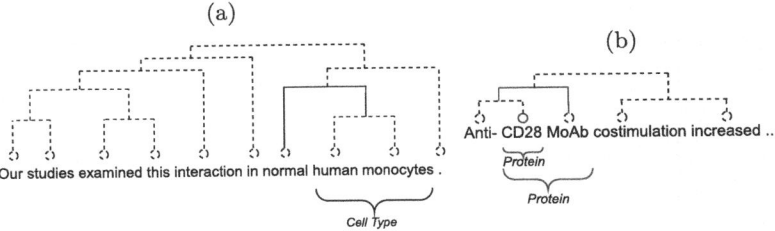

Fig. 5. Errors committed by SHACT on GENIA. Below the sentences is the ground truth, and the trees on top of the sentences are the predictions. Dashed circles/lines mean *null* class, while solid circles/lines entity predictions

5   Conclusions

In this paper, we proposed SHACT, a model for disentanglement of syntactic clusters from pre-trained transformer-encoders, such as BERT [3]. We proposed a feed forward network projecting from a concatenation of all the layers of the transformer to a latent space. In addition to the projection, we defined a loss function based on the minimization of inter-cluster distances and maximization of extra-cluster distances, where clusters are formed by multi-word spans. The optimization of the projection component, using a loss function, generates a latent vector space in which span words are closer together in comparison to the rest of the sentence. We complement the disentanglement with a classifier that uses the discovered syntax tree to classify the candidate spans.

We evaluated the model for flat and nested NER, as well as chunking. We observed that although the model does not perform better than all the state-of-the-art models in each task, the performance is competitive in across all tasks. We observed, as well, that the first component that builds the syntactic binary tree is successful in representing ground truth spans as clusters in the latent space, but the classification of these spans remains a challenging part of the model. We believe that this also illustrates the potential of the disentangled latent space that could also be exploited in other ways to improve the classification. By taking advantage of the separation between the syntactic and the semantic analysis of the spans, we can also analyze and explain the predictions of the model. In further experiments, we also tested the model on the task of full constituency parsing. Unfortunately, SHACT yielded poor results in the alignment between the binary trees and the full constituency trees. This observation is aligned to the findings in Wu et al. [20].

Our model was designed with the specific goal of disentangling nested syntactic representations. However, there are more syntactically relevant structures which are out of the scope of this paper. For instance, dependency trees like the ones studied by Hewitt and Manning [5]. We limited our experiments to the English language. Experimentation with other datasets in different languages and with richer and more fine-grained entity types are out of the scope of the paper and could be studied in future work.

Acknowledgments. This research was partially funded by the HPI Research School on Data Science and Engineering. We would like to thank Prof. Felix Naumann for the methodological advice.

Disclosure of Interests. The authors have no competing interests to declare that are relevant to the content of this article.

References

1. Chen, L., Liu, X., Ruan, W., Lu, J.: Enhance robustness of sequence labelling with masked adversarial training. In: Findings of the Association for Computational Linguistics: EMNLP 2020, pp. 297–302 (2020)
2. Chen, L., Ruan, W., Liu, X., Lu, J.: SeqVAT: virtual adversarial training for semi-supervised sequence labeling. In: Proceedings of the 58th Annual Meeting of the Association for Computational Linguistics, pp. 8801–8811 (2020)
3. Devlin, J., Chang, M.W., Lee, K., Toutanova, K.: BERT: pre-training of deep bidirectional transformers for language understanding. In: Proceedings of the 2019 Conference of the North American Chapter of the Association for Computational Linguistics, pp. 4171–4186 (2019)
4. Fu, Y., Tan, C., Chen, M., Huang, S., Huang, F.: Nested named entity recognition with partially-observed TreeCRFs. IN: Proceedings of the AAAI Conference on Artificial Intelligence. vol. 35(14), pp. 12839–12847 (2021)
5. Hewitt, J., Manning, C.D.: A structural probe for finding syntax in word representations. In: Proceedings of the 2019 Conference of the North American Chapter of the Association for Computational Linguistics: Human Language Technologies, vol. 1 (Long and Short Papers), pp. 4129–4138 (2019)
6. Lee, J., et al.: BioBERT: a pre-trained biomedical language representation model for biomedical text mining. Bioinformatics **36**, 1234–1240 (2019)
7. Lou, C., Yang, S., Tu, K.: Nested named entity recognition as latent lexicalized constituency parsing. In: Proceedings of the 60th Annual Meeting of the Association for Computational Linguistics (Volume 1: Long Papers), pp. 6183–6198 (2022)
8. Mareček, D., Rosa, R.: From balustrades to pierre vinken: looking for syntax in transformer self-attentions. In: Proceedings of the 2019 ACL Workshop BlackboxNLP: Analyzing and Interpreting Neural Networks for NLP, pp. 263–275 (2019)
9. Ohta, T., Tateisi, Y., Kim, J.D.: The Genia corpus: an annotated research abstract corpus in molecular biology domain. In: Proceedings of the Second International Conference on Human Language Technology Research, pp. 8286, HLT '02, San Francisco, CA, USA (2002)
10. Radford, A., Narasimhan, K.: Improving language understanding by generative pre-training (2018)
11. Sajjad, H., Durrani, N., Dalvi, F., Alam, F., Khan, A., Xu, J.: Analyzing encoded concepts in transformer language models. In: Proceedings of the 2022 Conference of the North American Chapter of the Association for Computational Linguistics: Human Language Technologies, pp. 3082–3101 (2022)
12. Shen, Y., Song, K., Tan, X., Li, D., Lu, W., Zhuang, Y.: DiffusionNER: boundary diffusion for named entity recognition. In: Proceedings of the 61st Annual Meeting of the Association for Computational Linguistics (Volume 1: Long Papers), pp. 3875–3890 (2023)

13. Shen, Y., et al.: Parallel instance query network for named entity recognition. In: Proceedings of the 60th Annual Meeting of the Association for Computational Linguistics (Volume 1: Long Papers), pp. 947–961 (2022)

14. Sohrab, M.G., Miwa, M.: Deep exhaustive model for nested named entity recognition. In: Proceedings of the 2018 Conference on Empirical Methods in Natural Language Processing, pp. 2843–2849 (2018)

15. Tan, C., Qiu, W., Chen, M., Wang, R., Huang, F.: Boundary enhanced neural span classification for nested named entity recognition. In: Proceedings of the AAAI Conference on Artificial Intelligence. vol. 34(05), pp. 9016–9023 (2020)

16. Tjong Kim Sang, E.F., Buchholz, S.: Introduction to the CoNLL-2000 shared task chunking. In: Fourth Conference on Computational Natural Language Learning and the Second Learning Language in Logic Workshop (2000)

17. Tjong Kim Sang, E.F., De Meulder, F.: Introduction to the CoNLL-2003 shared task: language-independent named entity recognition. In: Proceedings of the Seventh Conference on Natural Language Learning at HLT-NAACL 2003, pp. 142–147 (2003)

18. Vaswani, A., et al.: Attention is all you need. In: Proceedings of the 31st International Conference on Neural Information Processing Systems, pp. 60006010, NIPS'17 (2017)

19. Wang, X., et al.: Automated concatenation of embeddings for structured prediction. In: Proceedings of the 59th Annual Meeting of the Association for Computational Linguistics and the 11th International Joint Conference on Natural Language Processing (Volume 1: Long Papers), pp. 2643–2660 (2021)

20. Wu, Z., Chen, Y., Kao, B., Liu, Q.: Perturbed masking: Parameter-free probing for analyzing and interpreting BERT. In: Proceedings of the 58th Annual Meeting of the Association for Computational Linguistics, pp. 4166–4176 (2020)

21. Yang, S., Tu, K.: Bottom-up constituency parsing and nested named entity recognition with pointer networks. In: Proceedings of the 60th Annual Meeting of the Association for Computational Linguistics (Volume 1: Long Papers), pp. 2403–2416 (2022)

22. Zheng, C., Cai, Y., Xu, J., Leung, H.F., Xu, G.: A boundary-aware neural model for nested named entity recognition. In: Proceedings of the 2019 Conference on Empirical Methods in Natural Language Processing and the 9th International Joint Conference on Natural Language Processing (EMNLP-IJCNLP), pp. 357–366 (2019)

MaskPure: Improving Defense Against Text Adversaries with Stochastic Purification

Harrison Gietz[1]([envelope]) and Jugal Kalita[2]([ORCID])

[1] Louisiana State University, Baton Rouge, LA 70803, USA
harrygietz@gmail.com
[2] University of Colorado Colorado Springs, Colorado Springs, CO 80918, USA

Abstract. The improvement of language model robustness, including successful defense against adversarial attacks, remains an open problem. In computer vision settings, the stochastic noising and de-noising process provided by diffusion models has proven useful for purifying input images, thus improving model robustness against adversarial attacks. Similarly, some initial work has explored the use of random noising and de-noising to mitigate adversarial attacks in an NLP setting, but improving the quality and efficiency of these methods is necessary for them to remain competitive. We extend upon methods of input text purification that are inspired by diffusion processes, which randomly mask and refill portions of the input text before classification. Our novel method, MaskPure, exceeds or matches robustness compared to other contemporary defenses, while also requiring no adversarial classifier training and without assuming knowledge of the attack type. In addition, we show that MaskPure is provably certifiably robust. To our knowledge, MaskPure is the first stochastic-purification method with demonstrated success against both character-level and word-level attacks, indicating the generalizable and promising nature of stochastic denoising defenses. In summary: the MaskPure algorithm bridges literature on the current strongest certifiable and empirical adversarial defense methods, showing that both theoretical and practical robustness can be obtained together. Code is available on GitHub at https://github.com/hubarruby/MaskPure.

Keywords: Adversarial Robustness · Certified Robustness · Deep Learning

1 Introduction

Adversarial attacks have been studied in natural language processing for many years. With the increased use of large language models (LLMs) in real-world applications, it has become increasingly important to prevent adversarial inputs from causing incorrect or harmful outputs in these models; small changes in an input can lead to dramatic failures, such as misclassification, hallucination, and generally erroneous output, depending on the model and task.

© The Author(s), under exclusive license to Springer Nature Switzerland AG 2024
A. Rapp et al. (Eds.): NLDB 2024, LNCS 14762, pp. 379–393, 2024.
https://doi.org/10.1007/978-3-031-70239-6_26

Diffusion models have recently found great success in computer vision [6], and as a result, interest has grown in applying diffusion models to NLP tasks as well [38]. The intuition behind the generative portion of a diffusion model is that of "denoising" or purifying data. Because of this, in computer vision, these models have successfully been used to mitigate adversarial attacks, by adding and subsequently removing partial noise from an input [3, 27, 32].

Some limited initial work has explored employing diffusion-inspired defenses to mitigate adversarial attacks in the context of text [20], and previous studies have shown that incorporating randomness and stochastic purification has found success in improving robustness [30, 35]. Our purification method, MaskPure, is inspired by Li et al. [20] for improving robustness of text classification. Their approach randomly masks and refills tokens within multiple copies of an input text using BERT [7], followed by using a voting function to determine the final classification output. The idea behind this approach is that the masking and de-masking of tokens mimics the noising and de-noising that occurs in diffusion-based adversarial defenses in the image setting. MaskPure further explores and improves upon this stochastic purification of text by incorporating the use of different voting methods and fine-tuning unique models for mask-filling, rather than using one model for all parts of the purification and classification task.

We demonstrate the success of our method by testing BERT [7] on various adversarial attacks at the character and word levels, and comparing against recent work that leverages random perturbation-based defense [20, 35]. We find that MaskPure outcompetes previous methods when employing different voting-based recovery methods, and that it obtains these gains without any adversarial fine-tuning or any knowledge of attacker vocabulary. This is in contrast to works such as Ye et al. [33], which rely on knowledge of the attacks being performed in order to employ their defense. When defending against particularly-difficult modern attacks [10, 14], our method obtains accuracy-under attack scores as much as 25% higher than previous work (Table 3).

In addition, we leverage past results from Zeng et al. [35] to make certifiable guarantees on MaskPure's performance against adversaries. Our study serves as strong evidence in favor of the continued harnessing of stochastic purification methods to improve robustness, based on both positive theoretical and empirical results.

Overall, the contributions of this paper are the following:

- We introduce MaskPure, a novel diffusion-inspired defense mechanism, which enhances robustness against adversarial attacks in text classification by utilizing unique voting methods and a novel mask-filling approach, *without* requiring adversarial training.
- MaskPure is the first case of diffusion-inspired text purification we are aware of that is used to successfully defend against character-level attacks. At the same time, MaskPure outperforms previous works on empirical robustness when defending against word-level attacks.
- We demonstrate that MaskPure is provably certifiably robust, in addition to its strong empirical performance.

The rest of this paper starts by discussing related works, followed by establishing the problem of adversarial robustness in a formal manner and presenting the essence of the MaskPure algorithm. The paper continues with details of the experiments performed and results obtained on the AG News and IMDB datasets; first, empirical results are presented, followed by a proof of certified robustness and presentation of results from the experiments used to obtain robustness certificates.

2   Related Work

2.1   Adversarial Attacks in NLP

Recent surveys on adversarial robustness in NLP [1,11] describe many ways adversaries can be generated in NLP settings: for example by changing the input text at the character level (swapping, replacing), at the word level (insertion, deletion, swapping, substitution), and at the sentence level (deleting, injecting, paraphrasing). Among these, some of the most common and effective attacks include those that use a greedy search algorithm, such as Bert-Attack [19], TextFooler [14], DeepWordBug [10], and TextBugger [18]. Many of these attack styles are readily implemented in various forms in the TextAttack library [26], which we use to measure the robustness of our method when performing text classification. We test our defense method on one character-level attack, Deep Word Bug [10], and two settings of the word-level attack TextFooler [14].

2.2   Adversarial Defense in NLP

Many defense methods have been proposed to enhance the robustness of NLP models, including adversarial training [13,16,24,25,34,37], changes to model architecture [1,11,15,28], and add-ons such as spell-checking [2]. While adversarial training has shown effectiveness in enhancing robustness, it also presents challenges: it requires careful creation of adversarial examples and can significantly increase computational resources and training time. The presented defense method MaskPure avoids these potential issues, while also attaining stronger results than recent defenses that do utilize adversarial training (see Sect. 5 for comparison).

Recent approaches to defending against adversarial texts by incorporating randomness have shown promising results: Swenor and Kalita [30] demonstrated that adding random perturbations to adversarial inputs can bring classification model performance back to its original level. Additionally, Li et al. [20] demonstrate one of the first uses of diffusion-inspired purification in the text domain, by masking ("noising") and replacing ("de-noising") random tokens in the input. Both of these works show the potential utility of further exploring the use of randomness and purification for mitigating adversarial attacks in language settings.

Table 1 presents a comparison of the MaskPure defense method with other defenses in the literature. In the table, green denotes a positive aspect of the defense method compared to the others, red denotes a negative, and yellow denotes that the aspect of the defense method is neither explicitly positive nor negative compared to the others. "Defensive logit synthesis" refers to use of constructed logit scores (e.g. by majority voting or similar methods) rather than only defending with an averaged-logit voting approach. "Attack levels" refer to whether the method was tested and/or successful against both word and character-level attacks. "Fine-tuning requirements" denote whether or not the method requires fine-tuning of any models apart from the initial fine-tuning of the classifier for the tested dataset. With MaskPure, the masked LM is tuned depending on the task – this is denoted by "Per Dataset"; the method used by Li et al. [20] tunes the same model for masked language modelling and classifying, which requires the least fine-tuning among the listed approaches; for RanMASK, a new classifier must be fine-tuned depending on the relative quantity of the input text that is masked, as well as for each dataset; for SAFER, no fine-tuning is used apart from the classifier tuning.

Table 1. Comparison of MaskPure with other well-performing defenses. *SAFER's performance, although very strong, benefits from the usage of a synonym table (assuming knowledge of the attack type), making direct comparison unfair.

Property	MaskPure (ours)	Text Purification [20]	RanMASK [35]	SAFER [33]
Certifiably Robust	Yes	No	Yes	Yes
Uses Defensive Logit Synthesis	Yes	No	Yes	Yes
Adversarial Training	Not Needed	Yes	Yes	Yes
Attack Levels	Word & Char.	Word only	Word & Char.	Word only
Empirical Performance	Very Strong	Strong	Strong	Very Strong*
Uses Synonym Table	No	No	No	Yes
Fine-tuning Requirements	MLM, Per Dataset	Classifier and MLM, Together	Classifier, Per Dataset & Per Mask %	Classifier Only

3   Problem Formulation and Algorithm Design

Stochastic purification has a history of success in the continuous domain of computer vision [3, 27, 32], and preliminary promising results for defending against textual adversaries. Our study presents a novel method that improves

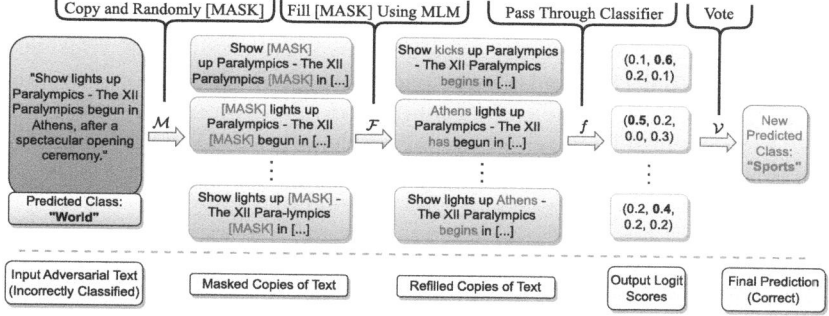

Fig. 1. The pipeline for the MaskPure purification process, as demonstrated using an example from the AG News dataset. In this illustrative example, the perturbed sample contains an adversarial word, "begun" that leads to misclassification. The masking, filling, and voting process allows the classifier to correctly recover the correct label, Sports.

stochastic text purification methods used to mitigate adversarial attacks. A formal description of the problem and our approach is provided below (Fig. 1).

3.1 Notation for Adversarial Examples

We use notation similar to Zeng et al. [35] and Levine and Feizi [17]: a dataset of texts, $\mathcal{X}$, has corresponding class labels, $y \in \mathcal{Y}$. Each $y \in \mathcal{Y}$ is an integer label from the set $C := \{1, 2, ..., c\}$, where c is the number of classes that can be predicted. Each $x \in \mathcal{X}$ is a sequence of "tokens" (typically words, but also including other characters, like punctuation) which can be passed into a trained classifier model, $f : \mathcal{X} \rightarrow \mathcal{Y}$. Hence, any text $x \in \mathcal{X}$ can be expressed as $x_1, x_2, ..., x_j$, where j is the number of individual tokens in the text.

To formulate the concept of an adversarial input, we consider what results from "perturbing" or changing d number of tokens within some x. If x is an input that can be correctly classified by f (i.e. $f(x) = y$, where y is the correct class), then a successful adversarial version of the input, called x', is a sequence that differs from x by d tokens while also satisfying $f(x') \neq y$. In other words, x' is a maligned version of x designed to fool the classifier f. We use Hamming distance $|| \cdot ||_0$ to denote the similarity of two input texts; saying that $||x - x'||_0 = d$ is equivalent to saying that x and x' have different tokens at d positions (while being the same in every other position). In this case, x and x' are of the same length, j.

We say that the model f is certified robust against d-sized adversaries on an input x if, with some (preferably high) probability, we know that $f(x') = y$. This definition applies for any x' satisfying $||x - x'||_0 \leq d$, meaning the model is robust against any and all changes to the text sequence x, so long as the number of changes is below or equal to the size d.

Next, we define the symbol $\ominus$ between two texts x and x', which represents the set of token indices where these texts differ. To illustrate this, consider the text x as "Quick Red Fox" and x' as "Quick Blue Fox", the set $x \ominus x'$ would be $\{2\}$ because the tokens at the second position in the two texts are different.

Furthermore, consider a set of indices $\mathcal{S}$, denoted as $\{1, \ldots, j\}$. Let $\mathcal{I}(j, k)$ be a set that contains all sets of k unique indices from $\mathcal{S}$. For example, for $\mathcal{S} = \{1, 2, 3, 4\}$ with cardinality $j = 4$, $\mathcal{I}(4, 2)$ might include subsets like $\{1, 2\}$, $\{1, 3\}$, and so on.

Lastly, let $\mathcal{U}(j, k)$ represent a uniform distribution over $\mathcal{I}(j, k)$. In other words, if we sample from $\mathcal{U}(j, k)$, we are effectively selecting k out of j indices without replacement, uniformly. As an example, if we draw a sample from $\mathcal{U}(7, 4)$, we might obtain a set like $\{2, 4, 6, 7\}$.

3.2   Notation for Text Processing

Our algorithm involves multiple steps prior to input to the classifier; first, we introduce a mask operation, denoted as $\mathcal{M}$, which maps pairs of texts and indices, $\mathcal{X}$ and $\mathcal{I}(j, k)$, to a new set $\mathcal{X}_{\text{mask}}$. $\mathcal{X}_{\text{mask}}$ is a similar set to $\mathcal{X}$, but some words in the texts are replaced by a [MASK] token. In particular, every word whose index does not correspond to a value in the input set of indices is converted to the [MASK] token. To illustrate this, consider the text "Hello Beautiful World" and the input indices $\{1, 3\}$; in such a case, $\mathcal{M}$ would transform the text to "Hello [MASK] World".

Next, we define a new function $\mathcal{F}$, which operates on $\mathcal{X}_{\text{mask}}$ and produces $\mathcal{X}_{\text{fill}}$ by replacing [MASK] tokens with predicted words from a masked language model (MLM).

Returning to our classifier, we use $f : \mathcal{X}_{\text{fill}} \to \mathcal{Y}$, as our base method for classifying texts, where the predicted class is represented by $y \in \{1, 2, \ldots, c\}$. In our case, f is a pre-trained BERT classification model from the textattack library.

To summarize, the pipeline for processing a single text involves the following mappings, in sequential order:

$$\mathcal{X} \times \mathcal{I}(j, k) \xrightarrow{\mathcal{M}} \mathcal{X}_{\text{mask}} \xrightarrow{\mathcal{F}} \mathcal{X}_{\text{fill}} \xrightarrow{f} \mathcal{Y}. \tag{1}$$

In practice, f can be considered to be composed of two parts, such that $f = f_c \circ f_l$. The first part of the function, f_l outputs a vector of c logit scores ranging from 0 to 1, which collectively sum to 1. Following that, f_c takes an argmax over the output of f_l to determine the index of the highest logit score, and this returned index is considered the predicted class $y = f(x)$.

Some of the voting methods employed using MaskPure (which are denoted by $\mathcal{V}$ and discussed later on) skip the final step of f_c, and instead use a collection of outputs of f_l to make the decision of the predicted class.

For ease of expressing and proving our claims about certified robustness, we re-frame this notation. Similar to [35], we simplify by defining $p_c(x)$ as the probability that, after randomly masking and filling, f returns the class c:

$$p_c(x) = \mathop{\mathbb{P}}_{\mathcal{H}\sim\mathcal{U}(j_x,k_x)} (f(\mathcal{F}(\mathcal{M}(x,\mathcal{H}))) = c).$$

In this equation, j_x is the cardinality (number of tokens) of x, and k_x is the number of tokens in x to be left unmasked. I.e. $k_x := r_{int}((1 - m) \cdot j_x)$, with m being the chosen proportion of tokens to be masked and $r_{int}(\cdot)$ indicating a nearest-integer rounding function. In our experiments, we set $m = 0.3$. Details surrounding hyperparameter selection are excluded due to space constraints.

Following similar steps to Zeng et al. [35], we then define a composite "smoothed" classifier $g(x)$ as:

$$g(x) = \mathop{\arg\max}_{c\in\mathcal{Y}} [p_c(x)].$$

Intuitively, $g(x)$ represents the most probable output from $f(x)$, if all but k_x words from x are randomly masked and re-filled before passing through the classifier.

3.3   Miscellaneous Notation

The following notation is used in the discussion of our algorithm below. Let $I_n = \{1, 2, ..., n\}$. For a set of n ordered text inputs, called X_n, and a set of n ordered samples $\mathcal{H} \sim \mathcal{U}(j, k)$ called H_n, define $\phi : I_n \to X_n \times H_n$ by $\phi(i) = (x_i, \mathcal{H}_i)$ for each $i \in I_n$.

3.4   MaskPure Algorithm

The purification method aims to be a simple algorithm leveraging an existing approach by Li et al. [20]. Note that the method is agnostically applied to all inputs, since in real life settings it is difficult to detect which inputs are adversarial or not. The general structure of the purification methods is as follows, for any one input:

1. Make v identical copies of the input x, such that we have a set of copies, $X = \{x_1, x_2, ..., x_v\}$; for each copy x_i, mask a proportion k_x of the input tokens according to the masking scheme, $\mathcal{M}$. That is, take v samples $\mathcal{H} \sim U(h_x, k_x)$, such that we have $H = \{\mathcal{H}_1, \mathcal{H}_2, ..., \mathcal{H}_v\}$; then, obtain a set of masked outputs, $\mathcal{M}(\phi(I_v))$. The function ϕ is defined as above.
2. Refill the masked tokens in each of the v copies, according to the mask-filling scheme, $\mathcal{F}$. In our case, $\mathcal{F}$ uses a masked language model to predict words to replace each [MASK] token.
3. Pass the new "re-filled" copies of the input text through the classification model f (in the case with averaged logit voting, only pass through f_l, instead of the entire composite function $f_c \circ f_l$). Then, use a voting function $\mathcal{V}$ to obtain a final set of output logit scores which conveys the top predicted class.

Hence, for a classification task with c output classes, the final predicted output $c' \in \{1, 2, .., c\}$ can be expressed as

$$c' = argmax\Big\{\mathcal{V}\Big(f\Big(\mathcal{F}\Big(\mathcal{M}(\phi(I_v))\Big)\Big)\Big)\Big\}. \tag{2}$$

4   Experiments

4.1   Datasets

We measure the model's robustness to adversaries on the AG News sentiment classification task [36] and the IMDB movie review classification task [23], since these are widely used tasks for classification models, making results easily comparable to other works. For AG News, we use the initial 1000 test samples for each dataset provided in the TextFooler Github repository [14], to replicate results from Li et al. [20]. For the IMDB task, 100 samples were randomly drawn from the test set used by Jin et al. [14]. This smaller sample number is due to the larger amount of text in each sample, which in turn requires more computational power and longer processing time.

4.2   Models

Classifications outputs are produced using *bert-base-uncased-ag-news*, available from the TextAttack library [26]; this model has been fine-tuned for text-classification on the AG News training corpus. To perform the mask-filling process, we use *bert-based-uncased* for masked language modelling, provided by Huggingface [31], and fine-tuned on the training data from the HuggingFace AG News dataset using a cross entropy loss function.

4.3   Implementation Details

One key variation behind our method compared to Li et al. [21] comes from fine-tuning the masked LM from step (2) on the dataset being tested on, rather than using the baseline BERT model. The intuition behind this is based on diffusion purification in computer vision; since the goal of an adversarial purification process is to remove noise and faults in a text, it makes sense for the purification process to bring the perturbed sample closer to the original distribution of data. Hence, we should expect the model used for mask filling to contribute to better performance if it is able to better fill masks according to the structure of the original data.

This is different from Li et al., [20], where the authors take a combined-training approach; in their method, the same model is used for both classification and mask filling, and it is trained on a joint loss function based on cross entropy; this cross entropy is calculated based on both classification and mask filling performance. We hypothesize that the reason for MaskPure's better performance may be that this combined training actually hinders performance when compared with fine-tuning two separate models on each task; the jointly-trained model is required to optimize for two distinct components of a loss function, which may compete against one another. Notably, using the alternative approach, MaskPure obtains improved performance on AG News and IMDB when compared with [20], and it does this *without* including adversarial-training of the classifier or mask-filling algorithm.

The other factor that differentiates MaskPure involves the voting process, $\mathcal{V}$. It is common practice for adversarial defense methods to use multiple modified copies of an input for classification, obtaining predictions from each copy, and using a voting process to combine the predictions [21,22,30,35]. Our result takes advantage of this approach, evaluating accuracy-under attack using different voting methods. These methods include logit averaging, majority vote-based logit scores, and a naive max or "one hot" majority vote-based logit scores. A description of each is provide below.

The logit averaging function takes the average of the n logit scores which are outputted by the classifier model. For example, assume there is a case with $n = 5$ vectors of logits, s_1 through s_5, where there are 2 classes scored in each vector. If the vectors are $\mathbf{s}_1 = (0.9, 0.1)$, $\mathbf{s}_2 = (0.76, 0.24)$, $\mathbf{s}_3 = (1, 0)$, $\mathbf{s}_4 = (0.81, 0.19)$, $\mathbf{s}_5 = (0.16, 0.84)$, then the averaged logits are $(0.726, 0.274)$, meaning the first class is the predicted output.

The majority vote-based logit scores are calculated by considering the top prediction of each of the n copies of the text, and then summing the total number of top predictions for each class. The final output is then normalized based on the number of voters. Using the same example logit scores, since there are 4 "votes" for the first class and only 1 vote for the second, that means the final logits outputted would be $(\frac{4}{5}, \frac{1}{5}) = (0.8, 0.2)$.

When using the naive max logit voting method, the result is very similar, but the output is not weighted. Instead, the output would simply be $(1, 0)$, with all of the weight put on the first class, since it won the majority vote.

Our results in Table 2 show that naive max logit scores perform better than basic majority voting, and that both of the majority voting methods perform better than the averaged logit voting. This informs the view that better majority-vote-resistant attacks need to be discovered to keep up with defenses that trick the typical greedy-search algorithms of attack methods (as also suggested by Devvrit et al. [8]).

5   Results

See Table 2 for results comparing MaskPure with other recent stochastic-based defenses. Following the terminology used by Zeng et al. [35], Cln% refers to the accuracy of the method used *before* attacking was conducted, while Boa% denotes "robust accuracy" of the model while under attack. Measuring both of these values allows us to see how MaskPure performs at defending against adversarial attacks, while at the same time measuring the extent to which it can retain baseline performance of the BERT model used.

Table 2. TAE after-attack accuracy for BERT on the IMDB and AG News datasets, using different defense methods. The performance of other defense methods are presented as reported by Li et al. [20].

Defense ↓ Attack →	DeepWordBug		TextFooler (50)		TextFooler (12)	
	Cln%	Boa%	Cln%	Boa%	Cln%	Boa%
IMDB ↓						
BERT (No Defense)	**92.7**	33.4	92.7	0.9	92.7	5.3
Adv-HotFlip [9]	-	-	95.1	8.0	95.1	36.1
FreeLB [37]	-	-	**96.0**	7.3	**96.0**	30.2
FreeLB++ [22]	-	-	93.2	45.3	-	-
Text Purification [20]	-	-	93.0	51.0	93.0	81.5
MaskPure: Averaged Logit	92.0	63.0	-	-	92.0	73.0
MaskPure: Majority-V Logit	91.0	71.0	-	-	91.0	75.0
MaskPure: Naive Max Logit	92.0	**78.0**	94.0	**64.0**	94.0	**82.0**
AG News ↓						
BERT (No Defense)	95.9	37.1	**95.9**	16.5	95.9	29.5
Adv-HotFlip [9]	-	-	91.2	18.2	91.2	35.3
FreeLB [37]	-	-	90.5	20.1	90.5	40.1
SAFER [33]	95.2	78.4	-	-	-	-
Text Purification [20]	-	-	90.6	34.9	90.6	61.5
RanMASK [35]	95.3	77.1	93.9	68.6	-	-
MaskPure: Averaged Logit	**96.3**	68.9	95.6	53.5	95.9	63.9
MaskPure: Majority-V Logit	95.9	79.2	95.6	69.3	**96.0**	76.3
MaskPure: Naive Max Logit	95.7	**87.8**	95.6	**84.0**	95.8	**85.8**

Informed by Si et al. [29], we use the standard Transfer Adversarial Evaluation, TAE (as opposed to Static Attack Evaluation, SAE) to measure the adversarial performance of our model. This evaluation method makes the defense more challenging, as new adversarial texts are generated for every defense type and variation, rather than using only one original set of adversarial texts for evaluation.

In Table 2, spaces marked with "-" mean that the test results were not available for that particular attack/defense combination. The value k (denoted with "TextFooler (k)") corresponds to the size of the synonym list used by the TextFooler attack. Note that [20] did not test their diffusion-inspired defense against DeepWordBug attacks, making MaskPure the first study we are aware of to test the capability of stochastic-purification on character-level attacks. Zeng et al. [35] did test against DeepWordBug, but their work only involved random masking without the diffusion-inspired mask-filling process.

The tests for MaskPure on AG News were conducted with the 1000-sample test set used by Li et al. [20], originally from Jin et al. [14]. Due to resource and time limitations, the tests for MaskPure on IMDB were conducted with 100 random samples from the IMDB test set. To obtain results for this table using MaskPure, the masking rate m is set to 0.3, and voting quantity v is set to 11.

Of particular note, MaskPure exceeds the performance of Li et al. [20] by over 25% when tested on TextFooler with a synonym list of size k = 12, while also retaining high clean accuracy. For all three attacks tested, the top MaskPure robust accuracy score was over 10% higher than the compared works. The only exception to this 10%+ robustness increase is when comparing against SAFER [33] on the AG News dataset; however, this comparison is not entirely fair, due to SAFER's assumed knowledge of attacker vocabulary (as discussed in an earlier section). Hence, MaskPure's ability to outperform SAFER at all (87.8 vs 78.4 Boa%), even without access to attacker vocabulary, is a testament to the method's effectiveness.

6   Certified Robustness of MaskPure

Recent work in computer vision has been able to demonstrate some theoretical justifications for the success of diffusion purification [27,32]. For instance, Nie et al. [27] prove that, under certain constraints, the L2 distance between a diffusion-purified adversarial sample and the original clean sample is bounded (with some probability) by a reasonably small value. Similar (though not entirely analogous) robustness findings have been shown for textual adversaries [33,35]. The approach used by Zeng et al. [35] demonstrates certifiable robustness for a classifier trained on samples of text that are partially masked (but not re-filled). Their work can easily be transposed to a similar result in our case, which also includes the "refilling" component of the text purification. Our theorem is a direct corollary of theirs, with the only difference being the definition of β. We demonstrate this below.

Theorem 1. *For an original text x and an adversarial text x', if $\|x - x'\|_0 \le d$, then:*

$$p_c(x) - p_c(x') \le \beta\Delta \tag{3}$$

$\forall c \in \mathcal{Y}$. *Here,*

$$\Delta = 1 - \frac{\binom{j_x - d}{k_x}}{\binom{j_x}{k_x}}, \tag{4}$$

$$\beta = \mathbb{P}\left(f(\mathcal{F}(\mathcal{M}(x, \mathcal{H}))) = c \mid \mathcal{H} \cap (x \ominus x') \ne \emptyset\right).$$

Proof. Recall that

$$p_c(x) = \mathbb{P}(f(\mathcal{F}(\mathcal{M}(x, \mathcal{H}))) = c) \text{ and } p_c(x') = \mathbb{P}\left(f\left(\mathcal{F}\left(\mathcal{M}\left(x', \mathcal{H}\right)\right)\right) = c\right). \tag{5}$$

Using the law of total probability, we can find that:

$$p_c(x) = \mathbb{P}\Big([f(\mathcal{F}(\mathcal{M}(x,\mathcal{H}))) = c] \wedge [\mathcal{H} \cap (x \ominus x') = \emptyset]\Big)$$
$$+ \mathbb{P}\Big([f(\mathcal{F}(\mathcal{M}(x,\mathcal{H}))) = c] \wedge [\mathcal{H} \cap (x \ominus x') \neq \emptyset]\Big),$$
$$p_c(x') = \mathbb{P}\Big([f(\mathcal{F}(\mathcal{M}(x',\mathcal{H}))) = c] \wedge [\mathcal{H} \cap (x \ominus x') = \emptyset]\Big)$$
$$+ \mathbb{P}\Big([f(\mathcal{F}(\mathcal{M}(x',\mathcal{H}))) = c] \wedge [\mathcal{H} \cap (x \ominus x') \neq \emptyset]\Big). \tag{6}$$

In the case where $\mathcal{H} \cap (x \ominus x') = \emptyset$ and $\mathcal{F}$ is deterministic (the latter of which we can assume), it is clear that x and x' hold the same values at each $i \in \mathcal{H}$. Hence, conditional on $\mathcal{H} \cap (x \ominus x') = \emptyset$, it is true that $\mathcal{F}(\mathcal{M}(x,\mathcal{H})) = \mathcal{F}(\mathcal{M}(x',\mathcal{H}))$. This gives us:

$$\mathbb{P}(f(\mathcal{F}(\mathcal{M}(x,\mathcal{H}))) = c \mid \mathcal{H} \cap (x \ominus x') = \emptyset) =$$
$$\mathbb{P}(f(\mathcal{F}(\mathcal{M}(x',\mathcal{H}))) = c \mid \mathcal{H} \cap (x \ominus x') = \emptyset) \tag{7}$$

The rest of the proof follows using the same steps as Zeng et al. [35].

Note that given the black-box nature of language models, it is intractable to precisely compute $p_c(x)$. Instead, we take a similar approach to [5,12], and [35], since we can estimate the guaranteed lower bound of the probability based on the one-sided exact (Clopper Pearson) interval [4]. More specifically, it is possible to obtain a lower bound on $p_c(x)$ by running the classifier f on n different masked and subsequently-filled copies of an input x. This lower bound holds true with a probability of at least $1 - \alpha$, and the estimation of the lower bound can be improved by increasing the number n of purified samples that are classified.

For n classification trials, denote the number of runs where the prediction is correct as $n_c \leq n$. Let $p := n_c/n$ and denote Beta$(\alpha; n, p)$ as the α-th quantile of a beta distribution with parameters n and p. If we (safely) assume that

$p, n_c \sim Binomial(n, p)$, then the Clopper-Pearson estimation [4] allows us to say:
$$min(p_c(x)) = \text{Beta}(\alpha; n_c, n - n_c + 1) \tag{8}$$

with probability of at least $(1 - \alpha)$.

This estimation will be useful in establishing a starting point for certifiable robustness. Based on Corollary 1.1 in [35], rearranging equation (3) tells us that

$$\mathbb{P}(g(x') = c \mid 0.5 < min(p_c(x)) - \beta\Delta) \geq 1 - \alpha. \tag{9}$$

Hence, if appropriate estimates for β and $min(p_c(x))$ can be obtained, then we can determine the conditions under which our classifier is robust against any d-perturbed adversary, x'; this robustness is guaranteed with a probably of at least $(1 - \alpha)$; in this work, we set $\alpha = 0.05$ for calculating robustness certificates, so that we can compare to Zeng et al. [35].

Table 3. Robustness certificates on AG News with different masking rates n.

Method	Rate $m\%$	Acc%	MCB	Method	Rate $m\%$	Acc%	MCB
RanMASK [35]	0.4	96.2	1	MaskPure (Ours)	0.1	96.0	1
	0.5	95.7	1		0.3	96.2	1
	0.6	95.7	2		0.4	96.2	1
	0.7	94.5	2		0.5	95.4	1
	0.8	92.0	3		0.6	94.0	2
	0.9	91.1	5		0.7	93.1	2

6.1 Empirical Evaluation of Robustness Certificates

To verify the certified robustness of MaskPure for any given input, it is possible to follow a similar process to Zeng et al. [35], using Monte Carlo methods to estimate values of $p_c(x)$. Informed by this work, we similarly approximate $\beta \approx p_c(x)$ and run a series of trials to find $p_c(x)$. Results are shown in Table 3. There, MCB is "Median Certified Robustness: the largest number, d, of perturbations that can be applied to samples in the dataset such that $> 50\%$ of the texts are still classified correctly.

In Table 3, for Zeng et al. [35], maximum median certified robustness (MCB) was achieved when using $m = 0.9$ or higher. For MaskPure, maximum MCB was achieved with a lower masking rate of 0.6, indicating the increased efficiency of MaskPure. Though the maximum MCB is a greater value for RanMASK, MaskPure obtains comparable MCB and accuracy when comparing at lower masking rates (i.e. RanMASK with $m = 0.4$ has approximately the same performance as MaskPure at $m = 0.1$), which is better for computational cost. Note that this comparison is not entirely fair, since Zeng et al. [35] used RoBERTA rather than BERT for their certificates.

7 Conclusion

Random purification has much potential for defending against adversarial inputs, as has been demonstrated in computer vision and by some pioneering works in NLP. By further exploring the effectiveness and benefits of stochastic purification in NLP, MaskPure contributes to filling this largely-unexplored gap in the literature. Our method demonstrates empirically-exceptional and certifiably-robust performance on the AG News and IMDB datasets when compared with previous defenses. This serves as a signal for future research to be conducted at the intersection of stochastic purification and improving robustness.

Acknowledgements. This material is based upon work supported by the National Science Foundation under Grant No. 2050919. Any opinions, findings, and conclusions or recommendations expressed in this material are those of the authors and do not necessarily reflect the views of the National Science Foundation.

References

1. Alshemali, B., Kalita, J.: Improving the reliability of deep neural networks in NLP: a review. Knowl.-Based Syst. **191**, 105210 (2020)
2. Belinkov, Y., Bisk, Y.: Synthetic and Natural Noise Both Break Neural Machine Translation (2018)
3. Carlini, N., Tramer, F., Dvijotham, K.D., Rice, L., Sun, M., Kolter, J.Z.: (Certified!!) Adversarial Robustness for Free! (2022)
4. Clopper, C.J., Pearson, E.S.: The use of confidence or fiducial limits illustrated in the case of the binomial. Biometrika **26**(4), 404–413 (1934)
5. Cohen, J., Rosenfeld, E., Kolter, Z.: Certified adversarial robustness via randomized smoothing. In: Proceedings of the 36th International Conference on Machine Learning, pp. 1310–1320. PMLR (2019). ISSN 2640-3498
6. Croitoru, F.A., Hondru, V., Ionescu, R.T., Shah, M.: Diffusion models in vision: a survey. IEEE Trans. Pattern Anal. Mach. Intell. 1–20 (2023)
7. Devlin, J., Chang, M.W., Lee, K., Toutanova, K.: BERT: pre-training of deep bidirectional transformers for language understanding. In: NAACL, pp. 4171–4186. Minneapolis, Minnesota (2019)
8. Devvrit, Cheng, M., Hsieh, C.J., Dhillon, I.: Voting based ensemble improves robustness of defensive models (2020). arXiv:2011.14031 [cs, stat]
9. Ebrahimi, J., Rao, A., Lowd, D., Dou, D.: HotFlip: white-box adversarial examples for text classification (2018). arXiv:1712.06751 [cs]
10. Gao, J., Lanchantin, J., Soffa, M.L., Qi, Y.: Black-box generation of adversarial text sequences to evade deep learning classifiers. In: 2018 IEEE Security and Privacy Workshops (SPW), pp. 50–56 (2018)
11. Goyal, S., Doddapaneni, S., Khapra, M.M., Ravindran, B.: A survey of adversarial defences and robustness in NLP. ACM Comput. Surv. 3593042 (2023)
12. Jia, R., Raghunathan, A., Göksel, K., Liang, P.: Certified robustness to adversarial word substitutions. In: EMNLP-IJCNLP, pp. 4129–4142. Association for Computational Linguistics, Hong Kong, China (2019)
13. Jiang, H., He, P., Chen, W., Liu, X., Gao, J., Zhao, T.: SMART: robust and efficient fine-tuning for pre-trained natural language models through principled regularized optimization. In: ACL, pp. 2177–2190. Association for Computational Linguistics, Online (2020)
14. Jin, D., Jin, Z., Zhou, J.T., Szolovits, P.: Is BERT really robust? A strong baseline for natural language attack on text classification and entailment (2020). arXiv:1907.11932 [cs]
15. Jones, E., Jia, R., Raghunathan, A., Liang, P.: Robust encodings: a framework for combating adversarial typos. In: ACL, pp. 2752–2765. Association for Computational Linguistics, Online (2020)
16. Kurakin, A., Goodfellow, I., Bengio, S.: Adversarial machine learning at scale (2017). arXiv:1611.01236 [cs, stat]
17. Levine, A., Feizi, S.: Robustness certificates for sparse adversarial attacks by randomized ablation. In: AAAI, vol. 34, no. 04, pp. 4585–4593 (2020)
18. Li, J., Ji, S., Du, T., Li, B., Wang, T.: TextBugger: generating adversarial text against real-world applications. In: NDSS, San Diego, February 2019. The Internet Society (2019)
19. Li, L., Ma, R., Guo, Q., Xue, X., Qiu, X.: BERT-ATTACK: adversarial attack against BERT using BERT (2020). arXiv:2004.09984 [cs]

20. Li, L.N., Song, D.N., Qiu, X.N.: Text adversarial purification as defense against adversarial attacks. In: Proceedings of the 61st Annual Meeting of the Association for Computational Linguistics (2023)
21. Li, Y., Zhou, K., Zhao, W.X., Wen, J.R.: Diffusion models for non-autoregressive text generation: a survey (2023). arXiv:2303.06574 [cs]
22. Li, Z., et al.: Searching for an effective defender: benchmarking defense against adversarial word substitution. In: EMNLP, pp. 3137–3147. Association for Computational Linguistics, Online and Punta Cana, Dominican Republic (2021)
23. Maas, A.L., Daly, R.E., Pham, P.T., Huang, D., Ng, A.Y., Potts, C.: Learning word vectors for sentiment analysis. In: ACL-HLT, pp. 142–150. Association for Computational Linguistics, Portland, Oregon, USA (2011)
24. Madry, A., Makelov, A., Schmidt, L., Tsipras, D., Vladu, A.: Towards deep learning models resistant to adversarial attacks (2019). arXiv:1706.06083 [cs, stat]
25. Miyato, T., Dai, A.M., Goodfellow, I.: Adversarial training methods for semi-supervised text classification (2021). arXiv:1605.07725 [cs, stat]
26. Morris, J.X., Lifland, E., Yoo, J.Y., Grigsby, J., Jin, D., Qi, Y.: TextAttack: a framework for adversarial attacks, data augmentation, and adversarial training in NLP (2020). arXiv:2005.05909 [cs]
27. Nie, W., Guo, B., Huang, Y., Xiao, C., Vahdat, A., Anandkumar, A.: Diffusion models for adversarial purification (2022). arXiv:2205.07460 [cs]
28. Sakaguchi, K., Duh, K., Post, M., Durme, B.V.: Robsut wrod reocginiton via semi-character recurrent neural network. In: AAAI. AAAI'17, pp. 3281–3287, San Francisco, California, USA (2017)
29. Si, C., et al.: Better robustness by more coverage: adversarial and mixup data augmentation for robust finetuning. In: Findings of ACL-IJCNLP 2021, pp. 1569–1576. Association for Computational Linguistics, Online (2021)
30. Swenor, A., Kalita, J.: Using random perturbations to mitigate adversarial attacks on sentiment analysis models. In: International Conference on Natural Language Processing (ICON), pp. 519–528. National Institute of Technology, Silchar, India (2021)
31. Wolf, T., et al.: HuggingFace's transformers: state-of-the-art natural language processing (2020). arXiv:1910.03771 [cs]
32. Xiao, C., et al.: DensePure: understanding diffusion models for adversarial robustness (2023)
33. Ye, M., Gong, C., Liu, Q.: SAFER: a structure-free approach for certified robustness to adversarial word substitutions. In: ACL, pp. 3465–3475. Association for Computational Linguistics, Online (2020)
34. Yoo, J.Y., Qi, Y.: Towards improving adversarial training of NLP models (2021). arXiv:2109.00544 [cs]
35. Zeng, J., Xu, J., Zheng, X., Huang, X.: Certified robustness to text adversarial attacks by randomized [MASK]. Comput. Linguist. 49(2), 395–427 (2023). https://doi.org/10.1162/coli_a_00476, https://aclanthology.org/2023.cl-2.5
36. Zhang, X., Zhao, J., LeCun, Y.: Character-level convolutional networks for text classification. In: Cortes, C., Lawrence, N., Lee, D., Sugiyama, M., Garnett, R. (eds.) NIPS, vol. 28. Curran Associates, Inc. (2015)
37. Zhu, C., Cheng, Y., Gan, Z., Sun, S., Goldstein, T., Liu, J.: FreeLB: enhanced adversarial training for natural language understanding (2020). arXiv:1909.11764 [cs]
38. Zou, H., Kim, Z.M., Kang, D.: Diffusion models in NLP: a survey (2023). arXiv:2305.14671 [cs]

SERIEMA: A Framework to Enhance Clustering Stability, Compactness, and Separation by Fusing Multimodal Data

Fillipe dos Santos Silva[1,2,3](✉), Julio Cesar dos Reis[1,3], and Marcelo S. Reis[1,2,3]

[1] Hub de Inteligência Artificial e Arquiteturas Cognitivas (H.IAAC),
Campinas, Brazil
[2] Artificial Intelligence Laboratory (Recod.ai), Campinas, Brazil
[3] Instituto de Computação, Universidade Estadual de Campinas (UNICAMP),
Campinas, Brazil
{fillipesantos,jreis,msreis}@ic.unicamp.br

Abstract. This article presents SERIEMA, a multimodal framework deSignEd to enhance clusteRIng stability, compactness, and separation by fusing catEgorical, nuMericAl, and textual data. We aim to overcome these critical challenges in clustering, which is essential for marketers to effectively provide targeted content to various consumer segments. SERIEMA aims to provide a more nuanced and comprehensive understanding of customer segments by leveraging a transformer-based embedding model for textual data analysis, a data fusion component, and a generative-based model. This integration overcomes the limitations of traditional methods that rely solely on structured data or text, facilitating precise segmentation and improved marketing strategies. The framework is evaluated using established stability measures and benchmarked against existing strategies across real-world datasets. The results highlight SERIEMA's superior effectiveness in enhancing clustering stability, compactness, and separation compared to traditional segmentation methods. The study's contributions are significant, marking a notable advancement in multimodal learning and customer segmentation.

1 Introduction

Customer segmentation provides valuable insights into customer preferences and behaviors, allowing for a more refined understanding of distinct consumer groups [26]. By acquiring these insights, marketers can tailor content to address each segment's unique needs and challenges [19]. Effective customer segmentation relies on stable clustering along with the creation of clusters characterized by high compactness and precise separation. Stable clustering ensures consistent identification of customer segments across datasets and, over time, is crucial for adapting marketing strategies to evolving consumer behaviors. Clusters with

A. Rapp et al. (Eds.): NLDB 2024, LNCS 14762, pp. 394–408, 2024.
https://doi.org/10.1007/978-3-031-70239-6_27

high compactness and clear separation enable marketers to discern distinct traits and preferences within the customer base, facilitating the creation of targeted messages that enhance engagement, satisfaction, and conversion rates [5, 29]. These elements, when combined, optimize the effectiveness of marketing efforts, contributing to both immediate success and the cultivation of long-term customer loyalty [1, 13].

The literature has proposed various methods to enhance clustering stability, compactness, and separation, explicitly focusing on structured data like categorical and numeric data [11, 13, 18]. A popular method is the Deep Embedding Clustering With Mixed Data Using Soft-Target Network (Mixed DEC + SU), an algorithm that leverages a deep learning framework for clustering [18]. This method uses a stacked autoencoder to learn latent feature representations and perform a clustering task using a soft assignment procedure. Although the Mixed DEC + SU strategy is quite effective, it faces challenges when applied to multimodal data encompassing structured and textual forms. Existing research suggests that combining structured data with textual data could improve overall data representation [2, 9, 28]. Structured data, such as age and purchase history, provides clear, quantifiable information, while textual data from social media reveals customer sentiments and preferences. We demonstrate that integrating these data types enhances cluster stability, compactness, and separation. We achieve a more comprehensive view of customers by combining objective metrics from structured data with textual insights. This allows for precise segmentation and more effective marketing, bridging the quantitative and qualitative data gap.

We introduce SERIEMA, a novel multimodal framework deSignEd to enhance clusteRIng stability, compactness, and separation by fusing catEgcrical, nuMericAl, and textual data. Our solution consists of three principal components: a transformer-based embedding model, a data fusion component, and a generative-based model. The transformer-based embedding model is essential for converting textual data into meaningful embeddings, capturing intricate patterns and relationships. The data fusion component fuses the derived embeddings with categorical and numerical data to form a comprehensive feature space. Taking its output, a generative-based model, such as Variational Autoencoder (VAE) or Generative Adversarial Network (GAN), is then employed to refine the clustering process further. By capturing the intricate relationships within the data, generative models ensure that clusters are cohesive and consistent, reducing variance and leading to more stable clustering outcomes [12, 31].

We employed five established stability measures to evaluate its effectiveness: Adjusted Rand Index (ARI), Adjusted Mutual Information Score (AMIS), BagClust (BG), Hierarchical Agglomerative Nesting (HAN), and Optimal Transport Alignment (OTA)—each one renowned for assessing cluster stability across varied contexts [17, 21, 22]. The Davies-Bouldin Score (DBS) metric also evaluates cluster compactness and separation. We selected the K-means algorithm for our evaluations due to its straightforward nature and acknowledged instability when juxtaposed with other methods, such as hierarchical techniques [32].

In our evaluation, we used real-world datasets, namely: Yelp Dataset. Melbourne Airbnb dataset, PetFinder.my, and Women's clothing reviews. To assess the robustness of our model, we benchmarked it against four prevailing strategies. The first strategy, **Structured**, strictly employs numerical and categorical data. The second, **Textual**, focuses exclusively on text embeddings. The third approach, **Combined Dataset - Structure Textual (CD-ST)**, integrates both structured and textual datasets, while the fourth, **Mixed DEC + SU**, assimilates mixed data categories to enhance convergence stability [18].

Our main contributions are as follows:

- We introduce SERIEMA, a novel framework that effectively integrates categorical, numerical, and textual data, significantly enhancing clustering stability, compactness, and separation in multimodal environments;
- We demonstrate that by integrating categorical and numerical data with textual data within our multimodal framework, we can significantly improve the stability of clustering algorithms;
- We achieve state-of-the-art clustering stability with our multimodal framework, advancing the field of multimodal learning through enhanced data integration techniques;
- To the best of our knowledge, we are the first to integrate categorical, numerical, and textual data in a multimodal framework, significantly enhancing clustering stability, compactness, and separation.

The remainder of this article is organized as follows. Section 2 presents a state-of-the-art synthesis and discussions. Section 3 presents SERIEMA. Section 4 outlines the experimental evaluations conducted. Section 5 presents the obtained results. Section 6 discusses our findings. Finally, Sect. 7 presents the conclusions and directions for future work.

2   Related Work

Various approaches have been proposed in the literature to improve clustering stability, quality and separation with emphasis on categorical, numeric, and text data [11, 18, 25, 30].

The development of a strategy to increase the stability of market segmentation solutions derived from binary empirical consumer data was proposed in [11]. Through the combination the variable selection method proposed in [4] and the global stability analysis introduced in [7], the strategy simultaneously selects the segmentation variables and the number of segments leading to high global stability levels. This can result in a less thorough understanding of market segments and lead to suboptimal marketing strategies.

A novel non-linear Deep Encoder-Decoder framework to capture the cross-domain information for mixed data types is proposed in [24]. The authors discuss the challenge of representing data that contain mixed variable types, such as numerical and categorical variables. However, the proposed model's non-linear space can introduce complexities when dealing with cross-domain information, particularly when incorporating unstructured text data. This complexity can hinder the overall performance of the model [2].

A Deep Fusion Clustering Network (DFCN) to enhance clustering performance by dynamically integrating autoencoder and graph autoencoder representations through a structure and attribute information fusion module is proposed in [25]. It employs a triplet self-supervision strategy and an improved graph autoencoder for consensus representation learning, showing superiority over state-of-the-art methods across various datasets.

A method called Deep Embedded Clustering (DEC) that simultaneously learns feature representations and cluster assignments using deep neural networks was proposed in [30]. However, if the difference between soft assignment and target values is significant, DEC applications may suffer from convergence problems.

The Deep Embedding Clustering With Mixed Data Using Soft-Target Network (Mixed DEC + SU), which leverages mixed data and soft-target updates from an enhanced deep Q-learning algorithm for more stable convergence, was proposed in [18].This integration of varied data and improved learning capabilities enhances clustering analysis, offering better assignments and deeper insights not previously achieved.

An adaptation of the DEC technique, termed X-DEC, designed to handle mixed data types effectively and enhance cluster stability and generalizability in critical care settings is proposed in [15]. By integrating an X-shaped variational autoencoder (XVAE) into the DEC framework, the study achieves improved cluster stability. The X DEC can produce stable and clinically relevant clusters, potentially enhancing patient care and resource allocation in intensive care environments. However, the study also notes potential overfitting risks associated with optimizing X-DEC's hyperparameters for cluster stability, which might oversimplify the model.

The strengths and weaknesses of these studies defined our approach. In particular, SERIEMA improves upon these efforts by incorporating categorical, numerical, and textual features, resulting in a more complete representation of the data and significantly enhanced clustering stability.

3   SERIEMA

SERIEMA has three key components: a transformer-based model, a data fusion component, and a generative-based model. Figure 1 provides a visualization of our framework. We describe in detail each component that follows:

1. **Transformer-based Model Component:** This component employs a pretrained transformer-based model, including, but not limited to, BERT, GPT-2.0, LLaMA, and others [3,6]. Without specialized heads, these models are exclusively for embedding purposes, leveraging their extensive pre-existing knowledge. We denote the output of this process as $\mathbf{x}$, which provides our framework with robust encoding capabilities for textual information, thereby delivering significant advantages [20].

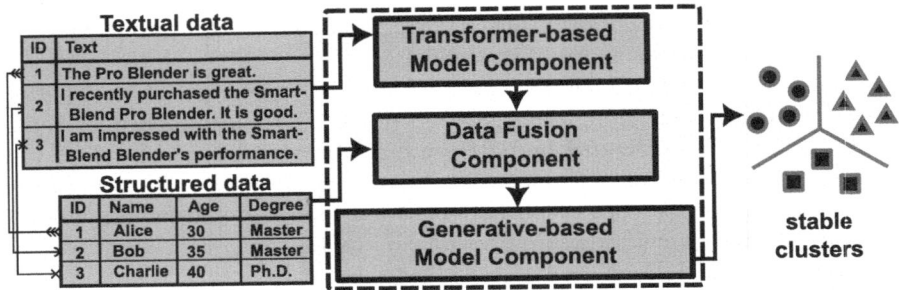

Fig. 1. SERIEMA combines text data with categorical and numerical features for enhanced clustering stability, compactness and separation.

For an input text $\mathbf{I}$, we use $\mathcal{T}$ to represent a pre-trained transformer model. The embedding process is succinctly captured as:

$$\mathbf{x} = \mathcal{T}(\mathbf{I}), \tag{1}$$

where $\mathbf{x}$ signifies the contextual embedding obtained from $\mathbf{I}$, used exclusively for embedding. This mechanism allows our framework to process and interpret the semantic depth of textual information efficiently.

2. **Data Fusion Component:** Let $\mathbf{x}$ represent the contextual embedding from a transformer-based model, and let $\mathbf{c}$ and $\mathbf{n}$ denote the categorical and numerical features, respectively. The process to integrate these inputs and produce an output $\mathbf{m}$, suitable for a generative-based model, is formalized as follows:

$$\mathbf{m} = \mathcal{F}(\mathbf{x}, \mathbf{c}, \mathbf{n}), \tag{2}$$

where $\mathcal{F}$ symbolizes the fusion method applied to combine the distinct feature types. We investigate eight distinct methods $\mathcal{F}_i, i \in \{1, 2, \ldots, 8\}$, each tailored to the unique properties of the integrated data, as detailed in Table 1. These methods range from basic concatenation to advanced approaches utilizing Multilayer Perceptrons (MLPs), aligning with recent innovations in multimodal data fusion.

3. **Generative-based Model Component:** Using the output $\mathbf{m}$ from the data fusion component, let $\mathcal{G}$ denote a generative model (e.g., VAE or GAN). The process for improved clustering is given by:

$$\mathbf{y} = \mathcal{G}(\mathbf{m}), \tag{3}$$

where $\mathbf{y}$ is the output, enhancing clustering stability and coherence by understanding data distributions via $\mathcal{G}$, aiming for robust and consistent clustering across different data scenarios.

4   Experimental Methodology

This section outlines our approach for evaluating the SERIEMA framework, covering datasets in Sect. 4.1, evaluation metrics in Sect. 4.2, model architecture in Sect. 4.3, baseline comparisons in Sect. 4.4, data fusion methods in Sect. 4.5, and the experimental procedure in Sect. 4.6.

Table 1. Feature integration methods. Uppercase bold letters represent 2D matrices, lowercase bold letters represent 1D vectors, and non-bold, lowercase letters are scalar values.

#	Method	Equation
1	text only	$\mathbf{m} = \mathbf{x}$
2	concatenation	$\mathbf{m} = (\mathbf{x}, \mathbf{c}, \mathbf{n})$
3	MLP on categorical then concatenate	$\mathbf{m} = (\mathbf{x}, MLP(\mathbf{c}), \mathbf{n})$
4	individual MLP on categorical and numerical features then concatenate	$\mathbf{m} = (\mathbf{x}, MLP(\mathbf{c}), MLP(\mathbf{n}))$
5	MLP on concatenated categorical and numerical features then concatenate	$\mathbf{m} = (\mathbf{x}, MLP(\mathbf{c}, \mathbf{n}))$
6	attention on categorical and numerical features	$\mathbf{m} = \alpha_{x,x}\mathbf{W}_x\mathbf{x} + \alpha_{x,c}\mathbf{W}_c\mathbf{c} + \alpha_{x,n}\mathbf{W}_n\mathbf{n}$ $\alpha_{i,j} = $ $\dfrac{exp(LeakyReLu(\mathbf{a}^T(\mathbf{W}_i\mathbf{x}_i, \mathbf{W}_j\mathbf{x}_j)))}{\sum_{k \in \{x,c,n\}} exp(LeakyReLu(\mathbf{a}^T(\mathbf{W}_i\mathbf{x}_i, \mathbf{W}_k\mathbf{x}_k)))}$
7	gating on categorical and features and then sum (Gating) [23]	$\mathbf{m} = \mathbf{x} + \alpha\mathbf{h}$ $\mathbf{h} = \mathbf{g}_c \odot (\mathbf{W}_c\mathbf{C}) + \mathbf{g}_n \odot (\mathbf{W}_n\mathbf{n}) + b_a$ $\alpha = min(\frac{\|\mathbf{x}\|_2}{\|\mathbf{h}\|_2}) * \beta, 1)$ $\mathbf{g}_i = R(\mathbf{W}_{gi}(\mathbf{i}, \mathbf{x}) + b_i)$, where β is a hyperparameter and R is an activation function
8	weighted feature sum on text, categorical, and numerical features (Weighted Sum)	$\mathbf{m} = \mathbf{x} + \mathbf{w}_c \odot \mathbf{W}_c\mathbf{c} + \mathbf{w}_n \odot \mathbf{W}_n\mathbf{n}$

4.1   Datasets

The first dataset is from the Yelp public dataset challenge[1], which is a collection of user reviews and other related details from the Yelp platform. It involves structured features such as user-generated numerical details, including review counts and average ratings, and unstructured elements represented by the review texts. Next is the Melbourne Airbnb Open dataset[2], which gives a detailed insight into

---

[1] www.kaggle.com/datasets/yelp-dataset/yelp-dataset.
[2] www.kaggle.com/datasets/tylerx/melbourne-airbnb-open-data.

Airbnb listings in Melbourne, Australia. It encompasses structured details like price, number of reviews, review scores, and unstructured data in the listing descriptions and host information. Following this, the PetFinder.my Adoption Prediction dataset[3] offers structured information detailing the numerical and categorical characteristics of pet listings, in addition to unstructured data captured in the pet descriptions penned by the caretakers. Lastly, the Women's E-Commerce Clothing Reviews dataset[4] comprises customer reviews and ratings of women's clothes sold online, including structured data such as age, rating, and categorical details like department and class name. It also contains unstructured data, which comes as detailed review texts. The richness and diversity of these datasets provide a solid ground for performing a robust stability analysis.

4.2   Evaluation Metrics

We utilized five stability metrics to assess SERIEMA's effectiveness, each offering unique insights into clustering performance. These metrics include ARI, AMIS, BG, OTA, and HAN.

ARI measures the similarity between two data clusterings, adjusted for chance, as expressed by:

$$\text{ARI} = \frac{\sum_{ij} \binom{n_{ij}}{2} - \left[\sum_i \binom{a_i}{2} \sum_j \binom{b_j}{2}\right] / \binom{n}{2}}{\frac{1}{2}\left[\sum_i \binom{a_i}{2} + \sum_j \binom{b_j}{2}\right] - \left[\sum_i \binom{a_i}{2} \sum_j \binom{b_j}{2}\right] / \binom{n}{2}}, \tag{4}$$

where $\sum_{ij} \binom{n_{ij}}{2}$ tallies pairs in the same cluster for both clusterings, $\sum_i \binom{a_i}{2}$ and $\sum_j \binom{b_j}{2}$ are the counts of within-cluster pairs, and $\binom{n}{2}$ is the total pair count. Variables n_{ij}, a_i, and b_j represent shared elements and cluster sizes. It scores from -1 (entirely disjoint) to 1 (identical clusterings) [14].

Derived from mutual information, AMIS corrects for chance, formulated as:

$$\text{AMIS} = \frac{2I(Y;C)}{H(Y)+H(C)} - E\left[\frac{2I(Y;C)}{H(Y)+H(C)}\right], \tag{5}$$

where $I(Y;C)$ represents mutual information, revealing shared knowledge between clusterings Y and C. Entropies $H(Y)$ and $H(C)$ measure each clustering's diversity.

BG uses resampling techniques to gauge clustering stability and a bootstrapped aggregation process to evaluate clustering robustness [8]. This method selects optimal clusters by randomly splitting the dataset D into learning set L and test set T for a specified maximum cluster number K. Clustering is applied to L to obtain partition P_L, then a classifier C builds a predictive model. C is applied to T to generate another partition P_T. The method can use PAM clustering with a linear discriminant analysis classifier [16]. Similarly, HAN provides a stability index for each data point in the cluster analysis [21].

---

[3] www.kaggle.com/competitions/petfinder-adoption-prediction.

[4] www.kaggle.com/datasets/nicapotato/womens-ecommerce-clothing-reviews.

Lastly, OTA compares clusterings using the theory of optimal transport:

$$\text{OTA} = \min_{\Pi \in \Pi(\mu,\nu)} \langle \Pi, C \rangle, \tag{6}$$

where $\Pi(\mu, \nu)$ denotes all potential transport plans between cluster distributions μ and ν. The optimal plan Π, minimizing cost $\langle \Pi, C \rangle$ where C is the cost matrix, measures the efficiency of converting one clustering to another. The AMIS, BG, HAN, and OTA metrics score from 0 (poor stability) to 1 (optimal stability).

Additionally, DBS was used to evaluate clustering compactness and separation:

$$\text{DBS} = \frac{1}{n} \sum_{i=1}^{n} \max_{j \neq i} \left(\frac{\sigma_i + \sigma_j}{d(c_i, c_j)} \right), \tag{7}$$

where n denotes the number of clusters, σ_i and σ_j are the average distances of points to the centroids of clusters i and j respectively, indicating intra-cluster compactness, and $d(c_i, c_j)$ represents the distance between the centroids of clusters i and j, reflecting inter-cluster separation; it aims for lower values, signifying compact and well-separated clusters.

All approach is further complemented by employing the K-means algorithm for cluster computation.

4.3   Model Architecture

The Bidirectional Encoder Representations for Transformers (BERT) model, recognized for its capability in text processing and tokenization [27], forms the core of our Transformer-based Model Component, mathematically denoted as $\mathcal{T}$. This component is pivotal for transforming input text $\mathbf{I}$ into contextual embeddings $\mathbf{x} = \mathcal{T}(\mathbf{I})$, from the pooled output of the last layer of the BERT model, specifically from the [CLS] token.

In conjunction with $\mathcal{T}$, the Data Fusion Component, symbolized as $\mathcal{F}$, is integral to our approach. It merges the contextual embeddings $\mathbf{x}$ from $\mathcal{T}$ with categorical $\mathbf{c}$ and numerical $\mathbf{n}$ features. The fusion operation is encapsulated as $\mathbf{m} = \mathcal{F}(\mathbf{x}, \mathbf{c}, \mathbf{n})$, enriching data representation.

For the Generative-based Model Component, represented by $\mathcal{G}$, we opt for a VAE model. This choice is strategic for refining the multimodal features into a more analyzable form. The transformation is formalized as $\mathbf{y} = \mathcal{G}(\mathbf{m})$, crucial for enhancing the framework's clustering efficiency through an in-depth understanding of data distributions.

The integration of $\mathcal{T}$, $\mathcal{F}$, and $\mathcal{G}$ enhances multimodal data analysis, aiming to improve clustering outcomes.

The loss function merges reconstruction loss with Kullback-Leibler (KL) divergence, adding structure to the latent space for better generalization. The VAE was designed with layers of 768, 500, 300, and 200 units. We divided the entire dataset into 80% for training, 10% for validation, and 10% for testing. An analysis of hyperparameters is provided in the Appendix.

The model was developed using PyTorch[5] and is made available at a GitHub repository[6]. It ran on a system equipped with two Titan X Graphics processing unit (GPU)s, each having 12 GB of Random Access Memory (RAM). The architecture, including the methods in the data fusion component, was inspired by Gu et al. [10].

4.4   Baselines

To benchmark our proposed model, we utilize four baseline strategies for comparison. The **Structured** baseline processes numerical and categorical data exclusively. The **Textual** baseline employs text embeddings generated by the bert-base-uncased model [6]. The **CD-ST** strategy specifically merges structured and textual data on a column-by-column basis for a detailed integration. Lastly, the **Mixed DEC + SU** approach aims to improve stability and convergence by using a mix of categorical and numerical data with soft-target updates [18]. These baselines are critical for assessing our proposed model's distinct advantages and effectiveness.

4.5   Evaluation of Data Fusion Methods

Building on the model architecture previously described, we evaluate the effectiveness of data fusion methods in the SERIEMA framework. We assess these methods' effectiveness across two sample sizes, 500 and the entire dataset, to identify the optimal method for integrating the diverse data processed by our BERT and VAE models. Specifically, 500 samples account for approximately 1.34% of Yelp, 4.52% of Melbourne Airbnb, 4.17% of Petfinder.my, and 2.70% of Women's E-Commerce Clothing Reviews. This smaller sample size analysis is essential to understand model behavior under data scarcity, common in real-world scenarios.

Table 2 shows each method's mean validation loss and 95% confidence interval, highlighting key results in bold. This comprehensive testing is essential to determine the most effective method of integration suited to the diverse characteristics of the data.

We excluded methods **3** (*MLP on categorical then concatenate*) and **4** (*individual MLP on categorical and numerical features then concatenate*) for the Yelp dataset due to their lack of categorical features. During our evaluation, method **7** (*gating*) emerged as the optimal approach for both the Yelp and Airbnb datasets, whereas method **5** (*MLP on concatenated categorical and numerical features, then concatenate*) and method **6** (*attention on categorical and numerical features*) performed best for the PetFinder.my and Women's Clothing Reviews datasets, respectively.

---

[5] pytorch.org.
[6] SERIEMA - GitHub.

4.6   Experimental Procedure

We begin with preprocessing, normalizing numerical data, encoding categorical data for machine readability, and cleaning textual data by removing emojis and non-textual elements.

Following the preprocessing phase, we delved into cluster analysis. We employed the silhouette coefficient to determine the optimal number of clusters, denoted as k, for each dataset and baseline model. This phase was pivotal in setting a benchmark for clustering stability, compactness, and separation, providing a solid foundation for subsequent comparisons.

Building on the model architecture previously described, we conducted a reevaluation to determine the ideal value of k (*e.g.*, with silhouette analysis) for each dataset provided as input. We meticulously selected hyperparameters during training, enhancing the model's adaptability and performance across different datasets and sizes, thereby improving the framework's clustering effectiveness.

Table 2. The mean validation loss, accompanied by a 95% confidence interval, is provided for all methods in the data fusion component across all sample sizes for all datasets, with the best results in bold. In this table, **M** refers to the feature integration method.

M	Yelp 500 s.	Yelp Entire dataset	Airbnb 500 s.	Airbnb Entire dataset	PetFinder.my 500 s.	PetFinder.my Entire dataset	Clothing 500 s.	Clothing Entire dataset
1	246.73 ± 7.3	239.41 ± 5.3	158.05 ± 7.7	136.27 ± 4.5	70.29 ± 6.5	66.05 ± 7.8	35.97 ± 9.0	38.58 ± 4.1
2	241.86 ± 5.4	232.50 ± 3.7	149.78 ± 9.8	122.78 ± 7.4	82.82 ± 8.6	77.45 ± 5.8	48.27 ± 5.5	44.63 ± 9.2
3	–	–	144.79 ± 4.6	119.92 ± 5.8	94.66 ± 3.5	88.82 ± 9.3	20.73 ± 6.7	23.77 ± 6.4
4	–		146.71 ± 6.7	120.18 ± 3.9	80.22 ± 7.3	80.54 ± 6.7	19.28 ± 8.2	17.64 ± 3.9
5	243.54 ± 5.1	237.57 ± 7.9	151.60 ± 7.7	123.60 ± 3.5	**45.28 ± 8.9**	**42.29 ± 8.2**	48.60 ± 8.4	50.10 ± 6.7
6	241.55 ± 3.4	231.79 ± 3.8	155.11 ± 5.1	129.63 ± 6.0	60.99 ± 5.4	57.34 ± 4.9	**14.88 ± 5.1**	**16.55 ± 6.7**
7	**189.09 ± 8.2**	**185.70 ± 5.2**	**107.10 ± 3.5**	**85.23 ± 3.8**	70.05 ± 6.1	66.59 ± 6.2	56.06 ± 5.6	54.21 ± 8.5
8	245.43 ± 9.0	239.57 ± 9.6	125.17 ± 8.5	105.86 ± 7.5	74.40 ± 6.8	68.59 ± 8.3	63.04 ± 8.3	62.25 ± 9.7

Further, we computed the stability, compactness, and separation of the clustering solutions for the model and the baselines across all datasets, employing the optimal k identified earlier. For all purposes, we utilized the *k-means* algorithm across all datasets and models, including those generated by our model. Details on silhouette score analysis are available in the Appendix for interested readers.

This rigorous experimental procedure allowed for a detailed comparison of our framework's clustering effectiveness, stability, compactness, and separation against the baseline models.

5   Results

In this section, we present the main results obtained with our methodology. In Table 3, we present the stability metric results for the test dataset, using both the 500 sample size and the entire dataset with strategies as follows: **A**: Structured; **B**: Textual; **C**: CD-ST; **D**: Mixed DEC + SU; and **E**: SERIEMA; values in bold indicate the best outcomes. We performed the experiment ten times for each sample and metric and reported the mean results with a 95% confidence interval. For the Yelp dataset, SERIEMA excelled in ARI and AMIS metrics for 500 samples and the entire dataset, showing robust clustering of multimodal data. It also outperformed in BG, HAN, and OTA metrics, emphasizing its proficiency in larger datasets. In the Airbnb dataset, SERIEMA demonstrated superior performance and consistency across ARI, AMIS, BG, HAN, and OTA metrics for 500 samples and the entire dataset, highlighting its precision and adaptability. For the PetFinder.my dataset, SERIEMA outshone alternatives in ARI, AMIS, BG, and HAN for both 500 samples and the entire dataset while ranking second in the OTA metric for 500 samples. In the Women's Clothing reviews dataset, SERIEMA showed robust scalability and robustness in ARI and AMIS for 500 samples and the entire dataset. It also maintained superiority in BG, HAN, and OTA metrics, confirming its effectiveness in handling complex datasets.

Table 3. Comparing the stability metrics of various strategies across different sample sizes on four distinct datasets on the test dataset. Values in bold indicate the best outcomes. The strategies are as follows: **A**: Structured; **B**: Textual; **C**: CD-ST; **D**: Mixed DEC + SU; and **E**: SERIEMA.

		Yelp		Airbnb		PetFinder.my		Clothing	
		500 s.	Entire Dataset	500 s.	Entire Dataset	500 s.	Entire Dataset	500 s.	Entire Dataset
ARI	A	0.56 ± .08	0.55 ± .10	0.77 ± .02	0.89 ± .02	0.50 ± .02	0.52 ± .05	0.54 ± .05	0.99 ± .00
	B	0.84 ± .02	0.96 ± .00	**0.93 ± .00**	0.95 ± .00	0.51 ± .02	0.67 ± .07	0.67 ± .06	0.89 ± .03
	C	0.51 ± .10	0.54 ± .10	0.80 ± .02	0.88 ± .02	0.49 ± .03	0.56 ± .03	0.60 ± .02	0.90 ± .03
	D	0.30 ± .02	0.93 ± .03	0.52 ± .03	0.79 ± .01	0.49 ± .02	0.52 ± .01	0.46 ± .07	0.70 ± .01
	E	**0.96 ± .01**	**1.00 ± .00**	0.87 ± .03	**1.00 ± .00**	**1.00 ± .00**	**0.99 ± .00**	**1.00 ± .00**	**1.00 ± .00**
AMIS	A	0.53 ± .07	0.52 ± .10	0.71 ± .02	0.83 ± .02	0.55 ± .01	0.58 ± .04	0.53 ± .02	0.98 ± .00
	B	0.78 ± .02	0.93 ± .01	**0.89 ± .01**	0.91 ± .00	0.60 ± .02	0.73 ± .05	0.63 ± .05	0.84 ± .03
	C	0.48 ± .10	0.51 ± .11	0.74 ± .01	0.83 ± .02	0.56 ± .02	0.63 ± .02	0.58 ± .02	0.85 ± .03
	D	0.26 ± .03	0.88 ± .03	0.59 ± .01	0.73 ± .01	0.57 ± .02	0.60 ± .02	0.40 ± .07	0.67 ± .01
	E	**0.93 ± .02**	**0.99 ± .00**	0.84 ± .03	**1.00 ± .00**	**1.00 ± .00**	**0.99 ± .00**	**1.00 ± .00**	**1.00 ± .01**
BG	A	0.92 ± .02	**1.00 ± .00**	0.93 ± .01	0.95 ± .05	0.72 ± .02	0.73 ± .13	0.79 ± .02	0.76 ± .06
	B	0.97 ± .01	0.99 ± .00	**0.99 ± .00**	**0.99 ± .00**	0.72 ± .02	0.83 ± .02	**0.93 ± .01**	**0.97 = .02**
	C	0.89 ± .04	0.94 ± .04	0.95 ± .01	0.97 ± .01	0.71 ± .02	0.76 ± .09	0.90 ± .01	**0.97 = .02**
	D	0.76 ± .02	0.99 ± .01	0.69 ± .02	0.94 ± .02	0.68 ± .02	0.78 ± .04	0.82 ± .02	0.83 ± .03
	E	**0.99 ± .01**	**1.00 ± .00**	0.97 ± .00	0.97 ± .01	**0.79 ± .04**	**0.85 ± .02**	0.90 ± .02	**0.97 = .05**
HAN	A	0.85 ± .07	0.97 ± .08	0.87 ± .01	0.94 ± .00	0.61 ± .03	0.63 ± .03	0.84 ± .03	0.92 ± .05
	B	0.92 ± .01	0.98 ± .00	**0.96 ± .00**	0.97 ± .00	0.61 ± .03	0.77 ± .01	0.86 ± .01	0.95 ± .01
	C	0.79 ± .04	0.81 ± .05	0.90 ± .01	0.94 ± .01	0.55 ± .03	0.63 ± .03	0.81 ± .03	0.95 ± .02
	D	0.61 ± .01	0.96 ± .01	0.58 ± .02	0.90 ± .01	0.54 ± .03	0.62 ± .04	0.70 ± .04	0.85 ± .02
	E	**0.99 ± .00**	**1.00 ± .00**	0.94 ± .02	**1.00 ± .00**	**0.85 ± .02**	**0.86 ± .02**	**1.00 ± .00**	**1.00 ± .00**
OTA	A	0.49 ± .01	0.50 ± .00	0.70 ± .05	0.73 ± .00	0.17 ± .03	0.13 ± .00	0.40 ± .08	0.40 ± .01
	B	0.73 ± .00	0.73 ± .01	**0.80 ± .01**	0.80 ± .01	0.37 ± .04	0.48 ± .02	0.60 ± .04	0.67 ± .03
	C	0.65 ± .05	0.50 ± .00	0.74 ± .01	0.73 ± .00	0.16 ± .05	0.45 ± .01	0.59 ± .04	0.67 ± .02
	D	0.54 ± .04	0.67 ± .00	0.20 ± .01	0.09 ± .01	0.25 ± .03	0.15 ± .05	0.59 ± .03	0.57 ± .01
	E	**0.88 ± .02**	**0.89 ± .00**	0.77 ± .01	**0.88 ± .01**	**0.60 ± .06**	**0.77 ± .23**	**0.64 ± .25**	**0.89 ± .01**

Table 4 presents the DBS for each strategy across different sample sizes; scores in bold indicate the best results. In the Yelp dataset, the Structured strategy reached a DBS score of 0.66 ± 0.08 for the entire dataset, while SERIEMA excelled with a score of 0.20 ± 0.01, indicating high efficacy. In the Airbnb dataset, the CD-ST method achieved its highest score of 2.79 ± 0.19 for 500 samples. SERIEMA showcased notable performance with a mean score of 0.10 ± 0.01 over the entire dataset, demonstrating its effectiveness in grouping similarity. For the PetFinder.my dataset, SERIEMA consistently decreased the DBS as the sample size grew, nearly reaching optimal clustering at the entire dataset level, signifying excellent adaptability and efficient cluster separation. SERIEMA demonstrated superior clustering efficiency and reliability in the Clothing dataset, indicated by the lowest and most consistent DBS scores across both 500 samples and the entire dataset.

Table 4. The DBS metric for each strategy across different sample sizes. Scores in bold indicate the best results.

Strategy	Yelp		Airbnb		PetFinder.my		Clothing	
	500 s.	Entire dataset	500 s.	Entire dataset	500 s.	Entire dataset	500 s.	Entire dataset
Structured	2.51 ± .12	0.66 ± .08	3.38 ± .17	3.43 ± .17	1.88 ± .03	1.96 ± .09	1.88 ± .13	1.84 ± .11
Textual	3.10 ± .21	3.14 ± .09	2.59 ± .10	2.63 ± .12	2.89 ± .11	3.01 ± .17	2.85 ± .17	2.87 ± .17
CD-ST	0.64 ± .10	0.84 ± .14	2.79 ± .19	2.66 ± .11	3.46 ± .16	3.52 ± .11	3.10 ± .19	3.08 ± .22
Mixed DEC + SU	2.39 ± .28	0.71 ± .21	1.57 ± .06	0.61 ± .03	1.53 ± .04	0.82 ± .03	2.19 ± .17	1.28 ± .10
SERIEMA	**0.30 ± .03**	**0.20 ± .01**	**0.13 ± .01**	**0.10 ± .01**	**0.02 ± .01**	**0.01 ± .01**	**0.48 ± .07**	**0.32 ± .08**

6   Discussion

Our proposed model demonstrated superior effectiveness in the metrics of the ARI and AMIS, consistently outperforming alternatives for 500 samples and the entire dataset. These consistently high scores highlight the model's robustness and precision, especially in handling large, complex multimodal datasets. This makes it ideal for applications requiring stable clustering and accurate information retrieval.

In the BG metric, SERIEMA was proficient for the entire dataset, indicating its ability to provide reliable and accurate clustering for extensive datasets. This affirms its effectiveness in scenarios demanding effective cluster separation and robustness. Our solution showed consistent superiority in the HAN metric for both 500 samples and the entire dataset. This underscores its capacity to generate stable and reliable clusters, proving its robustness and scalability and making it well-suited for various clustering tasks.

In the OTA metric assessment, SERIEMA emerged superior for the entire dataset, reaffirming its reliability and adaptability across different data volumes. Its consistent high OTA scores emphasize its suitability for maintaining clustering stability and agreement. Our proposed multimodal model displayed the lowest and most consistent DBS scores for 500 samples and the entire dataset, indicating its strong and consistent clustering patterns and making it a preferred choice for achieving clustering consistency and efficacy.

The SERIEMA framework improves clustering for multimodal data but has complexities due to its use of transformer models, data fusion, and generative models. This complexity can increase computational needs, such as more memory and longer processing times, challenging real-time or resource-limited applications. Also, its effectiveness is limited by how well models like BERT and GPT-3.5 match the target data and domain.

Data fusion challenges and the need for optimal integration of diverse data types can affect clustering performance. SERIEMA's potential is notable, but its generalization across various datasets and domains requires further validation, which could limit its effectiveness due to diverse data characteristics.

Scalability issues arise with large, complex datasets, and the risk of overfitting could hinder generalization. The model's tolerance to data imperfections, such as missing values or noise, remains untested, impacting its real-world use. Finally, hyperparameter tuning in the generative model requires time-consuming experimentation with potentially inconsistent results. Figure 2 shows the correlation between dataset size and execution time.

Fig. 2. Execution time correlates with dataset size.

Despite its limitations, the SERIEMA framework advances multimodal data clustering. By integrating transformer-based models, data fusion techniques, and generative models, it enhances clustering stability and efficiency, demonstrating superior performance across key metrics. This innovative approach addresses the complex needs of multimodal data analysis and sets a new benchmark for the field, establishing SERIEMA as a powerful solution for challenging clustering tasks.

7   Conclusion

This research presented SERIEMA, an innovative approach to customer segmentation that integrates structured and textual data. Our findings enhanced clustering stability, compactness, and separation, in heterogeneous data contexts by developing a novel multimodal model building on BERT and a unique data fusion component coupled with a VAE. This advancement tackles the challenge of clustering instability, which often affects traditional methods despite data preprocessing and normalization. Future efforts will focus on refining our model for broader industry applications, including images and audio, and enhancing text analysis with advanced language models like GPT and BERT.

Acknowledgements. This project was supported by the Ministry of Science, Technology, and Innovation of Brazil, with resources granted by the Federal Law 8.248 of October 23, 1991, under the PPI-Softex. The project was coordinated by Softex and published as Intelligent agents for mobile platforms based on Cognitive Architecture technology [01245.013778/2020- 21]. Additional support was provided by CAPES, CNPq, and FAPESP.

References

1. Akay, Ö., Yüksel, G.: Clustering the mixed panel dataset using gower's distance and k-prototypes algorithms. Commun. Stat.-Simul. Comput. **47**(10), 3031–3041 (2018)
2. Balducci, B., Marinova, D.: Unstructured data in marketing. J. Acad. Mark. Sci. **46**, 557–590 (2018)
3. Brown, T., et al.: Language models are few-shot learners. Adv. Neural. Inf. Process. Syst. **33**, 1877–1901 (2020)
4. Brusco, M.J.: Clustering binary data in the presence of masking variables. Psychol. Methods **9**(4), 510 (2004)
5. Cortez, R.M., Clarke, A.H., Freytag, P.V.: B2b market segmentation: a systematic review and research agenda. J. Bus. Res. **126**, 415–428 (2021)
6. Devlin, J., Chang, M.W., Lee, K., Toutanova, K.: Bert: pre-training of deep bidirectional transformers for language understanding. arXiv preprint arXiv:1810.04805 (2018)
7. Dolnicar, S., Lazarevski, K.: Methodological reasons for the theory/practice divide in market segmentation. J. Mark. Manag. **25**(3–4), 357–373 (2009)
8. Dudoit, S., Fridlyand, J.: A prediction-based resampling method for estimating the number of clusters in a dataset. Genome Biol. **3**, 1–21 (2002)
9. Fresneda, J.E., Burnham, T.A., Hill, C.H.: Structural topic modelling segmentation: a segmentation method combining latent content and customer context. J. Mark. Manag. **37**(7–8), 792–812 (2021)
10. Gu, K., Budhkar, A.: A package for learning on tabular and text data with transformers. In: Proceedings of the Third Workshop on Multimodal Artificial Intelligence, pp. 69–73. Association for Computational Linguistics, Mexico City (2021). https://doi.org/10.18653/v1/2021.maiworkshop-1.10. https://www.aclweb.org/anthology/2021.maiworkshop-1.10
11. Hajibaba, H., Grün, B., Dolnicar, S.: Improving the stability of market segmentation analysis. Int. J. Contemp. Hosp. Manag. **32**(4), 1393–1411 (2020)
12. Harshvardhan, G., Gourisaria, M.K., Pandey, M., Rautaray, S.S.: A comprehensive survey and analysis of generative models in machine learning. Comput. Sci. Rev. **38**, 100285 (2020)
13. He, Z., Yu, C.: Clustering stability-based evolutionary k-means. Soft. Comput. **23**(1), 305–321 (2019)
14. Hubert, L., Arabie, P.: Comparing partitions journal of classification 2 193–218. Google Scholar, 193–128 (1985)
15. de Kok, J.W., et al.: Deep embedded clustering generalisability and adaptation for integrating mixed datatypes: two critical care cohorts. Sci. Rep. **14**(1), 1045 (2024)
16. Van der Laan, M., Pollard, K., Bryan, J.: A new partitioning around medoids algorithm. J. Stat. Comput. Simul. **73**(8), 575–584 (2003)

17. Lall, S., Sinha, D., Ghosh, A., Sengupta, D., Bandyopadhyay, S.: Stable feature selection using copula based mutual information. Pattern Recogn. **112**, 107697 (2021)
18. Lee, Y., Park, C., Kang, S.: Deep embedded clustering framework for mixed data. IEEE Access **11**, 33–40 (2022)
19. Leung, F.F., Gu, F.F., Li, Y., Zhang, J.Z., Palmatier, R.W.: Influencer marketing effectiveness. J. Mark. **86**(6), 93–115 (2022)
20. Lin, T., Wang, Y., Liu, X., Qiu, X.: A survey of transformers. AI Open (2022)
21. Liu, T., Yu, H., Blair, R.H.: Stability estimation for unsupervised clustering: a review. Wiley Interdisc. Rev. Comput. Stat. **14**(6), e1575 (2022)
22. Peyvandipour, A., Shafi, A., Saberian, N., Draghici, S.: Identification of cell types from single cell data using stable clustering. Sci. Rep. **10**(1), 12349 (2020)
23. Rahman, W., et al.: Integrating multimodal information in large pretrained transformers. In: Proceedings of the 58th Annual Meeting of the Association for Computational Linguistics, pp. 2359–2369. Association for Computational Linguistics, Online (2020)
24. Sahoo, S., Chakraborty, S.: Learning representation for mixed data types with a nonlinear deep encoder-decoder framework. arXiv preprint arXiv:2009.09634 (2020)
25. Tu, W., et al.: Deep fusion clustering network. In: Proceedings of the AAAI Conference on Artificial Intelligence, no. 11 in 2, pp. 9978–9987 (2021)
26. Varadarajan, R.: Customer information resources advantage, marketing strategy and business performance: a market resources based view. Ind. Mark. Manag. **89**, 89–97 (2020)
27. Vaswani, A., et al.: Attention is all you need. Adv. Neural Inf. Process. Syst. **30** (2017)
28. Vo, N.N., Liu, S., Li, X., Xu, G.: Leveraging unstructured call log data for customer churn prediction. Knowl.-Based Syst. **212**, 106586 (2021)
29. Von Luxburg, U., et al.: Clustering stability: an overview. Found. Trends® Mach. Learn. **2**(3), 235–274 (2010)
30. Xie, J., Girshick, R., Farhadi, A.: Unsupervised deep embedding for clustering analysis. In: International Conference on Machine Learning, pp. 478–487. PMLR (2016)
31. Yang, L., Fan, W., Bouguila, N.: Clustering analysis via deep generative models with mixture models. IEEE Trans. Neural Netw. Learn. Syst. **33**(1), 340–350 (2020)
32. Zhou, S., et al.: A comprehensive survey on deep clustering: taxonomy, challenges, and future directions. arXiv preprint arXiv:2206.07579 (2022)

Exploiting Graph Embeddings
from Knowledge Bases for Neural
Biomedical Relation Extraction

Anfu Tang[1(✉)], Louise Deléger[2], Robert Bossy[2], Pierre Zweigenbaum[3],
and Claire Nédellec[2]

[1] Sorbonne Université, CNRS, ISIR, 75005 Paris, France
`tang@isir.upmc.fr`
[2] Université Paris-Saclay, INRAE, MaIAGE, 78350 Jouy-en-Josas, France
`{louise.deleger,robert.bossy,claire.nedellec}@inrae.fr`
[3] Université Paris-Saclay, CNRS, Laboratoire Interdisciplinaire des Sciences du
Numérique, 91405 Orsay, France
`pz@lisn.fr`

Abstract. Integrating external knowledge into neural models has been extensively studied to improve the performance of pre-trained language models, especially in the biomedical domain. In this paper, we explore the contribution of graph embeddings to relation extraction (RE) tasks. Given a pair of candidate entity mentions in a text, we hypothesize that the relations between them in an external knowledge base (KB) help predict whether a relation exists in the text, even if the KB relations are different from those of the RE task. Our approach consists of computing KB graph embeddings and estimating the plausibility that a KB relation exists between the candidate entities to better predict the target relation in the text. Experiments conducted on three biomedical RE tasks show that our method outperforms the baseline model PubMedBERT and achieves comparable performance to state-of-the-art methods. Our code is available at https://github.com/Bibliome/KBPubMedBERT.

Keywords: Relation Extraction · Knowledge Base · PubMedBERT

1 Introduction

Relation extraction (RE) is an important task in the domain of Natural Language Processing (NLP). It consists of predicting the existence of semantic relations and relation types given two entities and a text span, typically a complete sentence. An example is given in Fig. 1.

Transformer-based [29] pre-trained language models (PLMs) such as BERT [10] provide state-of-the-art (SOTA) performance on multiple NLP tasks. By self-supervised pre-training with objectives like Masked Language Modeling (MLM) on large-scale corpora, PLMs learn to produce contextualized vector representations at the word piece [32] level. To make BERT more suitable for

A. Rapp et al. (Eds.): NLDB 2024, LNCS 14762, pp. 409–422, 2024.
https://doi.org/10.1007/978-3-031-70239-6_28

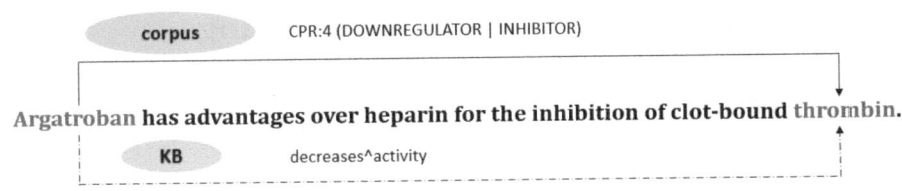

Fig. 1. An example from ChemProt [17]. A relation "downregulator | inhibitor" is annotated in the sentence between *Argatroban* and *thrombin*; A relation "decrease^activity" exists between the entities in an external knowledge base CTD [8].

domain-specific scenarios, researchers have created domain-specific BERT variants [14,18] by pre-training BERT on in-domain corpora.

Pre-training BERT on a text corpus does not have the explicit goal of learning factual knowledge. Injecting factual knowledge, especially knowledge from existing knowledge bases (KBs), has thus received much attention. Various studies such as [15,30] show that using a KB-related pre-training objective helps to inject factual knowledge. Others focus on using a KB to obtain additional training data for distant supervision [16] or pre-training [15]. Since graph embedding models such as [5,26,27] have been proposed to encode graph-structured data, some methods propose to leverage these graph embeddings in neural networks [34].

However, in the context of relation extraction from text, in-domain KBs often contain relations that are different from those searched in the text, though they may be relevant to them. For instance, the Comparative Toxicogenomics Database (CTD) [8] contains 134 chemical-gene interactions such as "*affects^stability*", while in the ChemProt [17] dataset the target classes are like "*downregulator | inhibitor*". Though both CTD relations and ChemProt relations describe interactions between chemicals and genes, CTD relations are more precise compared to ChemProt relations, as shown in Fig. 1. This leads us to hypothesize that leveraging these fine-grained KB relations can help detect coarser-grained relations in texts.

In this paper, we propose KB-PubMedBERT, a neural model specifically designed to extract biomedical relations by exploiting relations in an external KB, especially in the case where KB relations are different from the target relations in the RE tasks. Our model consists of the biomedical pre-trained PubMedBERT [14], and graph embeddings computed with RotatE [27]. We start from domain KBs that contain relations that are possibly semantically related to the target relations of RE tasks: we hypothesize that these KB relations may help improve RE performance. We use graph embeddings to estimate the plausibility that KB relations exist between two entity mentions. By adding this plausibility profile to the output of the pre-trained PubMedBERT, we make our model encode both textual and KB information. We observe that KB-PubMedBERT outperforms plain PubMedBERT on three RE tasks. To the best of our knowledge, we are the first to exploit KB relations that are not the same as the target biomedical RE task relations. Our method brings the following advantages:

1. No identity constraint on KB relation types: our method applies to scenarios where KB relations are not the same as target RE task relations;
2. Low cost: Our method requires no additional pre-training, and uses the existing RotatE graph embedding method to integrate KB information;
3. Effectiveness: We observe that our method consistently outperforms the KB-less baseline on three RE tasks in the biomedical domain.

2   Related Work

In this section, we present graph embedding methods through which we embed both KB concepts and relations into the vector space, then we focus on previous studies about the integration of KB information into BERT.

2.1   Graph Embedding Methods

Embedding graph nodes (concepts) and edges (relations) have been extensively studied by the representation learning community. Context-based graph embedding methods such as node2vec [13] consist of first applying random walks over a graph to create node sequences, then in a way similar to word2vec [22], training node embeddings using neighboring nodes as context. Some graph embedding methods embed graph edges as well. TransE [5] treats edges (relations) as translations in vector space: given a triple $(subj, r, obj)$, denoting the corresponding vectors by $(\mathbf{e}_{subj}, \mathbf{r}, \mathbf{e}_{obj})$, TransE expects that $\mathbf{e}_{obj} = \mathbf{e}_{subj} + \mathbf{r}$. RotatE [27] follows the same principle but instead of translations, it represents edges as rotations in the complex vector space:

$$\mathbf{e}_{obj} = \mathbf{e}_{subj} \circ \mathbf{r} \tag{1}$$

$\mathbf{e}_{obj} = \mathbf{e}_{subj} \circ \mathbf{r}$ where $\circ$ is the Hadamard (element-wise) product. In our work, we use RotatE to obtain both node and edge embeddings because it consistently outperforms TransE on multiple datasets, as reported in [27]. We leave the test of other graph embedding methods for further work.

2.2   Integration of KB Information Into BERT

Domain-specific knowledge bases usually contain verified, well-curated triples $(subj, r, obj)$ indicating that two entities $subj, obj$ are linked by a certain relation r. To the best of our knowledge, most previous KB-enhanced methods use the following three strategies, independently or together:

1. Collecting additional training data using the KB;
2. Infusing KB graph embeddings;
3. Updating pre-training objectives.

We detail them below.

Collecting Additional Training Data Using the KB. Traditional distant supervision methods for RE collect weakly labeled data by aligning entity pairs in a KB to entity pairs in texts. They assume that two entities co-occurring in a sentence denote the relation of the KB. For example, Iinuma et al. [16] proposed to collect distant supervision data by first extracting relation triplets from multiple knowledge bases, then collecting sentences from PubMed literature in which entity pairs are found to match those of KB triplets strictly. Two BERT models were then trained separately on distant supervision data and the target corpus. An architecture combining representations from the two models was then further fine-tuned. Though methods based on distant supervision may improve the relation extraction performance by increasing the amount of training data, the knowledge base is required to have the same relations as those of RE tasks. Besides, relational information about entities that are not directly linked is not exploited.

Infusing KB Graph Embeddings. Another solution for the integration of KB information into pre-trained LMs is to use pre-trained KB graph embeddings. In this section, we focus on methods that integrate pre-trained graph embeddings with no need for pre-training. Papaluca et al. [25] propose to first feed complete sentences to BERT, then average textual representations of tokens that belong to each entity to obtain entity textual representations x_{entity}^{BERT}. Final entity representations are the concatenation of textual representations and pre-trained TransE entity embeddings: $x_{entity} = [x_{entity}^{BERT}, x_{entity}^{graph}]$. Finally, the representations of subject and object entities are passed to a biaffine layer $\mathcal{B}$ for relation classification, where the function of a biaffine layer is: $\mathcal{B}(x_1, x_2) = x_1^T U x_2 + W(x_1 \| x_2) + b$. Asada et al. [3] propose to calculate knowledge graph embeddings over PharmaHKG [2], which is a heterogeneous knowledge graph. Descriptions and molecular structures are also regarded as nodes in PharmaHKG. Pre-trained BERT is used to initialize textual description nodes, and molecular structure nodes are initialized with a pre-trained Chem-BERTa [7] model. For each sentence, KB node placeholders that represent the two candidate entities are appended to the sentence, and share the same position embeddings with the corresponding entity tokens. At the output of BERT, KB entity token embeddings are concatenated with the [CLS] embeddings. That method explores the computation of entity embeddings from a rich, heterogeneous knowledge graph but does not explicitly represent the relations that may hold between a pair of entities in the KB.

Updating Pre-training Objectives. Originally, BERT was pre-trained to solve MLM and Next Sentence Prediction tasks [10]. Some studies propose to use a third KB-related pre-training objective to integrate KB information. In UmlsBERT, Michalopoulos et al. [21] updated the MLM task as follows: instead of randomly masking a single token and predicting it, they also predict tokens that share the same concept unique identifier as the masked token if this token is part of an entity from the UMLS Metathesaurus [4]. In ERNIE, Zhang et al.

[36] proposed a third pre-training objective associated with entity normalization between tokens and KB concepts: they randomly mask normalized concepts and make the model predict these masked concepts. However, these methods based on pre-training require more computing resources compared to fine-tuning. Our proposed method requires no specific or additional pre-training, therefore alleviating the need for large computing resources.

3   Methods

In this part, we present our proposed KB-enhanced model, KB-PubMedBERT. Our model contains two modules: a pre-trained domain-specific PubMedBERT model and a graph embedding module that consists of a concept embedding layer and a relation embedding layer. Different from previous KG embedding-based methods, our method does not seek to simply concatenate KG and sentence embeddings, but to exploit KG relation plausibility scores that are calculated from KG embeddings

3.1   Hypothesis

Most previous KB-enhanced models such as [33,36] focus on integrating KB entity information into pre-trained LMs. However, we argue that incorporating KB *relation* information is important as well, especially for RE tasks. One challenge that we are facing with KB relations is that in most cases, KB relations are different from the target relations of RE tasks. However, the relations in a domain-specific KB are likely to be semantically related to the task relations. Therefore, finding a way to link KB relations to task relations is crucial in building a KB-enhanced model for RE. For example, Iinuma et al. [16] used a manually created map to convert KB relations to target relations, and then build distant supervision data. We propose to take this idea further by removing the manual mapping and having the neural model learn the mapping automatically. We hypothesize that our neural model is capable of building a soft mapping between KB relations and task relations, and that adding these suggested, hypothetical relations on top of the PubMedBERT encoding of the text can improve RE performance. Another challenge is that given two entities found in a KB, none of the KB relations might be asserted between them. We hypothesize that the KB may nevertheless be leveraged to provide an estimate of how likely it is for each of the KB relations to hold between the two entities. This would thereby provide potentially useful relational knowledge for any two entities found in the KB.

3.2   Model Architecture

Figure 2 shows an overview of KB-PubMedBERT. Our proposed model takes two inputs: the input sentence s, and the concept identifiers of the subject and object entities $subj$, obj. The concept embedding layer and the relation embedding layer

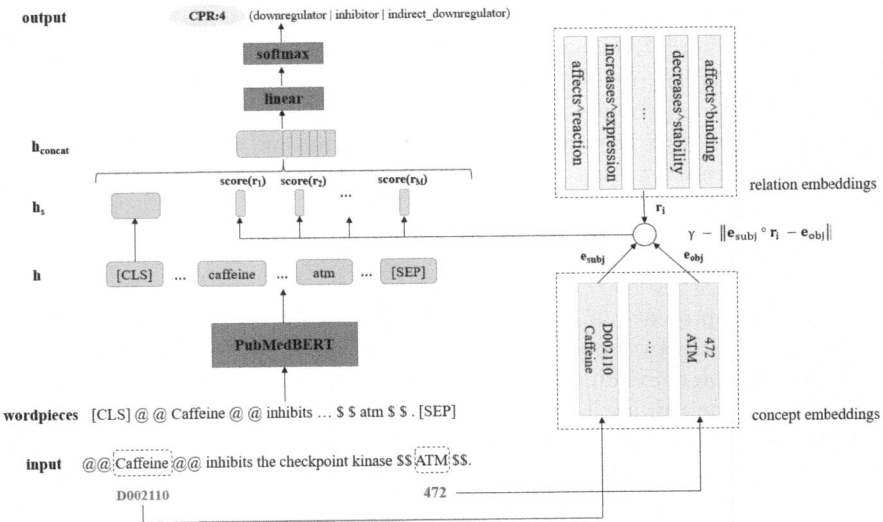

Fig. 2. Global architecture of KB-PubMedBERT.

are respectively initialized with pre-trained RotatE embeddings. After initialization, concept and relation embeddings are fine-tuned during model training. The data flow in our model is as follows. First, we obtain concept embeddings for the subject and object $\mathbf{e}_{subj}$, $\mathbf{e}_{obj}$ by looking up the concept embedding layer; then we obtain the M plausibility scores of Eq. 2:

$$score_i = \gamma - \|\mathbf{e}_{subj} \circ \mathbf{r_i} - \mathbf{e}_{obj}\| \tag{2}$$

where γ is a fixed margin, a hyperparameter set when training RotatE, $i = 1, 2, ..., M$, and M denotes the number of KB relations. According to the definition of RotatE, the distance $\|\mathbf{e}_{subj} \circ \mathbf{r_i} - \mathbf{e}_{obj}\|$ should be small for existing triples in KB, thus $score_i$ reflects the plausibility of the triple $(subj, r_i, obj)$. Following the convention of using the [CLS] embedding as the pooling vector to represent the sentence, denoting that vector by $\mathbf{h}_{[CLS]}$, we get the mixed representation:

$$\mathbf{h}_{concat} = [\mathbf{h}_{[CLS]}; \mathbf{h}_{score}] \tag{3}$$

where $[.;.]$ denotes vector concatenation, and $\mathbf{h}_{score}$ is an M-dimensional vector containing the KB relation scores. The mixed representation is then passed to a fully connected layer with the softmax activation that computes the probabilities of task relations at the output. The whole model is fine-tuned to minimize the cross-entropy loss, with non-frozen PubMedBERT weights.

4 Experiments

4.1 Datasets

We evaluate our proposed model on three biomedical RE corpora that are selected for the diversity of their characteristics. Table 1 summarizes the statistics of these corpora.

Table 1. Statistics of the ChemProt, DrugProt and BB-Rel$_p$ biomedical RE datasets: numbers of examples, number of relation classes.

	ChemProt	DrugProt	BB-Rel$_p$
# train	13,110	64,745	3,016
# dev	8,329	13,399	2,000
# test	10,990	238,694	2,473
# classes	6	14	2

1. ChemProt [17] annotates 6 high-level chemical-gene interaction relations, including one null relation, in PubMed abstracts. We use the BlurB [14] version of ChemProt because it is the version used by most recent studies.
2. DrugProt [23] classifies chemical-gene interactions into 14 relations including a null relation.
3. the BB-Rel dataset of the Bacteria Biotope shared task [6] annotates two relations: "lives_in" between microorganisms and habitats or geographical areas; and "exhibits" between microorganisms and phenotypes. Because we only have available knowledge bases covering microorganisms and habitats, we extract a subset of the BB-Rel dataset containing only entity pairs of (microorganism, habitat), which we denote by BB-Rel$_p$.

4.2 Experimental Setup

Pre-processing. In the same way as most previous studies on RE such as [14,18], we use two markers to mark the position of subject and object entities: "@@" is inserted before and after the subject entity, and "$$" before and after the object entity. The purpose of these markers is to provide positional information about candidate arguments to the model.

Entity Normalization. In a RE corpus, entities are not always normalized to KB concepts. In our experiments, in cases where entity normalization is not given, we use existing pre-trained models to align entities to KB concepts. We choose appropriate KBs for each corpus. For ChemProt and DrugProt, we chose the CTD [8] which contains normalized entities such as chemicals (normalized to MESH concepts), genes (normalized to NCBI Gene[1] concepts) and

---

[1] https://www.ncbi.nlm.nih.gov/gene.

134 chemical-gene interactions. For BB-Rel$_p$, we chose Omnicrobe [9], a KB aggregating information about microbial properties from diverse bioinformatics databases and strain collection catalogs. Omnicrobe contains normalized entities such as microorganisms (normalized to NCBI taxonomy [11] concepts) and habitats (normalized to OntoBiotope [24] concepts), and the relation "lives_in" linking these two entities. On Chemprot and Drugprot, we normalize entities to CTD concepts using BioSyn[2] [28]. On BB-Rel$_p$, we directly use gold normalization on the train and validation sets since they are available. On the test set, we use a regression model from the best participant [20] in the BB-Norm task [6] to normalize microorganism entities to NCBI species, and the state-of-the-art model C-Norm [12] to normalize habitat entities to OntoBiotope concepts. Table 2 summarizes the sources of entity normalization for each corpus.

Table 2. Sources of entity normalization for each corpus. *"gold"* refers to gold normalization annotations provided in BB-Norm [6]; *"regression"* refers to the regression model proposed in [20].

	ChemProt & DrugProt	**BB-Rel$_p$**
train	BioSyn	*gold*
dev	BioSyn	*gold*
test	BioSyn	C-Norm, *regression*

Baseline. We use the pre-trained PubMedBERT as a baseline, since it is the model from which our model is derived. On each task, that baseline model is fine-tuned to classify target relations. Comparing KB-PubMedBERT to the baseline directly shows whether integrating KB information helps to classify relations.

Table 3. Best learning rate for each (model, corpus) combination.

	ChemProt	DrugProt	**BB-Rel$_p$**
PubMedBERT	-	$3e^{-5}$	$5e^{-5}$
KB-PubMedBERT	$2e^{-5}$	$2e^{-5}$	$2e^{-5}$

Implementation Details. We use the official implementation[3] of RotatE [27] to calculate KB concept and relation embeddings. We keep the dimension of concept

---

[2] We use two public pre-trained models: biosyn-sapbert-bc5cdr-chemical for chemicals; biosyn-sapbert-bc2gn for genes.

[3] https://github.com/DeepGraphLearning/KnowledgeGraphEmbedding.

Table 4. F1 scores on RE tasks. We report a/b where a represents the average score of 5 runs with different random initializations; b represents the majority voting score. We report the two scores to better compare our results to the SOTA results. $\triangle$ indicates that we use the reported result on ChemProt from [14]. $*$ indicates statistically significant improvements with $p < 0.05$ under a t-test.

	ChemProt	DrugProt	**BB-Rel$_p$**
PubMedBERT [14]	$77.2^{\triangle}$ / -	75.8 ± 0.5 / 77.2	64.4 ± 0.7 / 65.3
KB-PubMedBERT	77.8 ± 0.1 / 79.2	77.6 ± 0.4 / 77.9	$\mathbf{65.7 \pm 1.0}^{*}$ / $\mathbf{66.5}$
SOTA	$\mathbf{80.0}$ / -	- / $\mathbf{79.7}$	- / 64.8

and relation embeddings at 200, γ at 24.0, and the learning rate at $1e^{-4}$. It might occur that some entities are normalized to concepts that do not exist in the KB, in these cases we randomly initialize the embeddings of these concepts. For all RE datasets, we use the model performance on the development set as the metric to find optimal hyperparameters. We only search the optimal learning rate from the set $(1e^{-5}, 2e^{-5}, 3e^{-5}, 5e^{-5})$. Table 3 provides the optimal learning rates. In the same way as most previous work such as [14], we use a slanted triangular scheduler for the learning rate, which consists in increasing the learning rate from 0 to a target value at the beginning of fine-tuning, then linearly decreasing to 0. We always use the first 10% steps for this learning rate warmup. For all models, we perform 5 runs using the same model architecture with different random seeds. We use a single NVIDIA Tesla V100 GPU for all our experiments. It is worth noting that changing GPU cards may lead to minor or in some cases even a 0.1 to 0.2 difference in F1-score, i.e. affecting the reproducibility of experimental results.

SOTA Methods. We compare KB-PubMedBERT to the state-of-the-art (SOTA) models on each corpus:

1. For ChemProt: BioM-BERT [1] which is a BERT model pre-trained on PubMed and PubMed Central (PMC) literature;
2. For DrugProt: an ensemble of 10 pre-trained RoBERTa-large-PM-M3-Voc [19] with chemical definitions curated from CTD [31];
3. For BB-Rel$_p$: A 12-layer Transformer model pre-trained on BooksCorpus, English Wikipedia, PubMed and PMC corpus. [35]

Evaluation. Micro F1-score excluding the null relation is the standard evaluation metric for the three datasets. For ChemProt, we calculate scores using the test set of the BLURB version as in [14]. On DrugProt and BB-Rel$_p$, we submit our predictions to the official evaluation kits[4].

---

[4] Official evaluation kits: https://codalab.lisn.upsaclay.fr/competitions/3293#participate (DrugProt); http://bibliome.jouy.inra.fr/demo/BioNLP-OST-2019-Evaluation/index.html (BB-Rel$_p$).

4.3   Main Results

Table 4 summarizes our experimental results. We observe that KB-PubMedBERT consistently outperforms the baseline model on all three corpora, which shows the effectiveness of injecting KB information.

Comparing our method to existing SOTA models, KB-PubMedBERT outperforms previous SOTA on BB-Rel$_p$. Though our model does not outperform SOTA models on ChemProt and DrugProt, the gap in performance might be explained by model sizes: both SOTA models have more layers and more parameters than KB-PubMedBERT.

4.4   Ablation Study

To verify how much the graph embedding module in our model is able to detect the target RE relations by itself, we conduct experiments in which we completely remove PubMedBERT from our model. This means that we only use the (subject, object) entity pair to predict the interaction type via RotatE graph embeddings. We compare the resulting relation classifier to a naive model that always predicts the most frequent non-null relation. Table 5 shows the results on the test set of the three corpora.

Table 5. Ablation study. KB-Pred denotes our proposed model without the PubMed-BERT embedding module, thus using only KB-derived information in its prediction. We report the average score of 5 runs. *naive* refers to a model that always predicts the most frequent non-null relation.

	ChemProt	DrugProt	**BB-Rel$_p$**
KB-Pred	23.8 ± 1.6	19.5 ± 1.0	26.6 ± 0.3
naive	17.3	12.3	38.3

We see that even with no context, our model significantly outperforms the naive model on ChemProt and DrugProt. This shows that the plausibility scores of fine-grained KB relations obtained from RotatE graph embeddings are helpful. On BB-Rel$_p$, the naive model can easily outperform our model because there is only one non-null relation.

4.5   Case Study

To get an insight into the behavior of our proposed model, we manually examine improved and degraded examples in the validation set of ChemProt and DrugProt, where an improved example refers to an example on which KB-PubMedBERT makes a correct prediction while PubMedBERT does not, and on the contrary a degraded example refers to an example on which PubMedBERT predicts correctly while KB-PubMedBERT makes a mistake. We observe that

PubMedBERT predicts the null relation for most of the improved examples, i.e. false negatives originally predicted by PubMedBERT can be corrected by KB-PubMedBERT. Besides, the KB relation between arguments of an improved example is found to be close to the true relation of the RE task. For example, KB relations "decreases^activity" and "decreases^reaction" are found to help predict the relation "inhibitor" and "increases^expression" helps predict the relation "activator". It demonstrates the effectiveness of inferred KB relations obtained from RotatE graph embeddings. However, KB relations are not always useful. Table 6 summarizes several degraded examples. We find that in the following cases, KB relations can be harmful:

Table 6. Case study on degraded examples in ChemProt and DrugProt. Red words refer to the subject entity (chemical) and blue words refer to the object entity (gene). The column "predictions" contains the relations predicted by the corresponding model, where a bold relation refers to a correct prediction. The last column contains relations found in the KB given the corresponding pair of entities.

sentence	KB?	predictions	KB relations
Ponatinib (AP24534) is a multikinase inhibitor with in vitro and clinical activity in tyrosine kinase inhibitor (TKI)-resistant chronic myeloid leukemia, irrespective of BCR-ABL KD mutation.	✗	**no_relation**	
	✓	downregulator |inhibitor	decreases^activity
Known VR1 antagonists (BCTC, thio-BCTC and capsazepine) were also able to block the response of TRPM8 to menthol (IC(50): 0.8+/-1.0, 3.5+/-1.1 and 18+/-1.1 microM, respectively).	✗	**downregulator |inhibitor**	
	✓	antagonist	decreases^reaction, increases^activity
Finally, PLA2 inhibitor methyl arachidonyl fluorophosphonate blocked the PUFA effects on COX-2 induction, promoter activity and arachidonic acid mobilization suggesting involvement of AA metabolites in PPAR activation.	✗	**inhibitor**	
	✓	indirect-downregulator	decreases^reaction

- False positives: KB-PubMedBERT can be biased to predict a relation that is close to a KB relation. In some cases (e.g. first example in Table 6), KB-PubMedBERT favors KB information over textual information, therefore predicting a non-null relation even though the relation is not expressed in the texts;
- Multiple KB relations: There may exist multiple KB relations for a given pair of entities. These KB relations seem to confuse KB-PubMedBERT when they are quite different from each other. For example, in the second example in Table 6, "decreases^reaction" and "increases^activity" describe two opposite chemical-gene interactions. The existence of "increases^activity" may prevent KB-PubMedBERT from predicting "downregulator | inhibitor", which is the gold relation.
- Lack of precision: For the last example in Table 6, KB-PubMedBERT predicts "indirect-downregulator" while the gold relation is "inhibitor". In ChemProt, the two relations are gathered together into a single class, while

in DrugProt they are taken as two separate classes. The prediction of KB-PubMedBERT may be biased to "indirect-downregulator" due to the KB suggestion "decreases^reaction", which is not false, but is not accurate enough.

5   Limitations

Though KB-PubMedBERT outperforms the baseline model PubMedBERT, we have not yet exhaustively investigated the effectiveness of our model architecture since we have only tested PubMedBERT as the base language model and RotatE as the graph embedding method. Besides, the analysis of degraded examples in the case study (Subsect. 4.5) shows that KB-PubMedBERT may focus more on KB suggestions and make erroneous predictions, ignoring textual information. This is likely due to the fact that in KB-PubMedBERT we simply concatenate KG and sentence embedding and the quantity of introduced KB information is not under control. Another problem is that multiple KB relations may exist between a pair of entities, and these relations may even be contradictory to each other (e.g. the second example in Table 6). In these cases, KB-PubMedBERT seems to be confused by KB suggestions. This phenomenon may be explained by the choice of graph embedding method. Since RotatE learns a relation-specific rotation in the complex space, it does not handle well the cases where multiple KB relations exist between the same entity pair. To handle the problem of pairs with multiple KB relations, KB suggestions should be context-dependent. We leave this investigation for future work.

6   Conclusion

In this paper, we propose the KB-PubMedBERT architecture which integrates knowledge base information into PubMedBERT to improve its performance in biomedical relation tasks. Unlike previous KB-enhanced models, we first estimate the plausibility that KB relations exist between the given entities using the RotatE graph embedding method, then use the plausibility scores to help predict target relations in texts. We conduct experiments on three biomedical RE corpora: the results show that KB-PubMedBERT consistently outperforms PubMedBERT, and at the same time gives performance close to or better than the previous state of the art. By conducting an ablation study, we further confirm the effectiveness of using KB relations to predict relations in text. In the future, we will extend our experiments to other datasets to further validate the applicability of our method.

Acknowledgements. We are grateful to the Saclay-IA platform of Université Paris-Saclay for providing computing and storage resources through its Lab-IA GPU cluster.

Disclosure of Interests. The authors have no competing interests to declare that are relevant to the content of this article.

References

1. Alrowili, S., Vijay-Shanker, K.: BioM-transformers: building large biomedical language models with BERT, ALBERT and ELECTRA. In: BioNLP workshop, pp. 221–227, Online, June 2021. ACL (2021)
2. Asada, M., Gunasekaran, N., Miwa, M., Sasaki, Y.: Representing a heterogeneous pharmaceutical knowledge-graph with textual information. Front. Res. Metrics Anal. **6**, 670206 (2021)
3. Asada, M., Miwa, M., Sasaki, Y.: Integrating heterogeneous knowledge graphs into drug-drug interaction extraction from the literature. Bioinformatics **39**(1), btac754, (2022)
4. Bodenreider, O.: The Unified Medical Language System (UMLS): integrating biomedical terminology. Nucleic Acids Res. **32**(Database issue), D267–270 (2004)
5. Bordes, A., Usunier, N., Garcia-Duran, A., Weston, J., Yakhnenko, O.: Translating embeddings for modeling multi-relational data. In: NEURIPS, pp.787–2795, Red Hook, NY, USA, 2013. Curran Associates, Inc (2013)
6. Bossy, R., Deléger, L., Chaix, E., Ba, M., Nédellec, C.: Bacteria biotope at BioNLP open shared tasks 2019. In: Proceedings of the 5th Workshop on BioNLP Open Shared Tasks, pp. 121–131 Hong Kong, China, November 2019. ACL (2019)
7. Chithrananda, S., Grand, G., Ramsundar, B., Chemberta: large-scale self-supervised pretraining for molecular property prediction. ArXiv:abs/2010.09885 (2020)
8. Davis, A.P., et al.: Comparative Toxicogenomics Database (CTD): update 2023. Nucleic Acids Res. **51**(D1):D1257–D1262 (2023)
9. Dérozier, S., et al.: Omnicrobe, an open-access database of microbial habitats and phenotypes using a comprehensive text mining and data fusion approach. PloS one **18**(1), e0272473 (2023)
10. Devlin, J., Chang, M.-W., Lee, K., Toutanova, K.: BERT: pre-training of deep bidirectional transformers for language understanding. In: NAACL, pp. 4171–4186, Minneapolis, Minnesota, June 2019. ACL (2019)
11. Federhen, S.: The NCBI Taxonomy database. Nucleic Acids Res. **40**(D1), D136–D143 (2011)
12. Ferré, A., Deléger, L., Bossy, R., Zweigenbaum, P., Nédellec, C.: C-Norm: a neural approach to few-shot entity normalization. BMC Bioinform. **21**(23), 579 (2020)
13. Grover, A., Leskovec, J.: node2vec: scalable feature learning for networks. In: SIGKDD, pp. 855–864, New York, NY, USA, 2016. ACM (2016)
14. Yu, G., et al.: Domain-specific language model pretraining for biomedical natural language processing. ACM Trans. Comput. Healthcare (HEALTH) **3**(1), 1–23 (2021)
15. Hao, B., Zhu, H., Paschalidis, I.C.: Enhancing clinical BERT embedding using a biomedical knowledge base. In: COLING, pp. 657–661, Barcelona, Spain (Online), December (2020)
16. Iinuma, N., Miwa, M., Sasaki, Y.: Improving supervised drug-protein relation extraction with distantly supervised models. In: BioNLP workshop, pp. 161–170, Dublin, Ireland, May 2022. ACL (2022)
17. Krallinger, M., et al.: Overview of the BioCreative VI chemical-protein interaction track. In: BioCreative Workshop, vol. 1, pp. 141–146 (2017)
18. Lee, J., et al.: BioBERT: a pre-trained biomedical language representation model for biomedical text mining. Bioinformatics **36**(4), 1234–1240 (2020)

19. Lewis, P., Ott, M., Du, J., Stoyanov, V.: Pretrained language models for biomedical and clinical tasks: understanding and extending the state-of-the-art. In: Clinical NLP Workshop, pp. 146–157, Online, 2020. ACL (2020)
20. Mao, J., Liu, W.: Integration of deep learning and traditional machine learning for knowledge extraction from biomedical literature. In: BioNLP Open Shared Tasks Workshop, pp. 168–173, Hong Kong, China, November 2019. ACL (2019)
21. Michalopoulos, G., Wang, Y., Kaka, H., Chen, H., Wong, A.: UmlsBERT: Clinical domain knowledge augmentation of contextual embeddings using the Unified Medical Language System Metathesaurus. In: NAACL-HLT, pp. 1744–1753, Online, June 2021. ACL (2021)
22. Mikolov, T., Chen, K., Corrado, G., Dean, J.: Efficient estimation of word representations in vector space. In: ICLR (workshop poster) (2013)
23. Miranda, A., Mehryary, F., Luoma, J., Pyysalo, S., Valencia, A., Krallinger, M.: Overview of DrugProt BioCreative VII track: quality evaluation and large scale text mining of drug-gene/protein relations. In: BioCreative Workshop, pp. 11–21 (2021)
24. Nédellec, C., Bossy, R., Chaix, E., Deléger, L.: Text-mining and ontologies: new approaches to knowledge discovery of microbial diversity. arXiv preprint arXiv:1805.04107 (2018)
25. Papaluca, A., Krefl, D., Suominen, H., Lenskiy, A.: Pretrained knowledge base embeddings for improved sentential relation extraction. In: ACL: Student Research Workshop, pp. 373–382, Dublin, Ireland, May 2022. ACL (2022)
26. Ribeiro, L.F., Saverese, P.H., Figueiredo, D.R.: struc2vec: learning node representations from structural identity. In: SIGKDD, pp. 385–394. ACM (2017)
27. Sun, Z., Deng, Z.H., Nie, J.Y., Tang, J.: RotatE: Knowledge graph embedding by relational rotation in complex space. In: ICLR, New Orleans, LA, USA (2019) OpenReview.net
28. Sung, M., Jeon, H., Lee, J., Kang, J.: Biomedical entity representations with synonym marginalization. In: ACL, pp. 3641–3650, Online, July (2020)
29. Vaswani, A., et al. Attention is all you need. In: NEURIPS, vol. 30, pp. 6000–6010, Red Hook, NY, USA, Curran Associates, Inc. (2017)
30. Wang, R., et al.: K-Adapter: infusing knowledge into pre-trained models with adapters. In: Findings of ACL-IJCNLP, pp. 1405–1418, Online, August 2021. ACL (2021)
31. Weber, L., Sänger, M., Garda, S., Barth, F., Alt, C., Leser, U.: Chemical–protein relation extraction with ensembles of carefully tuned pretrained language models. Database Nov 18 2022
32. Wu, Y., et al.: Google's neural machine translation system: Bridging the gap between human and machine translation. ArXiv: abs/1609.08144 (2016)
33. Yuan, Z., Liu, Y., Tan, C., Huang, S., Huang, F.: Improving biomedical pretrained language models with knowledge. In: BioNLP Workshop, pp. 180–190, Online, 2021. ACL (2021)
34. Zhang, N., et al.: Long-tail relation extraction via knowledge graph embeddings and graph convolution networks. In: NAACL-HLT, pp. 3016–3025, Minneapolis, Minnesota, June 2019. ACL (2019)
35. Zhang, Q., Liu, C., Chi, Y., Xie, X., Hua, X.: A multi-task learning framework for extracting bacteria biotope information. In: BioNLP Open Shared Tasks workshop, pp. 105–109, Hong Kong, China, November 2019. ACL (2019)
36. Zhang, Q., Liu, C., Chi, Y., Xie, X., Hua, X.: ERNIE: enhanced language representation with informative entities. In: ACL, pp. 1441–1451, Florence, Italy, July (2019)

DAHRS: Divergence-Aware Hallucination-Remediated SRL Projection

Sangpil Youm[1(✉)], Brodie Mather[2], Chathuri Jayaweera[1], Juliana Prada[1], and Bonnie Dorr[1]

[1] University of Florida, Gainesville, FL, USA
{youms,chathuri.jayawee,juliana.prada,bonniejdorr}@ufl.edu
[2] IHMC, Pensacola, FL, USA
bmather@ihmc.org

Abstract. Semantic role labeling (SRL) enriches many downstream applications, e.g., machine translation, question answering, summarization, and stance/belief detection. However, building multilingual SRL models is challenging due to the scarcity of semantically annotated corpora for multiple languages. Moreover, state-of-the-art SRL projection (XSRL) based on large language models (LLMs) yields output that is riddled with spurious role labels. Remediation of such hallucinations is not straightforward due to the lack of explainability of LLMs. We show that hallucinated role labels are related to naturally occurring divergence types that interfere with initial alignments. We implement *Divergence-Aware Hallucination-Remediated SRL projection* (DAHRS), leveraging linguistically-informed alignment remediation followed by greedy *First-Come First-Assign* (FCFA) SRL projection. DAHRS improves the accuracy of SRL projection without additional transformer-based machinery, beating XSRL in both human and automatic comparisons, and advancing beyond headwords to accommodate phrase-level SRL projection (e.g., EN-FR, EN-ES). Using CoNLL-2009 as our ground truth, we achieve a higher word-level F1 over XSRL: 87.6% vs. 77.3% (EN-FR) and 89.0% vs. 82.7% (EN-ES). Human phrase-level assessments yield 89.1% (EN-FR) and 91.0% (EN-ES). We also define a divergence metric to adapt our approach to other language pairs (e.g., English-Tagalog).

Keywords: semantic role labeling · hallucination remediation · explainability · divergences

1 Introduction

The natural language processing (NLP) task of semantic role labeling (SRL) captures *"who did what to whom"* for many downstream applications, e.g., machine translation, question answering, and summarization [14,21]. Semantic roles are central to inferring unstated information (e.g., stances [25,26] and emotional cues [3]) that are absent from the output of NLP tools such as dependency parsing.

© The Author(s), under exclusive license to Springer Nature Switzerland AG 2024
A. Rapp et al. (Eds.): NLDB 2024, LNCS 14762, pp. 423–438, 2024.
https://doi.org/10.1007/978-3-031-70239-6_29

Disappointingly, SRL has been studied primarily in English due to highly available English-specific SRL annotated datasets [12]. The scarcity of multilingual SRL-annotated corpora motivates the need for cross-language approaches that project semantic roles from English to other languages.

Many studies have explored pre-trained SRL models [28,34] and generative AI approaches for semantic tasks that include SRL [36]. These LLM-centric studies tend to focus exclusively on English. The associated LLMs thus introduce hallucinations without obvious recourse due to an inherent lack of explainability.

Our approach, "Divergence-Aware Hallucination-Remediated SRL Projection" (DAHRS) adopts a generalized characterization of divergence types [9,23] and corrects alignnments, remediating hallucinated semantic-role transfer from source to target languages (e.g., English-French and English-Spanish). We introduce a greedy "First-Come First-Assign" (FCFA) algorithm within DAHRS that projects roles from corrected initial alignments. FCFA also remediates the hallucinated lack of semantic role projections emerging from corrected initial alignments.

The key insight here is that leveraging linguistic knowledge overcomes deficiencies in current transformer-based alignment-projection approaches. Transformer-based alignment treats target words as a bag-of-words, frequently aligning source-language terms to hallucinated target-language terms. By contrast, DAHRS injects an awareness of naturally occurring language *divergences*, e.g., one-to-many/many-to-one translations or word/phrase order distinctions, into alignment. Straightforward correction of alignments that would otherwise lead to hallucinated *incorrect* roles supports effective and explainable transfer of semantic roles from the source language to the target language.

State-of-the-art XSRL [6] addresses a subset of language divergences explored in this paper: nominalizations and separable verb prefixes. In cases where the initial alignment is correct, XSRL fails to project valid roles in the context of other types of divergences, often hallucinating a *lack* of semantic role projections on the right-hand side. DAHRS is designed to address two types of hallucinations simultaneously: alignment and projection. The performance of DAHRS is compared to that of XSRL using data processed by both methods (see Sect. 5).

Hallucination remediation in DAHRS starts with token-level and phrase-level corrections to an initial transformer-based mBERT [11] alignment. Following this, additional hallucination remediation takes place during projection. Figure 1 illustrates two representative cases of *divergences* that have triggered hallucinations in prior work: *Light Verb* and *Structural*.[1] Square brackets '[]' indicate SRL projections, with unaligned words indicated by ϵ. The output shown at each stage explainably pin-points which sub-components fail or succeed (alignment or projection, or both).

(a) **Light Verb Divergence.** The single verb *fell* maps to a combination of a "light" verb (a) and content word "fallen" (*chuté*). Despite the correct

---

[1] Figure 1 inputs: (a) EN: The dow 's dive was the 12th - worst ever and the sharpest since the market fell 156.83 FR: La chute du dow jones a été la 12e - la pire et la plus forte depuis que le marché a chuté de 156.83. (b) EN: Some "circuit breakers" installed after the october 1987 crash failed their first test. FR: Certains "disjoncteurs" installés après l'écrasement d'octobre 1987 ont échoué leur premier test.

initial mBERT alignment, XSRL is unable to "see past" this divergence to project semantic roles to the target-language side. The inherent uninterpretability of the underlying models impedes the ability to determine what has gone awry, but we observe that this divergence type almost leads to a hallucinated *lack* of SRL assignments. By contrast, DAHRS correctly transfers labels V, ARG1 (EN *market* to FR *marché*), and ARG2 (EN *156.83* to FR *156.83*), leaving *a, de* appropriately unassigned. Also, *chuté* is an adjectival participle in French, but its verbal nature supports ARG1 assignments, so the V label is retained by design.

(b) Structural Divergence. A difference in source/target word order (*October 1987 crash* vs. *crash of October 1987*) combined with a bag-of-words design leads to an incorrect mBERT alignment. Here, *October* aligns to *Octobre* (October) and a (hallucinated) occurrence of *écrasement*, while *crash* aligns to a second occurrence of *écrasement*. The resulting XSRL projection includes *incorrect* role transfers, leaving *crash* unaligned and thus without a role. By contrast, DAHRS applies alignment remediation, mapping *crash* to *écrasement*, and *October* to *Octobre*, and correctly transferring ARGM-TMP to French.

DAHRS identifies divergence types, remediates hallucinations at both the token/phrase level, and applies greedy FCFA SRL projection. Divergence handling couples alignment remediation with FCFA, which is parameterized to include syntactic properties of the source language (e.g., English is head-initial) to accommodate proper SRL projection. This simple, efficient design transcends "yet another transformer" in both accuracy and explainability.

(a) Light Verb (Hallucinated *lack* of roles):
market fell 156.83 - marché a chuté de 156.83
mBERT-based Alignment:
```
  market  — marché
  ε       — a
  fell    — chuté
  ε       — de
  156.83  — 156.83
```
XSRL:
```
  [ARG1] market  — marché
  ε               — a
  [V] fell        — chuté
  ε               — de
  [ARG2] 156.83   — 156.83
```
DAHRS:
```
  [ARG1] market  — [ARG1] marché
  ε               — a
  [V] fell        — [V] chuté
  ε               — de
  [ARG2] 156.83   — [ARG2] 156.83
```

(b) Structural (Hallucinated *incorrect* roles):
october 1987 crash - écrasement d' octobre 1987
mBERT-based Alignment:
```
  october — écrasement
  october — octobre
  ε       — d'
  1987    — 1987
  crash   — ècrasement
```
XSRL:
```
  [ARGM-TMP] october — [ARGM-TMP] octobre
  ε                   — d'
  [ARGM-TMP] 1987    — [ARGM-TMP] 1987
  [ARGM-TMP] crash   — ε
```
DAHRS:
```
  [ARGM-TMP] october — [ARGM-TMP] octobre
  ε                   — d'
  [ARGM-TMP] 1987    — [ARGM-TMP] 1987
  [ARGM-TMP] crash   — [ARGM-TMP] écrasement
```

Fig. 1. Divergence cases corresponding to two hallucination types: (a) Light Verbs introduce one-to-many/many-to-one divergences that impede XSRL transfer of semantic roles even when the initial alignment is correct, thus hallucinating a *lack* of roles on the target-language side; (b) Structural divergences introduce word/phrase order distinctions that result in extra, spuriously aligned terms, thus hallucinating *incorrect* roles.

While numerous studies have focused on improving explainability in diverse NLP tasks and applications such as classification [22] or medical NLP [4] , to our knowledge, ours is the first to address explainability for SRL in NLP. Our visualization of alignment and projection decisions (see Fig. 1) displays accessible, linguistically relevant representations associated with SRL transfers (and predicates, indicated as "V"). These visualized linguistic representations display how and why each SRL projection is made, highlighting the handling of translation divergences throughout the entire process.

Below we present related work, followed by a description of DAHRS. We then present automated and human-validated evaluations. We demonstrate that DAHRS outperforms XSRL in accuracy (87.6% vs. 77.3% F1 (EN-FR), 89.0% vs. 82.7% F1 (EN-ES)). We discuss the potential for generalization to low-resource languages. We then conclude and explore future work.

2   Related Work

Early applications for annotation-projection include: dependency parsing [19]; part-of-speech taggers [38]; machine translation [33,39]; divergence-inspired alignment [10]; and creation of syntactic-dependency datasets for multiple languages [27]. We borrow the notion of annotation projection to produce explainable, cross-language SRL that advances the state of the art.

A contrasting SRL annotation projection approach is one where a source-language model is modified for direct applicability to a new language, using cross-lingually shared representations [20]. Such "model transferring" approaches do not align datasets across languages, but instead induce a separate dataset. By contrast, annotation projection approaches (including our own) propagate available information from one language to another via alignment.

Translation-based models provide an alternative approach for transferring SRL annotations. These have demonstrated promising performance due to recent improvements in neural machine translation (NMT) [12,13,17]. Translation-based projection involves tree-to-tree mappings to build cross-lingual SRL-annotated corpora [31], based on tree/graph-based representations [33]. By contrast, our approach aims to accommodate divergences for SRL projection via word-to-word mapping without relying on additional structure (e.g., trees or graphs).

Prior studies have demonstrated the benefits of embedding models in cross-language SRL projection. For example, Polyglot SRL [29] employs word vectors and is trained on the union of annotations between two languages. A cross-lingual encoder-decoder model is applied to simultaneously translate and apply SRL for resource-poor languages [5]. Adding a syntactic information layer to the embedding models demonstrates plausibility of transferring semantic roles [15]. By contrast, our approach enables improved SRL projection without additional vector-based machinery. Instead, we factor out syntactic variations, as these are not central to the transfer of semantic roles, and introduce a greedy SRL projection algorithm that is both accurate and efficient.

Translation divergences and associated alignment errors lead to considerable noise, often resulting in the implementation of intricate techniques. For example, projection probability distributions and gold-standard annotated data have been employed to improve alignment performance [1]. XSRL uses translations produced by DeepL [7], more than 10% of which are human-judged as improperly translated and removed. An mBERT [8] aligner is applied, followed by an additional transformer-based mechanism (BERT Score) [40], to project semantic roles to the target sentence. Although these approaches offer valuable SRL projection strategies, two major concerns are the added complexity (e.g., BERT-based scoring) and, in the case of XSRL, human filtering to remove noisy translations. The latter negatively impacts the resulting training data coverage.

While our approach involves projection, it differs from those above in that it operates on all translated sentence pairs (no human filtering) and produces a greedily induced SRL projection. The resulting annotations are consistent with translation divergence studies. Decisions on projected labels are made readily accessible and easily visualized, rather than hidden behind *black box* algorithms.

3   Divergence-Aware Hallucination-Remediated SRL Projection (DAHRS)

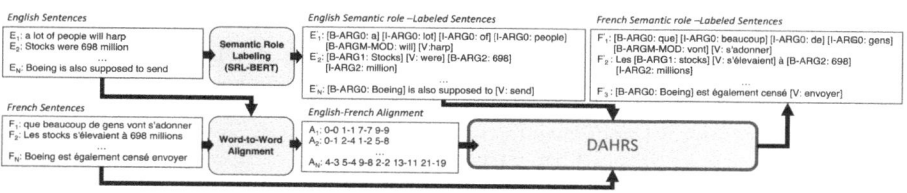

Fig. 2. *Divergence-Aware   Hallucination-Remediated   SRL   Projection* (DAHRS) pipeline from English to French

DAHRS's key contribution is its ability to compensate for potential semantic role errors emerging from hallucinated alignments that coincide with naturally occurring cross-language divergences. Leveraging source-language knowledge (e.g., English is head initial) coupled with a greedy FCFA algorithm, DAHRS transfers semantic roles to the target language.

Figure 2 illustrates the DAHRS step-wise pipeline with an English-to-French example. DAHRS's input is an initial mBERT-style alignment, as in XSRL, but prior to SRL projection it corrects hallucinated alignments and transfers semantic roles without additional transformer-based processing.

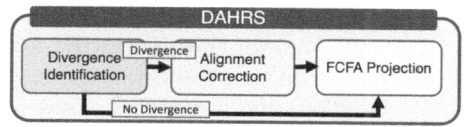

Fig. 3.   Divergence-Aware   Hallucination Remediated SRL Projection (DAHRS)

Figure 3 shows three key steps in DAHRS: divergence identification (see Sect. 3.1), alignment correction (DAHRS$_1$ and DAHRS$_2$, see Sect. 3.2), and

FCFA projection (DAHRS$_3$, also in Sect. 3.2). When divergence identification uncovers a divergence, DAHRS modifies the alignment prior to SRL projection. Otherwise it directly projects semantic roles through FCFA projection.

3.1 Divergence Identification

For divergence identification, DAHRS relies on a sub-categorization of divergences into three types, as shown in Fig. 4. For example, with regard to the divergences illustrated in Sect. 1, *Light Verb* divergences are associated with (a) one-to-many and (b) many-to-one sub-categories, and *Structural* divergences are associated with (c) the ordering sub-category.

The identification of these divergence sub-categories for a given source-target input pair relies on position-value pairs. These pairs indicate the tokens and phrases that are mapped singularly or repeatedly across the source and target inputs. Divergence types are identified across tokenized source and target sentences, where each token is assigned a position value starting from 0.

Consider the French sentence fragment *ordinateurs portable* (*laptops*) in Fig. 4(a). This string is associated with position values of 17 in English and 23,24 in French. Source and target word mappings are denoted by a hyphenated position-value pair. For example, 17–23 and 17–24 indicate the 17th English word (*laptops*) aligns with the 23rd and 24th word French words (*ordinateurs portable*). This case is identified as a one-to-many divergence, i.e., a single source token aligns with multiple target tokens. Analogously, a many-to-one divergence is identified when multiple source tokens align with a single target token, as in Fig. 4(b), where *fell*(4) and *apart*(5) align with *effondrée*(6).

(a) One-to-many
laptops —— ordinateurs ; 17-23
laptops —— portables ; 17-24
(b) Many-to-one
fell   —— effondrée ; 4-6
apart —— effondrée ; 5-6
(c) Ordering
october —— écrasement ; 9-7
october —— octobre ; 9-9
ϵ —— d' ; ϵ-8
1987   —— 1987 ; 10-10
crash   —— écrasement ; 11-7

Fig. 4. Three subcategories of divergences (token level): One-to-many, Many-to-one, and Ordering

An ordering divergence is detected when a single source token is mBERT-aligned with multiple target tokens (one-to-many) while one of those same target tokens aligns with a different source token (many-to-one). Returning to our earlier example, *October 1987 crash* (translated in French as *crash of October 1987*), as shown in Fig. 4(c): *october*(9) aligns with *écrasement*(7) and *octobre*(9), while one of target tokens, *écrasement*(7) also aligns with *crash*(11).

Although state-of-the-art (mBERT-based) word-to-word alignment establishes a reasonable source-to-target baseline, ordering divergences are not adequately handled, due to mBERT's bag-of-words design. These lead to incorrect alignments that must be remediated in order to avoid hallucinated SRL projections. We note that ordering distinctions have been a focus in statistical machine translation (SMT) for quite some time [32], but these have heretofore not been remediated for projection.

Subsequent to identifying divergence types, as described below, our approach remediates hallucinations due to divergences and projects semantic roles through FCFA SRL projection.

3.2   DAHRS Algorithms

DAHRS's three key steps each correspond to a component-level algorithm: alignment correction at the token level (Algorithm 1) and phrase level (Algorithm 2) to remediate hallucinated *incorrect* role projections, followed by FCFA SRL projection (Algorithm 3) which remediates hallucinated *lack* of role projections.

$DAHRS_1$: **Token-Level Hallucination Remediation.** We remediate alignment hallucinations at the token level, using $DAHRS_1$ (see Algorithm 1). Such hallucinations are discerned from input pairs for one-to-one (*tLevelOneToOne*), one-to-many (*tLevelOneToMany*), many-to-one (*tLevelManyToOne*) alignments. Additionally, a head-initial flag (*headInitialFlag*) ensures proper SRL projection. This algorithm outputs a list of remediated alignments (*remOneToOne*).

$DAHRS_1$ initializes remediated alignments (*remOneToOne*), inserting mBERT-aligned source-target token pairs specified in the *tLevelOneToOne* list (lines 4–5). Next the target tokens in the one-to-many pair list (*tLevelOneToMany*) are examined for alignment with other source tokens, preparing for hallucination remediation (line 6). If a target token is found to be aligned with an alternate source token, the hallucinated alignment is removed from the target token list (*tgtList*) (lines 7–10). This action remediates alignment hallucinations that emerge in the context of ordering divergences. For example, in

Algorithm 1. Token-level Hallucination Remediation ($DAHRS_1$)

Input tLevelOneToOne, tLevelOneToMany,
tLevelManyToOne, headInitialFlag
Output remOneToOne
1: **function** $DAHRS_1$(tLevelOneToOne,tLevelOneToMany,
    tLevelManyToOne,headInitialFlag)
2:     remOnetoOne ← []
3:     remTargetWords ← []
4:     **for** $(src, tgt) \in tLevelOneToOne$ **do**
5:         remOneToOne.insert((src, tgt))
6:     tgtOneOne ← targets of tLevelOneToOne
7:     **for** $(src, tgtList) \in tLevelOneToMany$ **do**
8:         **for** $tgt \in tgtList$ **do**
9:             **if** $tgt \in tgtOneOne$ **then**
10:                tgtList.delete(tgt)
11:            **else**
12:                remOneToOne.insert((src,tgt))
13:     srcOneOne ← sources of tLevelOneToOne
14:     **for** $(srcList,tgt) \in tLevelManyToOne$ **do**
15:         **if** $src \in srcOneOne$ **then**
16:             srcList.delete(src)
17:         **else**
18:             **if** $headInitialFlag \equiv True$ **then**
19:                 remOneToOne.insert((srcList[0],tgt))
20:             **else**
21:                 remOneToOne.insert((srcList[1],tgt))
22:     **return** remOneToOne

---

the earlier baseline alignment in Fig. 4(c), the word *october* is incorrectly aligned with *écrasement*. This is detected due to the simultaneous *october-octobre* alignment (where no other source word aligns with *octobre*). The spurious *october-écrasement* alignment is hypothesized to be a hallucination and is removed.

After remedying spurious alignments in the one-to-many pairs, $DAHRS_1$ proceeds to store the corrected source and target pairs in the output (*remOneToOne*) (lines 11–12). In the earlier baseline alignment in Fig. 4(a), $DAHRS_1$ correctly maps *laptops* to both *ordinateurs* and *portables*.

In the case of many-to-one alignment, $DAHRS_1$ examines the source tokens in the one-to-one pair list (*tLevelOneToOne*) for alignment with other target tokens, preparing for additional hallucination remediation (line 13). In this case, the algorithm addresses the potential for hallucinated (downstream) SRL projections due to the presence of particles or modifiers (e.g., *apart* in *fell apart*) that are aligned with the main verb.

Remediation removes such tokens from the source token list (*srcList*) (lines 14–16). For eaxample, in the earlier baseline alignment in Fig. 4(b), the *apart-effondrée* alignment is deleted. The remaining *fell-effondrée* alignment is retained and is positioned in the output (*remOneToOne*) according to the *headIntitalFlag*, where "True" indicates a head-initial language, selecting the first token and "False" indicates a head-final language (lines 17–21).

$DAHRS_2$: **Phrase-Level Hallucination Remediation.** $DAHRS_2$ shown in Algorithm 2 advances beyond the token-level processing of state-of-the-art (XSRL) in that it includes handling of phrases for SRL projection.

Phrase-level processing is similar to what is described above, but phrase identification is employed: BIO (Begin-Inside-Outside) tags are assigned to the source-language side via SRL-BERT [34].[2] These BIO-delineated phrasal units are brought together with alignment corrections for more robust alignment hallucination remediation. A phrase range is determined by arranging the source words in the order they appear within the sentence and employing BIO tags to identify phrases on the English side.[3]

Phrase information (start to end indices), encoded as a source phrase range (*srcPhRange*) and target phrase range (*tgtPhRange*), acts as phrase-level hallucination remediation input. Other inputs

---

Algorithm 2. Phrase-level Hallucination Remediation ($DAHRS_2$)

Input pLevelOneToOne, pLevelOneToMany, pLevelManyToOne , srcPhRange, tgtPhRange, funcWordIdx, headInitialFlag
Output remOneToOne
1: **function** $DAHRS_2$(pLevelOneToOne,pLevelOneToMany, pLevelManyToOne, srcPhRange, tgtPhRange, funcWordIdx, headInitialFlag)
2:     **if** $pLevelManyToOne = \emptyset$ and $pLevelOneToMany = \emptyset$ **then**
3:         remOneToOne ← pLevelOneToOne
4:         **return** remOneToOne
5:     **else**
6:         tgtOneOne ← targets index of pLevelOneToOne
7:         **for** $(src, tgtList) \in pLevelOneToMany$ **do**
8:             **for** $tgt \in tgtList$ **do**
9:                 **if** $tgt \notin tgtPhRange \mid tgt \in$ tgtPlevelOneOne **then**
10:                     tgtList.delete(tgt)
11:             **for** $tgt \in tgtList$ **do**
12:                 $remOneToOne$.insert((src,tgt))
13:         srcOneOne ← sources of pLevelOneToOne
14:         **for** $(srcList, tgt) \in pLevelManyToOne$ **do**
15:             **for** $src \in srcList$ **do**
16:                 **if** $src \notin srcPhRange \mid src \in srcOneOne \mid src \in funcWordIdx$ **then**
17:                     srcList.delete(src)
18:             **if** size of $srcList \equiv 1$ **then**
19:                 $remOneToOne$.insert(($srcList[0],tgt$))
20:             **else**
21:                 **if** $headInitialFlag \equiv True$ **then**
22:                     $remOneToOne$.insert(($srcList[0],tgt$))
23:                 **else**
24:                     $remOneToOne$.insert(($srcList[1],tgt$))
25:         $remOneToOne \leftarrow remOneToOne + pLevelOneToOne$
26:     **return** remOneToOne

---

[2] SRL-BERT achieves an F1 Score of 86.49 on the English Ontonotes dataset [37], and it can be used non-exclusively. https://allenai.org/terms.

[3] A phrase consists of a token that begins with a "B" tag and continues with tokens that have an "I" tag. The following token will have a new "B", an "O", or end of the sentence, indicating the end of the phrase.

are lists of phrase-level alignment pairs: one-to-one ($pLevelOneToOne$), one-to-many ($pLevelOneToMany$), many-to-one ($pLevelManyToOne$). To support remediation, a list of function words ($funcWordIdx$) and a head-initial flag ($headInitialFlag$) are also introduced. This algorithm returns lists of remediated mappings ($remOneToOne$).

First, $DAHRS_2$ examines whether the mBERT-aligned input is indicative of a one-to-many or many-to-one divergence within a given phrase (a BIO-tagged pair). If no such divergence is present, all the tokens in the phrase are returned as output ($remOneToOne$) without correction (lines 2–4).

The next step remediates a detected hallucinated alignment resulting from an ordering divergence (lines 7–10). For each target list of phrasal one-to-many alignments, two aspects are examined: whether any target tokens are outside the corresponding phrase range, and whether any target tokens are simultaneously aligned with other source tokens. Tokens meeting one of these conditions are removed from the target list ($tgtList$). After $DAHRS_2$ remediates spurious alignments in the one-to-many pair list, non-hallucinated source and target token pairs are stored in the output ($remOneToOne$) (lines 11–12).

Lastly, $DAHRS_2$ remediates hallucinated alignments arising from many-to-one divergences (lines 14–24). Three conditions are tested for each source token that aligns to a given target token: whether the source token is correctly located within corresponding range, whether it is aligned with another target token, and whether the source token is function word. Any source token matching

[I-ARG1] circuit	— ϵ
[I-ARG1] breakers	— disjoncteurs; **4-2**
[B-V] installed	— installés; **6-4**
[I-ARGM-TMP] after	— après; **7-5**
[I-ARGM-TMP] the	— l' ; **8-6**
[I-ARGM-TMP] october	— écrasement ; **9-7**
[I-ARGM-TMP] october	— octobre ; **9-9**
[I-ARGM-TMP] 1987	— 1987 ; **10-10**
[I-ARGM-TMP] crash	— **écrasement** ; **11-7**

Fig. 5. One-to-many (yellow) and Many-to-one (green) phrase-level alignments. (Color figure online)

one of those conditions is removed from the source list ($srcList$). Following this step, the algorithm opts for the first option if $headInitialFlag$ is true, or the second option otherwise.

We illustrate DAHRS$_3$ in Fig. 5, where the target token $écrasement$, has two distinct source token options ($october$ (9) and $crash$ (11)). Both fall within the correct source phrase range (7–30). Since the source token $october$ already maps to $octobre$, $october$ is removed from the source options for $écrasement$.

$DAHRS_3$: First-Come First-Assign (FCFA) SRL Projection. $DAHRS_3$ is a new greedy FCFA SRL projection that transfers semantic roles using the remediated alignments (one-to-one mappings, $remOneToOne$), as shown in Algorithm 3. Alignments are provided as an input along with corresponding role labels transferred from English ($srcSRLSet$).

Source side semantic roles are assigned to the remediated aligned target token (lines 3–9). Projection yields two outputs: a human interpretable alignment representation and a JSON formatted SRL representation. For example, in Fig. 6 (a), token-level FCFA projects label ("O") to *octobre* and *écrasement* from *october* and *crash* (ordering). In addition, the source label from *laptops* is projected to both *ordinateurs* and *portables*, leveraging the

---

Algorithm 3. First-Come First-Assign (FCFA) SRL Projection ($DAHRS_3$)

Input remOneToOne, srcSRLSet
Output tgtSRLList
1: **function** FCFA(remOneToOne, srcSRLSet)
2:    tgtSRLList ← []
3:    **for** $srcIdx, tgtIdx \in remOneToOne$ **do**
4:       srcSRL ← srcIdx th item of srcSRLSet
5:       **if** $tgtIdx \equiv eps$ **then**
6:          tgtSRL ← None
7:       **else**
8:          tgtSRL ← srcSRL
9:          tgtSRLList.insert((tgtIdx,tgtSRL))
10:    **return** tgtSRLList

---

correct (one-to-many) alignment. Advancing beyond state-of-the-art (XSRL), many-to-one handling results in the retention of V for *effondrée* and the elimination of the hallucinated $ARG4$ for *apart*.

Phrase-level projection operates similarly. In Fig. 6 (b), *october* aligns with *octobre* and "$ARGM$-TMP" transfers to *octobre* (one-to-many). Due to the correct alignment of *crash* with *écrasement*, "$ARGM$-TMP" is transferred to *écrasement* (many-to-one). Furthermore, phrase-level projection considers whether the source language is head-initial or head-final. For example, *[B-V-closed], [B-ARGM-MNR-down]—B-V-fermé*, DAHRS projects "V" from *closed*, rather than "$ARGM$-MNR" from *down*.

(a) Token-level FCFA SRL Projection
One-to-many
[O] laptop — [O] ordinateurs ; **17-23**
[O] laptop — [O] portables ; **17-24**
Many to one
[B-V] fall   — [B-V] effondrée; **4-6**
[B-ARG4] apart — ε
Ordering
[O] october — ε ; **9-7**
[O] october — [O] octobre ; **9-9**
[O] 1987   — [O] 1987 ; **10-10**
[O] crash   — [O] écrasement ; **11-7**
(b) Phrase-level FCFA SRL Projection
[I-ARG1] circuit   — ε
[I-ARG1] breakers   — [I-ARG1] disjoncteurs
[B-V] installed   — [B-V] installés
[B-ARGM-TMP] after   — [B-ARGM-TMP] après
[I-ARGM-TMP] the   — [I-ARGM-TMP] l'
[I-ARGM-TMP] october — [I-ARGM-TMP] octobre
[I-ARGM-TMP] 1987   — [I-ARGM-TMP] 1987
[I-ARGM-TMP] crash   — [I-ARGM-TMP] écrasement

Fig. 6. Token/phrase-level FCFA SRL projections

3.3 Explainability and Visualization

In contrast to blackbox LLMs, which do not elucidate the decisions behind language alignment and SRL projections, DAHRS builds readily visualized representations that explain how it arrives at its output. Whereas prior work [18] has proposed metrics such as 'goodness', 'user satisfaction', and 'understandability' as proxies for explainability, DAHRS integrates human-interpretable representations directly into alignment and projection.

Two visualized products of our implementation (with French, Spanish as our test case) are: (a) a set of linguistically annotated alignment representations (one for each predicate indicated as "V") that provides a window into why/how the system produces its output while elucidating errors that can be readily remedied, as depicted in Fig. 5; (b) a JSON formatted representation that specifies all semantic role-labeled tokens for each sentence, as depicted in Fig. 2 (*French semantic role-labeled sentence*). These examples showcase our handling of hallucination remediation in the face of divergences and highlight the assignment of predicates and corresponding semantic roles on the target side.

3.4 Model as a Diagnostic Tool

DAHRS employs a direct alignment-based source-to-target transfer mechanism, without requiring a filter or BERT Score (as implemented in XSRL). Moreover, the model based on this algorithm is an effective tool for assessing the accuracy of predicate and semantic role projection in longstanding community standard datasets. To illustrate this point, we explore a human-tagged English evaluation dataset from CoNLL-2009 [16], which has also been translated to French and Spanish data as part of XSRL's research [6].

Preliminary tests using these datasets for SRL projection yield a much lower precision for DAHRS than that of XSRL: *DAHRS: 65.9 (FR), 66.3 (ES), XSRL: 80.7 (FR), 85.4 (ES)*. Further investigation reveals that these data sets include a very large number of spurious V tags for non-predicates: 8341 (DAHRS) vs. 3777 (XSRL), 8401 (DAHRS) vs. 3870 (XSRL) for FR, ES, respectively. This is corroborated through analysis of part-of-speech (POS) attributes, which reveals that many verbs mislabeled as predicates do not have POS tag *V* or *VB(D)*.

This overabundance of incorrectly labeled non-predicates in the pre-existing English CoNLL-09 dataset (where spurious V-tagged tokens/phrases would more appropriately be labeled ARG0, ARG1, ARG2) leads to significantly corrupted projections. We thus leverage DAHRS as a diagnostic tool, paving the way for refinements of the CoNLL-2009 gold dataset. We automatically remove the Y (= Yes) flag for predicates that do not have part-of-speech *V* or *VB(D)*.[4] Correspondingly, incorrect transferal of falsely labeled predicates from the source is drastically reduced.

With this annotation refinement, we provide the updated new CoNLL-2009 dataset to the community. Correction of spurious predicate labels significantly improves the transferal of predicates and semantic roles during the application of DAHRS. In Sect. 4, all experiments use this newly updated dataset.

4   Data and Experimental Setup

We use our updated English CoNLL-2009 data for projecting semantic roles to French and Spanish datasets. Human-validated FR/ES datasets, parallel to the EN-CoNLL, are provided by XSRL. The original CoNLL-2009 data incorporates

---

[4] We have simplified the notion of *predicate* considerably in this discussion, focusing on verbs; however, other parts of speech may serve as predicates. For example, *destruction of the city* is a nominal phrase conveying a *destroy* event with a single argument: *the city*. Future work aims to explore other parts of speech as predicates.

semantic roles for headwords only. In our headword-level experiment, semantic roles from English headwords are projected to the headwords of the FR/ES datasets. Since phrase-level test datasets are unavailable, we employ AllenNLP's SRL-BERT to assign phrase-level semantic roles to the English corpora, which are then projected onto FR/ES corpora.

Phrasal-level semantic role assignment further enhances the accuracy of SRL, ensuring phrasal coverage-a significant advance over the head-word labeling in the original resource. For instance, without our phrase-level enrichment, the word *The* is considered a headword during SRL assignment in *The Dow Jones industrials closed at 2569.26.* The result is a single, inappropriate semantic role assignment of ARG1 to the word *The*. However, with our enrichment, an appropriate phrasal-level semantic role assignment is made possible: *[ARG1- The Dow Jones industrials] [V-closed] [ARGM-EXT at 2569.26]*. This corrected output yields a more thorough, accurate representation, which is crucial for downstream tools such as those enumerated in Sect. 1.

French and Spanish corpora, including their semantic roles, are projected from 2046 English sentences using XSRL (see details in Sect. 2) and DAHRS. Subsequently, we evaluate these against both the community standard ground truth CoNLL-2009 (headword) from XSRL and the human judgment (phrasal). Our experiments run on 3 cores of AMD EPYC 75F3 32-Core Processor and using a NVIDIA A100 GPU.

5   Results and Analyses

We explore the performance of two projection-based models: DAHRS and XSRL. DAHRS achieves higher F1 scores in comparison to XSRL on our test data in both word-level and phrasal-level (see Table 1). Performance improvements are obtained as well as explanability.

To evaluate the correctness of the French and Spanish projection outputs, we employ the ground truth data from CoNLL-2009 for the headword dataset. Linguistically trained human taggers

Table 1. Word/Phrase-level projection evaluation for French and Spanish: DAHRS vs. baseline (XSRL)

Model	Language	Level	P	R	F1
XSRL	French	word	80.7	74.2	77.3
DAHRS	French	word	86.8	88.3	**87.6**
XSRL	Spanish	word	85.4	80.3	82.7
DAHRS	Spanish	word	88.1	89.9	**89.0**
XSRL	French	phrase	91.9	74.4	82.2
DAHRS	French	phrase	98.9	81.1	**89.1**
XSRL	Spanish	phrase	99.4	78.3	87.6
DAHRS	Spanish	phrase	99.6	83.8	**91.0**

proficient in French and Spanish evaluate the phrasal output. Both evaluations use precision (P), recall (R), and F1 scores. Thus, we have achieved explainable transferability of semantic roles more efficiently and with more accurate outputs (P, R, F1).

We evaluate DAHRS against a human-validated CoNLL-2009 that assigns semantic roles only to headwords, per the original XSRL algorithm. We compare XSRL and a variant of DAHRS that produces only headword assignments against this same ground truth. In Table 1, DAHRS projection to headwords outperforms XSRL, with an F1 of 77.3 vs. 87.6 (FR), 82.7 vs. 89.0 (ES).

Furthermore, we conduct a post-analysis and evaluation of our phrasal-rich output against human judgment by French and Spanish proficient evaluators with linguistic training who evaluated 549 total labels (FR), and 582 total labels (ES). This analysis yields a F1 score (FR-89.1%, ES-91.0%, see Table 1). To our knowledge, this is the highest score achieved for this task, surpassing performance (accuracy) of single headword assignments without the overhead of human-labeled source data for French and Spanish.

6   Discussion: Beyond EN-FR/FR-ES

We explore hallucinations associated with linguistic divergences by considering language pairs beyond EN-FR / EN-ES. We consider Tagalog, a low-resource language notably influenced by Spanish at the word level [2], yet divergent from Spanish (and English) in that its subject follows the verb (VSO). Although our current study focuses on English as the source language, our future research focuses on Tagalog with both Spanish and English as source languages, further enriching our divergence exploration. This investigation aims to verify whether the pairs exhibit the divergent properties assumed by DAHRS and to provide a framework for testing longstanding hypotheses about cross-language divergences in the context of alignment.

We introduce divergence metrics that count the number of misalignments on both the source and target sides. When the target language demonstrates a higher number of misalignments, this typically indicates a one-to-many divergence case. Conversely, when the source side yields more misalignment, this typically corresponds to a many-to-one case. DAHRS effectively transfers semantic roles to the target language in both divergent cases, revealing the potential for generalizability to new language pairs.

As an early test case, we assess the applicability of our approach to English-Tagalog (EN-TL) or Spanish-Tagalog (ES-TL),[5] measuring misalignments on the source and target sides in both language pairs. Although mBERT alignment supports Tagalog, we are motivated to verify its effectiveness through this analysis, given that Tagalog is a low-resource language. We investigate alignment accuracy for EN-TL/ES-TL with the aid of a proficient human evaluator with ChatGPT [30] support. On average, 3.27 words (21.69%) and 4.04 words (26.77%) per sentence are corrected in EN-TL and ES-TL alignment, respectively.

After applying this alignment correction, we measure the misalignment in the source and target sides, revealing a decrease in misalignment of the EN-TL (3.94 (22.77%) to 3.0 (14.94%) words on the source side, 4.54 (34.82%) to 3.65 (26.05%) words on the target side). Notably, the findings demonstrate comparable misalignment in both language pairs (EN-TL and ES-TL).

Alignment regeneration and correction are prerequisites for employing DAHRS for low-resource languages like Tagalog. Base alignment (mBERT) is

---

[5] We use EN-ES-TL parallel data from LORELEI [35].

insufficient for aligning Tagalog with other languages such as English or Spanish necessitating meticulous customization of the alignment for such low-resource cases.

7 Conclusions and Future Work

We present a model for cross-language semantic role projection. Our work enhances semantically informed language processing with minimal overhead via a two-step process that rapidly identifies divergence cases and produces explainable, visualizable SRL output. We demonstrate performance improvements in accuracy without requiring a human-labeled French/Spanish corpus. Our evaluation relies on a community standard ground truth with SRL-tagged headwords (CoNNL-2009). Notable improvements are demonstrated when considering entire phrases, as evidenced by human judgments.

Future work will focus on expanding to other languages (Tagalog is underway) where hand-annotated labels are scarce. Although French and Spanish are investigated above, divergence-causing hallucinations, remediated by acknowledging the syntactic property of languages during DAHRS have been noted across many other languages, e.g., Spanish (categorial; [9]), Korean (structural; [23]), or German (light verb; [24]). As such, it is expected that DAHRS applies multilingually, both for mid-resource language pairs (e.g., English-Spanish/French) and for those that are low-resource language pairs (e.g., English-Tagalog).

Finally, our experiments reveal that a new model, DAHRS, improves the multilingual SRL projection task. We provide French and Spanish corpora, including SRL information per predicates. Additionally, we utilize DAHRS as a diagnostic tool to verify the accuracy of ground truth. Through this diagnostic tool, we identify errors in the data, enabling us to update and reproduce data for the language community. These data resources are not only beneficial for the SRL task but also may be leveraged for other tasks.

Acknowledgements. This research is based upon work supported by Defense Advanced Research Projects Agency (DARPA) under Contract No. HR001121C0186. Any opinions, findings and conclusions or recommendations expressed in this research are those of the authors and do not necessarily reflect the views of the US Government.

References

1. Akbik, A., Chiticariu, L., Danilevsky, M., Li, Y., Vaithyanathan, S., Zhu, H.: Generating high quality proposition banks for multilingual semantic role labeling. In: Proceedings of ACL-IJCNLP (2015)
2. Baklanova, E., Bellamy, K.: Spanish suffixes in tagalog: the case of common nouns. In: Traces of Contact in the Lexicon. BRILL (2023)
3. Campagnano, C., Conia, S., Navigli, R.: SRL4E - semantic role labeling for emotions: a unified evaluation framework. In: Proceedings of ACL (2022)

4. Danilevsky, M., Qian, K., Aharonov, R., Katsis, Y., Kawas, B., Sen, P.: A survey of the state of explainable AI for natural language processing. In: Proceedings of AACL-IJCNLP (2020)
5. Daza, A., Frank, A.: Translate and label! an encoder-decoder approach for cross-lingual semantic role labeling. In: Proceedings of EMNLP-IJCNLP (2019)
6. Daza, A., Frank, A.: X-srl: a parallel cross-lingual semantic role labeling dataset. In: Proceedings of EMNLP (2020)
7. DeepL SE: DeepL: neural machine translation software (2017)
8. Devlin, J., Chang, M.W., Lee, K., Toutanova, K.: Bert: pre-training of deep bidirectional transformers for language understanding. In: Proceedings of NAACL-HLT (2018)
9. Dorr, B.J.: Machine translation divergences: a formal description and proposed solution. Computational Linguistics (1994)
10. Dorr, B.J., Pearl, L., Hwa, R., Habash, N.: DUSTer: a method for unraveling cross-language divergences for statistical word-level alignment. In: Proceedings of the 5th Conference of the Association for Machine Translation in the Americas: Technical Papers, vol. 2499 (2002)
11. Dou, Z.Y., Neubig, G.: Word alignment by fine-tuning embeddings on parallel corpora. In: Proceedings of the EACL (2021)
12. Fei, H., Zhang, M., Ji, D.: Cross-lingual semantic role labeling with high-quality translated training corpus. In: Proceedings of ACL (2020)
13. Gehring, J., Auli, M., Grangier, D., Yarats, D., Dauphin, Y.N.: Convolutional sequence to sequence learning. In: Proceedings of ICML. vol. 3 (2017)
14. Genest, P.E., Lapalme, G.: Framework for abstractive summarization using text-to-text generation. In: Monolingual@ACL (2011)
15. Guarasci, R., Silvestri, S., Pietro, G.D., Fujita, H., Esposito, M.: Bert syntactic transfer: a computational experiment on Italian, French and English languages. Comput. Speech Lang. **71** (2022)
16. Hajič, J., et al.: 2009 conll shared task part 2 (2012)
17. Hassan, H., et al.: Achieving human parity on automatic Chinese to English news translation. arXiv preprint arXiv:1803.05567 (2018)
18. Hoffman, R.R., Mueller, S.T., Klein, G., Litman, J.: Metrics for explainable AI: challenges and prospects (2018)
19. Hwa, R., Resnik, P., Weinberg, A., Cabezas, C., Kolak, O.: Bootstrapping parsers via syntactic projection across parallel texts. Natural Lang. Eng. **11**, 311–325 (2005)
20. Kozhevnikov, M., Titov, I.: Cross-lingual transfer of semantic role labeling models. In: Proceedings of ACL (2013)
21. Liu, D., Gildea, D.: Semantic role features for machine translation (2010)
22. Liu, H., Yin, Q., Wang, W.Y.: Towards explainable NLP: a generative explanation framework for text classification. In: Proceedings of ACL (2020)
23. Maniyar, S.N., Kulkarni, S.B., Bhise, P.R.: Linguistic divergence in various language pair in machine translation perceptive. IOSR J. Comput. Eng. (IOSR-JCE) **23**(1) (2021)
24. Marzouk, S.: Chapter 3 german light verb construction in the course of the development of machine translation. In: Translation, Interpreting, Cognition: The Way Out of the Box. Language Science Press (2021)
25. Mather, B., Dorr, B.J., Dalton, A., de Beaumont, W., Rambow, O., Schmer-Galunder, S.M.: From stance to concern: adaptation of propositional analysis to new tasks and domains. In: Findings of the ACL (2022)

26. Mather, B., Dorr, B.J., Rambow, O., Strzalkowski, T.: A general framework for domain-specialization of stance detection. In: Proceedings of FLAIRS (2021)
27. McDonald, R., et al.: Universal dependency annotation for multilingual parsing. In: Proceedings of ACL (2013)
28. Mehta, S.V., Lee, J.Y., Carbonell, J.: Towards semi-supervised learning for deep semantic role labeling. In: Proceedings of EMNLP (2018)
29. Mulcaire, P., Swayamdipta, S., Smith, N.A.: Polyglot semantic role labeling. In: Proceedings of ACL (2018)
30. OpenAI: ChatGPT: Large-scale language model (2021)
31. Pražák, O., Konopík, M.: Cross-lingual srl based upon universal dependencies. In: Proceedings of RANLP (2017)
32. Rottmann, K., Vogel, S.: Word reordering in statistical machine translation with a pos-based distortion model. In: Proceedings of IEEE on TMI (2007)
33. Shen, Y., Chu, C., Cromieres, F., Kurohashi, S.: Cross-language projection of dependency trees with constrained partial parsing for tree-to-tree machine translation. In: Proceedings of the First Conference on Machine Translation (2016)
34. Shi, P., Lin, J.: Simple bert models for relation extraction and semantic role labeling. arXiv preprint arXiv:1904.05255 (2019)
35. Tracey, J., et al.: Lorelei (low resource languages for emergent incidents) tagalog representative language pack (2023)
36. Tsai, H.C., Kuo, C.W., Huang, Y.F.: Llamaloop: enhancing information retrieval in llama with semantic relevance feedback loop. Preprint at Reserch Square (2023)
37. Weischedel, R., et al.: Ontonotes release 5.0 (2013)
38. Yarowsky, D., Ngai, G.: Inducing multilingual pos taggers and np bracketers via robust projection across aligned corpora. In: Second Meeting of the NAACL (2001)
39. Zhang, M., Jiang, H., Aw, A., Li, H., Tan, C.L., Li, S.: A tree sequence alignment-based tree-to-tree translation model. In: Proceedings of the ACL-HLT (2008)
40. Zhang, T., Kishore, V., Wu, F., Weinberger, K.Q., Artzi, Y.: Bertscore: evaluating text generation with bert. arXiv preprint arXiv:1904.09675 (2019)

EpidGPT: A Combined Strategy to Discriminate Between Redundant and New Information for Epidemiological Surveillance Systems

Edmond Menya[1,2,3(✉)] ⒾⒹ, Mathieu Roche[3,4] ⒾⒹ, Roberto Interdonato[3,4] ⒾⒹ,
and Dickson Owuor[2] ⒾⒹ

[1] Université de Montpellier, Montpellier, France
[2] Strathmore University, Nairobi, Kenya
{emenya,dowuor}@strathmore.edu
[3] TETIS, Univ Montpellier, AgroParisTech, CIRAD, CNRS, INRAE, Montpellier,
France
{mathieu.roche,roberto.interdonato}@cirad.fr
[4] CIRAD, UMR TETIS, 34398 Montpellier, France

Abstract. Textual documents such as online news articles have become a key source in epidemiological surveillance such as being used in the detection of new and re-emerging diseases. However, such sources suffer redundancies with the need to automate the process of identifying novel information. In this paper, we propose a framework for learning novel thematic information in epidemiological news documents. Our approach involves both extraction and classification of new, duplicate, additional and/or missing pieces of relevant information in epidemiological news documents. Firstly, we propose an initial step to solve the limited data problem where fewer gold labelled datasets exists for training text-based epidemiological surveillance systems. This initial step is built using extractive question answering technique whereby we automate the process of extracting relevant thematic features inclusive of disease and host names, location and date of reported events and reported number of cases in order to create a large silver labelled dataset. We then propose a main step where we build a novelty information classification model that is trained using our large silver labeled dataset. We then test our novelty classifier model alongside competitive ones on the challenge of detecting whether there is novel, redundant and/or missing information in a target epidemiological news article. We later carry out ablation studies on the most informative document segments in epidemiological news articles.

Keywords: Novel Information Extraction · Extractive Question Answering · Text Mining

1   Introduction

Documents such as online news articles, social media posts, blogs and emails serve as a rich data source for epidemiological surveillance. Such systems take in vast amount of online textual data in real time and output relevant emergency signals [3,19,27,31]. These surveillance signals, aid in the achievement of early warning systems that first responders rely on to help mitigate disasters including but not limited to epidemic disasters (pandemics, endemics), ecological catastrophes (wildfires, drought, floods), extreme weather events (thick smog, heatwaves) and geographical disasters (earthquakes, volcano eruptions) [1,12].

However, these online text sources (majorly online news articles) contain a lot of redundant information that occurs as a consequence of journalistic writing styles and the fundamental questions that journalists ask when producing news [11,16]. Whenever disaster strikes, the online space is flooded with redundant news containing unstructured pieces of information about a given event of interest (location, date, time, number of reported cases, type of disaster).

> **Doc 1:** African swine fever alert in Arad. Hundreds of pigs will be slaughtered The Local Center for Disease Control (CLCB) Arad approved a plan of measures to prevent the spread of the disease ... The Romanian authorities decided that Pig housing buildings and equipment will be disinfected...
>
> ---
>
> **Doc 2:** An outbreak of African swine fever has been confirmed in a farm with over 300 pigs in Frumusani commune, Aluniş village , Arad county, county authorities announced today, Friday – August 18 , which specified that all animals will be euthanized.

Fig. 1. Example of introduction sentences of two news articles (Doc 1 and Doc 2) from PADI-Web, both articles are reporting on the same event on the same day (18th August 2023). Novel information types are highlighted in different colors i.e. new disease (e.g. African swine fever), new location (e.g. Arad), new date (today, Friday - August 18) and new case (over 300).

Novelty detection tasks can be applied to solve the aforementioned problems. This task involves finding a target text source that has significant new information compared to other previously seen sources (Fig. 1). This technique has been applied in key language processing tasks such as plagiarism detection, text summarization, news development tracking and computing the impact value of research articles [9,10,24]. Several approaches exists for novelty detection in text sources that rely on text summarization techniques [14], deep learning [20], textual entailment [8] and attention techniques [6].

Learning novel epidemiological information and eliminating redundancies seats at the heart of improving epidemic intelligence (EI) and several approaches have been tried by [5,9]. This task of mining for novel information in epidemiological textual data is related to fundamental language processing tasks such as information extraction, named entity recognition, and thematic feature extraction which have largely been improved thanks to the adoption of deep learning approaches. New information is critical in the EI framework especially in the signal verification stage [30]. For instance, the detection of new information can elevate classification index of a given disaster (e.g. from moderate to critical) helping first responders to prioritize on emergencies requiring immediate attention.

In this paper we propose a new classification model for novelty classification in epidemiological corpora, trained on silver labeled data. Originality of our work is thus the proposal of novelty classification in epidemiology using silver labeled data approach:

- We propose an initial step that uses extractive question answering for automatically mining thematic features from news articles using five proposed questions. In this step, we use *hard prompt fine tuning* using a gold labeled dataset to train a model for automatic extraction of thematic features. This trained model is then used to generate silver labeled dataset. This technique eliminates the need to have human experts to manually label the training data to be used for our main step.
- We propose a multi-label novelty classifier model for detecting new, redundant and/or missing thematic information in epidemiological text sources. This model is trained on silver labeled dataset from our first step.

The rest of this paper is organized as follows: Sect. 2 outlines related work majorly reviewing existing novelty detection models and our major contributions; Sect. 3 introduces our approach to novelty detection in epidemiology surveillance, our adopted architecture and data used; Sect. 4 discusses empirical results from comparing competitive baselines with our models as experimented on curated datasets; Sect. 5 presents ablation study findings on key aspects of both our models and datasets and finally Sect. 6 presents a summary of the entire paper and proposed future works.

2   Related Works

Novelty Detection in Documents: Our proposed work relates greatly with the task of finding novel information in text data. The use of neural networks in detecting novelty in documents was introduced by [7] who trained a deep Convolution Neural Network model (CNN) to classify documents into novel and non-novel classes while later, [20] experimented over CNN-LSTM performance over the same problem. [6] used the Attention technique to mine novel information in documents that contain semantic level redundancies. The attention based models do not require manually labeled features thus can work well with vastly available unstructured datasets. [8] studies document level novelty detection and uses pre-trained textual entailment to improve detection. This approach improves semantic level novelty detection in documents that have less

Pigs are seized from Sverdlovsk colonies due to an outbreak of
African plague

Pigs are seized from colonies no. 6 and no. 12, located in nizhny tagil . the blame for
this is the outbreak of African plague ...

Q: "When did this event take place?" A: No answer	
Q: "Where did this event take place?" **A: Sverdlovsk**	
Q: "What event is being reported?" **A: outbreak of African plague**	
Q: "What was the cause of the event?" **A: Pigs**	
Q: "How many cases were reported?" A: No answer	

Fig. 2. A document with two segments shown (document title and first paragraph) with questions posed on the first segment with 3/5 questions answered and 2/5 missing information.

lexical overlaps as experimented over benchmarks presented by [9]. All the above focuses on document level novelty. Novelty at the sentence level has also been widely studied. For instance, [34] studies how named entity patterns can be used to identify novelty in sentences, while [26] used knowledge based approach to further enriched this process of relevant sentence retrieval. [28] studied different novelty control measures comparing word-based against named entity-based vector models over news articles concluding that focusing on named entities as opposed to all words in a sentence improves novelty detection. Our approach is also an extension of epidemiological thematic features proposed by [19] and extended by [18] where thematic features are classified into different classes of novelty.

Extractive Question Answering: Also (in order to address the challenge of limited training data in epidemiology surveillance) we propose an initial step that involves extracting thematic features automatically from new articles. In this initial step, our adopted approach specifically relates to the task of using span extraction question answering techniques which traditionally requires a context, a paused question and an extracted answer which must an extract of the given context. To this regard, we set thematic features (disease names of reported outbreaks, host names, location, date and number of cases) as the gold label answers and news article segments as contexts. Span extractive question answering has been studied widely with datasets and benchmarks like SQUAD 1.0 [23] which consists of questions asked on Wikipedia documents and all questions are assumed to have an answer span within the given context. SQUAD 2.0 introduces questions which do not have an answer within a given context [22] and a related technique is employed by [29] under the QNLI task which extracts answer span from a given context if-and-only-if the question is answerable else the model abstains from answering (predicting null answers).

When?	Where?	What?	Cause?	How Many?
-	Sverdlovsk	African plague	Pigs	-

Fig. 3. Event Structure of 1st segment showing three answered question (existing information) with two other questions unanswered (missing information)

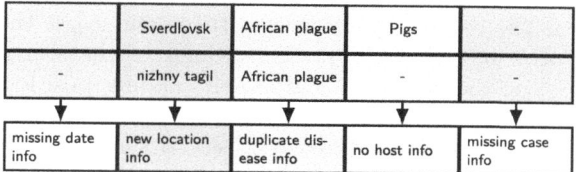

-	Sverdlovsk	African plague	Pigs	-
-	nizhny tagil	African plague	-	-
missing date info	new location info	duplicate disease info	no host info	missing case info

Fig. 4. Comparing Event Structures of 1st and 2nd segments showing one new location information and one duplicate disease information. Three questions are unanswered in this 2nd segment (missing information)

3   Methodology

In this section we present the formal definition of our proposed model starting with our initial step that uses extractive question answering for silver labeled data generation followed by our novelty classification model.

3.1   Formal Model Definition: EpidGPT

Extractive Question Answering: In order to generate silver labeled data, we propose a set of five prompt questions as we show in Fig. 2 whose generated answers are thematic feature (names of disease, location, date etc.). This proposed task is formally defined as follows: given a set of news articles D and a set of text segments $S = \{s_1, \ldots, s_i\}$ belonging to the same document $d \in D$, set up a model to learn automatic thematic feature extraction by prompting a series of five questions, with similar question at a time, on $(s_i, S)\forall S$ from which the model extracts answers $A = \{a_1, \ldots, a_n\}$ for every paused question as demonstrated in Fig. 2. Using the generated set A our model then builds thematic-feature information structure for each S as demonstrated in Fig. 3 and then compares these event structures over $(s_i, S)\forall S$ and automatically labels s_i

into *either, none* or a *subset* of the target classes C made up of $\mathcal{I} := \{1, \ldots, N\}$ representing the set of N thematic information types (e.g. new or duplicate information) and $\mathcal{H} := \{1, \ldots, M\}$ representing the set of M thematic features such that $C = \mathcal{A} \times \mathcal{B}$ and $\mid C \mid = 20$ (e.g. a segment can be labelled as having "new disease information" and/or "duplicate date information" in a multi-label fashion). We propose hard-prompt fine-tuning approach using our gold labeled data which contains context-question-answer triples with our model learning by minimizing the cost function:

$$NLL = \sum_{(\mathcal{C}_i, q_i, a_i)}^{|\mathcal{N}_b|} -log(P(a_{i_{start}} \cdot a_{i_{end}})) - \alpha[e \cdot log(P(a_i))$$
$$+ (1 - e)log(1 - P(a_i))]$$

where $(\mathcal{C}_i, q_i, a_i)$ is the context-query-answer triple and $\mathcal{N}_b$ is the train set size with batch size of b. $a_{i_{start}}$ is the predicted logit of the starting position of answer a and $a_{i_{end}}$ is the predicted logit for its ending position. $P(a_p)$ is the probability that the answer a exists. α is a hyperparameter that controls the degree of detecting null answers, when it is set to zero then null answers are not detected (the first half of the NLL loss computes the answer prediction loss while the second half computes the null answer prediction loss).

Novelty Detection Model: We propose a main method for novelty classification in epidemiological news articles trained on silver labeled data as demonstrated by Fig. 4. This task we formally define as; given a news article $d \in D$ subdivided into segments $S = \{s_1, \ldots, s_i\}$ our model learns to maximize the probability (i.e. minimizing the fraction of labels that are incorrectly predicted) $p(c_j | (s_i, S)) \forall S$ where $c_j \in C$. Our model thus minimizes the hamming loss cost function:

$$L = \frac{1}{\mid \mathcal{N}_b \mid\mid \mathcal{L} \mid} \sum_i^{|C|} \sum_j^{|\mathcal{N}_b|} XOR(y_{ij}, (z_{ij}))$$

where $\mathcal{N}$ is the train set size and $\mathcal{L}$ is the set size of the target class while b is the batch size, y_{ij} is the true label vector z_{ij} is the predicted label vector. We use parameter efficient fine-tuning on a pre-trained language model to achieve this text classification task.

3.2   Used Models

We fine-tune generative pre-training (GPT-3) [2] based model for our tasks. We fine-tuned our initial model for generating silver labeled data using hard-prompt fine tuning on our gold labeled dataset and we name the model $EpidGPT_{QA}$. We then fine-tune our main model using parameter efficient fine tuning (PEFT) on our silver labeled dataset and we name our model $NovelEpidGPT$. We compare both our initial and main models with competitive models namely $BERT$, $XLNET$, and $RoBERTa$ models trained using general English corpus [4,33] and also *BioELECTRA*, *BioBERT*, and *PubMedBERT* models trained using biomedical domain corpora [13,15,25] in order to experiment how different pre-training strategies affects our tasks.

Table 1. Summary of our Datasets and the model they train. Column #**Docs** is number of documents, #**Segs** is number of segments, **Generates** is the respective data that is generated from one dataset and **Trains** is the respective model trained on the given dataset.

Dataset	#Docs	#Segs	Generates	Trains
Gold Data				
PADIWeb$_{gold}$	800	-	PADIWeb$_{QA}$	-
PADIWeb$_{QA}$	800	11,500	PADI-Web$_{novel}$	$EpidGPT_{QA}$
Silver Data				
PADI-Web$_{novel}$	3,500	36,000	-	$NovelEpidGPT$

3.3 Data

For our initial question answering step, we use [21] ($PADIWeb_{gold}$) expertly labeled epidemiological news articles to create our corpus set consists of $11,500$ generated question-answer-context triples out of which $4,200$ questions are answerable with the provided context and $7,300$ questions that are unanswerable. We name this dataset $PADIWeb_{QA}$ and we use it as our gold labeled dataset to train and test our model ($EpidGPT_{QA}$) in order to use it to generate our silver labeled dataset.

For our main experimental stage, we generate silver labels using our model from the initial stage (EpidGPT$_{QA}$) on $3,500$ epidemiological news articles from [17] dataset and we obtain $36,000$ document segments. We then use prediction entropy regularization technique to de-bias the generated labels [32]. Document segments in this new dataset are automatically labeled as either containing new, duplicate, additional or missing information (one document segments can have multiple labels). We name this new dataset $PADIWeb_{novel}$ and out of these, we use 60% as train set, 20% as held-out corpus set and 20% as test set to train and test $NovelEpidGPT$ novelty classification model. We summarize our datasets and the models they train in Table 1.

4 Experiments

4.1 Experimental Set Up

We experiment our model training, testing and hyperparameter settings on the NVIDIA V-100 GPU with 32 GB memory and 112 TFlops tensor performance.

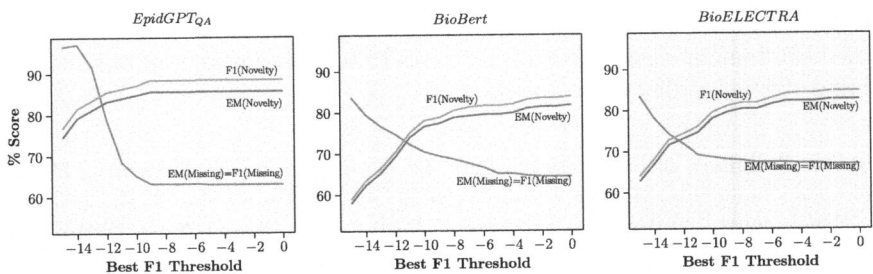

Fig. 5. Effect of choosing different values of $\mathcal{T}$ on EM and F_1 scores of novel versus missing information in $PADIWeb_{QA}$ held out corpus. This shows how we pick the Best F1 Threshold to use in decision of predicting null answers. $EpidGPT_{QA}$ produces the highest intersection points.

4.2 Hyperparameter Setting

We perform grid search hyperparameter tuning and we adopt embedding sizes of 768, 12 Attention Heads and 12 Transformer blocks. We set a batch size of 16 and a sequence length of 128 and experiment with 50 epochs. We experiment with dropout rates of 0.05, 0.1 and 0.2 to avoid model overfitting. We adopt Adam optimizer with decoupled weight decay (AdamW) with $\beta_1 = 0.9$ and $\beta_2 = 0.999$, we set $\epsilon =$1e-8 and weight decay $= 0.01$ and initial learning rates of 1e-5 and 2e-5.

4.3 Evaluation Strategies

Evaluating Label Generation Model: To evaluate our initial-step model ($EpidGPT_{QA}$), we compare the score of a null answer s_{null} with that of the best answer $s_{i,j} = max(a_{start:end}) \forall S$ and we predict null answer (missing information) when $S_{i,j} > S_{null} + \mathcal{T}$ where $\mathcal{T}$ is a threshold we set from the best F_1 score as in Fig. 5. We evaluate a predicted answer a_i by cross checking set membership in the set of gold answers A using Exact Match (EM) score as of Eq. 1 then we average them over the count of all answers.

$$f(a_i, A) = \begin{cases} 1, & \text{for } a_i \in A \\ 0, & \text{otherwise} \end{cases} \tag{1}$$

We then compute the overlap ratios between the predicted and gold answer sets after which we measure precision as the ratio of the count of shared answers to the size of predicted answer set, and recall as the ratio of the count of shared answers to the total size of gold answer set. F_1 score is then computed as the harmonic mean of precision and recall.

Evaluating Classifier Model: We evaluate our main model ($NovelEpidGPT$), which is a multi-label novelty classifier, using Exact Match Ratio (EMR) defined as $\frac{1}{n}\sum_{i=1}^{n} I(y_i = z_i)$ such that we check which members of the predicted subset class match the ones in the silver subset class and assigning scores similar to Eq. 1. We additionally compare $NovelEpidGPT$ with other competitive models by evaluating with micro averaged precision and micro averaged recall. To this respect, micro averaged precision is calculated as $Pr^{micro}(s_i \in S) = \frac{\sum_{c_i \in C} TP_{c_i}}{\sum_{c_i \in C} TP_{c_i} + FP_{c_i}}$ where we sum up the individual true positives and false positives and compute their average. Micro averaged recall is in turn calculated as $Pr^{micro}(s_i \in S) = \frac{\sum_{c_i \in C} TP_{c_i}}{\sum_{c_i \in C} TP_{c_i} + FN_{c_i}}$ having true positives and false negatives values summed and averaged. F_1 Score is the harmonic mean of the precision and recall values.

Table 2. Results Table comparing competitive model performances in epidemiological extractive question answering task. Models are compared on their skill in extracting novel information (first column) verses extracting missing information (middle column) and their performance is averaged (last column). Model best performances are in **Bold**.

Model	Novel Answer Extraction		Missing Answer Extraction		Average Scores	
	EM	F_1%	EM	F_1%	EM	F_1%
$BioBert(PubMed + Squad_{v2})$	78.48	79.53	72.07	72.07	74.37	74.75
$PubMedBERT(PubMed + Squad_{v2})$	74.69	75.51	98.85	98.85	90.20	90.49
$BioELECTRA(Squad_{v2} + PubMedAbstracts)$	83.21	84.05	**99.45**	**99.45**	93.57	93.87
$XLNET_{QA}$	40.47	42.87	75.29	75.29	62.25	63.15
$RoBERTa_{QA}$	75.0	77.06	98.33	98.33	89.59	90.37
$EpidGPT_{QA}(Squad_{v2} + PADIWeb_{novel} + WebCorpus)$	**89.11**	**90.69**	98.62	98.62	**95.03**	**95.63**

4.4 Results and Discussions

Data Generation Through Question Answering Results: Table 2 presents results of our proposed initial step for automating data generation process for thematic feature labelling in news articles. In this table we compare $EpidGPT_{QA}$ verses competitive models in their performance on the test set of $PADIWeb_{QA}$ gold dataset. Our model, $EpidGPT_{QA}$ is pre-trained on general English corpus (CC-News, STORIES and OPENWEBTEXT) and fine-tuned on wikipedia question answering dataset (SQUAD2.0) followed by hard prompt fine tuning on the train set of our question answering dataset $PADIWeb_{QA}$.

We compare our model with other language models pre-trained on general English ($XLNET, RoBERTa$) and BioMedical ($BioBERT$, $BioELECTRA$, $PubMedBERT$) domain datasets. We also compare with models pre-trained using different strategies (masked vs unmasked language modelling) to track how this affects the answer extraction task (i.e. difference between $BERT$, $ELECTRA$ and GPT). We evaluate all the models by tracking metrics outlined in Sect. 4.3 and we indicate the best recorded scores in bold.

Novelty Classification Results: Table 3 presents results after training and testing our competitive models on our silver labeled dataset. In this table, wee compare $NovelEpidGPT$ with other competitive models on their skill of detecting novel information in $PADIWeb_{novel}$ dataset. Our adopted model is pre-trained using generative pre-training strategy (GPT-3) [2] and fine tuned using PEFT strategy. We set up competitive models similar to our first experimental stage with models pre-trained on general English ($BERT$, $RoBERTa$) and BioMedical ($BioBERT$, $BioELECTRA$) and we compare their results.

Table 3. Results Table comparing competitive model performances in novelty detection in $PADIWeb_{novel}$ dataset. Models are compared on their skill in detecting novel information between two corpus segments by predicting one or many C labels depending on the type of information contained in the segments. Model best performances are in **Bold**.

Model	Prec%	Rec%	F_1%	EMR	ROC-AUC
$BERT$($PADIWeb_{novel}$ + $BookCorpus$)	81.49	79.63	80.55	53.86	86.80
$RoBERTa$($PADIWeb_{novel}$ + $BookCorpus$)	80.94	79.53	80.23	52.68	86.64
$BioBERT$($PADIWeb_{novel}$ + $PubMedAbstracts$)	85.67	87.34	86.50	80.83	88.64
$BioELECTRA$($PubMed$ + $PADIWeb_{novel}$)	90.67	88.34	89.49	**95.83**	87.64
$NovelEpidGPT$($WebCorpus$+ $PADIWeb_{novel}$)	**92.89**	**91.23**	**92.05**	92.93	**91.12**

Discussions As observed in Table 2 results recorded on all models show that they perform well in predicting missing answers labels as compared to novel information labels (new, additional, duplicate). It is essential to note that this effect is influenced by the choice of *best F_1 threshold* as described in Sect. 4.3. We track this effect in Fig. 5 and record different EM and F_1 scores on different best F_1 thresholds on three of the most competitive models. $EpidGPT_{QA}$ outperforms all the competitive models in answer generation on epidemiological article contexts by achieving $+6.64$ F_1 score on novel answer extraction and $+1.76$ average F_1 score above $BioELECTRA$ which performs as second best. This performance can be attributed to the advantages of generative pre-training approach as opposed to masked language modelling which benefits downstream tasks such as epidemiological extractive question answering (with answers here taken as generated silver labels for our synthetic dataset). Such advantages include causal language modeling (CLM) objective which predicts current tokens by only attending to the past tokens in a given context with CLM tending to help $EpidGPT_{QA}$ to be coherent during answer span extraction (silver label generation). Absolute position embeddings is another key advantage as outlined by [2] where segments are paded on the right as opposed to the left, since in our approach segments are usually shorter than the whole document, this technique tends to help all segment information to be captured during answer extraction.

Epidemiological domain is closely related to BioMedical domain by which it shares some vocabularies such as disease names and host names, however, we do observe that pre-training a language model using datasets from the BioMedical domain doesn't necessarily improve our epidemiological answer extraction task. We observe $PubMedBERT$ a BioMedical domain language model fine-tuned on question answering dataset underperforming by -15.18 on novel F_1 score points compared to $EpidGPT_{QA}$. Furthermore, we do note that increasing sequence length severely impacts performance making $XLNET_{QA}$ to underperform below all models trailing $EpidGPT_{QA}$ by -34.94 and -23.33 in novel answer extraction and missing answer extraction F_1 scores respectively.

From Table 3 we observe the results of our multi-label novelty classification model termed $NovelEpidGPT$ and we compare its performance to other competitive models. We note that, $NovelEpidGPT$ outperforms all models in F_1 score and $ROC - AUC$ metric scores with $+2.56$ and $+3.48$ points above $BioELECTRA$. This shows the models' skill in balancing precision and recall having benefited from generative pre-training strategy similar to the advantages impacting $EpidGPT_{QA}$. However, we note that $BioELECTRA$ outperforms $NovelEpidGPT$ on EMR score, this can be attributed to the fact that both $BioELECTRA$ and $BioBERT$ greatly benefited from their underlying pre-training strategy of using biomedical data. Unlike in our previous extractive question answering task for data label generation, the pre-training data and pre-training strategy used in a model seems to boost epidemiological novelty classification.

5   Ablation Studies

In this section we present the findings of our ablation experiments carried out to understand two key aspects; the value that fine-tuning brings to our approach and the most informative segments in a given epidemiological document

5.1 Effect of Fine Tuning

To test if fine tuning relevant pre-trained models improves our main work, we compare our fine-tuned $NovelEpidGPT$ models vs the respective base none fine-tuned $GPT - 3$ model and we capture these comparisons in Fig. 6. From this figure we note that the validation loss of $NovelEpidGPT$ model is below that of GPT meaning that $NovelEpidGPT$ model is learning our respective tasks much significantly than the base GPT model. We interpret the gap between the validation losses as the added fine-tuning value that makes $NovelEpidGPT$ outperform other competitive models as discussed in Sect. 4.4.

Table 4. Tracking novel verses missing information frequencies in the first four segments of documents in $PADIWeb_{novel}$ dataset.

Segment No.	DIS Novel	DIS Miss.	LOC Novel	LOC Miss.	HOST Novel	HOST Miss.	DATE Novel	DATE Miss.	CASE Novel	CASE Miss.
1	**55.88**	44.12	**64.71**	35.29	**47.06**	52.94	**58.82**	41.18	**55.88**	44.12
2	0.0	69.7	9.09	**60.61**	6.06	**63.64**	21.21	39.39	15.15	**57.58**
3	16.13	**70.97**	12.9	48.39	9.68	58.06	16.13	32.26	16.13	35.48
4	6.67	60.0	6.67	53.33	6.67	60.0	6.67	**46.67**	6.67	56.67

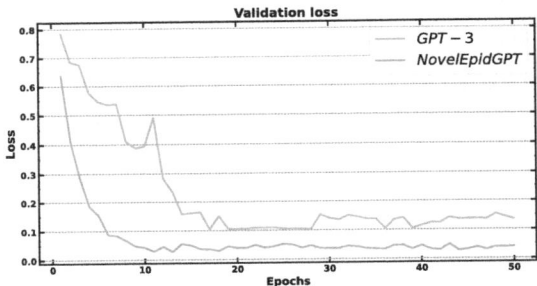

Fig. 6. Train Loss scores of $NovelEpidGPT$ compared to $GPT - 3$ on epidemiology extractive question answering task.

5.2 Most Important Document Segments

We investigate results of our multi-label novelty classification experiment to understand which document segments were found to have the most novel information and of which kinds. We observe from Table 4 and Fig. 7 that for all thematic features *new information* is mostly found in the first segments of a document. Important thematic features such as disease, host and location have their novelty levels dwindle almost close to zero in segments found deep into the document as less and less new information is being mentioned. Other features such as the date and number of reported cases tend to have their novelty distributed fairly in all segments.

We also note from Fig. 7 that *additional* and also *duplicate* information forms most of the rest of an epidemiological news article as they tend to occur from segment three on-wards. *Missing disease information* tends to majorly occur in the middle of an epidemiological news article. From our ablation studies we also observe that the last segments of an epidemiological news article mostly contains additional and duplicate information. This is a critical observation since it could underlie that the quality of data used to train text-based epidemiological surveillance systems doesn't necessarily have to be long documents. To speed up training of such systems, train corpus can be truncated and still state-of-the-art results can be achieved. This technique could help improve tasks such as epidemiological news summarization, question answering and novel information mining.

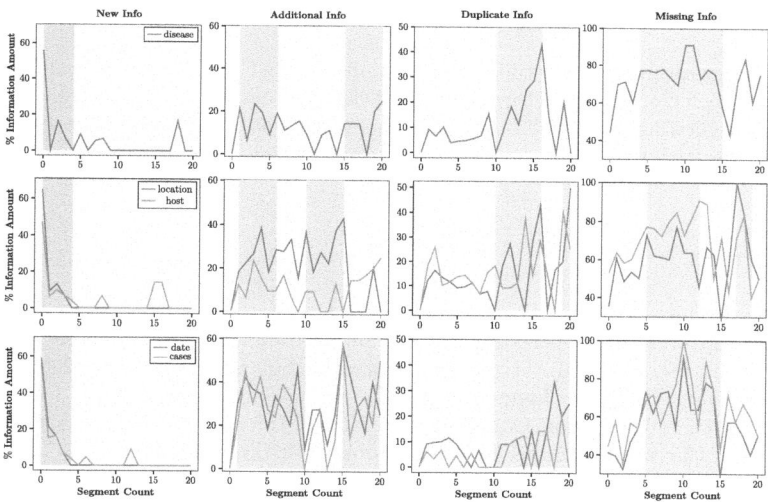

Fig. 7. Thematic features Information chats showing where new, addition, duplicate and missing information are located in $PADIWeb_{novel}$ documents. The first row focuses on disease feature with the second row comparing location and host and the last row compares date and cases frequency distributions.

6   Conclusion and Future Works

This paper proposes a novelty classification approach in epidemiological news articles. Our approach also proposes an initial model to automate the process of mining epidemiological thematic features from news articles using extractive question answering technique. These automatically mined thematic features (disease, location, host, date and number of reported cases) form silver labels in our synthetic dataset. The synthetic dataset is then used in training and testing a multi-class novelty classification model in order to classifiers epidemiological news article segments as having new, redundant or missing thematic information. This paper also studies the most informative article segments in epidemiological news articles. From our experimentation and ablation studies, we found out that generative pre-trained models achieve state-of-the-art performance on both our data label generation and novelty classification. We also found out that most *new information* is found at the beginning of an epidemiological news article with *additional* and *duplicate information* found at the end of such articles. *Missing information* is majorly found at the center of such articles. As a future work, we propose the task of entity linking in order to have thematic information linked to a particular event. We also propose a study on duplicate and additional information and their contribution to redundancies and a further experimentation on diverse datasets to test extractive question answering as an approach to generate synthetic data of large amounts in order to train epidemiological classification systems.

Acknowledgements. This study was partially funded by "Ambassade de France - Nairobi", French General Directorate for Food (DGAL) and by EU grant 874850 MOOD and is catalogued as MOOD089. The contents of this publication are the sole responsibility of the authors and do not necessarily reflect the views of the European Commission.

References

1. Boulton, C.A., Shotton, H., Williams, H.T.P.: Using social media to detect and locate wildfires. In: Proceedings of the International AAAI Conference on Web and Social Media (2016). https://api.semanticscholar.org/CorpusID:20838800
2. Brown, Tom B., E.A.: Language models are few-shot learners. In: Proceedings of the 34th International Conference on Neural Information Processing Systems. NIPS'20, Curran Associates Inc., Red Hook, NY, USA (2020)
3. Brownstein, J.S., Freifeld, C.: Healthmap: the development of automated real-time internet surveillance for epidemic intelligence. Weekly Releases (1997–2007) **12**(48), 3322 (2007)
4. Devlin, J., Chang, M., Lee, K., Toutanova, K.: BERT: pre-training of deep bidirectional transformers for language understanding. CoRR **abs/1810.04805** (2018). http://arxiv.org/abs/1810.04805
5. Färber, M., et al: Towards monitoring of novel statements in the news. In: Sack, H., et al (eds.) The Semantic Web. Latest Advances and New Domains (2016)
6. Ghosal, e.: Is your document novel? let attention guide you. an attention-based model for document-level novelty detection. Nat. Lang. Eng. **27**(4), 427-454 (2021). https://doi.org/10.1017/S1351324920000194
7. Ghosal, T., Edithal, V., Ekbal, A., Bhattacharyya, P., Tsatsaronis, G., Chivukula, S.S.S.K.: Novelty goes deep. a deep neural solution to document level novelty detection, pp. 2802–2813, August 2018. https://aclanthology.org/C18-1237

8. Ghosal, T., Saikh, T., Biswas, T., Ekbal, A., Bhattacharyya, P.: Novelty detection: a perspective from natural language processing (2022)
9. Ghosal, T., Salam, A., Tiwari, S., Ekbal, A., Bhattacharyya, P.: TAP-DLND 1.0 : a corpus for document level novelty detection (2018). https://aclanthology.org/L18-1559
10. Gipp, B., Meuschke, N., Breitinger, C.: Citation-based plagiarism detectionâĂŕ: practicability on a large-scale scientific corpus. J. Am. Soc. Inf. Sci. **65**(8), 1527–1540 (2014)
11. Hamborg, F., et al.: Giveme5w: main event retrieval from news articles by extraction of the five journalistic w questions. In: Chowdhury, G., et al (eds.) (2018)
12. Huang, L., Shi, P., Zhu, H., Chen, T.: Early detection of emergency events from social media: a new text clustering approach. Nat Hazards (Dordr) (2022)
13. Kanakarajan, K.R., Kundumani, B., Sankarasubbu, M.: BioELECTRA: pretrained biomedical text encoder using discriminators (2021)
14. Kumar, S., Bhatia, K.K.: Semantic similarity and text summarization based novelty detection. SN Appl. Sci. **2**(3), 332 (2020)
15. Lee, J., et al.: BioBERT: a pre-trained biomedical language representation model for biomedical text mining. Bioinformatics **36**(4), 1234–1240 (2019)
16. Lejeune, G., Brixtel, R., Doucet, A., Lucas, N.: Multilingual event extraction for epidemic detection. Artif. Intell. Med. **65**(2), 131–143 (2015)
17. Menya, E., Interdonato, R., Owuor, D., Roche, M.: PADI-web corpus used for the EpidBioELECTRA approach (2023). https://doi.org/10.18167/DVN1/WD1UC2
18. Menya, E., Interdonato, R., Owuor, D., Roche, M.: Explainable epidemiological thematic features for event based disease surveillance. Expert Syst. Appl. **250**, 123894 (2024). https://doi.org/10.1016/j.eswa.2024.123894
19. Menya, E., Roche, M., Interdonato, R., Owuor, D.: Enriching epidemiological thematic features for disease surveillance corpora classification. In: Calzolari, N., (eds.) Proceedings of the Thirteenth Language Resources and Evaluation Conference, pp. 3741–3750. European Language Resources Association, Marseille, France, June 2022. https://aclanthology.org/2022.lrec-1.399
20. Nandi, D., Basak, R.: A quest to detect novelty using deep neural nets. In: 2020 11th International Conference on Computing, Communication and Networking Technologies (ICCCNT), pp. 1–7 (2020)
21. Rabatel, J., Arsevska, E., de Goër de Hervé, J., Falala, S., Lancelot, R., Roche, M.: PADI-web corpus: news manually labeled (2017)
22. Rajpurkar, P., Jia, R., Liang, P.: Know what you don't know: unanswerable questions for SQuAD. In: Association for Computational Linguistics, July 2018
23. Rajpurkar, P., Zhang, J., Lopyrev, K., Liang, P.: SQuAD: 100,000+ questions for machine comprehension of text (2016). https://aclanthology.org/D16-1264
24. Shibayama, S., Yin, D., Matsumoto, K.: Measuring novelty in science with word embedding. PLoS ONE **16**(7), e0254034 (2021)
25. Tinn, R., et al.: Fine-tuning large neural language models for biomedical natural language processing. CoRR **abs/2112.07869** (2021). https://arxiv.org/abs/2112.07869
26. Tsai, F.S., Chan, K.L.: An intelligent system for sentence retrieval and novelty mining. Int. J. Knowl. Eng. Data Min. **1**(3), 235–253 (2011)
27. Valentin, S., et al.: Padi-web 3.0: a new framework for extracting and disseminating fine-grained information from the news for animal disease surveillance, p. 100357 (2021)
28. Verheij, A., Kleijn, A., Frasincar, F., Hogenboom, F.: A comparison study for novelty control mechanisms applied to web news stories (2012)

29. Wang, A., Singh, A., Michael, J., Hill, F., Levy, O., Bowman, S.: GLUE: a multi-task benchmark and analysis platform for natural language understanding (2018)
30. WHO: early detection, assessment and response to acute public health events: implementation of early warning and response with a focus on event-based surveillance: interim version. World Health Organization (2014)
31. Woodall, J.P.: Global surveillance of emerging diseases: the promed-mail perspective. Cad. Saude Publica **17**, S147–S154 (2001)
32. Wyatte, D.: De-biasing weakly supervised learning by regularizing prediction entropy(2019)
33. Yang, Z., Dai, Z., Yang, Y., Carbonell, J.G., Salakhutdinov, R., Le, Q.V.: Xlnet: generalized autoregressive pretraining for language understanding. CoRR **abs/1906.08237** (2019). http://arxiv.org/abs/1906.08237
34. Zhang, Y., Tsai, F.S.: Combining named entities and tags for novel sentence detection (2009)

Towards Generating High-Quality Knowledge Graphs by Leveraging Large Language Models

Morteza Kamaladdini Ezzabady[1(✉)], Frederic Ieng[2],
Hanieh Khorashadizadeh[3], Farah Benamara[1,4], Sven Groppe[3], and Soror Sahri[2]

[1] IRIT, University of Toulouse, Toulouse, France
{morteza.ezzabady,farah.benamara}@irit.fr
[2] Université Paris Cité, Paris, France
{frederic.ieng,soror.sahri}@u-paris.fr
[3] University of Lübeck, Lübeck, Germany
{hanieh.khorashadizadeh,sven.groppe}@uni-luebeck.de
[4] IPAL, CNRS-NUS-A*STAR, Singapore, Singapore

Abstract. Knowledge graph creation requires relation extraction (RE) tools often trained on annotated data either manually or by distant supervision. Recent approaches operate at the model level to handle new domains with unseen relations, relying on transfer learning or generative approaches in few/zero-shot learning scenarios. In this paper, we adopt a different strategy by operating instead at the level of dataset creation. We, for the first time to the best of our knowledge, investigate the ability of prompt-based models to build high-quality RE datasets relying on GPT4 to extract triples from sentences. Our approach is further enhanced by linking our knowledge graph to Wikidata, a step that enriches our dataset and ensures its interoperability. This strategy has been successfully employed in two use cases: COVID and health relation extraction.

Keywords: Knowledge Graph · Relation Extraction · Data Quality

1 Introduction

Knowledge Graphs (KG) encode domain knowledge using a graph-based abstraction of knowledge where nodes are entities that can be real-world objects or abstract concepts and edges the relationships that represent the relation between these entities [12,14]. KGs have become a valuable resource for many downstream applications, such as reasoning and decision-making [20].

KG construction from texts heavily depends on the performances of entity recognition, entity linking, and relation extraction (RE) tools, the latter task being our focus here. To this end, RE datasets are crucial to train and evaluate RE classification models. Existing resources are either built manually following a predefined set of generic or domain-specific relations of interest [26] or by distant

© The Author(s), under exclusive license to Springer Nature Switzerland AG 2024
A. Rapp et al. (Eds.): NLDB 2024, LNCS 14762, pp. 455–469, 2024.
https://doi.org/10.1007/978-3-031-70239-6_31

supervision leveraging knowledge bases such as Wikipedia pages or Wikidata [18]. While this last approach is an elegant solution to overcome human efforts due to manual annotations, significant errors in automatic annotation may occur, leading to noisy training data, which may hurt models' precision [33].

To handle new domains with unseen relations, recent approaches operate *at the model level* relying on few/zero-shot learning strategies [9]. Recently, prompt-based models have been proposed as an alternative for entity-relation triples generation when evaluated on benchmarks RE datasets [5,6,15,31,40]. However, manual annotation is still needed to ensure wide-coverage data quality [3]. This is particularly salient when building domain-specific KGs in domains that lack annotated data and where the set of relations to be extracted has to be designed by experts [1].

To reduce the amount of supervision, we adopt a different strategy that addresses these shortcomings at the beginning of the process, i.e., *at the level of dataset creation*. We explore for the first time, as far as we know, the potential of recent advances in large language models (LLM) exemplified by GPT-4 [22] to answer the following questions: *Does a prompt-based approach work well for resource creation in domains with limited resources? Does this approach ensure the correctness and completeness of the generated KG? And more importantly, can this approach be transferred to other domains?* To this end, we design an iterative approach that first defines an initial domain-specific taxonomy of relations of interest and then generates triples from reliable sources while ensuring KG refinement. The core of our research lies in introducing a novel methodology that leverages LLMs to facilitate the entire KG creation process, from defining ontologies to annotating triples. It is important to note that our primary objective is not to build a comprehensive RE datasets but to show that (1) a generative approach for triple extraction is feasible, (2) a coherent set of triples can subsequently aid the RE task. Our contributions are as follows:

1. Investigate the ability of prompt-based models in building high-quality KG. We showcase the proposed approach on the specific use case of the COVID-19 domain in which a massive amount of unstructured (and potentially unreliable) data has been produced. However, most available KGs are (bio) medical-based with less effort on other aspects of the disease [16]. In addition, most current COVID-19-KGs rely on open RE without predefined relation taxonomy, showing many errors in RE prediction [13]. Therefore, RE COVID-19 datasets become primordial to improve the quality of KG and overcome the lack of evaluation standards [21]. Our approach results to **the first dataset annotated for COVID-19 relations.**[1]
2. Perform a qualitative intrinsic evaluation of our dataset relying on standard KG quality dimensions [11] that have never been used to evaluate a RE dataset as far as we know.
3. Demonstrate the utility of this novel resource for the task of relation classification. Our results show that prompt-based dataset creation achieves an accuracy of 87.43% compared to gold labels.

---

[1] The annotated dataset will be available for research purposes upon request.

4. Show that the proposed approach is portable to a new domain while drastically reducing human efforts due to manual annotations.

This paper is structured as follows. We first present related work on LLM-based approaches for resources creation with a focus on RE as well as knowledge graph validation. Section 4 presents our methodology for generating our knowledge graph. Section 5 presents the intrinsic evaluation while Sect. 6 our experiments on automatic relation classification. We discuss our results focusing in particular on qualitative error analysis together with a study of the portability of our approach to an unseen domain. We conclude this paper highlighting our main findings as well as limitations and directions for future work.

2   Related Work

2.1   LLMs for Resource Creation

The realm of synthetic data generation has witnessed transformative changes with the integration of LLMs, especially in contexts where authentic data is limited. Recently, LLMs have been used for generating training data in various NLP tasks, including database [2,24] and reasoning [25]. Some approaches augment existing datasets with automatically generated examples like ZeroShotDataAug [28] and AugGPT [7]. These approaches however require an already-existing labeled dataset. For example, when applied on the medical domain, AugGPT might yield inaccurate augmentations because most general-purpose LLMs lack specialized domain knowledge. The reader can refer to [17] for comprehensive overview of the use of LLMs as labeler or data generator.

2.2   LLMs for Relation Extraction

Relation extraction (which entails discerning semantic interrelations between textual entities) has been significantly augmented by the capabilities of LLMs. For example, [34] introduced two strategies to utilize LLMs for relation extraction: 1) in-context learning relying on prompts designed to consider task definition, relation labels, and entity types, and 2) data generation guided by instance descriptions along with some example instances. [30] evaluated the ability of large language models to perform few-shot relation extraction via in-context learning. They found out LLMs can achieve performance equivalent to SOTA methods by providing some demonstration examples. They augmented target RE labels with Chain of Thought (CoT) style explanations elicited from GPT-3 and used this to fine-tune Flan-T5. In [6], which is close to our work, the aim is to train a model for RE in the zero-shot setting. They proposed the RelationPrompt paradigm and showed that language models can effectively generate synthetic training data through relation label prompts to output triples. This is one difference with our work, because we extract triples from the text. Finally, [38] proposed LLMaAA as a new alternative to low-quality issues of the generated data but still requires hundreds of annotated examples to achieve good performances.

Compared to these works, and due to the lack of annotated resources (i.e., triples) in the COVID domain, our approach uses zero-shot learning, therefore creating the KG from scratch, starting from ontology definition to triple annotation. The first advantage of our method is reducing the need for extensive pre-existing data, making it particularly beneficial in low resources domains. Furthermore, by automating the KG creation process, our approach minimizes the manual effort traditionally required in these tasks.

2.3 Data Quality Criteria for KG Validation

Assessing KG is a crucial task to assure that the KG is exploitable, there are several quality metrics that can help assess KG quality [37]. The metrics can be grouped in different dimensions: accuracy, consistency, completeness, timeliness, trustworthiness, and availability [32]. Most metrics can be manually checked. However, it became tedious as the KG grew larger. Some work uses the sampling method instead of assessing the whole KG to make the assessment more realistically feasible [8]. In this paper, we manually assess every triplet to guarantee the highest quality assessment. We mainly focus on the most important issues: inaccurate triplet (accuracy) and incomplete triplet (completeness).

3 Methodology

Our methodology is automatic, in the sense that most parts of the process are driven by LLMs and guided by carefully crafted prompts. Manual inspection is needed but only at the validation step, which is essential to evaluate the effectiveness of our approach. We provide below a summary of the main steps, highlighting ones that rely on manual annotations:

1. *Ontology Definition*: This step generally requires a domain expert to design the main concepts and relations linking them. Although this approach will reduce the risk of mistakes, it is costly and experts are not always available. We therefore choose to rely on LLMs to build our initial ontology. This ontology is not evaluated per se, but the purpose of it was to guide the LLM to understand the domain we were focusing on.
2. *Ontology Expansion*: Utilizes the LLM alongside the preliminary ontology to extract triples from the data source.
3. *Ontology Pruning*: This phase emphasizes the refinement of relations, i.e., grouping relations that share similar characteristics or meanings under the same top-level relation. We streamline the ontology by merging semantically akin relations and eliminating those that are infrequent or nonsensical. Human intervention is mainly required in this stage. While some manual effort is essential, especially in the early stages of ontology building, it is notably less labor-intensive than starting data annotation from scratch. As we explain in depth in Sect. 4.3, because of $|relations| < |triples|$, we believe human efforts would be less than constructing a KG all manually.

4. *Intrinsic evaluation*: This step is not part of the process in itself and is only needed to report the quality of the generated triples.
5. *Extrinsic evaluation* via RE Task: We employ our generated dataset to fine-tune a relation classification model. This step shows how our dataset can be used in a classification task.

Steps 2 and 3 are applied to all the input data as an iterative process, i.e., we split our dataset into batches then step 2 and 3 are looped until all the batches have been processed. This iterative approach ensures that each instance receives individual attention, allowing for more precise adjustments and refinements to the ontology. Overall, only step 3 requires manual validation as part of the process. Manual quality evaluation (i.e., step 4) allows for a better linguistic analysis of the generated triples. We illustrate the three key steps of our methodology on the COVID-19 domain (see Fig. 1 and Table 1), but it is generic enough to be applied to other domains as well. We detail below each of these steps.

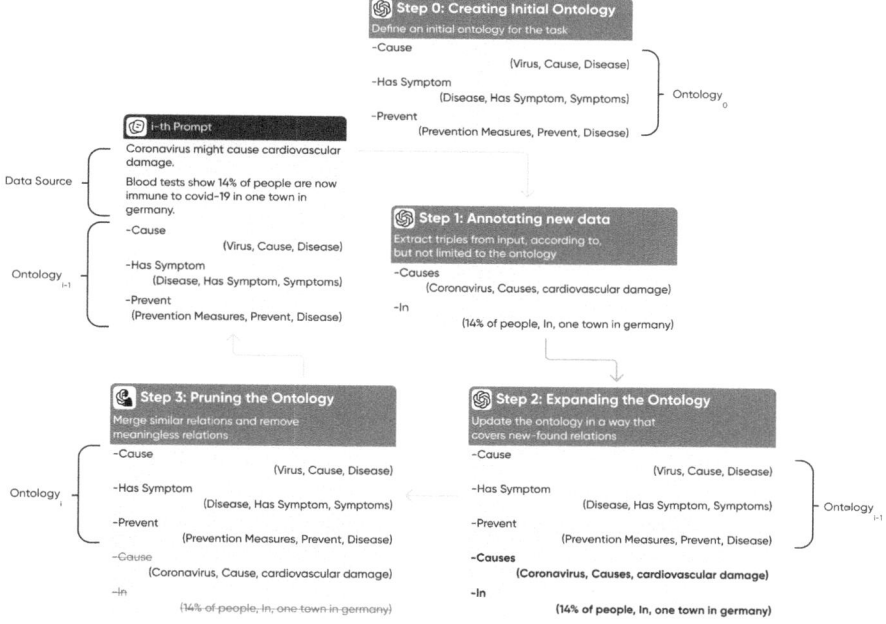

Fig. 1. KG Construction.

4 KG Construction

4.1 Ontology Definition

In traditional knowledge representation, an "ontology" typically refers to a structured framework that defines entities, concepts, and their inter-relationships within a specific domain. However, in our approach, we deviate from this strict

Table 1. Prompts and Responses.

Step	Prompt	Response
Initiate Ontology	I want to create a knowledge graph about COVID-19 facts and information. This knowledge graph contains triples (head entity, relation, tail entity). Build an ontology by defining possible relation and entity types.	... Entity types: - Virus - Disease - Symptoms ... Relation types: - Cause - Has_Symptom - Treat ...
Annotate Data	Now according to the ontology, for each sentence extract triples. [..., "Fujifilm tests favipiravir as covid-19 treatment", ...]	... (Fujifilm, Test, Favipiravir), (Favipiravir, Treat, Covid-19), ...
Expand Ontology	Update the ontology with the extracted relations.	... Relation types: - Cause - Has_Symptom - Treat - Test - In ...
Prune Ontology	Try to reduce the number of relations of ontology by grouping similar relations or changing them. Then update the ontology.	... Relation types: - Cause - Has_Symptom - Treat - Test ...
Augment Data	I'll give you a list of triples, generate a sentence for each representing that relation and containing both entities. [..., {'head': 'Moderna', 'tail': 'COVID-19 Vaccine', 'relation': 'develops'}, ...]	... Moderna, a biotechnology company, develops a COVID-19 Vaccine to help curb the spread of the virus. ...

definition. We categorize our triples solely based on their relation token, completely ignoring the types of each instance's entities. This flexibility is a deliberate design choice to accommodate the dynamic nature of the data we handle. Given the vast and evolving nature of data, especially in domains like healthcare, it is essential to have a system that can accommodate new entities and relationships without requiring significant restructuring. Our framework can seamlessly integrate new information by not strictly defining entity types for a given relation. For example:

1. Relation: "Treat"
   - Traditional Ontology: Medicine Disease (e.g., "Paracetamol" treats "Fever")
   - Our Framework: Entity (e.g., "Paracetamol" treats "Fever" or "Exercise" treats "Depression")
2. Relation: "Cause"
   - Traditional Ontology: Disease Symptom (e.g., "COVID-19" causes "Fever")

– Our Framework: Entity (e.g., "COVID-19" causes "Fever" or "Loud Noise" causes "Hearing Loss")

4.2   Ontology Expansion

The second step is to define a first core ontology. Existing Covid-KGs have been built for different purposes, either from scientific articles or biological databases covering various relations such as disease-symptom, drug-drug or drug-disease interactions [4]. In our case, we do not assume any prior set of relations as we aim to cover a wide range of relations beyond a medical use case, including regulations, policies, and everyday statistics about the pandemic. To this end, we used GPT-4, prompting it to define an initial core ontology covering domain entities (e.g., "virus", "country", "policy") and the potential relationships between them. This results in 12 initial relations (e.g., "cause", "have symptom", " affect").

Guided by this core ontology, we deploy the generative model to automate the extraction of triples (e_1, R, e_2) (i.e., entities and their relations) from external textual data while extending it to cover new relations through an iterative process. The data was chosen according to two criteria: (a) cover a comprehensive range of COVID-19-related information reflecting various aspects of the pandemic, and (b) contain verified information to guarantee the quality of the information encapsulated in the KG.

Among the huge amount of existing sources about Covid, we rely on Covid-Fact [23], a dataset of 4,086 sentences, among them 1,296 are scientific and simplified media claims, manually annotated as evidence for the claims, and 2,790 automatically generated refuted claims. For example, from the claim "$[Alcoholism treatment]^1$ is potentially effective against $[covid - 19]^2$", the triple (e1, Affect, e2) was generated, e1 (resp. e2) being the entities denoted by the linguistic expressions "Alcoholism treatment" (resp. "covid-19").

Our study aims to show that triple generation, along with domain ontology building, is feasible only when a small proportion of input data is provided. Hence, in comparison to benchmarks RE datasets (e.g., 106,264 sentences in TACRED [39]), we only relied on the 1,296 verified evidence (i.e., each one composed of one sentence with an average of 12 tokens) from CovidFact and arrived at 1,556 generated triples corresponding to 170 relations, among which 1,435 appear more than twice for a total of 61 relations.

4.3   Ontology Pruning

As the iterative expansion progresses, the ontology captures a wide range of relations, leading to a significant increase, totaling 170 relations. While this comprehensiveness is advantageous, it can pose challenges for subsequent classification and knowledge representation. Therefore, pruning and structuring these relations into a coherent taxonomy become imperative [10]. To this end, we employed generation together with manual review to combine relations that are semantically similar (such as "cause" and "lead to") while eliminating others. The discarded relations were either uninformative about the pandemic, infrequent, or

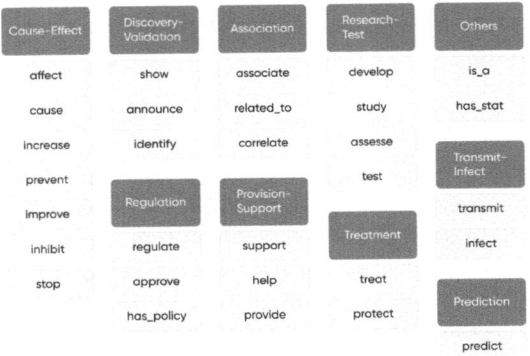

Fig. 2. CovidFact relations hierarchical structure.

comprised of illogical or incomprehensible connections, such as (e1, In, e2), generated from the statement "$Blood tests show [14\% of people]^1$ *are now immune to covid-19 in* $[one town in Germany]^2$".

Notably, the manual evaluation in this pruning step offers a more efficient approach than complete manual annotation. The focus shifts from extracting each triple to evaluating the relations, with $|relations| < |triples|$ streamlining the manual effort involved. The remaining relations have been hierarchically organized by grouping relations that share similar characteristics or meanings (e.g., "improve" and "increase") under the same top-level relation (e.g., "Cause-Effect"), as shown in Fig. 2. Finally, since some relations are rare, we removed triples with their relations appearing in less than 25 instances to reduce noise due to extreme data imbalance. In the end, we arrived at a total of 1,164 instances corresponding to 10 top-level relations (see Table 2).

For a detailed account of the exact prompts used to interact with GPT-4 and the corresponding responses for different steps in our study, see Table 1.

5   KG Intrinsic Evaluation

Qualitative and rigorous evaluation is a significant challenge when constructing KGs [11]. Despite its importance, intrinsic evaluation has never been employed in NLP to evaluate a RE dataset. We rely on key determinant quality dimensions developed within the KG community [37], focusing, in particular, on those that can negatively impact the performances of RE models [27,32], namely:

(a) *Semantic accuracy* refers to the degree of correctness of facts in a KG [32]. For our cases, we have identified the following types of errors:

– *Incorrect entities* (Inc_E) are defined as errors in either the head or the tail of the triple. For example, in "$[stanford researchers]^1$ *test* $[3,200 people]^2$ *for covid-19 antibodies"* → (e1, Tests, e2), the tail (e2) should be: "covid-19 antibodies" or "3,200 people for covid-19 antibodies".

– *Inaccurate relations* (INC_R) are defined as errors in the relation of the triple. For example, in "*[Dutchscientists]*[1] *find[new role for ACE2 receptors in Covid disease process]*[2]" → (e1, Develop, e2), the relation "identify" should be more appropriate as "dutch scientists" did not develop anything but they identified "new role for ACE2 receptors in Covid disease process".

– *Incorrect triples* (INC_T) are defined as error in the whole triple, as in "*[Coronavirusvaccines]*[1] *leap through [safetytrials]*[2]" → (e1, Develop, e2), which suggests that coronavirus develops safety trials, which is incorrect.

(b) *Completeness* refers to the extent to which a KG covers the knowledge of interest [32]. For our case, we have identified the following issues:

– *Missing triples* (MIS_T): some information is not properly extracted; hence, some data is missing, as in "*[Antibodytest]*[1] *for COVID − 19 could help to [control virus spread]*[2], *says Singapore med-tech firm*", where the triple (e1, Helps, e2) was not generated. This happens quite often for very long sentences.

– *Missing entities* (MIS_E): some information is only partially extracted and needs more information to be complete, like in "*[different mutationsinSARS − CoV − 2]*[1] *associate with severe and/mild outcome]*[2]" where the underlined tokens are ignored for the triplet extraction. This often happens when multiple triples overlap on all but one element.

During the quality evaluation, we noticed that on the linguistic side, the most common errors concern entity extraction, especially when entities are acronyms or span over nonconsecutive tokens. Triples involving these entities (totaling 185) have been removed for the next classification experiments, leaving these complex cases for future work. We manually evaluated the remaining triples (970) in the next step according to these four quality dimensions. We observed that around 12.36% have quality issues split into correctness (6.54%) and completeness (5.82%): 3.12% are about INC_T, 1.25% INC_R while MIS_T concerns 5.1% of the triples vs. 0.52% for MIS_E. Overall, we observed that relation extraction in long sentences is more challenging. These observations align with those reported in generative KG construction [35].

It should also be noted that this step is not part of the process in itself and is only needed to report the quality of the generated triples.

6   KG Extrinsic Evaluation

We now show how the generated RE dataset can be used to train supervised RE classifiers. Following the general trend in the field, entities are given as input to the model. We rely on LUKE [36], a state-of-the-art RE model that we fine-tuned on our annotated dataset.

6.1 Relation Extraction on the Covid Domain

Evaluation Settings. Our dataset is highly imbalanced, with certain classes (or types of triples) being underrepresented (less than 20% of the triples). These minority classes posed a challenge to the model's learning process. To rectify this and ensure a balanced training set, we employed a data augmentation strategy. Specifically, we augmented all classes, expect the majority class and arrived at three training sets as follows:

- COV: Represents the original triples extracted using GPT-4. This setting serves as our baseline, capturing the raw knowledge extraction capability of GPT-4 without any augmentation or external data sources.
- GEN: Combines the original triples from COV with augmented data generated by GPT-4 (see the last row in Table 1).
- DB: Merges the original triples from COV with triples from an external data source. This setting provides a hybrid approach, leveraging both GPT-4's extraction capabilities and external, possibly domain-specific, knowledge. It uses a random set of 308 tuples from a publicly available structured database about the daily statistical updates and policy actions of different countries in response to the pandemic [19]. We then transform each tuple into coherent sentences, mimicking the data format found in the CovidFact dataset. For instance, from the tuple (`USA, 5000 new cases, 05-09-2023`), the sentence "*On August 05, 2023, the USA reported 5000 new COVID-19 cases*" is generated.

Data in DB are regularly published by reputable health organizations and governmental bodies, which guarantees the reliability of the generated sentences. GEN resulted in 889 new sentences covering all the classes except "Cause-Effect", our majority class. DB, on the other hand, allows a significant augmentation of "Regulation" and "Others", which are among the less frequent (see Table 2).

Results and Error Analysis. Results are shown in Table 3 in terms of macro-averaged F1-score when tested on the COV test set, considering generated labels as gold. Best scores have been achieved by models trained on the augmented dataset, GEN being the most productive with 75.20. When compared to COV, the performances of all minority classes have been increased except for "Transmit-Infect" and "Prediction". This is more salient for "Treatment", "Regulation", and "Research-Test". DB achieved interesting results, particularly in classes like "Regulation" which has been considerably augmented. Although results on the class "Others" are less compared to COV, adding more instances from this class contributed to the other classes as well. These findings suggest incorporating reliable external structured data sources can be a reliable data augmentation strategy with less cost. A qualitative evaluation of the best classifier (i.e., GEN) shows that most errors occur between "Cause-Effect" and "Association", and "Research-Test" and "Discovery-Validation", suggesting potential linguistic similarities causing confusion.

Table 2. Original vs. augmented Train-Test split. We made the split randomly while keeping the same distribution of instances in each class.

	# Triples			Train			Test
	Cov	Gen	Db	Cov	Gen	Db	Cov
Cause-Effect	393	393	393	309	309	309	84
Disc.-Vali.	136	322	136	117	303	117	19
Association	109	287	109	78	256	78	31
Research-Test	103	258	103	87	242	87	16
Treatment	50	140	50	41	131	41	9
Others	43	111	200	35	103	153	8
Transmit-Infect	37	110	37	32	105	32	5
Provision-Supp.	37	84	37	26	73	26	11
Prediction	32	80	32	26	74	26	6
Regulation	30	74	181	25	69	152	5
Total	**970**	**1,859**	**1,278**	**776**	**1,665**	**1,021**	**194**

Table 3. Model performances on the COV test set. We repeated the process 5 times and these numbers are the average.

	Cov	Gen	Db
Cause-Effect	84.52	**87.65**	83.53
Discovery-Validation	75.00	80.95	**85.71**
Association	75.00	73.68	**75.41**
Research-Test	41.67	**71.43**	62.07
Treatment	31.58	**64.00**	35.29
Others	80.00	**87.50**	75.00
Transmit-Infect	61.54	55.56	**71.43**
Provision-Support	50.00	**66.67**	58.82
Prediction	**100.00**	90.91	92.31
Regulation	66.67	**90.91**	88.89
Macro F-score	66.60	**76.93**	72.85

To further evaluate our model, we manually labeled the whole 194 triples[2] from the Cov test set and then compared manual labels first with the ones generated by our approach, then with the ones predicted by Gen. We obtained an accuracy of 87.43% for GPT-4 vs. human and 81.15% for Gen vs. human.

In Table 4, we show examples from our dataset with labels that different settings predicted alongside the human annotation.

---

[2] Two of the authors of this paper annotated the data to have gold labels to evaluate performance of our approach to create a dataset. As we are not specialists we used common sense and if needed google search for this task.

Table 4. Examples from Test set with different model predictions. Blue and orange blocks indicate head and tail entities respectively.

	HUMAN	GPT-4	LUKE (COV)	LUKE (GEN)
fda authorizes 15-minute coronavirus test.	Regulation	Regulation	Regulation	Regulation
high incidence of venous thromboembolic events in anticoagulated severe covid-19 patients.	Cause-Effect	Cause-Effect	Association	Cause-Effect
anticoagulant treatment is associated with decreased mortality in severe coronavirus disease 2019 patients with coagulopathy.	Association	Cause-Effect	Cause-Effect	Association
polish doctor treats covid19 symptoms within 48h with amantadine.	Treatment	Treatment	Cause-Effect	Treatment
more than 80 clinical trials launch to test coronavirus treatments.	Research-Test	Research-Test	Research-Test	Research-Test

6.2   Portability to Unseen Domain

We now demonstrate the portability of our relation classifier to a new unseen domain, reducing therefore human efforts due to manual annotations. We rely on HealthFC [29], a curated collection of health claims designed explicitly for evidence-based medical fact-checking. Comprising 750 claims, this dataset offers a rich source of medical assertions that can be leveraged to test the robustness and adaptability of knowledge graph models in the medical domain. It is important to note that HealthFC was not part of the iterative phase and we just evaluated fine-tuned LUKE on our generated dataset (see previous section), on HealthFC.

From the HealthFC dataset, we meticulously extracted 109 triples. The extraction process was guided by the criteria of compatibility of the claims with our model's training data, which means relations of these selected triples could be categorized within our model's relations. For the experiment, we employed our best-performing model which is fine-tuned on GEN, results are presented on Table 5. We obtain an average F-score of 65.05%, the best performing was the majority relation Cause-Effect. Except Association which achieves low score (28.57%– which can be explained by the very low number of instances in the test set), all the remaining relations achieved very good score (> 80.00%).

Table 5. Model performances on the unseen HealthFC dataset.

	# Triples	Macro F-score
Cause-Effect	76	93.06
Discovery-Validation	7	80.00
Association	1	28.57
Research-Test	1	00.00
Treatment	6	80.00
Others	4	85.71
Transmit-Infect	0	-
Provision-Support	14	88.00
Prediction	0	-
Regulation	0	-
Average	109	65.05

Overall, we can conclude that our approach can be a good alternative to alleviate the need of human annotation in a zero-shot evaluation scenario.

7   Future Work

Future work will explore the use of open-source models, which could offer significant improvements. While we focused on key determinant quality dimensions developed within the KG community, we also identified issues with entity consistency. Emphasis will be placed on entity linking to unify related entities under common concepts, thereby enhancing the knowledge graph's coherence and effectiveness. Additionally, Entity Evaluation will be a critical area of focus, as entities extracted by LLMs can sometimes be of low quality and include pseudo-sentences. Refining entity extraction methods to better capture complete contexts, especially in complex sentences, will be another important direction for improvement.

8   Conclusion

In this paper, we proposed a generative approach for RE dataset creation leveraging recent generative models. Our approach has been illustrated on the COVID-19 domain and evaluated relying on two quality dimensions criteria. We also demonstrated that with a very small subset of existing unstructured data, we can build a new dataset that can be used to train a robust state-of-the-art RE classifier. While our method involves some manual efforts, it is judiciously optimized for maximum effectiveness, representing a significant advancement in knowledge graph creation in under-resourced domains. However, there are also drawbacks. Our reliance on a specific LLM means that our results are contingent on the capabilities and limitations of that model. Additionally, while our method reduces manual labor, it doesn't eliminate it entirely, as human validation is still crucial, particularly in the ontology pruning phase. We believe these minimal efforts are still needed when dealing with new domains which lack good quality linguistic resources.

Our approach relies on external source of data (CovidFact claims) that have been used as input to prompt the model. Therefore our RE dataset can be potentially biased towards those claims. However, the approach has been designed to be domain-agnostic and can be easily transferred to other use cases for which reliable external sources are available, such as scientific papers, news articles, or encyclopedic knowledge (e.g., Wikipedia). Its generalization to generic as well as other domain-specific relations are important directions for future work.

Acknowledgments. This work is jointly funded by the French National Agency QualityOnt ANR-21-CE23-0036-01, and the Deutsche Forschungsgemeinschaft (DFG, German Research Foundation) - Project-ID 490998901.

References

1. Abu-Salih, B.: Domain-specific knowledge graphs: a survey. J. Network Comput. Appl. (2021)
2. Borisov, V., Seßler, K., Leemann, T., Pawelczyk, M., Kasneci, G.: Language Models are Realistic Tabular Data Generators (2023)
3. Cabot, P.L.H., Tedeschi, S., , Navigli, R.: RED^{FM}: a filtered and multilingual relation extraction dataset. In: ACL (2023)
4. Chen, C., Ebeid, I.A., Bu, Y., Ding, Y.: Coronavirus knowledge graph: a case study (2020)
5. Chen, X., et al.: Knowprompt: knowledge-aware prompt-tuning with synergistic optimization for relation extraction. In: Proceedings of the ACM Web Conference 2022 (2022)
6. Chia, Y.K., Bing, L., Poria, S., Si, L.: RelationPrompt: leveraging prompts to generate synthetic data for zero-shot relation triplet extraction. In: Findings of the Association for Computational Linguistics: ACL 2022 (2022)
7. Dai, H., et al.: AugGPT: Leveraging ChatGPT for Text Data Augmentation (2023)
8. Gao, J., Li, X., Xu, Y.E., Sisman, B., Dong, X.L., Yang, J.: Efficient knowledge graph accuracy evaluation. arXiv preprint arXiv:1907.09657 (2019)
9. Gao, T., et al.: FewRel 2.0: towards more challenging few-shot relation classification. In: EMNLP-IJCNLP (2019)
10. Han, X., Yu, P., Liu, Z., Sun, M., Li, P.: Hierarchical relation extraction with coarse-to-fine grained attention. In: Proceedings of the 2018 Conference on Empirical Methods in Natural Language Processing (2018)
11. Hofer, M., Obraczka, D., Saeedi, A., Köpcke, H., Rahm, E.: Construction of knowledge graphs: State and challenges (2023)
12. Hogan, A., et al.: Knowledge graphs. ACM Computing Surveys (CSUR) (2021)
13. Jaradeh, M., Singh, K., Stocker, M.e.a.: Information extraction pipelines for knowledge graphs. Knowledge Information Systems (2023)
14. Ji, S., Pan, S., Cambria, E., Marttinen, P., Yu, P.S.: A survey on knowledge graphs: Representation, acquisition and applications (2020)
15. Jimenez Gutierrez, B., et al.: Thinking about GPT-3 in-context learning for biomedical IE? think again. In: Findings of the Association for Computational Linguistics: EMNLP 2022 (2022)
16. Khorashadizadeh, H., Tiwari, S., Groppe, S.: In: Proceedings of the EAI International Conference on covid-19 knowledge graphs and their data sources. In: Proceedings of the EAI International Conference on Intelligent Systems and Machine Learning (EAI ICISML 2022) (2022)
17. Lee, D.H., Pujara, J., Sewak, M., White, R., Jauhar, S.: Making large language models better data creators. In: EMNLP 2023, pp. 15349–15360 (2023)
18. Martinez-Rodriguez, J.L., Hogan, A., Lopez-Arevalo, I.: Information extraction meets the semantic web: a survey. Semantic Web (2018)
19. Mathieu, E., et al.: Coronavirus pandemic (covid-19). Our World in Data (2020)
20. Melnyk, I., Dognin, P., Das, P.: Knowledge graph generation from text. In: Findings of the Association for Computational Linguistics: EMNLP 2022 (2022)
21. Nguyen, H., Chen, H., Chen, J., Kargozari, K., Ding, J.: Construction and evaluation of a domain-specific knowledge graph for knowledge discovery. Information Discovery and Delivery (2023)
22. OpenAI: Gpt-4 technical report (2024)
23. Saakyan, A., Chakrabarty, T., Muresan, S.: COVID-fact: fact extraction and verification of real-world claims on COVID-19 pandemic. In: Proceedings of the 59th Annual Meeting of the Association for Computational Linguistics (2021)

24. Schick, T., Schütze, H.: Generating datasets with pretrained language models. In: Proceedings of the EMNLP 2021 (2021)
25. Shao, Z., Gong, Y., Shen, Y., Huang, M., Duan, N., Chen, W.: Synthetic prompting: generating chain-of-thought demonstrations for large language models. In: ICML 2023 (2023)
26. Stoica, G., Platanios, E.A., Póczos, B.: Re-TACRED: Addressing Shortcomings of the TACRED Dataset (2021)
27. Trajanoska, M., Stojanov, R., Trajanov, D.: Enhancing knowledge graph construction using large language models (2023)
28. Ubani, S., Polat, S.O., Nielsen, R.: ZeroShotDataAug: Generating and Augmenting Training Data with ChatGPT (2023)
29. Vladika, J., Schneider, P., Matthes, F.: HealthFC: a dataset of health claims for evidence-based medical fact-checking (2023)
30. Wadhwa, S., Amir, S., Wallace, B.: revisiting relation extraction in the era of large language models. In: Proceedings of the 61st Annual Meeting of the Association for Computational Linguistics (Volume 1: Long Papers) (2023)
31. Wan, Z., et al.: Gpt-re: in-context learning for relation extraction using large language models (2023)
32. Wang, X., et al.: Knowledge graph quality control: A survey. Fundamental Research (2021)
33. Xie, C., Liang, J., Liu, J., Huang, C., Huang, W., Xiao, Y.: Revisiting the negative data of distantly supervised relation extraction. CoRR (2021)
34. Xu, X., Zhu, Y., Wang, X., Zhang, N.: How to Unleash the Power of Large Language Models for Few-shot Relation Extraction? (2023)
35. Xu, X., Zhu, Y., Wang, X., Zhang, N.: How to unleash the power of large language models for few-shot relation extraction? arXiv preprint arXiv:2305.01555 (2023)
36. Yamada, I., Asai, A., Shindo, H., Takeda, H., Matsumoto, Y.: LUKE: deep contextualized entity representations with entity-aware self-attention. In: EMNLP 2020 (2020)
37. Zaveri, A., et al.: Quality assessment methodologies for linked open data. Submitted to Semantic Web Journal (2013)
38. Zhang, R., Li, Y., Ma, Y., Zhou, M., Zou, L.: LLMaAA: making large language models as active annotators. In: EMNLP 2023, pp. 13088–13103 (2023)
39. Zhang, Y., Zhong, V., Chen, D., Angeli, G., Manning, C.D.: Position-aware attention and supervised data improve slot filling. In: Proceedings of the 2017 Conference on Empirical Methods in Natural Language Processing (EMNLP 2017) (2017)
40. Zhu, Y., et al.: Llms for knowledge graph construction and reasoning: recent capabilities and future opportunities (2023)

DeepCodeGraph: A Language Model for Compile-Time Resource Optimization Using Masked Graph Autoencoders

Federico Cichetti[✉][ID], Emanuele Parisi[ID], Andrea Acquaviva[ID], and Francesco Barchi[ID]

University of Bologna, 40126 Bologna, BO, Italy
federico.cichetti@studio.unibo.it,
{emanuele.parisi,andrea.acquaviva,francesco.barchi}@unibo.it

Abstract. Analysing source code using deep learning aids compile-time decisions affecting performance in embedded devices. We propose Deep-CodeGraph, a general graph-based language model, which learns patterns to identify better compilation strategies, optimal hardware configurations and software transformations. DCG includes i) A large-scale dataset containing over 100k graphs. ii) A graph neural network to implement a graph-based language model. iii) A self-supervised pre-training framework leveraging Masked Graph Autoencoders. The performance of DCG is evaluated on two downstream tasks: heterogeneous device mapping and thread block size prediction. DCG outperforms previous graph-based state-of-the-art improving previous results by 3%.

Keywords: Masked graph autoencoder · Source code analysis · Compile-time decisions

1 Introduction

Contemporary computing systems frequently feature diverse hardware units, including CPUs, GPUs, or TPUs, making them *heterogeneous* devices. These devices can accelerate some classes of operations, but conventional compiler heuristics may struggle to adapt to the range of possible mapping options to fully leverage the potential of all platforms. Furthermore, optimal performance on a given compute unit can often only be achieved after rigorous exploration of device configuration parameters.

Statistical modelling and deep learning techniques applied to source code have been recently considered to address this complexity [1]. Notably, Language Models (LMs) and other Natural Language Processing (NLP) techniques are frequently deployed thanks to their ability to identify useful patterns for their designated task. In the domain of source code, these patterns may encapsulate knowledge regarding good software engineering practices, and its acquisition could facilitate the development of more intelligent, data-driven software engineering tools.

A. Rapp et al. (Eds.): NLDB 2024, LNCS 14762, pp. 470–484, 2024.
https://doi.org/10.1007/978-3-031-70239-6_32

Techniques based on NLP handle source code files as language artefacts on the basis of a similarity between natural and programming languages [1]. However, source code inherently carries patterns related to the causal and temporal dependencies between data (e.g. variables and constants) and instructions, which can be challenging to identify in sequential formats. In fact, recent studies demonstrate that Large Language Models (LLMs), widely used to analyze natural language, can be ineffective when dealing with source code optimization and analysis [9,18]. It is also unclear whether existing training methodologies designed for LLMs of source code can effectively leverage the knowledge derived from this data type [22]. Graph-based representations can instead enhance understanding of high-level code concepts [15].

In recent years, the deep learning community has seen a transition from end-to-end models to transfer learning techniques. In this methodology, models undergo an initial pre-training phase on a significant dataset and are then fine-tuned for specific tasks of interest. This approach distinguishes the learning of a problem's solution from the extraction of inherent patterns in the data, allowing the general knowledge acquired during pre-training to be reused across multiple tasks. Following this trend, we aim to empirically validate the efficacy of graph-based learning by employing a self-supervised pre-training technique tailored for Graph Neural Networks (GNNs) and measuring the improvements that a pre-trained model introduces across two downstream tasks: i) mapping computational kernels to compute units (heterogeneous device mapping) and ii) determining the most efficient thread block size for a GPU kernel (thread block size prediction).

To this end, we develop "DeepCodeGraph" (DCG), a procedure for building a general language model for graph-based representations of source code. The key component of our methodology is an adaptation of the Masked Graph AutoEncoding (MGAE) framework. This technique involves masking a selection of random elements from an input graph and tasking the model with their reconstruction using the remaining information. While being a popular technique in other settings, to the best of our knowledge, prior research has not explored the utilisation of MGAEs as a pre-training method in the context of language models for source code analysis.

DeepCodeGraph outperforms prior graph-based techniques and pre-training procedures designed for code optimisation, improving state-of-the-art results on the aforementioned downstream tasks. In particular, we achieved an average accuracy of more than 87% on heterogeneous device mapping, improving the scores of previous graph-based models by 3.2%. Additionally, we obtained a 3% enhancement in thread size prediction, with a top-3 accuracy of over 19%.

The rest of this work is structured as follows: Sect. 2 reviews the main solutions found in the literature related to both source code analysis and MGAE techniques. Section 3 describes our DCG methodology. Section 4 examines pre-training and fine-tuning results, proposing different tests determined to evaluate the benefits introduced by our method. Lastly, Sect. 5 wraps up the work and highlights future directions.

2   Background and Related Works

The focus of this work is on the integration of probabilistic source code models into optimization tools, specifically addressing *heterogeneous device mapping* and *thread block size prediction*. These tasks optimize compile-time choices to enhance program efficiency. Heterogeneous device mapping identifies the most efficient device for executing a code segment, a crucial task in embedded systems with diverse hardware configurations. Thread block size prediction, instead, targets GPU-powered applications and aims to select the optimal thread size for a given kernel depending on the input matrix size. Both tasks require extensive experimentation and expertise due to elements such as dependencies on memory parallelization, cache usage and so on.

2.1   Source Code Techniques

Pioneering works for solving heterogeneous device mapping borrow techniques and models from the field of NLP. DeepTune [11] is a simple model composed of two LSTM layers producing a final dense semantic representation for a sequence of tokens extracted from tokenized OpenCL source code. Vavaroutsos et al. [29] improved the design of DeepTune by introducing a Bidirectional LSTM, including an initial convolutional layer and a final attention layer to emphasise and reweigh information before extracting a global representation.

More recently, several works have leveraged LLVM-IR source code as an alternative to high-level languages [2–4,8] showing impovements in results. LLVM-IR is a low-level, flexible and human-readable Intermediate Representation used for program analysis and optimisation within the LLVM compiler suite [23]. Relying on intermediate representations offers enhanced representational power and the ability to create language models independent of a specific source language. LLVM-IR explicitly includes memory-related operations (e.g., `alloca`, `load`, `store`), supports control flow analysis through ϕ-expressions and facilitates data flow analysis with Static Single Assignment (SSA) form [16].

Graph representations of source code have also been explored, as during compilation, source code transforms into different tree-based and graph-based forms. Abstract Syntax Trees (ASTs) depict syntax, while Control Flow Graphs (CFGs) and Data Flow Graphs (DFGs) represent code operations. A branch-free code segment ("basic block") can be represented as a DFG, while CFGs delineate the order of instructions and the conditions for the branches connecting the basic blocks. Novel source code graph representations can be created by combining these definitions, such as the Control and Data Flow Graph (CDFG) or the Code Property Graph [31].

Brauckmann et al. [8] integrate CDFGs with Graph Neural Networks (GNNs), specialised networks for graph data processing. Ben-Nun et al. [4] employed "conteXtual Flow Graphs" (XFGs) for learning an embedding space for LLVM-IR instructions (*inst2vec*) through the *skip-gram* approach.

More recently, ProGraML [15] has enabled parsing LLVM-IR files and transforming them into *directed multigraphs*. In these graphs, nodes correspond to *instructions*, *variables*, and *constants* in code, while edges denote dependencies among them. These dependencies can be of three distinct types: *control* and *data*, reflecting control and data flow respectively, or *call*, symbolizing function calls and return-to-caller relations. Moreover, edges are enhanced with numerical values, providing positional information for distinguishing among parameter ordering or different CFG branches. Our work brings this exploration of source code representations for code analysis to the next step, proposing a framework for pre-training a general graph-based language model that can be fine-tuned to improve performance on several downstream tasks.

2.2   Masked Autoencoders on Graphs

Self-supervised learning (SSL) is a versatile concept applicable in various ways based on input data and tasks. Essentially, SSL enables the extraction of valuable knowledge directly from data, eliminating the need for costly manual labelling. This feature becomes especially attractive as the demand for data in training deep learning models continues to grow.

Contrastive Self-Supervised Learning (SSL) is widely used in graph data [30], emphasising the generation of multiple perspectives or "views" for each graph through carefully designed data augmentation. Models are then trained to maximise an agreement measure within the same graph views while minimising it between different graphs. However, criticism exists due to heavy reliance on the design of data augmentations and negative sampling techniques for pre-training. This dependency can be resource-intensive, time-consuming, and may not readily transfer across diverse graph types [20,24,30].

Contrarily, "Generative SSL" focuses on training models through a direct reconstruction of input graphs. This task is comparatively simpler and can be easily integrated into existing models. Encoder-decoder techniques are usually employed: the encoder network translates input graphs into a latent space, while the decoder reconstructs the masked elements of the original graph from the embedding. In order to avoid trivial mappings and enhance generality, the latent representation may have lower dimensionality or introduce noise to corrupt the input before encoding. In MGAEs, masking serves as the noise, hiding node and edge content by replacing embeddings with a "mask" token or removing connections.

Our approach, aligned with recent studies [20,21,24,27,28], leverages MGAEs as effective pre-training methods. We establish a novel connection between source code analysis and MGAEs, using them as a viable pre-training methodology for the specific data type of graph-based representations of source code. The learned LM then serves as an encoder in downstream tasks.

3   The DeepCodeGraph Methodology

In this section, we present DeepCodeGraph (DCG), the pipeline we designed for pre-training a graph-based language model using graph representations of

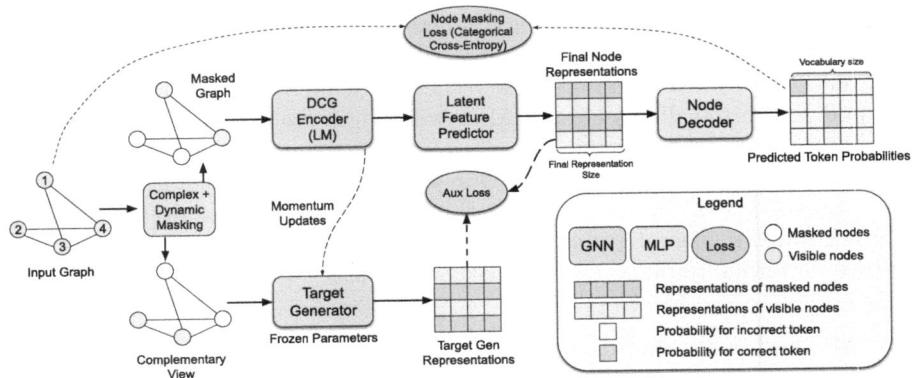

Fig. 1. DCG pre-training architecture.

source code and employing MGAEs as a pre-training framework. Additionally, we introduce the DCG dataset, a large collection of compiled OpenCL, C, and C++ source codes taken from different open-source benchmarks and projects. Lastly, we explain how our LM can be tailored for the downstream tasks outlined in Sect. 2.

3.1   Preliminaries

A graph representation can be expressed as a tuple $G = (V, E)$, where V is the set of nodes and E is the set of edges. Every node $v \in V$ represents an element from a dictionary of n possible tokens and can be mapped to a learnable feature vector h_v^0 by lookup in a fixed-size embedding table $D \in \mathbb{R}^{n \times d}$. Edges $e \in E$ can also contain information depending on the chosen graph format. For instance, edges in ProGraML [15] carry the *type* information (a categorical value specifying the kind of dependency among DATA, CONTROL or CALL) and the *position* information (an unbounded value representing operands order). Given an edge $e_{v,w}$ from node v to node w, these can be accessed by functions $\text{Type}(e_{v,w})$ and $\text{POS}(e_{v,w})$.

3.2   Model Description

The MGAE model implemented in this project is a modified version of RARE [28] introducing numerous optional components inspired by other works in the field. An overview of the whole architecture can be seen in Fig. 1. The model first randomly partitions the group of nodes into *masked* and *visible* nodes. Masking a node changes its initial features to those of a special [MASK] token. *Masked* nodes are selected with a probability p_{mask} that increases as training progresses (*dynamic masking*). There is also a lower probability $p_{rand} \leq p_{mask}$ that rather than a [MASK] token, the node is replaced by another random node from the vocabulary (*complex masking*). Both of these advanced masking techniques were inspired by HGMAE [27].

Subsequently, the masked graphs are input into our language model, which, during pre-training, serves as the encoder within the architecture. The language model is a GNN processing the input graphs through a local aggregation mechanism called *message passing*, repeated for a number of steps T. For the architecture of the GNN, we follow the design of [15]. At each step, $t \in [0, \ldots, T-1]$, three fundamental operations are executed: i) *Message emission*: A message for each pair of neighboring nodes (v, w) is generated based on current source features h_v^t, edge information and learnable matrix A:

$$msg_{v,w} = A_{\text{Type}(e_{v,w})}(h_v^t \odot \text{POS}(e_{v,w})) \tag{1}$$

ii) *Message aggregation*: Nodes receive messages from each incoming connection and aggregate them (e.g. by sum). iii) *Update*: Function U_t decides how to update the current set of features based on the current state and the aggregated message m_v^{t+1}.

$$h_v^{t+1} = U_t\left(h_v^t, m_v^{t+1}\right) \tag{2}$$

In this work, U_t is implemented as a Gated Recurrent Unit (GRU) cell [10]. At the end of message passing, node representations contain contextual information for their T-step neighbourhood. A final *readout operation* is used to obtain a global representation for the whole graph:

$$\hat{G} = \sum_{v \in V} \sigma\left(g_m(h_v^0, h_v^T)\right) \odot f_m(h_v^T) \tag{3}$$

After the LM, another small GNN (called *latent feature predictor* in [28]) further processes the representations. Concurrently, a third neural component with the same architecture as the LM, the *target generator*, computes representations for a complementary graph view (i.e. where masked nodes are visible and vice-versa). The *target generator* parameters ξ are not trained by backpropagation; instead, *momentum update* is used to manually update the weights from those of the LM (θ) every N training steps:

$$\xi \leftarrow \tau\xi + (1 - \tau)\theta \tag{4}$$

The representations of the *target generator* are compared with those of the *latent feature predictor*, generating a self-supervised loss (mean squared error) that acts as regularisation for the primary training task of masked node reconstruction. Finally, a *decoder* (a simple multi-layer perceptron) is tasked to reconstruct the original node embeddings from the outputs of the *latent feature predictor*.

The original paper suggests utilizing a *reconstruction loss* based on the angle misalignment between the vectors of original and predicted node features [28]. However, we observed exceedingly poor pre-training results and low fine-tuning accuracy following this or similar approaches (e.g. [20,21]). We conjecture that by training both the embedding matrix D and the rest of the model, the loss minimization problem could lead to a naive solution, mapping all initial embeddings towards a singular point (e.g. 0) and pushing the decoder to consistently output values close to this cluster. To address this issue, we propose to re-frame the problem as a node token *classification*, similarly to the approach used in BERT

[17]. In this way, the model naturally learns discriminative embeddings in order to distinguish the correct option between all tokens in the vocabulary. To reflect the new task, the decoder was re-designed to produce probability distributions over the vocabulary, and the loss was changed to a standard cross-entropy, where the target is a one-hot encoding of the original token.

3.3 Codebase

To achieve generality, the LM must be exposed to a large collection of source code representations during the self-supervised training phase. The internet provides convenient access to an immense quantity of source code samples. However, as our representation relies on LLVM-IR, it is also necessary that the collected samples can be compiled using tools from the LLVM toolchain.

To this end, we introduce the DCG Dataset, a large, heterogeneous collection of compilable C/C++ and LLVM-IR code sourced from a wide range of open-source projects and publicly available benchmarks. This dataset encompasses various libraries for scientific computation, biological-oriented projects, and executable code from popular GitHub repositories. LLVM-IR source code files were obtained from pre-compiled collections (e.g., the CompilerGym project [14]) or were compiled from scratch using Clang [23]. The latter operation required, for each project, the adaptation of the compilation procedure. The ProGraML Python library [15] was then utilised to produce graph representations.

We discarded source code files that resulted in compilation errors and LLVM-IR files that took longer than 5 s to convert into graphs. Moreover, to ensure meaningful samples and stabilize the training process considering memory constraints, we excluded graphs with fewer than 5 or more than 3,000 nodes. These thresholds were selected on the basis of the distribution of unfiltered graph nodes, ensuring that not more than 10% of the graphs would be removed. Table 1 provides an overview of the source code distribution within the dataset.

3.4 Data Analysis

Vocabulary. The dataset was split into a training (80%), a validation (10%) and a test (10%) set. Particularly, POJ104 [25] was split per-problem, avoiding to include codes from the same problem in the different sets. The training set was used for data analysis and to collect a representative vocabulary of tokens for the graph transformation. While 99.5% of our training dataset can be covered with a dictionary of only 341 tokens, we further increased the size of the vocabulary up to 2,220 tokens for fair comparison with other vocabularies in literature (e.g. Cummins et al. use 2,230 tokens [13]). An additional "[UNK]" token is added for elements that are not found in the vocabulary.

Back Edges. In our analysis, we discovered that 6.1% of nodes lacked incoming connections. This scenario typically indicates variables and constants that are defined manually (i.e. not outputs of prior operations). Consequently, a significant portion of the graphs may never be influenced by the message-passing mechanism. To address this issue, we propose to introduce a fourth type of

Table 1. DCG Dataset description, indicating source project, number of source code, LLVM-IR and graph files.

Name	C Files	Compiled	Graphs
Blas	300	300	216
bowtie2	57	57	25
bwa-mem	24	24	15
cBench	23	23	9
clang	711	711	66
CLGen	996	996	996
eigen	4,998	4,998	3,368
gemm_synth	3,700	3,700	3,072
Gromacs	1,249	1,205	828
JotaiBench	5,535	5,535	5,535
Linux	13,920	13,920	8,585
LLVM	21,371	21,371	17,598
MiBench	40	40	38
OpenCV	442	442	254
POJ104	49,816	49,815	49,804
stencil_synth	12,800	12,800	12,721
Tensorflow	1,985	1,985	683
Total	**117,967**	**117,922**	**103,813**

edge, BACK, connecting all targets of DATA dependencies back to their sources. BACK edges enable data nodes to be aware of the operations they are involved in, enriching the node representation and increasing communication within the graph with no additional parameters.

3.5 Models for Downstream Tasks

At the end of pre-training, we retain the parameters of the LM and remove the other components. Then, we adapt the LM to the downstream tasks by attaching some output layers learning to draw conclusions from the expressive graph representations.

The pipeline for heterogeneous device mapping is represented in Fig. 2a. We employ the DevMap dataset introduced in [11,12]. It contains a total of 256 OpenCL kernels paired with two dynamic values: the *OpenCL Work Group size* (affecting the amount of kernel parallelism) and the *Data* or *Payload size* (affecting the transfer time of data from host to device). Different values of workgroup/data size are used for some of the kernels, bringing the total number of samples to 680. These auxiliary inputs are normalized and processed into a tensor with fixed dimensionality that is concatenated to the graph representation output by the LM, following the procedure by [26]. Then, a MLP acts as a binary classifier, producing a probability distribution over the 2 allocation choices (CPU or GPU). The prediction is evaluated by binary cross-entropy loss against a one-hot encoded vector representing the fastest option.

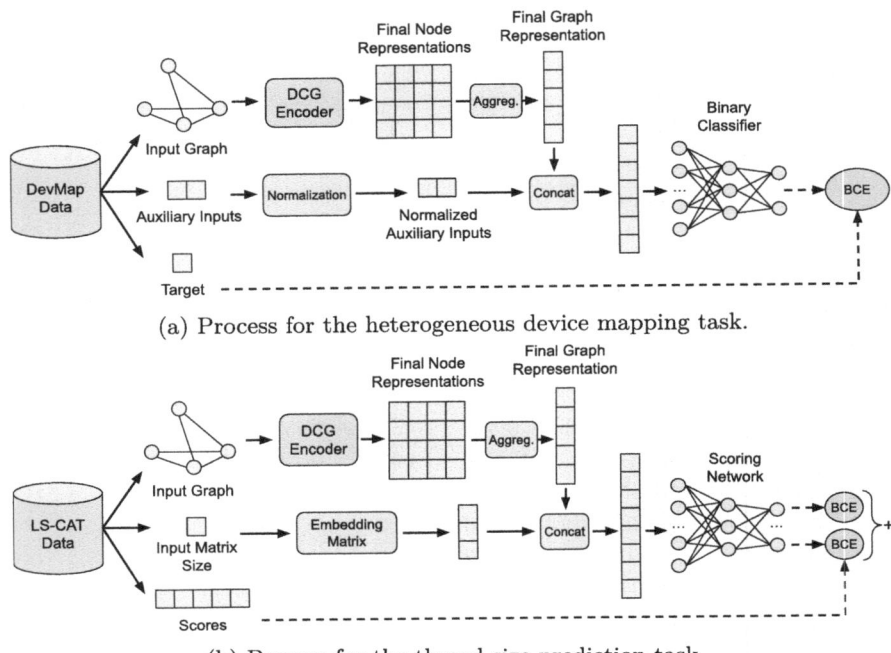

(a) Process for the heterogeneous device mapping task.

(b) Process for the thread size prediction task.

Fig. 2. Input/output processing steps for the downstream tasks.

For thread size prediction we follow a similar approach (see Fig. 2b) and employ the recently introduced LS-CAT dataset [6]. The dataset focuses on auto-tuning in CUDA, specifically on the task of thread size prediction. Each CUDA kernel in the dataset is paired with an input matrix size, which is treated as an auxiliary input for the model and mapped to learnable features through an embedding matrix. The features are then concatenated to the final code graph representation. An MLP performs multi-label classification, assigning a score to each of the available thread sizes. Since the label for this task is a "performance score" for each of the thread sizes (see Sect. 4.3), the loss function is a sum of binary cross-entropy losses applied to the individual options.

4   Experimental Results

In this Section, we report the results of our experiments with the DCG pipeline, with a focus on the improvements that are obtained on the aforementioned downstream tasks.

4.1   Setup

Experiments. Depending on how the pre-trained components are handled, we define four tests that aim at exploring the quality of our methodology. The tests

Table 2. Configuration studies for fine-tuning.

	Pre-Training			Model init in DevMap	
Test	Dataset	CodeRepr	Model	Embedding	Encoder
A1	DCG	ProGraML*	DCG	PreTrained	PreTrained
A2				PreTrained	Random
B	NCC	ProGraML*	DCG	PreTrained	PreTrained
C	NCC	XFG	inst2vec	PreTrained	n.a.

are summarised in Table 2 and can be described as follows: i) For *Test A*, we pre-train our DCG LM parameters and embedding matrix D by applying the self-supervised training framework of MGAE on the graphs of the DCG dataset During subsequent fine-tuning, we either load the set of pre-trained weights as the initial values of parameters (Test A1) or initialize them randomly (Test A2); however, the pre-trained embedding matrix D is always loaded. ii) In *Test B*, we apply the same methodology as Test A1, but pre-train the model on a best-effort reconstruction of the NCC dataset [4]. The vocabulary for this experiment was extracted from this dataset following our methodology and contains the same amount of tokens as the one described in Sect. 3.4. The objective of this test is to compare the NCC and DCG datasets: the latter is 4.5x larger, so the LM is expected to exhibit better loss and accuracy values. iii) In *Test C*, we use the inst2vec vocabulary and pre-trained embedding space [4] as external components. As model weights are not produced during pre-training, the fine-tuning phase always trains the model parameters from random initialization. This test aims to evaluate the quality of our DCG embeddings with respect to inst2vec.

Implementation. We implemented our models and data processing procedures with PyTorch Geometric [19]. For all experiments, we use $T = 6$ steps of message passing, a hidden dimensionality of 256 and an Adam optimizer. The initial embedding dimension $d = 200$ was chosen to have the same size of inst2vec embeddings [4]. We pre-train for 20 epochs with a mask rate increasing from 0.5 to 0.7 and a batch size of 32. Since the NCC dataset is approximately 4.5x times smaller, for test B the model is pre-trained for 90 epochs keeping all other hyperparameters the same to ensure a fair comparison. We then fine-tune on device mapping for 100 epochs and on thread size prediction for 40 epochs, with a learning rate of 2.5×10^{-4} reduced by a factor of 0.05 on loss plateaus. Device mapping employs a label smoothing factor of 0.05 for regularisation purposes.

4.2   Heterogeneous Device Mapping

The DevMap dataset reports, for each kernel, execution times on CPU and GPU for two separate heterogeneous devices. The devices share the same CPU but are equipped with different GPUs (NVIDIA and AMD). However, the version of the

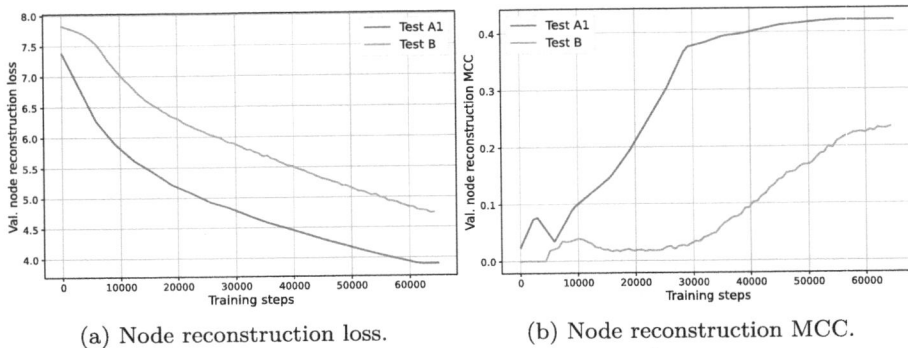

(a) Node reconstruction loss.

(b) Node reconstruction MCC.

Fig. 3. Validation loss and MCC score trends during training steps for pre-training configurations A1 and B.

dataset which is typically distributed contains undefined external functions and constants. To capture the full complexity of the kernels, the missing elements were reconstructed by hand using the source code from the original benchmarks as reference. This operation introduces greater complexity into the dataset but enables a more realistic analysis scenario.

The dataset is notoriously small, so *stratified K-fold cross-validation* (SKF) is employed for training and evaluating our models, averaging results across ten test folds. To ensure robustness against different random seeds, we report an average of ten experiments. As the dataset has a noticeable class imbalance [26], class weights are assigned to samples of the two classes in order to downweigh the loss for GPU samples (the most frequent). Table 4 shows the accuracy results of the different model configurations.

The results are all very similar and fall within the same confidence interval, except for test C, which exhibits a considerable drop in performance. In particular, in test A1, we reach outstanding results on the AMD subset of DevMap and obtain a slightly better average performance (.8713) than on test A2 (.8705) and test B (.8683).

We further study the difference between tests A1 and B. Purely in terms of pre-training results, we notice that pre-training on the DCG dataset allows the LM to produce more expressive representations, as can be seen by the lower decoding loss and higher node classification MCC score in Fig. 3. However, fine-tuning results show that the LM is able to quickly pick up on the downstream tasks even after pre-training on a less varied dataset. This does not make our dataset redundant, as test B still yields a lower performance with respect to A1 and A2. Note that the NCC dataset includes a partial overlap with the DevMap dataset, whereas the DCG dataset, by design, does not contain any code present in the DevMap dataset. Thus, these results support the hypothesis that the deployed MGAE approach has indeed provided the model with general and transferrable knowledge, giving it an edge with respect to other solutions.

Table 3. Comparison between prior works and our accuracy results on DevMap.

Model	Ref.	NVIDIA	AMD	Mean
DeepTune	[11]	.805	.814	.810
Inst2vec	[4]	.820	.828	.824
ProGraML	[15]	.800	.866	.833
DeepLLVM	[3]	.823	.853	.838
CDFG	[8]	.814	.864	.839
DeepTune-Exp	[29]	.815	.874	.844
DCG-A1 (Ours)		**.852**	**.890**	**.871**

Table 4. Results of our DevMap experiments.

T	NVIDIA		AMD	
	Mean	CI$_{95\%}$	Mean	CI$_{95\%}$
A1	**.8524** ± .0020		**.8901** ± **.0018**	
A2	**.8553** ± **.0042**		.8856 ± .0018	
B	.8500 ± .0028		.8865 ± .0042	
C	.8146 ± .0034		.8591 ± .0019	

In Table 3, we compare our methodology with prior approaches in terms of average test accuracy. DCG improves upon all previous graph-based source code analysis models, setting a new state-of-the-art in heterogeneous device mapping.

4.3 Autotuning (LS-CAT)

The LS-CAT dataset [6] comprises over 20K CUDA kernels collected from larger GitHub projects. The kernels have been isolated and processed in order to allow their compilation and execution as stand-alone functions. The authors provide average execution times on a Tesla T4 GPU. Each kernel is executed with 7 different input matrix sizes, serving as auxiliary input, and 20 thread block sizes, constituting the decision space. Since non-optimal choices are still able to achieve improvements with respect to the average scenario, [6] proposes to assign penalties to the model based on a *performance* metric measuring the distance between the predicted and the optimal choice in a 0–1 range:

$$p_{(k,i,b)} = \frac{\min_x T_{(k,i,x)}}{T_{(k,i,b)}} \tag{5}$$

where T are times, k, i and b are respectively kernels, input sizes and block sizes.

While useful for evaluation, this metric tends to have high values for almost all choices. For this reason, performance scores are further processed with a transformation, aimed at raising the entropy in predicted probability distributions:

$$m_{(k,i,b)} = \frac{e^{Cp_{(k,i,b)}}}{\sum_x e^{Cp_{(k,i,x)}}} \qquad l_{(k,i,b)} = \frac{m_{(k,i,b)}}{\max_x m_{(k,i,b)}} \tag{6}$$

where C is a constant set to 12 and l represents the actual training labels. Finally, the loss function is a sum of binary cross-entropy terms for each of the options evaluating the alignment between the performance labels and the outputs.

One-tenth of the dataset is held out as a test set, one-tenth as a validation set, while the remaining 80% is used as a training set. The model that performs best on its validation fold is evaluated against the test set. To the best of our

Table 5. Test metrics for thread size prediction on LS-CAT.

Name	Top-1 Acc.	Top-3 Acc.	Perf.
Random Selection	0.050	0.150	0.92
Fixed Selection (1D, 1024)	0.056	0.160	0.93
fastText+LSTM	n.a.	n.a.	0.94
DCG-A1 (Ours)	0.069	0.191	0.93

knowledge, only another work by Bjertnes et al. [5] currently reports results on LS-CAT, although they only provide the performance metric of their model. Their best approach is token-based, using fastText [7] embeddings for LLVM-IR tokens and a simple LSTM-based LM. We compare our best configuration (A1) against theirs, reporting top-1, top-3 and performance results averaging over five different experiments with varying random seeds in Table 5. We also report the same metrics for random and fixed selection (i.e. always choosing the largest thread block size). We achieved comparable state-of-the-art results on the task, with a performance of 0.93 and a top-3 accuracy of over 19%.

5   Conclusions

Modern computing systems pose challenges for traditional compiler heuristics due to increasing complexity and diverse hardware specialisation. Recent studies leverage machine learning, particularly neural networks, for compile-time decisions. This paper introduces a novel language model for source code analysis, employing a Graph Neural Network pre-trained with a Masked Graph Autoencoding (MGAE) technique. Our approach, called DeepCodeGraph (DCG), utilizes an expanded ProGraML format for code processing. We adapt and extend RARE [28], a MGAE technique, enhancing its suitability for source code. DCG has been evaluated on two tasks: heterogeneous device mapping and thread size prediction. We observed a 3% improvement in DevMap test accuracy when comparing DCG to similar techniques. We also report a 3% enhancement in LS-CAT top-3 accuracy with respect to a fixed selection policy. Additional contributions include expanding the dataset for heterogeneous device mapping through the re-introduction of external elements, and creating the DCG dataset, a collection of approximately 100k graph representations of source code which is 4.5x larger than similar datasets in literature (i.e. NCC [4]).

References

1. Allamanis, M., et al.: A survey of machine learning for big code and naturalness. ACM Comput. Surv. **51**(4), 81:1–81:37 (2018). https://doi.org/10.1145/3212695
2. Barchi, F., et al.: Code mapping in heterogeneous platforms using deep learning and llvm-ir. In: Proceedings of the 56th Annual Design Automation Conference 2019. Dac '19. Association for Computing Machinery, New York (2019). https://doi.org/10.1145/3316781.3317789

3. Barchi, F., et al.: Exploration of convolutional neural network models for source code classification. Eng. Appl. Artif. Intell. **97**, 104075 (2021). https://doi.org/10. 1016/j.engappai.2020.104075

4. Ben-Nun, T., et al.: Neural code comprehension: A learnable representation of code semantics. In: Advances in Neural Information Processing Systems 31: Annual Conference on Neural Information Processing Systems 2018, NeurIPS 2018, December 3-8, 2018, Montréal, Canada, pp. 3589–3601 (2018). https://proceedings.neurips. cc/paper/2018/hash/17c3433fecc21b57000debdf7ad5c930-Abstract.html

5. Bjertnes, L., et al.: Autotuning cuda: Applying nlp techniques to ls-cat. In: Norsk IKT-konferanse for forskning og utdanning, pp. 72–85. No. 1 (2021)

6. Bjertnes, L., et al.: LS-CAT: A large-scale CUDA autotuning dataset. CoRR abs/2103.14409 (2021). https://arxiv.org/abs/2103.14409

7. Bojanowski, P., et al.: Enriching word vectors with subword information (2017)

8. Brauckmann, A., et al.: Compiler-based graph representations for deep learning models of code. In: CC '20: 29th International Conference on Compiler Construction, San Diego, CA, USA, February 22-23, 2020, pp. 201–211. ACM (2020). https://doi.org/10.1145/3377555.3377894

9. Chen, Z., Fang, S., Monperrus, M.: Supersonic: Learning to generate source code optimisations in c/c++. arXiv preprint arXiv:2309.14846 (2023)

10. Cho, K., et al.: Learning phrase representations using RNN encoder-decoder for statistical machine translation. CoRR **abs/1406.1078** (2014). http://arxiv.org/ abs/1406.1078

11. Cummins, C., et al.: End-to-end deep learning of optimization heuristics. In: 26th International Conference on Parallel Architectures and Compilation Techniques, PACT 2017, Portland, OR, USA, September 9-13, 2017, pp. 219–232. IEEE Computer Society (2017). https://doi.org/10.1109/pact.2017.24

12. Cummins, C., et al.: Synthesizing benchmarks for predictive modeling. In: 2017 IEEE/ACM International Symposium on Code Generation and Optimization (CGO), pp. 86–99 (2017). https://doi.org/10.1109/cgo.2017.7863731

13. Cummins, C., et al.: Deep data flow analysis (2020)

14. Cummins, C., et al.: Compilergym: Robust, performant compiler optimization environments for AI research. CoRR **abs/2109.08267** (2021). https://arxiv.org/abs/ 2109.08267

15. Cummins, C., et al.: Programl: A graph-based program representation for data flow analysis and compiler optimizations. In: Meila, M., Zhang, T. (eds.) Proceedings of the 38th International Conference on Machine Learning. Proceedings of Machine Learning Research, vol. 139, pp. 2244–2253. Pmlr, June 2021. https://proceedings. mlr.press/v139/cummins21a.html

16. Cytron, R., et al.: Efficiently computing static single assignment form and the control dependence graph. ACM Trans. Program. Lang. Syst. **13**(4), 451–490 (1991). https://doi.org/10.1145/115372.115320

17. Devlin, J., et al.: BERT: pre-training of deep bidirectional transformers for language understanding. CoRR abs/1810.04805 (2018). http://arxiv.org/abs/1810. 04805

18. Fang, C., et al.: Large language models for code analysis: Do llms really do their job? (2024)

19. Fey, M., et al.: Fast graph representation learning with PyTorch Geometric. In: ICLR Workshop on Representation Learning on Graphs and Manifolds (2019)

20. Hou, Z., et al.: Graphmae: Self-supervised masked graph autoencoders (2022)

21. Hou, Z., et al.: Graphmae2: A decoding-enhanced masked self-supervised graph learner (2023)

22. Karmakar, A., Robbes, R.: What do pre-trained code models know about code? In: 2021 36th IEEE/ACM International Conference on Automated Software Engineering (ASE), pp. 1332–1336 (2021). https://doi.org/10.1109/ASE51524.2021.9678927

23. Lattner, C., et al.: Llvm: A compilation framework for lifelong program analysis & transformation. In: Proceedings of the 2004 International Symposium on Code Generation and Optimization (CGO'04). Palo Alto, California, March 2004

24. Li, J., et al.: What's behind the mask: Understanding masked graph modeling for graph autoencoders (2023)

25. Mou, L., et al.: Convolutional neural networks over tree structures for programming language processing (2015)

26. Parisi, E., et al.: Making the most of scarce input data in deep learning-based source code classification for heterogeneous device mapping. IEEE Trans. Comput. Aided Des. Integr. Circuits Syst. **41**(6), 1636–1648 (2022). https://doi.org/10.1109/tcad.2021.3114617

27. Tian, Y., et al.: Heterogeneous graph masked autoencoders. In: Williams, B., Chen, Y., Neville, J. (eds.) Thirty-Seventh AAAI Conference on Artificial Intelligence, AAAI 2023, Thirty-Fifth Conference on Innovative Applications of Artificial Intelligence, IAAI 2023, Thirteenth Symposium on Educational Advances in Artificial Intelligence, EAAI 2023, Washington, DC, USA, February 7-14, 2023, pp. 9997–10005. AAAI Press (2023). https://doi.org/10.1609/aaai.v37i8.26192

28. Tu, W., et al.: Rare: Robust masked graph autoencoder (2023)

29. Vavaroutsos, P., et al.: Towards making the most of nlp-based device mapping optimization for opencl kernels. In: 2022 IEEE International Conference on Omni-layer Intelligent Systems (COINS), pp. 1–6 (2022). https://doi.org/10.1109/coins54846.2022.9855002

30. Wu, L., et al.: Self-supervised learning on graphs: Contrastive, generative,or predictive (2021)

31. Yamaguchi, F., Golde, N., Arp, D., Rieck, K.: Modeling and discovering vulnerabilities with code property graphs. In: 2014 IEEE Symposium on Security and Privacy, pp. 590–604 (2014). https://doi.org/10.1109/SP.2014.44

Design and Implementation of a Natural Language Interface for Controlling the Web of Things Devices

Zhou Gui$^{(\boxtimes)}$, Layla Kuty , and Andreas Harth

Friedrich-Alexander-Universität Erlangen-Nürnberg, Nürnberg, Germany
{zhou.gui,layla.kuty,andreas.harth}@fau.de

Abstract. We present a systematic workflow for developing a Natural Language Interface (NLI) using Knowledge Graphs (KGs) and the Web of Things (WoT) specification as an abstraction layer. We first synthesize a data corpus from a given device interface description using manually created templates and parameter sheets. Then we paraphrase the synthesized data corpus with pre-trained Large Language Models (LLMs). The resulting corpus serves as training data for a text-to-code encoder-decoder neural network model, enabling the mapping of diverse natural language commands into an executable code format. To the best of our knowledge, no existing data corpus or NLI system has been tailored for WoT device interactions. Our work provides a baseline and can be extended to a broader range of real world WoT use cases.

Keywords: Natural Language Interface · Knowledge Graphs · Large Language Models · Web of Things

1 Introduction

With the increasing applications of Internet of Things (IoT) devices across diverse domains, the demand for user-friendly Natural Language Interfaces (NLIs) has been on the rise. In recent years, commercial virtual assistants like Apple's Siri and Amazon's Alexa have incorporated natural language interfaces, enabling users to issue commands via voice-based interface. Despite their growing popularity and technological advancements, these virtual assistants have several limitations.

One significant limitation is their inability to seamlessly integrate with arbitrary IoT devices, as they are specifically designed to interact with particular IoT platforms and devices. For instance, Siri is compatible with the Eve Home ecosystem, whereas Alexa works with the Ring ecosystem. The issue extends beyond these specific virtual assistants. The heterogeneous characteristic of IoT devices in terms of protocols and data encodings [14], creates a significant barrier for developing a universal solution that can enable natural language interactions with any device. This challenge is particularly acute when developers seek to

© The Author(s), under exclusive license to Springer Nature Switzerland AG 2024
A. Rapp et al. (Eds.): NLDB 2024, LNCS 14762, pp. 485–499, 2024.
https://doi.org/10.1007/978-3-031-70239-6_33

integrate new IoT devices from different manufacturers. Another concern is data privacy and security. User data, including users' commands to interact with their devices and information about their devices, is stored and processed in the cloud databases of these large companies. The data is not exclusive to the user but may be accessed by service providers.

To address the challenges of device interoperability, data privacy, and resource limitations, we propose the deployment of a lightweight, locally-hosted NLI system based on the Web of Things (WoT) specifications. However, creating a NLI for controlling multiple IoT devices on a single local machine is challenging, as natural language has various ways to express a single intention, for example, *turn on the light*, *switch the light on*, and *power up the light* all imply the lights being switched on. Traditional setups for such systems require extensive resources including data collection, annotation, as well as high-performance hardware likes GPU clusters.

To address this variability, we create a set of templates covering diverse natural language expressions and the corresponding parameter sheets for interactions that are commonly found in IoT devices. The templates and parameter sheets are used to synthesize a compact size of training corpus. Afterwards, we use Large Language Models (LLMs) to paraphrase the corpus, augmenting both the size and diversity of our training data.

Our NLI system uses a device description Knowledge Graph (KG) [9] using the Thing Description (TD) ontology, which is specified by the WoT architecture [12] to enable interaction with arbitrary devices. In the WoT context, the device interface description KG is referred to as Thing Description. Our proposed system comprises two phases: the development phase and the inference phase.

During the development phase, the developers can either find a Thing Description from the WoT community or prepare the Thing Description of a device on their own. Once the Thing Description is ready, our system can generate a data corpus from the Thing Description. The data corpus will be used for the training of neural network models and the trained model will be converted and saved for later inference. In the inference phase, the trained model processes user's input in natural language and predicts it into executable code. To improve accuracy before execution, we use a syntax parser to parse the predicted code into abstract syntax tree conforming to the code grammar definition. Only if the code successfully passes the syntax code check is it sent to our WoT execution engine. In summary, the paper makes the following contributions:

- We introduce a systematic workflow for building a NLI tailored for controlling IoT device using the WoT architecture as an abstraction layer.
- We present a specialized data corpus for IoT device interactions and a data corpus generator that can produce new corpus based on the Thing Description KGs of the device.
- We demonstrate an end-to-end implementation of the proposed NLI system, which is publicly accessible through a web interface.

2   Running Example

We use a Philips Hue smart lamp and a Elgato Stream deck Mini as our running example in this paper. The lamp, which uses Bluetooth Low Energy to communicate, can be switched on and off, has adjustable brightness, and can change light color. The Stream Deck Mini has six buttons to display color and each button press can trigger an event. The Stream Deck Mini can be used either as a standalone device, allowing color and brightness changes on its buttons, or in combination with the Philips Hue lamp, for instance, pressing the top left button (designated as button number one) can power on or change color of the Philips Hue lamp. These interaction capabilities, in conjunction with additional static data, are semantically represented in a KG that adheres to the WoT Thing Description specification. More information on WoT interactions is explained in Sect. 3.

Table 1. Example of primitive command and code pairs

Command	Code
Please switch on the Philips Hue.	philipshue.writeProperty('power', 1);
Turn off Hue lamp.	philipshue.writeProperty('power', 0);
Dim Hue to half the brightness.	philipshue.invokeAction('dim', 127);
Change the color of Philips Hue to red.	philipshue.writeProperty('color', {red:255,green:0,blue:0});
I want Streamdeck color be blue.	streamdeck.writeProperty('color', {red:0,green:0,blue:255});
Decrease brightness of Streamdeck to half.	streamdeck.writeProperty('brightness', 127;

Table 2. Example of compound command and code pairs

Command	Code
If button five is pressed in Streamdeck, set Hue color to white.	streamdeck.subscribeEvent('buttonPress', [false, false, false, false, false, true]) ⇒ {philipshue.writeProperty('color', White)};
Activate Philips Hue once Streamdeck button two is pushed.	streamdeck.subscribeEvent('buttonPress' [false, false, true, false, false, false]) ⇒ {philipshue.writeProperty('power', 1)};
Dim Philips Hue to half brightness when Streamdeck button one is pressed.	streamdeck.subscribeEvent('buttonPress', [false, true, false, false, false, false]) ⇒ {philipshue.writeProperty('brightness', 127)};

Table 1 and Table 2 illustrate examples of natural language commands and their corresponding executable code format for interactions with a single device and multiple connected devices, respectively. The goal is to enable users to interact with devices such as a Philips Hue lamp or a Elgato Stream Deck mini (for primitive commands), and a combination of both devices (for compound commands) through natural language alone. For example, a user can simply say, *Change the Philips Hue color to red*, and watch the light turn red, eliminating the need to worry about the technicalities such as the specific URI where the updated color value needs to be sent, or how the word *red* is mapped to its RGB value equivalent. Another use case is the event triggered interaction like *If the button number five is pressed in Streamdeck, set Hue color to white.*, simplifying the control of connected devices.

In the sections that follow, we introduce the system architecture step by step, explain how to build a natural language interface using Knowledge Graphs compliant with the WoT TD specification, and illustrate the role of encoder decoder deep neural networks in developing a light-weight NLI for WoT devices.

3   Background and Related Work

3.1   WoT Interaction Model

The Web of Things Architecture, introduced by the World Wide Web Consortium (W3C), aims to address the interoperability challenges of the IoT by using semantic interface descriptions in the form of RDF Knowledge Graphs, known as Thing Descriptions [10], to semantically describe the APIs of connected devices, called Things. A TD graph describes the API, relationships and static data of a Thing and groups the available interactions into property affordances, action affordances, and event affordances.

- Property affordances expose the states of IoT devices. Some devices offer read-only properties, while others offer both read and write properties. For instance, the `power` state of a lamp is modeled as a read/write property because the state of the lamp can be both read and updated.
- Action affordances are used to trigger long-lasting processes of IoT devices that manipulate states. Examples of actions include dimming a light.
- Event affordances are used to expose event sources of IoT devices. When an event occurs, data is asynchronously pushed to all event subscribers. Examples of an event is a button is pressed.

Information within the TD can be encoded in different level of abstractions. Table 3 shows the supported interactions of a Philips Hue lamp and Elgato Streamdeck represented in both high and low level abstractions. As a human user, we are more likely to refer to a Philips Hue lamp using high level terms such as "hue lamp" or even more specific like "my office lamp" when multiple devices are involved. However, the hardware implementation requires the low-level data representation e.g., the MAC address to execute the function. Similar with data values, natural language refer to the high level color name "red" while in the low-level the HEX value or the RGB value is required. Our hypothesis is that, high-level data representation is more compact and better suited for the code format compared to the low-level ones.

Table 3. Low and high level representation of device and data value in Philips Hue and Elgato Stream Deck

		Low-level (hardware implementation)	High-level (human expression)
Philips Hue	device	mac address(F5:FF:7A:3D:AA:64)	hue lamp
	brightness	128/64	half/quarter
	color	{red:255,green:0,blue:0}/#FF0000	red
	power	1/0	on/off
Elgato Stream Deck	device	mac address(3C:6A:9D:13:5D:92)	stream deck
	brightness	128/64	half/quarter
	color	{red:255,green:0,blue:0}/#FF0000	red
	button	[true, false, false, false, false, false]	0

3.2 Natural Language Interfaces for IoT Systems

Conversational natural language interfaces offered by Amazon Alexa and Google Home have experienced great commercial success in the realm of home automation applications. However, these interfaces are often bound by constraints within their respective platforms, restricting both the hardware and software options available.

Genie [3] has provided an open-source virtual assistant implementation. Genie provides users with a natural language interface to interact with a wide range of IoT devices and web services. The Genie team has developed their own logical form representation for natural language understanding and execution called ThingTalk [13]. Genie supports applications over different domains such as social networks, web API services, and home automation. However, it has a focus on web service automation with only six out of 45 supported services are about IoT devices. Also, Genie does not utilize WoT as unified abstraction layer, thus developers are still required to understand the specifications and communication protocols of each individual device when getting started. In the early phrase of development [2], the Genie team constructed a dataset of total size 7488 commands (3511 are primitive and 3977 are compound) for text to code learning. Among which 4466 are paraphrase set that are crowd-sourced by Mechanical Turk workers.

Snips.ai [4] was another open-source Natural Language Understanding (NLU) platform with a primary focus on building voice-based natural language interfaces for IoT devices. The platform allows users to create customized and privacy-preserving voice assistants that ran entirely on edge devices. Users can define custom voice commands, intents, and actions to suit their specific application domains. However, Snip.ai has been acquired by Sonos[1] in 2019 and is no longer open source available.

---

[1] https://www.sonos.com/.

4   System Architecture

The system architecture depicted in Fig. 1 has two main phases: the development phase and the inference phase. There are two stages in the development phase: corpus generation and model training. We will describe each component below in detail.

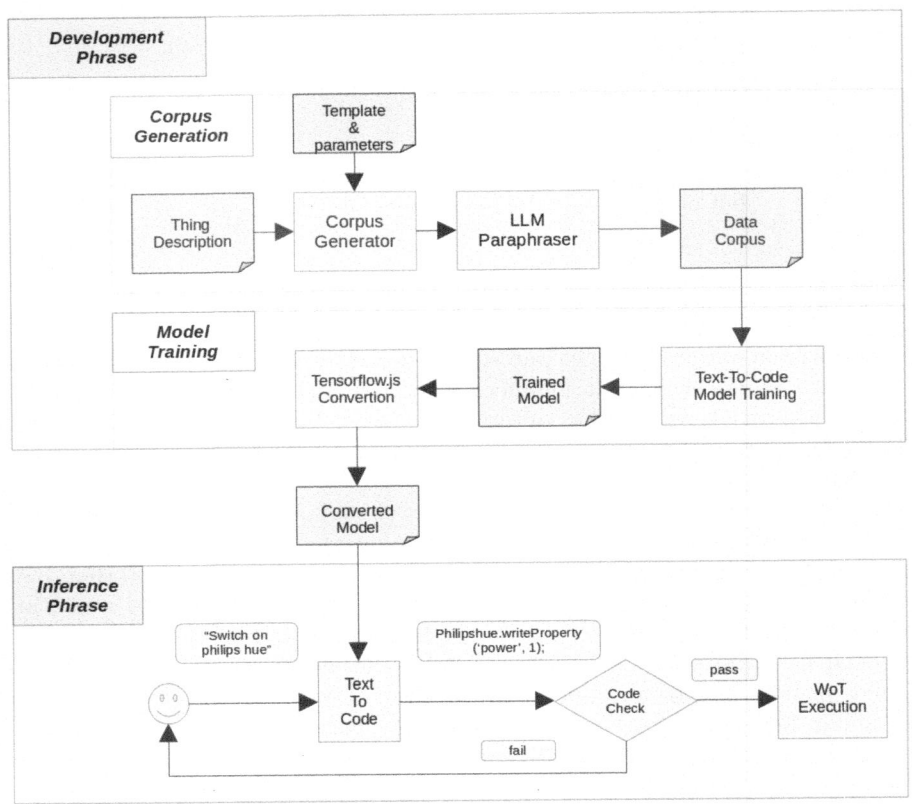

Fig. 1. System architecture of the proposed NLI

4.1   Corpus Generation

The corpus generation stage involves creating a data corpus for the training of the text-to-code model. The corpus is generated from Thing Description, which provides a structured representation of the IoT device's capabilities and functionalities together with prepared templates and parameter sheets.

Firstly, we built template for each interaction operation, and associated parameter sheets are linked in the Thing Description. These templates and parameter sheets can be reused across multiple devices, as many IoT devices share similar functionalities such as power, color, and brightness. The corpus generation module takes the Thing Description as input, parses all the relevant information, for example, the name of the device, interaction type, and synthesize an initial data corpus based on the detected interactions and their corresponding templates. For instance, in the Philips Hue Thing Description, the module identifies the *power* property, along with its corresponding template for power containing various command expressions related to *power* and the parameter sheet that maps power status *on* to 1 and *off* to 0. Users can flexible expand the template and parameter to meet their individual requirements.

Algorithm 1. Paraphrase and Rank

1: Input file: P
2: Output file: Q
3: Paraphrase model: $Model$
4: SBERT ranking model: S_Model
5: Semantic textual similarity score: S
6: Threshold: T
7: **for** p in P **do**
8:     $Q \leftarrow Model(p)$
9:     **for** q in Q **do**
10:         $S \leftarrow S\_Model(p, q)$
11:         **if** $S \geq T$ **then**
12:             $P \leftarrow P + q$ ▷ Attach q at the end of P
13:             **return** P

Secondly, to increase the diversity and expressibility of natural language utterances, we use pre-trained large language models to paraphrase the synthesized corpus instead of manual effort. We experimented with three paraphrase models: Parrot [5], Pegasus [20], and T5ChatGPT [18]. The corpus paraphrase process is described in Algorithm 1. Parrot model is a paraphrase based utterance augmentation framework pre-trained on multiple datasets including Google PAWS, ParaNMT, Quora question pairs, SNIPS commands. Pegasus paraphraser is pre-trained on multiple datasets such as HugeNews and C4. And the T5ChatGPT is fine-tuned for the task of paraphrasing, trained on the Chat-GPT paraphrase dataset (Quora paraphrase question, texts from the SQUAD 2.0 and the CNN news). As our goal is to achieve a time efficient and high quality paraphrasing process, we select a subset covering all interactions from the synthesized output as the input for paraphrase models. The paraphrased outputs will be ranked by a semantic textual similarity measurement score from SBERT [16]. Based on our experiment, we only keep those paraphrased outputs with a semantic textual similarity score higher than threshold 0.75 to ensure output quality.

Table 4 shows the size of input file, the paraphrased output file, and the filtered output. Examples of paraphrased sentence by the three models can be found in Table 5.

Table 4. Number of sentences in input file, output file and filtered file

Model	# of Input	# of Output	# after Filtering
Parrot	130	1280	1245
Pegasus	130	2115	1545
T5chatGPT	130	3495	2725

Table 5. Examples of paraphrased outputs for input sentence "change the color of Philips-Hue to blue."

Model	Paraphrased Output
Parrot	Make philips hue blue. Can you change the color of the philips hue to blue? can you turn philip shue blue? If I want to change the color of my philips to blue, can I? I want to change the color of the philips to blue.
Pegasus	The color of Philips-Hue should be blue. The color of Philips-Hue should be changed to blue. The color of Philips-Hue is supposed to be blue. The Philips-Hue should be painted blue. The Philips-Hue needs to be blue.
T5chatGPT	Can you please change the color of Philips-Hue to blue? Is it possible for you to convert the color of Philips-Hue to blue? Could you consider changing the blue color of Philips-Hue? May I request that Philips-Hue be colored blue? Are you able to modify the color of Philips-Hue to blue?

4.2   Text-to-Code Model Training

After the data corpus generation is finished, we can proceed to the training of the text-to-code model. As the resource limitation is a critical issue for us, we do not consider training or fine-tuning the large language models for text to code mapping. The task of translating natural language text into machine-executable code is typically achieved through two approaches. The first approach involves a classical natural language understanding technique: intent detection and slot filling [19], while the second approach is an end-to-end sequence-to-sequence model inspired by machine translation tasks [15]. In our work, we use a sequence-to-sequence model for transforming text to code. The model comprises an encoder and a decoder, both containing LSTM [8] layers. The encoder processes the input sequence token by token and encodes the input into a fixed-length hidden state, also known as a context vector. The context vector captures essential information from the input sequence. The decoder takes the context vector and decoder hidden states to generate the output sequence token by token.

Before using the data corpus for model training, we conduct several text preprocessing steps, including tokenization, converting all inputs to lowercase, and removing stop words. During the training phase, the input to the model is both the input text and output code. The encoder iterates over the data corpus in batches for multiple epochs, aiming to minimize the loss function between the model's predicted output and the ground truth. We use the Adam [11] algorithm as an optimizer due to its adaptive learning rate. Once the training is finished, the model stores the optimal parameters learned from the training data and is prepared for inference on new inputs.

We also apply modified network structures on top of the base sequence-to-sequence model to compare its performance. The Bidirectional LSTM processes input data in both forward and backward directions, providing a better context understanding of the input. The attention mechanism [1] improves model training by assigning higher weights to the most relevant tokens in the input sequence, helping the decoder to focus better. While there are other enhancements that can increase the complexity and capacity of the model, for instance, using transformer [17] architecture instead of using traditional recurrent networks, our data corpus is relatively small, making it challenging for training a complex and large language model.

As our execution engine is implemented in Node.js, we convert the trained model using Tensorflow.js[2] for inference and execution in the inference phase.

4.3 Inference Phase

After sufficient training of the text-to-code model, the trained model is able to translate new, unseen text into executable code, conforming to the syntax of the reference implementation of the WoT Scripting API, node-wot[3]. During the inference phase, the input to the model is only user-given text.

Text to Code. When a user provides a natural language command, for instance, *Switch on Philips Hue*, the input undergoes the same preprocessing steps as described in the model training section. The trained text-to-code model will then predict the input into code format: `philipshue.writeProperty('power', 1)`. The trained model is capable of handling a wide range of natural language expressions as it has been trained on various examples during the development phase.

---

[2] https://www.tensorflow.org/js.
[3] https://github.com/eclipse/thingweb.node-wot.

Listing 1.1. EBNF grammar notation for executable code

```
1   program ::= primitive | compound
2   primitive ::= thing '.' interaction ';'
3   compound ::= eventProperty | eventAction
4   thing ::=  'philipshue' | 'streamdeck' | ...
5   interaction ::= event | property | action
6   /* Events */
7   event ::= 'subscribeEvent(' eventName [',' value ]')'
8   eventName ::= 'overheat' | 'inputreport(buttonPress)'
9   /* Properties */
10  property ::= readProperty | writeProperty
11  readProperty ::= 'readProperty(' rpName ')'
12  rpName ::= 'power' | 'brightness'
13  writeProperty ::= 'writeProperty(' wpName ',' value ')'
14  wpName ::= 'power' | 'color' | 'brightness'
15  /* Actions */
16  action ::= 'invokeAction(' actionName ',' value ')'
17  actionName ::= 'dim'
18  value ::= 1st | integer
19  1st ::= '{' 'red:' integer ',' 'green:' integer ',' 'blue:' integer '}'
20  integer = digit {digit}
21  digit = '0' | '1' | '2' | ... | '8' | '9'
22
23  /* event and property */
24  eventProperty ::= event '=>' '{' property '}' ';'
25  /* event and action */
26  eventAction ::= event '=>' '{' action '}' ';'
```

Code Check. We define the formal grammar of the generated code adhering to the W3C EBNF notation[4] (see Listing 1.1). Users have the flexibility to extend the grammar to match their own specifications of IoT devices. Before executing the generated code, we implement a code checking module to verify the code's syntax against the defined grammar. If the generated code can be parsed into an abstract syntax tree using the provided grammar, it successfully passes the syntax check and proceeds to the execution engine; otherwise, a notification indicating that the generated code contains syntax errors is sent to the user and the generated code will not be executed. Note that the code check module only verifies the syntactic correctness of the predicted code but not the semantics, meaning the predicted code may pass the syntax check while containing incorrect data values. For our future work, a conversational component can be integrated in order to validate the semantic correctness.

WoT Execution. Our WoT execution engine is implemented in JavaScript and built upon the WoT Scripting API reference implementation, node-wot[5]. Freund et al. [6] have developed and included protocol bindings for Bluetooth Low Energy in the execution engine, which allows us to describe Bluetooth LE devices in a Thing Description and control them using the WoT abstraction. The execution engine contains predefined templates for property, action, and event affordances. The NLI-generated JavaScript source code is automatically

---

[4] https://www.w3.org/TR/n-quads/#sec-grammar.

[5] https://github.com/eclipse/thingweb.node-wot.

inserted into the correct template, creating a WoT compliant script, which is directly executed by the execution engine. A demo of the running example and all code artifacts can be found here[6]

5   Evaluation

In this section, we evaluate the performance of our text-to-code neural network model using the generated data corpus for interacting with Philips Hue and Stream Deck. The data corpus covers all the interactions specified in Thing Descriptions and in forms of pairs of natural language commands and its corresponding code, comprising approximately 9k for primitives and 21k for compound commands.

We first log the validation loss along with training epochs of the three models trained on the primitive set: base sequence-to-sequence model (Base), Bi-directional LSTM model (Bi-LSTM) and attention mechanism enhanced model (Attention). To demonstrate that the training is lightweight and feasible even without a powerful GPU, we also record the runtime (in second) for text to code model training on an Intel Core i7-8565U CPU. Note that the runtime serves as a general indicator of training time and is not intended to provide an exact measurement, as it can be influenced by many factors, including system activity.

Table 6. Validation loss and runtime (in second) over training epochs

Epochs		3		6		9	
		Val. Loss	Runtime	Val. Loss	Runtime	Val. loss	Runtime
Base	high	0.09	10.13	0.02	17.21	0.02	25.56
	low	0.15	12.62	0.06	24.11	0.05	33.01
Bi-LSTM	high	0.03	19.88	0.02	30.74	0.01	48.36
	low	0.33	26.12	0.17	44.42	0.09	67.26
Attention	high	0.09	11.61	0.03	18.39	0.02	26.44
	low	0.24	15.91	0.12	23.95	0.07	35.95

We set the learning rate to 0.01, dropout to 0.5, and use L2 regularization for the training as they are the best configurations during training observations. As shown in Table 6, training a text-to-code model on the generated corpus takes less than one minute. Note that bi-directional LSTM model requires the longest training duration because of its loss calculates in both forward and backward directions. On the high level data corpus, all three models tend to converge after 3-4 epochs while on the low-level data corpus it take longer training epochs for models to learn.

---

[6] https://anonymous.4open.science/r/NLI4WoT-945D.

Table 7. Text to code performance based on two levels of data representation corpus

		Exact Match(%)	Loose Match(%)	Avg. Sentence BLEU
Base	high	93.33	100	0.97
	low	92.50	100	0.97
Bi-LSTM	high	90.41	100	0.94
	low	89.58	100	0.92
Attention	high	94.17	100	0.98
	low	93.75	100	0.97

After sufficient training of each model, we use three metrics to evaluate the trained model prediction performance on the test set: Exact Match, Loose Match, and average sentence BLEU score. Exact match calculates the ratio of precise matches between the predicted code sequence and the corresponding ground truth code. Loose Match accounts for the ratio of syntactically correct predicted code, even if it includes incorrect entity values. Loose match counts as correct as long as the predicted code can be successfully parsed into an abstract syntax tree. BLEU score is a common evaluation score for machine translation task that measures the similarity of the model predicted output to its ground truth. We randomly choose samples from the generated corpus and paraphrased examples to build a test set of size 240. The result is shown in Table 7. All three models are able to learn the syntactic structure of the code effectively after sufficient training, but they struggle at predicting the exact entity values.

6   Discussion

In this section, we discuss the limitations of our proposed system and potential improvements.

6.1   Trade-Off Between Capacity and Cost

A trade-off exists between model capacity and training cost. While larger language models may offer more sophisticated conversational interfaces, our goal is to develop a lightweight NLI system tailored for controlling IoT devices rather than a universally applicable, general NLI.

Our NLI system is resource efficient by leveraging reusable templates and parameter sheets and paraphrasing corpus with LLMs instead of costly and labor-intensive manual paraphrasing. As we directly use fine-tuned LLMs for paraphrasing, the paraphrasing process requires minimal additional computing resources and is completed within seconds.

Additionally, we implement a simple rule-based mechanism to filter out completely irrelevant inputs by comparing the input tokens with training vocabulary. If there is no overlap between user's input and vocabulary, our model will

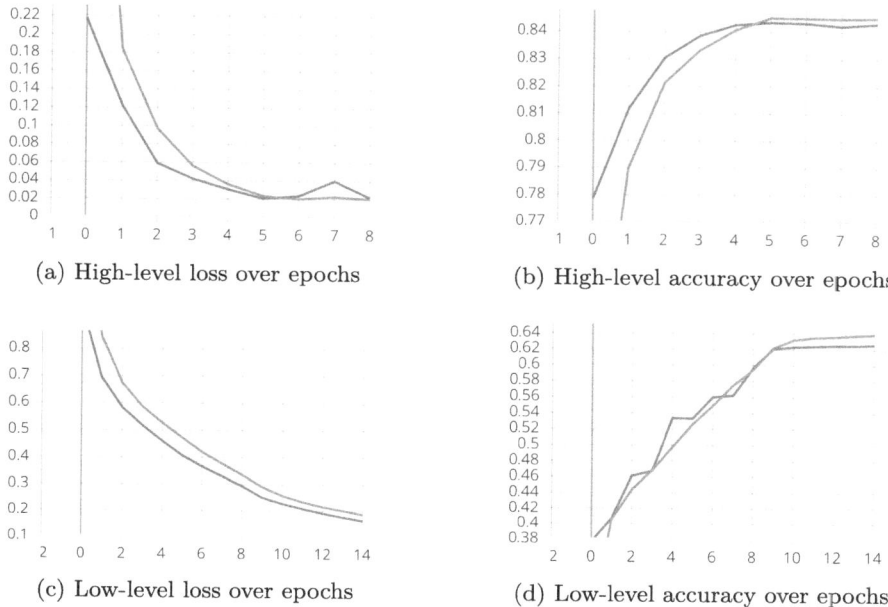

Fig. 2. Training loss and model accuracy plot on high-level and low-level data representation corpus with basemodel (blue: validation, orange: train) . (a) High-level loss over epochs. (b) High-level accuracy over epochs. (c) Low-level loss over epochs. (d) Low-level accuracy over epochs. (Color figure online)

respond directly "Sorry, I don't understand you" without passing the input to the trained model.

6.2 Data Representation Levels

The impact of data representation on the learning efficiency of text-to-code model aligns with our hypothesis: high-level data representation converges faster during training compared to the low-level data representation and thus is the preferred format for code. Based on Fig. 2, our model's training loss converges at around the 4th epoch on high-level data representation corpus while the low-level representation corpus requires more than twice the number of epochs to reach a similar level of convergence. Furthermore, the high-level representation enables the integration of a copy mechanism [7] to address out-of-vocabulary (OOV) issue. The copy mechanism allows the model to choose from when to generate words from its target vocabulary and when to directly copy words from the input sequence, which is especially beneficial for handling OOV words or specific entities such as color names and numbers.

6.3   Scalability and Error Analysis

One challenge comes with scaling up the NLI systems to support more IoT devices is the identification of individual devices, especially when multiple devices of the same type are integrated in the system. Assuming the scenario that two Philips Hue lamps are connected, our text to code models need to know which lamp the user meant. To address this, we can modify the Thing Description by assigning distinct names, unique id, or location information to individual devices. As the data is generated based on parsed information from Thing Description, the differentiation of devices of the same type is also included within the generated data corpus. Table 7 shows a few examples of user input that the model struggles to predict correctly.

Table 8. Example cases of not supported commands

Type	Input	Prediction	Ground Truth
Irrelevant	How are you?	Sorry I don't understand.	None
Incomplete	Hue color on.	philipshue.writeProperty ('color',olive);	None
Ambiguous	Hue lamp off?	philipshue.writeProperty ('power', 0);	philipshue.writeProperty ('power', 0); or philipshue.readProperty ('power');
Unsupported	Make sound in hue.	philipshue.writeProperty ('power', 1);	None

6.4   Real World Data as Test Set

At the moment of development, the data corpus is synthesized from templates created by the authors and paraphrased by large language models, we acknowledge the manual effort and subjectivity limitation in the corpus construction process. We plan to use openly hosted website to crowdsource a broader, more diverse, and more realistic data corpus for testing our system in the future.

7   Conclusion and Future Work

In this paper, we introduce the workflow of building a natural language interface for IoT devices leveraging Knowledge Graphs and the WoT specification. Our proposed system generates a data corpus directly from the Thing Description of a device, and the training of the text-to-code model is efficient and lightweight for local deployment.

We demonstrated a small running example with a Philips Hue smart lamp and showcased the process of generating data corpus for arbitrary new device given a device thing description. The generated corpus can be re-used for training or fine-tuning of other language models.

We are currently working on expanding the number of supported devices and interactions, as well as improving the identification of multiple devices of the same type through additional knowledge graphs. Also, we are developing a more comprehensive composition rules such as the ECA rule to achieve a more practical NLI for IoT system with diverse use cases.

References

1. Bahdanau, D., Cho, K., Bengio, Y.: Neural machine translation by jointly learning to align and translate. In: 3rd International Conference on Learning Representations. ICLR (2015)
2. Campagna, G., Ramesh, R., Xu, S., Fischer, M., Lam, M.S.: Almond: the architecture of an open, crowdsourced, privacy-preserving, programmable virtual assistant. In: International World Wide Web Conferences Steering Committee (2017)
3. Campagna, G., Xu, S., Moradshahi, M., Socher, R., Lam, M.S.: Genie: a generator of natural language semantic parsers for virtual assistant commands. In: Proceedings of the 40th ACM SIGPLAN Conference on Programming Language Design and Implementation
4. Coucke, A., et al.: Snips voice platform: an embedded spoken language understanding system for private-by-design voice interfaces
5. Damodaran, P.: Parrot: paraphrase generation for NLU (2021)
6. Freund, M., Dorsch, R., Harth, A.: Applying the web of things abstraction to bluetooth low energy communication. arXiv preprint arXiv:2211.12934 (2022)
7. Gu, J., Lu, Z., Li, H., Li, V.O.K.: Incorporating copying mechanism in sequence-to-sequence learning (2016)
8. Hochreiter, S., Schmidhuber, J.: Long short-term memory. Neural Comput. (1997)
9. Hogan, A., et al.: Knowledge graphs. ACM Comput. Surv. (CSUR) (2021)
10. Kaebisch, S., McCool, M., Korkan, E., Kamiya, T., Charpenay, V., Kovatsch, M.: Web of things (WOT) thing description 1.1 (2023)
11. Kingma, D.P., Ba, J.: Adam: a method for stochastic optimization (2017)
12. Lagally, M., et al.: Web of things (wot) architecture 1.1 (2023)
13. Lam, M.S., Campagna, G., Moradshahi, M., Semnani, S.J., Xu, S.: Thingtalk: an extensible, executable representation language for task-oriented dialogues (2022)
14. Noura, M., Atiquzzaman, M., Gaedke, M.: Interoperability in internet of things: taxonomies and open challenges (2019)
15. Sutskever, I., Vinyals, O., Le, Q.V.: Sequence to sequence learning with neural networks. In: Advances in Neural Information Processing Systems (2014)
16. Thakur, N., Reimers, N., Daxenberger, J., Gurevych, I.: Augmented sbert: data augmentation method for improving bi-encoders for pairwise sentence scoring tasks. arXiv preprint arXiv:2010.08240 (2020)
17. Vaswani, A., et al.: Attention is all you need (2023)
18. Vladimir Vorobev, M.K.: A paraphrasing model based on chatgpt paraphrases (2023)
19. Weld, H., Huang, X., Long, S., Poon, J., Han, S.C.: A survey of joint intent detection and slot filling models in natural language understanding (2022)
20. Zhang, J., Zhao, Y., Saleh, M., Liu, P.J.: Pegasus: pre-training with extracted gap-sentences for abstractive summarization. In: Proceedings of the 37th International Conference on Machine Learning (2020)

IndEL: Indonesian Entity Linking Benchmark Dataset for General and Specific Domains

Ria Hari Gusmita[1,2]([✉]), Muhammad Faruq Amiral Abshar[2][iD],
Diego Moussallem[1,3][iD], and Axel-Cyrille Ngonga Ngomo[1][iD]

[1] Paderborn University, Warburger Street 100, Paderborn, Germany
{ria.hari.gusmita,diego.moussallem}@uni-paderborn.de, axel.ngonga@upb.de
[2] The State Islamic University Syarif Hidayatullah Jakarta, Ir. H. Juanda Street 95,
Ciputat, South Tangerang, Banten, Indonesia
ria.gusmita@uinjkt.ac.id, faruq.abshar19@mhs.uinjkt.ac.id
[3] Jusbrasil, Salvador, Brazil
https://dice-research.org/team/

Abstract. In recent years, there has been a surge in natural language processing research focused on low-resource languages (LrLs), underscoring the growing recognition that LrLs deserve the same attention as high-resource languages (HrLs). This shift is crucial for ensuring linguistic diversity and inclusivity in the digital age. Despite Indonesian ranking as the 11th most spoken language globally, it remains under-resourced in terms of computational tools and datasets. Within the semantic web domain, Entity Linking (EL) is pivotal, linking textual entity mentions to their corresponding entries in knowledge bases. This process is foundational for advanced information extraction tasks, including relation extraction and event detection. To bolster EL research in Indonesian, we introduce IndEL, the first benchmark dataset tailored for both general and specific domains. IndEL was manually curated using Wikidata, adhering to a rigorous set of annotation guidelines. We used two Named Entity Recognition (NER) benchmark datasets for entity extraction: NER UI for the general domain and IndQNER for the specific domain. IndQNER focused on entities from the Indonesian translation of the Quran. IndEL comprises 4765 entities in the general domain and 2453 in the specific domain. Using the GERBIL framework, we use IndEL to evaluate the performance of various EL systems, such as Babelfy, DBpedia Spotlight, MAG, OpenTapioca, and WAT. Our further investigation reveals that within Wikidata, a significant number of NIL entities remain unlinked due to the limited number of Indonesian labels and the use of acronyms. Especially in the specific domain, transliteration and translation processes performed to create the Indonesian translation of the Quran contribute to the presence of entities in a descriptive form and as synonyms.

Keywords: entity linking benchmark dataset · Indonesian · general and specific domains

© The Author(s), under exclusive license to Springer Nature Switzerland AG 2024
A. Rapp et al. (Eds.): NLDB 2024, LNCS 14762, pp. 500–513, 2024.
https://doi.org/10.1007/978-3-031-70239-6_34

1 Introduction

In recent years, there has been a surge in Natural Language Processing (NLP) research focused on low-resource languages (LrLs), underscoring the growing recognition that LrLs deserve the same attention as high-resource languages (HrLs). This shows that the shift is crucial for ensuring linguistic diversity and inclusivity in the digital age. In the rapidly evolving field of NLP, Entity Linking (EL) serves as a pivotal bridge, connecting raw textual mentions to structured entities within knowledge bases, such as DBpedia, YAGO, and Wikidata. Sentences *Affandi bergabung dengan kelompok Lima Bandung sekitar tahun 30-an* (Affandi joined Lima Bandung group around the 30 s) and *Affandi berhasil memaksimalkan peran badan amil zakat kabupaten* (Affandi succeeded in bringing a district amil zakat foundation to its top performance) have one identical text mention i.e. *Affandi*. To help with the disambiguation of the two names, by leveraging Wikidata, EL can distinguish them. The first *Affandi* is recognized as a famous painter (wd: Q2826050), and the second one is identified as a regent (wd: Q20426359).

Indonesian, the lingua franca of the Indonesian archipelago, is spoken by over 278 million individuals[1]. Yet, the NLP resources tailored for it, remained underdeveloped until 2020. This is partly due to the absence of a robust benchmark dataset that can cater to both the general linguistic characteristics of Indonesian and its domain-specific nuances. Since 2020, noticeable efforts have been done to address the gap. Indonesian benchmark datasets for various NLP fundamental tasks in the general domain were presented along with the Indonesian pre-trained language model, IndoBERT [6,15]. More than 140 datasets for Indonesian NLP tasks were introduced as a result of the collaborative initiative to collect and unify existing resources for Indonesian languages [1]. Furthermore, [4] presents IndQNER as the first Named Entity Recognition (NER) benchmark dataset for Indonesian in a specific domain. However, to the best of our knowledge, no EL benchmark datasets are available for Indonesian both in general and specific domains.

To bridge this gap, we introduce IndEL, a meticulously crafted EL benchmark dataset tailored to Indonesian. We leveraged Wikidata, which encompasses a broad range of topics and domains, as the Knowledge Base (KB) to link entities within our dataset to their corresponding entries. IndEL caters to both general and specific domains, ensuring wide applicability across various use cases. Using NER UI[2], one of the Indonesian NER benchmark datasets, we extracted entities from the general domain, while IndQNER helped us identify entities in the specific domain[3]. The annotation process was conducted manually, adhering to a rigorous set of guidelines to ensure precision and consistency. IndEL contains 4765 and 2453 entities for general and specific domains, respectively. With the

---

[1] https://www.worldometers.info/world-population/indonesia-population/#google_vignette.

[2] https://github.com/indolem/indolem/tree/main/ner/data/nerui.

[3] https://github.com/dice-group/IndQNER/tree/main/datasets.

GERBIL benchmarking system, we use IndEL to evaluate cutting-edge EL systems, including Babelfy, DBpedia Spotlight, MAG, OpenTapioca, and WAT. Our evaluations underscore the dataset's potential as a foundational tool for advancing EL research in Indonesian, both in general and specific domains. Through this initiative, we contribute to advancing Indonesian as a developing-resource language.

2   Related Work

We outline some works in creating EL datasets in particular or multilingual settings.

[16] reported that the EL research for Chinese text is still in its early stages, and lacks publicly available annotated datasets and evaluation benchmarks. Existing Chinese corpora for EL are primarily constructed from noisy short texts, such as microblogs and news headings. Long texts, which represent a broader range of real-life scenarios, have been largely overlooked. The authors introduced CLEEK, a Chinese corpus of multi-domain long text for EL. CLEEK aims to promote the advancement of EL in languages other than English. CLEEK comprises 100 documents from various domains and is publicly accessible.

The first EL corpus for Icelandic was presented by [3]. Corpus annotation was conducted leveraging a multilingual entity linking model (mGENRE) combined with Wikipedia API Search (WAPIS). mGENRE is used to obtain record suggestions in Wikidata to expedite the EL labeling process in an Icelandic corpus. Meanwhile, WAPIS is leveraged to further enhance the labeling process, since it involves a search query run on the Wikipedia API. This method combination achieved a 53.9% coverage on the corpus, which was superior to the 30.9% coverage using only WAPIS.

In 2018, [12] presents the VoxEL dataset, a gold standard for EL in five European languages: German, English, Spanish, French, and Italian. The dataset is based on multilingual news, with 15 corresponding news articles for each language (75 articles in total). Two versions of VoxEL are created: a strict version focusing on traditional entity definitions (*Person, Place, Organization*) and a relaxed version considering a broader range of entities described by Wikipedia. Using the VoxEL dataset, the authors evaluate various EL systems to compare performance across systems and languages. They also compare the performance of EL systems for specific languages against results produced by translating the text to English using machine translation.

KORE^{DYWC} was introduced as an extension of the KORE 50 data set to include YAGO, Wikidata, and Crunchbase [10]. The goal is to provide an evaluation data set that addresses the limitations of existing data sets and can be easily used by other developers. The KORE 50 data set was chosen as a foundation because it is popular and covers a broad range of topics in English. Three sub-data sets are released for each KB: YAGO, Wikidata, and Crunchbase. YAGO and Wikidata cover general knowledge, while Crunchbase focuses on technology and business. To perform the annotation, the authors used WebAnno, a web-based annotation tool, to manually annotate the KORE 50 data set using entities from different KBs. Each document was manually annotated by searching for entities in the respective KB. The annotations were exported using the WebAnno TSV3 format. There are some peculiarities of the annotation. Some entities were available in YAGO and Wikidata, but not in Crunchbase. YAGO offers a larger number of resources for annotation compared to DBpedia. Wikidata provides information for a broader range of mentions than DBpedia. Crunchbase has a tech-focused domain, resulting in fewer entities compared to DBpedia.

DocRED-FE was introduced as an English dataset that enhanced DocRED but with a redesigned entity type schema [14]. The new schema includes 11 coarse-grained types and 119 fine-grained types, providing richer contextual information. An example document is provided to illustrate the differences between the original DocRED and the new DocRED-FE schema. The authors used WebAnno for manual annotation, linking each entity to Wikidata to determine its types. The annotations were based on a new schema that was designed through a bottom-up, data-driven approach. The schema was refined through iterative exploratory annotation, with feedback from annotators leading to adjustments in the schema. Some entities were available in multiple types, and the authors had to make decisions on which type to assign based on context. The new schema was more precise and expressive compared to the original DocRED schema. The authors provide a comparison of DocRED-FE with other well-known datasets, highlighting the unique features of their dataset. They also analyze the distribution of entity types in their dataset, noting the top and least frequent types. The authors conducted experiments to evaluate JERE models on both DocRED and DocRED-FE. They found that DocRED-FE posed a greater challenge to existing models, but the fine-grained entity information improved relation classification performance.

3   Datasets Construction

In this section, we detail the development process of IndEL. We begin by discussing the document sources, from which we extracted entities for both the general domain (NER UI) and the specific domain (IndQNER). Subsequently, we shed light on the challenges posed by the entities from NER UI. We then delve into the crafting of the annotation guidelines, the manual annotation process, and the resultant findings.

3.1   Document Source of IndEL

Given the limited resources, we utilized two benchmark datasets for Indonesian NER, NER UI[4] and IndQNER[5], to obtain entities. NER UI and IndQNER

---

[4] https://github.com/indolem/indolem/tree/main/ner/data/nerui.

[5] https://github.com/dice-group/IndQNER/tree/main/datasets.

are designed to aid the benchmarking of Indonesian NER systems in general and specific domains, respectively. NER UI is from the news domain, and contains 5055 entities from *Person* (1870 entities), *Organization* (1949 entities), and *Location* (1236 entities) classes. Out of two Indonesian NER benchmark datasets introduced in 2020, NER UI has been shown as the best dataset as IndoBERT fine-tuning performed with it yields the highest F1 score of 90.1% [6]. Meanwhile, IndQNER is the first Indonesian NER benchmark dataset in a specific domain, the Indonesian translation of the Quran. It was presented with 3117 sentences and 2475 entities from 18 entity classes as explained in [4]. An evaluation of BiLSTM and CRF-based Indonesian NER system performed with IndQNER obtains an F1 score of 98% [4].

3.2   Challenges from Document Source

The NER UI dataset, while valuable as a document source for the general domain, presents several challenges that can impact the performance of EL systems. These challenges can be categorized into misspelled entities, incorrect entity spans, and missing entities.

Misspelled entities - Misspellings in entity names can hinder the ability of EL systems to correctly identify and link them to the appropriate entries in KBs. Table 1 provides examples of such misspellings from the NER UI dataset. The entities *Lea Iacocca* (the first example) and *Lentang* (the second example) are incorrectly spelled and should be written *Lee Iacocca* and *lenteng*, respectively.

Incorrect entity spans - The dataset sometimes incorrectly labels spans of text as entities or fails to capture the full span of an entity. Table 2 showcases this issue. In the first example, *Fakultas Ekonomi* (Economics Faculty) is labeled as a common noun, while *Universitas Indonesia* (the University of Indonesia) is identified as a proper noun. However, in the given context, both entities should be combined to form a single entity: *Fakultas Ekonomi Universitas Indonesia* (Economics Faculty at the University of Indonesia). A similar issue arises with the entities *Pemkot* (city/local government) and *Surabaya* in the second example, which should be combined as *Pemkot Surabaya*.

Missing entities - There are instances where valid entities are entirely overlooked in the dataset. Table 3 highlights such omissions, including entities like *Hye-kyo* (*Person*) and *Korea Times* (*Organization*) in the first example, and *Kabinet Kerja* (*Organization*) in the second example.

3.3   Annotation Guidelines

To help the annotators with the same knowledge of how to do the annotation, we designed the annotation guidelines meticulously.[6] The guidance presents information pertaining to two aspects as follows.

---

[6] https://github.com/dice-group/IndEL/blob/main/Annotation_guidelines_%20in_%20English.pdf.

How to Annotate. The manual annotation is performed using a semantic annotation platform, INCEpTION [5]. Annotators are tasked with identifying entities within the text and associating them with the corresponding Wikidata entries. INCEpTION facilitates this process by allowing annotators to search for entities directly on Wikidata. It is crucial for annotators to verify that the links they find correspond accurately to the entities mentioned in the text and that these links include Indonesian labels.

What to Annotate. Before beginning the annotation process, all annotators are provided with two types of documents: one containing raw text with sentences and another with the same text pre-tagged with entities. The raw text serves as the workspace for annotators to locate and tag entities, while the pre-tagged document is intended to guide the annotators by highlighting the specific sections of text that are entities. Annotators can simply use the search function to link entities to the correct entries on Wikidata if they are certain of the refer-

Table 1. Examples of misspelled entities in the document source of the general domain dataset.

First Example	Second Example
\<entity\>**Lea Iacocca**\</entity\> mampu secara cepat membenahi \<entity\>Chrysler\</entity\> karena dia mempunyai wewenang penuh melakukan konsolidasi, termasuk membawa beberapa kolega lamanya dari \<entity\>Ford\</entity\>.	Itu bukan etika \<entity\>PDIP\</entity\>, ujar \<entity\>Hasto\</entity\> di sela pelatihan manajer kampanye kader \<entity\>PDIP\</entity\> di kantor DPP, \<entity\>Jl **Lentang** Agung\</entity\>, \<entity\>Jakarta Selatan\</entity\>, Kamis (7/4/2016).

Table 2. Examples of incorrect entity spans in the document source of the general domain dataset.

First Example	Second Example
Mantan Dekan \<entity\>**Fakultas Ekonomi**\</entity\> \<entity\>**Universitas Indonesia**\</entity\> ini mengatakan ...	... capaian yang sudah dilakukan \<entity\>Risma\</entity\> dan \<entity\>**Pemkot**\</entity\> \<entity\>**Surabaya**\</entity\> terhadap kepedulian ...

Table 3. Examples of missing entities in the document source of the general domain dataset.

First Example	Second Example
"Dia memerankan karakternya dengan sangat bagus, menarik, bahkan membuat saya berdebar," kata **Hye-kyo** lagi, yang dikutip oleh **Korea Times**, Rabu (20/4/2016).	Sinyal akan dilakukannya reshuffle **Kabinet Kerja** oleh Presiden \<entity\>Joko Widodo\</entity\>terus berhembus.

ences based on the sentence context. If the names are incomplete or the context does not provide enough information for a confident identification, annotators are instructed to use Google's document retrieval function to search for the names within documents. If no relevant documents are found, the names remain untagged. To obtain correct links on Wikidata, annotators must disambiguate the entries by navigating them using the provided descriptions.

3.4   Human Annotation and Results

The manual annotation was initially carried out by six non-volunteer native speakers, with four annotators focusing on the general domain and two on another domain. Specifically, for the specific domain, the annotators were fourth-year bachelor's students from the Quran and Tafseer department at the State Islamic University Syarif Hidayatullah Jakarta. Each of the two annotators labeled the same document according to the designed annotation guidelines. Therefore, we had two groups of annotators labeling the general domain dataset, and one group was assigned to label the specific domain dataset. Furthermore, we had a third annotator that was tasked with verifying the annotation results manually. We started by conducting the trial annotation process to observe whether all annotators have the same understanding of the annotation process. In this stage, the annotators were asked to label all entities in 20 sentences from another Indonesian NER benchmark dataset, NER UGM. The actual annotation was done after all annotators demonstrated their common understanding of the annotation.

According to the analysis of the actual annotation results, we distinguished the labeled entities into three categories. They are *Agreed*, *Disagreed*, and *OneNo-Link*. *Agreed* is used in the case when two annotators provide the same links for an NE. Different links from annotators will make an NE classified as *Disagreed*. When only one annotator provides a link for an NE, then it will be grouped in the last category, *OneNoLink*. This happens when another annotator does not think of the name as an NE, or overlooks it. Table 4 depicts the number of entities from all categories in both general and specific domains. In the case of the number of *OneNoLink* entities, we summed the number of entities that were annotated only by each of the annotators.

We performed the second annotation to resolve *OneNoLink* entities. We asked the respective annotators to relook at the document and decide whether the names must be labeled or remain as non-entities. At this point, although the number of entities in the *OneNoLink* group remained small, we obtained new entities in other groups. This altered the distribution of entities, as displayed in Table 5. To handle the remaining *OneNoLink* entities in the general domain, we first selected valid entities among them by checking whether the entities exist in the document source, NER UI. We obtained 114 and 122 valid entities from the first and second groups of annotators, respectively. The remaining entities were termed NE candidates. Both valid entities and NE candidates were presented with the link provided by the respective annotators in the second annotation stage. The third annotator verified the NE candidates as well as the proposed links manually. In the case of valid entities, the third annotator just checked whether the proposed links were correct. Table 6 shows the results of the manual verification. In the section of *Valid Named Entities*, we term entities with correct proposed links as *Taken* where most annotators have the highest number of them. We also found valid entities that are actually common nouns, and thus we categorized them as *Invalid entities*. These entities mostly exist in the results of the first annotator in both groups. In the *Named Entity Candidates* section, *Taken* category is used to state NE candidates that were verified as valid entities and that the proposed links were correct. More than 59% of new entities could be identified by the majority of annotators. However, the first annotator in *Group 1* contributed the highest number of invalid entities. Furthermore. only the proposed links from the second annotator in *Group 1* needed to be corrected.

Table 4. Distribution of entities in Agreed, Disagreed, and OneNoLink categories for general and specific domains.

Domain	Agreed	Disagreed	OneNoLink
General-group 1	1975	246	527
General-group 2	1905	191	258
Specific	2266	179	34

Table 5. Distribution of entities in Agreed, Disagreed, and OneNoLink categories for general and specific domains after the second annotation.

Domain	Agreed	Disagreed	OneNoLink
General-group 1	2035	411	299
General-group 2	1905	276	191
Specific	2296	179	4

To resolve the *Disagreed* annotation results, the third annotator manually checked different proposed links on Wikidata from two annotators to determine the correct one. If no correct link was found, the annotator searched for the link manually, following the annotation guidelines. From this process, not only did we find the correct links, either from the proposed links or those suggested by the third annotator, but we also identified Not in Lexicon (NIL) and invalid entities. Table 7 describes the results of manual checking to handle *Disagreed* entities. Generally, we distinguished the checking results according to the source of the correct link. There are three categories of them, i.e. from one of the annotators, from the third annotator (term *New Link*), and no correct link available. The latter is divided into NIL entities and invalid ones. In *Group 1*, more than 50%

Table 6. Manual verification results on valid entities and entity candidates for the general domain

Verification Results Category	Group 1		Group 2	
	1st Annotator	2nd Annotator	1st Annotator	2nd Annotator
Valid Named Entities				
Taken	77.9%	26.3%	73.1%	75%
NIL Entities	15.8%	57.9%	15.4%	6.25%
Invalid Entities	1%	36.8%	3.8%	15.26%
New Link	5.3%	15.8%	7.7%	3.1%
Named Entity Candidates				
Taken	70.6%	0.75%	75.9%	60%
Invalid Entities	25.5%	99.3%	24.1%	40%
New Link	3.9%	-	-	-

Table 7. Manual checking results on *Disagreed* category for general domain.

Results Checking Category	Group 1	Group 2
Taken from 1st annotator	25.4%	64.2%
Taken from 2nd annotator	52.5%	27.4%
New Link	2.8%	2.8%
NIL Entities	1.8%	4.2%
Invalid Entities	18%	1.4%

correct links were taken from the 2nd annotator, while the 1st annotator in *Group 2* contributed more than 64% of the correct links. In both groups, we had the same portion of entities with new links as many as 2.8%. Moreover, the existence of invalid entities in *Group 1* has much more portion than in *Group 2* where they numbered 18%.

In the specific domain, the third annotator manually checked four entities that were still in the *OneNoLink* category and found no correct links for all of them. To handle entities in *Disagreed*'s, the annotator went through all two different proposed links and selected correct links as many as 73.2% from the 1st annotator and 26.8% from the 2nd annotator.

We applied the same procedure on entities in the *Agreed* category to maintain the annotation quality of IndEL. We first checked whether every NE was a valid one, and we found 119 entities do not appear in NER UI. Therefore, we categorized them as NE candidates. The third annotator performed manual checking to determine whether the NE candidates were entities and whether the proposed links were correct. Finally, we collected 4765 and 2453 entities for general and specific domains, respectively. Details of the number of NIL entities and the number of entities affected by the challenges in the source document are provided in the repository.[7]

Deal with the Challenges in the Source Dataset. To overcome challenges found in NER UI (Sect. 3.2), we extended the aim of manual verification that we have explained in Sect. 3.4. For example, when we performed a selection of two proposed links in *Disagreed* category, if we found no correct link we further checked if the entity falls in one issue in NER UI. If this is the case, we will make the appropriate corrections, such as finding the correct name (for misspelled entities), combining entities (for incorrect entities' span), and providing correct links on Wikidata (for missing entities).

Dataset Analysis, Format, and Usage. Table 8 presents the distribution of the number of unique entities, sentences with nested entities, and the average number of entities in each sentence in IndEL for general and specific domains. As expected, the general domain contains a substantially wider range of entities, as evidenced by the presence of 31% unique entities. It also has more sentences containing nested entities compared to the specific domain. An average appearance of 2.4 entities in sentences within the general domain denotes a more complex sentence structure than is typical in the specific domain. The lower number of unique entities and lower average number of entities per sentence in the specific domain support the fact that it has focused content. To meet the need for widely used EL benchmark datasets, IndEL was created in the NLP Interchange Format (NIF).[8] Furthermore, to facilitate the evaluation process of multilingual EL systems, IndEL has been integrated into the GERBIL platform [13]. This integration enables researchers to efficiently test and compare the performance of various EL systems across multiple languages.[9]

Table 8. Distribution of unique entities, sentence with nested entities, and entities in sentences.

Domain	Total Entities	Unique Entities	Sentence with Nested Entities	Entities in Sentence
General	4767	1488	55	2.4
Specific	2453	141	16	1.6

4   Experiments and Analysis

We performed experiments using IndEL to examine the performance of cutting-edge EL systems in multilingual contexts. These experiments aimed to understand how these EL systems operate and perform when dealing with the Indonesian language, thereby providing insights into their effectiveness and adaptability in diverse linguistic settings. In doing so, we use GERBIL, a framework that

---

[7] https://github.com/dice-group/IndEL/tree/main.
[8] https://github.com/dice-group/IndEL/tree/main/datasets.
[9] https://gerbil.aksw.org/gerbil/.

enhances the ease of comparing and analyzing different EL systems [13]. It allows a more uniform and efficient evaluation process by standardizing the way the systems are accessed, and their results are processed. GERBIL is also capable of translating identifiers across various KBs, ensuring compatibility and integration between different systems. We used micro-measures for precision, recall and F1 to show the performance over the set of all annotations inside the dataset.[10] From the systems integrated on GERBIL, only Babelfy [8], DBpedia Spotlight [7], MAG [9], OpenTapioca [2], and WAT [11] yielded results in our experiments.

Table 9 showcases the results of the experiments with all systems in both general and specific domains. It is observed that systems generally achieve greater precision within the specific domain compared to the general domain. DBpedia Spotlight excels in the specific domain but experiences a marked decline in its performance when used in the general domain. Conversely, OpenTapioca demonstrates superior performance in the general domain compared to the specific domain, where its precision outperforms all other systems. Babelfy maintains consistent precision across domains, but has a notable drop in recall when transitioning from the specific to the general domain. MAG shows a considerable increase in performance across all metrics when moving from the specific to the general domain. In contrast, WAT demonstrates considerably better results in the specific domain as compared to the general domain, particularly its F1 score, which surpasses all others. At this point, WAT emerges as the top-performing EL system for Indonesian text, securing the highest F1 score in both domains. These findings indicate that Indonesian entities in the Indonesian translation of the Quran may have more clear-cut entities, facilitating accurate identification by the systems. However, the inherent diversity of Indonesian entities in the general domain presents a greater challenge for multilingual EL systems. Furthermore, we provide details of the evaluation results as well as the performance of the mentioned EL systems on other benchmarks in the repository.[11]

Table 9. GERBIL evaluation of Babelfy, DBpedia Spotlight, MAG, OpenTapioca, and WAT in the general and specific domains of IndEL

Metrics	Babelfy	DBpedia Spotlight	MAG	OpenTapioca	WAT
General Domain					
Precision	0.7278	0.6750	0.4265	**0.7984**	0.6118
Recall	0.3719	0.3577	0.4166	0.4105	**0.5549**
F1	0.4923	0.4676	0.4215	0.5423	**0.5820**
Specific Domain					
Precision	0.8049	**0.8471**	0.1523	0.6179	0.7715
Recall	0.4725	0.6731	0.1508	0.0310	**0.7501**
F1	0.5954	0.7501	0.1515	0.0590	**0.7606**

---

[10] https://github.com/dice-group/gerbil/wiki/Precision,-Recall-and-F1-measure.
[11] https://github.com/dice-group/IndEL/blob/main/README.md.

To further investigate the impact of how Indonesian entities are presented on Wikidata on the performance of EL systems, we conducted an additional experiment using MAG, the EL system with the lowest F1 score both in general and specific domains. The experiment was aimed at the identification of NIL entities within both domains. Specifically, we explored if NIL entities are acknowledged as either entry names or as labels in the Indonesian language within Wikidata, which could potentially affect the EL systems' ability to correctly link entities. For this purpose, we randomly selected 55 NIL entities from each domain. Our findings indicated that only 14.5% of NIL entities in the general domain are listed as entry names, with the number slightly lower at 10.9% in the specific domain. In contrast, 29.1% of NIL entities in the specific domain are represented as Indonesian labels, compared to only 12.7% in the general domain. The main reason for the scarce appearance of NIL entities as entry names and Indonesian labels on Wikidata in the general domain is the use of acronyms. In the specific domain, 22.2% of the 81.8% of NIL entities that do not appear as entry names exist as Indonesian labels. Additionally, approximately 60% of NIL entities that do not appear as entry names lack Indonesian labels because they are defined descriptively. For example, the entity *Allah* appears as *Tuhan dalam Islam* (God in Islam). Another reason is the use of corresponding synonyms for NIL entities in the Indonesian label section of Wikidata. Some examples are *Ummul Qura* vs. *Makkah* (Mecca), *Hari Akhir* vs. *Yaumul Qiyamah* (Qiyama), *Baitullah* vs. *Ka'bah* (Kaaba), and *Israil* vs. *Ya͟qub* (Jacob in Islam). Based on the findings, several recommendations can be made to improve the performance of EL systems in linking Indonesian entities on Wikidata as follows:

1. Increasing the number of Indonesian labels for entities can enhance the accuracy of EL systems.
2. Standardizing terminology for entities, particularly those defined descriptively, will promote more consistent linking. This is especially relevant for entities in the specific domain due to the transliteration and translation process from the original Qur'an, which is written in Arabic, to the Indonesian translation.
3. Recognizing and incorporating synonyms in Indonesian will ensure comprehensive label inclusion.
4. Developing better methods to handle acronyms, especially in the general domain, will reduce the number of unlinked NIL entities.

5   Conlusion and Future Works

We have introduced a pioneering benchmark dataset specifically crafted to evaluate EL systems targeting the Indonesian language, covering both general and specific domains. The general domain entities were sourced from one of Indonesian NER benchmark datasets, NER UI. Meanwhile, IndQNER, which was built from the Indonesian translation of the Quran, was used to obtain entities in the specific domain. All entities in IndEL are provided with their corresponding links on Wikidata. A GERBIL benchmarking process demonstrates that IndEL can be employed as an appropriate evaluation metric for assessing the performance of EL systems in Indonesian, both in general and specific domains. However, we recognize the challenges posed by the limited scope of IndEL and the fact that many entities remain unlinked, primarily due to the insufficient quantity of Indonesian labels on Wikidata. To address the former, we plan to enrich the dataset by incorporating additional entities from various Indonesian NER benchmark datasets, such as NERGrit, NERP, NER UGM, etc.[12] To address the latter as well as to develop KB agnostic EL systems for Indonesian, we intend to broaden the range of entity links within IndEL to establish connections with other KBs, such as BabelNet, DBpedia and YAGO. This expansion aims to facilitate the seamless integration of Indonesian entities with broader semantic knowledge resources, contributing to improved accuracy and versatility of EL systems.

Acknowledgements. We acknowledge the support of the German Federal Ministry of Education and Research (BMBF) within the project COLIDE (01IS21005D), the European Union's Horizon Europe research and innovation programme within the project ENEXA (101070305), the German Federal Ministry of Education and Research (BMBF) within the project KIAM (02L19C115), the Deutsche Forschungsgemeinschaft (DFG, German Research Foundation) within the project SFB-TRR 318 (TRR 318/1 2021 - 438445824), and Mora Scholarship from the Ministry of Religious Affairs, Republic of Indonesia.

References

1. Cahyawijaya, S., et al.: NusaCrowd: open source initiative for Indonesian NLP resources. In: Findings of the Association for Computational Linguistics: ACL 2023, pp. 13745–13818. Association for Computational Linguistics, Toronto, Canada, July 2023. https://doi.org/10.18653/v1/2023.findings-acl.868, https://aclanthology.org/2023.findings-acl.868
2. Delpeuch, A.: Opentapioca: Lightweight entity linking for wikidata. ArXiv **abs/1904.09131** (2019). https://api.semanticscholar.org/CorpusID:125953443
3. Friðriksdóttir, S.R., et al.: Building an Icelandic entity linking corpus. In: Proceedings of the Workshop on Dataset Creation for Lower-Resourced Languages within the 13th Language Resources and Evaluation Conference, pp. 27–35. European Language Resources Association, Marseille, France, June 2022. https://aclanthology.org/2022.dclrl-1.4
4. Gusmita, R.H., Firmansyah, A.F., Moussallem, D., Ngonga Ngomo, A.C.: IndQNER: Named Entity Recognition Benchmark Dataset from the Indonesian Translation of the Quran, vol. 2. Springer Nature Switzerland (2023). https://doi.org/10.1007/978-3-031-35320-8_12
5. Klie, J.C., Bugert, M., Boullosa, B., de Castilho, R.E., Gurevych, I.: The inception platform: Machine-assisted and knowledge-oriented interactive annotation. In: Proceedings of the 27th International Conference on Computational Linguistics: System Demonstrations, pp. 5–9. Association for Computational Linguistics, June 2018. http://tubiblio.ulb.tu-darmstadt.de/106270/, event Title: The 27th International Conference on Computational Linguistics (COLING 2018)

---

[12] https://indonlp.github.io/nusa-catalogue/index.html.

6. Koto, F., Rahimi, A., Lau, J.H., Baldwin, T.: IndoLEM and IndoBERT: a benchmark dataset and pre-trained language model for Indonesian NLP. In: Proceedings of the 28th International Conference on Computational Linguistics, pp. 757–770. International Committee on Computational Linguistics, Barcelona, Spain (Online), Dec 2020. https://doi.org/10.18653/v1/2020.coling-main.66, https://aclanthology.org/2020.coling-main.66

7. Mendes, P.N., Jakob, M., García-Silva, A., Bizer, C.: Dbpedia spotlight: Shedding light on the web of documents. In: Proceedings of the 7th International Conference on Semantic Systems, I-Semantics '11, pp. 1–8. Association for Computing Machinery, New York (2011). https://doi.org/10.1145/2063518.2063519

8. Moro, A., Raganato, A., Navigli, R.: Entity linking meets word sense disambiguation: a unified approach. Trans. Assoc. Comput. Ling. **2**, 231–244 (2014). https://aclanthology.org/Q14-1019

9. Moussallem, D., Usbeck, R., Röeder, M., Ngomo, A.C.N.: Mag: a multilingual, knowledge-base agnostic and deterministic entity linking approach. In: Proceedings of the Knowledge Capture Conference. K-CAP 2017. Association for Computing Machinery, New York (2017). https://doi.org/10.1145/3148011.3148024

10. Noullet, K., Mix, R., Färber, M.: KORE 50DYWC: an evaluation data set for entity linking based on DBpedia, YAGO, Wikidata, and crunchbase. In: Proceedings of the Twelfth Language Resources and Evaluation Conference, pp. 2389–2395. European Language Resources Association, Marseille, France, May 2020. https://aclanthology.org/2020.lrec-1.291

11. Piccinno, F., Ferragina, P.: From tagme to wat: a new entity annotator. In: Proceedings of the First International Workshop on Entity Recognition & Disambiguation, ERD 2014, , pp. 55–62. Association for Computing Machinery, New York (2014). https://doi.org/10.1145/2633211.2634350

12. Rosales-Méndez, H., Hogan, A., Poblete, B.: Voxel: a benchmark dataset for multilingual entity linking. In: Vrandečić, D., et al. (eds.) The Semantic Web - ISWC 2018, pp. 170–186. Springer, Cham (2018)

13. Verborgh, R., Röder, M., Usbeck, R., Ngonga Ngomo, A.C.: Gerbil - benchmarking named entity recognition and linking consistently. Semant. Web **9**(5), 605-625 (2018).https://doi.org/10.3233/SW-170286

14. Wang, H., Xiong, W., Song, Y., Zhu, D., Xia, Y., Li, S.: Docred-fe: a document-level fine-grained entity and relation extraction dataset. In: ICASSP 2023 - 2023 IEEE International Conference on Acoustics, Speech and Signal Processing (ICASSP), pp. 1–5 (2023). https://doi.org/10.1109/ICASSP49357.2023.10095786

15. Wilie, B., et al.: IndoNLU: Benchmark and resources for evaluating Indonesian natural language understanding. In: Proceedings of the 1st Conference of the Asia-Pacific Chapter of the Association for Computational Linguistics and the 10th International Joint Conference on Natural Language Processing, pp. 843–857. Association for Computational Linguistics, Suzhou, China, December 2020. https://aclanthology.org/2020.aacl-main.85

16. Zeng, W., Zhao, X., Tang, J., Tan, Z., Huang, X.: CLEEK: a Chinese long-text corpus for entity linking. In: Proceedings of the Twelfth Language Resources and Evaluation Conference. pp. 2026–2035. European Language Resources Association, Marseille, France, May 2020. https://aclanthology.org/2020.lrec-1.249

Semantic Multi-concept Annotation for Tabular Data in Financial Documents

Rungsiman Nararatwong[1]([✉]), Yuting Shi[2], Natthawut Kertkeidkachorn[2], and Ryutaro Ichise[1,3]

[1] National Institute of Advanced Industrial Science and Technology, Tokyo, Japan
r.nararatwong@aist.go.jp
[2] Japan Advanced Institute of Science and Technology, Ishikawa, Japan
{syting,natt}@jaist.ac.jp
[3] Tokyo Institute of Technology, Tokyo, Japan
ichise@iee.e.titech.ac.jp

Abstract. Tables in financial documents provide structured data for various analyses, such as the company's financial health. However, their heterogeneous structures complicate data extraction and narrow the scopes of the analyses. Semantic annotation solves this problem by standardizing the meanings of tabular data, making it fully structured and machine-readable. Although previous research has explored and enhanced semantic annotation, they mainly focus on singular or hierarchical concepts within a table cell, which is insufficient to annotate financial filings. Therefore, we present a more challenging task of annotating multiple non-hierarchical concepts in financial tables. This new task requires a model to identify different concepts describing a table cell. We created a dataset of 10,000 samples and benchmarked seven language models through prompting and fine-tuning. The results demonstrate the challenges of the task, even for large language models, offering the opportunity for future research.

Keywords: Semantic Annotation · Tabular Data · Financial Domain

1 Introduction

In financial documents, tabular data contains valuable information, such as revenue and liabilities, in a structured manner that makes it easy for analysts, investors, and stakeholders to assess the company's status. Although tabular data offers a wide range of potential usages, it is difficult to use in practical applications due to heterogeneous schema, and vocabulary issues [11].

One solution for these issues is semantic annotation, which assigns standardized meanings to table elements, enhancing machine interpretability and data integration across domains by linking to ontologies or taxonomies. There have been many studies [6,10] on semantic annotation for tabular data. Previous research assumed that a cell in tabular data contains one concept, or hierarchical concepts (sub-concepts) related to the main concept. Nevertheless, a cell

A. Rapp et al. (Eds.): NLDB 2024, LNCS 14762, pp. 514–529, 2024.
https://doi.org/10.1007/978-3-031-70239-6_35

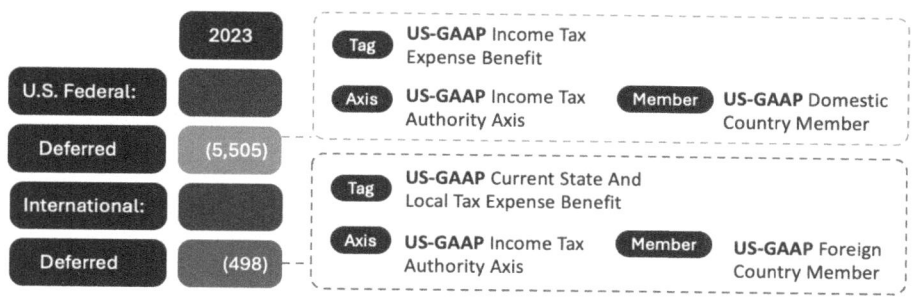

Fig. 1. An example of a table in financial document with semantic annotation. We omitted other parts of the table (and tables in other figures) due to space limitation.

of a table in financial documents could contain one main concept (called a tag, according to the U.S. Securities and Exchange Commission's standard) alongside non-hierarchical multi concepts in the form of axes and members, as illustrated in Fig. 1. In Fig. 1, the tag in the blue cell is "Income Tax Expense Benefit"; however, the cell also contains the 'Income Tax Authority Axis' concept as the axis and the "Domestic Country Member" concept as the member. The red cell, on the other hand, has a different tag (Current State and Local Tax Expense Benefit) and member (Foreign Country Member) but the same axis (Income Tax Authority Axis). The structure of axes and members varies depending on the content of the table. To the best of our knowledge, the investigation of multi-concept semantic annotation in this context has not yet been studied.

In this paper, we introduce a novel semantic multi-concept annotation task for tabular data in the financial domain. Our contributions are as follows: (1) A novel semantic multi-concept annotation for tabular data, (2) a large-scale dataset for training[1], and (3) two baseline approaches (prompting and fine-tuning) with extensive experiments and in-depth analyses.

2   Related Work

Researchers have proposed many resources for semantic concept annotation in tabular data. Limaye et al. introduced four semantic annotation datasets of tabular data constructed from various sources, including HTML tables from a web crawl [8]. Ritze et al. proposed T2D.V2 for evaluating web table matching systems [13]. Bhagavatula et al. annotated a gold standard for semantic tabular annotation from Wikipedia tables [2]. SemTab[2] is a series of semantic web challenges that provide benchmarks for annotating tables with knowledge graphs [3]. SemTab also provides benchmarks for specific domains, such as Biodiversity [1]. Nguyen et al. proposed multiple tabular annotation approaches that achieved high scores on SemTab using helpful tabular information [11]. Fan et

---

[1] Available upon request.
[2] https://www.cs.ox.ac.uk/isg/challenges/sem-tab/.

The table below summarizes fair value information about our derivative...

Fig. 2. A tag and multiple axis-member pairs describing a table cell. The model must correctly identify all the heterogeneous concepts.

al. also studied dataset discovery from data lakes using the tables' contextual semantic information [4]. Later, Nararatwong et al. introduced a semantic annotation benchmark for tabular data in financial documents [9]. The tabular data, extracted from 10-K reports, are annotated with ontology concepts from the financial knowledge graph [5].

Previous studies have focused on annotating a single entity per cell or a concept per column. However, in financial documents, a cell within a table can include a main tag along with multiple associated axis-member pairs, thereby presenting more challenge for annotation than standard semantic annotation practices for tabular data. To the best of our knowledge, no study has yet focused on the semantic annotation of multiple concepts within tabular data.

3 Multi-concept Table Annotation

3.1 Problem Definition

Given an Ontology $O = \langle \Omega, R \rangle$, where Ω consists of a set of tags C, a set of axes A, and a set of members M, and R represents a set of relations, the objective of the semantic multi-concept annotation is to annotate each cell c_{ij} in table T with a tag t from C, associating it with a set of axis-member pairs $p_{c_{ij}}$ corresponding to the cell c_{ij}. The formal definition is as follows:

$$F(c_{ij} \mid O, T, D) \rightarrow \{(t_{c_{ij}}, p_{c_{ij}}) \mid t_{c_{ij}} \in C,$$
$$p_{c_{ij}} = \{(a_1, m_1), ...(a_x, m_x)\}, a \in A_{c_{ij}}, m \in M_{c_{ij}} \tag{1}$$

where $F(\cdot)$ denotes the function that maps a cell $c_{ij} \in T$, given the ontology O, tabular data T, and context description D, to a tuple consisting of a tag $t_{c_{ij}}$ and a set of axis-member pairs $p_{c_{ij}}$. The subset $A_{c_{ij}}$ specifies that $A_{c_{ij}}$ is a subset of axes related to the cell c_{ij}. Similarly, $M_{c_{ij}}$ is a subset of members related to the cell c_{ij}.

Figure 2 shows an example of a prediction. The task is predicting the tag and axis-member pairs describing to the bottom-right cell of the table with the value "(44)." The model must understand the structure of the table and the technical meaning of the value. It must then find the correct concept (Derivative Liabilities) and all four pairs of axes and members. Failing to identify any element will result in an incorrect interpretation of the value in downstream tasks.

3.2 Dataset Construction

We focus on companies featured in FinKG [5], which includes 3,000 of the largest U.S.-traded stocks according to the Russell 3000 Index as of 2021. We collected financial documents for these companies from the publicly accessible database of the U.S. Securities and Exchange Commission (SEC)[3]. Our investigation was limited to annual reports (10-K) in the XBRL format[4]. A 10-K report is an annual document that provides a comprehensive overview of a company's financial performance over the year. In total, we obtained 487,903 tables from 9,843 reports of 2,806 companies. Note that the number of companies is less than 3,000 because some companies did not provide their data in the XBRL format.

We used the 2023 version of the US GAAP taxonomy available on the SEC website[5]. We collected the labels and documentation of all the concepts (including tags, axes, and members) defined in the taxonomy. However, the standard taxonomy does not cover all the concepts found in the filings. Companies also define their concepts to adapt to specific business terminologies and accounting requirements. During prediction, the model must consider these custom concepts addition to the standard concepts. The taxonomy contains 20,650 US GAAP concepts and 661,812 company-defined (custom) concepts. Thirteen companies do not create their internal concepts. The average number of custom concepts is 235.86 (SD = 192.14), with a maximum count of 3,529, meaning that the model must choose from up to 24,179 concepts (including the US GAAP concepts). We stored the taxonomy in a JSON file separated into the standard US GAAP and custom sections of key-value pairs, where the key is an identifier (e.g., "us-gaap: Assets"), and the value consists of a label (e.g., "Assets") and documentation.

Next, we identified tables that contained XBRL tags, which describe a concept of a specific value (e.g., a number in a table cell). Specifically, we searched for tables where each candidate table cell contained exactly one XBRL tag and no additional content. We collected all such tables that met our criteria for XBRL tagging. To ensure diversity in our dataset, we then randomly selected XBRL tags for inclusion. This selection process allowed for table overlap; however, we guaranteed that the selected table cells were unique to prevent data redundancy.

Following table and XBRL tag selection, we converted the tables, XBRL tags, and the texts surrounding the tables into a JSON format. This conversion

---

[3] https://www.sec.gov.

[4] https://www.xbrl.org.

[5] https://www.sec.gov/edgar/information-for-filers/standard-taxonomies.

Table 1. Statistical summary of cells, companies, reports, tables, tags, axes, and members in the dataset.

	Training	Validation	Testing	All
# Annotated Cell	8000	1000	1000	10,000
# Companies	2,411	782	792	2,510
# Reports	3,590	836	841	3,999
# Tables	7,292	982	985	8,910
# Tags	1,856	606	593	2,064
# Axes	248	107	112	272
# Members	3,031	558	563	3,587

Table 2. Overlapping ratio of cells within the same table across training, validation, and testing subsets (common tables that appear in multiple splits of the dataset).

Tags			
	Training	Validation	Training and Validation
Validation	501/606 (82.67%)	–	–
Testing	485/593 (81.79%)	279/593 (47.05%)	490/593 (82.63%)

Axes			
	Training	Validation	Training and Validation
Validation	97/107 (90.65%)	–	–
Testing	98/112 (87.50%)	75/112 (66.96%)	98/112 (87.50%)

Members			
	Training	Validation	Training and Validation
Validation	282/558 (50.54%)	–	–
Testing	279/563 (49.56%)	156/563 (27.71%)	283/563 (50.27%)

process included the extraction of texts within 10 HTML tags above and below the tables to capture contextual information effectively. Lastly, we divided the collected data into training, validation, and test sets. This step was crucial for preparing the dataset for machine learning applications, ensuring that we had distinct sets of data for model training, parameter tuning, and final evaluation.

3.3 Statistics of the Dataset

After completing the construction process, our dataset comprises 10,000 cells, each annotated with a tag, axes, and members. In the semantic multi-concept annotation task for tabular data, a cell can be annotated with more than one concept. The numbers of samples with axis-member pairs from one to six are: 8,323, 1,411, 234, 28, 3, and 3, respectively.

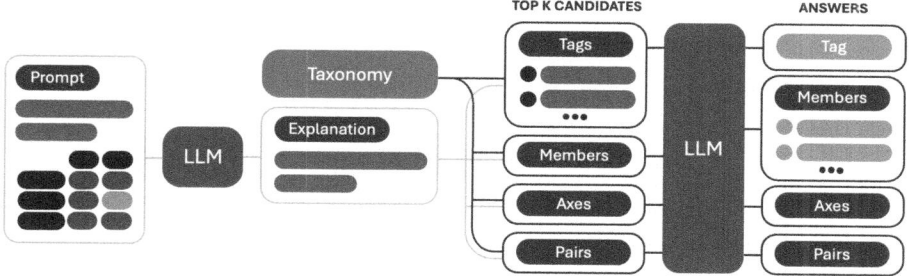

Fig. 3. The proposed pipeline with a retrieval module for prompting language models.

To ensure consistency in future evaluations, we divide the dataset into training, validation, and testing subsets by randomly assigning cells across the subsets in an 8:1:1 ratio. For an in-depth understanding of our dataset, we conducted an analysis detailing the number of companies, reports, tables, tags, axes, and members, presented in Table 1. Additionally, Table 2 shows the overlapping ratio of cells within the same table in the training, validation, and testing subsets.

4 Baselines

We tested two larger models using prompting and five small models using fine-tuning. The larger models are capable of zero-shot prediction but, for our task, require an additional retriever. The smaller models need a large training corpus but can make end-to-end predictions directly. Our experiment compares these two settings and provides analyses of the different training/prediction strategies.

4.1 Prompt-Based Large Language Model

The prompt-based large language model aims to provide an explanation of the cell and then compare this explanation with the definitions of the concepts in the taxonomy to annotate tags and axis-member pairs, as shown in Fig. 3. Specifically, we use the large language model with a zero-shot prompting strategy. The prompt requires the information of the target cell, its corresponding table, and the context surrounding the table, which significantly increases the prompt's size. Therefore, it is difficult to employ a few-shot prompting strategy.

After obtaining the explanation of the cell, we need to compare this explanation with the definitions of the concepts. Nevertheless, our taxonomy contains too many concepts making it difficult to exhaustively compare all definitions using the large language model. Therefore, we employ the BM25 algorithm to select the top k candidates of tags and axis-member pairs in the taxonomy that are most similar to the explanation. To determine the final tag for the cell, we use the large language model to select the most similar one from the top-k tags. Since the cell could contain many axis-member pairs, we use the large language model with a prompt to classify whether the definition of the axis concept and the definition of the member match the cell explanation. This final step cross-checks the definitions to ensure the concepts align with the meaning of the cell.

4.2   Fine-Tuned Pretrained Language Model

We fine-tuned sequence-to-sequence language models by inputting the table and surrounding texts and training the models to generate the tag, axes, and members. The autoregressive approach allows the models to output multiple axes and members in a simple end-to-end process without specific changes to the models' architecture or an ensemble of models. First, we flattened the table into a sequence, followed by the closest text (extracted from an HTML tag) above the table, then the one below, before moving one by one further from the table in an alternate above-and-below iteration. The input is in the following format: $< table > cell_{1,1}... < mention > cell_{ij} < /mention > ...cell_{rc} < /table >$ $text_1^{Above}...text_n^{Below}$, where r and c are the numbers of rows and columns, i and j indicate the target cell for prediction, and n is the number of texts (equal between above and below the table). We did not use additional tokens since the <table> and <mention> tags can effectively separate the table from the texts and point the model to the target cell. We use tab characters (\t) to separate table cells and new line characters (\n) for rows and texts.

The output format is as follows: $t_i, |a_1 = m_2|...|a_x = m_x$, where $t_{i,j}$ is the tag, $a \in A_{c_{ij}}$ are the axes, and $m \in M_{c_{ij}}$ are the members. The post-processing algorithm uses "|" to separate the output sequence into a list of answers. It recognizes an answer containing "=" as an axis-member pair; the rest are candidate tags. Although there is only one tag in the label, the model often outputs multiple non-pair answers. The model searches each answer in the taxonomy and chooses the last one it finds. It then tries to find matching axis and member concepts in the taxonomy. As there can be multiple axis-member pairs, the algorithm does not remove any axes or members. This approach allows us to evaluate the model's ability to predict axes and members individually in addition to the pairs.

5   Evaluation

5.1   Experimental Setting

Prompting. We prompted the March 2024 version of GPT 3.5 via OpenAI's API[6] and Llama 2 via Replicate[7]. We crafted two prompts, one instructing the large langauge models (LLMs) to explain the table cell and the other asking them to choose the axes and members from the candidates. The first prompt is:

> Given a specific cell with row, column and value in a financial report table, the detailed information for this cell is as follows: Table: ..., Text

---

[6] https://openai.com.

[7] https://replicate.com/meta/llama-2-70b.

Table 3. Hyperparameter settings and training environments for fine-tuning.

	Number of Params	Learning Rate	Batch Size	Max Epochs	GPU (NVIDIA)	Appx. Training Duration
BART base	139M	5e-5	32	10	TITAN RTX	2 hrs 49 min
BART large	406M	5e-5	32	10	RTX A6000	4 hrs 29 min
T5 small	60.5M	1e-3	32	10	TITAN RTX	45 min
T5 large	737M	2e-4	16	10	RTX A6000	6 hrs 2 min
MVP	406M	1e-4	32	10	RTX A6000	5 hrs 42 min

Above Table: ..., Text Below Table: ..., Cell: row ..., column ..., Value ... Please analyze the cell, focusing on: 1. Axes, which classify facts in an XBRL instance, like 'Time Period', 'Business Segment', 'Geographical Location'. 2. Members, representing possibilities within a domain in dimensional modeling (e.g., specific fiscal years, named company segments, individual countries). 3. Concepts in XBRL, referring to specific financial reporting items (e.g., "Revenue", "Net Income") with attributes like name, balance type, and data type.

Next, we selected the top five candidates for axes and members using the prompting output and BM25 to search the taxonomy. The second prompt asks the LLMs to select the axes and members:

Given the explanation of a specific cell within a financial report table, and a list of 5 possible concepts(axises/members). your task is to identify one concept (one to five axises/members) that are most relevant and logically consistent with the provided details. Explanation: ... State your chosen concept(axises/members) without any instructions.

Fine-Tuning. We fine-tuned three language models ranging from 60.5M to 737M parameters. These models include BART [7], T5 [12], and MVP [14], all of which are autoregressive. The BART and T5 models have been evaluated extensively in various tasks. On the other hand, MVP is relatively new but has achieved remarkable success in natural language generation (NG) tasks. The authors pre-trained and published multiple model variations from their corpus containing 77 datasets over 11 diverse NLG tasks. Specifically, we used their MTL-data-to-text variant[8] since the authors designed it for data-to-text generation, including table-to-text. Although the model supports table-to-text generation, we fine-tuned it to fit our task's input and output formats. The summary of the hyperparameter settings and training environments is in Table 3.

---

[8] https://huggingface.co/RUCAIBox/mtl-data-to-text.

5.2   Evaluation Metrics

The problem setting necessitates two main evaluation metrics. The model must choose a tag from up to 24,179 concepts, including the standard US GAAP and company-defined custom concepts. This number depends on the number of custom concepts defined by the company that generates the table. Therefore, we used the standard accuracy metric to evaluate this subtask, i.e., the number of correctly predicted tags divided by the number of all samples in the dataset split. However, the axes and members are more complicated since there can be more than one correct pair. Thus, we employed the precision, recall, and F1 scores calculated for each sample instead of simple accuracy.

Given the predicted axis-member pairs $\hat{P}_{c_{ij}} = \{(\hat{a}_1, \hat{m}_1), ..., \hat{a}_y, \hat{m}_y)\}$, where $\hat{A}_{c_{ij}}$ represents the predicted axes, $\hat{M}_{c_{ij}}$ represents the predicted members, $\hat{a} \in \hat{A}_{c_{ij}}$ and $\hat{m} \in \hat{M}_{c_{ij}}$, the metric calculates the pair-precision score as the ratio of correctly predicted pairs to all predicted pairs. Similarly, the pair-recall score is the ratio of correctly predicted pairs to all correct pairs $P_{c_{ij}}$:

$$precision_{pair} = \frac{\hat{P}_{c_{ij}} \cap P_{c_{ij}}}{\hat{P}_{c_{ij}}}, recall_{pair} = \frac{\hat{P}_{c_{ij}} \cap P_{c_{ij}}}{P_{c_{ij}}} \qquad (2)$$

We also calculated the axes and members' precision, recall, and F1 scores separately. We found that the models sometimes predict either the axis or member correctly but not both. These scores eliminate the dependency between axes and members and evaluate the models' abilities to predict them individually:

$$precision_{axis} = \frac{\hat{A}_{c_{ij}} \cap A_{c_{ij}}}{\hat{A}_{c_{ij}}}, recall_{axis} = \frac{\hat{A}_{c_{ij}} \cap A_{c_{ij}}}{A_{c_{ij}}} \qquad (3)$$

We calculated $F_{1_{axis}}$ the same way as $F_{1_{pair}}$. Similarly, $precision_{member}$, $recall_{member}$, and $F_{1_{member}}$ follows those of the axes. In addition to the main evaluation, isolating the axes and member scores helps us conduct a more detailed analysis. Lastly, we average the precision, recall, and F_1 scores across each dataset split and report them as the final scores.

5.3   Results

The results in Table 4 show that fine-tuning yields better performance than prompting. The limitation of prompting is that the LLMs do not have direct access to the entire taxonomy. It needs a retrieval module to find the most likely answers, which, in this case, is the BM25 algorithm. The highly complicated definitions of financial concepts, often with minor differences distinguishing them from each other, put the LLM-retrieval approach at a disadvantage. The candidate selection module, while necessary, contributes further to the inferior performances, as seen from the significant gap in the scores of GPT-3.5 and Llama 2 between tag prediction accuracy and the rest of the metrics.

Comparing the fine-tuned models, T5-large outperforms the other models by a significant margin. The smaller version of the model also performs reasonably well, surpassing the rest on most metrics. Interestingly, the MVP model ranked worst among the large models. This issue could be due to the different training objectives between the variant of MVP and ours. Nevertheless, compared to the BART-large model, which is approximately the same size, the performance margins on the test set across all metrics are relatively small (between 0.1–2.2).

We reported the training scores in Table 5. While the models can learn from the training data reasonably well, they struggle to generalize to the test set. The tags are the most challenging to predict since all concepts are general (US GAAP). While there are more unique members (3,587) than tags (2,064), 19.5% are company-defined, which could be less challenging to predict since they are specific to the company's business. Another potential reason is the member concepts could be more similar or relevant to the table content or the context. The axes are the easiest, most likely due to their small numbers (272).

Table 4. Experimental results on the test set (Tag Acc = Tag Accuracy).

		Tag	Axis			Member			Pair		
		Acc	P	R	F1	P	R	F1	P	R	F1
Prompting	Llama2 70b	0.9	0.1	0.4	0.1	0.1	0.7	0.2	0.0	0.0	0.0
	GPT 3.5	10.6	0.4	3.0	0.6	0.3	2.3	0.5	0.1	0.8	0.2
Fine-tuning	BART base	33.8	70.3	64.4	66.2	40.5	37.1	38.2	37.4	34.3	35.2
	BART large	_37.4_	71.0	65.7	67.3	42.5	39.8	40.7	38.6	36.2	36.9
	T5 small	35.9	_73.6_	_72.8_	_72.1_	_44.6_	_44.1_	_43.9_	_42.7_	_42.3_	_42.1_
	T5 large	**39.0**	**74.9**	**74.6**	**73.6**	**48.0**	**48.0**	**47.3**	**45.8**	**46.0**	**45.3**
	MVP	35.2	71.0	65.4	67.2	41.3	38.4	39.3	37.6	35.1	35.9

Table 5. Fine-tuning results (Mem F1 = Member F1)

	Train				Val				Test			
	Tag	Axis	Mem	Pair	Tag	Axis	Mem	Pair	Tag	Axis	Mem	Pair
	Acc	F1	F1	F1	Acc	F1	F1	F1	Acc	F1	F1	F1
BART base	80.8	85.4	76.5	73.4	29.2	66.7	37.2	34.7	33.8	66.2	38.2	35.2
BART large	76.1	84.6	74.3	70.4	_33.3_	67.3	39.5	35.6	_37.4_	67.3	40.7	36.9
T5 small	_81.3_	_94.6_	_84.7_	_83.6_	32.9	_70.4_	_42.4_	_40.4_	35.9	_72.1_	_43.9_	_42.1_
T5 large	**87.0**	**96.6**	**89.0**	**88.3**	**35.8**	**74.2**	**45.8**	**44.1**	**39.0**	**73.6**	**47.3**	**45.3**
MVP	69.2	83.7	69.4	65.7	32.1	68.1	37.0	34.6	35.2	67.2	39.3	35.9

6   Analysis and Discussion

6.1   Ablation Study on Fine-Tuning

We fine-tuned the models to predict the tags, axes, and members at once in the output sequence. While this method is more practical and cost-effective than predicting them separately, it is unclear how much the multi-concept prediction affects the models' performances. Therefore, we conducted an ablation study where we fine-tuned multiple variants of the models to predict individual concept types separately. In Fig. 4, each table reports the performances of the models trained to predict the respective concept type. For example, Fig. 4 A reports the results of the models trained to predict the tags. The numbers in the table are the changes in the scores (accuracy or F1) compared to the models in the main experiment, which predict all concept types. The results show that separate prediction generally benefits the performances, with a notable exception in the BART-base models' accuracy, where the tag prediction benefits from the axis and member prediction but not the other way around.

We summarize the ablation study's scores in Table 6. The T5-large model maintains the lead across all metrics, with BART-large outperforming T5-small in more cases. The highest tag accuracy on the test set increases from 39.0 to 42.7 when predicted separately, with an average increase among the five models of 1.2. The maximum F1 score for the axes increases from 73.6 to 73.9 (average = +1.2). While the maximum F1 scores for the members and pairs decrease from 47.3 to 46.5 and 45.3 to 45.0, their averages increase by 2.2 and 1.3.

(A) Tag prediction only

Tag Acc	Train	Val	Test
BART base	-8.9	-2.6	-4.5
BART large	+1.2	+3.6	+3.8
T5 small	+2.6	-0.2	+0.5
T5 largs	+0.5	+3.4	+3.7
MVP	-0.5	0	+2.4

(B) Axis prediction only

Axis F1	Train	Val	Test
BART base	+4.4	+3.2	+2.6
BART large	+4.5	+2.8	+3.3
T5 small	+1.1	+3.6	-0.8
T5 largs	+0.2	-1.3	-1.6
MVP	+4.1	+3.5	+2.7

(C) Member prediction only

Member F1	Train	Val	Test
BART base	+9.1	+4.8	+4.5
BART large	+7.4	+5.7	+3.7
T5 small	+1.6	-0.8	-1.4
T5 largs	+3.2	+0.8	-0.8
MVP	+8.1	+6.1	+4.8

(D) Axis-member pair prediction only

Pair F1	Train	Val	Test
BART base	+7.4	+4.7	+3.9
BART large	+1.5	+1.6	-0.2
T5 small	+5.1	+2.2	+0.2
T5 largs	+1.0	+0.2	-0.3
MVP	+6.3	+4.6	+3.0

Fig. 4. Ablation study results, where we fine-tuned the models to output the tag, axes, members, and axis-member pairs separately. The numbers indicate the differences between the scores of the modified objectives (individual concept predictions) and the original objective (all concept predictions in one sequence)

Table 6. Ablation study results, where we fine-tuned the models to output the tag, axes, members, and axis-member pairs separately.

	Tag			Axis			Member			Pair		
	Train Acc	Val Acc	Test Acc	Train F1	Val F1	Test F1	Train F1	Val F1	Test F1	Train F1	Val F1	Test F1
BART base	71.9	26.6	29.3	89.8	69.9	68.8	85.6	42.0	42.7	80.8	39.4	39.2
BART large	77.2	36.9	41.2	89.1	70.1	70.6	81.6	45.2	44.4	71.9	37.3	36.7
T5 small	83.9	32.7	36.4	95.7	**73.9**	71.3	86.3	41.5	42.5	88.8	42.6	42.3
T5 large	**87.5**	**39.2**	**42.7**	**96.8**	72.9	**72.1**	**92.2**	**46.5**	**46.5**	**89.3**	**44.3**	**45.0**
MVP	68.7	32.1	37.6	87.8	71.6	69.9	77.4	43.1	44.1	72.1	39.2	39.0

Consolidated Statements of Changes in Stockholders' Equity

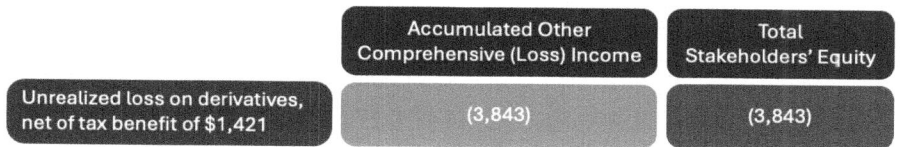

Fig. 5. The source table for an example of GPT-3.5's incorrect explanation.

Table 7. An example of GPT-3.5's incorrect explanation.

Tag

Generation: The cell value (3,843) may correspond to a specific financial reporting item or concept within the financial statements. In this context, it could represent the 'Unrealized loss on derivatives' for the year ended December 31, 2019. This concept would have attributes like name ('Unrealized loss on derivatives'), balance type (debit or credit), and data type (numeric value).

Ground truth: **[US GAAP]** Other Comprehensive Income (Loss), Unrealized Gain (Loss) on Derivatives Arising During Period, Net of Tax

Axes

Generation: Time Period: The cell value (3,843) could be classified under the 'Time Period' axis, representing a specific point in time within the financial report (December 31, 2019).

Ground truth: **[US GAAP]** Equity Components [Axis]

Members

Generation: Domain: The domain for the 'Time Period' axis could include specific fiscal years (2019, 2018, 2017), which are the possible members within this axis. The cell value (3,843) corresponds to the member '2019' within the 'Time Period' axis.

Ground truth: **[US GAAP]** AOCI Attributable to Parent [Member]

Table 8. Examples of incorrect predictions by fine-tuned models.

Tag
[US GAAP] Business Combination, Recognized Identifiable Assets Acquired and Liabilities Assumed, Current Liabilities, Accounts Payable
Prediction
[US GAAP] Business Combination, Recognized Identifiable Assets Acquired and Liabilities Assumed, Current Liabilities, Long-Term Debt

Tag
[US GAAP] Income (Loss) from Subsidiaries, Tax Expense (Benefit)
Prediction
[US GAAP] Income Tax Expense (Benefit)

Tag
[US GAAP] Stock Issued During Period, Shares, New Issues
Prediction
(None of the models predicted tags in the taxonomy)

6.2   Error Analysis

Prompting. We found that it is common for LLMs to output information not directly related to the concepts as part of their explanation. For example, we prompted GPT-3.5 to explain the highlighted cell in Fig. 5. The model's explanation in Table 7 contains the relevant information: "Unrealized Loss on Derivative." However, the rest of the output makes finding the correct tag in the taxonomy difficult. Worst yet, the model failed to explain the axes and members entirely, simply interpreting them as time dimensions. In other cases, we observed that the LLMs did not mention relevant information or only provided a general explanation with no specificity.

Fine-Tuning. Table 8 shows three common cases where the models made incorrect predictions. The first case involves the models failing to distinguish subtle differences among similar concepts. In this case, most parts of the two concepts (Business Combination, Recognized Identifiable Assets Acquired, and Liabilities Assumed) are identical. Only the last part (Accounts Payable and Long-Term Debt) is different, and the model fails to recognize the difference. The second case involves insufficient detail in prediction. The correct label (Income (Loss) from Subsidiaries, Tax Expense (Benefit)) describes a more detailed concept than the broader Income Tax Expense (Benefit). Figure 6 also shows a similar case, where the model fails to specify "Sale of Other" in "Gain (Loss) on Sale of Other Investment." Lastly, there are many cases where the models fail to output a sequence of tokens matching any concepts in the taxonomy.

Fig. 6. An example of a fine-tuned model's incorrect prediction.

6.3   Data Characteristics and Model Performances

In the previous section, we mentioned the problem of subtle differences in the concepts leading to the models' misclassification. We also observed that many concepts tend to be very long, which could make them harder to predict since all predicted tokens must be correct. Similarly, more axis-member pairs could make the prediction more challenging. Therefore, we conducted analyses of the models' performances based on concept length and number of axis-member pairs.

Figure 7 (A) shows the averages of the models' performances on the test set in terms of tag accuracy and axis/member F1 score (averaged from axis, member, and pair F1 scores). We calculated the distribution of word lengths from all tags, axes, and members in the test set but decided to report up to 15 words since there are few samples with more than 15 words (2.2% with each length having less than ten samples). There is no clear trend for tag accuracy, likely because the tag concepts are hard to predict regardless of the length. However, the axis/member F1 scores are generally lower for long concepts. This score drop could be due to the long length and the sparsity of the samples.

The downward trends are much more noticeable in Fig. 7 (B), where samples with more axis-member pairs are more difficult to predict. A part of these drops may be due to the sparsity of the samples. Nevertheless, this analysis informs future research on the problems of subtle differences among the concepts, the effect of multiple axis-member pairs, and the sparsity of these hard samples.

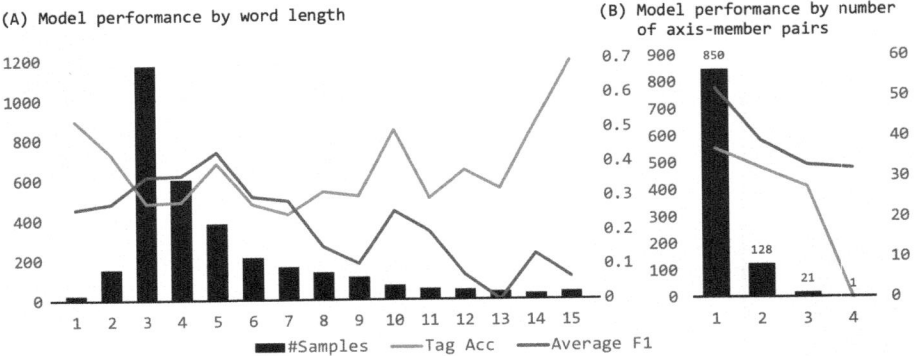

Fig. 7. Fine-tuned models' performances by word length and number of axis-member pairs on the test set. We averaged the axis, member, and axis-member pair's F1 scores to simplify the charts.

7   Conclusion

We introduce a new semantic multi-concept annotation task for financial tables. The task requires a model to identify multiple non-hierarchical concepts describing a table cell. We created a large-scale dataset of 10,000 samples and evaluated two prompt-based and five fine-tuned models. While the fine-tuning approach yields significantly better results than prompting, the results show considerable space for improvement, making this task challenging. Future research direction may focus on improving the retrieval module for the prompting method and different model architectures for fine-tuning. Other semantic annotation tasks in any domain that involve complex hierarchical tabular structures will also benefit from our proposed task and models.

Acknowledgment. This paper is partially supported by the New Energy and Industrial Technology Development Organization (NEDO).

References

1. Abdelmageed, N., Schindler, S., König-Ries, B.: BiodivTab: a table annotation benchmark based on biodiversity research data. In: Proceedings of the Semantic Web Challenge on Tabular Data to Knowledge Graph Matching, pp. 13–18 (2021)
2. Bhagavatula, C.S., Noraset, T., Downey, D.: TabEL: entity linking in web tables. In: Arenas, M., et al. (eds.) ISWC 2015. LNCS, vol. 9366, pp. 425–441. Springer, Cham (2015). https://doi.org/10.1007/978-3-319-25007-6_25
3. Cutrona, V., Bianchi, F., Jiménez-Ruiz, E., Palmonari, M.: Tough tables: carefully evaluating entity linking for tabular data. In: Pan, J.Z., et al.: (eds.) ISWC 2020. LNCS, vol. 12507, pp. 328–343. Springer, Cham (2020). https://doi.org/10.1007/978-3-030-62466-8_21

4. Fan, G., Wang, J., Li, Y., Zhang, D., Miller, R.J.: Semantics-aware dataset discovery from data lakes with contextualized column-based representation learning. VLDB Endowment **16**(7), 1726–1739 (2023)
5. Kertkeidkachorn, N., Nararatwong, R., Xu, Z., Ichise, R.: FinKG: a core financial knowledge graph for financial analysis. In: Proceedings of the IEEE International Conference on Semantic Computing, pp. 90–93. IEEE (2023)
6. Khurana, U., Galhotra, S.: Semantic concept annotation for tabular data. In: Proceedings of the ACM International Conference on Information and Knowledge Management, pp. 844–853 (2021)
7. Lewis, M., et al.: BART: denoising sequence-to-sequence pre-training for natural language generation, translation, and comprehension. arXiv preprint arXiv:1910.13461 (2019)
8. Limaye, G., Sarawagi, S., Chakrabarti, S.: Annotating and searching web tables using entities, types and relationships. VLDB Endowment **3**(1–2), 1338–1347 (2010)
9. Nararatwong, R., Kertkeidkachorn, N., Ichise, R.: Evaluating tabular and textual entity linking in financial documents. In: Proceedings of the IEEE International Conference on Semantic Computing, pp. 130–133. IEEE (2024)
10. Nguyen, P., Kertkeidkachorn, N., Ichise, R., Takeda, H.: MTab: matching tabular data to knowledge graph using probability models. In: Proceedings of the 14th International Workshop on Ontology Matching (2019)
11. Nguyen, P., Kertkeidkachorn, N., Ichise, R., Takeda, H.: MTab4D: semantic annotation of tabular data with dbpedia. Semantic Web (Preprint), pp. 1–25 (2022)
12. Raffel, C., et al.: Exploring the limits of transfer learning with a unified text-to-text transformer. J. Mach. Learn. Res. **21**(140), 1–67 (2020)
13. Ritze, D., Bizer, C.: Matching web tables to dbpedia-a feature utility study. In: Proceedings of the International Conference on Extending Database Technology, pp. 210–221 (2017)
14. Tang, T., Li, J., Zhao, W.X., Wen, J.R.: MVP: multi-task supervised pre-training for natural language generation. In: Findings of the Association for Computational Linguistics, pp. 8758–8794 (2023)

Author Index

A. Rapp et al. (Eds.): NLDB 2024, LNCS 14762, pp. 531–534, 2024.
https://doi.org/10.1007/978-3-031-70239-6

GPSR Compliance

The European Union's (EU) General Product Safety Regulation (GPSR) is a set of rules that requires consumer products to be safe and our obligations to ensure this.

If you have any concerns about our products, you can contact us on ProductSafety@springernature.com

In case Publisher is established outside the EU, the EU authorized representative is:

Springer Nature Customer Service Center GmbH
Europaplatz 3
69115 Heidelberg, Germany

The manufacturer's authorised representative in the EU is Springer
Nature Customer Service Centre GmbH, Europaplatz 3, 69115 Heidelberg,
Germany. If you have any concerns regarding our products, please
contact ProductSafety@springernature.com

Printed and bound by CPI Group (UK) Ltd, Croydon, CR0 4YY

29/04/2026

02099533-0005